STATE FORMATION I
EARLY MODERN ENGL.
c. 1550–1700

This book examines the development of the English state during the long seventeenth century. The main emphasis is on the impersonal forces which shaped the uses of political power, rather than the purposeful actions of individuals or groups – it is a study of state formation rather than of state building.

The author's approach does not however rule out the possibility of discerning patterns in the development of the state, and a coherent account emerges which offers some new answers to relatively well-established questions. In particular, it is argued that the development of the state in this period was shaped in important ways by social interests – particularly those of class, gender and age. It is also argued that this period saw significant changes in the form and functioning of the state which were, in some sense, modernising. The book therefore offers a narrative of the development of the state in the seventeenth century in the aftermath of revisionism.

MICHAEL J. BRADDICK is a Senior Lecturer in History, University of Sheffield.

STATE FORMATION IN EARLY MODERN ENGLAND
c. 1550–1700,

MICHAEL J. BRADDICK, 1962-

CAMBRIDGE
UNIVERSITY PRESS

PUBLISHED BY THE PRESS SYNDICATE OF THE UNIVERSITY OF CAMBRIDGE
The Pitt Building, Trumpington Street, Cambridge, United Kingdom

CAMBRIDGE UNIVERSITY PRESS
The Edinburgh Building, Cambridge CB2 2RU, UK   http://www.cup.cam.ac.uk
40 West 20th Street, New York, NY 10011–4211, USA   http://www.cup.org
10 Stamford Road, Oakleigh, Melbourne 3166, Australia
Ruiz de Alarcón 13, 28014 Madrid, Spain

First published 2000

Printed in the United Kingdom at the University Press, Cambridge

Typeface 11/12½ Baskerville [VN]

A catalogue record for this book is available from the British Library

Library of Congress cataloguing in publication data
Braddick, M. J. (Michael J.), 1962–
State formation in early modern England, *c.* 1550–1700/Michael J. Braddick.
p.   cm.
Includes bibliographical references.
ISBN 0 521 78346 1 (hb) – ISBN 0 521 78955 9 (pbk.)
1. Great Britain – Politics and government – 17th century.   2. Great Britain – Politics and
government – 1558–1603.   I. Title.

JN191.B73 2000
320.941'09'031 – dc21   00-023623

ISBN 0 521 78346 1 hardback
ISBN 0 521 78955 9 paperback

Contents

Acknowledgements

In the course of writing this book I have worked at three universities and held fellowships at a number of other institutions. As a result I have incurred a large number of intellectual debts which are too numerous to detail, but some must be acknowledged here. In particular, Jonathan Clark gave me the initial encouragement to write a book of this kind and read the first draft. John Walter, throughout the time that I have been working on these issues, has been both a friendly and demanding critic. Most of the initial writing was done while living in London and during that period I was very fortunate to have the benefit of almost daily advice and criticism from Justin Champion. I wish that I knew how to thank Emma Davies.

Among the many others to whom I owe considerable debts of gratitude Ann Hughes and John Morrill figure prominently. They both read drafts of the whole book and I am grateful to them, and to the anonymous readers for Cambridge University Press, for their very helpful suggestions about revision. Particular chapters have benefited from critical readings by Dan Beaver, Erika Bsumek, Nicholas Canny, Andrew Gamble, Julian Goodare, Michael Kenny, Ian Kershaw, Peter Lake and Anthony Milton. What I have written also owes much to discussions of the larger questions with Erika Bsumek. For discussions of particular issues I am especially grateful to Tom Cogswell, Faramerz Dabhoiwala, Mark Greengrass, Steve Hindle, Ian Kershaw, Peter Lake, Stephen Salter, Bob Shoemaker, John Styles, Nicholas Tyacke, Tim Wales, Simon Walker, John Watts and Amanda Vickery. Papers outlining the argument of the book, or of parts of it, have been presented at St Peter's College, Oxford, the Huntington Library, the London Group of Historical Geographers, All Souls College, Oxford, the Department of History at the University of York and the Department of Archaeology at the University of Sheffield. I have also spoken on these themes at conferences held at the Institute for European History, Mainz, the

Charles Warren Center at Harvard University and Birkbeck College, London. The final version has benefited considerably from the many helpful comments that were made on those occasions.

Work on this book has been made possible by a number of grants. Between 1991 and 1992, I held a British Academy Postdoctoral Fellowship and the British Academy has also furnished a small research grant. I have also held both a Mayers Fellowship and an Andrew W. Mellon and Fletcher Jones Fellowship at the Huntington Library. The book, in the form in which I eventually wrote it, was planned at the Huntington Library and I profited immensely from the opportunity to work in such a stimulating intellectual environment and on such rich documentary sources. Between 1995 and 1996, I held a Nuffield Foundation Social Science Fellowship and it was during that year that I completed the first draft of the book. Without that fellowship I suspect that the book would never have been written. The final version of the manuscript was produced while I was a fellow at the Max-Planck-Institut für europäische Rechtsgeschichte in Frankfurt. My Department at the University of Sheffield kindly granted me a period of study leave and two periods of special leave which allowed me to take up these fellowships, as well as a number of small sums which greatly facilitated the research and writing of this book. More importantly it has provided a stimulating and challenging intellectual environment in which to develop my ideas on these issues. I am grateful to the staffs of the British Library, Chester City Record Office, the Public Record Offices at Chancery Lane and Kew, the Huntington Library, the Max-Planck-Institut für europäische Rechtsgeschichte, the Institute of Historical Research and the University Libraries in Cambridge and Sheffield. Finally, it has been a pleasure to work with Cambridge University Press. In particular I am grateful to Bill Davies for his patience and sensitivity in seeing the manuscript into press; and to Sheila Kane for her expert and thorough copy-editing once it was there. I am also grateful to the Press for permission to reproduce some material first published in my article 'The early modern English state and the question of differentiation, from 1550 to 1700', *Comparative Studies in Society and History*, 38, 1 (1996), 92–111.

With so many people to thank I ought to be able to blame the remaining flaws and errors on someone else. Sadly, I must take responsibility for those.

Abbreviations and conventions

APC	*Acts of the Privy Council of England*, ed. J. R. Dasent, 46 vols. (London, 1890–1964)
BIHR	*Bulletin of the Institute of Historical Research*
BL	British Library
CCRO	Chester City Record Office
CSPD	*Calendar of State Papers, Domestic Series*
EcHR	*Economic History Review*
EHR	*English Historical Review*
HEH	Henry E. Huntington Library
HJ	*Historical Journal*
HMC	*Historical Manuscripts Commission*
HP	Hartlib Papers, Sheffield University Library
JBS	*Journal of British Studies*
PP	*Past and Present*
PRO	Public Record Office
SR	*Statutes of the Realm* (London, 1963)
TRHS	*Transactions of the Royal Historical Society*

NOTE ON DATES AND TRANSCRIPTIONS

Dates are given old style but with the new year taken to begin on 1 January. Where possible original spelling has been preserved in quotations. Punctuation has been added in some cases in order to clarify the meaning.

NOTE ON BIBLIOGRAPHY

A list of secondary works cited is available on the worldwide web at www.shef.ac.uk/~hri/braddick/

General introduction

This book examines the development of the English state in the long seventeenth century. It is based on a relatively flexible definition of the state which allows for its use in relation to political forms quite different from the nation states of the nineteenth and twentieth centuries. The emphasis of the analysis is on the impersonal forces which shape the uses of political power rather than the purposeful actions of individuals or groups – it is, in short, a study of state formation, rather than of state building. Such an approach does not rule out the possibility of discerning patterns in the development of the state, however. On the basis of this flexible definition of the state, it is possible to tell a coherent story about state formation in this period and to offer some new answers to relatively well-established questions. In particular, it is argued that the development of the state in this period was shaped in important ways by social interests – particularly those of class,[1] gender and age. It is also argued that the long seventeenth century saw important changes in the form and functioning of the state, changes which were to some extent modernising.[2] Overall, therefore, this book offers a grand narrative of the development of the state in the seventeenth century, seeking to address long-standing questions about the relative autonomy of the state and the importance of this particular period in its longer-term history.

[1] This is a controversial term, of course. I use it here in the sense outlined by Keith Wrightson:

> If we use a fairly eclectic definition of social class to describe a loose aggregate of individuals of varied though comparable economic position, who are linked by similarities of status, power, lifestyle and opportunities, by shared cultural characteristics and bonds of interaction, then I would argue that social classes, so defined, can be discerned in early modern England

'The social order of early modern England: three approaches', in L. Bonfield, R. M. Smith and K. Wrightson (eds.), *The World We Have Gained: Histories of Population and Social Structure. Essays Presented to Peter Laslett on his Seventieth Birthday* (Oxford, 1986), 177–202, quotation at p. 196. Class was not an exclusive consciousness, however, but a language of 'differentiation'. There were other languages (those of 'identification') which cut across class distinctions – such as neighbourliness, kinship, religious identity or the relationship between patron and client, for example: ibid., p. 199. Similar caveats should be entered regarding the use of the term gender, which was also unfamiliar to contemporaries but which has explanatory value none the less.

[2] For a discussion of this term see below, pp. 97–8.

1

An account of the development of the state was implicit in the Whig
and Marxist narratives of the seventeenth century. The political crises of
the 1640s and 1650s, and of 1688/9, were once seen as crucial to the
development of the modern state, but in recent writings on the political
history of the seventeenth century this question has largely fallen from
view. Older narratives of the rise of bourgeois political power or of
constitutional liberty have been demolished without replacement, and
for most political historians the most interesting questions have been
about the causes of the English civil war rather than its consequences.
But one reason why the civil war loomed so large in narratives of English
history was because of associated claims about the importance of the
experience of the mid-seventeenth century to the development of
the English state. For some historians the functional incapacity of the
state has replaced ideological difference or social conflict as part of the
explanation for political breakdown. There has been an allied account
of functional failure in the early work of the 'county-community school'
too, in this case attributed to the structural problem of local resistance to
central authority. More recently, the discussion of the problem of the
multiple kingdoms has, again largely implicitly, located the English
experience in the context of broader debates about the early modern
state. On the whole, however, the state has not been, explicitly, at the
centre of the debate. What follows is in one sense a belated attempt to
'bring the state back' into our picture of the seventeenth century.

Even as it receded to the background in the writing of the political
history of the century before 1640, however, the state was coming to
prominence in social histories of the period. Village studies and social
histories of crime, social and moral regulation and the prosecution of
witchcraft have all made reference to, and illustrated, 'the rise of the
state' in early modern England. Such accounts have not focused on
formal constitutional arrangements but instead on the functioning of the
state. Whereas the Whig and Marxist accounts were preoccupied with
explaining tensions over the power to make decisions and to initiate
legislation, this social history has been concerned with the actual exercise of state authority in the locality. But there is more than one contrast
here: not only has the state figured more prominently in social than
political histories, it has also been portrayed as a functional and institutional success. Where political historians of the period before 1640 have
made reference to the state it has generally been as an explanation for
political dysfunction: structural failure and incapacity are the most
prominent features of the state in the work of Russell, Morrill and

others. Claims about the weakness of the state are also implicit in religious histories of the sixteenth century – the functional incapacity of the government forms part of the explanation for the slow progress of Protestantism, the growth of Protestant sectarianism, and the survival and revival of Catholicism, for example. In the work of social historians such as Wrightson, however, the century before 1640 is said to have seen a great growth in the authority of the state and historians of crime have placed considerable emphasis on the displacement of informal means of dispute resolution by the use of the law.[3]

Historians of eighteenth-century Britain have been more explicitly interested in the development of the state than their seventeenth-century colleagues. Recent work has drawn attention to the state and to the importance or otherwise of the Glorious Revolution in its development. But here, too, there are contrasting accounts of the nature and purpose of the state. In much of this literature, fiscal-military functions are given great emphasis, as they are in much recent writing on many other European states in the early modern period. Typical of such accounts is Tilly's claim that 'war made the state and vice versa': that the escalating cost and complexity of warfare forced the development of elaborate bureaucratic systems, and the successful development of such systems enabled further bellicosity. This set of interests has been most clearly laid out for eighteenth-century Britain by Brewer in his influential study of the *Sinews of Power*. Clark, by contrast, has drawn attention

---

[3] For excellent accounts of the debate about the causes of the civil war, see A. Hughes, *The Causes of the English Civil War* (London, 1998 edn), esp. chs. 1, 3; and R. Cust and A. Hughes (eds.), *The English Civil War* (London, 1997), Introduction. For the functional incapacity of the state, see C. Russell, *The Causes of the English Civil War* (Oxford, 1990), ch. 7; Russell, 'Monarchies, wars, and estates in England, France and Spain, *c.* 1580–*c.* 1640', in Russell, *Unrevolutionary England, 1603–1642* (London, 1990), 121–36; Russell, 'The British Problem and the English Civil War', ibid., 231–51, esp. pp. 233–4; J. Morrill, *Revolt in the Provinces: The People of England and the Tragedies of War 1630–1648* (London, 1999), esp. 'Introduction'. For the effectiveness of state authority in local life see K. Wrightson, 'The politics of the parish in early modern England', in P. Griffiths, A. Fox and S. Hindle (eds.), *The Experience of Authority in Early Modern England* (London, 1996), 10–46, esp. pp. 25–31; K. Wrightson and D. Levine, *Poverty and Piety in an English Village: Terling, 1525–1700*, 2nd edn (Oxford, 1995), esp. pp. 201–3. For an overview of the history of crime in the light of the 'growth of the state', see J. A. Sharpe, *Crime in Early Modern England 1550–1750* (London, 1984), ch. 8. For Europe as a whole, see B. Lenman and G. Parker, 'The state, the community and the criminal law in early modern Europe', in V. A. C. Gatrell, B. Lenman and G. Parker (eds.), *Crime and the Law: A Social History of Crime in Western Europe since 1500* (London, 1980), 11–48. For social regulation see, now, S. Hindle, *The State and Social Change in Early Modern England c. 1550–1640* (London, 2000). I am grateful to Dr Hindle for letting me see this book prior to publication. R. B. Manning, *Religion and Society in Elizabethan Sussex: A Study of the Enforcement of the Religious Settlement 1558–1603* (Leicester, 1969); M. C. Questier, *Conversion, Politics and Religion in England, 1580–1625* (Cambridge, 1996).

to the importance of Tory-Anglican ideology to the legitimation of political authority in the eighteenth century, and there are few points of contact between these interpretations. Clark's account, for example, gives emphasis to the transformative effects of Catholic emancipation and parliamentary reform in the early nineteenth century as the moments in the modernisation of the state, rather than to the functional and institutional changes consequent upon the Glorious Revolution.[4]

Implicit in much work on the early modern state, of course, are such arguments about modernity and modernisation. We might discern two terminal dates for claims about the modernisation of the English state – Elton's claims for the 1530s and Clark's for the 1820s.[5] In the intervening 300 years a number of other periods have been singled out as particularly important in this respect. The seventeenth-century revolutions, in particular, are often said to be important in the development of the modern state. It has been claimed, for example, that the 1640s and 1650s saw the assertion of constitutional safeguards of individual liberty, through a reduction in the executive power of the monarch. Those decades have also been seen as crucial to the rising political influence of agrarian and merchant capitalists, who took greater control over legislative authority.[6] The 1690s too have been seen as significant in the triumph of capital or constitutionalism, and also in bringing the military revolution to England.[7] The contrast, here as elsewhere, is not so much a result of empirical disagreement (although there is, of course, plenty of empirical disagreement about the importance of the 'Tudor

---

[4] J. Brewer, *The Sinews of Power: War, Money and the English State, 1688–1783* (London, 1989); L. Stone (ed.), *An Imperial State at War: Britain from 1689–1815* (London, 1994); C. Tilly, *Coercion, Capital and European States, AD 990–1992* (Oxford, 1992); T. Ertman, *Birth of Leviathan: Building States and Regimes in Medieval and Early Modern Europe* (Cambridge, 1997); B. M. Downing, *The Military Revolution and Political Change: Origins of Democracy and Autocracy in Early Modern Europe* (Princeton, 1992); J. E. Thompson, *Mercenaries, Pirates and Sovereigns: State-Building and Extra-Territorial Violence in Early Modern Europe* (Princeton, 1994). It should be noted, of course, that Brewer is well aware of issues arising from legitimation. J. C. D. Clark, *English Society 1688–1832: Ideology, Social Structure and Political Practice during the Ancien Régime* (Cambridge, 1985); Clark, *Revolution and Rebellion: State and Society in England in the Seventeenth and Eighteenth Centuries* (Cambridge, 1986).

[5] For a sense of this debate, see G. R. Elton, *The Tudor Revolution in Government: Administrative Changes in the Reign of Henry VIII* (Cambridge, 1953); C. Coleman and D. Starkey (eds.), *Revolution Reassessed: Revisions in the History of Tudor Government and Administration* (Oxford, 1986); and J. Guy, *Tudor England* (Oxford, 1988), ch. 6.

[6] For the debate about the civil war, see Hughes, *Causes*; Cust and Hughes (eds.), *English Civil War*. For the importance of the 1640s for the propagation of a new concept of the state and of political obligation, see R. Tuck, *Philosophy and Government 1572–1651* (Cambridge, 1993). A similar case is made by K. Sharpe, 'A commonwealth of meanings: languages, analogues, ideas and politics', reprinted in Sharpe, *Politics and Ideas in Early Stuart England: Essays and Studies* (London, 1989), 3–71.   [7] For the fiscal-military state see Brewer, *Sinews*.

revolution in government'). Instead, it arises from contrasting assumptions about what a discussion of the state involves. Elton's concern, for example, is with the bureaucratisation of decision-making at the centre of government; Clark's with the legitimation of political power; others are more concerned with the effectiveness of its expression in relation to particular functions.

On the basis of these accounts quite different conclusions arise about the functions of the English state, its institutional forms and the chronology of its development. In social histories emphasis is given to the domestic functions of the state carried out by the institutions of county and parish governance – magistrates, constables and vestries. The operations of these institutions were closely tied to vested social interests. In these accounts, then, the state appears to have been far from autonomous and its institutional forms and legitimating languages were far from 'modern'. In political histories, by contrast, emphasis is given to the enforcement of confessional identities and the pursuit of fiscal-military effectiveness. Discussion of fiscal-military change gives emphasis to emerging bureaucracies and the increasingly modern languages of political legitimation. The state, in such accounts, appears to be relatively autonomous of social interest and there is an emphasis on the relative modernity of state forms. These accounts are sometimes difficult to reconcile. For example, Tilly's account, with the exception of its sensitivity to the variations in the economic resources available to fund military effort, imputes a degree of autonomy to the state which contrasts sharply with the account of patriarchal, magisterial government in many social histories. Other such accounts, which include discussion of the English case, are equally indifferent to domestic governance and legitimation. The accounts of social historians, on the other hand, have given much greater emphasis to these issues, but hardly any to the importance of fiscal-military developments.

Behind these historiographical debates, therefore, lie a number of more fundamental questions. Clearly there are varying accounts of what the state was used for and who benefited from its activities – the functional purpose and degree of autonomy of state power. Secondly, a related problem, there is clearly disagreement about what or who drove the development of state institutions. Here there are combinations of relatively determinist explanations or relatively ideological explanations. For example, explanations of the upheavals of the 1640s and 1650s in terms of class interest, or of those of the 1690s in terms of changing military technology, are open to charges of determinism. On the other hand, some explanations of the civil war and both seven-teenth-century revolutions give much greater emphasis to the indepen-dent power of ideology, concentrating instead on arguments about how to secure political liberty. Similarly, changing conceptions of the proper sphere of legitimate political activity or the necessity of propagating and enforcing the true religion place the pressure for political change more clearly in the realm of ideas. In practice, of course, explanations (includ-ing the current one) pick a path somewhere between these rather stark extremes. Thirdly, there are varying accounts of which were the key moments in the development of the state and these disagreements are related to arguments about its 'modernity'. All the periods of develop-ment singled out for particular attention in the historiography have been said to be important to the development of the 'modern' state. Finally, for reasons particular to the way in which the history of this period has been written, these questions consistently raise the issue of the relationship between centre and locality, or between state and community. This book addresses these four related issues arising from these historiographical disputes: the nature of the relationship between centre and locality; the changing institutional form of the state (includ-ing its modernisation); the uses and degree of autonomy of state power; and the need for a more satisfactory chronological framework for the analysis of its development.

Clearly, in trying to readdress these questions, it is first necessary to tackle the problem of defining the state. The difficulty is to arrive at a definition which is useful in an early modern context, but which does not empty the term of meaning for us. In chapter 1 the state is defined as a 'coordinated and territorially bounded network of agents exercising political power', a definition which is coherent in modern sociological terms but sufficiently flexible to comprehend pre-modern state forms. Crucial to this definition is the idea that there is a distinct kind of 'political' power. The state is a network of agencies distinguished by the kind of power that they exercise, rather than the precise form of these agencies (there is no insistence that they be bureaucratic, for example) or the ends to which they were employed. Thus, the definition of the state as a general category is separate from the description of the institutions that comprised the state in early modern England. Having defined the state in general terms, therefore, chapter 1 goes on to describe the institutions which comprised the early modern state.

The principal concern of this book, however, is to describe how the institutions of the state were used, with what effect and by whom.

Because the process of state formation is continuous, to describe the uses of political power is simultaneously to describe changes in the form and uses of the state. Chapter 2 outlines a model of political change to explain these changes. Looking at the whole range of institutions embodying political power, it is clear that no single will, or group interest, lay behind all the uses made of these offices. Different groups, responding to a variety of challenges and opportunities, sought to make use of the resources at their disposal. They attempted to redefine the scope of existing offices, or to invent new ones, and in doing so they appealed to legitimating ideas current in society at large. As a consequence, the uses of existing offices changed and it was the shortcomings of existing offices that called forth the creation of new ones. This process was undirected, there was no defined end in view and, in the absence of a single blue-print or design, the term 'state building' seems inappropriate. Instead, the more neutral term 'state formation' is preferred. But, although they were not the result of conscious design there were, none the less, patterns in these developments. Firstly, there were regularities in the kinds of challenges and opportunities which prompted new uses of political power. There were also regularities in the kinds of task for which particular forms of office were useful and for which particular legitimating languages proved most effective. We can, therefore, trace affinities between particular kinds of functional purpose, particular forms of office and the legitimating languages which offered the most effective explanations or justifications. This model does not presume that innovation derived only from the centre and at the expense of the locality, that there was a single pressure for change, or that a single interest or will lay behind it. It therefore provides the basis for a narrative of the changing form of the state in seventeenth-century England, but it is a narrative free of the weaknesses usually attributed to the Marxist and Whig accounts of this issue.

The first part of the book, therefore, is unavoidably concerned with issues of definition and with the conceptual underpinnings of the argument that follows. The rest of the book sets out to analyse the development of the state, so defined, in the long seventeenth century. Not all the agencies of state power were performing similar functions and neither were they legitimated in the same way, so that within the total network of offices we can discern semi-distinct sub-sets of offices or administrative initiatives. Three distinct 'crystallisations' of political power within the network of state agencies in England are distinguished – the patriarchal, military-fiscal and confessional states – each of which was

experienced differently in the localities. In each case, differing patterns
in development can be discerned – in the material conditions prompting
innovation, the forms of office through which power was exercised and
the languages in which this was legitimated. In each case different
conclusions arise about the origins of the impetus for change, its chronology, the interests that lay behind the use of political power and the
degree to which change was modernising. An important characteristic
of political power is that it is territorially based, and a dramatic change
in the early modern state was the transformation of the scale of this
territorial base. Part v therefore considers this expansion, the development of the 'dynastic' state. In this expansion can be seen the working
out of similar processes over new territories – in particular, parallels can
be drawn with the experience of the patriarchal and fiscal-military states
in the English core.

These categories are, of course, terms of art and they would have had
little meaning for contemporaries. While useful for the analytic purposes
laid out here, the main purpose of this book is to argue not for the
usefulness of these particular categories, but for the model of political
change laid out in chapter 2. The conclusion, in addition to drawing the
threads of the analysis together in order to answer the questions set out
above, also seeks to knit the understanding of political power back
together again. Clearly, this model of political change provides a means
to integrate quite disparate kinds of history – of social policy, financial,
military and religious history, for example – but also to make connections between largely separate national historiographies – of the three
kingdoms, Wales and the Americas. Of course, the treatment of all these
historiographies is partial, driven as it is by a particular set of questions,
and more than one narrative of the seventeenth century is possible.
'Bringing the state back in' in this way, however, not only offers some
new answers to old questions but also provides a fruitful way of thinking
across the boundaries set by our professional specialisations.

PART I

State formation in early modern England

Introduction

In seeking to 'bring the state back in' this book draws on a wealth of specialised work dealing with a great variety of aspects of seventeenth-century government. The state has been discussed in a variety of contexts, and quite different conclusions have been drawn about its form, the uses of state power, the chronology of its development and the interests that it represented. At the same time, some historians would deny the usefulness of the term in discussing early modern government altogether. Chapter 1 therefore sets about the problem of definition – in what sense was there a 'state' in early modern England? The answer offered here is that there was a coordinated and territorially bounded network of agencies exercising political power, and this network was exclusive of the authority of other political organisations within those bounds. It is argued both that it is reasonable to refer to this as a state in terms of modern social theory – it is not a definition which empties the term of meaning for us – and that it is a view that would have been comprehensible to increasing numbers of contemporaries. What separates the early modern polity from the modern one is not the absence of a state, but the specific forms of political power embodied in the state. This chapter also, therefore, describes the offices that made up the early modern state, and their responsibilities. In doing so, it defines the limits of the present study, describing which institutions are the proper subject of a study of the state in early modern England.

The definition of political power is, clearly, crucial to this approach since the control of political power is the essence of definition of the state. Political power is distinctive in being territorially based, functionally limited and backed by the threat of legitimate physical force. Other kinds of power may have one or more of these qualities, but political power is unique in its combination of all three. Normally, compliance with political power does not result from the use of force but from a recognition of the essential legitimacy of the action in hand. For these reasons, chapter 2 gives a more detailed account of legitimation, and of how the uses of their office by individual officeholders were represented as legitimate. In legitimating exercises of political power individuals justified their activities both in terms of the formal limits of their office and in terms of beliefs current in society at large. In order for this latter justification to be credible their actions had to be made to conform to some extent to those claims. Officeholders who claimed to be defenders of the Protestant religion, for example, had to sustain their credibility by acting in ways which appeared to do that. In effect, legitimation gave force to ideas whose generally understood meanings were not determined by the officeholders themselves. As a result, the extent to which individual and group interests could be given free rein was limited. Secondly, some forms of legitimation were more useful for particular purposes than others, and some were more modern than others, so that an account of the legitimation of administrative acts helps to explain both the effectiveness of state power in relation to particular functions, and the pressures leading to changes in the forms of state office. A discussion of legitimation, therefore, introduces the approach to the principal questions to be addressed – what gives shape and purpose to these offices of the state? Whose interests lay behind the use of state power and what were the important periods in its development? Some of the embodiments of the state in early modern England pretty clearly served particular interests, some of them were relatively autonomous and some were coming to resemble more closely the forms of the modern state. In exploring the ways in which political power was legitimated chapter 2 therefore lays out a model of political change in early modern England.

CHAPTER I

The embodiment of the state

> The State is a dream ... a symbol of nothing at all, an emptiness, a mind without a body, a game played with clouds in the sky. But States make war, don't they, and imprison people?[1]

Although, or perhaps because, the state has not been at the centre of discussions of seventeenth-century English history there is a great variety of views about its nature, uses and development. Many of these accounts rest on contradictory (and usually unstated) definitions of the state. This chapter therefore sets out a definition of the state which allows us to reconcile these competing accounts and to place in context the importance of the seventeenth century to the development of the English state. In doing so, however, it takes issue to some extent with the definitions of the state which seem to inform these varying accounts of its development. The state is not defined here in terms of its form, or a particular set of functions, but in terms of the kind of power that it represents. Having defined the state as a general category, the network of offices which comprised the state in early modern England will be described.

DEFINITIONS OF THE STATE

Arguments are shaped by their premises, and this is particularly true of discussions of the state about the definition of which there is little agreement. Sabine's rather gloomy conclusion reflects these difficulties:

the word commonly denotes no class of objects that can be identified exactly, and for the same reason it signifies no list of attributes that bears the sanction of common usage. The word must be defined more or less arbitrarily to meet the

---

[1] J. Le Carré, *Call for the Dead* (London, 1995), 28.

11

exigencies of the system of jurisprudence or political philosophy in which it occurs.[2]

Certainly, the varying accounts of the development of the early modern English state outlined in the general introduction are only partly matters of empirical disagreement – clearly many of these authors are discussing quite different aspects of the state or are working with quite different ideas of what the state is.

An argument mounted by Mann exemplifies one strand of writing about the early modern state. He defined the state as 'a centralized, differentiated set of institutions enjoying a monopoly of the means of legitimate violence over a territorially demarcated area'. This led him to examine the functions of the 'state at Westminster', the coordinating centre of the '"ultimate" authority over violence employed within England/Britain'.[3] While acknowledging that this was only a partial account of the pre-modern state, he none the less proceeded to examine the functions performed by '*this* state', through an analysis of exchequer revenue totals. He found that exchequer revenues consistently increased in periods of warfare, and concluded that 'the functions of the state appear overwhelmingly military and overwhelmingly international rather than domestic'.[4] Only in the more recent past has state spending reflected a concern with welfare and social order.

There is, however, a problem of circularity here. One of the principal functions of the exchequer was to raise and administer war revenues, and so it is unsurprising to learn that the level of this activity increased in wartime – the specification of a particular institutional form has also in this case specified the functional purposes revealed. Moreover, not all government activities were paid for in cash, not all money was circulated through the centre and, in the absence of a bureaucracy, not all the functions of the state at Westminster cost money. Indeed, the arbitration of disputes was an onerous task, and something from which governments secured significant prestige. It was not, however, a charge on government coffers. In fact, the role of the exchequer itself increased in this respect from about 1590 onwards, with the rapid expansion of its equity jurisdiction, but this is not reflected in the accounts.

Mann's concern, and perhaps the underlying definition of the state, is

---

[2] G. H. Sabine, 'State', in E. R. A. Seligman (ed.), *The Encyclopaedia of the Social Sciences* (New York, 1934), vol. XIV, 328–32, at p. 328.

[3] M. Mann, 'State and society, 1130–1815: an analysis of English state finances', in M. Zeitlin (ed.), *Political Power and Social Theory*, vol. I (1980), 165–208, quotation at p. 166. Much of the material and argument was incorporated into his book, *The Sources of Social Power*, I, *A History of Power from the Beginning to AD 1760* (Cambridge, 1986).   [4] Mann, 'State and society', p. 196.

similar to that of the historiography of 'state building' in early modern Europe. Under the impact of inflation, escalating military costs and heightened international tensions, the finances of early modern governments were put under severe strain. In response to this they were forced to seek new powers to tax and to raise troops and to create new bureaucratic institutions capable of dealing with these administrative demands.[5] The historiography of seventeenth-century England has been little affected by this concept of state building driven by war (the 'military revolution') except in the negative sense, that the failure of state building under Elizabeth and the early Stuarts is seen as a component in the collapse of the political system in 1640–2. There was, it has been said, a 'functional breakdown' in the seventeenth-century state and, according to most historians of the period, the real problem in this respect lay in the localities. Local elites refused to assess adequate amounts of taxation or to implement militia measures with the necessary efficiency, preferring to act as good neighbours rather than as effective representatives of the national governmental interest. To this one could add the failure of government in the pursuit of religious uniformity, another policy issue of central importance that foundered, to some extent, on the problems of local enforcement.[6]

Clearly the role of local officeholders is crucial to an understanding of the seventeenth-century English state but by concentrating on the differentiated institutions at Westminster, this important dimension of early modern government is obscured. However, although most historians are sensitive to the functioning of local government, the state is still frequently associated with 'the centre' and its functions are presumed to be those of the centre. This gives rise to considerable emphasis on warfare, at the expense of consideration of the domestic and internal pressures driving the development of the state. Some such definition, for

---

[5] G. Parker, *The Military Revolution: Military Innovation and the Rise of the West, 1500–1800* (Cambridge, 1996); C. Tilly, *Coercion, Capital and European States, AD 990–1992* (Oxford, 1992); T. Ertman, *Birth of Leviathan: Building States and Regimes in Medieval and Early Modern Europe* (Cambridge, 1997); B. M. Downing, *The Military Revolution and Political Change: Origins of Democracy and Autocracy in Early Modern Europe* (Princeton, 1992). For applications to the English case see J. Brewer, *The Sinews of Power: War, Money and the English State, 1688–1783* (London, 1989); M. Duffy, 'The Foundations of British Naval Power', in Duffy (ed.), *The Military Revolution and the State*, Exeter Studies in History, no. 1 (Exeter, 1980), 49–85.

[6] This approach can be found in the work of Conrad Russell, for example. See, most recently, his *The Causes of the English Civil War* (Oxford, 1990). Russell prefers other terms, such as 'kingdom', 'monarchy' or 'political system': for example, 'the breakdown of a financial and political system in the face of inflation and the rising cost of war', *Causes*, p. 213. Cogswell provides a corrective about the potential impact of military reform prior to 1640: T. Cogswell, *Home Divisions: Aristocracy, the State and Provincial Conflict* (Manchester, 1998). For religion see Russell, *Causes*, ch. 4; below, ch. 7.

example, seems to inform Sharpe's view that 'the best starting point in attempting to understand the nature of the European state in this period is to regard it as a vast machine designed essentially to raise money and finance warfare'.[7] In essence, a particular institutional form is specified for the state – centralised differentiated institutions enjoying a monopoly of the means of legitimate violence – and the functions and development of those institutions are then investigated.

This raises the problem, of course, of the relationship between these institutions and others which also exercised political power. This problem is noted by Mann: 'centralized institutions which we intuitively recognize as "states" in feudalism . . . sometimes did *not* possess a monopoly of the means of legitimate violence (either of judicial or military force)', instead, they shared their powers with other institutions – church, manor and borough.[8] The problem here seems to be the identification of the state as the institutions at the 'centre' – there is an elision here of 'centralized' and 'centrally located'. Clearly, though, the institutions of a centralised state are not all centrally located. By the same token, the institutions of local government can, in principle at least, be component parts of a centralised state. In another context, Mann argued that pre-modern states had a 'penumbra' of poorly defined institutions through which they sought to realise their ends.[9] An alternative is to think of the state as a network of agents which embraces this 'penumbra'. These local institutions were coordinated from the centre, but were not located there – they were (weakly) centralised, but they were not centrally located. In this view, state power is not something 'central', but rather something that is extensive.

Accounts which associate the state with centrally located, differentiated institutions tend to concentrate on the fiscal and military functions of the state. In the sixteenth and early seventeenth centuries this leads to an emphasis on weakness, while accounts relying on another definition of the state are radically different, painting a picture of an active and increasingly intrusive state apparatus. This alternative view of the state

---

[7] J. A. Sharpe, *Early Modern England: A Social History 1550–1760* (London, 1987), 101.

[8] Mann, 'State and society', p. 166.

[9] In his paper at the Anglo-American Conference of Historians, 1990. Goldstone suggests a different solution to this difficulty: he 'follows Weber and Mann in ascribing to [early modern] states the centralized national rule-making and rule-enforcing authority, but ... differs [from them] in recognizing that the state shares political space with other actors and authorities'. Following from this it is possible to argue that the 'monopoly of legitimate force ... is a false characterization of early modern states, which existed in tension with semiautonomous sources of legitimate authority at the regional level or among groups subject to religious law': J. A. Goldstone, *Revolution and Rebellion in the Early Modern World* (Berkeley, 1991), 5 n.

in the historiography of early modern England is based on a far more elastic definition of the state, which seems similar to that used in some anthropological studies. An influential theme in writing on political anthropology is a typology of rule, which places the state at one end of a spectrum, distinct from such other means of regulating social life as the tribe, lineage or warrior band. The state is viewed as a recent phenomenon in human societies, distinguished by the continuous public power above ruler and ruled, in which authority is divorced from the personality of the leader. Krader, for example, defines the state as 'a nonprimitive form of government. Unlike primitive forms of government the agencies of government by the state are usually explicit, complex, and formal.' It is associated with large and stratified populations, and provides a means of integration and coordination.[10] From this rather different point of departure some strikingly different conclusions flow. Such typologies might, for example, emphasise law rather than warfare as a significant feature of states.[11] The state is not defined here in terms of very specific institutional forms, but its function is central to the definition. Again, then, the question of what the state does is to some extent foreclosed by the definition of the state – the functions of the state are not the subject of the inquiry but among its premises. For example, in controversies over 'hydraulic civilisation' or the relationship between the origins of the state and of social stratification, the function of the state is central to its definition. In the first case, the state is seen as a response to the needs of agriculture based on irrigation, and so it is a regulatory and coordinating institution. In the latter, the state emerges to protect property and social order in settled agricultural societies of a particular level of complexity. In these views the state is defined partly institutionally, but these institutions are not separated from their functional purposes – the state is both an institutional and functional form.[12]

In current social histories of England between 1550 and 1640 (which owe much to village studies informed by anthropological methods) the state is portrayed as something altogether more active and effective than in the accounts of fiscal-military state building. In Wrightson's view, for example, 'it is surely beyond serious contention that the "increase in

---

[10] L. Krader, *Formation of the State* (Englewood-Cliffs, 1968), 13.

[11] See, for example, S. Roberts, *Order and Dispute* (London, 1979).

[12] The literature here is extensive. See, among others, R. Cohen and E. R. Service (eds.), *Origins of the State: the Anthropology of Political Evolution* (Philadelphia, 1978) and H. J. M. Claessen and P. Skalnik (eds.), *The Early State* (The Hague, 1978). For a recent account of Welsh state formation informed by this literature, see R. A. Jones, 'Problems with medieval local administration – the case of the *maenor* and the *maenol*', *Journal of Historical Geography*, 24 (1998), 135–46.

governance" under Elizabeth and the early Stuarts enhanced the "infrastructural strength" and effective presence of the early modern state in the localities'.[13] The emphasis here is not so much on institutional change as on increased functional efficiency and competence. Again, the key figures are local elites, but in this context they appear to have been increasingly active and effective. In this respect the state was responding to domestic rather than international pressures.

Before 1640, fiscal-military failure provides a contrast with the effectiveness of social regulation. Both depended, ultimately, on local officeholders, who were responding to different demands with contrasting effects. Rather than accept that one set of functions represent the activities of the 'state' and that the other did not, the approach adopted here is to seek a definition of the state which embraces local officeholders. Even though these offices were not centrally located or modern in form, they embodied political power which was coordinated from a single centre. From this starting point, their role in the functioning of the state can be more easily embraced. But more importantly, by expanding the definition of the state in this way, a wider range of functions is revealed, and an account of the state emerges which is much less concerned with the 'centre'. Initiatives relating to the use of these offices arose both in the localities and at the centre, in relation to both domestic and international needs, and could reflect either ideological or material interests. If, then, we broaden the institutional definition of the state to include local officeholders, we are struck by a contrast in the period before 1640 between the failure of the state in some functions and its success in others, a contrast not revealed by a concentration either on the institutions of government located at the centre or on a narrower range of functions of government. The crucial question, therefore, is whether these local officers can be said to have been agents of the state.

A MIND WITHOUT A BODY: THE STATE AND POLITICAL POWER

Weber, whose name is often invoked in discussions of the state, argued that the essence of the state is the control of political power. What distinguishes the state from other organisations is the distinctive kind of power that it represents, not any particular functional purpose or institutional form.

Sociologically, the state cannot be defined in terms of its ends. There is hardly any task that some political association has not taken in hand, and there is no

---

[13] K. Wrightson and D. Levine, *Poverty and Piety in an English Village: Terling, 1525–1700*, 2nd edn (Oxford, 1995), 201.

task that one could say has always been exclusive and peculiar to those associations which are designated as political ones: today the state, or historically, those associations which have been the predecessors of the modern state. Ultimately, one can define the modern state sociologically only in terms of the specific *means* peculiar to it, as to every political association, namely, the use of physical force . . . Of course, force is certainly not the normal or the only means of the state – nobody says that – but force is a means specific to the state.[14]

An agent of state authority has access to a distinctive kind of power and it is that which distinguishes him or (rarely in our period) her from other individuals. Local officeholders exercised political power and were part of a territorially bounded, centrally coordinated network of such offices. These offices were not bureaucratic in form but the whole network is, it will be argued, recognisable as a kind of state. This definition is defensible both in terms of modern sociological theory and also later sixteenth-century usage. An obvious implication is that the issue of the precise form and function of the state is left open – what form state power assumed and to what ends it was directed are matters of inquiry rather than of initial definition.

In what sense, then, did local officeholders exercise political power? Or, to put it another way, what distinguished the power exercised by a constable (say) from the power of a landlord or a father, given that one man might have been all three? Firstly, political power resides in offices, not persons. In practice, particular personal attributes are usually necessary to hold office, but the authoritative power depends on holding the office and not on the possession of particular attributes – when an individual loses office s/he loses the power that goes with it. The power exercised by an officeholder is a collective resource, embodied in, but not deriving from, the individual.

Secondly, offices are defined in terms of specific functions and territories.[15] It is not possible to define political power in relation to any particular function, but it is possible to say that it is always functionally limited and territorially bounded.[16] Constables, fathers and landlords all had legitimate powers, but those of a father were exercised over

---

[14] M. Weber, 'Politics as a vocation', reprinted in H. H. Gerth and C. Wright Mills (eds.), *From Max Weber: Essays in Sociology* (London, 1991), 77–128, quotation at pp. 77–8. See also G. Poggi, *The State: Its Nature, Development and Prospects* (Oxford, 1990), 14.

[15] See also Giddens' discussion of the control of 'allocative resources': A. Giddens, *The Nation-State and Violence* (Oxford, 1985), ch. 1.

[16] For territory as an intrinsic feature of the state, see Weber, 'Politics as a vocation', esp. p. 78. For an interesting case study, developing some of the implications of this, see Jones, '*Maenor* and *maenol*'. For a stimulating discussion of the relationship between authority over people and over territory, see P. Seed, 'Taking possession and reading texts: establishing the authority of overseas empires', *William and Mary Quarterly*, 3rd series, 49 (1992), 183–209.

relations, and a landlord had power over those in a contractual relationship with him. The constable, by contrast, had power over all the inhabitants of a territory, in relation to particular functions – unlike a father or landlord, he exercised a kind of power that had specified territorial and functional bounds. The nature of those territorial and functional bounds can vary considerably, but the fact that the scope of an office is defined in this way distinguishes the power of offices from other kinds of power. It was the definition of those bounds that gave definition to the office and within those limits the officeholder's power was backed by the threat of legitimate force.

Thirdly, therefore, the threat of legitimate force is also an important feature of political power. Force is not the usual means by which the state acts, but it is particular to the state. It is also significant that Weber defined the state in terms of the *legitimate* use of force.[17] States do not have monopolies of force, even of legitimate force, however. Individuals such as parents, for example, can exert force generally recognised to be legitimate. But the state is the ultimate arbiter of what *constitutes* legitimate force within its territory and as a consequence its own ultimate sanction is force. It is the combination of these features – territoriality, functional definition and the ultimate threat of legitimate force – that distinguishes political power. One man acting as a constable was playing a different social role, and had access to a different kind of power, than the same man acting as a father or as a landlord.

Local officeholders exercised a distinctively political power – it was territorially and functionally specific, and within those bounds it was backed up by legitimate force. Collectively, these offices constituted a 'state' in the sense that they were part of a territorially bounded and coordinated network, which was exclusive of the authority of rival political organisations within those limits. They were all legitimated with reference to, and coordinated by, a single centre and constituted, collectively, a single political organisation. The crucial issue, here, is that the state is not being defined in terms of form – for example, bureaucracy or centrally located institutions – or in terms of particular functions – making war or keeping the peace, for example. It is defined instead by the kind of power that is distinctive to it. The forms assumed by this power, and the uses to which it was put, are the object of the enquiry, rather than part of the definition of its terms.

[17] 'The state is a human community that (successfully) claims *the monopoly of the legitimate use of physical force* within a given territory': Weber, 'Politics as a vocation', p. 78 (emphasis in the original). Legitimate force is not simply force, *per se*. This is, therefore, a distinct position from that taken by Poggi: Poggi, *State*, esp. pp. 4–6.

There was a state in England in 1550 in the sense that there was a network of offices wielding political power derived from a coordinating centre by formal means – commission, charter or specific command (warrant). The network was exclusive of other political powers within particular territorial bounds under the Tudor crown, and it makes sense to analyse this network as a whole. The authority of all these bodies derived from a centre – it was an integrated and weakly centralised network – but they were not centrally located. What is usually taken to be a Weberian definition of the state, in terms of centralised, differentiated institutions, is here considered an ideal-type of the *modern* state – a theoretical construct against which to compare observed social realities. Divergences from this ideal-type can reveal what was not modern about the early modern state, for example that it was only a partially differentiated and weakly coordinated state. As a coordinated network of territorially bounded offices exercising political power it is, none the less, recognisable to us as a kind of state.[18]

This rather abstract view is justifiable in terms of twentieth-century social theory, but also in terms of early modern understanding, for it was in this period, it has been persuasively argued, that such a notion took shape in European thought.[19] The English-speaking world was not immune to this development.

It is striking that, whereas in 1500 the word 'state' had possessed no political meaning in English beyond the 'state or condition' of the prince or the kingdom, by the second half of Elizabeth's reign it was used to signify the 'state' in the modern sense. In the reigns of Henry VII and Henry VIII politicians had spoken only of 'country', 'people', 'kingdom', and 'realm', but by the 1590s they began to conceptualize the 'state'.[20]

---

[18] For differentiation see Poggi, *State*, pp. 20–1. It would be possible to argue that this network was not a state, but some other kind of political association. In the passage cited above, pp. 16–17, Weber is distinguishing between the modern state and the forms of political association that preceded it. I am suggesting here that the subject of this study is the early modern state – a political association resembling the ideal-type of the modern state but diverging from it. Readers offended by the term 'state' in this context might substitute the phrase 'territorially bounded and coordinated network of agents exercising political power'. In that case this study might be glossed as a discussion of the rise of the state from among a collection of other political institutions – in effect, a narrative of the emergence of the state as a distinctive form of political association. In a sense this is not a matter of crucial importance because the story being told here would be essentially the same – in order to understand the rise of the state it would be necessary to understand the functioning and weaknesses of the forms of political association that preceded its emergence.

[19] Q. Skinner, *The Foundations of Modern Political Thought*, 2 vols. (Cambridge, 1976). For the comparison with Weber, see esp. I, pp. ix–x.

[20] J. Guy, *Tudor England* (Oxford, 1988), 352. The emergence of the term in England is discussed ibid., ch. 13. A broadly similar case is made for England by Skinner, *Foundations*, II, esp. pp. 356–8.

The term appears in a recognisably modern sense with some frequency in privy council correspondence of the 1590s[21] and royal proclamations of the 1620s used it with some familiarity. So, for example, in proclaiming against public discussion of foreign affairs in 1620, James I condemned 'lavish and licentious speech in matters of state'.[22] In 1625, in justifying the assumption of direct responsibility for the government of Virginia, in place of the Virginia Company, Charles I proclaimed that 'the Government of the Colonie of Virginia shall immediately depend upon Our Selfe and not to be committed to any Companie or Corporation, to whom it may be proper to trust matters of Trade and Commerce, but cannot be fit or safe to communicate the ordering of State-affaires be they of never so meane consequence'.[23] The sphere of action which is being studied here can be defined as activities and matters of state, and that definition would have been comprehensible to increasing numbers of contemporaries.

EMBODIMENTS OF THE STATE: POLITICAL OFFICES IN EARLY MODERN ENGLAND

The state, as a general category, is defined by the kind of power that it exercises, rather than the specific uses made of that power or the institutional forms through which it is expressed – it is, in a general sense, a mind without a body. The state is embodied in political offices whose form and purpose vary between states and over time. The particular institutional forms of these agencies and uses made of this power in any particular context are an open question, rather than part of the definition of the state itself. What is to be explained is not the rise or growth of 'the' state, but the changing forms of state power – for example, the development of the 'modern' or, perhaps, the 'postmodern' state. Although we are primarily interested in the functions of the state, we have not made a particular set of functions part of our definition of the state itself. Instead, the issue of how a 'mind without a body' was embodied in early modern England is a matter of empirical enquiry.

---

[21] For examples, see below, pp. 29 n.43, 56, 288, 321. Q. Skinner, 'The state', in T. Ball, J. Farr and R. L. Hanson (eds.), *Political Innovation and Conceptual Change* (Cambridge, 1989), 90–131.

[22] Quoted in T. Cogswell, *The Blessed Revolution: English Politics and the Coming of War, 1621–1624* (Cambridge, 1989), 20.

[23] Quoted in R. M. Bliss, *Revolution and Empire: English Politics and the American Colonies in the Seventeenth Century* (Manchester, 1990), 19–20. Of course, companies continued to exercise governmental functions long after 1625: see below, ch. 9.

The state is embodied in offices, and differences between states over time and between places are differences in the forms of office. It is argued here that there are three dimensions of the 'form' of an office or institution – its functional purpose, its territorial competence, and the characteristic ways in which it is legitimated. The first two points, about territorial and functional definition of offices, require little elaboration, of course. Less familiar is the claim that forms of legitimation shape offices. For example, in a modern bureaucracy, impersonal norms distance the individual from his or her exercise of office – bureaucrats have no personal control over their actions, they are simply implementing the rules or 'doing their job'. A civil servant implementing such rules is acting in a role, which makes clear the distance between the individual and their office – bureaucratic legitimation requires from individuals particular performances and languages of justification. Early modern magistrates, acting as fathers of their country, explained and justified their actions with reference to different values, and in order to appear credible had to act in different ways. The languages and performances which legitimated their actions, therefore, gave to their offices a distinctive form. Legitimacy is not simply about the formal limits of office, but also about appropriate behaviour and comportment on the part of officeholders – the expression and legitimation of political power has a cultural and intellectual dimension. Early modern officeholders generally used different languages to legitimate their activities and this gave their offices a distinctive 'form', quite different from the rational, differentiated bureaucracies of modern states. But they were, none the less, exercising political power.[24]

Some of these abstract arguments can be illustrated with reference to the central offices of the early modern state, and this serves also to introduce the empirical discussion which follows in the rest of the book. At the centre of the early modern state were offices which conferred legal validity on administrative action. They legitimated decisions and crucial to this was the depersonalisation of authority and the taking of counsel. Kings could not make law by their will alone, and were expected to act in the light of advice. The English monarchy was limited (but also enabled) by formal procedures which gave legal validity to particular kinds of action, and by adherence to less formal expectations about appropriate behaviour. What separated a tyrant from a monarch was, in part, adherence to the legal forms which the incumbent swore to

---

[24] The idea of offices as social roles is discussed below, pp. 71–8.

uphold at his or her coronation. The obligation to take advice, 'counsel', was of similarly crucial significance. In all, the crown operated within limits set by legal forms and by more informal expectations about what constituted good government. In practice, royal charisma – the sacred authority of the monarch – was routinely represented in writs of standard form circulating throughout the realm.

One way of glossing a standard theme of seventeenth-century history is by saying that these formal legitimations became more routine and more codified. The debate about the Tudor revolution in government has tended to downplay the suddenness or coherence of the changes in central administration during the 1530s, but at the heart of claims for modernisation was precisely this issue – the formalisation of procedure which had the effect of limiting the impact of the personal wishes of the monarch. Constraints had been imposed earlier, and monarchical caprice continued to be important thereafter, and the emphasis of most accounts is now on more protracted and complex adjustments.[25] None the less, over this period as a whole the formal constraints on the powers of monarchs did increase. Commands might be authenticated by a variety of seals or warrants, and the rules governing these legitimations were complex, the preserve of specialists commanding technical knowledge.[26] The monarchy, as a network of offices, was increasingly powerful, although the personal power of the monarch had been reduced. To this might be added the less familiar example of the development of public borrowing.[27]

Alongside these formal legitimations monarchs were also constrained by less formal conventions, in particular the expectation that they would take counsel: 'Few things, if anything, were more central to medieval political thought than the belief that a good ruler took counsel from a wide variety of sources.'[28] There was a variety of more or less institutional means by which this counsel was offered. The royal court, the privy council and parliament provided, in Elton's famous phrase, 'points of contact' between the Tudor monarchs and their subjects. The court, for example, served to focus political ambition on the person of

---

[25] G. R. Elton, *The Tudor Revolution in Government: Administrative Changes in the Reign of Henry VIII* (Cambridge, 1953); C. Coleman and D. Starkey (eds.), *Revolution Reassessed: Revisions in the History of Tudor Government and Administration* (Oxford, 1986); Guy, *Tudor England*, ch. 6.

[26] For discussions of these arrangements see G. R. Elton, *The Tudor Constitution: Documents and Commentary* (Cambridge, 1960), esp. ch. 3; P. Williams, *The Tudor Regime* (Oxford, 1979), ch. 1.

[27] For which see below, ch. 6.

[28] C. Russell, 'The nature of a parliament in early Stuart England', in H. Tomlinson (ed.), *Before the English Civil War: Essays on Early Stuart Politics and Government* (London, 1983), 123–50, 202–6, quotation at p. 129.

the monarch and thereby neutralised alternative power centres. But it also created stability. 'Government . . . cannot work unless it obtains obedience and (preferably) consent from the governed' and 'any system needs to include organized means – public structures – to provide for the ambitions at the centre of affairs of such persons as can, if those ambitions remain unsatisfied, upset that stability'.[29] The court offered place and employment, particularly in the Household, but more importantly gave access to the monarch. Those with influence at court acted as mediators between petitioners and the king and therefore enjoyed power. Among these people alliances formed, seeking to influence decision-making. The result was that Tudor monarchs were 'managed at worst, and manoeuvred at best, by the purposeful groupings of interest that articulated the nation's politics'.[30] The court was thus a means of integrating not just ambition but also opinion into politics.

Two other institutions also served as 'points of contact' in this way – the privy council and parliament. By the late sixteenth century it is reasonable to talk of a privy council in generalised, functional terms, although there is some debate about when such a body had emerged. Like the court, it provided an avenue for ambition and a channel of communication, but it was to a degree open to men of lower social status. Its deliberative and administrative functions were poorly differentiated: on any given day the council might deal with a great variety of issues, from mundane matters of local administration to discussion of foreign policy. It was this pressure of business that prevented effective oversight of the activities of local governors in the 1620s and, probably, earlier.[31] Parliament, of course, offered contact with the broadest spectrum of opinion: 'Parliament, as all agreed, represented the nation', and it was axiomatic in law that the consent of parliament was the consent of the whole realm.[32] But this representation was brought to bear intermit-

---

[29] G. R. Elton, 'Tudor Government: the points of contact', reprinted in Elton, *Studies in Tudor and Stuart Politics and Government*, vol. III, *Papers and Reviews 1973–1981* (Cambridge, 1983), 3–57, quotations at pp. 2, 4.

[30] Ibid., p. 50. For the concept of 'faction' see E. W. Ives, *Faction in Tudor England* (Historical Association Pamphlet, 1979). The importance of faction in the formulation of policy is, of course, controversial.

[31] For the origins of the privy council: J. A. Guy, 'The privy council: revolution or evolution?' in Coleman and Starkey, *Revolution*, 59–85; and D. Starkey, 'Introduction: court history in perspective', in D. Starkey *et al.*, *The English Court from the Wars of the Roses to the Civil War* (London, 1987), 1–24. For the administrative pressures and inefficiencies, see D. Hirst, 'The privy council and the problem of enforcement in the 1620s', *JBS*, 18 (1978), 46–66; B. W. Quintrell, 'Government in perspective: Lancashire and the privy council, 1570–1640', *Transactions of the Historic Society of Lancashire and Cheshire*, 131 (1982 for 1981), 35–62.

[32] Elton, 'Points of contact', p. 22; Russell, 'Nature of a parliament'.

tently. Parliament's powers of legislation and taxation were considerable, but that did not give the Houses control over policy, and that does
not appear to have been an ambition of the members, either.[33] None the
less, parliament provided a resource for local interest groups – lobbies
could secure statutory backing for particular local initiatives.[34]

All this implies, of course, that there was much more to the agency of
the state than monarchical will. The apparatus of central government
authenticated decisions by delivering them in legal form and at the same
time channelled advice, petitions and counsel. The result was government through, rather than by, the monarch and the impetus for political
action could come from a variety of sources. Courtiers, councillors and
members of parliament, responding to a wider circle of clients and
petitioners, raised issues of concern and suggested legitimate means of
dealing with them. This was true in the localities too, as officeholders
responded to perceived challenges and opportunities with initiatives of
their own. The poor law, as we will see, grew out of such local initiatives
and is a good illustration of the fact that the development of the state was
not a matter of central, still less monarchical will – the poor law of the
later sixteenth century were Elizabethan, not Elizabeth's.

As a means of legitimation much of this seems unfamiliar to modern
eyes. Counsel mitigated the views and passions of the monarch. It was
given on the basis of a sense of representation but what was being
represented was, in theory, not a range of opinion.[35] Counsel was
intended to be disinterested and those with the power to offer advice laid
claim to moral authority, rather than a popular or party mandate. As a
consequence, criticism of these people was frequently expressed in these
terms, rather than articulating more obviously political objections to
details of policy. Courtiers, councillors and members of parliament all
filled social roles defined in terms of wider values and expectations and
political attacks often took the form of social or moral criticism. Un-

---

[33] Although these brief remarks are relatively uncontentious, they conceal considerable controversy. For summaries see M. A. R. Graves, *The Tudor Parliaments: Crown, Lords and Commons,
1485–1603* (London, 1985); P. Williams, *The Later Tudors: England 1547–1603* (Oxford, 1995),
135–41.

[34] D. Dean, *Law-Making and Society in Late Elizabethan England: The Parliament of England, 1584–1601*
(Cambridge, 1996); I. W. Archer, 'The London lobbies in the later sixteenth century', *HJ*, 31
(1988), 17–44.

[35] J. Guy, 'The rhetoric of counsel in early modern England', in D. Hoak (ed.), *Tudor Political Culture*
(Cambridge, 1995), 292–310. Before the later seventeenth century 'opinion' was frequently
juxtaposed to 'judgement' and 'truth' – to be governed by opinion was a danger to the
commonwealth. See, for example, D. Freist, *Governed by Opinion: Politics, Religion and the Dynamics of
Communication in Stuart London 1637–1645* (London, 1997), 1–5.

popular privy councillors were said to be socially unfit for office, rather than politically misguided or ineffective, and subversive comment about monarchs frequently took the form of commentary on their moral qualities. As Henry, 5th earl of Huntingdon, told his household, the issue of household order was central to his capacity to govern:

for makinge the worlde to carry a providente opinion of me in this which in proportion doth nearest resemble the government in publicke offices which men of my rancke are verie often called unto and do most com[m]only happen unto them for as a learned writer sayeth as of molle hils are made mountaines so of divers families are made Cities so of Cities com[m]onwealthes therfore if I faile in the lesse then the which ther can be no greater dishonor it followeth of necessitie I shall never be capable of the greater.[36]

This was not, then, a bureaucratic state – the legitimacy that such people enjoyed was not that of a rational bureaucracy. None the less, some of the offices of state were closer to that model of authority, depending on a close formal specification of their powers and of due process. Legislation and the administration of justice were crucial to early modern government, with the result that law and government were intimately related. 'Lawyers could expect to be involved in government primarily because government was carried on in legal institutions and according to legal forms . . . public administration was inextricably caught up in the terminology and procedures of the law.'[37] The crown was the fount of justice as well as of patronage and honour, and its will was normally expressed through legal documents. The management of the crown's resources was carried out by courts of law, particularly the exchequer, and the other great courts were also closely connected with government. Chancery authenticated royal commands with the Great Seal, for example, and Star Chamber originated in the privy council sitting judicially. Executive will was expressed through a complex of offices – the signet, the privy seal and the Great Seal – and alongside them the secretaries of state and the privy council. All these offices gave voice and form to monarchical authority, with varying degrees of formality. In all they formed a kind of bureaucracy, a 'central machine',[38] and around this core of London government there developed a range of full-time functionaries, among them professional lawyers.

[36] HEH, HAP Box 14 (18), Henry, fifth earl of Huntingdon, a draft set of instructions to his household regarding behaviour in his absence.
[37] W. R. Prest, *The Rise of the Barristers: A Social History of the English Bar 1590–1640* (Oxford, 1986), 236–7.
[38] For concise discussions see, Williams, *Tudor Regime*, pp. 39–43; Williams, *Later Tudors*, pp. 141–4.

These formal and impersonal procedures provided agreed and routine means by which to legitimate particular kinds of decisions.

By this period a range of institutions had developed which carried out carefully defined functions, and whose relationships were governed by elaborate and repetitive procedures. Counsel was taken, decisions made and commands issued according to complex (and of course contested) rules. The central courts not only offered justice to the subject but authenticated and executed administrative decisions. In part this served to authenticate commands, or to provide the means to ensure that commands of particular kinds had been made by agreed means, through the proper channels. The receipt and issue of money, for example, was governed by complex rules, interpreted by specialists holding offices that had evolved over a very long period. Royal commands were made, or were delegated, by agreed means and approved under a variety of seals to signify compliance with accepted procedures. To those who oversaw their operation, and to those who were subject to it, these institutions had a life of their own. Legitimacy, and legal form, were intersubjective – they were the outcome of collective agreements, often enshrined in complicated procedural rules, and were not under the control of individuals. It is the growing importance of the impersonal, intersubjective, legitimation and authentication of decision-making that lies at the heart of Elton's claims about the Tudor revolution in government. Whatever the merits of Elton's thesis this essential proposition is sound – that routinisation and bureaucratisation depersonalised political authority. The 'course of the exchequer', for example, was thought to be something, once underway, which could not be diverted by individual effort.[39] The absence of discretion was of crucial importance to the legitimacy of these kinds of office.

In all, the centre of the early modern state was small. The privy council consisted of a dozen or so people, the court a few dozen more, and parliament a few hundred. Many of these people held local office and, particularly members of the House of Commons, would not necessarily have identified themselves as representatives of the centre. Alongside the court, council and parliament, institutions which were to some extent empowered by social prestige, rather than formal rules, were more bureaucratic institutions. The operation of these latter offices

[39] M. J. Braddick, *Parliamentary Taxation in Seventeenth-Century England: Local Administration and Response*, Royal Historical Society, Studies in History, 70 (Woodbridge, 1994), 30–8, 161–2; Braddick, 'Resistance to the royal aid and further supply in Chester, 1664–1672: relations between centre and locality in restoration England', *Northern History*, 33 (1997), 108–36, esp. p. 120.

was in the hands of functionaries of various kinds, representing collectively a kind of proto-bureaucracy. 'Bureaucracy' because there were broad similarities between the means of entry and preferment and in the forms of remuneration between separate institutions. 'Proto'-bureaucracy because these terms were relatively informal. Office was secured through patronage and preferment, remuneration received in fees charged on the subject rather than in the form of a salary paid for service.[40] The size of this proto-bureaucracy was also small. During Elizabeth's reign there were probably fewer than 1,000 officials receiving salaries or fees from the crown, of whom some hundreds were in the localities rather than London.[41]

Although these forms of office are quite alien to modern eyes, they are recognisable as component parts of a kind of state. In describing the actions of these offices, that is, the functioning of the state, we are actually describing decisions and actions taken by particular people. The history of these institutions and offices is therefore the history of individuals, but individuals who were acting as officeholders – their behaviour was constrained by the formal and informal limits of their office played out in a collectively understood social role. The exercise of political power depended on the action of individuals, but these people did not act freely. The state was embodied in individuals who, in exercising an office, laid claim to a distinctively political power and were both empowered and constrained by that claim.

THE EMBODIMENT OF THE STATE IN THE LOCALITIES

This book is principally concerned with the impact of the state in English villages and wards. Examination of this level of politics reveals a new set of constraints on government: the formal and informal limits of action imposed on the agents of state authority in the localities. Once an initiative had legal form it became, to an extent, a matter of policy, sanctioned by the executive. This 'governmental will' operated through local officeholders who were, in this sense 'intermediaries', mediating policy in the light of local interests. In addition to mediating governmental will, however, groups in the localities sought legal validity for their own political innovations – there were local initiatives alongside central initiatives. Both kinds of initiative were, of course, mediated and this allowed for further local influence, of a more informal kind. In

[40] G. E. Aylmer, *The King's Servants: The Civil Service of Charles I, 1625–1642* (London, 1961), esp. chs. 2–4.   [41] A. G. R. Smith, *The Government of Elizabethan England* (London, 1967), 54.

numerous ways, then, the legitimation of local office affected the ways in which state power was actually used in the localities. In effect, local agents of state authority constantly exercised discretion in implementing their formal powers: there is another level of political decision-making here.

Most government activities were carried out with the cooperation of pre-existing elites through the hierarchy of officeholding. Whereas territorial potentates and great magnates might aspire to positions at court and in council, ambitious village notables aspired to positions at the bottom end of the hierarchy of local officeholding. In addition to this hierarchy of officeholders, however, there were other local agencies, empowered by charter or licence. If decision-making involved participation as a result of more or less formal requirements to take counsel, the execution of policy depended on a variety of intermediaries who were also responding to pressure when they interpreted their duties in the light of local circumstances. Here, again, a notable feature of the system was participation. A corollary of this was that the terms on which participation was forthcoming affected, intimately and crucially, what could be achieved through these intermediaries or, to put it another way, how ordinary people experienced the power of the state.

Much attention has been paid to local officeholding in recent years and there is no need to discuss it in detail here.[42] At the head of the county administration was the lord lieutenant, primarily, but not only, a military office. This office was characteristic of local offices in a number of ways, not least in the fact that it was evolving in this period. As in the case of the account of the institutions of government at the centre, what is offered here is a snapshot of a continually evolving network: a 'static approximation' of the later sixteenth-century state. The lieutenancy had an intermittent existence in the early Tudor period, but after 1549 the office lapsed. The real impetus for the establishment of a lieutenancy in each county came from 1585 onward, in response to the military demands of the Spanish war, the threat of invasion and internal subversion.[43] However, during the 1590s it was

---

[42] For a good recent summary of the early Stuart position, see M. Kishlansky, *A Monarchy Transformed: Britain 1603–1714* (London, 1996), ch. 2.

[43] G. S. Thomson, *Lords Lieutenants in the Sixteenth Century* (London, 1923). For a convenient summary, see Smith, *Government*, pp. 86–90. His account differs slightly from that of Fletcher, who dates the full emergence of the lieutenancy to the early Stuart period: A. Fletcher, *Reform in the Provinces: The Government of Stuart England* (London, 1986), 282. In the autumn of 1586, in the aftermath of the Babington plot, existing lieutenants were required to undertake searches for Jesuits and priests and it was suggested that they should be appointed in every county: J. Goring and J. Wake (eds.), *Northamptonshire Lieutenancy Papers and other Documents 1580–1614*, Northamptonshire Record Society, 27 (Northampton, 1975), xvii; J. S. Nolan, 'The muster of 1588', *Albion*,

not thought necessary for every county to have a lord lieutenant.[44]

Under Elizabeth all lords lieutenant were peers and some were privy councillors too. A number of lieutenants had charge of more than one county and because of their pre-eminence it was necessary to hand over some of the more routine matters of administration to deputies, particularly in the 1590s. Deputies were appointed by lords lieutenant and numbers varied according to local need. Unlike some of their superiors, however, deputy lieutenants held office in only one county. In addition to its military duties – organising the militia and raising troops for service abroad – the lieutenancy was also an agency for the raising of loans – lieutenants were responsible for the provision of a list of men of substance along with estimates of what they might be required to lend. They also served as monitors of local government, for example, reporting on the conduct of the justices of the peace or the imposition of the penal laws against Catholic recusants. The attraction of the office may not be obvious, but the lords lieutenant commanded an important channel of information between the privy council, which oversaw their activity, and the locality – the compensation for performing unpleasant tasks under the direct supervision of the privy council was that in doing so their local status was confirmed. Their access to the privy council and the weighty nature of their tasks confirmed the status which was the basis for their selection. The lieutenancy is thus characteristic of much Elizabethan local government in several ways. Firstly, service was regarded as a confirmation of standing and a source of further status. Secondly, because this was the case, the social hierarchy and the political hierarchy were very close, a recipe for stability. Further, we will examine later an implication of this for the system as a whole: that if social standing was jeopardised by the execution of an administrative task then that service might not be performed.[45]

---

23 (1991), 387–407; HEH, HM 30881, fos. 32–6 (1586); *CSPD, 1581–90*, p. 352. They were also to encourage the justices to control false rumours by having a due regard 'to such as at tymes of faiers, marketts or any other assemblies of people in Inns or Alehouses, shall give out any matter that either directlie or indirectlie maye tend to the disquieting of the state, or ingendring of any misconceipt in the peoples mindes': HEH, HM 30881, fo. 20v. Certainly, Lambarde thought the lieutenancy a temporary expedient. The extra-ordinary conservator of the peace of Edward III's reign, 'as he was endowed with an higher power, so was he not ordinarily appointed, but in the times of great troubles only, much like as the Lieutenants of Shires are now in our days': W. Lambarde, *Eirenarcha Or of the Office of Iustice of the Peace, in Foure Bookes* (London, 1599), 18. A similar passage appears in earlier editions.

44 Goring and Wake (eds.), *Northamptonshire*.

45 For a general view of this tension posed by the duties of the lieutenancy, see V. L. Stater, *Noble Government: The Stuart Lord Lieutenancy and the Transformation of English Politics* (Athens, Ga., 1994), Introduction and ch. 1. For important local studies: A. H. Smith, *County and Court: Government and Politics in Norfolk 1558–1603* (Oxford, 1974); T. G. Barnes, *Somerset 1625–1640: A County's Government during the 'Personal Rule'* (Chicago, 1982); Cogswell, *Home Divisions*.

Theoretically superior to the lord lieutenant, but in practice next in line, was the sheriff.[46] This was an office of very ancient origin, and the sheriff was in principle the chief legal representative of the crown in the county. The importance of the office was declining but this did not mean that the labours of the sheriff were any less burdensome. He presided over the monthly court, which increasingly dealt only with small claims, outlawries and the management of elections. Sheriffs also empanelled juries, oversaw the production of defendants and the carrying out of sentences. When royal writs were issued to individuals within the county they were directed through the sheriff and he was responsible for the ancient revenues. He was thus responsible for some onerous judicial and administrative functions, and yet had little executive power. As a result, the shrievalty became unpopular, still more so because the incumbent ended up out of pocket for his pains. Sheriffs had to pay a fine on entry to the office and a fee to settle their account at the exchequer, as well as the salary of the undersheriff and hospitality for visiting dignitaries.[47] The only times when the shrievalty was really attractive was during a parliamentary election, the oversight of which was a responsibility of the sheriff. In these circumstances the sheriffs had considerable power, but for the most part the position was onerous and offered few compensations. In some counties there was such reluctance to serve that among the leading gentry appointment to the shrievalty could be used as a punishment – if a gentleman was chosen for the shrievalty, he could not serve in the more attractive position of justice of the peace. But the shrievalty could also offer a means for aspiring gentry to establish themselves among the county elite.

The backbone of Elizabethan local government was the commission of the peace, and its individuals members, the justices of the peace.[48] Commissions of the peace tended to grow in both size and importance in this period. At the beginning of the Tudor period there were about ten justices per shire, by the middle of Elizabeth's reign about forty or fifty and by the end of the sixteenth century commissions were larger still. Not all the men named to the commissions were active, however, and the increase in size reflected not just the growing pressure of work but also a growing demand for place. Service as a justice was a mark of

---

[46] For general accounts, see Smith, *Government*, ch. 7; Barnes, *Somerset*, ch. 5. For the civil war period, see J. Mather, 'The civil war sheriff: his person and office', *Albion*, 13 (1981), 242–61.

[47] The president of the Council of the Marches in the later seventeenth century, for example, received a large number of requests for exemption from service: HEH, EL 7079, 7101, 7146, 7172, 7175, 7180, 7197, 7199, 7204–06, 7227, 7236, 7253, 7274–75, 7288.

[48] For general accounts see Smith, *Government*, pp. 90–7; Fletcher, *Reform*, esp. chs. 1, 3.

social distinction and to be left off the commission could be a great snub for eminent gentlemen. None the less, the increasing size of the commissions was paralleled by an expansion of the range of duties too. In 1599, 306 statutes placed duties on the shoulders of the justices. Of these, 133 dated from before 1485, 60 from the period 1485–1547, 38 from the period 1547–58, and a further 75 from the period 1558–97.[49]

A single justice had wide summary powers over a range of misdemeanours and some civil jurisdiction over disputes between masters and apprentices and cases of bastardy, for example. They were also, by the later sixteenth century, important in the policing of Catholicism and to the implementation of the legislation concerning poverty. In tandem with another justice they had power over more serious criminal acts – riot, for example – and the range of administrative functions was also increasing – for example, licensing alehouses, regulating the grain trade and overseeing the accounts of the sheriffs. All these powers were subordinate to those wielded by the members of the commission acting together, the bench. In most counties the bench assembled collectively four times each year to hear a variety of business, especially criminal and administrative, at the quarter sessions. The bench could try murder, assault, burglary, witchcraft, disorderly conduct, vagrancy and a host of minor offences. It had the power to impose the death penalty, at least until the 1580s when this was restricted, if not eliminated. The administrative powers covered the whole range of social policies from wage rates to oversight of the houses of correction. In addition to filling continuous offices such as the commission of the peace, county gentlemen also acted in response to *ad hoc* commissions. For example, commissioners for parliamentary subsidies were likely to be drawn from the same group as the justices of the peace,[50] and the most active county magistrates tended to be involved in a variety of administrative duties.

During the seventeenth century, particularly after the restoration, but also earlier, the increasing amount of business handled collectively by the commission led to the development of petty sessions – divisional meetings held in parts of the county between general quarter sessions. This development owed much to local initiative.[51] Another example of

---

[49] Smith, *Government*, p. 91.   [50] Braddick, *Parliamentary*, pp. 65–71.
[51] For the development of institutional forms below the level of general sessions see F. A. Youngs, 'Towards petty sessions: Tudor JPs and the divisions of counties', in D. J. Guth and J. W. McKenna (eds.), *Tudor Rule and Revolution: Essays for G. R. Elton from his American Friends* (Cambridge, 1982), 201–16. For the later seventeenth century, see also below, p. 167; N. Landau, *The Justices of the Peace, 1679–1760* (Berkeley, 1984); and J. R. Kent, 'The centre and the localities: state formation and parish government in England circa 1640–1740', *HJ*, 38 (1995), 363–404.

the adaptability of local administration is the development of an informal forum for county business in Lancashire. There were no county
sessions and so the activities of the divisional sessions were not easy to
coordinate. This function was assumed by meetings of the justices at the
sheriff's table during assizes week. This was originally a means by which
the circuit judges could impress on the magistracy what were the
concerns of the crown. Increasingly, however, the meetings began to
acquire the initiative and they became a forum for the discussion of
administrative business affecting the county as a whole, making up for
the absence of general quarter sessions in the county.[52] These are,
therefore, significant examples of institutional change that occurred in
response to local demand.

All this activity was overseen by the monarch and the privy council,
who issued the commissions. The supervision could not be too strict,
however. Justices served voluntarily and yet they were essential to
government. The stick wielded by the central government was the status
which service as a justice brought. If a justice made himself so unpopular
with the privy council or with local rivals that he was dismissed, this was
a personal calamity. On the other hand, justices also responded to local
pressures and if these were very general, affecting all of them, the privy
council could do little about it – the privy council could not get rid of all
of the justices. This was the problem with taxation – local consensus that
accurate assessment was bad could not be circumvented. For example,
Leicestershire justices threatened with dismissal for failing to bring their
personal subsidy assessments to a level in line with a newly specified
minimum, sought to call the privy council's bluff. Those rated below the
specified level, it was said, 'think it too burthensome for their small
estates to be so rated, considering the daily charge they undergo by their
pains in his Majesty's several services. And therefore submit themselves
to your lordships' pleasure for the continuance of their places.'[53] This
essential office was more effective for some purposes than others, therefore, as there were limits to what could successfully be asked of these
officeholders.

[52] B. W. Quintrell (ed.), *Proceedings of the Lancashire Justices of the Peace at the Sheriff's Table during Assizes Week, 1578–1694*, Record Society of Lancashire and Cheshire, 121 (Chester, 1981). In Suffolk, in the later sixteenth century, 'general county meetings' developed, supplementing the work of the assizes. Again this development was at local initiative: D. MacCulloch, *Suffolk and the Tudors: Politics and Religion in an English County 1500–1600* (Oxford, 1986). For the assizes, see below, pp. 37–8.
[53] Quoted in J. Thirsk and J. P. Cooper (eds.), *Seventeenth-Century Economic Documents* (Oxford, 1972), 608. In April 1626 William Capell, a Somerset JP, claimed that he would positively welcome the prospect of dismissal as relief from the onerous duties that a place on the commission entailed: Barnes, *Somerset*, pp. 302–3.

In all cases these commissions were dependent on the activities of lesser officeholders, particularly the high constables and below them the village constable. High constables controlled a division of a county – a hundred, lathe or wapentake. They were selected by the justices of the peace from the ranks of the lesser gentry or even of the yeomanry. High constables were responsible for apportioning the burden of county-wide rates between townships, reporting to the quarter sessions or the assizes on local grievances and abuses, and overseeing the lowest level of administration, the petty or parish constables.[54] Petty constables have usually been given bad press, from Shakespeare onwards, but as the lowest representative of the state they deserve serious consideration. The constable, it has been suggested, 'seems to have been a kind of village headman, a leader of the township who enjoyed various responsibilities within its bounds, often of an agrarian nature, and who acted as its agent in its dealings with outsiders'.[55] The constables had their share in the stacks of statutes, dealing with crime, highways, poor relief, alehouses and regulation of the sale of meat, for example. It was also the constables who made presentments – reporting wrong-doers to the courts. They were not just the agents of justices of the peace, however, since the lieutenancy also depended on them: it was the constables who were responsible for ensuring attendance at musters and the maintenance of arms. Still more importantly, all taxation came through the constables – the subsidy, the fifteenth and tenth, county rates, ship money, purveyance. Without the cooperation of the constables none of the most important government policies could have been achieved, and in addition to these regular duties the constables also undertook all manner of other kinds of business, for example, administering the Protestation Oath of 1641. In that instance, constables were responsible for the appearance of all the inhabitants of their township to swear an oath to uphold the Protestant religion, the liberty of parliament and the unity between the three kingdoms of England, Scotland and Ireland.

[54] Less is known about high constables than about parish constables. There are some observations about the Cheshire high constables in J. S. Morrill, *The Cheshire Grand Jury, 1625–1659: A Social and Administrative Study*, Leicester University Department of English Local History, Occasional Papers, 3rd series (Leicester, 1976), 59–60. See also J. R. Kent, *The English Village Constable 1580–1642: A Social and Administrative Study* (Oxford, 1986), *passim*. For an (undated but probably late sixteenth-century) example of a charge to the high constables see HEH, EL 2525. It required them to pay particular attention to felonies, vagabonds, recusants and the regulation of alehouses. They were to 'take an accompte and reckoninge once everie fortnight or three weekes of the pettie Constables and other inferiour officers' and to report to the justices every month or six weeks. This charge is accompanied by articles which constables should present to the assizes: EL 2526.   [55] Kent, *Constable*, p. 15.

'While such duties did not constitute a very large, or perhaps very significant, part of the office, they further attest to the role of the constables in providing a link between the central government and local communities.'[56]

The people who filled such offices were thus crucial to the whole system. In some places the office went to holders of particular tenements, elsewhere constables were elected, or it was an office held in rotation among a group of householders. Formally they could be removed by a justice of the peace, but in practice they were representatives of local interests chosen without much direction from above. In many cases, 'Not only were constables usually chosen by local bodies, but they were also formally accountable to the local community.'[57] They were usually from the most substantial section of local society, and they were often literate.[58] They frequently held a series of offices in succession, as churchwardens, for example. In exercising their office constables responded both to administrative command and to local expectations of appropriate behaviour: 'the fact that the constable occupied a position where two distinct hierarchies of authority intersected, probably enhanced his ability to mediate between them, but it also made his position a focus of conflict'.[59] As with the higher offices of local government, local social status was enhanced or compounded by service as constable. In the villages of early modern England, all functions of government were mediated by officeholders whose role was conceived in broad, social terms which did not necessarily sit easily with all their tasks.

There are two observations about these local officeholders that are crucial for our purposes. Firstly, there was a great variety of commissions and writs but they were often acted upon by literally the same people. For example, militia and subsidy commissions were aimed at the same group of county gentlemen who provided the justices of the peace. Within this group there were more and less active people, and in a number of counties historians have discerned the evolution of a group of 'professional' magistrates. None the less, they were not specialised functionaries. An active local officeholder might, for example, have acted as administrator of the poor law, militia and taxation, as a judge and as a licenser of alehouses. Secondly, not only were these offices

---

[56] Ibid., p. 50. For the Protestation, see A. Hughes, *The Causes of the English Civil War* (London, 1998), 162–3.   [57] Kent, *Constable*, p. 63.

[58] Ibid., ch. 4 and pp. 284–6. Wrightson is less sure on this point: K. Wrightson, 'Two concepts of order: justices, constables and jurymen in seventeenth-century England', in J. Brewer and J. Styles (eds.), *An Ungovernable People? The English and their Law in the Seventeenth and Eighteenth Centuries* (London, 1980), 21–46, 312–25, at pp. 26–7.   [59] Kent, *Constable*, pp. 55–6.

unspecialised, the distinction between public and private authority was very blurred. Analytically the authority of a magistrate was distinct from the authority of a substantial local gentleman, but in practice the former depended on the latter. Fitness for office was appraised not simply in administrative but also in social terms. In both senses, measured against the Weberian ideal-type of the modern state, this state was only partially differentiated.

In the counties most political power lay with men drawn from among a group of 'natural' governors.[60] This was empowering since it lent to their activities as magistrates and constables a sense of legitimacy which did not derive from their office alone. In tying the administrative hierarchy so closely to social status it reduced the possibility that an influential social group could be entirely excluded from political power. However, there was a potential tension in the holding of office, and this is something to which we will return on many occasions. Office not only reflected social status but also confirmed it and this was a motive, sometimes perhaps the chief one, for seeking office. Clearly, administrative tasks would be undertaken assiduously when and where assiduity would enhance local social standing. Where implementation of an administrative task was likely to be unpopular, active officeholders faced the prospect of losing rather than gaining prestige. Officeholding could become counter-productive, perhaps even wholly so. For example, some county gentry made themselves very unpopular by trying to enforce more accurate subsidy valuations and there is some evidence that the pressure on constables responsible for the collection of ship money had, by the later 1630s, become so substantial that it was difficult to find men willing to serve.[61] These more informal expectations shaped the way in which offices were perceived and set limits to administrative action. In this way, the legitimation of offices gave political force to wider social values, such as neighbourliness, and local standards of order.

Much local government in the counties and towns was conducted through offices which reflected wider social values and status, rather than specialised functionaries. This was true also of the incorporated towns, although with the complicating factor of the borough charter. Boroughs were towns with legal privileges granted by charter which included individual arrangements for administration. There was a great

---

[60] Although in the later sixteenth century, increasingly, Protestantism became a criterion of selection too. See below, pp. 300–1, 303.
[61] Braddick, *Parliamentary*, pp. 113–14, 120–3; Kent, *Constable*, pp. 242–8, 305–6.

diversity among forms of borough organisation, varying from the great complexity of London government to that of small towns whose significance had decreased following the grant of their charter. In London perhaps one in ten of the adult male population held some office, and this created a tradition of urban self-government and independence remarked upon by contemporaries. The range of functions attached to urban government was very large and it was in the towns that many administrative initiatives originated. It was Norwich that first used a compulsory poor rate, and the measures taken in London to cope with poverty by the late sixteenth century were in advance of much of the rest of the country. These administrative measures were given teeth by the plethora of local officers charged with enforcement. London poor-relief measures, for example, generated a large body of records through the efforts of local officers.[62] In late Elizabethan Ipswich, constables visited inns and tippling houses on Sundays in order to flush out absentees from church.[63]

Borough government points up two further aspects of local government. Firstly, it was intimately connected with particular legal liberties and privileges. Law and administration were very closely allied in this period so that, for example, debtors to the crown were not invoiced but served with a writ to appear before the court of exchequer (or chancery). Who was responsible for serving the writ in each case was dependent on local liberties. In other words, law was an active arm of government. Secondly, boroughs demonstrate again how early modern government was, in some sense, representative. This representation may have been direct, through election. More frequently it was a more elusive kind of representation, reflecting a set of social rather than political expectations: 'In early modern England, political choice was subsumed within a wide system of social relations.' There was 'a kind of social ecology in which elevation to titles and honours, appointments to the bench, the lieutenancy, or the assumption of corporate responsibility marked out the thriving species'.[64] On the other hand, however, office was a means to influence, offering a hand up to those anxious to reinforce or increase

---

[62] For London see I. W. Archer, *The Pursuit of Stability: Social Relations in Elizabethan London* (Cambridge, 1991); S. Rappaport, *Worlds within Worlds: Structures of Life in Sixteenth-Century London* (Cambridge, 1989); V. Pearl, *London and the Outbreak of the Puritan Revolution: City Government and National Politics 1625–43* (Oxford, 1961).

[63] P. Collinson, *The Religion of Protestants: The Church in English Society 1559–1625* (Oxford, 1982), 170–1.

[64] M. A. Kishlansky, *Parliamentary Selection: Social and Political Choice in Early Modern England* (Cambridge, 1986), quotations at pp. 12, 22.

their social standing.[65] Not all gentlemen held office and some, such as the Catholics, were systematically excluded. Political effectiveness rested on social standing but, although status and office were closely connected, they were, none the less, separate things. In the boroughs, however, officeholders were sometimes selected by a process that was open to more political manipulation. It was possible, at least, that the 'natural governors' of the town might be excluded from power by political opponents. This was true also of county benches (and may have been true of parish office) but it was probably more true of the boroughs.

Judicial and political authority were closely intertwined in other bodies too. In some parts of the country special tribunals, for example the Councils in the North and in the Marches, combined legal and executive authority in order to bring good governance to localities remote from London.[66] In these and other institutions 'Government . . . was largely channeled through legal forms, and as a result the boundaries between judicial and administrative action were far less clearly drawn than is the case today.'[67] Another illustration of this connection is provided by the assizes. By 1550 there were six circuits, each ridden by two justices, twice a year. They were usually judges in the superior courts[68] and in this sense they represented central law. It has been suggested that 'the justices looked to the visiting justices for legal and procedural advice. Their willingness to attend assizes and learn the law at the judges' side was one test of their diligence.' Assizes thus complemented quarter sessions, confirming decisions or responding to requests for advice. On controversial matters of rating or of alehouse regulation the confirmation of quarter sessions decisions at the assizes could be crucial.[69] In general, assizes were concerned with business similar to that of the quarter sessions – the regulation of local administration and the trial of a mixture of criminal and civil business. The assizes, though, were the principal criminal courts in the country until 1971. For example, trials for felony were a virtual monopoly of the assizes by the

---

[65] As, for example, the fifth earl of Huntingdon, whose precarious social position goes some way to explaining the energy with which he pursued the office of lieutenant in Leicestershire and Rutland: Cogswell, *Home Divisions*.

[66] P. Williams, *The Council in the Marches of Wales under Elizabeth I* (Cardiff, 1958); Williams, 'The attack on the Council in the Marches, 1603–1642', *Transactions of the Honourable Society of Cymmrodorion* (1961), 1–22; R. R. Reid, *The King's Council in the North* (London, 1921); C. Cross, *The Puritan Earl: The Life of Henry Hastings, Third Earl of Huntingdon 1536–1595* (London, 1966), chs. 5–7.

[67] M. Ingram, *Church Courts, Sex and Marriage in England, 1570–1640* (Cambridge, 1987), 27.

[68] J. A. Sharpe, *Crime in Early Modern England 1550–1750* (London, 1984), 23.

[69] Fletcher, *Reform*, pp. 92–4, quotation at p. 93.

late sixteenth century. Thus, the quarter sessions and the assizes gradually differentiated – burglary, homicide, witchcraft, arson, rape and grand larceny were all assize offences and quarter sessions took up much of the more minor business.

The assizes also fulfilled broader political functions. As a great social occasion, at which the county gentry met and formed solidarities, they were crucial to local politics and to the ritual display of social and political order. Judges were met at the county border by trumpeters and the sheriff's bailiff. The sheriff himself, with other officers and county gentlemen, met them several miles from the assize town.

The ensuing cavalcade . . . was one of some magnificence, attended by pike- and liverymen specially clothed for the occasion. Welcomed into town with bells, music, and occasionally, a Latin oration, the judges went first to their lodgings. There they received leading members of the local gentry who probably reported briefly on the state of the county. Thus forewarned, the judges, now robed and again attended by the sheriff and his men, passed to the church where the local minister read prayers and the sheriff's chaplain delivered a sermon.[70]

This 'atmosphere of majesty, spectacle and ceremony' led one observer in 1678 to declare 'that the "awful solemnities" accompanying assizes might overawe defendants of "low and common education"'.[71] For those of the better sort this meant 'good company' and sumptuous living. For the poorer sort, it was the awful majesty of the law – something which was an important part of the deterrent effect of the eighteenth-century legal system. Assizes were of political significance because they were addressed by the judges reporting general political concerns and they were also marked by a sermon. Like the pulpit, the assize courts were a means of publicising royal policy and projecting the authority of the crown. Sir Edward Coke, for example, told his audience at Norwich assizes early in the reign of James I, that 'the king "is over us the lord's anointed, and in these his realms and dominions, in all causes, and over all persons, as well ecclesiastical as civil next under Jesus Christ our supreme governor"'.[72] The assizes were, therefore, organs of both central and local politics, and they exemplify the intimate and ambiguous relationship between the state and the legal system. The implementation of the law was both a function and a means of government, and the activities of the courts were often 'political'.

Lawyers were not agents of the state, however, and this is not a history

---

[70] J. S. Cockburn, *A History of English Assizes 1558–1714* (Cambridge, 1972), esp. Introduction, quotation at p. 65.　　[71] Sharpe, *Crime*, p. 23.　　[72] Williams, *Tudor Regime*, p. 358.

of the law. The relatively bureaucratic institutions in London operated with the help of what was, according to Prest,[73] one of the oldest professions. Law was a system of rules binding social action within a territory whose interpretation was in the hands of individuals with specialist knowledge. This system was constitutive of the state – one of the principal means by which political power was legitimated was by reference to the law – and the source of all justice was the king. In criminal cases, however, the king was a party, because it was his peace that was being disturbed, and as a result there were procedural devices to ensure that it was not the king who instituted proceedings. This was delegated to officers or to individuals exhibiting informations or making appeals of felony. Thus, the courts were royal organs, administering royal justice, but they were independent of the will of the monarch. Lawyers themselves represented an independent profession – they served the court, not the state. Justice legitimated political power at an overarching level and it was the duty of the monarch to foster both, but it legitimated, rather than served, the state. There was a fundamental difference between an official of the state and a lawyer although in practice they might be party to the same political act. Lawyers were not 'state functionaries' in the way that, for example, commissioned officers or excisemen were.

None the less, law was a means of administrative action and offices were formally empowered by legal instruments. Much local authority was held by commission in the ways described above, but there were a number of other such instruments – charter, warrant and licence, for example – each of which created vested interests. On the whole, county and borough government was conducted by dominant social groups whose prestige lent authority to public administration. But in operating this way the public and private were enmeshed to an extent which limited as well as empowered them. This harnessing of essentially private resources (social prestige in this case) had analogies with other forms of government action: it was not only boroughs that had charters. Durham, Lancaster and Cheshire had palatinate charters granting particular jurisdictional authority to hold their own courts with varying degrees of independence of the Westminster courts.[74] In the north and the marches, as we have seen, there were regional councils offering local

---

[73] Prest, *Barristers*, pp. 1–3.

[74] W. J. Jones, 'Palatine performance in the seventeenth century', in P. Clark, A. G. R. Smith and N. Tyacke (eds.), *The English Commonwealth 1547–1640: Essays in Politics and Society Presented to Joel Hurstfield* (Leicester, 1979), 189–204.

courts of law and taking on some of the duties of administrative oversight associated with the privy council in other areas of the country.[75]
These charters had been a means of bringing border areas within the
general ambit of royal authority and they continued to be used in this
way. For example, Lord Baltimore was granted powers to govern
Maryland by a charter expressly modelled on the Durham palatinate
charter of the fourteenth century. Elsewhere in America, trading companies, which had been granted charters in order to help them to raise
capital for their ventures, also assumed governmental authority.[76] Here,
again, the relationship between centre and locality was complicated.
National government coordinated the grant of charters, it was the
source of legal validity, and was, hence, a crucial resource for chartered
authorities. Boroughs maintained recorders and colonial government
sent agents to London in order to protect or increase their liberties.[77]
But, on the other hand, these chartered authorities were also sensitive to
any threat from the centre, and were sometimes forced to choose
between compliance with initiatives originating at the centre of the
polity and local interest and opinion. The same tension was manifest in
the relationship between commissioners or licensees and the source of
their licence or commission, but the formality and permanence of a
charter seems to have increased the consciousness of these ambiguities.

In these cases, the relationship between private and public interest
was obviously ambiguous – if there was ambiguity in the relationship
between private benefit and public service in relation to officeholders,
this was far more manifest in the case of trading companies. Beyond
such charters lay areas that were yet more grey. Particular people, or
groups of people, were given licences for limited purposes, often to fulfill
tasks for which officeholders were ineffective. These were usually financial, and frequently had financial consequences. Such government by
licence was used, for example, to raise money from domestic industrial
production (through patents of monopoly) or to try to maximise revenues (through the appointment of customs farmers, for example).[78]

---

[75] Williams, *Council in the Marches*; Reid, *Council in the North*.   [76] See ch. 9.

[77] For recorders see Prest, *Barristers*, esp. pp. 240–52; for agents, see G. J. Milne, 'New England
agents and the English Atlantic, 1641–1666', Ph.D. Dissertation, Edinburgh University
(1993).

[78] It has been suggested that this created a conflict of interest between privileged merchants,
enjoying the benefits of crown concessions, and others trading on their own who tended to
favour freer trade and to oppose the authority of the crown: R. Brenner, *Merchants and Revolution:
Commercial Change, Political Conflict and London's Overseas Traders, 1550–1653* (Cambridge, 1993). In
fact, though, there were also conflicts of interest between those enjoying crown concessions. For
a critique of some aspects of an earlier version of Brenner's argument, see R. Ashton, 'Conflicts

These relationships could be more or less informal, in fact, as in the role of intermediaries in government borrowing.[79] Perhaps the most loosely connected agents of the state were common informers. Misdemeanours could be brought before the courts by information exhibited by individuals *qui tam* (acting for themselves and for the king). This provided the means by which to reward those who reported infringements of the law, particularly economic regulations. Informers could claim a share of the fines for infringements or enter into a composition with offenders under licence from the court. In some cases the crown gave the exclusive right to present particular infringements to individuals or consortia. In these ways, informing came to provide a significant income for some individuals. The suspicion that these people were acting out of self-interest and not for the public good was, of course, acute. As one historian has put it, it 'was the marriage of justice with malice or avarice which helped to discredit common informers in the eyes even of those who were not lawbreakers'.[80]

These agencies were much more specialised than those of the office-holding hierarchy, but they do not conform to the Weberian ideal-type of a modern bureaucracy in other ways. There is clearly a distinction to be made between a salaried official and someone seeking to maximise private profit under crown licence. These licensees attracted characteristic forms of opposition in accusations of avarice and cheating – the favoured terms of abuse for these people were those implying greed or dishonesty, such as rogue, caterpillar or knave. Those taking up supplies for the crown – purveyors and saltpetremen – often found themselves in this position. Saltpetremen, for example, were often thought to be 'officious in their demands, negligent about property rights, slow to fill in their excavations and quick to resent the less than total cooperation given them by locals'. The requisitioning of carts for royal service by these men ('cart-taking') was also resented 'because they often forced the

of concessionary interest in early Stuart England', in D. C. Coleman and A. H. John (eds.), *Trade, Government and Economy in Pre-Industrial England: Essays Presented to F. J. Fisher* (London, 1976), 113–31. See also L. L. Peck, *Court, Patronage and Corruption in Early Stuart England* (London, 1990), ch. 6, esp. p. 159.   [79] See pp. 251–2, 257–8, 266–7.

[80] M. W. Beresford, 'The common informer, the penal statutes and economic regulation', *EcHR*, 2nd series, 10 (1957), 221–38, quotation at p. 221. For proceedings by information see J. H. Baker, 'Criminal courts and procedure at common law, 1550–1800', in J. S. Cockburn (ed.), *Crime in England 1550–1800* (London, 1977), 15–48, 299–309 at pp. 20–1. See, in general, Peck, *Corruption*, ch. 6. For informers see also Williams, *Tudor Regime*, pp. 148–51; M. Ingram, 'Communities and courts: law and disorder in early-seventeenth-century Wiltshire', in Cockburn (ed.), *Crime*, 110–34, 321–8 at pp. 122–3, 134. For attempts to restrain their activities, see D. R. Lidington, 'Parliament and the enforcement of the penal statutes: the history of the Act "In restraint of Common Promoters" (18 Eliz. I *c*. 5)', *Parliamentary History*, 8 (1989), 309–28.

local farmers to drive them and their cargoes long distances for little remuneration and the carts were seldom in the same condition at the end of the duty as at the start'. As Robert Bowyer put it:

Abuse of such as have commission to make Salt Peeter is exceeding great to the Subject in digging up their Dove Houses at unseasonable tymes, and other Houses at their Pleasure; And in takeinge their carts, and their wood up and other things in more violent and unlawfull sort now, then in tyme of warr.

Functional effectiveness was here being achieved at some political cost. The activities of purveyors were also a source of acute suspicion in many places.[81]

Another group inhabiting this twilight world of government and self-service were those who made a profit by seeking out encroachments on crown lands, and false titles, the hunters after concealed lands. Sir Thomas Sherley of Wiston, Sussex, was licensed by James I for this purpose in September 1617. The king had been informed that 'manye alienacons aswell of estats of Inherytaunce as for lyves of mannors lands and tenements holden in Chiefe' had been made since the end of the reign of Elizabeth. Sherley, accordingly, was given licence to track down such alienations, which effectively defrauded the king of revenue. It was, thus, 'iust and honorable', to empower Sherley to undertake this work, and he was given power to do so for fifteen years from that Michaelmas. But Sherley and his deputies were also given power to compound with offenders, while two-thirds of the proceeds were reserved to him as his reward. Sherley was to have power to release those holding alienated lands, a substantial right. In return he was to pay an annual rent of £400. Such arrangements, effectively seeking to govern by licence, gave individuals a clear vested interest in the implementation of a government policy and were frequently awarded as a means of reward. But in tying self-interest so closely to government, they opened up the licensee to charges of corruption.[82] In 1579, commissions to hunters were re-

[81] R. W. Stewart, *The English Ordnance Office: A Case-Study in Bureaucracy*, Royal Historical Society, Studies in History, 73 (Woodbridge, 1996), 82; Bowyer quoted ibid., p. 82 n. 6. See also C. Russell, 'Monarchies, wars and estates in England, France and Spain, *c.* 1580–*c.* 1640', reprinted in *Unrevolutionary England, 1603–1642* (London, 1990), 121–36, at p. 127; and K. Sharpe, *The Personal Rule of Charles I* (London, 1992), 491–4. For resentment of purveyors, see A. Woodworth, *Purveyance for the Royal Household in the Reign of Queen Elizabeth*, Transactions of the American Philosophical Society, 35 (Philadelphia, 1945), esp. pp. 18–26, 37–8; Smith, *County and Court*, pp. 293–302.

[82] H. Hope Lockwood, 'Those greedy hunters after concealed lands', in K. Neale (ed.), *An Essex Tribute: Essays Presented to Frederick G. Emmison* (London, 1987), 153–70; C. J. Kitching, 'The quest for concealed lands in the reign of Elizabeth I', *TRHS*, 5th series, 24 (1974), 63–78. For Sherley's warrant see HEH, EL 1452. For a full list of complaints about the effects of the hunters, in this case relating specifically to lands currently held by the church, see *CSPD, 1591–94*, pp. 325–6.

voked on the grounds of their 'great misusage' which had led the queen to perceive that by pretence of law 'a great multitude of her loving subjects . . . in many cases (though not offending) to have been greatly vexed and molested, and the laws not thereby anything the better executed . . . nor any such profit recovered or obtained to her highness' use'.[83]

In the light of such suspicions, precision, rather than discretion, was more likely to render their activities legitimate. Indeed, the modernisation of the early modern state took the form not just of the development of more specialised and differentiated offices, but also of the reduction of discretion in the exercise of these more specialised functions. Bureaucratisation, enshrining precision, accuracy and predictability, can be understood in terms of legitimation, as a means of rendering political authority acceptable. By reducing the discretion available to specialised state functionaries, and by specifying their rewards more closely, the emphasis on precision and regularity helped to secure more ready consent to their activities.

We began with the natural leaders of society and ended with the caterpillars that fed upon it, but all government offices depended on private energies and resources, coordinated and harnessed by a variety of more or less formal means. Whereas the gentry commissioners and village officers were constrained by social expectations and their own perception of the appropriate use of their office, groups and individuals operating under particular licences depended more closely on legal powers and were constrained in different ways. Their brief was usually more specialised and they usually had a clearer vested interest in implementing it efficiently. Informers, for example, were particularly significant in the enforcement of economic regulations. By the same token, however, it was particularly difficult to disentangle their private benefit from their public role: their importance to the implementation of the apprenticeship laws was considerable and hostility to their activities resulted in considerable pressure to find some more acceptable means of public enforcement.[84] Monopolists, chartered companies, informers, tax farmers and hunters were all suspect in a way that officeholders generally were not.

---

[83] P. L. Hughes and J. F. Larkin (eds.), *The Royal Proclamations*, II, *The Later Tudors (1553–1587)* (London, 1969), 451–3, at pp. 451–2, dated 15/12/1579. Another example of this government by licence was the issue of letters of marque to privateers in wartime. In this way private enterprise (the pursuit of armed trade and piracy by individual merchants) might be made to serve a broader public purpose. For privateering, see below, pp. 205–8, 218, 224.

[84] M. G. Davies, *The Enforcement of the English Apprenticeship Laws: A Study in Applied Mercantilism 1563–1642* (Cambridge, Mass., 1956), chs. 1–6. For the latter point see esp. p. 157.

This variety of offices, none of them 'modern' in form, were all exercising a distinctively political power coordinated (weakly) from a single centre. The boundaries of the state, however, are difficult to draw in relation to the church. This is not an idly chosen example of conceptual difficulty, of course, for this was a central question for contemporaries too. The issue is complicated for several reasons. Firstly, states sought symbolic legitimation for their political power by claiming to determine and protect 'true religion'. Churches were therefore implicated in state activities as a means by which they could be legitimated. Secondly, churches had political power which could resemble that of the state or was actively drawn upon by the state (in using the pulpit to propagate ideas legitimating political power or mobilising clerical resources for taxation or militia service, for example).[85] Thirdly, the creation of a national church in England exaggerated both these features of the church while also making the organisation and offices of the church formally dependent on the head of the state. Thus, the organisational power of the church was, to a degree, at the disposal of the head of state, who might seek to control the content of the symbolic message that it communicated. Fourthly, because the political and symbolic power of the church was tied to that of the state, the enforcement of compliance with the symbolic message being propagated became defined as a secular matter. Heterodoxy was punished by secular officers and was defined, in part at least, as a threat to political order, not solely as a jeopardy to the salvation of particular souls.[86]

For these reasons some historians would consider the established church to be a department of state: 'The ubiquitous agency of the State was the Church, quartering the land not into a few hundred constituencies but into ten thousand parishes, impinging on the daily concerns of the great majority, supporting its black-coated army of a clerical intelligentsia, bidding for a monopoly of education, piety and political ac-

---

[85] Indeed, Wolter has argued that the 'office', a 'central element of the modern state was formed within the organization and law of the Church in the Middle Ages': U. Wolter, 'The *officium* in medieval ecclesiastical law as a prototype of modern administration', in A. Padoa-Schioppa (ed.), *Legislation and Justice* (Oxford, 1997), 17–36, quotation at p. 17.

[86] See Questier's view:

> In that the Church is an institution in which power is exercised by some over others, an organised form of ecclesiastical society as well as a religious concept, it has political characteristics, and the things which it does (even the way that it expresses doctrine) are affected by political considerations. In addition, because religious opinion affects the way that people behave, those who exercise authority on behalf of the State cannot ignore people's opinions about religion. In late-sixteenth- and early seventeenth-century England, attitudes to Rome incorporated not just a series of doctrines about grace but also a view of the relationship between the Church and the State.

M. C. Questier, *Conversion, Politics and Religion in England, 1580–1625* (Cambridge, 1996), 2.

ceptability.'[87] There is much to commend such a view, but the clergy will be treated here as an independent professional group whose services were very valuable to secular government. They possessed distinctive skills, promoted in a way which increasingly resembled a modern profession, but access to the profession was not solely controlled by the government. To an extent, like the legal profession, it was self-regulating and independent of secular government.[88] Moreover, although churches had political power as defined above, their ultimate sanction was not legitimate force, but damnation. The effective power of the church depended not on its prisons or armies but on the strength of its claim to give access to the means of salvation – its power rested, ultimately, upon the expression of symbolic or ideological power. Churches and states were alike, and their power was particularly entwined in this period even if, analytically, they embodied different kinds of power. Churches had political power and states made spiritual claims which helped to legitimate their political power. They were, thus, similar and this blurring was accentuated by developments in the early modern period, but they are analytically distinct. The church only features in this study in so far as its political power was deployed on behalf of the state. Religion is discussed here in so far as political power was utilised to secure some religious end. This is a history of the state, not of the church, but a peculiarity of this particular state (and a common feature of many early modern states) was its very close relationship to the church.[89]

The state in early modern England was, according to the definition adopted here, a network of offices exercising political power. The forms of these offices – their functional purpose, territorial limits and modes of legitimation – were quite varied, but they are all recognisable as

[87] J. C. D. Clark, *English Society 1688–1832: Ideology, Social Structure and Political Practice During the Ancien Régime* (Cambridge, 1985), 277. He is referring to the period after 1688, of course, but it is a view consistent with his account of the earlier period: *Revolution and Rebellion: State and Society in England in the Seventeenth and Eighteenth Centuries* (Cambridge, 1986), 104–11.

[88] The distinction is made in another context by M. Gray, 'An early professional group? The auditors of the land revenue in the late sixteenth and early seventeenth centuries', *Archives*, 87 (1992), 45–62, esp. p. 52. For some sceptical reflections about the 'professionalisation' of the clergy see M. Hawkins, 'Ambiguity and contradiction in "the rise of professionalism": the English clergy, 1570–1730', in A. L. Beier, D. Cannadine and J. M. Rosenheim (eds.), *The First Modern Society: Essays in English History in Honour of Lawrence Stone* (Cambridge, 1989), 241–69.

[89] This distinction would also allow for the application of this definition of the state to medieval polities. It is possible to discern bounded and coordinated networks of agencies of political power in medieval England, and the distinction between the state and the church allows for the description of these networks as 'states' despite the spiritual jurisdiction of the church, which penetrated the territorial bounds of these 'states', and despite the complexity of jurisdictional relations within these networks.

agencies of political power. These forms extend to include all the commissioned, chartered and licensed agencies discussed above, but do not include independent professions – particular the lawyers and clergy. Overall, this network of offices did not conform to the Weberian ideal-type of a modern state – in particular, it was weakly coordinated and relatively undifferentiated by comparison with the bureaucratic states of Weber's day. None the less, it makes sense to describe the whole network as a state, a description justifiable in terms of modern sociological theory and emerging sixteenth-century practice. Defining the state in terms of political power, rather than specific institutional forms or particular functional purposes, leaves open questions about what forms state offices took, what they did and whose interests they served. By comparison, accounts concentrating on relatively differentiated, specialised institutions, or accounts which define the state in terms of a particular function (such as preserving order), appear partial. Having defined the subject of study, chapter 2 will consider what the state was used for, with what success, by whom and at what times.

The uses of political power in early modern England

Chapter 1 was primarily definitional – setting out a definition of the state and describing the institutions that comprised it. The main purpose of this book, however, is to examine the *history* of the early modern state – changes in its form and functioning over time – and to try to reconcile competing accounts of that history. In particular, we are interested in patterns in the forms and use of state power – the degree of the autonomy of the state, the relationship between centre and locality, and the chronology of its development. These patterns were not given by a central will, or by a single function. In examining state formation, as opposed to state building, patterns will be sought in three general sources of pressure on the exercise of political power. Firstly, the uses of political power were patterned by the kinds of end for which political power was characteristically found appropriate. Secondly, the definition of these opportunities and challenges, and of appropriate responses to them, was shaped by patterns of participation in the system. Finally, the limits on what could legitimately be done were also set, in part, by the availability of languages appropriate to the legitimation of the action in hand.

In this chapter we will first consider the general pressures which called forth new or increased uses of state power. In responding to these pressures, legitimate uses and forms of office had to be found. The key concept here, then, is legitimacy which will be considered in some detail in the second section of the chapter. Agents of state power had to demonstrate that their actions fell within the formal limits of their office but also sought to justify these actions with reference to beliefs current in society at large. This gave force to those ideas, and set limits on the range of administrative action. Different kinds of office, naturally, were legitimated in different ways. Since there were limits to what could be done within the limits of particular offices, some forms of office were more useful for some functions than others. This affinity between form and function is briefly introduced in the third section of the chapter. In the fourth the threads of the discussion in Chapters 1 and 2 are brought together in a discussion of the issue of the agency of the state; to explain how a state can acquire agency is at once to account for its functional purpose and the interests it served.

THE USES OF POLITICAL POWER

Emerging contemporary practice defined the state as the 'omnipotent yet impersonal power' within a particular territory.[1] The state was omnipotent in the sense that there was no superior political power, but it was also omnipotent (or nearly so) in another sense – as Weber recognised, the state might, potentially, be used to do almost anything. So, what was this network of agents used for? The emphasis here is on practicalities; the answer to this question, for our purposes, lies in what they did, not in contemporary visions of what government was for. Even with this drastic simplification the issues are still complex, but we can isolate four general areas of administrative concern. Measures were taken to preserve social order; to enforce and protect established religion; to protect the territorial and trading base of government; and to secure the financial, administrative and military resources necessary to do these things. It is immediately apparent that these are overlapping concerns, of course, but they provide some general categories with which to outline the practical concerns of early modern English government. The initiatives which are described in the following chapters can be understood as combinations of one or more of these four general pressures and none of these general influences can be collapsed entirely into any of the others.

Measures to preserve social order were in part a response to changing material conditions. During the first part of our period, down to the mid-seventeenth century, rapid population growth created both economic opportunities and social problems. Crude economic indicators paint a stark picture indeed. In 1561 the population of England and Wales was just below 3m, by 1601 it had risen to 4.1m and by 1651 to over 5.2m. This was an increase of nearly 75 per cent.[2] Price data seem to demonstrate that this created an increase in demand which the economy could not supply. Price series indexed against prices in the

---

[1] Q. Skinner, *The Foundations of Modern Political Thought*, 2 vols. (Cambridge, 1976), II, 258.
[2] E. A. Wrigley and R. S. Schofield, *The Population History of England 1541–1871: A Reconstruction* (Cambridge, 1989), table 7.8, 208–9.

period between 1451 and 1475 reveal significant inflation, particularly for food stuffs. For the decade beginning in 1561 the index for food stuffs stood at 298, in 1601 at 527, and in 1651 it had reached 687. There was, clearly, a general rise in prices throughout the period and in some years the effects were more dramatic. For example, the decade beginning 1591 saw average prices at 530, a substantial increase over the average of 389 for the previous decade. Prices after 1631 stood, on average, at 687 by contrast with the 585 of the previous decade. The rate of inflation was not the same for all commodities, however. In particular, price rises for industrial and livestock products were slower: in 1651 the index of industrial prices stood at only 327.[3] As a result of the close relationship between population and price curves, and because of the differential rate of inflation between various kinds of product, historians have tended to explain this in terms of the relationship between supply and demand – to favour a real rather than a monetary explanation for this inflation. For example, when population increase slowed down, after about 1650, so too did prices – population pressure was no longer pushing levels of demand beyond levels of supply. Secondly, the fact that there was differential between price increases for staple foods (grain) and relative luxuries (livestock and industrial products) is best explained by the relative inelasticity of demand for food. As prices rose patterns of consumption shifted away from relative luxuries such as meat and clothing, with the result that the general rise in demand for those commodities was more muted. Finally, rapid price rises in the 1590s and 1630s occurred in decades of poor harvests, adding short-term pressure on supply and thus compounding the general pressure described here. Changes in money supply – the debasements of the mid-sixteenth century and the subsequent influx of bullion – must have exacerbated these developments but they offer a less persuasive explanation for the general rise in prices and its patterns.[4]

The price rise was not accompanied by similar increases in wage rates – population growth was increasing the labour supply faster than economic growth was creating employment. The result was an over-supply of labour and declining real wages: according to one influential estimate, wages for agricultural workers in the south of England in 1596/7 were worth only 29 per cent as much as they had been at the turn of the sixteenth century, and over the 1590s as a whole, only about

[3] R. B. Outhwaite, *Inflation in Tudor and Early Stuart England* (London, 1969), 10.
[4] Ibid.; C. G. A. Clay, *Economic Expansion and Social Change England 1500–1700*, 2 vols. (Cambridge, 1984), I, ch. 2.

50 per cent. Again, short-term factors could produce really serious problems: bad harvests such as those in the late 1590s meant not just high prices but a reduced demand for labour.[5]

Population, price and wage data therefore provide evidence for a compelling case that population growth outstripped economic growth, and that this created potential hardship. However, when population growth began again in the eighteenth century there was no rapid inflation in food prices – the link between population growth and rising prices had been broken. In the meantime, it seems, the carrying capacity of the land must have increased markedly. This was a product of greater efficiency, on the whole, rather than simply an increase in the amount of land under cultivation (although this was also a factor). Between 1550 and 1700, we may conclude, there was economic change which resulted in declining living standards, particularly for wage earners and for those who bought food. However, alongside this increase in 'poverty' there was also 'progress' since, ultimately, the productivity of English agriculture increased.

There is some question about the real extent of both poverty and progress, however.[6] The stark picture painted here depends on three indicators: population, prices and wages. Of these, the population figures are much the most reliable. An alternative price series to that quoted above has been constructed for London in the sixteenth century. It suggests that inflation was slower, more affected by monetary factors, and that changes in relative prices were less like those associated with over-population. The fall in the value of wages was less marked too; by the end of the seventeenth century they had fallen by only 29 per cent, and such a decline might have been offset by comparatively modest changes in consumption. By making such minor adjustments (eating rabbit rather than other kinds of red meat, for example) real wages

---

[5] Wrigley and Schofield, *Population*, table A9.2, pp. 642–4. See also P. J. Bowden (ed.), *Economic Change: Wages, Profits and Rents 1500–1750: Chapters from the Agrarian History of England and Wales*, I (Cambridge, 1990), 167.

[6] For a sceptical view of the claims for an agricultural revolution prior to 1750 see M. Overton, *Agricultural Revolution in England: The Transformation of the Agrarian Economy 1500–1850* (Cambridge, 1996), esp. ch. 5. His case is not that there was no improvement in the seventeenth century, but that it was less significant to the development of English agriculture than improvements in the later eighteenth century. They were, though, significant. Improvements in net yield (i.e. the yield available for consumption) might increase more rapidly than gross yield, and so market supplies might increase rapidly without an agricultural revolution. For the implications of the difference between gross and net yields, and the implications for food supply, see E. A. Wrigley, 'Some reflections on corn yields and prices in pre-industrial economies', in J. Walter and R. Schofield (eds.), *Famine, Disease and the Social Order in Early Modern Society* (Cambridge, 1989), 235–78.

might have fallen by only 17 per cent.[7] This is important evidence because London experienced very rapid population growth in this period, as a result of immigration. It contained a substantial proportion of the total population, and was particularly 'harvest-sensitive' – virtually all of its food was produced elsewhere and procured through the market.

There are other reasons for caution in accepting the gloomiest views of economic change in this period. Estimates for wage levels are based partly on a series of wages paid to builders, but the meaning of this wage is not straightforward. Builders did not depend entirely on cash but were probably paid at least partly in kind. More importantly, perhaps, they were more like small businessmen than wage earners. They supplied raw materials, employed labour and were likely to have other employments, such as a smallholding. Wages paid to them are not a good indication of their overall income, therefore, particularly for large-scale contracts which would have included deals for raw materials and employees. This was probably true of many other trades, too.[8] None the less, bearing all these difficulties in mind, 'there can be no doubt that real wages did decline until the middle of the seventeenth century'.[9]

A related question, again one to which there is no agreed answer, is (to paraphrase Laslett) how often did peasants starve? It seems that there were famine-related mortality crises, but they were not very frequent: one recent survey of the material suggests that there were more than local crises in 1557–8, 1596–8, 1622–3. On the other hand, despite successive harvest failures (and heavy taxation) there is little evidence of widespread starvation between 1647 and 1650 or between 1697 and 1699. Famine had disappeared from England by the late seventeenth century and had been a regional problem before that date.[10] It has been argued that the chronology and geography of famines 'shows that they were generally diminishing both in intensity and in geographical range, rather than worsening as population increased'. As a result, there are

[7] S. Rappaport, *Worlds within Worlds: Structures of Life in Sixteenth-Century London* (Cambridge, 1989), ch. 5, figures quoted from p. 160. See also Walter and Schofield, 'Famine, disease and crisis mortality in early modern society', in Walter and Schofield (eds.), *Famine*, 1–73, at pp. 44–5.

[8] D. Woodward, 'Wage rates and living standards in pre-industrial England', *PP*, 91 (1981), 28–46, quotation at p. 45. For a full account see Woodward, *Men at Work: Labourers and Building Craftsmen in the Towns of Northern England, 1450–1750* (Cambridge, 1995), esp. ch. 2. See also D. M. Palliser, 'Tawney's century: brave new world or Malthusian trap?', *EcHR*, 2nd series, 35 (1982), 339–53, at pp. 349–50.

[9] D. Woodward, 'The determination of wage rates in the early modern north of England', *EcHR*, 2nd series, 47 (1994), 22–43, quotation at pp. 24–5. See also Woodward, *Men at Work*, esp. ch. 7.

[10] Walter and Schofield, 'Famine', pp. 28–37.

good grounds for doubting that population growth in England was so far outstripping production that regular Malthusian checks were applied by famine.[11]

Thus, there is some doubt about the true extent and depth of poverty in this period, the real social costs of population growth and associated economic change. The weaknesses of price and wage data, and the absence of general starvation, suggest that we should be cautious about accepting the most apocalyptic accounts of economic change in this period. But there are two points to make about this revision: it has only shown that things were not as bad as was previously thought; and the attitude of influential contemporaries was, it seems, less optimistic. Even the optimists among modern historians acknowledge that there were years when people died for want of food (or, perhaps more terrible, for want of the means to get access to food), and the most hopeful view of living standards is that with adjustments in consumption the value of a wage might have fallen by only 17 per cent. The second point is more important for our purposes. Contemporary fears drove some radical extensions of the power of government: to intervene in food and labour markets, to enforce donations for the poor and drastically to limit the movement of the migrant poor, for example. How widely implemented these measures were is considered below, but it is clear that important measures were taken and that they were prompted, to a significant extent, by fear of the worst consequences of economic and social change.

These economic changes had profound social consequences. It is clear that the changing balance of prices and wages created both opportunities and hardships. Rising prices and falling wages meant increased profit margins for farmers who regularly produced a marketable surplus and employed labour. For those who were dependent on the market to supplement their own production, and who also sold their labour, the opposite was true. In arable areas, those at subsistence level or below in terms of their own food production found it increasingly difficult to break even, and came to depend on other sources of income.[12] This, presumably, would have further depressed the value of

---

[11] Palliser, 'Tawney's century', p. 345.

[12] Clay, *Economic Expansion*, I, pp. 92–9. In fact, because of the effect of short-run fluctuations on price, even producers who met their own subsistence needs, on average, were under pressure. In a bad year, when they resorted to the market to supplement their shortfall, prices might be very high. On the other hand, in a good year, when they were in a position to sell, prices were poor. If they sold the same amount in good years as they bought in bad, they would be out of pocket. As a result, farmers producing exactly as much as was consumed in their household would, in an

wages. Over the period as a whole, large numbers of smallholders lost out, and their lands were taken up by the prospering market-oriented farmers. In such cases the increase in poverty was considerable, but so too was the potential for agricultural improvement. Larger holdings generated the income necessary to support experimentation, and farmers further away from subsistence level were freer to try new crops and new methods of cultivation, or to specialise in particular kinds of production.[13]

The extent to which occupiers of the land benefited, as opposed to its owners, depended on leasing arrangements and the flexibility of rent levels.[14] This makes the picture more complicated. So, too, does regional variation in inheritance customs. Where partible inheritance was practised (that is, where an estate might be divided between a number of beneficiaries) population increase might result in sub-division of holdings and the creation of a large group of near landless cultivators dependent on other activities for subsistence. In some areas primogeniture, that is inheritance of the land by a single descendant, ideally the eldest son, was practised. In such areas population increase should have had less effect on the size of landholdings, but would have resulted in the creation of an entirely landless group. For these people the options were to find wage labour, enter service locally, or to migrate.

In many areas of the country it was possible for smallholders to find enough sources of income to survive. Notably, in fen and forest regions common lands provided subsistence and other resources, and rural industries provided further possibilities to make up the shortfall in household income. Population growth in such areas could actually result in increasing numbers of smallholdings, particularly since these areas also tended to practise partible inheritance. For the inhabitants of fen and forest regions the consequences of price rises and declining real wages may have been less stark, or at least the poor in those districts were not quite so much at their mercy.[15] But, at the same time, agricultural improvement in these areas was also likely to be more restricted. Finally, such districts were extremely harvest-sensitive:

average ten years, accumulate a debt. This would have to be paid for by some other activity or it might result in rent arrears and, ultimately, bankruptcy. The effects on prices of short-run variations in yield are discussed in Wrigley, 'Some reflections'. This makes it clear that runs of either high or low prices were not simply a reflection of runs of bad or good harvests. For influential local studies of changing patterns of landholding see K. Wrightson and D. Levine, *Poverty and Piety in an English Village: Terling, 1525–1700*, 2nd edn (Oxford, 1995); M. Spufford, *Contrasting Communities: English Villagers in the Sixteenth and Seventeenth Centuries* (Cambridge, 1974).

[13] Clay, *Economic Expansion*, I, ch. 4.   [14] Ibid., pp. 85–91.

[15] Spufford, *Contrasting*, ch. 5; Clay, *Economic Expansion*, I, pp. 99–101

they were, in general, net importers of grain and therefore extremely vulnerable to short-term movements in prices.[16] This regional variation in economic experience is another reason why historians are uncertain about how much poverty and how much progress this period witnessed.[17]

Despite these complexities, it is clear that in many arable parishes there was a redistribution of land. This almost certainly led to migration to areas where the possession of land was less central to subsistence. Fen and forest areas thus faced yet more population pressure while the urban population grew faster than that of the country as a whole. Urban population growth was largely the result of the massive growth of London, which was home to 2 per cent of the country's population in 1520, and 8 per cent by 1650 at which point its population had increased from 60,000 to 575,000.[18] In itself, as we will see, this migration was regarded with suspicion by settled and prosperous observers. This unease was heightened by the association of migration with the growth of cottager and squatter communities in the suburbs and at the edges of fen and forest areas. Social differentiation implied not just a polarisation of wealth, therefore, but also diversification. We can find contrasting communities not just in differing kinds of agricultural community but also between, for example, settlements dominated by weavers in the Stour Valley, miners in the High Peak district of Derbyshire and coal miners on Tyneside.[19]

These developments resulted in improved agricultural productivity

[16] J. Walter, 'The economy of famine in early modern England', *Bulletin of the Society for the Social History of Medicine*, 40 (1987), 7–10. For an influential local study see B. Sharp, *In Contempt of All Authority: Rural Artisans in the West of England, 1586–1660* (Berkeley, 1980).

[17] For a clear discussion of regional variations in agrarian economies see J. Thirsk, *England's Agricultural Regions and Agrarian History, 1500–1750* (London, 1987).

[18] Clay, *Economic Expansion*, I, ch. 6. For London population figures see ibid., p. 197. For London's economic and demographic significance see E. A. Wrigley, 'A simple model of London's importance in changing English society and economy, 1650–1750', reprinted in Wrigley, *People, Cities and Wealth: The Transformation of Traditional Society* (Oxford, 1987), 133–56. For the effect on suburban settlement see R. Finlay and B. Shearer, 'Population growth and suburban expansion', in A. L. Beier and R. Finlay (eds.), *London 1500–1700: The Making of the Metropolis* (Harlow, 1986), 37–59.

[19] The classic statement of differentiation interpreted primarily in terms of polarisation is K. Wrightson, 'Aspects of social differentiation in rural England *c.* 1580–1660', *Journal of Peasant Studies*, 5 (1977), 33–47. For contrasting agricultural communities see Spufford, *Contrasting*. For the industrial and mining regions mentioned see J. Walter, *Understanding Popular Violence in the English Revolution: The Colchester Plunderers* (Cambridge, 1999), ch. 7; A. Wood, 'Industrial development, social change and popular politics in the mining area of north west Derbyshire', Cambridge Ph.D., 1994; D. Levine and K. Wrightson, *The Making of an Industrial Society: Whickham 1560–1765* (Oxford, 1991). Examples of local variation could, of course, be multiplied.

over the period as a whole, but in the meantime there was a cost in declining living standards for broad sections of the population, increased landlessness and migration. Additionally, short-term problems such as harvest failure, the disruption of trade or visitations of the plague could result in even greater hardship. Thus, there were a number of related social problems – poverty, landlessness, migration, and the rapid growth of some communities which often lacked what were taken to be the means to maintain social and political order. Throughout our period, but especially before 1640, many of England's governors were acutely aware of these things and frequently acted to preserve what they saw as the foundations of social and political order. National policies to relieve, discipline and provide work for the poor, and to contain the perceived threats arising from migration, provided the framework for the 'poor law' until the early nineteenth century. Wages were regulated, and markets policed, in order to ensure that subsistence was possible. These perceptions of potential disorder also coloured the elaborate measures developed to contain the effects of epidemic disease.[20] These measures were being implemented by local officeholders likely to be drawn from precisely those groups prospering as a result of economic change.

The 'real' extent of poverty or volume of migration are not the central point, here. To some extent, contemporaries were responding to 'objective' problems, but this response was filtered through perceptions of what constituted social order. As we will see, measures to deal with poverty were closely associated with campaigns against sin and disease. This conflation of problems reflected more generalised notions of order, drawing on humanist and Protestant thought.[21] In some places, at least, the changing distribution of wealth seems to have opened a cultural gap between those influenced by these ideals and their poorer neighbours, so that social problems were perceived from a cultural distance.[22] Responses were partly designed to promote civility, therefore, not simply to tackle material problems. Fears were prompted by changes in material conditions, but it was the fears rather than the material conditions which really shaped social policy.

Perceived threats to what were taken to be the bases of social order were an important source of political innovation in this period. They

---

[20] See below, ch. 3.
[21] See ch. 3; P. Slack, *From Reformation to Improvement: Public Welfare in Early Modern England* (Oxford, 1998).
[22] K. Wrightson, *English Society 1580–1680* (London, 1982), ch. 7; Wrightson and Levine, *Terling*, ch. 6. For the debate see ibid., pp. 197–220.

were related to a second general pressure, the consequences of religious reformation. Haigh distinguishes between the official and Protestant reformations in this period. We might say that the official reformation gave the English state a Protestant identity which had to be defended internationally and against internal subversion. Legitimate authority was used to enforce and to exploit this process of religious reformation. At the same time, the Protestant reformation, because it did not wholly succeed, made for internal division. It promoted an exclusive form of religion which was not open, or acceptable, to all. According to Haigh, the result was that by the end of the reign of Elizabeth there were four different kinds of religious practice: godly Protestants; recusant papists; parish Anglicans; and 'old Catholics'.[23] This had a number of consequences, not the least of which was that the theoretical religious identity of the state was in practice considerably compromised.

No early modern state could afford to ignore religion. 'Virtually no public proponent of religion in Elizabethan England believed in, or found it possible to approve of, a state of religious pluralism.'[24] As Bishop Sandys put it in a speech at the opening of parliament in 1571:

This liberty, that men may openly profess diversity of religion, must needs be dangerous to the commonwealth . . . One God, one King, one faith, one profession, is fit for one monarchy and one Commonwealth. Division weakeneth; concord strengtheneth . . . Let conformity and unity in religion be provided for, and it shall be a wall of defence unto this realm.

As an assize judge put it in his address to the grand jury at Stafford in 1683: 'Where disagreement is admitted in the church there could be no agreement in the state.'[25] The church was not an arm of state, but considerable influence was exercised over it by the national government. It was an agency, it need hardly be said, of 'religion' in a period when that term involved much more than private belief. Its activities and personnel, and the message it preached, were unavoidably political. To take an extreme, but illuminating, example from the end of our

---

[23] C. Haigh, *English Reformations: Religion, Politics and Society under the Tudors* (Oxford, 1993), esp. pp. 285–95.

[24] P. Collinson, 'William Shakespeare's religious inheritance and environment', reprinted in Collinson, *Elizabethan Essays* (London, 1994), 219–52, quotation at p. 228.

[25] For a general account see C. Russell, 'Arguments for religious unity in England, 1530–1650', reprinted in Russell, *Unrevolutionary England 1603–1642* (London, 1990), 179–204. Sandys is quoted in J. W. Martin, 'Toleration 1689: England's recognition of pluralism', in G. J. Schochet, P. E. Tatspaugh and C. Brobeck (eds.), *Restoration, Ideology and Revolution* (Washington, DC, 1990), 67–82, at p. 68. Sandys apparently made pointed reference to the French Wars of Religion in his speech: ibid., p. 80 n. 1.

period, it was not possible to hold office in Ireland without swearing against belief in the real presence in the communion.[26]

The interpenetration of church and state in this period operated at several levels. The church lent sacred legitimacy to the authority of the monarch. But this cut the other way too: those who did not accept the message of the church might have a reduced or compromised sense of the legitimacy of monarchical authority. Moreover, the religious identity of the English state after 1563, at the latest, cut across those of other states, and the existence of domestic religious plurality posed the threat of subversion. In 1584, following a revelation of Catholic plots against Elizabeth's life, a Bond of Association was drawn up and enforced across the country.[27] The reality of this internal threat,[28] or the sincerity of protestations of religious war, are not really the issue here. The fear of these things was clear enough in government rhetoric. In June 1588 lieutenants were urged, in a letter signed by the queen, to impress on those liable for militia duty or payments that no effort should be spared 'Considering these great preparacons and arrogant Threatenings now burst oute into accion upon the seas, tending to a conquest wherein every man's particular estate is in the highest degre to be touched, in Respect of Country, lyberty, wyfe, childeren, lyf and that which is speciallie to be regarded for the profession of the trew and sencere religion of Christ.'[29] On the other hand, in 1599 Adelantado of Castilla, captain general of the galleys and the army of the sea, justified the campaign against the Tudor crown in England and Ireland in terms of the obligation his monarch, 'his Catholic majesty', had 'received of God to defend his holy faith and the Roman Church'. The impending attack would free Catholics from their bondage to the heretics, and English Catholics, or those who declared themselves to be Catholic,

---

[26] 'Act excluding papists from public trust in Ireland', reprinted in A. Browning (ed.), *English Historical Documents, 1660–1714* (London, 1953), 772–6.

[27] For the bond see D. Cressy, 'Binding the nation: the Bonds of Association, 1584 and 1696', in D. J. Guth and J. W. McKenna (eds.), *Tudor Rule and Revolution: Essays for G. R. Elton from his American Friends* (Cambridge, 1982), 217–34. It is also discussed in P. Collinson, 'The Elizabethan exclusion crisis and the Elizabethan polity', *Proceedings of the British Academy*, 84 (1993), 51–92, esp. pp. 63–71. The text of the Bond taken in Pontefract, on 14 November 1584, made no direct reference to Catholicism, emphasising instead the duty of natural born subjects to protect the life of their sovereign. It did, however, note that one of the many benefits that had been enjoyed under Elizabeth was 'godlie governement': HEH, HAP 0/5 3 (27).

[28] Greaves suggests that English Protestants had turned their backs on resistance theory during Elizabeth's reign: R. L. Greaves, 'Concepts of political obedience in late Tudor England: conflicting perspectives', *JBS*, 22 (1982), 23–34. By the 1590s most Catholics are said to have adopted a quietist position, too: J. Bossy, 'The character of Elizabethan Catholicism', reprinted in T. Aston (ed.), *Crisis in Europe 1560–1660: Essays from Past and Present* (London, 1965), 223–46, esp. 227–9. See below, pp. 304–5.   [29] HEH, HM 30881, fo. 88r.

would be secure in their estates and liberties.[30] In the 1620s blood-curdling cries against the threat of popery were raised once more.[31]

Religious rhetorics therefore destabilised national and international order. 'The rituals of the parish church were blueprints for a relationship with God which prescribed in turn the roles of social and political behaviour.' Consequently, conflicts over ritual forms 'encompassed personal religious discipline, the rules of social interaction and the values structuring the use of political power'.[32] Locally, however, religious plurality could be very diverse, and this diversity could lead to conflict when activists managed to make local headway. For example, godly Protestants often led attempts at a 'reformation of manners', which aimed at reformation and the preservation of social order. This led them into conflict with other values, those associated with the 'festive sociability' of many English villages. This attempt to reform behaviour was not confined to godly Protestants, but they may have been disproportionately represented among its proponents.[33] In any case, disagreements over religious order encompassed broad aspects of social life. Social order was physically represented in the seating arrangements in church. The disposition of pews reflected the local hierarchy, and disputes over pews reflected larger conflicts over precedence.[34] Urban

[30] *CSPD, 1598–1601*, pp. 184–85.

[31] T. Cogswell, *The Blessed Revolution: English Politics and the Coming of War 1621–1624* (Cambridge, 1989); Cogswell, 'Phaeton's chariot: the parliament-men and the continental crisis in 1621', in J. F. Merritt (ed.), *The Political World of Thomas Wentworth, Earl of Strafford, 1621–1641* (Cambridge, 1996), 24–46; C. Russell, 'Sir Thomas Wentworth and anti-Spanish sentiment, 1621–1624', in ibid., 47–62; P. Lake, 'Antipopery: the structure of a prejudice', in R. Cust and A. Hughes (eds.), *Conflict in Early Stuart England: Studies in Religion and Politics 1603–1642* (London, 1989), 72–106.

[32] D. Beaver, 'Conscience and context: the Popish Plot and the politics of ritual, 1678–1682', *HJ*, 34 (1991), 297–327, quotation at p. 326. For a general account of the role of religious ritual and symbol in the creation of community see Beaver, *Parish Communities and Religious Conflict in the Vale of Gloucester 1590–1690* (Cambridge, Mass., 1998). This is an important study, applying the insights of cultural anthropology in seeking to understand the meaning of early modern religious practices.

[33] Wrightson and Levine, *Terling*, ch. 7. For an account of the debate, see ibid., pp. 197–220.

[34] For the significance of pews to the understanding of local history and hierarchy see R. Gough, *The History of Myddle*, ed. D. Hey (London, 1981), 67–249; A. Flather, *The Politics of Place: A Study of Church Seating in Essex, c. 1580–1640*, Friends of the Department of English Local History, University of Leicester, Friends' Papers no. 3 (Leicester, 1999); S. Pittman, 'The social structure and parish community of St. Andrew's church, Calstock, as reconstituted from its seating plan', *Southern History*, 20–1 (1988–9), 44–67. Disputes are discussed in D. Underdown, *Revel, Riot and Rebellion: Popular Politics and Culture in England 1603–1660* (Oxford, 1985), 29–33; M. Ingram, *Church Courts, Sex and Marriage in England, 1570–1640* (Cambridge, 1987), esp. pp. 111–22. For some other local examples see: Beaver, *Parish Communities*, p. 80; N. Alldridge, 'Loyalty and identity in Chester parishes 1540–1640', in S. J. Wright (ed.), *Parish, Church and People: Local Studies in Lay Religion* (London, 1988), 85–124, esp. pp. 94–7; N. Evans, 'A scheme for re-pewing the parish church of Chesham, Buckinghamshire, in 1606', *Local Historian*, 22 (1992), 203–7; J. Merritt, 'The social context of the parish church in early modern Westminster', *Urban History Yearbook* (1991), 20–31.

parishes were units of both civil and spiritual administration and they continued to act as the focus for civic loyalties and conflicts as well as for spiritual life.[35] 'Religious policy' was not just about 'religion', then, but about an overlapping sense of order and hierarchy.[36] Religious division might disrupt these other representations of social and political relationships. The desire to shore up this order was partly a domestic concern, but also one of international politics. For these reasons it was extremely difficult to enforce – the range of 'religious' claims in early modern English society was huge. Moreover, a consequence of religious plurality was that cooperation was not guaranteed in the localities, while the promotion of a Protestant policy internationally might impose costs that were unpopular at home. Support for the war, if not for its costs, was vocal in the 1620s in the light of the threat to Protestantism in the Palatinate. But for war against the covenanting Scots in the later 1630s there was much less vocal enthusiasm.

There were more mundane, institutional or practical elements of the relationship between church and state. For example, churchmen were active at all levels of politics and administration – in the privy council, the House of Lords, on the commissions of the peace. Churchwardens had common law obligations, being regarded as a corporation managing moveable property on behalf of the parish. They might have resort to common law for robbery and trespass in relation to these duties, and were accountable for their conduct under the law. Moreover, they had duties imposed on them by statute, which were quite wide-ranging. They included, for example, responsibilities in relation to the maintenance of the highways and the extermination of vermin. They might be required to act as overseers of the poor, and were central to the enforcement of secular laws relating to church attendance.[37] The church was a very rich corporation, even after the age of plunder, and its financial resources were regularly drawn upon by the government in taxation and, for example, in attempts to make the church contribute to the militia effort.[38] Control of the church also gave access to an

---

[35] Alldridge, 'Loyalty'; J. Barry, 'The parish in civic life: Bristol and its churches', in Wright (ed.), *Parish*, 152–78; M. Goldie and J. Spurr, 'Politics and the restoration parish: Edward Fowler and the struggle for St Giles Cripplegate', *EHR*, 109 (1994), 572–96. For a rural example see P. Collinson, 'Cranbrook and the Fletchers: popular and unpopular religion in the Kentish Weald', in P. N. Brooks (ed.), *Reformation Principle and Practice: Essays in Honour of Arthur Geoffrey Dickens* (London, 1980), 171–202.   [36] See Beaver, 'Conscience', for example.

[37] W. Lambarde, *The Duties of Constables, Borsholders, Tithingmen, and such other low Ministers of the Peace* (London, 1583), 42–52.

[38] C. G. Cruickshank, *Elizabeth's Army*, 2nd edn (Oxford, 1966), 30–2; J. J. N. McGurk, 'The clergy and the militia 1580–1610', *History*, 60 (1975), 198–210; C. M. Hibbard, 'Episcopal warriors in

infrastructure of communication that was invaluable to government. In 1579, perturbed that subjects might be uneasy regarding their rights in relation to the new military obligations being imposed upon them, the privy council turned to the pulpit to overcome this problem of presentation. Lords lieutenant were asked to ensure 'either by announcements in Church or in some other way' that a planned general muster was not a preliminary to sending people on an expedition.[39] During the 1640s Samuel Hartlib appears to have considered the possibility that important political questions could be put to the people via the pulpit in regular referenda.[40]

In most villages the church was the only building large enough to hold a meeting of the inhabitants. It was in the church at Burton Agnes that Henry Griffith took accounts for purveyance to the queen's household in 1598, and when Robert Downes, a recusant, complained that he had been overtaxed in the fifteenth and tenth in Great Melton, Norfolk, he was told 'that he might come to church and hear what was done, and do as they did'.[41] Church courts provided another resource for securing local order, particularly moral and spiritual offences, and they depended on local participation for the presentment and prosecution of offenders.[42] Religious change had profound implications for overarching conceptions of legitimacy and for more routine matters of government and administration. It posed a fundamental challenge for government, and yet that very profundity made any successful administrative solution all but impossible to design. The consequences of religious change pervaded political life throughout this period.

A third general pressure making for political innovation was inflation in military costs. War was a fact of early modern political life, perhaps increasingly so. It has been suggested that the sixteenth century saw thirty-four wars in Europe, averaging 1.6 years in duration, and that there was a war somewhere in Europe 95 per cent of the time. The seventeenth century was a little more pacific: only twenty-nine wars, but

the British wars of religion', in M. C. Fissel (ed.), *War and Government in Britain, 1598–1650* (Manchester, 1991), 164–92; P. Carter, 'Clerical Taxation during the civil war and interregnum', *Historical Research*, 67 (1994), 119–33. Only in the eighteenth century was clerical taxation used to promote improvements in clerical livings and standards: I. Green, 'The first years of Queen Anne's Bounty', in R. O'Day and F. Heal (eds.), *Princes and Paupers in the English Church 1500–1800* (Leicester, 1981), 231–53. For the plunder of the church, see W. G. Hoskins, *The Age of Plunder: The England of Henry VIII 1500–1547* (London, 1976), ch. 6.

[39] Cruickshank, *Elizabeth's Army*, p. 12.   [40] HP 28/1/10a–10b, Hartlib's Ephemerides, 1649.

[41] P. Laslett, *The World We Have Lost – Further Explored*, 3rd edn (London, 1983), 72–3; HEH, HM 50657, fo. 62v. For purveyance in Yorkshire see below, pp. 248–9. PRO, E134/9 Jas I/M 28 fo. 6.

[42] See below, pp. 298–300.

each lasted 1.7 years, and so there was a war somewhere about 94 per cent of the time.[43] The great frequency of wars in this period was accompanied by an increase in their intensity. Roberts suggested, famously, that this period witnessed a military revolution in which changes in battlefield tactics transformed the nature of armed forces and the relationship between war and society. The adoption of gunpowder weapons changed the way that infantry were used, requiring greater discipline and expertise. Cavalry were also used more systematically and this had strategic and logistical consequences. As a result, the conduct of war became more terrible – larger armies wreaked greater physical and economic destruction.

By 1660 the modern art of war had come to birth. Mass armies, strict discipline, the control of the state, the submergence of the individual had all arrived; the conjoint ascendancy of financial power and applied science was already established in all its malignity . . .[44]

Subsequent research has tended to focus on the consequences of changes in battlefield tactics, in particular the growing size and permanency of armed forces, the greater cost of sustaining them as well as the bureaucratic and administrative innovation necessary to support this increased mobilisation. In the process, the chronological boundaries have moved – back into the fifteenth century and forward into the eighteenth – and geographical variations elaborated to the point that some now question the usefulness of the term 'revolution'.[45]

The difficulty with finding a single moment when such a process affected the whole of Europe is, of course, that there was no point at which all European states were belligerents simultaneously. Individual states faced the consequences of these changes at different points in time. In each case the challenge had changed slightly in the light of previous developments elsewhere and according to local strategic and logistical considerations. For individual states the process of adjustment could be extremely painful, and concentrated in a short space of time, but each state had a different experience. The costs of failure were significant, however. In 1500 there were about 500 independent political entities in Europe. By 1789 this had fallen to 350.[46] A minor example

[43] Quoted in C. Tilly, *Coercion, Capital and European States AD 990–1992* (Oxford, 1992), 73.
[44] M. Roberts, 'The military revolution, 1560–1660', reprinted in Roberts (ed.), *Essays in Swedish History* (Minneapolis, 1967), 195–225, at p. 218.
[45] See J. Black, *A Military Revolution? Military Change and European Society 1550–1800* (London, 1991).
[46] Quoted in M. Greengrass, 'Conquest and coalescence', in Greengrass (ed.), *Conquest and Coalescence: The Shaping of the State in Early Modern Europe* (London, 1991), 1–24, at p. 1.

of the scale of the task is provided by the case of Hesse-Cassel, a small German principality. At the end of the Thirty Years War it had paid off and reduced its forces to 600 infantry and 40 landsknechts. By 1688 it was felt necessary to have an army of 10,000, which was supported by subsidies from England and the United Provinces until the end of the 1720s. At that point its armed forces cost more than its total tax revenues.[47] Not all areas of Europe were affected in this way, obviously, and England is often said to stand at the opposite end of the spectrum, protected, as it was, by the sea rather than massed ranks of infantry and heavy fortifications. Whatever the problems of periodisation and geographical variation, though, it is still reasonable to conclude that 'the scale of warfare in early modern Europe was revolutionized, and this had important and wide-ranging consequences'.[48] Although a number of historians have suggested that the process was too protracted and dispersed to be a revolution, few have denied this essential proposition.

The Elizabethan privy council, at least, would probably have agreed. According to a set of militia instructions, dated 28 August 1583, it was imperative that horsemen be equipped to greatest effect, both offensive and defensive. The reason, it was said, lay in the fact that 'all forrain princes, beinge neighbours to this Realme be in armes, and that the manner of the present warres doe differ from warres in former tymes'.[49] Elizabethan and early Stuart military commitments were comparatively limited, but engagement was not avoidable indefinitely. In Elizabeth's reign, for example, the 'war effort increased steadily as the reign progressed ... after the official armed intervention in the low countries in 1585 the curve went rapidly up'.[50] A new kind of war meant a new scale of mobilisation, particularly of supplies and equipment. It is, perhaps, only a slight exaggeration to claim that in meeting the challenge of military engagement the 'government's main struggle was not with the French, or the Spaniards, or the rebels in occupied Ireland. It was against its own citizens, whose enthusiasm for military service, never great, diminished in direct proportion to the demands made on them.'[51]

England avoided major military commitments on land more effectively than most European powers, at least before the 1690s, but the pressure to reform was felt none the less. As we will see in chapter 5,

[47] Ibid., p. 6.
[48] G. Parker, 'The military revolution, 1560–1660 – a myth?', *Journal of Modern History*, 48 (1976), 195–214, at p. 214.
[49] HEH, EL 6253 fo. 1r. Quoted in J. Goring and J. Wake (eds.), *Northamptonshire Liutenancy Papers and other Documents 1580–1614*, Northamptonshire Record Society, 27 (Northampton, 1975), 7.
[50] Cruickshank, *Elizabeth's Army*, p. 16.   [51] Ibid.

from the 1570s onwards consistent pressure was applied to establish a well-armed and well-trained militia capable of meeting the threat of invasion. The demands were constantly changing, however. For example, during the Elizabethan period the trained bands were being encouraged to adopt the caliver. By 1618, however, the privy council was writing to lords lieutenant that as 'your lordship well knoweth ... the moderne use doth altogether exclude the caliver as unserviceable and not to be allowed upon any musters of arms'. The caliver had already been superseded by the musket.[52] For fairly complex reasons the naval build-up required less direct activity by the national government, but here too, by the 1630s, there was pressure for major reform. This caused, notoriously, domestic political and administrative problems. Military expeditions before 1640 were unimpressive on the whole, and certainly unambitious, with the exception of the Irish campaigns. But preparations against invasion and the aggressive acquisition of commercial interests produced military commitments with increasing political and administrative consequences.

A fourth general pressure for political change in this period was the growing complexity of the crown's territorial and trading interests. Political authority is territorially defined and all states have territorial interests. This might have been driven by dynastic ambition too, the pursuit of resources or glory in the name of the head of state. Of course, such interests were by no means peculiar to the sixteenth and seventeenth centuries, and the union of England and Scotland by dynastic means reflected the normal pattern of European politics. However, during this period English overseas trade was transformed, and this too had implications for government – the later Stuart state spread much more widely than, say, the Angevin state had. The territorial interests of a number of European states were becoming global in this period and this produced an expanding territorial commitment. As a direct result of the pursuit of trade the Tudors and Stuarts acquired territorial interests in the West Indies and America. Indirectly, the expanding range of European trade also transformed the geography of dynastic politics – the Stuarts acquired Tangier and Bombay through marriage, for example. Trade was an important source of revenue (customs duties produced 30–40 per cent of total revenues throughout the period)[53] and

---

[52] Privy council to the lords lieutenant, 25 April 1618, *APC, 1618–1619*, p. 118. For a local case study see T. Cogswell, *Home Divisions: Aristocracy, the State and Provincial Conflict* (Manchester, 1998), esp. pp. 42–52.

[53] M. J. Braddick, *The Nerves of State: Taxation and the Financing of the English State, 1558–1714* (Manchester, 1996), 49.

so governments had an interest in promoting it. The expansion of trading interests was also a source of prestige and an extension of competition with other European states. For this latter reason the expansion of overseas trade had military implications, as we will see. By the late seventeenth century fairly conscious steps were taken to promote trade and these were quite explicitly acknowledged to be at the expense of rivals.

At the beginning of the period England's trade was unimpressive.[54] Exports were dominated by semi-finished woollen cloth, leather and tin. These were essentially primary materials, since the profits of finishing the cloth accrued to foreign producers. In return, English merchants imported a range of manufactured goods which domestic industry was unable to supply. Moreover, most of the trade was handled by foreign merchants and carried in foreign ships. In these ways 'England's place in the international economic order was not many degrees removed from that of the colonial economy, dependent upon sales of primary products to more advanced regions and purchasing manufactures and services from them'.[55] In the first part of the sixteenth century cloth exports had expanded rapidly, at the expense of wool, but by the mid-sixteenth century this trade was stagnating. This was partly due to the disruption of England's principal markets in north west Europe and Iberia, and this was only partly offset by the development of new markets (for example the Baltic and Russia). One interest of national government in this period was, therefore, to promote the development of these new markets. This was all the more important because England was importing increasing amounts of luxury goods, and import merchants began to trade directly with Mediterranean ports to satisfy this demand. The result of the 'insatiable appetite of England's well-to-do for luxury goods, was a spectacular widening of the geographical horizons of English foreign trade'.[56] Some of it was to regions with which English merchants had had no previous contact, not least, in the early seventeenth century, with the East Indies. A final impetus to this expansion of the geographical range of trade was the lure of the new world and here competition with other European powers was of great importance: preying on Spanish shipping, for example, came to be regarded by some as a patriotic activity.[57]

[54] For an excellent general account see Clay, *Economic Expansion*, II, ch. 9.　　[55] Ibid., p. 103.
[56] Ibid., p. 126.
[57] K. R. Andrews, *Trade, Plunder and Settlement: Maritime Enterprise and the Genesis of the British Empire, 1480–1630* (Cambridge, 1984), esp. pp. 34–7.

The commercial consequences of this were extremely important. Accelerating change after 1630, and especially after 1660, transformed England's place in world trade. The development of new kinds of finished cloth exports opened up new export markets in the Mediterranean and increased domestic profits. There was also an expansion in the export of English manufactures, but the most important changes were in the import and re-export trades. English merchants secured significant shares of world trade in new commodities from new markets – notably sugar and tobacco. These trades provided an important leg of the famous triangular trades, while the East India trade began to produce substantial returns, in part from the rapid expansion of the silk trade. These new imports were re-exported to European markets with the result that, by 1700, England stood at the heart of a global trading network. This was supported by sophisticated financial services and a greatly enlarged shipping industry. These developments were enabling for government – providing revenue, for example, or the financial expertise to support ever more complex credit operations. They were, for that reason, fostered by government: the promotion of overseas trade was more or less deliberately encouraged throughout our period, by various means. But they also, by the same token, imposed new burdens on government. England's trade was more complex, and so regulation was more demanding, and the range of English 'strategic interests' was greatly increased. Thus, in the 'western design' of the 1650s, a blow against Spanish, Catholic power was to be struck not on land in Europe but at sea in the Caribbean. In fact, much of the privateering, contraband and plundering activity of the English pioneers in the Americas was justified and perhaps even motivated by patriotic and religious interests.[58] This expansion of the commercial and strategic interests of the English government posed, in particular, a challenge to the naval resources of the country.

Keeping up with military technology and organisation had financial consequences. So did, potentially at least, responses to threats to social order, to religious order and attempts to regulate trade. As a result, in practical terms, much of the energy of government was devoted to designing, agreeing and imposing a variety of taxes and rates to support

---

[58] For the complexities of foreign policy, see S. C. A. Pincus, *Protestantism and Patriotism: Ideologies and the Making of English Foreign Policy, 1650–1668* (Cambridge, 1996); Pincus, 'England and the World in the 1650s', in J. Morrill (ed.), *Revolution and Restoration England in the 1650s* (London, 1992), 129–47; and for the mixture of motives among colonisers and adventurers see K. O. Kupperman, *Providence Island 1630–1641: The Other Puritan Colony* (Cambridge, 1993); Andrews, *Trade*, pp. 30–40.

the activities of local and national government. This was a fruitful period for national initiatives aiming to fund areas of expenditure such as military expeditions or the supply of the household and court. In the localities elaborate rating systems were developed to cope with these charges, and those imposed directly by local government, such as rates for the poor, the gaols, the highways or the militia. In individual villages these ratings had to be harmonised with those for the church. Thus, at all levels of government raising money was a constant concern, but these efforts were simply the sharp end of governmental commitments on a number of fronts.

Revolutions have been claimed in prices, military organisation and commerce, and each gave opportunities to England's rulers while also posing challenges. The upheaval in the nation's spiritual life generally merits the comparatively modest title of reformation, but its effects were scarcely less momentous. These processes intersected in complex ways, too. For example, the price revolution produced a mixture of poverty and progress resulting from diverging economic fortunes of particular regions and social groups. Economic distance was often compounded by cultural change – the better sort (a revealing self-description in this context) disposed of their income in ways that separated them even more clearly from their social inferiors. They dressed themselves and furnished their houses more elaborately, for example, and were more likely to be enjoying the fruits of the growing empire. But more significantly, it has been suggested that because they were more educated they imbibed new and aggressive social values. In many of the areas where economic differentiation occurred, therefore, a much more profound social differentiation took place, reflected in patterns of education, recreation and consumption. In some villages, at least, this cultural differentiation was also associated with religious change. In such places, hotter Protestants among the prospering middling sort came to see the use of office to secure reformation and social discipline as an extension of their religious practice. In this, no doubt, they had allies among the gentry and the respectable poor, but the coincidence of economic prosperity and religious change might give, in many localities, a particular colouring to their initiatives in relation to social problems.[59]

---

[59] For godly magistracy, see P. Collinson, *The Religion of Protestants: The Church in English Society 1559–1625* (Oxford, 1982), ch. 4; D. Underdown, *Fire from Heaven: The Life of an English Town in the Seventeenth Century* (London, 1992); Slack, *Reformation to Improvement*, ch. 2. Active magistracy was not always godly, of course, and not all the godly were active magistrates: M. Spufford, 'Puritanism and social control?', in A. Fletcher and J. Stevenson (eds.), *Order and Disorder in Early Modern England* (Cambridge, 1985), 41–57; F. Heal and C. Holmes, *The Gentry in England and*

The second Dutch war provides another example of the complex interactions between these developments. Its causes, and the way it was promoted domestically, conflated religious and commercial interests along with fears for domestic political order which also had religious origins. The Dutch, as opponents of bishops and kings, were claimed to be in league with subversives at home. Their strength, and their threat to England's power, was commercial. The war was not simply commercial in origin – mercantile interests were potentially threatened by the disruption of trade consequent on war, and it was advocated for religious and political reasons. But, just as the Spanish had been weakened by attacking their commercial interests in the Americas, so too, could the Dutch be weakened by the pursuit of commercial rivalry.[60] When the war came, the cost of the mobilisation was enormous by Elizabethan standards: £5 million was raised in taxes in three years, about half as much again as Elizabeth's campaigns had cost in the period 1590–1603. In order to meet this cost the heaviest tax of the seventeenth century prior to 1688 was raised, the combined royal aid and further supply, and a general excise was proposed.[61] In order to raise the credit necessary to mobilise for war, innovations were made, changing the security of government loans by guaranteeing repayment in the order in which the debt had been contracted. To make this stick parliamentary powers of audit and appropriation were extended. These innovations in borrowing were of long-term significance and, along with the short-term financial costs and proposals, had further domestic political consequences. The constitutional implications were further interpreted in the light of the threat of previous innovations and the association of popery with arbitrary government.[62] The effects of the military and commercial revolutions, and of religious change, intertwined here in complex ways.

Wales 1500–1700 (London, 1994), 181–3. The most comprehensive review of the evidence of social regulation in England's local courts in the period before 1600 argues that the desire to exercise social control cannot be attributed to puritanism, but 'supports Wrightson's emphasis on the distinctiveness of social regulation when implemented by committed Puritans': M. K. McIntosh, *Controlling Misbehavior in England, 1370–1600* (Cambridge, 1998), quotation at p. 14. She goes on to point out that this distinctive approach, and an insistence on particular issues, often served to disrupt a consensus about the broad uses of the court.

[60] Pincus, *Protestantism*, pt. III. See also P. Seaward, 'The House of Commons Committee of Trade and the origins of the second Anglo-Dutch war, 1664', *HJ*, 30 (1987), 437–52.

[61] C. D. Chandaman, *The English Public Revenue 1660–1688* (Oxford, 1975), 30, 44, 86–7, 228; Braddick, *Nerves*, pp. 28–9, 148–9; Braddick, 'Resistance to the royal aid and further supply in Chester, 1664–1672: relations between centre and locality in restoration England', *Northern History*, 33 (1997), 108–36.

[62] J. P. Kenyon, *The Stuart Constitution 1603–1688: Documents and Commentary* (Cambridge, 1966), 388–9; H. Roseveare, *The Financial Revolution 1660–1760* (London, 1991), 14–15.

It is possible to discern four distinct sources of pressure for political innovation, therefore: social change, the transformation of military technology, the political consequences of the reformation and the expansion of overseas trade. One set of patterns in the development of the state derived from these underlying pressures, although in practice, of course, the effects intertwined, producing complex pressures for political innovation. The success of responses to these problems and opportunities depended on the success with which concrete actions taken by agents of state power could be legitimated. Activists, at the centre and in the localities, designed and promoted new administrative measures in the light of these pressures. In order to implement their innovations it was necessary to find legally valid ways of dealing with these challenges. More than this, however, in order to secure compliance these measures required a broader legitimacy. Further patterns in political development derived, therefore, from regularities in the ways that political innovations were legitimated, and the characteristic strengths and weaknesses of particular kinds of legitimation.

LEGITIMATION, RESISTANCE AND FUNCTIONAL EFFECTIVENESS

As we have seen, legitimacy is a key term in the sociological definition of political power and, therefore, of the state. A discussion of how legitimacy is claimed, established and sustained also helps to elucidate several of the key issues being addressed here: in particular, the relationship between ideas and political action; the extent and origins of the autonomy of the state; and the sources of administrative and political initiative.

For these reasons legitimacy is a crucial concept, but it is also a slippery one. It cannot be reduced simply to legal validity, not least because it is plainly the case that political actions can be legal without being regarded as legitimate, or vice versa. On the other hand, attempting to define more generalised standards of legitimacy founder on the fact that some regimes enjoy legitimacy even though the values by which their actions are justified are unacceptable in many other societies. One solution is to argue that a regime is legitimate where it is believed to be so, but this allows no moral content to the idea of legitimacy.[63] In response to these difficulties Beetham has suggested that, 'A given power relationship is not legitimate because people

---

[63] D. Beetham, *The Legitimation of Power* (London, 1991), 1–10. See also R. Barker, *Political Legitimacy and the State* (Oxford, 1990), for a lucid discussion of these problems.

believe in its legitimacy, but because it can be *justified in terms of* their beliefs.' The force of this distinction is that it leads us to compare how far the actions of a regime conform to the beliefs in terms of which its activities are justified. We are comparing its practices with its claims rather than reporting on a level of belief.[64]

The next problem, then, is how to measure this. In practice, legitimacy is not only about belief. Actions can confer legitimacy on a regime, implying acceptance of its claims and helping to make them good in practice.[65] Compliance is difficult to interpret, of course, since it might derive from approval or the lack of a viable alternative: at this minimal level legitimacy might simply mean acquiescence. However, it might also derive from positive approval or from a mixture of motives. Accepting unpleasant acts of state might, for example, be the price of enjoying the benefits of other acts of state or it might simply be the force of habit, what Morrill has termed the 'momentum of obedience'.[66]

The real difficulty here lies in the attempt to recover the motives of an individual from a study of their actions, a problem made even more difficult since they themselves may not have been clear about their motives. For present purposes, however, the *motivation* of an individual is not the key issue, but the generally understood *meaning* of their actions. Rather than discuss individual motivation, Beetham concentrates on the meaning of political action (or consent to it), not for the actor, but in terms of broader social conventions. Within such conventions actions with diverse motivations can confer legitimacy: 'what is important for legitimacy is evidence of consent expressed through actions *which are understood as demonstrating consent* within the conventions of the particular society'. This might include 'concluding an agreement or entering a contract with a superior party; swearing an oath of allegiance; joining an acclamation; voting in an election or plebiscite; and so on'. An important feature of such acts, though, is that they imply a mutual acceptance of the obligations on both sides.[67] 'Legitimate government is a relationship between state and subjects.'[68]

In this view then, legitimacy can be measured against three yardsticks: legal validity; the justifiability of the regime in terms of the beliefs and values current in the given society; and the evidence of consent derived from actions taken to be expressive of it. In the case of each of

---

[64] Beetham, *Legitimation*, pp. 10–11, quotation at p. 11.   [65] Ibid., p. 12.

[66] Both John Morrill and I believe the phrase to be his, but neither of us has been able to find it in his published work. For 'habitual legitimacy', a similar concept, see Barker, *Legitimacy*, pp. 29–40.

[67] Beetham, *Legitimation*, pp. 12, 25–6 (emphasis added).   [68] Barker, *Legitimacy*, p. 2.

these three criteria there is an obverse. Firstly, obviously, actions may be illegal. Secondly, there might be a mismatch between the actions of a regime and the beliefs in terms of which they are justified. On a larger scale, expressed against offices or functions rather than individuals, such a mismatch ('legitimacy deficit') might result from changed beliefs but also from changed circumstances of political action. Finally, there are varieties of action implying a lack of, or only measured, consent, from non-cooperation to forceful demonstration.[69] There are degrees of legitimacy and the degree of legitimacy enjoyed by particular actions and offices will affect the quality of the performance of a regime. In fact, the quality of the performance becomes almost an indicator of the degree of legitimacy enjoyed.[70] Exercises of political power that fail, or succeed only partially, may be presumed to have enjoyed measured legitimacy, reflected in partial or grudging consent.

The process of legitimation acted as a constraint on officeholders and limited their freedom to pursue their own interests, narrowly conceived. In order for legitimating ideas to have this force it is not necessary that they be the genuine motives for action, of course. They may not explain why a person is acting in a particular way, but they are none the less among the things that constrain those actions. Legitimating ideas are 'inter-subjective': their meaning 'is a property of the words in standard use; not something bestowed on them by the conventional, individual user'.[71] The representation of a political action as legitimate involves an attempt to reconcile the action in hand with these wider values, not simply the assertion of its legitimacy, and failure to justify action in this way limits its effectiveness. At the same time, having laid claim to a particular justification other actions become necessary in order to sustain the credibility of that justification. Even if the ideas are not the real motives for action, therefore, they set limits to what can or cannot be done subsequently. Ideas are constraining because there are limits to the sphere of action that can plausibly be justified with reference to particular values: 'to recover the nature of the normative vocabulary available to an agent for the description and appraisal of his conduct is at the same time to indicate one of the constraints on his conduct itself'.[72] Legitima-

---

[69] Beetham, *Legitimation*, pp. 16–20.   [70] Ibid., pp. 25–37.

[71] J. Tully, 'The pen is a mighty sword: Quentin Skinner's analysis of politics', in J. Tully (ed.), *Meaning and Context: Quentin Skinner and his Critics* (Princeton, 1988), 7–25, 289–91, quotation at p. 13.

[72] Q. Skinner, 'Language and social change', reprinted ibid., 119–32, 311–13, quotation at p. 132. See also his argument that Namierites and behaviourists

   have in effect been involved in a non sequitur. It does not, as they have tended to suppose, follow from the fact that an agent's professed principles may be *ex post facto* rationalizations that they have no role to play in

tion does not necessarily offer a guide to motivation, but it reveals some of the constraints on the actions of individuals and some of the meanings attached to those actions.

Legitimacy is, in short, 'an historically observable set of justified relationships rather than a normatively awarded status'.[73] Officeholders laid claim not just to legal validity, but to legitimacy. In doing so they tried to justify their actions in terms of beliefs in society at large, and a measure of their success was compliance. The degree to which compliance was forthcoming is a rough measure of the degree to which legitimacy was established. In the following pages, therefore, legitimacy is not seen as an all-or-nothing property, but a matter of degree. In response to the general pressures for political change outlined above, administrative innovations were proposed and designed, legitimated with reference to wider beliefs and implemented with degrees of success. Both legal validity and wider legitimacy could empower officeholders but each set limits to their competence – the sphere of action which could plausibly be claimed to lie within their limits. Legitimation gives force to ideas and beliefs. The difficulty of establishing and sustaining credible legitimations shapes the exercise of political power, and offers means to resist it. The success of strategies of legitimation is reflected in functional effectiveness.

We will see in what follows how a variety of legitimating languages were mobilised to justify political action, but some more concrete illustration might be useful here. For many officeholders, office, honour, reputation and status were closely linked. As James I put it to the judges in 1616, the justice was 'the King's eyes and ears in the Country' and the office 'a place of high honour and great reputation ... [as] minister of the King's justice in service of the commonwealth'. Good justices were those who were 'careful to attend the service of the King and country for thanks only of the King and love to their country, and for no other respect'.[74] In general, those who sought office in order to promote their own interests were castigated and the government propagated an

explaining his behaviour. [T]his argument ignores the implications of the fact that any agent possesses a standard motive for attempting to legitimate his untoward social or political actions. This implies first of all that he will be committed to claiming that his apparently untoward actions were in fact motivated by some accepted set of social or political principles. And this in turn implies that, even if the agent is not in fact motivated by any of the principles he professes, he will nevertheless be obliged to behave in such a way that his actions remain compatible with the claim that these principles genuinely motivated him.

Q. Skinner, 'Some problems in the analysis of political thought and action', reprinted ibid., 97–118, 309–11, quotation at p. 116.   [73] Barker, *Legitimacy*, p. 29.
[74] J. R. Tanner (ed.), *Constitutional Documents of the Reign of James I A.D. 1603–1625* (Cambridge, 1952), 19–21, quotations at pp. 19, 20.

'ideology of public service', emphasising the 'solemn duty to be exercised for the public good'. It was important to be impartial and energetic in providing justice – this, it was said, was a duty of gentility. As John Newdigate put it in 1608, the magistrate was to be the 'champion of justis, the patron of peace, the father of thy country and as it were as other god on earth'. This was not restricted to the puritan gentry and by the 1630s a mixture of positive propaganda and the punishment of those who erred had given these ideas wide currency.[75]

These ideals of governance were not confined to the magistracy, of course. For William Lambarde, a widely published contemporary authority on local government, constables were more junior officers of the peace, appointed to serve the same ideals as the justices, and a number of studies have shown how village elites were active in the promotion of order.[76] In fact, parishes with a resident gentleman were in a minority and the success of many administrative initiatives in this period depended in part on at least willingness among village worthies. But like their seniors, petty constables were sensitive to the expectations not just of their superiors but of their neighbours. This was true even of their implementation of criminal law. Local mediation might prevent formal prosecutions of offenders and, in fact, analysis of quarter sessions indictments seems to reveal a consistent bias in favour of local offenders, who benefited from local expectations of mercy and neighbourliness.[77] On the other hand, like the villagers from whose ranks they were drawn, constables were often petty offenders themselves.[78] Over-zealous constables ran the risk of an accusation of 'business', or unneighbourliness, and were subject to considerable pressures to mediate and mitigate the

[75] Heal and Holmes, *Gentry*, pp. 177–84, quotations at pp. 177, 179, 180.
[76] Lambarde, *Duties of Constables, passim*; Lambarde, *Eirenarcha Or of the Office of Iustice of the Peace, in Foure Bookes* (London, 1599 edn), 14–15. For some influential accounts of the importance of village elites see M. Ingram, 'Communities and courts: law and disorder in early-seventeenth-century Wiltshire', in J. Cockburn (ed.), *Crime in England, 1550–1800* (London, 1977), 110–34, 321–8; J. A. Sharpe, '"Such disagreements betwyx neighbours": litigation and human relations in early modern England', in J. Bossy (ed.), *Disputes and Settlements: Law and Human Relations in the West* (Cambridge, 1983), 167–87; Sharpe, 'Enforcing the law in the seventeenth-century English village', in V. A. C. Gatrell, B. Lenman and G. Parker (eds.), *Crime and the Law: The Social History of Crime in Western Europe since 1500* (London, 1980), 97–119; Wrightson and Levine, *Terling*, chs. 4–7; Spufford, 'Puritanism and social control'; J. R. Kent, *The English Village Constable 1580–1642: A Social and Administrative Study* (Oxford, 1986).
[77] K. Wrightson, 'Two concepts of order: justices, constables and jurymen in seventeenth-century England', in J. Brewer and J. Styles (eds.), *An Ungovernable People? The English and their Law in the Seventeenth and Eighteenth Centuries* (London, 1980), 21–46, 312–15; Ingram, 'Communities and courts', pp. 128–34.
[78] Sharpe, 'Crime and delinquency in an Essex parish 1600–1640', in Cockburn (ed.), *Crime*, 90–109, 316–21, esp. pp. 95–7.

impact of particular initiatives.[79] They had to make their behaviour conform to local standards as well as to the ideals laid out by their superiors. Their effectiveness locally depended on establishing and sustaining this legitimacy.

At all levels of local officeholding, performance in the office was appraised in terms of more general expectations and values, but it is more difficult to document this at village level. In this respect we are fortunate in the survival of the 'Swallowfield articles', agreed by the chief inhabitants of Shepperidge Magna, Shepperidge Parva, Farleigh Hill and Didsham in Wiltshire. They were agreed on 4 December 1596,

for that the Justices are farr of This we have don to the end we may the better & more quyetly lyve together in good love & amytie to the praise of God And for the better servynge of her Majesty when wee meete together about any Sessments or other Besynes of her Majestie what soever, or any mater or cause concernynge the Churche, the poore or the parrishe.[80]

Such an agreement appears to have been necessary because these townships, although lying within the boundaries of Berkshire, were for administrative purposes part of Wiltshire. As a consequence of this administrative anomaly they were, to an extent, cut off from the normal routine of local government.[81] This is not a typical case, therefore, but the articles offer a detailed picture of an ideal of orderly village society which gives an impression of some of the principal concerns of village elites revealed by village studies.

There are many specific concerns, such as a wish to avoid burdening the parish by the settlement of illegitimate children, to combat minor crime, to enforce sabbath observance and to prevent drunkenness. Clearly, too, the concern was informed by a godly commitment that cannot be assumed to have been 'typical'. For example, the inhabitants were to ensure the attendance of their servants at church 'in due tyme to learne & put in practize that whiche shall ther be delyverd by the Mynyster out of the word of God for their edifycation', and not to send them on 'their worldly besynes as is to muche practysed'.[82] But what is

[79] Wrightson, 'Two concepts'; Kent, *Constable*, esp. pp. 233–79.

[80] HEH, EL 6162 fos. 34av–36ar, quotation at fo. 34av. This agreement might be comparable to those made by a number of Essex vestries in the late sixteenth and early seventeenth centuries: W. Hunt, *The Puritan Moment: The Coming of Revolution in an English County* (Boston, Mass., 1983), 82–3.

[81] P. Collinson, 'The monarchical republic of Queen Elizabeth I', *Bulletin of the John Rylands Library*, 69 (1986–87), 394–424, at p. 395. Swallowfield was the chapelry comprised by the settlements of Sheepbridge and Farley Hill, hence the reference to the 'Swallowfield articles'.

[82] HEH, EL 6162 fo. 36ar. An exception was made for those preparing dinner.

more striking about the document is the commitment to neighbourliness, participation, deference and order. This included meetings of the chief inhabitants themselves, where every man was to be heard 'quyetly one after another' without interruption, and each man 'as he is fyrst in accompt, and so in order, that therby the depthe of every mans Judgment with reason may be concedered'. Rules of debate were laid out, and the signatories undertook to strive to prevent fallings-out and resort to law. Thus, the whole company was to be privy to any grievances so that 'all stryfes may be ended before any mallece take roote'. Anyone who failed to accept these precepts and act 'as neighbours', and the cause not affecting the crown or freehold, 'shall not be accompted one of our Companye' since he had thereby effectively refused to co-operate with measures for 'our better quyet and orderynge of our selves and the whole inhabitantes'. Meetings had to be conducted without malice or affection, and the individual was to be ruled by the whole or the majority part of it. In short, the chief inhabitants were to act 'as helpers, assisters & Councellors of one another And all our doynges to be good, honest, lovyng and iuste one to an other.'[83]

The chief inhabitants, thus united, could act as leaders of village society, seeking to prevent the need to present offenders to court and promising to do their best 'to end all stryfes which shall happen between neighebor and neighebour be they poore or Ryche'. This was obviously not a democratic vision. Any of the poorer inhabitants who 'malapertlye compare with their betters and sett them at nought' were to be warned to 'lyve & behave them selves as becomethe them'. Failure to amend would result in their being considered 'Common disturbers of peace & quyetnes', and reported to the justices that they 'may be reformed by the severetie of the lawe in suche case provyded'.[84] This insistence on proper relations of deference was accompanied by the commitment to respect for official duties too: 'the offycers shall not be dislyked of for the doynge of theyr offyce, & in furtherynge her Majesties service, or any other busynes of the Tythinges . . . but shalbe used with all gentellnes bothe in word and deed'.[85] Clearly, social and political authority were recognised as being distinct and requiring separate defence. Household order was crucial, too. The chief inhabitants were, it will have been noticed, men. Within the village they were to take a special care 'to speake to the mynyster to stay the maryage of suche as wold mary before they have a convenyent house to lyve in, accordynge to their callynge'.[86]

[83] Ibid., fo. 35ar.   [84] Ibid., fo. 35av.   [85] Ibid., fo. 35av.   [86] Ibid., fo. 35av.

In these Wiltshire villages, as elsewhere in England, there was a clear preference for the regulation of social life without resort to the formal sanctions of the law.[87] None the less, two of the signatories were to attend each sessions 'to make the Justices privey to the mysorders & to present the deffaultes that ar amongest us, yf upon warnynge to the offendors they persist in their wilffull & vyle synns'. To this end, monthly meetings were to be held 'to use the best means for to keepe dowen Synne, & all of us to be contrybutory to the Charges thereof, yf those parties shall be wilffull & stubborne agaynst the peace'.[88] This desire for self-sufficiency and order had a corollary in the defence of the collective interest of the tithings against others. It was a duty of the inhabitants, if they remembered anything which would save the tithings from harm or danger, to inform the whole company and have it entered in the record. This was part of the same localism, for it was intended thereby 'that in Charetye & truthe everye of us shall take all honest care one of an other, And of the wronges, that may aryse amongest us or agaynste us, especyally of our duties or Servece towards her majesty'.[89] It was not a localism necessarily in tension with the interests of national government, but there was a clear insistence on local norms of order and self-sufficiency. Offices were part of a broader, organic, set of social roles. The priority was the preservation of a local interaction order – norms of interaction between neighbours, relations of deference and paternal responsibility – rather than an abstract legal and political order.[90]

This agreement has been quoted at some length because it exemplifies so many features of village politics identified by social historians. There was a clear concern to defend personal credit and repute, and to link this with the defence or preservation of local community and order. Concern for local order shaded into defence of the collective interest of the tithings against outside interests. To protect these collective interests

---

[87] Sharpe, 'Enforcing the law'; Ingram, 'Communities and courts'; T. C. Curtis, 'Quarter sessions appearances and their background: a seventeenth-century regional study', in Cockburn (ed.), *Crime*, 135–54, 328–31. For the social significance of the increasing resort to law, see C. Muldrew, 'The culture of reconciliation: community and the settlement of economic disputes in early modern England', *HJ*, 39 (1996), 915–42.   [88] HEH, EL 6162 fo. 36ar.

[89] Ibid., fo. 35ar.

[90] For 'interaction order' see E. Goffman, 'The interaction order', *American Sociological Review*, 48 (1983), 1–17. For a broader account see T. Burns, *Erving Goffman* (London, 1992), esp. ch. 2; and P. Drew and A. Wootton (eds.), *Erving Goffman: Exploring the Interaction Order* (Oxford, 1988), esp. 'Introduction'. According to Drew and Wootton, the interaction order 'was more than rules . . . which permit people to interact with each other . . . The technical mechanisms of interaction . . . were only of sociological significance insofar as they were the vehicles for the participants *moral* enterprises . . . the world of interaction was a moral one which could generate in people a sense of effectiveness or ineffectiveness, success, disenchantment, fraud and so on': ibid., p. 6.

the signatories agreed to 'join together in purse, travell and Credett'.[91] Such conflicts were noted to be possible in relation to 'her Majesties service', and it was implicitly acknowledged that officeholders could become unpopular by virtue of their actions in that office. The magistracy was seen as a means of securing harmony and order. In all these respects it was probably a manifesto representative of the aspirations of villagers elsewhere, although the vision of a Christian commonwealth, the association of order and ministry and of disorder and sin, might suggest a hotter-than-average brand of Protestantism.

These ideals legitimated the power of officeholders, but also offered a means by which they could be held to account. They were an important part of the definition of local offices in terms of a social role. 'The normative constraints of society are . . . tangibly represented in a system of roles for performance in which the individual is socialized, which subsequently define his rights, privileges and social relationships.'[92] Roles, as predictable forms of behaviour patterned by the expectations of their performers and their audiences, connect the abstract order of society with the actual experience of everyday life. Class, gender and age relations, for example, are abstractions which describe the performance of particular, relatively regularised, social roles – the gender order of society is *experienced* in terms of patterns of behaviour common to people of similar status within it. Offices, as varieties of social role, connect the abstract political order with the experience of political power in everyday life. In early modern England state power pervaded social interactions through appeals made to it by officeholders. In the Essex village of Terling, in the sixteenth and seventeenth centuries, for example, energetic political action was explained and justified in terms of a much more general language of reformation. '[Parish officers] slipped comfortably into the rhetoric of reformation when presenting swearing and alehouse offences', for example, and 'the godly ideals of the Reformation era were a powerful element in their own perception of what their initiatives *meant*'.[93]

The distance between the individual and the office was, therefore, established not simply by formal warrant but also by a variety of performances. State power was exercised in face-to-face contexts, which is 'where most of the world's work gets done',[94] and in those contexts individuals had to secure compliance with their actions. These offices were 'institutions of the state' because when people acted in them the

---

[91] HEH, EL 6162 fo. 35av.   [92] J. A. Jackson (ed.), *Role* (Cambridge, 1972), 1.
[93] Wrightson and Levine, *Terling*, p. 203.   [94] Erving Goffman quoted in Burns, *Goffman*, p. 18.

ultimate means of securing compliance was the possibility of exercising legitimate force. But these offices were deeply embedded in the social fabric. This was true institutionally because it was true in the minds of local officials – local governors did not always perceive themselves as such. When asked to act *qua* governor, officeholders frequently chose to act as neighbours instead. Not only was there some lack of clarity in the differentiation of public and private activities, but the institutions of the state were not clearly differentiated one from another. Gentlemen assessing taxes and implementing poor laws were acting under different commissions, but neither they nor their neighbours appear to have regarded these activities as separate, insisting instead on a broader appraisal of legitimate magisterial activity. To a greater extent than in a modern context the activities of many of the agents of the early modern state were constrained by wider social expectations – their offices were envisioned as broader social roles, in which particular patterns of behaviour were expected, in conformity with wider cultural values.

When an early modern officeholder laid claim to political power, he or she made claims about their formal powers, but also appealed to these wider social values. That appeal, in order to be credible, might require them to temper their demands, or undertake tasks that they had not initially envisaged. Legitimation gave force to ideas, and set limits on the individual officeholder's ability to use office exclusively in their own interests. The success of their claims to legitimacy was reflected in the quality of compliance that they elicited. The overall institutional form of the state was the bundle of ways in which the exercise of political power was made routinely legitimate. Again, this was done with reference not just to the formal limits of office but to a wider social role and was asserted through the reproduction of relatively standardised performances – almost literally, early modern gentlemen wore their 'magistrate's hat' when attending to state business. Through these performances an individual could therefore be identified as acting the role of constable rather than neighbour, or a stranger could quickly be recognised as, for example, a justice. Particular offices represented particular social roles, justified with reference to specific sets of beliefs, entailing distinctive sets of performances, and warranted in different ways. 'Institutional practice' was, in these terms, cultural performance. Legitimacy was asserted and conveyed through a repertoire of symbolic texts and performances.[95] Evidence of this understanding, if not of the

[95] For warrants and legal papers as symbols of power, see J. M. Rosenheim, 'Documenting authority: texts and magistracy in restoration society', *Albion*, 25 (1993), 591–604, although he is

actual practice, of political power, is the arrest of the Lancashire witches
by the constable in Heywood and Broome's *Late Lancashire Witches*. The
supernatural power of the witches, the audience is told, is of no avail
against the officer, since it is one of the devil's tricks to 'leave you all to
the Law, when you are once seized on by the tallons of Authority'. This
authority was conveyed by the 'Common-wealth Characters upon his
staffe', which enabled him 'in spite of all your bugs-words, to stave off
the grand Divell for doing any of you good till you come to his
Kingdome to him'.[96] In more ordinary transactions of political power
the signifiers of 'state magic' were, no doubt, less dramatic but of equal
importance to its exercise.[97]

The effectiveness of political authority, or of resistance to it, rested on
the outcome of the projection of this image of authority. Individual
officeholders, entering a public arena in which political power was to be
transacted, presented a 'self'. This was defined by the formal powers of
their office but also by the wider expectations held about the conduct of
officeholders. Presentation of this self was part of the process of government – failing to project and defend this face successfully could lead to
political or administrative difficulty. Early modern officeholders were
sensitive to such challenges to their face and easily put off their stroke,
for example, by 'violent words'. For example, John Harman's public
contempt for subsidy collectors in London in the early seventeenth
century apparently limited their effectiveness. Harman 'with great scorn
and contemptuously refused to pay demanding in a proud and scornful
manner who were the assessors'. Told that they were common council-
men he 'openly replied and said in contempt and discountenance of
your highness's service and in disgrace of his Majesty's officers therein
employed that they were all blockheads and fools saying further had the
beetle headed asses nothing else to busy their beetle heads withall but to
assess him'. This open contempt for the collectors' public representation

---

surely wrong to limit the importance of such texts to the restoration period. For cultural
differences in the representation of authority, see W. Palmer, 'That "Insolent Liberty": honor,
rites of power and persuasion in sixteenth-century Ireland', *Renaissance Quarterly*, 46 (1993),
308–27; P. Seed, 'Taking possession and reading texts: establishing the authority of overseas
empires', *William and Mary Quarterly*, 3rd series, 49 (1992), 183–209.

[96] T. Heywood and R. Broome, *The Late Lancashire Witches* (London, 1634), reprinted in J. Pearson
(ed.), *The Dramatic Works of Thomas Heywood*, vol. IV (London, 1874), 166–262, quotation at
p. 257. I am grateful to Clive Holmes for drawing my attention to this scene. This reflects the
doctrine of inviolability – that, since the power of offices was divinely ordained, it must be greater
than the powers of the servants of Satan. For this see S. Clark, *Thinking with Demons: The Idea of
Witchcraft in Early Modern Europe* (Oxford, 1997), ch. 38.

[97] For state magic see P. Bourdieu, *The State Nobility: Elite Schools in the Field of Power*, trans. L. C.
Clough (Oxford, 1996), esp. pp. 374–7.

of themselves robbed them of their ability to perform their duty. Later in the century Richard Prickard, hearth tax collector in the North Riding of Yorkshire, was effectively stopped in his work by an even more stunning humiliation. Called before two justices of the peace, his warrant was denied and 'in the face and hearing of all the people there' was called 'a cheat and not fit to be trusted with the king's money'. It was the public nature of the insult which mattered in such cases. Thomas Taylor, the constable of Skipton, refused to deliver to gaol a man who would not pay the excise. The effect of this refusal was much increased by the fact that he did so 'very peremptorily . . . in the open market'.[98] In exercising political power early modern officeholders and officers were embroiled in negotiation, and built into the functioning of the state was a sensitivity to expectations outside the ranks of the formally empowered.

Appeal to these values created expectations which officeholders had to fulfill in order to appear credible. The meaning of these ideas was inter-subjective and not, therefore, within their control. Instead they had to try to make their behaviour conform to the generally understood meaning of these ideas. The political influence of the earl of Shrewsbury was threatened, in the mid-sixteenth century, by the strained relations he had with his tenants in Glossopdale and Ashford, and with his wife. These failings as head of his household and father of his country were, it seems, used by his opponents to undermine his position at court. A lengthy and complicated feud with Sir John Zouch was played out in conflicts over the patronage of offices in local government. It became a court issue because Zouch, and the tenants of Glossopdale, took their grievances there. Shrewsbury corresponded anxiously with both Leicester and Burghley and a lengthy report from his son at court betrayed extreme sensitivity to perceptions of his father at court and the extent of his father's popularity or unpopularity. It seems that there was indeed some threat to his position, for Burghley himself was dispatched for a visit. In the course of all this, Leicester said to Shrewsbury's son that what was most likely to persuade the queen to take away Shrewsbury's charge of guarding Mary Queen of Scots, was not the dispute with the tenantry, but reports 'that there were not good agreement betwixt my lord & my ladie and that it was informed the Queen & others that there

---

[98] M. J. Braddick, *Parliamentary Taxation in Seventeenth-Century England: Local Administration and Response*, Royal Historical Society, Studies in History, 70 (Woodbridge, 1994), esp. pp. 120, 218, 255. For other examples see ibid., pp. 117–24, 151–8, 163–5, 169–223, 252–66. For some reflections on these issues see E. Goffman, *The Presentation of Self in Everyday Life* (New York, 1959), esp. ch. 1.

was a secret division betwixt your doeings'.[99] This threatened loss of political authority was to be justified in terms of his supposed shortcomings as head of his household and perhaps as landlord. He was failing to conform to a broadly defined social role, associated with his office.

The definition of these roles put pressure on individual officeholders, both from their audience and from their superiors. The crown, of course, made constant reference to the duty of officeholders to act conscientiously. The privy council registers could be opened more or less at random for choice quotations, but a few illustrations will suffice. In 1598 Yorkshire justices of the peace were rebuked for failing to implement a number of statutes made in the previous parliament 'for the good and benefet of the whole State of the Realme', in particular those to relieve the poor and maimed soldiers, to punish rogues and vagabonds and to maintain tillage. The response had been unimpressive, however, and the queen was concerned 'at the remessness that hath bene used generallie by the Justices of the Peace in manie parts of the Realme' despite 'the gret good that maie in sewe' from proper attention, especially considering 'thes licenteous tymes'. The stick that the government wielded was that justices garnered prestige from their office, and dismissal held some terror. Accordingly, they were warned, 'if you shall necklect the same her majesty cannot but accompt you to be unmett and unworthie for the auchtoritie and places which you hould under her'. Thus, report was to be had of which justices were regular and disinterested attenders, as opposed to the other sort who attended only when 'they have special Causes of there owne or there friendes to treat uppon'. In the light of this information she could 'enter into Consideration howe to Reforme the neckligence' of the less diligent.[100] James I acknowledged that some justices fell short of the ideals he laid out for them. There were 'idle slow-bellies, that abide always at home, given to a life of ease and delight, liker ladies than men'. Others were 'busy-

---

[99] HEH, HM 41954, p. 346. For the dispute see S. E. Kershaw, 'Power and duty in the Elizabethan aristocracy: George, earl of Shrewsbury, the Glossopdale dispute and the council', in G. W. Bernard (ed.), *The Tudor Nobility* (Manchester, 1992), 266–95. There is more material in the earl's letter book at the Huntington Library: HEH, HM 41954, pp. 283–357. It has been suggested that members of parliament were representative in this broader sense, reflecting an aspiration for communal harmony. Members of parliament were selected, rather than elected, their qualifications being their capacity to stand for their country and its interests rather than their advocacy of party political positions – they represented the interest of their locality or corporation: M. Kishlansky, *Parliamentary Selection: Social and Political Choice in Early Modern England* (Cambridge, 1986). This interpretation has been contested by R. Cust, 'Politics and the electorate in the 1620s', in Cust and Hughes (eds.), *Conflict*, 134–69.

[100] HEH, HM 50657, vol. I, fos. 77r–77v.

bodies, and will have all men dance after their pipe and follow their greatness'. These 'proud spirits' needed to learn 'that the country is ordained to obey and follow God and the King, and not them'. Thirdly, he claimed, there were justices 'that go seldom to the King's service but when it is to help some of their kindred or alliance; so as when they come it is to help their friends or hurt their enemies, making justice to serve for a shadow to faction, and tumultuating the country'. Finally there were those 'of great worth in their own conceit' who sought to 'snatch against' the monarchy and its prerogatives by acting to protect the liberty of the people. This 'itching after popularity' was frequently castigated in the early Stuart period.[101] This sense of duty was propagated deliberately but it was in the nature of the relationship between privy council and magistrate that interests might clash. Both were parties to a negotiation, a fact demonstrated by the response of the Leicester magistrates to the demand to act more diligently as tax assessors.[102] One common criticism of the justices was that they pursued private interests and neglected the public good. In 1597 the archbishop of York, president of the Council in the North, had received a letter complaining at the 'slender regard had to this her majesty's servis'. In this case it was the composition for purveyance which had caused those in London to 'marvail' but there were many such complaints in all parts of the country in this period.[103]

There was no single vision of an ideal magistrate, but what was common to all accounts was a conception of magistracy as a broad social role, embracing values and responsibilities beyond the formal duties of the office. Administrative innovation might lack legitimacy because it was illegal or because it was thought unjustifiable. Certainly, magistrates and constables were as constrained by the latter as by the former consideration. Social fitness was essential to the position, and office confirmed it. For these reasons gentlemen sought office or sought

---

[101] Tanner, *Constitutional Documents*, pp. 19–21, quotations at pp. 20–1. James added that if there was no monarch, as a result of the actions of the populists, 'they would be less cared for than other men': ibid., p. 21. See D. Underdown, *A Freeborn People: Politics and the Nation in Seventeenth-Century England* (Oxford, 1996), ch. 2. See also Tooker's complaints about subsidy commissioners who 'to gather applause of their own friends and the common people affect popularity in all their actions'. Such men, he said, 'talk popularly or pleasingly' in pursuit of a 'vain popularity': quoted in Braddick, *Parliamentary*, p. 113. There were echoes of it in the Privy Council's correspondence with magistrates in the 1660s too: ibid., pp. 252–66. In a letter to the justices in Gloucester and Gloucestershire of 30 November 1665, for example, the privy council castigated those who 'affect popularity': BM Add MS 33589, fos. 33–34, at 33r.

[102] See p. 32.

[103] HEH, HM 50657, vol. I, fo. 79r. See also the further letters on fos. 79r–80r. These letters were not, of course, privy council letters.

to oust their rivals from it.[104] Those with insufficient private wealth could not be trusted to act for the public good. John Bonnifant, a subsidy collector in Cornwall in the 1590s, was hindered by the assertion that he was not a man of 'competent estate and livelihood', but was a tailor, drunkard and molester of married women. It was suggested that tax-payers would be reluctant to pay any money to him, he 'being a man of so small means and credit'. Credit is the key term here, reflecting a more general sense of social fitness. His status and personal conduct, it was suggested, made him unfit for administrative office.[105] As we have seen, those accused of being unfit for office might often have made enemies by their administrative actions, but they were abused in social terms.[106] In early Stuart Yorkshire, accusations of personal misconduct were the stuff of gentry rivalries, played out through the commissions of the peace. At the same time, 'allegations of misuse of judicial powers ... were frequently no more than a pretext used to undermine the credit of fellow-justices seen as rivals'.[107] Posthumus Hoby, a newcomer to the Yorkshire commission of the peace in the early seventeenth century, 'was abused as a "scruvy urchen" and "spindle-shanked ape". He was widely condemned as a busybody and was described on one occasion as "the busiest, saucie little Jacke in all the Contrie": another man called him "a busye and giddy-headed justice." Sir Hugh Cholmley ... de-clared that he was "a troublesome and vexatious neighbour".'[108] In all then, for these men their 'reputation was the very essence of their ability to govern'.[109]

Officeholders were empowered as much by their status as by their formal powers – their capacity to govern was a product of both social and legal authority. Discretion was expected of them, but this also gave room to suspicions of corruption and self-service.[110] The constant repeti-

---

[104] A. J. Fletcher, 'Honour, reputation and officeholding in Elizabethan and early Stuart England', in Fletcher and Stevenson (eds.), *Order and Disorder*, 92–115.

[105] Braddick, *Parliamentary*, p. 33.   [106] Above, pp. 24–5, 78–81.

[107] G. C. F. Forster, 'Faction and county government in early Stuart Yorkshire', *Northern History*, 11 (1976 for 1975), 70–86, quotation at p. 85.   [108] Ibid., p. 74.

[109] Fletcher, 'Honour, reputation and officeholding', p. 115.

[110] Lambarde was at great pains to explain that the discretion allowed to justices in statutes had a strictly limited legal meaning. Statutes could not predict every particular circumstance so that 'they do many times leave to be supplied (by the discretion of the *Executioner* of the law) that thing which was not conveniently comprehended before hand, by the wisdom of the author of the law'. But such '*Discretion*' was not the same as '*discretion*'. The former was 'necessary to the execution of the law' and operated within its bounds. Lambarde clearly felt, however, that it was used by some justices to 'arrogate unto themselves authoritie to use their *discretion*, and to play (as it were) *Chancellors* in every cause that cometh before them'. In other words, the judgement of a

tion of laments about corrupt or partial administration of justice is testimony to the perceived lack of effect, of course. These failures form the subject of later chapters and more detailed consideration follows. However, we should note that we need not regard officeholders as entirely self-seeking and lacking in any sense of obligation. Certainly, some of the most dramatic innovations in response to perceived threats to social order originated in the ranks of these officeholders, particularly but not exclusively among the godly social activists on county benches and in town corporations. This sense of duty is more difficult to document in the case of lowlier officeholders: we do not have constables' letter books or memoranda. But it is evident that constables spent time, energy and money on public engagements, such as tax collection, military organisation or the enforcement of law and order, which can have had little to do with their immediate self-interest. Although they did not always conform to national practice, it was because they had conflicting responsibilities rather than because they were irresponsible. In Wrightson's terms, they were pulled between two concepts of order,[111] rather than being unmoved by the need for it.

Officeholders acted in wider social roles, therefore. Gentlemen and aristocrats advised their sons about a fully rounded social role, explaining the behaviour expected of them in relation to their family, neighbours, superiors and inferiors. Conduct at table and in the field was recommended and, within this broad advice about the presentation of the self in public situations, how to conduct oneself if called to office. The fifth earl of Huntingdon's advice to his son listed all these things as 'public' concernments, including the choice of wife and conduct towards her. Among all these roles the public presentation of self was clearly of pre-eminent significance: 'There is nothing will more increase or lessen thy esteeme then thy carriage abroad for men that cannot judge of thee nor p[er]chance thou shalt ever see againe will censure of thee by thy outward behaviour.' On the other hand, 'This applause is not very hard for putting of thy hatt, takeinge of them by the hande,

---

justice did not, as that of a judge of equity, supplement the common law. The justice executed, but did not make, law and the justice who wished to appear to have true discretion would bear in mind that he was '*lex loquens*' and 'contain himself within the lists of the law, and (being soberly wise) do not use his own *Discretion* but only where both the law permitteth and the present case requireth it': *Eirenarcha*, p. 59. For the chancellor and equity see J. H. Baker, *An Introduction to English Legal History*, 3rd edn (London, 1990), 122–3. For an example of an exhortation to moderation in the exercise of judicial power by magistrates, drawing on classical and biblical sources, see HEH EL 1163.   [111] Wrightson, 'Two concepts'.

callinge them by their names, in thy answers a kinde and courteous speech winne mens affections exceedingly.'[112]

Individuals 'acting as' magistrates or constables were constrained not just by the formal limits on their offices, but by less formal expectations about what such roles entailed. It was through the definition of these social roles that ideas such as 'godly magistracy' became a programme of political action, legitimating offices in the performance of new tasks. 'Institutional form', as the discussion of social roles implies, is here understood to be the means by which an individual was successfully and routinely represented as an agent of legitimate political authority. The everyday activities of states are these activities of political power, ultimately backed by force but in the normal course of events recognised unproblematically as legitimate. Normally, of course, they were routine and lacking in drama – the arbitration of a dispute over poor rates by a magistrate, or the binding of a neighbour to keep the peace or to be of good behaviour. In many cases, too, the power exercised was not that of one individual over another, but a collective resource enabling the achievement of a public end. This is not to suggest that it was independent of particular interests of course – the public being served was almost always smaller than the total population.[113]

The process of legitimation was empowering but also embedded the state in the wider network of social relationships and values. Minor forms of resistance, and minor gestures of dissent, could undercut the authority of officeholders, and the fear of these responses from their neighbours served as a restraint upon them. The effect of this, of the necessity of negotiating authority, is written into the account of the state in the chapters that follow. A measure of the success of these legitimations is the quality of compliance which administrative actions elicited, and behind the accounts of grudging and partial compliance outlined in the following chapters lies the discomfort of innumerable officeholders

---

[112] HEH, HAP 15 (8), 'Certaine directions for my sonne to observe in the course of his life'; Heal and Holmes, *Gentry*, pp. 243–7; R. Cust (ed.), *The Papers of Sir Richard Grosvenor, 1st Bart. (1585–1645)*, Record Society of Lancashire and Cheshire, 134 (Stroud, 1996), xxiv, 26–38. See also HEH, HAM, Box 53 (5): papers relating to the attempt to exclude Mr Bale from the commission of the peace on the grounds of his low birth, poor education, ambition, avariciousness as a landlord and incontinent living. It was these wider social attributes that made men fit or otherwise for office.

[113] See, for example, the use of local offices to determine rights of settlement and of access to communal resources. In effect, these were exercises of power legitimated with reference to a public good, but they entailed, by definition, a process of exclusion: S. Hindle, 'Exclusion crises: poverty, migration and parochial responsibility in English rural communities, *c.* 1560–1660', *Rural History*, 7 (1996), 125–49.

in the face of the hostility of their neighbours. The success of responses to the pressures for political innovation was a product of the success of harmonising the proposed measures with these wider legitimating beliefs. At the same time, the necessity of legitimating offices, and sustaining their legitimacy, meant that offices and their holders were responsive to local, as well as central, interests. Moreover, in seeking to justify the exercise of political power with reference to wider beliefs and attitudes, officeholders not only gave administrative force to these ideas but also submitted political authority to a test which could serve to limit the power of vested interests to affect the activities of the state.

POLITICAL INNOVATION: CHANGING FORMS OF OFFICE

A discussion of legitimation provides a way into some of the larger themes of this book – the autonomy of the state and the uses of state power, for example. It is also the starting point for another – the 'modernisation' of the state or, more neutrally, the changing forms and uses of state power in early modern England. Agreements about the legitimate bounds of particular offices, and the more informal terms in which their authority is expressed, are not fixed. Innovation in political life might be achieved in several ways. For example, by changing the agreed competence of an office, a new class of actions might become possible – constables might take on new responsibilities such as the collection of a compulsory rate for the relief of the local poor, for example. An alternative would be to argue successfully that a new class of actions fell within the agreed sphere of legitimate action. For example, under Elizabeth and the early Stuarts, a number of financial measures were taken which tested the limits of existing conventions about monarchical authority. The powers being claimed were not new in constitutional terms, but their application in these particular ways was questionable. Thirdly, innovation might result in the establishment of an entirely new office, such as specialised revenue agents to collect a new tax. These are all changes in the forms of office – their functional and territorial competences and the languages in which their actions are legitimated. In each case, these kinds of innovation might be contested legally, or in terms of their justifiability, and the functional success of an innovation constrained by the effect of this contestation.

There were limits on what particular forms of office could plausibly and effectively be used for. Different offices were justified in different ways, and so were subject to distinctive kinds of constraint. It follows from this that particular kinds of office were effective for particular kinds of action: there was an affinity (not, it must be emphasised, a perfect correlation) between institutional form in this broad sense and functional purpose. The development of particular forms of office is associated with pressures to use political power for particular ends.

Officeholders, for example, were unreliable tax assessors, since their official duty was difficult to reconcile to their wider social obligations. Where officeholders were thought inappropriate or ineffective, more specialised agents were employed, but they tended to lack the generalised sense of legitimacy commanded (or claimed) by the fathers of their country, the patriarchal justices and their juniors. It has been noted in another context that 'there had long been a contradiction between the authority of those who in some way were born to power by being a gentleman with commissions and the authority of those who had to make themselves powerful in their particular domain by years of experience and learning and who served under warrant'. To some extent this captures the difference between the powers of officeholders, with relatively wide powers and a broadly conceived social role, and licensees with more closely defined and formally specified powers. 'The Commission, direct from the Crown, in some way displaced the person commissioned, leaving much more room for a sense of public altruism in its rhetoric. The Warrant, a certificate of some personal capital in knowledge and skill outside the gift of the Crown, was much more privatising and entrepreneurial.'[114] Warrants reflected the fact that an individual possessed specific technical skills. They did not create a king in miniature, a lesser magistrate.

Monopolists, saltpetremen, purveyors, patentees, licensees, hunters after concealed lands and informers all carried out specialised functions with formally prescribed powers. But their personal interest made them objects of hostile comment and attack. For example, considerable effort was put into devising ways in which the powers of purveyors could be limited, ensuring that their appraisal of local resources was accurate and that the full benefit of purveyance went to the crown. The House of Commons Apology of 1604 captured this sense that strict surveillance was necessary for such people: 'But a general, extreme, unjust, and crying oppression is in cart-takers and purveyors, who have rummaged

---

[114] G. Dening, *Mr Bligh's Bad Language: Passion, Power and Theatre on the Bounty* (Cambridge, 1992), quotations at pp. 21–2. Dening is referring specifically to patterns of authority in the English navy in the eighteenth century, of course, and constables did not act under Commission from the Crown. None the less the distinction has some force here.

and ransacked since your Majesty's first coming in far more than any of your royal progenitors: there hath been no prince since Henry III except Queen Elizabeth who hath not made some one law or other to repress or limit them.'[115] John Culpeper famously said of the monopolists in 1641 that they are a 'nest of wasps, a swarm of vermin which have overcrept the land . . . like the frogs of Egypt they have gotten possession of our dwellings . . . these are the leeches that have sucked the common wealth so hard it has almost become hectical'. To that extent their experience epitomised a more general suspicion of those executing a legal warrant but lacking broader authority. Later in the seventeenth century they were joined by professional revenue agents, the excisemen, and they too were criticised in biblical terms: 'what malignant ill-affected persons, what enemies, pests, vipers, locusts and caterpillars to the kingdom and nation' as one writer put it in 1653.[116] The price of functional efficiency might very well be increased hostility and it is easy to see how precise definition of their powers offered reassurance about the potential abuse of their office. Precision about such things was the aim of much statutory regulation – discretion was the last thing that would legitimate such offices.

A cash-poor monarchy did not reward all its functionaries directly, but put them in positions from which they could derive benefits. This was justified by a language of patronage which represented the crown as a fountain of bounty, wisdom and justice. In return for access to its waters clients offered loyalty and political or other services. Such a relationship was ambiguous, however, and the waters could be corrupted by self-interest and greed. In the early Stuart period these suspicions were particularly acute, and this may have reflected a real change in standards of behaviour. Alongside a language of patronage there devel-

---

[115] Tanner, *Constitutional Documents*, p. 227.

[116] Quoted in Braddick, *Nerves*, pp. 208–9, 221–2. For purveyors see ibid., pp. 202–6; A. Woodworth, *Purveyance for the Royal Household in the Reign of Queen Elizabeth*, Transactions of the American Philosophical Society, 35 (Philadelphia, 1945). For hunters see H. Hope Lockwood, 'Those greedy hunters after concealed lands', in K. Neale (ed.), *An Essex Tribute: Essays Presented to Frederick G. Emmison* (London, 1987), 153–70; C. J. Kitching, 'The quest for concealed lands in the reign of Elizabeth I', *TRHS*, 5th series, 24 (1974), 63–78. For informers, L. L. Peck, *Court, Patronage and Corruption in Early Stuart England* (London, 1990), 145 and M. W. Beresford, 'The common informer, the penal statutes and economic regulation', *EcHR*, 2nd series, 10 (1957), 221–38, esp. pp. 222, 226, 232. There are some interesting reflections on the relationship between private profit and public good in D. H. Sacks, 'Private profit and public good: the problem of the state in Elizabethan theory and practice', in G. J. Schochet, P. E. Tatspaugh and C. Brobeck (eds.), *Law, Literature and the Settlement of Regimes* (Washington, DC, 1990), 121–42. For saltpetremen see R. W. Stewart, *The English Ordnance Office: A Case-Study in Bureaucracy*, Royal Historical Society, Studies in History, 73 (Woodbridge, 1996), esp. pp. 80–5; above, pp. 40–3.

oped one of corruption, and this was a serious political difficulty for the Jacobean and Caroline regimes.[117] In Weberian terms the modernisation of these offices would take the form not just of specialisation and differentiation (in contrast to officeholding) but in the replacement of government by licence with government by bureaucracy. What marks out modern forms of administration is not just specialisation and differentiation but a system of reward for precise implementation of agreed rules.[118] The rewards for licensees were set by how far they could push their powers, rather than by an agreed salary scale reflecting the appraisal of their performance by their superiors. Modernisation occurred at the expense not just of officeholders but of government by licence.

The changing form of the state was not the result of a conscious act of will by an individual or particular social group, but the net effect of numerous attempts to find legitimate ways of achieving particular ends. The process of legitimation, and the patterns in the effectiveness of particular forms of office, moulded the development of state forms. This was partly a matter of legal competence, but was also a matter of broader legitimating ideas. What might legally be done might not always legitimately be done, and there might be serious disagreement about how to classify a particular kind of action. For example, it was widely acknowledged that the king had absolute prerogative powers which supplemented, rather than rivalled, the common law. In places where the common law did not apply the exercise of the absolute prerogative was acceptable and posed no threat to the rights of the subject. In the early seventeenth century, duties collected on imported currants were imposed by prerogative authority and this caused political conflict within a wider consensus. The issue revolved around whether these 'impositions' affected property – in which case they should be regulated by the common law – or whether they related to the high seas and external relations and thus were beyond the reach of the common law. The issue was not the relationship between common law and the prerogative, but whether the crown could successfully argue that a particular class of action – the impositions – should be a matter for the prerogative or the common law. The '"Jacobean consensus" ... co-existed with sharp disagreements over political policy and acts', there-

---

[117] Peck, *Corruption*. For standards of behaviour among officeholders see G. E. Aylmer, *The King's Servants: The Civil Service of Charles I 1625–1642* (London, 1961), ch. 4, esp. pp. 178–82; and Aylmer, *The State's Servants: The Civil Service of the English Republic 1649–1660* (London, 1973), 139–67. For a favourable verdict on the later period in this comparison see ibid., esp. pp. 328, 341–2.   [118] G. Poggi, *The State: Its Nature, Development and Prospects* (Oxford, 1990), 20–1.

fore. Political conflict was fought out within agreed languages of legitimation.[119] In what follows the concern will be the effect of these
'disagreements over policy and acts' – functional measures of the degree
of legitimacy enjoyed by particular political measures. Legitimacy is
clearly not an all-or-nothing affair; political contestants were able to
communicate with each other in a shared language but they were, none
the less, contestants. The concern here is with which of these contests
could be won, and how easily, as measures of the success of strategies of
legitimation.[120]

There were patterns in the effectiveness of particular forms of office.
There is a broad distinction to be made between relatively specialised
agents of state authority acting under licence or warrant and the
hierarchy of local officeholders wielding more general influence. An
important part of the overall argument is the affinity between form and
function, the suggestion that the pursuit of particular kinds of political
purposes was most effectively achieved through particular forms of
office. Magistrates and constables were characteristically able to achieve
some things and unable to achieve others, or at least only able to achieve
them with difficulty. Written into their actions was the effect of wider
expectations and values – invisible lines of force were revealed by
patterns in the way in which the state as a whole operated. The warrants
and powers of other officers such as purveyors were more closely
specified and regulated. Such people exercised their office for financial
benefit and so were clearly pursuing their own interests as well as those
of the Commonwealth. As a consequence, their actions were closely
monitored to restrain their corrupt intent. Their authority rested more
clearly on their legal powers and if their specialised function was
disliked, their unpopularity was not diluted by a more generalised sense
of worthy public duty and trust. Demands for innovation in these forms
of office, or their competence, might originate at the centre or in
the localities in response to a wide range of functional challenges or

---

[119] G. Burgess, *The Politics of the Ancient Constitution: An Introduction to English Political Thought 1600–
1642* (London, 1992), ch. 6, quotation at p. 139. For impositions see esp. pp. 140–4.

[120] Following here Skinner:

the task of the innovating ideologist is a hard but an obvious one. His concern, by definition, is to legitimate a
new range of social actions which, in terms of the existing ways of applying the moral vocabulary prevailing in
his society, are currently regarded as in some way untoward or illegitimate. His aim must therefore be to show
that a number of existing and favourable evaluative-descriptive terms can somehow be applied to his
apparently untoward actions.

Skinner, 'Political thought and action', quotation at p. 112. For the current purposes we might
substitute the term 'innovating political actor' for 'innovating ideologist'.

opportunities. The development of these offices was patterned, however. Particular offices, and legitimating languages, were better suited to
meeting particular kinds of challenge, and we can discern some consist-
encies in the kinds of challenges that were perceived to be worth
responding to. The development of the state was shaped by the inter-
relationship between the available legal forms of office, patterns of
participation, the available languages of legitimation and patterns in the
uses to which these resources were put.

THE AGENCY OF THE STATE

The state was a coordinated network of agencies exercising political
power. The precise form assumed by these agencies was a product of
their territorial and functional bounds, but also of the wider beliefs in
terms of which their activities were justified. Particular forms of office
were more effective for particular functions than for others – there was
an affinity between form and function. The state has not been defined
here in terms of particular forms of office, or particular functional
purposes, but in more abstract terms. But this abstract definition of the
state is a preliminary to an analysis of what forms it actually took, and
what uses were made of its institutions. In the following analysis the
principal concern is with the effects, and effectiveness, of state action.

In the Introduction (pp. 5–6) we noted four related issues in the
historiography of the forms and uses of state power in early modern
England: the relationship between centre and locality; what forces drove
its development; the uses of its power and the degree of its autonomy;
and the need for a more satisfactory chronological framework in which
to narrate its development. The first three of these questions might be
expressed more concisely: how did the state acquire agency? How does
a mind without a body come to make war and imprison people? The
answer proposed here lies in the process by which offices were defined
and redefined. In that process, social interest, and the interest of the
centre, were important, but not unconstrained. Similarly, a study of the
process by which the state acquired agency is simultaneously a study of
the uses of state power.

We often read that the state did things and even sometimes that it
wanted things, and yet the state is not something that can be touched or
seen, let alone questioned about its motives. It is argued here that the
state does not want or do things; people want the state to do things, and

they have varying degree of success in achieving their ends. But it is the offices of the state, rather than individuals, which act.[121] It is the definition of office that gives form and purpose to the state. The pressure for political change came from officeholders and those who had power over them – those who could grant legal validity and those who could extend a more general sense of legitimacy. Activists inside and outside government sought to respond to functional challenges and opportunities as they perceived them, seeking to negotiate legitimate means of doing so. Interests – those of particular social groups or particular lobbies – might therefore lie behind the pressure for political innovation. In this way, the definition of offices gives purpose and form to the state and also connects the exercise of political power with particular interests. Because access to office was not open in the early modern period, and because the beliefs in terms of which power was justified served the interests of some social groups rather better than others, there was a differential capacity to define these problems and challenges. These challenges were defined in relation to some kind of objective reality but, it need hardly be said, the important thing for this analysis is contemporary perception. Political power was exercised not just through the definition of offices but through the definition of what were important functional challenges and opportunities. In these ways the definition of offices built into the functioning of the state interests and values which favoured particular groups.

However, the need to legitimate political power served to temper those interests and was a source of autonomy in the state – they were justified in terms of beliefs which were not at the command of particular groups. The justification of an office, or a particular use of political power with reference to a particular set of ideas, offered to those who might wish to resist a means to hold agents of the state to account. Moreover, particular forms of behaviour were assumed to be appropriate to particular offices and in early modern England many officeholders were expected to fulfill broad social roles rather than specialised administrative functions. The definition of offices, in this broad sense, enshrined particular values in political practice – ideas were given force as a consequence. Legitimacy enabled and constrained, and could be relatively successful or unsuccessful. Finally, initiatives, once adopted as 'state policy', became binding on all agents of state power, whether or

---

[121] For a discussion of how the state has agency independent of its servants see A. Vincent, *Theories of the State* (Oxford, 1987), esp. pp. 8–9.

not the policy was in their immediate self-interest. The execution of such policy might have become a condition of continued service and these demands of office were, in particular cases, independent of the wishes of individual officeholders. From the point of view of an individual office-holder the interests of the state were relatively autonomous, therefore, and might have required them to do things not in their direct self-interest and even, perhaps, against their self-interest. Activists gave agency to the state – the state was not self-activating – but no particular individual or group wholly dictated its form and functioning. The interests of these activists compounded state power with social or ideological interests, but the necessity of legitimating state power, of securing compliance and bringing initiatives within the remit of the formal demands of offices, set limits on those interests. In these ways legitimation was a source of autonomy in the state.

By the same token, political innovation is not just a product of the centre. In much writing about the development of the state it is presumed that the process is driven from the centre, and even that the growth of the state depends on a victory over the localities. It is this kind of presumption, for example, that explains historians' puzzlement that restoration England could be closely governed without regular central oversight.[122] The view that there was a division between centre and locality has been seen as problematic for a number of reasons. For example, there were conflicts within localities between different communities; there were solidarities between local and central interests; there were institutions such as the assizes (or parliament) in which local and central identities mingled; and administrative innovations arose in the localities as well as in Westminster or Whitehall (hereafter, 'London').[123] Conceiving of the state as the whole network of political institutions coordinated in London reveals how they served to integrate central and local interests. The state as defined here was distinct from the locality, not by being central but by being more extensive than the locality – it was one of the things common to a number of localities rather than an alien and hostile central body. The state, as we will see,

---

[122] Braddick, 'Royal aid'. For further reflections on this issue, see P. D. Halliday, '"A clashing of jurisdictions": Commissions of Association in restoration corporations', *HJ*, 41, 2 (1998), 425–55.

[123] A. Hughes, *Politics, Society and Civil War in Warwickshire, 1620–1660* (Cambridge, 1987), esp. ch. 1; Hughes, 'The king, the parliament and the localities during the English civil war', reprinted in R. Cust and A. Hughes (eds.), *The English Civil War* (London, 1997), 261–87; C. Holmes, 'The county community in Stuart historiography', *JBS*, 19 (1980), 54–73; Braddick, *Parliamentary*, esp. introduction, ch. 6.

was useful to all sorts of people in early modern England and far from having to penetrate the localities was frequently invited in – state power pervaded the localities, embodied in the actions of innumerable individuals invoking its authority.

Mann's distinction between distributive and collective power is useful in thinking about this relationship between the centre and the localities.[124] Distributive power is that of one person or group over another, whereas collective power reflects the potential power of an organised group. The routine exercise of administrative power involves both getting people to do things that they would not otherwise do (distributive power) and increasing the collective capacity of groups of people (collective power). The exercise of political power, however, is not a zero-sum game played between competing groups and individuals. For example, regularisation of measures relating to poor relief might involve statutory action, or codification by the privy council. To that extent it increased the distributive power of those institutions, but it also increased the collective power of groups of people to deal with the perceived consequences of economic and social change.

The centre provided an agreed source of legal validation, authority which could be called upon for a variety of purposes. This was a source of power for the centre, but not a power necessarily in conflict with the localities. Moreover, legitimacy was achieved and conferred by appeal to more diffuse beliefs and practices, so that the localities were powerful too. The essential point, however, was that the changes in the legitimate scope of political power were not necessarily achieved by the centre at the expense of the localities. Examining the activities of the entire network of agents of political power de-centres the account of the state and draws attention to the arenas in which policies succeeded or failed. Officials and officeholders in the localities took up or ignored administrative initiatives, as well as generating administrative innovation themselves. Changes in the form and functioning of the state did not derive solely from the 'centre'. Legitimation involved local negotiation and political power was invoked for local as well as general or central purposes.

Agency was given to the state by those who sought to use it. In doing so they responded to perceived problems, defining political issues and proposing solutions to them. The range of such initiatives was very wide – embracing matters to do with social order, economic regulation,

---

[124] Mann, *Sources*, I, esp. pp. 6–7.

religious orthodoxy and territorial or commercial expansion. In recent historical sociology, as well as in the recent historiography of early modern Europe and eighteenth-century England, much attention has been devoted to the role of war in driving the development of the state.[125] But by concentrating on the everyday use of political power through the whole network of its agents a larger range of functional uses emerges. This tends, as we will see, to give less prominence to war and the autonomy of the state and more to problems of social order and the importance of vested social interests. Similarly, the central concern with legitimation integrates the history of ideas more closely with the history of institutions. This helps to soften what might be taken to be the technological determinism of some accounts of state formation which take as their motive force the impact of the 'military revolution'.

The early modern English state was a coordinated and territorially bounded network of agents exercising political power. Agency was given to this network by a variety of social interests, both at the centre and in the localities. As a result of the successful initiatives of activists a wide range of uses was found for political power and a variety of institutional forms was found for its expression. Patterns in the development of the state were the net effect of this activism. The degree of autonomy was a product of the tension between the strength of social interests and the need to establish and sustain legitimacy. Institutional form was also a product of the need to do this – particular languages of legitimation, or kinds of performance, were more effective than others in justifying particular uses of state power. For example, appeal to patriarchal values was more effective as a legitimation for innovation in poor relief than for militia reform. As a consequence, there was an affinity between patri-archal forms of government and a particular set of functional purposes – the preservation of domestic social order. By the same token, mobilisa-tion for war called forth other forms of office, reinforcing the sense that there is some affinity between form and function. Finally, therefore, political innovation was shaped by the underlying patterns in what it was used for – the general problems or opportunities which consistently attracted the attention of activists. In the rest of the book these complex issues will be disentangled by considering different crystallisations of political power separately. Four distinct 'states' will be discussed, all of them contained within the overall network of political agencies. These states are defined by the underlying challenges with which they were

---

[125] See above, ch. 1, n. 5.

concerned, and by the characteristic forms of office and languages through which they were expressed. In this way, patterns can be discerned in a process lacking overall design. Regularities in the ways that political power was used – its functional purposes – created regularities in the forms in which it was expressed.

Conclusion

The state, as a general category, is characterised by the control of political power. There was a network of agencies exercising a distinctively political power in early modern England, but the precise forms assumed by that power were very varied. These forms can be defined in formal terms – the territorial and functional bounds of office – but also by the beliefs in terms of which their authority was justified. These justifications enjoyed varying degrees of success, and this made the offices more or less effective in relation to the functions being demanded of them. In the following pages the complexities of these patterns will be simplified by looking at crystallisations of power within the early modern state – patriarchal, fiscal-military and confessional. Part V adds a spatial dimension to the analysis by considering the development of a British state and a British empire. Since the 1970s revisionist scholarship has demolished the grand narratives of the seventeenth century without establishing an alternative view. The overall purpose of this attempt to bring the state back in is to offer one such narrative in the aftermath of revisionism.

This is a book about state formation rather than state building. Changes in the form of the state are seen as the net effects of the uses made of state power by innumerable individuals and groups throughout the territories of the Tudor and Stuart crowns. There were patterns in these effects, but they were not the result of a single, conscious will – the state did not want or do things, but there were patterns in the ways in which the state was used. The state was responsive to a range of vested interests – class, gender and age, for example – and also to a range of ideological commitments – such as the pursuit of the true religion, for example. In revealing a patterned, but unplanned process of change, this book is offering a grand narrative rather than an account of one damn thing after another. But the explanation of political change that emerges is free of some of the weaknesses usually imputed to the Whig and Marxist master narratives of political change in the seventeenth century. It is not determinist, reducing political change to an outgrowth of social conflict. Neither is it teleological, assuming that the events it describes are important primarily because they led inevitably to a particular outcome, and it is certainly innocent of any charge that it collapses the distinction between change and progress. Finally, it is not intentionalist – there is no claim that the pattern of political change that is described here was the result of a conscious act of will.[1]

The emphasis here is on the experience of state authority in the localities, the ways in which its routines impinged on ordinary lives. The concern is with government rather than politics for it is government that affects social life more continuously and more intimately. The uses of political power modulated continuously in the light of changing conditions and demands in all the territories of the English crown. This argument also therefore has implications for the chronological patterns discerned in the process of state formation. For example, it is clear that the claims made about the modernisation of the state in the 1530s, 1640s, 1690s or 1820s apply only to particular parts of the state, or particular aspects of its functioning. This book examines the long seventeenth century, and gives some prominence to developments in the 1640s and 1690s, but is not concerned exclusively with those decades. A corollary of this, therefore, is that no particular period or moment was crucial for the development of all the institutions or all the functions of the state – a more integrated account leads to a more complex chronology.

Between 1550 and 1700 people living in the territories of the Tudor and Stuart crowns were subject to some novel, and even spectacular, claims for state authority. Some of the forms of office which proved useful appear to be more modern – in particular bureaucratised, differentiated and specialised offices justified with reference to the requirements of an impersonal political order. These 'modern' forms were more effective for meeting some of the challenges defined by activists in this period. But modernisation is not the central concern of this study. The term itself, of course, is problematic, given both the impact of postmodernism in the academy and the changes in modern states which make it more difficult to accept nineteenth-century conceptions of the

---

[1] For an outline of the revisionist hostility to these aspects of the grand narratives of political development in seventeenth-century England see J. Morrill, *Revolt in the Provinces: The People of England and the Tragedies of War 1630–1648* (London, 1999), Introduction.

essence of the modern state. What is intended by the term here is simply a greater resemblance to the Weberian ideal-type. Secondly, the account here of state formation places those changes in a wider context. Modernisation of the state is not exclusively associated with any particular moment, nor with the vision of any particular individual. In drawing attention to the wider process of state formation this account also draws attention to a more abiding question – the relationship between the power of the state and the life of the individual. Questions about the emergence of the modern state are less easy to pose now that we are less certain about what the modern state is, but the impact of state power on individual lives retains its interest. The development of institutions of state power which were more modern in form is a part of a wider story of the changing impact of all forms of state power in this period. As we will see, modernisation is particularly associated with the impact of warfare, but contemporaries would have been at least as aware of other changes in the forms and functions of political power.

This raises the problem of measuring the success or failure of political action. For example, is the measure of policies designed to prevent starvation whether or not people starved? The problem here is that the absence of starvation may not result from government activity. Equally, the failure to implement the dearth orders in any given locality was not necessarily a failure of the policy, it might simply reflect the absence of dearth in that locality. Functional success in the following pages is assessed in terms of the degree and quality of compliance with particular political measures. What we can measure (albeit crudely) is how far their activities were met with actions understood to be indicative of consent. The effectiveness of the state is measured against the goals being set, and in terms of compliance as a (rough-and-ready) measure of legitimacy. Of course, there were wide local variations in these things. In making claims about the power of the state we are talking about the net outcome of a myriad of local negotiations – thousands of requests to release part of a store of grain onto the market, for example. In this context, an idea or set of ideas was mobilised in order to legitimate an act of power by individuals adopting a particular social role. However, at this quantum level of state activity there is a potentially alarming degree of indeterminacy – local variations in the outcomes of these negotiations might be considerable. The form and function of the state as a whole, therefore, is a net effect of innumerable local negotiations, and statements about general patterns of political change are always subject to qualification on the basis of experience in particular localities at particular times.

Certainty about the overall institutional form and functional effectiveness of the state is statistical rather than absolute.

In many ways this government was weak – lacking in even the most basic information about the size and composition of the population, or the sources of wealth available for taxation, for example. The degree of coordination over the everyday activities of local agencies of the state was also poor. However, a more significant measure of the power of the state is its impact on individuals. In response to the perceived threat of vagrancy, of witches or of the plague, for example, local officeholders were given dramatic new powers. By 1700, the national government was comfortably the largest employer in the country and a large and increasing proportion of national wealth circulated through government.[2] This was just the most tangible of a number of ways in which the power of government over the individual had increased by that date. Whether or not this had the desired effect, or whether the effects were really desirable, are not the issues here. The concentration on innovation is not intended to suggest that the power of the state was 'increasing' in a naive sense, or that this was the only period in which the claims of political power over the lives of individuals increased, or that this was a uniform process.

The emphasis here is on the continuous expression and modulation of political power and the chronological limits of this study are rather unconventional. The seventeenth century has long occupied a place of central importance in the history of the English state and this book clearly grows out of that tradition. But the definition of the state used here leads to a greater awareness of continuities in the development of the English state and 1550 is in that sense an arbitrary starting point. In this account political change is understood to be the unplanned but none the less patterned outcome of negotiating legitimate responses to functional challenges and opportunities. This is a continuous process and the chronological limits for this study are set by functional challenges rather than constitutional crises. These limits embrace a period of rapid population growth and associated social change; of increasing pressure for changes in military resources; of a sustained commitment to the idea of a Protestant state; and of the growth and elaboration of the territorial limits of crown authority. Putting it this way, however, draws attention to the ways in which the study could go beyond these chronological limits – many of these challenges were not unique to this period.

[2] M. J. Braddick, *The Nerves of State: Taxation and the Financing of the English State, 1558–1714* (Manchester, 1996), 6–12, 100–1, 188–202.

Political power was legitimated in different ways and its institutional expressions and functional purposes modulated variously and pretty continuously over a much longer period. The concentration on this important period does not imply a claim that it was the only formative stage.

Subsequent chapters narrate the impact of functional challenges on available institutions, and the pressures which explain the creation of new forms of political office or the reinterpretation of the role of old ones. Part II examines political innovations intended to preserve what were taken to be the bases of social order. The vision of order on which these definitions were based, and the beliefs which justified the offices of those charged with implementing the resulting initiatives were, broadly speaking, patriarchal. Part III examines measures taken in the light of changing military technology. These pressures exposed weaknesses in the capacity of patriarchal officeholding. As a result new institutions developed, which were more specialised and differentiated and were justified with reference to distinctive political languages. Part IV examines the confessional state, emphasising the limited effect of appeals to the defence of the true religion in legitimating the specific measures that were being taken. The problem of legitimation here led to local divergences from national norms. These divergences ultimately subverted the aims of activists to the extent that, at the end of the period covered here, the ambitions for the confessional state were tempered. In each case legitimacy was asserted with reference to distinctive general languages. The purchase of these languages, or the plausibility of their application in these particular circumstances, shaped political innovation. Where innovations could not be made within existing constraints they might be abandoned, or new languages and institutions might be used instead. Finally, political power is territorial, and by 1700 the authority of the state coordinated from London was much more extensive than it had been in 1550 – stretching throughout Britain and Ireland, across the Atlantic and to toeholds in Africa and Asia. Part V explores this process, drawing out parallels between state formation in England and the wider territories of the Tudor and Stuart crowns.

PART II

The patriarchal state

Introduction

A large number of administrative initiatives during the Elizabethan and early Stuart periods were prompted by a set of interrelated concerns about social order. In part this was a response to objective conditions – for example, the growth of poverty – but the response was informed by broader concerns. These initiatives also reflected a growing social distance between, on the one hand, the gentry and the middling sort, who occupied many of the positions of local government, and the poorer sort on the other, with whom a number of social problems came to be identified. It was widely accepted that personal morality was a public matter (and one which was the proper concern of the magistracy), and for some officeholders this intersected with an association of sin with disease and poverty. The result was that many initiatives in relation to the social order came to target the poor. Another important feature of contemporary social thought was the importance of patriarchy to social order, which rested on 'the family and household, on schooling and apprenticeship and on the formal and informal institutions of control in the parish. Relations between husbands and wives, parents and children and heads of households and their dependants and servants were deemed to be central to the maintenance of a well-regulated society.'[1] As a result, threats to social order were also associated with those outside the bounds of patriarchal order – young men, scolding or single women, for example. These interests were expressed fairly directly in the formulation of policy, but were also powerfully reinforced by its implementation. The uses of state authority operated disproportionately in particular directions, to target those perceived to be most threatening to these values. In short, measures to preserve social order were not determined solely by material conditions.

[1] A. J. Fletcher and J. Stevenson, 'Introduction', in Fletcher and Stevenson (eds.), *Order and Disorder in Early Modern England* (Cambridge, 1985), 1–40, at pp. 31–2.

These measures found expression, among other things, in the poor law, dearth orders and plague orders, and these are the subject of chapter 3. These administrative measures were shaped by presumptions about the basis of social order, and their implementation gave further reinforcement to this vision. Fears about social order were also manifest in the uses of the criminal law, which in some respects became an instrument of social discipline. Chapter 4 considers the ways in which the operation of the law had this effect, but the law, particularly the civil law, was more than this. Chapter 4, accordingly, will also consider the broader uses of the courts. These broader uses of the courts represent, in a sense, an increase in the role of political power in the localities, as legitimate authority was invoked in order to resolve local disputes, but it was not driven simply by respectable fears or targeted solely on the weak and the marginal.

None the less, changing material conditions prompted fears among the respectable. In particular the growth of poverty among the able-bodied and of long-distance subsistence migration fed fears about an escalating moral and normative threat to social order. Similarly, harvest failure and disease, both 'real' aspects of the material environment, were associated with poverty and were interpreted partly in moral and normative terms. Through an examination of the ways in which these threats were defined we can come to a clearer understanding of what vision of social order the state was being used to protect. The legitimation of the power of officeholders lay in a complex and changing vision of social order, but a consistent element of it was 'patriarchy' – a pattern of hierarchy and subordination which subsumed class, status and gender relations. The forms of the offices through which these measures were taken, and the ways in which these measures were targeted, reflect the power of these patriarchal ideas. It is suggested here, therefore, that the administrative measures taken in the face of these threats reflect a vision of social order that can usefully be described in these terms, and chapters 3 and 4 offer an outline of a 'patriarchal state' in early modern England.

CHAPTER 3

Social order: poverty, dearth and disease

Social historians of early modern England have been impressed by the increasing range of administrative measures undertaken by local governors in order to preserve social order. This chapter considers these administrative measures – the development of the poor law and crisis measures taken in response to dearth and outbreaks of the plague – as manifestations of an increasing use of state power in the localities. Behind these measures lay material conditions such as increasing levels of poverty and increased vulnerability to famine. However, the precise measures that were taken, and the ways in which formal requirements were interpreted in practice, draw attention to the ideals of order which defined and legitimated these actions. The impact of these uses of state power on the lives of individuals was sometimes dramatic – they represent significant aspects of the development of the state in this period – but they did not result from central initiatives alone, and cannot be embraced by a model of the exercise of state power which depends for its motive force on central will. For the history of these administrative developments it was the three generations before the civil war that were most important. In the later seventeenth century, innovation is less striking than consolidation, and the tone of magistracy changed – in Landau's phrase patriarchs were giving way to patricians. This consolidation took place largely at local initiative and the regular routine of local administration ensured that England was closely governed in these respects, despite the absence of routine oversight from the centre. The first two sections of the chapter consider the development of the poor law and the dearth and plague orders. The final section outlines the importance of local initiative, and widely disseminated views about social and political order, in shaping the development and implementation of these measures.

THE POOR LAW

The pre-eminent concern for many early modern magistrates was poverty and its consequences, and during Elizabeth's reign a body of legislation developed which provided the means to tackle the problems as they were perceived. Firstly, a regularised system of relief developed, allowing for short- and long-term alleviation. Alongside this were measures to provide work for those thought fit for it and discipline for those thought to be undeserving. A new kind of institution, the bridewell or house of correction, was introduced to discipline and reform the poor. Relief and the provision of work increasingly depended on the collection of regular local rates, and in order to tackle acute problems measures were taken to ensure that food prices could be controlled. The success of the implementation of these measures was by no means uniform. For example, it might have been the case that by the 1670s only a third or so of English parishes had poor rates, although they were likely to be the most populous.[1] Even by this yardstick, however, this is impressive – in 3,000 parishes unpaid officeholders were regularly imposing rates in line with statutory provision. In fact, as we will see, it is possible to make a stronger case for administrative success. The case of poverty demonstrates the strengths of government by officeholders, and in some ways the responsiveness of national government to influential local groups.

We saw in chapter 2 that there is some debate about how seriously the living standards of the poorer sort declined during this period. In trying to measure levels of poverty there is, of course, a problem of sources. Older estimates based on tax returns from the 1520s and 1660s painted a desperate picture, of perhaps between one-third and one-half of the population living in poverty. However, such estimates are certainly too credulous about the meaning of tax exemptions – assessment for taxation was by no means rigorous in this period, and exclusion from the taxpaying population cannot be equated with destitution. Because of these uncertainties, and in the light of the absence of general mortality crises, a number of historians have become sceptical about high estimates of the level of poverty.[2]

---

[1] P. Slack, *Poverty and Policy in Tudor and Stuart England* (London, 1988), 170. This is a consciously conservative estimate.

[2] T. J. Tronrud, 'Dispelling the gloom. The extent of poverty in Tudor and Stuart towns: some Kentish evidence', *Canadian Journal of History*, 20 (1985), 1–21. Slack echoes this: *Poverty*, p. 47. For some of the difficulties of using tax records to estimate levels of poverty in the later seventeenth century, see T. Arkell, 'The incidence of poverty in England in the later seventeenth century', *Social History*, 12 (1987), 23–47.

The experience of poverty was diverse and this again makes it difficult simply to count the poor. Censuses of the poor, or other records generated by the administration of the poor law, reveal not just raw numbers of the 'poor' but also complex patterns of poverty. Clearly, a broad group of potentially vulnerable poor existed, a group for whom real destitution might easily result from economic or family misfortune. Estimates of the number of poor based on snapshots taken at particular times underestimate the effect of the life-cycle – individuals moving into and out of poverty during their lives – and of the effects of particularly hard times – harvest failure, trade depression, disease mortality and so forth. A number of local studies have demonstrated how those at the lower end of village society derived income from a variety of sources – by-employments, charity, smallholdings and so on. Moreover, many depended on a household, rather than an individual income. Formal relief was only one source of income among many for those eking out a living in this economy of makeshifts. The characteristic form of poverty was probably this – chronic vulnerability to sudden change that could disrupt the household economy. Particularly vulnerable were those in households below or above an optimum size – widows and widowers, orphans or families 'overcharged' with children.[3] In many parishes, particularly rural parishes, formal and regular rates might not have been necessary. Here 'the poor were . . . an easily recognized and normally small minority, [and so] traditional attitudes could persist longer than in the more transient and less easily monitored society of the towns'.[4] A key variable, of course, will have been the availability of private charity and of endowments for the poor.[5] Treatment of the sick and mentally

---

[3] T. Wales, 'Poverty, poor relief and the life-cycle: some evidence from seventeenth-century Norfolk', in R. M. Smith (ed.), *Land, Kinship and Life-Cycle* (Cambridge, 1984), 351–404; A. L. Beier, 'Poverty and progress in early modern England', in A. L. Beier, D. Cannadine and J. M. Rosenheim (eds.), *The First Modern Society: Essays in English History in Honour of Lawrence Stone* (Cambridge, 1989), 201–39, esp. pp. 203–26. See also Beier, 'The social problems of an Elizabethan country town: Warwick, 1580–90', in P. Clark (ed.), *Country Towns in Pre-Industrial England* (Leicester, 1981), 45–85, esp. pp. 54–64. It is possible that the north-west European preference for nuclear households increased the vulnerability of the population as a whole to life-cycle poverty: see P. Laslett, 'Family, kinship and collectivity as systems of support in pre-industrial Europe: a consideration of the "nuclear hardship" hypothesis', *Continuity and Change*, 3 (1988), 153–75. For sickness and poverty see M. Pelling, 'Illness among the poor in an early modern town: the Norwich census of 1570', *Continuity and Change*, 3 (1988), 273–90; Pelling, 'Healing the sick poor: social policy and disability in Norwich 1550–1640', *Medical History*, 29 (1985), 115–37.　　[4] Slack, *Poverty*, p. 63.

[5] I. W. Archer, *The Pursuit of Stability: Social Relations in Elizabethan London* (Cambridge, 1991), 163–82 offers a detailed account of the role of private charity in late sixteenth-century London. See also Beier, 'Warwick', pp. 64–73. For rural England see B. Sharp, 'Common rights, charities, and the disorderly poor', in G. Eley and W. Hunt (eds.), *Reviving the English Revolution: Reflections and*

disabled could also, no doubt, be handled with discretion.[6] The English economy was characterised by marked regional variations, and the crises that might precipitate such people into subsistence problems varied likewise. In all, therefore, counting the poor is problematic not just because of the difficulty of sources, but because of the diversity of the experience of poverty.

Behind these issues lies a more fundamental one: what is poverty? It is difficult to arrive at a definition which will hold for all societies and which can be easily measured. This is one of the difficulties with the use of tax records: exemption from taxation has been used in the past as an unproblematic definition of poverty, but it is not at all clear that the grounds for exemption can be equated easily with an external criterion for gauging poverty.[7] Secondly, some relative measure of deprivation can be used, although there are difficulties of documentation here. This does have the advantage of taking into account contemporary perceptions, however. A final alternative is to adopt contemporary views of poverty in their entirety, and here the records of poor relief are helpful because they are the outcome of just such perceptions.[8] One of the difficulties in interpreting such sources is that embedded in their categorisations of poverty are assumptions about entitlement – those listed as receiving regular relief, for example, will be definitely those who were thought to deserve it, but might not be all those who we might think needed it. For that very reason, though, these records are very helpful for particular kinds of question. On the other hand, these records of poor law administration often give only snapshots of the problems of poverty, and cannot give a clear sense of the ways in which individuals experienced hardship over time, moving into or out of dependence through their life-cycle or as economic conditions changed.[9] Since the experience of poverty was very diverse, and the contribution of poor relief to household subsistence equally varied,

Elaborations on the Work of Christopher Hill (London, 1988), 107–37; and, in crisis conditions, J. Walter, 'The social economy of dearth in early modern England', in J. Walter and R. Schofield (eds.), *Famine, Disease and the Social Order in Early Modern Society* (Cambridge, 1989), 75–128. For an impressive overview see Slack, *Poverty*, pp. 162–73.

[6] For a local study of the later period see P. Rushton, 'Lunatics and idiots: mental disability, the community, and the poor law in North-East England, 1600–1800', *Medical History*, 32 (1988), 34–50.   [7] See Arkell, 'Incidence', for example.

[8] Tronrud, 'Dispelling'. For general discussions of the problem see B. Stapleton, 'Inherited poverty and life-cycle poverty: Odiham, Hampshire, 1650–1850', *Social History*, 18 (1993), 339–55; J. Henderson and R. Wall, 'Introduction', in Henderson and Wall (eds.), *Poor Women and Children in the European Past* (London, 1994), 1–28, esp. pp. 1–4.

[9] See, for example, Beier's criticisms of the 'optimistic' evaluations of poverty levels: 'Poverty and progress', pp. 203–26.

counting poor rates offers only a very rough guide to the numbers of the poor and the effectiveness of poor relief.

In the light of these evidential and methodological problems, Slack proposes distinctions between background and crisis levels of poverty, and between deep and shallow poverty. In the first case, bad years might raise levels of poverty by a factor of four or five. The second distinction is important as a way of thinking about the nature of the problem: '[s]ome people may be starving while others simply lack fuel or clothes'. Thus, the number of poor does not really reveal the intensity of poverty. If the number of those experiencing shallow poverty rises more quickly than the number in deep poverty falls, then the number of poor increases but the intensity of poverty does not. The best evidence of deep poverty is starvation, and this was increasingly rare in the seventeenth century; but the sixteenth century had probably seen an increase in shallow poverty. The evidence of wage levels is not good, but it would have to be really terribly flawed to invalidate the claim that general living standards for the poorer sort fell during the sixteenth century. This remained true for many in the seventeenth century: 'It seems probable that the number of people in deep poverty – those in danger of starvation – markedly declined, while the number in shallow poverty – those who might be described as "poor" – increased by at least as much . . . In terms of intensity, poverty was ameliorated in the seventeenth century; in terms of numbers it was not.'[10] An important component of this new poverty in sixteenth- and seventeenth-century England was long-distance migration, driven by subsistence problems, and this migration frequently ended in the suburbs of large towns and cities or on marginal or waste ground of the fen and forest.[11]

Against this background of increasing poverty and long-distance migration, a number of important initiatives were taken before 1640, dealing with both deep and shallow poverty, informed by humanist ideals of commonwealth and order.[12] For the poor the Elizabethan statutes laid out a coherent programme of relief, punishment and

---

[10] Slack, *Poverty*, p. 39.
[11] For migration see P. Clark and D. Souden (eds.), *Migration and Society in Early Modern England* (London, 1987). For the problems of the suburbs J. Boulton, *Neighbourhood and Society: A London Suburb in the Seventeenth Century* (Cambridge, 1987); Beier, 'Warwick'; P. Clark and J. Clark, 'The social economy of the Canterbury suburbs: the evidence of the census of 1563', in A. Detsicas and N. Yates (eds.), *Studies in Modern Kentish History Presented to Felix Hull and Elizabeth Melling* (Maidstone, 1983), 65–86. For fen and forest see Sharp, 'Common rights'.
[12] For the ideals behind these initiatives see Slack, *Poverty*, ch. 6 *passim* and P. A. Fideler, 'Poverty, policy and providence: the Tudors and the poor', in P. A. Fideler and T. F. Mayer (eds.), *Political Thought and the Tudor Commonwealth: Deep Structure, Discourse and Disguise* (London, 1992), 194–222.

provision of work, and they did so partly in response to local initiatives. Many of the features of late Tudor legislation had precedents before 1550.[13] For example, statutes of 1495 and 1531 had sought to regulate begging, imposing licences and punishments, with whippings for vagrants. This disciplinary and regulatory project was accompanied by positive measures too – a statute of 1536 encouraged contribution to poor rates and the children of the poor were to be taught a trade and found work. The most striking feature of this early legislation, however, was the desire to control begging and vagrancy. The 1547 act, which defined as vagrant anyone unemployed for three or more days, imposed particularly savage (in fact unenforceable) punishments: vagrants were to branded with a 'v' and enslaved to the informant for two years.[14] This was repealed because it was too savage, but the legislation of 1531 is almost as striking. This made it lawful to take 'any man or woman being whole and mighty in body and able to labour' but who 'can give none reckoning how he doth lawfully get his living' before a justice of the peace. That justice should then cause the vagrant to be taken to the nearest market town 'and there to be tied to the end of a cart naked and be beaten with whips throughout the same market town . . . till his body be bloody by reason of such whipping'. Having suffered thus, the vagrant was to take an oath to return to where he last dwelled 'and there put himself to labour like as a true man oweth to do'.[15]

Clearly, the explanation for such measures does not lie in material conditions alone, but in the interaction between those conditions and contemporary thinking about the nature of social order. At the centre of much social and economic policy in this period was a view of the moral and political worth of labour and a calling. As William Tyndale told lowly kitchen servants, 'God hath put thee in that office.' Social responsibility flowed, in Tyndale's view, from the proper fulfilment of the functions to which God had called the individual: 'Let every man therefore wait on the office wherein Christ hath put him, and therein serve his brethren.' If that was a place of low degree, 'let him patiently therein abide, till God promote him, and exalt him higher'. But it was

---

[13] This was true of local initiatives too: M. K. McIntosh, 'Local responses to the poor in late medieval and Tudor England', *Continuity and Change*, 3 (1988), 209–45. For an account of these initiatives in the broader context of social regulation by local courts, see McIntosh, *Controlling Misbehavior in England, 1370–1600* (Cambridge, 1998), esp. ch. 3. For mid-Tudor initiatives see P. Slack, 'Social policy and the constraints of government, 1547–58', in J. Loach and R. Tittler (eds.), *The Mid-Tudor Policy c. 1540–1560* (London, 1980), 94–115, 206–10.

[14] C. S. L. Davies, 'Slavery and Protector Somerset: the Vagrancy Act of 1547', *EcHR*, 2nd series, 19 (1966), 533–49. For the provisions see pp. 533–4.

[15] Quoted in J. Pound, *Poverty and Vagrancy in Tudor England*, (2nd edn, London, 1986), 96.

equally true of the kitchen servant's social superiors. Kings and head officers had a duty 'to seek Christ in their offices, and minister peace and quietness unto the brethren; punish sin, and that with mercy'.[16] These notions of social order were closely related to a sense of the proper ordering of the household, and of relations between men and women and between the old and the young. To lack a calling was to be without place or purpose in a divinely ordained social order.

To have a calling and not to fulfil it – for example, to be able to work but none the less to be idle – was a moral offence. In contemporary thinking about poverty, therefore, the key categories among the poor were in one sense the 'able' and 'impotent', and these had a moral content. The able but idle were worthy of discipline, indeed they required it since they were clearly failing to fulfil the purpose intended for them. The impotent and poor were the proper objects of relief. These distinctions are plain in the legislative measures that were taken. The imposition of a poor rate in 1572 was an evolution from earlier exhortations to contribute and, in 1563, a compulsory contribution enforced by quarter sessions. This systematisation of relief was accompanied by equally systematic discipline for the undeserving. Vagrants were to be whipped and have their ears bored for the first offence, their second offence was to be considered a felony and a third offence was punishable by death. The clearer definition of entitlement clearly had a disciplinary obverse. But this is too simple: as the legislation was developed (and even more as it was interpreted)[17] it was increasingly recognised that the poor might be both able and willing, but also unemployed. The 1572 statute had excepted some categories of the able-bodied from definition as vagrants and a statute of 1576 called for the provision of work for the able-bodied from parish stocks of raw materials. Thus, a third strand of the response was established, alongside relief and discipline.

These strands of provision, relief and discipline were codified in the legislation of 1598. Vagrants were to be arrested, whipped and sent home where, if they were able-bodied, they were to be put into service. For the recalcitrant, houses of correction were to be established, and real trouble-makers could be banished. Return from banishment was a capital offence. At the same time, duties for the relief of the deserving were outlined in detail. Rates were to supply not only relief for the impotent but also work for the able-bodied. Children were to be taught

---

[16] William Tyndale reprinted in C. H. Williams (ed.), *English Historical Documents 1485–1558* (London, 1971), 292–5, quotation at p. 293.   [17] See below, p. 114.

habits of industriousness through apprenticeships and quarter sessions were to enforce the collection of the rates by distraint. All this would make begging unnecessary, and it was made illegal.[18] Giving the poor (putting them in) their place was the essence of the measures. Everyone was to have an employment (a place in the social hierarchy) and a place of settlement. To lack both was to become the object of a stern disciplinary intent. The administrative burden fell on magistrates in and out of quarter sessions, and on the constables who collected and administered the rates in the villages and wards. It was these people, the better sort, who drew upon state power to enforce decisions about entitlement and respectability. The ideas which legitimated their offices served also to legitimate their position in the social order – here was a happy coincidence between the legitimation of a set of administrative measures and of the offices charged with their execution.[19]

This legislative programme grew out of local initiatives and reflected much broader notions about poverty, disorder, disease and decay. It was informed also by a desire for civic harmony and order that owed much to renaissance ideals.[20] There were important changes in perceptions of poverty during the sixteenth century and the first half of the seventeenth century. Traditional values emphasising the obligations of the rich to the poor ('tribute') were transformed as harsher views of poverty ('marginality') gained ground. By comparison, views of the poor which emphasised the economic resource that they represented ('labour') were of more muted importance before the 1640s. Thus, a traditional view of the poor 'as an integral part of a Christian commonwealth, necessary stimuli if the rich were to practise virtue and useful examples of humility',[21] was applied more sparingly and critically. 'Discrimination and public relief made it necessary to define private charity, and in the process it became exclusive, calculating and deliberate', particularly from the late sixteenth century onwards.[22] Those discriminated against, as it were, became regarded as marginal to, or outside, society, rather than an integral part of it. Groups among the poor were regarded as subversive of social values and dangerous to social and political order. It was comparatively late in the development of policy that surveys of the poor 'uncovered people who did not fit neatly into either the impotent or the idle category'.[23] These were

---

[18] Pound, *Poverty*, pp. 51–3.   [19] For the legitimation of these offices see above, pp. 71–85.
[20] Slack, 'Social policy'. See, now, P. Slack, *From Reformation to Improvement: Public Welfare in Early Modern England* (Oxford, 1998), esp. ch. 1.   [21] Slack, *Poverty*, p. 19.   [22] Ibid., p. 22.
[23] Ibid., p. 27.

people willing to work but unable to find it, or whose household income was insufficient to support their families: a Tudor and Stuart equivalent of the labouring poor.[24]

Perhaps the most dramatic response to the problem of poverty, however, was the bridewell or house of correction. A reformative and penal institution, designed to tackle the problem of an anti-society, it originated in a number of urban experiments in the third quarter of the sixteenth century. By the end of the century about a quarter of English counties had them and in 1630 there were probably about seventy in rural England, with dozens more in cities and towns. Life inside was regimented to discipline the recalcitrant and to enable the willing to work, but their capacity was limited. Although the high hopes for their reformative potential were not realised, they provided a blueprint for workhouses later established by corporations of the poor, for example the scheme for a corporation in London in the 1640s.[25] They also provided another option for magistrates in dealing with poverty, vagrancy or bastardy, and in that they probably had a long-term influence on behaviour.[26] In the later seventeenth century houses of correction appear to have been an important part of the labour policy employed by magistrates around the country.[27]

The legislative programme chimed with contemporary perceptions about the nature of poverty. Moreover, many of the specific measures enacted drew on local experience: 'The Tudor poor law . . . was founded on local experiments, and the contacts between councillors and the counties and towns where they had an interest continued to direct their view of national problems and potential solutions.'[28] Most famously, the corporations of Norwich, Salisbury and London implemented schemes which were subsequently taken up nationally. It was probably in London that measures against vagrancy developed – branding, whipping, licensing and badging were all ways of controlling begging and vagrancy

---

[24] Ibid., ch. 2.

[25] J. Innes, 'Prisons for the poor: English bridewells, 1555–1800', in F. Snyder and D. Hay (eds.), *Labour, Law, and Crime: An Historical Perspective* (London, 1987), 42–122. The Lancashire house of correction had only fifty places in the early seventeenth century: W. J. King, 'Punishment for bastardy in early seventeenth-century England', *Albion*, 10 (1978), 130–51, p. 131. A. L. Beier, *Masterless Men: The Vagrancy Problem in England 1560–1640* (London, 1985), 164–9, is sceptical about their achievement. For the London scheme see below, pp. 132–3.

[26] Innes, 'Prisons for the poor'. For their use in relation to bastardy: King, 'Punishment'. For bastardy in general see below, pp. 143–5.

[27] A. Fletcher, *Reform in the Provinces: The Government of Stuart England* (London, 1986), 219–28.

[28] P. Slack, 'Books of Orders: the making of English social policy, 1577–1631', *TRHS*, 5th series, 30 (1980), 1–22, quotation at p. 7. See, for the earlier period, McIntosh, 'Local responses'.

in London by the 1520s. By 1533 poor rates were being raised, antici-
pating national legislation by twenty-five years. Such measures were
reproduced in other large towns – Bristol, Canterbury, York and
Ipswich, for example. But perhaps the most notable local experiment
was that undertaken in Norwich in 1570. Faced with rising numbers of
poor the corporation undertook an elaborate census which revealed the
presence of 2,300 poor people in the city. Begging was forbidden, and
poor relief was organised systematically, to include the provision of
work for the able-bodied; and this was supported by regular funding
and sustained attempts at enforcement. This administrative reform,
particularly the rate, became the basis for discipline too. The undeserving were sent to the bridewell. Children were to be educated, the aged to
be given alms. This was, in contemporary terms, a comprehensive
response, and it was a model too. The chief architect of the Norwich
scheme, John Aldrich, sat on the committee whose deliberations informed the national legislation of 1572.[29] In the towns the pressure of
poverty led corporations to experiment, and this was probably the case
in some rural parishes – those that had a growing pauper population
and a group of prospering farmers able to support regular rates.[30] In
both cases there were other influences such as renaissance civic ideals or
concerns at the supposed decline of hospitality in the countryside.[31]
None the less, local initiatives were no doubt important because the
local experience of poverty was pressing and sometimes acutely felt.

Naturally, the implementation of these measures was not instant. It is
difficult to measure, but it seems that local officeholders were flexible in
their implementation of the poor law.[32] Statutes in relation to social
order were evidently regarded in practice as, to use a modern term,
'permissive legislation'.[33] There was reluctance to pay rates when they
were introduced in the late sixteenth century, and by the early 1590s
measures against vagrancy were considered by some to be too harsh.[34]
Even in the 1620s some areas resisted rates on principle, justices around
Ormskirk agreeing in 1624 that as long as the impotent were orderly
and did not wander, they should be 'at liberty to ask and have reasonable relief . . . not troubling any house above once a week'.[35] Rates were

---

[29] Pound, *Poverty*. For Aldrich see Slack, *Poverty*, p. 149, and for local initiatives, ibid., pp. 148–56.
[30] Beier, 'Poverty and progress', esp. p. 239.
[31] Slack, *Poverty*, ch. 6; F. Heal, *Hospitality in Early Modern England* (Oxford, 1990), chs. 1, 3.
[32] For local case studies revealing discretion, see P. Slack, *Poverty in Early-Stuart Salisbury*, Wiltshire
   Record Society, 31 (Devizes, 1975); and Beier, 'Warwick', pp. 75–8.
[33] Much the same applies to the broader programme represented by the dearth and plague orders,
   for which see below, pp. 118–28.   [34] Slack, *Poverty*, pp. 125–6.   [35] Ibid., pp. 128–9.

not always essential to achieving the ends envisaged by the poor laws. In Hanworth, Norfolk, in 1645 and 1646, it appears that no poor rates were raised and in 1647 this was definitely the case. But this was not an indication that the poor laws were being neglected: in 1647 it was noted 'it being held fitter by our Minister to provide for the Poor rather by voluntary contributions than by rates and collections there have been divers several sums of money contributed and distributed these and other poor persons within the said parish'.[36] The implementation of rates is a crude and perhaps inadequate indication of compliance, therefore.

According to Beier the 1590s and the 1620s were the crucial periods in the enforcement of the poor laws. 'Before 1590 official action taken to relieve the poor was sporadic, and largely confined to the larger towns and a few rural parishes.' From the mid-1590s, however, 'the evidence of more widespread action is impressive'.[37] In Gloucester and Canterbury there were important innovations during the 1590s,[38] and evidence from a number of towns reveals innovations in the introduction of corn stocks, the regularisation of poor relief and the discipline of the migrant poor. In sum, the 1590s might have seen a 'crisis contained'.[39] In the counties, poor relief was being 'widely enforced from the end of Elizabeth's reign, but especially after 1620 when the numbers of poor began to rise again'.[40] The distractions of the 1640s do not appear to have disrupted administration. Indeed, if hard times in the 1590s and 1620s had prompted the regularisation of poor relief in many areas, the 1640s seem to have been similarly significant. In the absence of central direction local officeholders in a number of counties jumped to provide relief. Five bad harvests in succession was the worst run since the 1590s. In Wiltshire, Cheshire, Huntingdonshire and Lancashire dearth orders were applied rigorously, suggesting that 'the magistracy coped

[36] Quoted in Wales, 'Life-cycle', p. 359.
[37] Beier, 'Poverty and progress', p. 234.
[38] P. Clark, '"The Ramoth-Gilead of the Good": urban change and political radicalism at Gloucester 1540–1640', in P. Clark, A. G. R. Smith and N. Tyacke (eds.), *The English Commonwealth 1547–1640: Essays in Politics and Society Presented to Joel Hurstfield* (Leicester, 1979), 167–87, 253–60, pp. 175–6; Clark and Clark, 'Canterbury', pp. 85–6.
[39] P. Clark, 'A crisis contained? The condition of English towns in the 1590s', in Clark (ed.), *The European Crisis of the 1590s: Essays in Comparative History* (London, 1985), 44–66. For an exemplary account of the means by which London escaped serious disorder in this period, Archer, *Pursuit*, especially, for the current purposes, ch. 5.
[40] Beier, 'Poverty and progress', p. 235, based on the cases of Kent, Sussex, Lancashire and Shropshire. In Lincolnshire and Somerset implementation probably came rather later, in the 1620s and 1630s. Slack places greater weight on developments later in the century: *Poverty*, p. 170.

triumphantly'.[41] In Devon, administration at the lowest levels was, to a significant degree, self-activating during the 1640s, and in Yorkshire too, the interregnum saw the magistracy operating pretty much as usual.[42] Elsewhere the experience of the 1640s prompted local elites to switch their efforts from informal to formal relief. In many places, of course, poor relief was well established before 1640, and it may have been the case that the dearth of 1647 to 1650 was a 'decisive factor in the institutionalisation of the poor law where this had not yet occurred'.[43] During the 1650s it is unlikely that less than £100,000 was being raised in poor rates in England and Wales.[44]

Local officeholders were undoubtedly quick to take up aspects of these measures, but were slow to implement the full range – they seem to have used their discretion in judging the appropriateness of general measures to particular local conditions. It was the discretion of local authorities that created the space for a third kind of response to poverty, between punishment and relief.[45] It was probably marked in relation to the sick poor, too.[46] However, this is best viewed as the flexible implementation, or creative interpretation, of a programme whose broad outlines were largely unquestioned. Down to 1640 the magistracy was often energetic in pursuing aspects of a policy which was not necessarily applicable in its entirety. By 1660, it is safe to say that 3,000 parishes in England and Wales (and probably the most populous parishes) were accustomed to raising rates for the poor, rates being an indicator of virtually full implementation of the legislation.

There is also evidence of considerable energy being directed towards the implementation of wage and apprenticeship laws.[47] As we have seen, employment was more than a means of subsistence, it was a means of securing a place in society. Apprenticeship was clearly one means by which young migrants were absorbed into new communities, although

---

[41] Fletcher, *Reform*, pp. 199–200, quotation at p. 199. For Cheshire, J. S. Morrill, *Cheshire 1630–1660: County Government and Society during the English Revolution* (Oxford, 1974), 249–52; for Lancashire, J. Walter and K. Wrightson, 'Dearth and the social order in early modern England', *PP*, 71 (1976), 22–42, esp. pp. 38–40. For poor relief in London see R. W. Herlan, 'Poor relief in London during the English revolution', *JBS*, 18/2 (1979), 30–51.

[42] S. K. Roberts, *Recovery and Restoration in an English County: Devon Local Administration 1646–1670* (Exeter, 1985), p. 3; G. C. F. Forster, 'County government in Yorkshire during the Interregnum', *Northern History*, 12 (1976), 84–104.

[43] Fletcher, *Reform*, p. 187, based on evidence from Cheshire, Lancashire, Warwickshire and Devon. See also Wales, 'Life-cycle', esp. p. 359.   [44] Slack, *Poverty*, p. 171.

[45] Ibid., p. 29.   [46] Pelling, 'Illness'; Pelling, 'Healing'; Rushton, 'Lunatics'.

[47] M. G. Davies, *The Enforcement of the English Apprenticeship Laws: A Study in Applied Mercantilism 1563–1642* (Cambridge, Mass., 1956); D. Woodward, 'The determination of wage rates in the early modern north of England', *EcHR*, 2nd series, 47 (1994), 22–43. For some further discussion see S. Foot, *The Effect of the Elizabethan Statute of Artificers on Wages in England*, Exeter Research Group Discussion Paper, no. 5 (Exeter, 1980).

its significance in that respect was probably declining over this period.[48] This may not have been explicitly the concern of magistrates regulating apprenticeship and employment, but it seems clear that it was at the back of their minds. The predominance of private interests in the enforcement of the apprenticeship laws before 1642 makes it difficult to discern a coherent 'policy'. But it is clear that the dominant concern motivating justices of the peace to enforce the laws 'was the preservation of order and status'.[49] In bad years cloth-masters were enjoined not to drive wages too low, for example. The provision of work for the poor was a moral as much as an economic programme, and even vagrants were thought to have specialised trades in their counter-culture.[50] Quarter sessions were willing to intervene to protect apprentices from abuse, again reflecting the importance of the institution as a means of socialisation.[51] The children of the poor were bound into apprenticeships in large numbers – 1,506 in a particularly zealous initiative in Hertfordshire in 1619, for example. There were questions about the legality of forcing people to take apprentices which were not really resolved until it was given statutory backing in 1697.[52] Long before this, however, it was an established part of the armoury for dealing with poverty and the lack of uniformity was not necessarily a failure of initiative. In the case of the apprenticeship laws, for example, the privy council explicitly acknowledged that the provisions might not be appropriate in all circumstances.[53]

Allied to this initiative was magisterial regulation of wages, restraining excess wages in order to encourage employment. This was based on clauses in the 1563 statute of artificers, reinforced by a statute of 1597, and there is evidence of considerable activity before 1640 in many parts of the country.[54] The effect of this energy is difficult to gauge. A recent survey of wage rates in northern towns, for example, suggests that the period when wage regulation was most effective was the first half of the sixteenth century. Magisterial activity in the second half of the century may have helped to stabilise wages, although on the whole the effect of regulation on wage levels was probably marginal. None the less, there is

---

[48] P. Clark, 'Migrants in the city: the process of social adaptation in English towns, 1500–1800', in Clark and Souden (eds.), *Migration*, 267–91, at pp. 269–70.

[49] Davies, *Enforcement*, quotation at p. 255.   [50] See below, p. 151.

[51] P. Rushton, 'The matter in variance: adolescents and domestic conflict in the pre-industrial economy of north-east England, 1600–1800', *Journal of Social History*, 25 (1991), 89–107.

[52] Fletcher, *Reform*, pp. 215, 217.   [53] Davies, *Enforcement*, pp. 257–8.

[54] Fletcher, *Reform*, pp. 212–27. For evidence of regulation prior to 1563 see D. Woodward, 'Labour regulation at Hull, 1560: select document', *Yorkshire Archaeological Journal*, 51 (1979), 101–4.

evidence of intent.[55] Here again, it is not clear how to measure the 'effectiveness' of this policy, but certainly it does not appear to have caused significant friction between privy council and magistracy.

It is certainly the case that the restoration period saw the complete adoption of the poor law system. By 1700, according to Slack, the practice of raising taxes for the poor 'was well-nigh universal'.[56] A survey by the Board of Trade in 1696 established that £400,000 per annum was collected in poor rates in England and Wales (£40,000 in London).[57] This was an impressive sum – almost one-twelfth as much as was raised by national taxes during the 1690s – and it supported doles to large numbers of people. It might have paid doles to support 4.4 per cent of the population, or food for 4.8 per cent.[58] Again, experience varied from place to place, but it is not inappropriate to suggest that there was 'a machine of social welfare which was well established by the later seventeenth century and which was still expanding'.[59] Indeed, it continued to expand even though the problem of poverty was to some extent easing. In the later seventeenth century the threat of crisis mortality caused by dearth was receding and prices in general were levelling off. As a result, the problem of deep and acute poverty was reduced but the number of people in shallow poverty probably did no more than stabilise at a high level. The poor law mediated social relations between those who were prospering and their less fortunate neighbours, chronically vulnerable to hardship and likely to become dependent at points in their life-cycle. In the villages of late seventeenth-century England most inhabitants were definable either as contributors to, or beneficiaries from, poor rates. And built into the relationship, of course, were notions of entitlement which carried with them a freight of social expectation. In Wrightson's view, the poor law gave 'in its balance of communal identification and social differentiation, a powerful reinforcement of habits of deference and subordination'.[60]

And yet there was little legislative action in relation to poverty in the

[55] Woodward, 'Determination', pp. 26–8. See, more generally, D. Woodward, *Men at Work: Labourers and Building Craftsmen in the Towns of Northern England, 1450–1750* (Cambridge, 1995), esp. ch. 6. Foot, reviewing printed sources, is also sceptical about the impact of regulation: *Effect*.

[56] Slack, *Poverty*, p. 170. In the north-east the response to the Elizabethan legislation had been slow, but by 1700 the poor law seems to have been as well established there as anywhere else: P. Rushton, 'The poor law, the parish and the community in north-east England, 1600–1800', *Northern History*, 25 (1989), 135–52.

[57] Slack, *Poverty*, pp. 170–1.   [58] Ibid., pp. 172–3.   [59] Ibid., p. 182.

[60] K. Wrightson, *English Society 1580–1680* (London, 1982), 181. In Odiham, Hampshire, a complex system of relief supported families that were poor from generation to generation, rarely experiencing the good times presumed by accounts of life-cycle poverty: Stapleton, 'Odiham', pp. 339–55. Habits of deference and subordination must be understood in a broader context than simply the operation of the poor law, of course: Walter, 'Social economy'.

later seventeenth century. This completion of the Elizabethan poor law resulted from a local embrace of existing measures and this was largely in the absence of privy council oversight too. In this respect the poor law captures effectively a marked paradox about the government of post-restoration England. The localities were freer of central direction and interference than at any time in the period covered here, and yet they were closely governed. The resolution of this paradox is, of course, that much government by officeholders was dependent on and derived from local initiative. In the case of poor relief this strength was built into the operations of the machine. The only really significant legislation after 1660 was the passage of the settlement acts. This legislation was the natural corollary of the vagrancy laws, which had presumed that everyone should have a place of residence. The 1662 Act clarified how this was to be determined and authorised two justices to remove any migrant likely to become chargeable, if complaint was received within forty days of their arrival and they rented a house worth less than £10 per annum. This was too restrictive, and was subsequently amended, but in essence it completed the legislative framework for the control and relief of the poor.

So powerful was the parochial basis of relief and control of the poor that a second wave of enthusiasm for corporations of the poor, in the late 1690s and early eighteenth century, foundered on parochial non-cooperation. Large towns hosted schemes to house, train and discipline the poor, but it was almost impossible to secure parochial cooperation in securing the necessary rates. Parochial control institutionalised relations between the rich and those in shallow poverty, and it became a self-perpetuating and very resilient feature of English life. Routinisation and the passing of the worst years for the poor resulted in a domestication of government in the localities.[61] The network of bridewells was consolidated and, particularly after 1690, extended. This extension was partly a response to hard times, now perceived quite accurately by monitoring levels of poor relief: publicly funded relief was now such a routine feature of local life that changes in its level served as an indicator of changing levels of deprivation. Pressure on officials from below resulted in constantly increasing levels of relief and the adoption of bridewells may have been intended as a deterrent.[62] In that case, it is further testimony to the importance of the poor law in mediating social

[61] Slack, *Poverty*, ch. 9. See also V. Pearl, 'Puritans and poor relief: the London Workhouse, 1649–1660', in D. Pennington and K. Thomas (eds.), *Puritans and Revolutionaries: Essays in Seventeenth-Century History Presented to Christopher Hill* (Oxford, 1978), 206–32.

[62] Innes, 'Prisons for the poor', esp. pp. 79–82. For the responsiveness of the administration to pressure from below see Wales, 'Life-cycle'.

relations in the later seventeenth century. This increasing level of provision was enabled by the apparently draconian settlement legislation.[63] Routinisation was also associated with quantification and surveillance – there was a mercantilist strand of thought in relation to the poor, in which they were regarded as idle resources more than a moral threat. In any event, a system of relief had developed which now shaped local social identities and embraced all, or nearly all, of the population as contributors or recipients. This was a dramatic development of state power, whose roots lay in the generations before the civil war, and in an identification of interests between the centre and the locality.

CRISIS MEASURES: THE DEARTH AND PLAGUE ORDERS

Local initiative led the development of these uses of state power, informed by a set of values which we can, loosely, term 'patriarchal'. These values imposed obligations on the poor if they were to be considered deserving but they also imposed obligations on their more prosperous neighbours. The people who filled the offices charged with the implementation of these measures – constables and magistrates – were drawn from exactly those groups whose position was reinforced by their administration. The obligations of the better sort are more evident in relation to the dearth orders. In addition to their statutory obligations, local officeholders received privy council directions, a principal aim of which was to provide a framework of action in the face of dearth. This dearth programme also had a statutory basis – a series of statutes provided the means to retain grain in England in order to supply domestic demand. This was done by imposing export bans when grain prices were above specified floor levels. Thus, when domestic demand was great, prices would rise and a ban on exports come into force. This stopped prices rising further and therefore protected the poorer sort, at least to some extent. It was against the interests of producers, however, since they would like to have found the market offering the best price. It seems that there was a general pressure from the landowning interest in parliament to raise these floor prices, allowing them to export more

[63] J. S. Taylor, 'The impact of pauper settlement, 1691–1834', *PP*, 73 (1976), 42–74. This assertion seems to have survived the debate about the role and importance of the settlement legislation: K. D. M. Snell, 'Pauper settlement and the right to poor relief in England and Wales', *Continuity and Change*, 6 (1991), 375–415, at pp. 40–1; N. Landau, 'Who was subjected to the laws of settlement? Procedure under the settlement laws in eighteenth century England', *Agricultural History Review*, 43 (1995), 139–59, at p. 159. See also J. S. Taylor, 'A different kind of Speenhamland: non-resident relief in the industrial revolution', *JBS*, 30 (1991), 183–208.

freely. This pressure was effective particularly, but not exclusively, in periods of relative plenty when the livelihood of the poorer sort was less threatened. It was at such times that export markets could most persuasively be argued to be the salvation of tillage at home – producers with assured profits could continue to grow corn and provide the basis of a stable social order.[64]

This was only one of a range of measures to regulate the supply of grain, however. After 1587 the privy council issued, periodically, 'a sprawling set of regulations' referred to as the Books of Orders.[65] An important strand in these orders was extensive powers of search, vested in justices of the peace, in order to prevent hoarding and to ensure a flow of domestic stocks of grain to the market at affordable prices. This was called for 'whenever the harvest failed between 1527 and 1630'.[66] Thus, 'corn supplies were to be kept in the country, carefully husbanded and distributed to those most in need'.[67] It is striking that these calls to energetic action blamed dearth not on the weather but on human agency. It was the operations of the market which caused price rises – shortage was good business for market-oriented farmers. In this way, 'searches and surveys of corn supplies undertaken by public authorities with a view to the regular and ordered provision of the open market' offered a means to avert famine. This policy derived from humanist ideals, at least in the 1520s, but it chimed with the suspicions of the poorer sort, who were most sensitive to the effects of the harvest on the market. Hardship was explained partly by the 'doctrine of judgements', which attributed it to divine judgement on human sinfulness, but the council 'always' emphasised the operation of the market in explaining dearth.[68]

The persuasiveness of this explanation probably lay in the fact that

---

[64] Floor prices were raised in 1555, 1563, 1593, 1604, 1624, 1656 and 1663. In 1624 and 1663 the immediate background was not plenty, and in 1604 the memories of the bad years of the 1590s must have been fresh. 'The fact that an immediate background of dearth could be overridden in these ways suggests the power of the parliamentary interests working for such revisions': R. B. Outhwaite, 'Dearth and government intervention in English grain markets, 1590–1700', *EcHR*, 34 (1981), 389–406, esp. pp. 389–92, quotation at p. 392.

[65] Ibid., p. 393. The measures are also described in Outhwaite, 'Food crises in early modern England: patterns of public response', M. Flinn (ed.), *Proceedings of the Seventh International Economic History Congress*, 2 vols. (Edinburgh, 1978), II, 367–74.

[66] Searches were ordered in 1527, 1544, 1549, 1550, 1556 and by books of orders in 1587, 1594, 1595, 1600, 1608, 1622 and 1630. There was similar action in at least parts of the country in 1534, 1562, 1573 and 1586: P. Slack, 'Dearth and social policy in early modern England', *Social History of Medicine*, 5 (1992), 1–17, esp. pp. 1–2, quotation at p. 2.   [67] Ibid., p. 1.

[68] Ibid., p. 6. For the doctrine of judgements, see Walter and Wrightson, 'Dearth', esp. pp. 28–34.

famine was a localised phenomenon.[69] To modern historians it appears to have been the problem of upland pastoral areas, which were dependent on grain imports and often had large and growing land-poor populations. These areas were highly vulnerable to sharp increases in grain prices and this was a serious social cost of economic specialisation.[70] Another indication of this is the highly patterned distribution of grain riots during the period, aiming to prevent the movement of grain through, or out of, areas of scarcity to meet demand in more lucrative markets. Moreover, the actions of rioters seem to reflect their sense that they were making up for the failure of local authorities to intervene in the agreed manner.[71] Thus, recent work pointing to the relative infrequency of general famine may offer an explanation for government action: a small problem was more susceptible to alleviation. In seeking to ensure that surpluses flowed to these deficient areas the council's policy reinforced ideals of order with which we are now familiar. Popular views 'derived from customary expectations of the ideal ordering of economic transactions, firmly centred on the market-place, informed by the notions of the just price and conscionable course of dealing and governed by the imperative of maintaining neighbourly harmony and well-being'. The government, in its pronouncements and favoured policy, 'offered in trenchant terms a confirmation of traditional economic presuppositions permeated by moral and religious overtones'.[72] Of course, urban populations were also vulnerable to price movements and town corporations were also likely to have been active in the policing of markets.[73] In London, those infringing market regulations were subject not just to fines but also to shaming punishments.[74] These bear similarities to informal sanctions on those who offended

---

[69] J. Walter, 'The economy of famine in early modern England', *Bulletin of the Society for the Social History of Medicine*, 40 (1987), 7–10, p. 7; Slack, 'Dearth', esp. pp. 7–9; R. B. Outhwaite, 'Progress and backwardness in English agriculture, 1500–1650', *EcHR*, 2nd series, 39 (1986), 1–18, esp. pp. 16–17; D. Palliser, 'Tawney's century: brave new world or Malthusian trap?', *EcHR*, 2nd series, 35 (1982), 339–53, esp. pp. 344–6.   [70] Walter, 'Economy of famine', pp. 7–8.

[71] J. D. Walter, 'The geography of food riots 1585–1649', in A. Charlesworth (ed.), *An Atlas of Rural Protest in Britain 1548–1900* (London, 1983), 72–80; Walter and Wrightson, 'Dearth'.

[72] Walter and Wrightson, 'Dearth', p. 31.

[73] For London, R. M. Benbow, 'The Court of Aldermen and the Assizes: the policy of price control in Elizabethan London', *Guildhall Studies in London History*, 4 (1980), 93–118; and Archer, *Pursuit*, esp. pp. 200–3; see also Beier, 'Warwick', pp. 75–7. For the scheme for a municipal storehouse supplying victuals at cost price see Slack, *Salisbury*, pp. 8–15. It operated using tokens issued to the poor in order to try to prevent the poor spending their money on drink. It was a characteristic of many such initiatives that they aimed both to relieve and improve.

[74] Benbow, 'Court of Aldermen', pp. 109–11. For contacts between official and unofficial shaming punishments more generally, Ingram, 'Ridings, rough music and the "reform of popular culture" in early modern England', *PP*, 105 (1984), 79–113.

against neighbourly or communal values in other ways and further suggest that the authorities were responding to the expectations of the governed in imposing market regulations.

However, in the third quarter of the seventeenth century there was a reversal of government grain policy. Down to 1663 controls had meant that exports were frequently restricted. Successive statutes raised the price floor, but in 1670 it was removed altogether, ending a significant effort at control. In 1672 a bounty was introduced to encourage exports, and made permanent in 1689. Domestic prices were given further support by heavy import duties on grain below a certain price.[75] This meant, effectively, that government intervention was now intended to support prices in periods of plenty – to protect the producer – rather than keeping them down to protect the consumer. In a way this represents a triumph for landed interests in parliament – pressure to support domestic production by freeing exports had been fairly consistent over the previous hundred years.[76] The change of policy was apparent too in the domestic regulation of the market by the privy council. Despite local footdragging 'one would be hard pushed to find any flagging of Conciliar intent before the early 1630s'.[77] But disengagement was apparent during subsequent dearths. The policy of searching for private stocks of grain culminated in a bang in 1630, followed by a 'prolonged whimper'. Aspects of the dearth policy were implemented in the hard year of 1649 and informers took advantage of the legislation subsequently. Essentially, however, dearth orders were observed with less and less frequency in the later seventeenth century.[78]

In order to explain this we need to look a little more closely at the chronology of this slow death. It has been suggested that the Books of Orders disappeared with the privy council after 1640, but this fails to explain why the privy council failed to act in the face of dearth in 1637/8. In the light of that inaction 1631 emerges more clearly as an endpoint for the policy, and it is tempting to believe that the unpopularity of the measures in those years fatally weakened the system. An important part of the explanation, therefore, is 'the volume of criticism which searches had attracted in 1630, when they were probably unnecessary, and still more in the harvest year 1631–2 when they were

---

[75] Outhwaite, 'Dearth', pp. 391–2. For a brief account of government policy in the context of the development of the grain trade see A. H. John, 'Agricultural improvement and grain exports, 1660–1765', in D. C. Coleman and A. H. John (eds.), *Trade, Government and Economy in Pre-industrial England: Essays Presented to F. J. Fisher* (London, 1976), 45–67, esp. pp. 47–8.
[76] Outhwaite, 'Dearth', pp. 389–92.   [77] Ibid., p. 395.
[78] Ibid., 395–6. Quotation from Slack, 'Dearth', p. 16.

certainly so'.[79] Hostility came not from the poor but from the farmers, and we should note an important feature of this. 'Social policy is an expression of power.'[80] This power was legitimated to the poor, as we have seen, by appeal to a powerful rhetoric of communal and neighbourly responsibility. For those who found it unpalatable, however, there were means (albeit unconvincing ones) available to question this legitimacy, this time in formal terms. The orders rested on the legal authority of the queen-in-council and at least by 1586 (only eight years after the first book was issued) unease was being expressed. Searches and surveys, after all, dealt with private property. By 1631 such doubts were common enough that the council cited statute in support of its orders, whenever possible. 'By 1638 it may well have lacked the confidence to go beyond them', given the unpopularity of the measures of 1631.[81] There were many more examples of this sort of problem of legitimation in fiscal and military matters, as we will see. None the less, the policy continued to work without privy council enforcement. In the bad harvest years of the late 1640s justices of the peace were active in the localities and the crisis year of 1649 saw aspects of the dearth orders implemented. Lancashire, for example, saw vigorous action.[82] As we have seen in relation to the poor law, the absence of the privy council oversight did not mean the absence of activity. However, after 1660 national government was reluctant to use prerogative authority, and when the books of orders were reprinted in 1662 it was the House of Commons that asked for a revival of the search policy.[83] Certainly, the popular mandate for such action was evident, albeit to an extent that is debated, well into the eighteenth century.[84]

There are other factors then, beyond the unpopularity of the measures of 1630–1 and a reluctance to use privy council power after 1660. One is the abandonment of support for the orders by the city of London – which contained the largest concentration of the 'harvest-sensitive' in the country. Another is surely the end of the long downward pressure on the living standards of the poor. The incidence of famine diminished rapidly later in the seventeenth century, reducing the likelihood of calls for a resumption of the orders. In itself, however, it does not really explain the chronology, particularly if we take 1631 rather

[79] Ibid., p. 14. The suggestion was Outhwaite's: 'Dearth', pp. 398, 404–5.
[80] Slack, 'Dearth', p. 1.   [81] Ibid., p. 15. See also Slack, 'Books of Orders', pp. 18–21.
[82] Slack, 'Dearth', p. 15. Walter and Wrightson, 'Dearth', pp. 39–40.
[83] Slack, 'Dearth', p. 15.
[84] For a contribution to, and overview of, the debate about the moral economy see J. Stevenson, 'The "moral economy" of the English crowd: myths and realities', in A. Fletcher and J. Stevenson (eds.), *Order and Disorder in Early Modern England* (Cambridge, 1985), 218–38.

than 1649 to be the endpoint.[85] By the later seventeenth century too, poor rates were better established and these transfers offered a better prospect of securing subsistence. This compounded other developments, notably the 'progress' discussed in chapter 2. '[A]gricultural productivity was high enough to supply corn for the whole population virtually every year, and . . . both a market network and system of poor relief were well enough developed to take care of its distribution.'[86] It was this general improvement, after all, that lay behind the switch to a policy of price support.

Down to 1630, at least, dearth orders were implemented to secure social order, and behind this lay the paternalism which helped to legitimate the authority of local officeholders. A second great challenge to early modern society was the plague, and another notable administrative innovation in the face of crisis conditions was the set of orders designed to limit the effects of plague visitations. There was, though, a political problem with the plague orders in that they made manifest a potential conflict of values. Visitations were appalling in their impact and must have been terrifying to experience, but there were patterns in the impact of the plague that encouraged attempts to limit its effects. The disease can kill very quickly and in large numbers. In our period it did both. In 1563 one-third of London's population died (20,000) and there were further major outbreaks in 1578, 1582, 1593 and 1603. The latter carried off 30,000, that of 1625 killed between 40,000 and 50,000, and the most famous plague of all, in 1665, killed around 70,000 people. The deaths were highly concentrated though. In 1664, for example, there were four deaths. Between 1 January and 27 January 1665 there were two more. In the four weeks ending 25 August, however, there were 16,455.[87] Obviously such epidemics had an enormous economic

[85] Outhwaite, 'Dearth', pp. 396–405.   [86] Slack, 'Dearth', p. 14.
[87] J. A. Sharpe, *Early Modern England: A Social History 1550–1760* (London, 1987), 53–4. The central work on the plague is P. Slack, *The Impact of the Plague in Tudor and Stuart England* (Oxford, 1990). For accounts of the local impact of plague outbreaks see: I. G. Doolittle, 'The effects of the plague on a provincial town in the sixteenth and seventeenth centuries', *Medical History*, 19 (1975), 333–41; J. Howells, 'Haverfordwest and the plague, 1652', *Welsh History Review*, 12 (1985), 411–19; J. A. I. Champion, *London's Dreaded Visitation: The Social Geography of the Great Plague in 1665*, Centre for Metropolitan History, Historical Geography Research Series, no. 31 (London, 1995); Champion (ed.), *Epidemic Disease in London* (London, 1993); C. B. Phillips, 'The plague in Kendal in 1598: some new evidence', *Transactions of the Cumberland and Westmorland Antiquarian and Archaeological Society*, 94 (1994), 135–42; J. Taylor, 'Plague in the towns of Hampshire: the epidemic of 1665–6', *Southern History*, 6 (1984), 104–22. Willan takes a sceptical view of the seriousness of the impact on the basis of an examination of a particular outbreak in Manchester: T. S. Willan, 'Plague in perspective: the case of Manchester in 1605', *Transactions of the Historic Society of Lancashire and Cheshire*, 132 (1983), 29–40.

impact, and affected the demographic regime. But they were often geographically localised, affecting the towns disproportionately.[88]

The plague challenged people's faith, their understanding and their normal social values. Desire for self-preservation might easily cut across other obligations to community, neighbourhood or family, and rumours of visitations were damaging to the commercial life of towns.[89] There was, however, a pattern to the way that the plague struck, and this made it more clearly related to other social problems in the minds of contemporaries than we might otherwise have expected. Slack's careful reconstruction of the impact of the disease demonstrates that it was not entirely unpredictable, there were in fact 'regularities in the geographical and social incidence of the disease'.[90] The combination of unpredictable and predictable features of visitations moulded reactions, and encouraged the belief that some counter-measures might be effective, although there was no effective medical response to the disease. On the whole, though, it was an urban problem to which the poorer districts were more liable. It was clearly not associated with harvest failure. Gradually, 'It was becoming possible to view plague not as a catastrophe of immeasurable proportions, but as the particular problem of certain social groups and localities.'[91]

In this way the plague became viewed as another social problem, akin to poverty and vagrancy, and treated in similar ways. A set of plague orders developed, beginning slightly earlier than the dearth orders in 1577. In 1578 they were incorporated into a printed book of orders which was reissued without major alteration until 1636. The only major revision, in fact, came in 1666, the last outbreak of the plague.[92] Unlike the poor laws, however, the plague orders were of central, not local,

---

[88] Slack, *Plague*, p. 194.

[89] For the anxiety of the Chester corporation to quash rumours of visitations in 1609 see CCRO, ML/2/229; ML/6/31. In January 1614 assurances were sent to the mayor of Dublin that there was no plague, and had not been for some years, ML/6/89. In 1610 the corporation of Ruthin wrote in response to the fact that it 'is commonly reported that the city of Chester is visited with the sickness of the plague'. Accordingly, they requested that the corporation should not 'suffer any of yr city to repair' to the fair at Ruthin, ML/6/55. See also the assurance of the mayor to a correspondent in the county that the visitation in April 1654 had only affected eight families, living away from any of the main routes into the city, ML/3/376.   [90] Slack, *Plague*, p. 192.

[91] Ibid., p. 195. For some more general reflections on the relationship between epidemic disease and social presumptions see P. Slack, 'Introduction', in T. Ranger and P. Slack (eds.), *Epidemics and Ideas: Essays on the Historical Perception of Pestilence* (Cambridge, 1992), 1–20, esp. pp. 8–14. For an example of the interpretation of the plague as a judgement, see E. M. Wilson, 'Richard Leake's plague sermons, 1599', *Transactions of the Cumberland and Westmorland Antiquarian and Archaeological Society*, 75 (1975), 150–73.

[92] Slack, *Poverty*, p. 139. Books were issued in 1592, 1593, 1603, 1625, 1630 and 1636. For 1666 see below, p. 128.

provenance and reflected political and international aspirations as much as they did responses to the impact of disease. The measures are particularly associated with politicians anxious to demonstrate the reality of royal paternalism: Thomas Wolsey, William Cecil or Charles I's council during the 1630s, for example. The measures were also inspired by foreign models. They centred on policies of isolation – shutting up the houses of the victims, confining the infected to pest houses. Clothes and possessions of those who died were destroyed, and the ceremonial life of the town was restricted in order to reduce contact. Even funeral rites were curtailed. These measures of isolation and control affected the poor disproportionately – it was in those districts that the plague arrived and was confined. Flight was more an option for the rich. In a sense then, these measures sought to seal off areas – the poor back alleys and suburbs – which were also areas of poverty, vagrancy and the social problems that were perceived to go along with these things.

These measures posed a challenge to local government. Novel taxes were imposed and novel constraints were placed on the lives of local people, and there is plenty of evidence of resistance.[93] The most dramatic of these constraints was confinement. The papers of Sir Richard Grosvenor include a complaint about the 'gracelesse and Lawlesse' people in London and Southwark in 1603 who 'will not Endure ther dores wher the sicknesse ys to be shutt up', and resisted or ignored other preventive measures.[94] 'The incarceration of whole families in infected houses characterised English policy between 1578 and 1665', and behind the policy lay powerful legal sanction. The 1604 statute specified that 'anyone with a plague sore found wandering outside in the company of others was guilty of felony and might be hung; anyone else going out could be whipped as a vagrant'. These powers were invoked too, and large numbers of people were incarcerated during outbreaks of the plague. In Shrewsbury in 1604, for example, one fifth of the population was confined.[95]

Confinement was the most spectacular, but by no means the only, restraint imposed during visitations. 'Opportunities for mutual support and consolation were severely curtailed by the restrictions which local and central governments tried to impose on popular behaviour and popular assemblies during epidemics.' Popular games and processions

---

[93] Slack, *Plague*, p. 295.   [94] CCRO, Grosvenor of Eaton MSS, Box 1, 2/1.

[95] P. Slack, 'The response to plague in early modern England: public policies and their consequences' in Walter and Schofield (eds.), *Famine*, 167–87, at pp. 170–1. For a brief description of the powers of government in relation to the plague see ibid., pp. 168–74.

were prohibited, and even church attendance was restricted. In Nottinghamshire men gathered to play football in order to flout these commands during one visitation, and there are numerous other examples of such resistance. Interference in burial customs – not allowing the corpse into the church but taking it straight to the burial ground – were much resented. There was a consistent campaign against large public funerals, and in 1666 there were special burial grounds for the victims of the plague. Officials arriving to shut up the houses of the infected were frequently attacked, and pesthouses were too.

In many respects popular disturbances during epidemics were like crowd behaviour in other circumstances, like food riots in the eighteenth century, for example. They had similar motives, similar participants, and similar claims to legitimacy. They often sought, or were accorded, the approval of people in authority.[96]

In the end, in order to overcome popular hostility to the plague regulations, it was often incumbent upon magistrates and nobles to risk death by staying put. Charles I insisted in 1636 that the bishop of Carlisle should not leave his diocese because 'he thought it unreasonable that a main pillar of the country should be absent in such needful times'. Wentworth stayed in York, in 1631, believing that the populace were much comforted by his presence.[97]

Not all magistrates passed this test, of course, and the notion of duty cut both ways. This is demonstrated by the response of East Riding justices to appeals for help for the town of Scarborough, visited by the plague in 1598. The queen had written to the archbishop of York, concerned to 'avoide the daunger which mighte insewe to others of our subjects elswhere, & for the restrainte of the inhabitants of that Towne from wandring abroad, and also for their better releif'. Accordingly a rate was to be raised 'for the use of the infected & poorer sorte of that Towne': 569 of the inhabitants were, apparently, dependent 'onlie upon releif by want of traffique' and 'throughe wante & necessitie are likelie to starve, or in daunger to go abroad to seek releif'. The rate had not been fully collected and now further action was required.[98] The need was plain, and the interest of the surrounding areas in providing relief, but this was in tension with other concerns. Firstly, Christopher Hildyard, justice of the peace in the East Riding, sought to protect his division of the Riding from bearing what he saw as a disproportionate share of the

[96] Slack, *Plague*, p. 300.   [97] Ibid., p. 303.
[98] HEH, HM 50657, vol. I, fos. 36r–36v, quotations at fo. 36r.

burden: 'I see no reason to chardge the Contrie further, untill other places haithe paid asmuche.'[99] Rather obnoxious as this might be, it is of a piece with other 'public' concerns expressed by officeholders in this period. Secondly, the obligations were seen to be reciprocal. Hildyard's brother William was unwilling to co-operate having heard that Thomas Heddon of Scarborough had been at Preston, Holderness, 'verie sore sick and not able neither to gett upp of his horse nor ride'. The chief constable had 'ridd after him to thend if he should staie att any place the house should be shutt upp'. But the lesson was clear: 'you maie see thei deserve littill att our hands that suffers there people soe to endanger the cuntrie'. '[B]ut what did become of him', he added, 'as yet I doe not heare.'[100]

This certainly prompts us to think worse of the Hildyard brothers, but it does demonstrate that even here, what seems to have been pretty naked self-interest was operating through a language of representation and mutual obligation. The appeal for help, and the refusal to comply further, were not made in terms of concern, pity or charity, but of order and mutual responsibility. The responsibility was to fall on all local areas and was to include the sick themselves. William Hildyard may have been unusually hard-hearted, but in being so he was able to exploit a language of public duty.

When they did stay put and overcame the other problems of implementation early modern magistrates were motivated by concern for 'order' and this had both a class and a religious component.[101] 'Central and local governors were preoccupied during epidemics with concepts, not of neighbourliness, but of "order".' This concern conveyed command and direction, but also 'tidiness, peace and quiet'. Magistrates were enjoined to stay by appeal to their magisterial, not their neighbourly, duties. In York in 1604, for example, it was said 'The infection doth so greatly increase in this city that unless we the magistrates have great care and do take pains in the governing and ruling of this city, and in taking order for the relieving of them, the poorer sort will not be ruled.'[102] The desire to regulate was not restricted to the disease alone, but was also related to other concerns for 'order' – the body politic and good order. The association of sin with disease, and sin and the poor, also linked these problems and godly magistrates in particular had theological and moral purposes in seeking to regulate social life during visitations. In all, then, this was a complex response. It did not represent class interest in any straightforward way, but prevailing notions of order

[99] Ibid., fo. 36v.   [100] Ibid., fo. 38r.   [101] Slack, *Plague*, p. 303.   [102] Ibid., p. 304.

and new visions of moral well-being. It was akin to the vision of order propagated by the poor law and dearth orders, but here it was contested: 'there was an alternative concept of order: not order in the sense of tidiness and command, but order as harmony between the several parts of the body politic, each with reciprocal rights and duties'. This latter sense of order could be deployed against the socially divisive plague regulations. Unlike the dearth orders, the plague orders conflicted, to some extent, with the wishes of the poorer sort.[103] None the less, the implementation of the plague orders did not simply reflect self-interest on the part of the magistracy.

The plague orders were issued for the last time in 1666, in response to the outbreak of plague in London. On this occasion it was a delayed response, reflecting again some of the unease about prerogative authority that we noted in relation to the dearth orders: 'The Council . . . hesitated before revising and republishing the book of plague orders in the epidemic of 1665–66, hoping that parliament would supply a solution. The political caution was palpable.'[104] There was a growing confidence even here, that plague was not irresistible: 'Human action could mitigate the divine punishments of pestilence and famine.'[105] In the absence of privy council direction, the metropolitan authorities appear to have acted energetically.[106] In the event this was the last outbreak, and so we will never know for sure, but it is possible that here, as in the case of the poor, the localities were to a great extent self-regulating. Officeholders, wielding legitimate authority, were largely self-activating and provided the means for securing an agreed social order.

IMPLEMENTATION: DISCRETION, LOCAL INITIATIVE AND
REGULARISATION

In the three generations before 1640 considerable efforts were made to control the effects of plague and famine, and to provide for a regularised response to the problem of poverty. These measures reflected material realities but were clearly shaped by contemporary perceptions of what constituted social order, and threats to it. After 1640 the crisis measures were abandoned, as plague and famine disappeared from England, but the implementation of the poor laws became universal, or nearly so. In all this the role of local initiative was crucial. National initiatives fre-

---

[103] Slack, *Poverty*, p. 144.   [104] Ibid., p. 147.   [105] Ibid., p. 148.
[106] For an excellent account of this visitation see Champion, *London's Dreaded Visitation*.

quently followed local ones, and the implementation of the poor laws in the 1640s was undertaken without prompting – national government collapsed in civil war and revolution, but the local routine of poor relief does not seem to have gone with it. After the restoration local government action in relation to the poor law was largely self-activating – there was something of a structural differentiation between local government offices concerned with social problems and national government institutions preoccupied with war, empire and international trade.[107] But this differentiation merely confirms the impression formed from a consideration of earlier measures – that the impetus for measures to control perceived threats to social order was as much local as it was central.

Gauging the effect of these measures – the poor laws, dearth orders, regulation of apprenticeship and of wages – is extremely difficult but in particular cases the impact might be dramatic. As we have seen, during the visitation of the plague in 1604 one-fifth of the population of Shrewsbury was confined. The impact could be no less dramatic for the individuals taken up as vagrants or denied poor relief. In 1608 the justices of the peace in Flint wrote to the corporation in Chester about a poor woman who had been 'lurking' in Hanmer for about six months. Alice Trevor alias Bradesby had been born in Chester and had been sent on there. The constables, however, had refused to admit her to the city because her passport had been signed only by a vicar, not by the justices. Following receipt of the letter from Flint, the corporation took action. The poor, impotent woman, unable to labour for her living, was examined and it was found that she had indeed been born in the city, but had not lived there for forty years, having married and gone elsewhere. The city was the resort of many people like her and the corporation was anxious to prove that she had not lived in the city since her marriage. Alice does not seem to have told them where she had been, although it was clear that she had resided in one place for twenty years.[108] Perhaps she was confused. She was certainly elderly and had obviously been moved on not just in Flint and Chester but from other places too. Her experience certainly tells us something about the potential effectiveness of these measures – of the 'strength' of the state.

More generally, the implementation of these measures can be considered effective in the sense that activists proposing these innovations could expect to see most of their provisions imposed in most of the country at least some of the time. Local initiative fed central action and

[107] N. Landau, 'Country matters: *The Growth of Political Stability* a quarter-century on', *Albion*, 25 (1993), 261–74, at p. 267.   [108] CCRO, ML/2/219; ML/6/8, 9.

local discretion could be harmonised with general prescriptions – there was a general unity of purpose behind these measures. The image of a harmonious relationship between national and local governors is easily overstated, of course. Attempts to enforce uniformity of local practice caused some friction, and this was exacerbated by the perceived weakness of the warrant for some of these actions, for example, in response to the dearth orders. In the late sixteenth and early seventeenth centuries 'one can find frequent examples of that well-known gap between Privy Council intentions and their actual realization'.[109] Indeed, localised famine and widespread hardship demonstrated that 'the policy had failed'.[110] As we have seen, there were a number of problems, not least the resistance of corn producers, who complained that searches overstated their stocks or that the policy was being implemented unnecessarily. In some localities laying up stocks, or preventing exports, was an inappropriate response to shortage. For grain importers, for example, laying up stocks in good years could be regarded as a means of supporting the livelihood of producers. In grain-rich areas, by contrast, preventing exports exacerbated the problem of distribution which, it was thought, lay behind dearth. In fact, it was a common complaint from provincial towns that the dearth orders were being used to choke off their supply by magistrates in surrounding areas. Movement across county boundaries or along rivers was often essential, and the council sought to explain that the orders were not intended to interfere with such movement. Moreover, it was frequently objected that the problem was not getting the corn to market, but that the poor had no money to buy it. Finally, by encouraging the keeping of stocks the government was actually encouraging a practice that it sought to remedy.[111] Failures to comply, or partial compliance, do not necessarily reflect resistance therefore. Discretion does not imply resistance to the spirit of the regulations.[112]

---

[109] Outhwaite, 'Dearth', pp. 394–5.   [110] Slack, 'Dearth', p. 9.

[111] Ibid., pp. 10–14. See also Slack, 'Books of Orders', pp. 12–13.

[112] See, for example, Cheshire justices' report to the privy council on 17 February 1587 in response to a letter enjoining action in the face of dearth. They noted that there was not enough grain to feed the county until the next harvest without imports: obviously then, some movement across county boundaries was necessary. In general, most producers had only small stocks of grain beyond their own subsistence needs and their requirements. Those who did have significant marketable surpluses were willing to maintain both the local markets and to sell grain to their poor neighbours who lacked money or carriage at the usual market rate on credit. As a consequence, the magistrates were not taking formal action to force stores to be brought to market. They had also suppressed large numbers of alehouses and prevented people from buying grain in order to sell it again. As result prices were somewhat amended and 'the poorest sorte much better served': HEH, EL 6265. Here, clearly, discretion was in harmony with the spirit of privy council instructions.

The measures were not appropriate in all cases, therefore, and this explains some of the reluctance to implement them. But there is enough evidence of selective implementation to support the view that considerable use was made of these powers. In part it was prompted by pressure from below. We have noted already that the diagnosis of the causes of dearth implicit in the orders – and the moral, social and political vision that lay behind that diagnosis – found resonance among those vulnerable to movements in grain prices. Actual disorder often represented an attempt to jog the authorities into action, and it could do so.[113] Perhaps more often the fear of disorder prompted justices to implement the measures.[114] We cannot read success from the absence of starvation, but neither can we really claim that the dearth orders did not save some lives.[115] It was not only the most assiduous magistrates that acted, although their actions may have been misguided. Perhaps the real measure of the success of the dearth orders, though, is their expression of solidarity with the plight of the poor. Society emerged from dearth 'intact, with its values and structure of authority reinforced, for dearth highlighted the former and reinforced the latter's legitimacy'.[116] In fact the wider measures taken to prevent starvation, the 'social economy of dearth', served to re-inforce habits of deference and point to the need to locate 'state' activity in the context of wider social relations. It was not just dearth orders that contributed to the avoidance of starvation,[117] but a local officeholder, legitimating his position with reference to values of patriarchal order, would have had difficulty finding plausible reasons to resist pressure to implement them during bad years.

Where these measures – the poor law, dearth and plague orders – were felt necessary they were generally imposed. The only real frictions that emerged did so in areas or periods where the privy council tried to enforce generalised measures where they were inappropriate to particular circumstances. It was the detail of the application that was at stake. The programme as a whole reflected, indeed to an extent grew out of, local initiatives. We should certainly be wary of making too much of reluctance, for although cases of full implementation of every detail were no doubt rare, almost any surviving documentation of quarter

---

[113] Walter and Wrightson, 'Dearth', pp. 32–4, 35–8; J. Walter, 'Grain riots and popular attitudes to the law: Maldon and the crisis of 1629', in J. Brewer and J. Styles (eds.), *An Ungovernable People? The English and their Law in the Seventeenth and Eighteenth Centuries* (London, 1980), 47–84, 315–26.

[114] Walter and Wrightson, 'Dearth', pp. 39–40.

[115] For a particularly illuminating discussion of these issues see J. Walter and R. Schofield, 'Famine, disease and crisis mortality in early modern society', in Walter and Schofield (eds.), *Famine*, 1–73, at pp. 41–8, 57–61.   [116] Walter and Wrightson, 'Dearth', p. 42.

[117] Walter, 'Social economy'.

sessions or magisterial papers will reveal action in relation to some parts of this programme. Discretion rather than resistance characterised the response of local officeholders. For example, the 1630 Book of Orders was once regarded as a measure of centralisation unacceptable in the localities. In some localities, it is true, there was resistance, but the effect was that the Book had a varied impact. This is not a sign of resistance, perhaps, so much as the fact that 'local circumstances were crucial to its implementation'.[118] The inappropriateness of the dearth orders may have been crucial to their demise, as we have seen. But overall, from 'many corners' of the country and across 'a range of business there is clear evidence that it succeeded in, to use the Council's own term, "quickening" the magistrate'.[119] The patchwork implementation, therefore, is testimony to the potential of the partnership between centre and locality; its success 'owed much to the coincidence of interest of the magisterial class with the programmes of central government'.[120]

Compulsory poor rates were also viewed with discretion, adopted or not in the light of local conditions. There is evidence of their implementation in Bedfordshire from the 1560s and yet in Northumberland the poor law was probably not implemented before 1640. As a national scheme, then, 'it was slow to get off the ground', but clearly it was acted upon where it was felt appropriate.[121] The final achievement of national uniformity, therefore, was a 'triumph of local initiative, a response to felt need'.[122] In part, too, this was dependent on local economic factors: 'The enforcement of the poor laws presupposed a body of tax-payers, who were the beneficiaries of progress, but also considerable numbers of paupers, who were its casualties.'[123] The impact of economic and social change was highly variable geographically and so we should expect the governmental response to be equally so.

Pretty clearly, these measures reflected a generalised set of assumptions about the social order. To that extent, provision of relief or work were as much measures of social discipline as were the punishments inflicted on vagrants. This is increasingly clear as the provision of work for the able-bodied became more important and the apparatus of poor relief more complex. A good example is the response of Samuel Hartlib to the endowment of a London corporation of the poor in 1647, and its further endowment in 1649. The remit and function of the corporation

---

[118] K. Sharpe, *The Personal Rule of Charles I* (London, 1992), 486.
[119] Ibid., p. 486. For the end of the dearth orders see above, pp. 121–3.   [120] Ibid., p. 486.
[121] Fletcher, *Reform*, pp. 183–4, quotation at p. 184. For government and administration in Northumberland see S. J. Watts and S. J. Watts, *From Border to Middle Shire: Northumberland 1586–1625* (Leicester, 1975), chs. 5–7; for the adoption of the poor law see Rushton, 'Poor law', at p. 137.
[122] Fletcher, *Reform*, p. 187.   [123] Beier, 'Poverty and progress', p. 239.

was not clear and it provided Samuel Hartlib with the opportunity to suggest one. He published a manifesto for the care of the poor in which he called for petty criminals to be put to work 'the better to make them serviceable to the Common-wealth, by reforming their ungodly life'. Children were to be educated and given religious instruction along closely specified lines – both the contents of sermons and the nature of the central doctrines to be taught were described out. Appropriate forms of behaviour between the children were described and the schoolmaster was to be given extensive duties, including moral and academic instruction. The purpose was to keep children 'under a godly and civill Government, to the great joy of good peopl'. Charity embraced not just relief but measures of discipline and socialisation. The scheme aimed at a Godly and practical education intended to render the orphans serviceable to the commonwealth in their calling. What was being addressed was a culture of poverty.[124] In fact, 'Tudor and Stuart schools were just as much concerned to inculcate religion, civility, good behaviour and obedience as academic learning.'[125] Thus, the definitions of the precise challenge that was posed by these changing material conditions gave administrative force to ideas about the basis of social order. These ideas operated differentially, marking out particular groups for discipline and punishment and shaping administrative action to serve the ideas and interests of dominant groups. On the other hand, legitimation in terms of these wider values also offered a means of holding particular office-holders to account – as grain rioters sometimes did, for example.

The completion of the poor law built on these shared values to the extent that it occurred in the absence of central oversight. It was associated with changes in magisterial activity, in particular a routinisation of their activities. The relatively radical and godly regimes of the 1650s had failed to remake England in their image, although the presence of activists certainly affected local life in some areas at least.[126]

---

[124] Samuel Hartlib, *LONDONS Charity inlarged STILLING The Orphans Cry* (London, 1650), esp. pp. 10–12, 14, 20–1, quotations at title page and p. 10.

[125] A. J. Fletcher and J. Stevenson, 'Introduction', in Fletcher and Stevenson (eds.), *Order and Disorder*, 1–40, at p. 35. There are some interesting observations on this theme in C. J. Sommerville, 'The distinction between indoctrination and education in England, 1549–1719', *Journal of the History of Ideas*, 44 (1983), 387–406.

[126] D. Hirst, 'The failure of Godly rule in the English Republic', *PP*, 132 (1991), 33–66; K. V. Thomas, 'The puritans and adultery: the act of 1650 reconsidered', in Pennington and Thomas (eds.), *Puritans*, 257–82; A. Coleby, *Central Government and the Localities: Hampshire 1649–1689* (Cambridge, 1987), chs. 1–3, esp. pp. 51–63. In Warwickshire, however, there was a change in the balance of magisterial concern. Although a new Jerusalem was not achieved, the claims of godly rule were not completely without effect: A. Hughes, *Politics, Society and Civil War in Warwickshire, 1620–1660* (Cambridge, 1987), esp. pp. 282–90; Hughes, *Godly Reformation and its*

The reality instead seems to have been the continuation, self-activated, of already established policies and procedures. This regularisation involved the completion of a number of longer-term trends. So, for example, there had been a tendency over much of the period for justices to meet outside sessions in smaller numbers to regulate the affairs of divisions of their counties. The process was not uniform, and in some counties policy was reversed. However, many of the counties which had been slower off the mark caught up after the restoration, leaving quarter sessions freer of minor business.[127] The benches themselves were increasing in size, particularly after 1690. Where there had been 1,200 JPs in 1600 there were over 3,000 by 1714.[128]

Membership of the benches was subject to much more systematic regulation, on the grounds of political acceptability, after the restoration and in particular after 1680. But these purges represented changes in personnel rather than in procedure: membership of the bench was a means of developing an interest and this had become politicised. The battles being fought out were conducted in terms of debates about the proper ordering of religious and political life. The actual business of the benches was increasingly regularised, for example in the administration of consolidated county rates for various purposes.[129] Concentration on a relatively narrow range of tasks probably helped efficiency.[130] The increasing size of the bench meant that gentry of lower status were being

Opponents in Warwickshire, 1640–1662, Dugdale Society Occasional Papers, 35 (Stratford-upon-Avon, 1993), esp. pp. 5–6, 10–18; C. D. Gilbert, 'Magistracy and ministry in Cromwellian England: the case of King's Norton, Worcestershire', *Midland History*, 23 (1998), 71–83.

[127] Local initiatives of this kind were made in response to successive new burdens on the commissions from the reign of Henry VIII onwards. The development of the subsidy, the militia, and the variety of administrative duties demanded under Elizabeth served successively as stimulants to such local initiatives. It was the addition of judicial duties that led from these experiments in divisional activity to petty sessions: F. A. Youngs, 'Towards petty sessions: Tudor JPs and divisions of counties', in D. J. Guth and J. W. McKenna (eds.), *Tudor Rule and Revolution: Essays for G. R. Elton from his American Friends* (Cambridge, 1982), 201–16. For petty sessions see also T. G. Barnes, *Somerset 1625–1640: A County's Government During the 'Personal Rule'* (Chicago, 1982), 80–5; G. P. Higgins, 'The government of early Stuart Cheshire', *Northern History*, 12 (1976), 32–52, at pp. 39–40, A. H. Smith, *County and Court Government and Politics in Norfolk 1558–1603* (Oxford, 1974), 103–5. For post-restoration developments: L. K. J. Glassey, 'Local government', in C. Jones (ed.), *Britain in the First Age of Party 1680–1750: Essays Presented to Geoffrey Holmes* (London, 1987), 151–72, at pp. 161–3; N. Landau, *The Justices of the Peace 1679–1760* (Berkeley, 1984), ch. 7; G. C. F. Forster, 'Government in provincial England under the later Stuarts', *TRHS*, 5th series, 33 (1983), 29–48, at pp. 37–8. Fletcher, *Reform*, pp. 122–35, gives an excellent overview.   [128] Fletcher, *Reform*, p. 39.

[129] Glassey, 'Local government', pp. 153–65. For the purges see L. K. J. Glassey, *Politics and the Appointment of Justices of the Peace 1675–1720* (Oxford, 1979). See also J. M. Rosenheim, 'County governance and elite withdrawal in Norfolk, 1660–1720', in Beier, Cannadine and Rosenheim (eds.), *First Modern Society*, 95–125, esp. pp. 100–18; Forster, 'Government in provincial England'.   [130] Forster, 'Government in provincial England', esp. pp. 37–8.

appointed and, increasingly, magnates withdrew from active service. The routinisation of county business, and its insulation from party politics, meant that membership of the bench, rather than service on it, became the important thing. In the last quarter of the seventeenth century there was a quite dramatic withdrawal of the county elite, ceding the running of routine county business to lesser gentry. Petty sessions business before clerical magistrates and even trading justices (men making a profit from magistracy) replaced the patriarchal rule exercised by the great gentry such as Richard Grosvenor in the early seventeenth century. County grandees began to look elsewhere for means to build their political influence, the lieutenancy or London, for example.[131] In Landau's view patriarchs, or kings in miniature, were replaced by patricians, applying rules in the manner of legal administrators.[132] Administrative reform, building on solidarities between those with legislative power and those holding local offices, had produced a stable routine of measures to cope with material problems in the light of widely disseminated values of order, deference and obligation.

[131] Rosenheim, 'County governance'. For trading justices, see R. B. Shoemaker, *Prosecution and Punishment: Petty Crime and the Law in London and Rural Middlesex, c. 1660–1725* (Cambridge, 1991), esp. pp. 14, 93–4, 229–30. For Grosvenor see R. Cust and P. Lake, 'Sir Richard Grosvenor and the rhetoric of magistracy', *BIHR*, 54 (1981), 40–53. For an account of the career during the 1660s of an energetic justice drawn from the lower ranks of the gentry see J. M. Rosenheim, 'Robert Doughty of Hanworth, a restoration magistrate', *Norfolk Archaeology*, 38 (1983), 296–312. Forster's account of the fitful and intermittent activities of North Riding justices in the early seventeenth century provides a contrast with the routine administration portrayed in accounts of restoration magistracy: 'North Riding Justices and their sessions', *Northern History*, 10 (1975), 102–25. [132] Landau, *Justices*.

CHAPTER 4

The courts and social order

Order and discipline were at the core of parliamentary and privy council concerns and clearly lay behind the actions of active local officeholders. There was, in the development of the administrative measures considered in chapter 3, considerable local participation and they were guided to a notable degree by local experiment. The importance of this local initiative in the preservation of order was even more marked in other initiatives. For some people, particularly perhaps the godly, the pursuit of order also found expression in a campaign for moral reformation. These measures represented a concerted attempt to use the courts to promote higher standards of moral behaviour, to promote civility. We have already noted the close relationship between law and government, and between perceptions of crime and of sin, in this period. Church courts also offered a forum specifically designed to allow the correction of moral offenders.[1] These perceptions, and the high degree of participation in the administration of the law were crucial to its use as a means of social discipline.[2] The first section of this chapter

[1] M. J. Ingram, 'Communities and courts: law and disorder in early-seventeenth-century Wiltshire', in J. S. Cockburn (ed.), *Crime in England 1500–1800* (London, 1977), 110–34, 321–8; Ingram, *Church Courts, Sex and Marriage in England, 1570–1640* (Cambridge, 1987), 27–34; J. A. Sharpe, 'Crime and delinquency in an Essex parish 1600–1640', in Cockburn (ed.), *Crime*, 90–109, 316–21; Sharpe, 'Enforcing the law in the seventeenth-century English village', in V. A. C. Gatrell, B. Lenman and G. Parker (eds.), *Crime and the Law: The Social History of Crime in Western Europe since 1500* (London, 1980), 97–119. For other recent accounts of church courts see C. Cross, 'Sin and society: the northern high commission and the northern gentry in the reign of Elizabeth', in C. Cross, D. Loades and J. J. Scarisbrick (eds.), *Law and Government under the Tudors: Essays Presented to Sir Geoffrey Elton Regius Professor of History in the University of Cambridge on the Occasion of his Retirement* (Cambridge, 1988), 195–209; J. Addy, *Sin and Society in the Seventeenth Century* (London, 1989).

[2] This is a well-developed theme in relation to the presentment and prosecution of criminal offences. A characteristically elegant summary of criminal procedure is offered by J. H. Baker, 'Criminal courts and procedure at common law, 1550–1500', in Cockburn (ed.), *Crime*, 15–48, 299–309. For the practical significance see, among many others: K. Wrightson, 'Two concepts of order: justices, constables and jurymen in seventeenth-century England', in J. Brewer and J. Styles (eds.), *An Ungovernable People? The English and their Law in the Seventeenth and Eighteenth Centuries*

outlines the ways in which participation patterned the uses of the courts. We will then consider two particular cases of the use of the law to achieve moral reformation – the disciplinary initiatives against loose living often referred to as the puritan reformation of manners – and, thirdly, we will examine the use of the courts to prosecute deviant figures – in this case beggars and witches. These prosecutions again point up the potential power of, broadly defined, 'patriarchal' ideas. These measures, resting as they did on participation, provide further testimony to the usefulness of these ideas for all sorts of people in early modern England. But the use of the courts did not just serve to enforce adherence to patriarchal ideals and to cement the position of the powerful. The courts were used to pursue other ends too, and the fourth section of the chapter considers the great increase in civil litigation as a reminder to the limitations of the characterisation of these institutions simply as patriarchal. Finally, the last section of the chapter considers at greater length the implications of the routinisation of local government discussed in chapter 3.

PARTICIPATION AND INITIATIVE IN THE USE OF THE LAW

Legal redress and protection was available in a great variety of jurisdictions in early modern England. Much attention has been paid to quarter sessions and assizes in recent years, but it is also clear that more local jurisdictions, such as leet and manorial courts, were active in both civil and criminal matters. Indeed, many administrative initiatives in relation to poverty were taken through leet courts during the early sixteenth century.[3] These jurisdictions were, however, gradually superseded by

(London, 1980), 21–46, 312–15; J. S. Morrill, *The Cheshire Grand Jury, 1625–1659: A Social and Administrative Study*, Leicester University Department of Local History, Occasional Papers, 3rd series, no. 1 (Leicester, 1976); T. C. Curtis, 'Quarter sessions appearances and their background: a seventeenth-century regional study', in Cockburn (ed.), *Crime*, 135–54, 328–31; C. B. Herrup, 'Law and morality in seventeenth-century England', *PP*, 106 (1985), 102–23; Herrup, 'New shoes and mutton pies: investigative responses to theft in seventeenth-century East Sussex', *HJ*, 27 (1984), 811–30; Herrup, *The Common Peace: Participation and the Criminal Law in Seventeenth-Century England* (Cambridge, 1987); J. B. Samaha, 'Hanging for felony: the rule of law in Elizabethan Colchester', *HJ*, 21 (1978), 763–82.

[3] For the role of these courts down to 1600 see: M. K. McIntosh, *Controlling Misbehavior in England, 1370–1600* (Cambridge, 1998). By 1600 most of the offences being considered here (broadly comparable to McIntosh's 'disorder cluster' of offences) were being handled by quarter sessions and the other 'intermediate' courts: ibid., p. 11. For local courts see also McIntosh, 'Local responses to the poor in late medieval and Tudor England', *Continuity and Change*, 3 (1988), 209–45; McIntosh, 'Social change and Tudor manorial leets', in J. A. Guy and H. G. Beale (eds.), *Law and Social Change in British History*, Royal Historical Society, Studies in History, 40 (London, 1984), 73–85; K. C. Newton and M. K. McIntosh, 'Leet jurisdiction in Essex manor courts during the Elizabethan period', *Transactions of the Essex Archaeological Society*, 13 (1981), 3–14;

quarter sessions[4] and the emphasis of this discussion will be on these sessions and the church courts.

It is a well-remarked feature of early modern justice that considerable discretion was observed in the capture of offenders and the resort to the formal processes of the law. Moreover, even if a formal prosecution was set in train, the operation of the law was open to influence. The key feature of the common law in this respect was that the courts only considered what was brought before them, they did not instigate prosecutions. Prosecutions for felonies could be brought privately by appeal of felony or by indictment in the name of the king. Misdemeanours were brought before the courts by information or by indictment. Indictments were made by twelve or more laymen, constituting a jury, sworn to inquire on the king's behalf. In practice these juries were often not the initiators of indictments but considered bills presented to them by others. They could find the bills true (worthy of trial) or *ignoramus* (not true). Not only then were courts dependent on business being brought before them, but there was an important further filter on what was eventually answered for in court. Informations were made by individuals *qui tam* (for themselves and the king) or *ex officio* (if they were law officers). At trial juries could be judges of law, too, resisting strained interpretations of the law or government-minded judges. Juries were also known to commit 'pious perjury' by, for example, undervaluing stolen goods in order to reduce the seriousness of the offence being tried. Judgement could be stayed on a number of grounds and even if found guilty the accused felon stood a good chance of securing a pardon. In fact, it was a peculiarly unlucky or frightening offender who failed to escape prosecution at any of these stages.[5]

W. J. King, 'Leet jurors and the search for law and order in seventeenth-century England: "Galling Persecution" or reasonable justice?', *Histoire Sociale/Social History*, 13 (1980), 305–23; King, 'Early Stuart courts leet: still needful and useful', *Histoire Sociale/Social History*, 23 (1990), 271–99. For manorial courts, C. Harrison, 'Manor courts and the governance of Tudor England', in C. Brooks and M. Lobban (eds.), *Communities and Courts in Britain 1150–1900* (London, 1997), 43–59. Sharpe, 'Crime and delinquency', emphasises the range of courts available to early modern villagers. For the use of manorial courts for the implementation of a 'reformation of manners' in the fourteenth century see M. Spufford, 'Puritanism and social control?', in A. Fletcher and J. Stevenson (eds.), *Order and Disorder in Early Modern England* (Cambridge, 1985), 41–57. For the fifteenth century see M. Ingram, 'Reformation of manners in early modern England', in P. Griffiths, A. Fox and S. Hindle (eds.), *The Experience of Authority in Early Modern England* (London, 1996), 47–88.

[4] In effect, government by franchise was supplanted by commission, a more direct form of government. This might be interpreted as a degree of 'modernisation'. It is more clearly evident in the development of governance across the Tudor/Stuart territories more generally: see below chs. 8 and 9.

[5] Baker, 'Criminal courts', esp. pp. 14–25, 32–45. The classic local study of the operation of this discretion is Herrup, *Common Peace*. For church courts see below, pp. 298–300.

Alongside these court procedures stood justices exercising a summary jurisdiction, acting outside quarter sessions. Here, obviously, the scope for flexible interpretation of the offence and of the law was considerable. In Lambarde's view the flexible use of the criminal law represented potentially damaging indulgence.

If you would complain of unlawful gaming in the day, of untimely walking in the night, and of unseemly appareling all the year, you should hew and cut in sunder the first steps, as it were, of those stairs which do lead up to pickery, theft and robbing. The same might be said almost of all other offenses, the which of small seeds at the first wax in time to be great weeds by your too long sufferance and forbearing.[6]

Thus, influential local opinion was crucial in moulding the activities, and effectiveness, of government in these areas – it was essential that everyone was active in combating these minor offences.

There was a widely diffused sense of the identity of sin and crime, so that moral behaviour became a matter of public concern. At the same time, the officers of the peace were entrusted with a duty to combat sin. As Lambarde put it:

All men do see, and good men do behold it with grief of mind, that sin of all sorts swarmeth and that evildoers go on with all licence and impunity. If the cause be searched for it shall never be found in the want of laws, for sin in this age and light of gospel is not only detected by the mouth of the preacher but also prohibited by the authority of the prince.[7]

As a result, the law was a means of government, and that government aimed at combating vice, policing many aspects of behaviour now regarded as private matters. Sin, according to Lambarde, flourished not just because of the minds of the sinners but also the 'remiss dealing of those persons that are put in trust with the execution of such laws as we have'. Thus, if officers of the peace should

find out the disorders of alehouses, which for the most part be but nurseries of naughtiness, then neither should idle rogues and vagabonds find such relief and harborow as they have, neither should wanton youths have so ready means to feed their pleasures and fulfil their lusts, whereby, besides infinite other mischiefs they nowadays do burden all the country with their misbegotten bastards.[8]

In the use of the law in this way, however, there was a high degree of participation and considerable scope for discretion. Constables, grand

---

[6] Quoted in L. A. Knafla. '"Sin of all sorts swarmeth": criminal litigation in an English county in the early seventeenth century', in E. W. Ives and A. H. Manchester (eds.), *Law, Litigants and the Legal Profession*, Royal Historical Society, Studies in History, 36 (London, 1983), 50–67, at p. 66.
[7] Quoted in Knafla, 'Sin', p. 50.   [8] Quoted ibid., pp. 50, 65–6.

juries and trial juries all had the capacity to prevent formal prosecution or punishment, and this allowed many potential convicts to escape.[9] In order for the formal powers of the law to operate, there had to be considerable local participation and cooperation. Written into the details of its operation, therefore, are powerful local ideals of order and discipline.

THE REFORMATION OF MANNERS: ALEHOUSES AND BASTARDY

The law was brought to bear on a range of offences, encouraging some historians to refer to a 'puritan reformation of manners' in Elizabethan and Stuart England. It is often associated with the regulation of alehouses and attempts to police sexual behaviour. These initiatives were not unique to the godly, but they were closely associated with the vision of many of them. 'For many ministers and magistrates religious reform and social reform were inextricably intertwined and the poor were obvious raw material for both.'[10] Ale and the alehouse were central to the lives of the poor. The drink itself was an important dietary supplement and for the poor, particularly elderly women, ale-brewing was an important by-employment. Most villages had an alehouse, supplied by ale-wives, and it was, for example, estimated that there was one alehouse for every twenty households in Essex in 1646. Alehouses were central to the social life of the poor, but had other functions too: labour was often hired there, and village business discussed. However, alehouses were distinctively the preserve of the poor. Richer drinkers frequented inns or taverns, and it is here that the growing cultural separation of rich and poor becomes relevant. Alehouses came to be regarded with acute suspicion, as centres of a counter-culture.[11] For 'the gentry and those in authority . . . [the alehouse] was a nursery of vice, a place where petty crime was planned, stolen goods were received, prostitution was organised, idle political talk went unchecked, riot might be contemplated; a place where violence, which so easily accompanied

---

[9] See also Curtis, 'Quarter sessions appearances'; Ingram, 'Communities'; Sharpe, 'Enforcing'; Wrightson, 'Two concepts'; Herrup, 'Law and morality'.

[10] P. Slack, *Poverty and Policy in Tudor and Stuart England* (London, 1988), 26.

[11] K. Wrightson, 'Alehouses, order and reformation in rural England, 1590–1660', in E. Yeo and S. Yeo (eds.), *Popular Culture and Class Conflict, 1590–1914: Explorations in the History of Labour and Leisure* (Brighton, 1981), 1–27; P. Clark, 'The alehouse and the alternative society', in D. Pennington and K. Thomas (eds.), *Puritans and Revolutionaries: Essays in Seventeenth-Century History Presented to Christopher Hill* (Oxford, 1978), 47–72; P. Clark, *The English Alehouse: A Social History, 1200–1830* (London, 1983), ch. 7.

the effects of drink, was common'.[12] This sense of the alehouse as a threat to order informed a desire to regulate, an impulse further encouraged by the need to restrict unnecessary consumption of grain in years of hardship. Moreover, while brewing consumed grains perhaps better employed for other forms of consumption, the money spent at the alehouse might also be better spent in hard years.

A number of pressures came together around the issue of the control of alehouses, therefore. Some of them are revealed in a letter from John Clenche and Fr. Rodes to Richard Brereton on 18 March 1589 about the 'excessyve number of Alehowses & bakers' in Manchester and the need for 'reformacion thereof by persons of good Credite'. They requested that Brereton go to Manchester and call before him all alehouse-keepers and bakers 'And to take such order theare for the suppressyon of all all [sic] such as youre helpes shall thinke goode And for the Alowynge of such as shalbe thought metest for that purpose.' Clearly, since the target was both alehouses and bakers, concern about grain consumption must have been part of the motivation. But also at stake was Brereton's honour, to be secured through combating vice.

Herein you shall not onely do good service to the Common wealthe by reason that these houses are the verye nurses of all malefactors & harbors for all lewde & evil disposed persons But also you shall geave us iuste cause in reformacion of this enormytie to thinke the better of your good service therein & also to geave you Condigne thankes for the paynes you shall take in the same.

The matter was left to Brereton's 'sircumspet [sic] dealinge', but they were anxious that Brereton report to the next assizes how many he had suppressed or allowed. Those that were allowed were to be given 'certen orders to be observed' in the conduct of their business.[13] Brereton's credit with Clenche and Rodes was clearly related to his service of the commonwealth in combating vice.

The results of these various pressures could be spectacular attempts at regulation through licensing. In Essex between 1620 and 1680 there were 1,682 quarter sessions presentments and 873 indictments at quarter sessions and assizes. Regulation might also have had a revenue purpose, however, and this could be an obstruction to the implementation of effective control. Reformers though, sometimes responded to this tension creatively – establishing a common brewery whose profits went

---

[12] A. Fletcher, *Reform in the Provinces: The Government of Stuart England* (London, 1986), 230.
[13] HEH, EL 6297.

to support the poor.[14] The attempt to impose licences in Chester in 1608 and 1609 met with an impressive display of solidarity from the alehouse-keepers, who refused to enter compositions for licences on the grounds that they were too poor. The result was that, at least in the short term, they were suppressed and no licences were issued. It may have been, however, that the corporation was not whole-hearted in its determination to make the scheme work – that was certainly the suspicion of the privy council.[15] Sir Robert Johnson complained to Thomas Egerton in March 1615 that as a result of lax administration in London there were 1,000 'superfluous' alehouses 'within the space of ii miles distant frome the Cittie'.[16] Certainly, in practice, unlicensed alehouses continued to operate in large numbers across the country throughout the period, subject to periodic waves of activity. At other times the issue seemed less pressing, the need for alehouses more significant or the issue of a licence too important to revenue or the exercise of patronage.[17]

Once again, then, conciliar pressure did not meet with a uniform response. But where regulation was effective in the successful, periodic, campaigns of regulation at various times throughout the country, it was because of initiatives from within the villages and towns. In the early seventeenth century, in counties widely dispersed around the country 'substantial yeomen, husbandmen and tradesmen' and grand juries sought regulation through the quarter sessions. In general, it was south-ern and western counties that saw concerted efforts before the civil war,[18] but again inactivity is not a measure of 'failure'. The great strength of government by officeholders was this discretion – fitting central policy to local needs. On the whole, though, this kind of initiative appealed to particularly active or godly officeholders, not village and county elites as a whole. 'The victories won during the early Stuart period against alehouse proliferation, drunkenness and disorder

---

[14] P. Slack, *Poverty in Early Stuart Salisbury*, Wiltshire Record Society, 31 (Devizes, 1975), 10–12; Slack, 'Poverty and politics in Salisbury, 1597–1666', in P. Clark and P. Slack (eds.), *Crisis and Order in English Towns, 1500–1700: Essays in Urban History* (London, 1972), 164–203 at pp. 182–3, 190–1; D. Underdown, *Fire from Heaven: The Life of an English Town in the Seventeenth Century* (London, 1992), 113–15.   [15] CCRO, ML/6/21, 35.

[16] HEH, EL 272. The principal reason for laxity, he thought, was that licensing business was handled in a single day and licences were renewed unless 'notorious objection be against it, by some of the inhabitaunts, but that is verie seldome'.

[17] See, for example, S. K. Roberts, 'Alehouses, brewing, and government under the early Stuarts', *Southern History*, 2 (1980), 45–71. For the discretion of leet courts in the enforcement of licensing in Lancashire see W. J. King, 'Regulation of alehouses in Stuart Lancashire: an example of discretionary administration of the law', *Transactions of the Historic Society of Lancashire and Cheshire*, 129 (1979), 31–46.   [18] Fletcher, *Reform*, pp. 239–43.

associated with intoxication were usually victories won by individual gentry or by groups of parish notables.'[19]

A second important component of moral reformation was the regulation of sexual behaviour. This focused, in particular, on the poor and on illegitimacy. It seems clear that in the villages of England sex was permissible before formal marriage, on the basis of a relatively informal promise.[20] Marriage was also restricted by economic opportunities – the predominance of the nuclear household presupposed economic independence prior to marriage. For economically vulnerable individuals it was possible that such opportunities might recede so that an informal promise followed by sex resulted in an illegitimate birth. As a consequence illegitimacy rates rose after particularly difficult years. In fact, in our period, they seem to have peaked around 1600 when 4.5 per cent of all births in a sample of twenty-four parishes were illegitimate. It seems fairly clear that in the boom years following a period of economic hardship large numbers of spousals were made, but that marital opportunities for the poorer sort were volatile. As a result of these unstable arrangements a number of unfortunates could be added to the list of bastard-bearers.[21] They thereby increased levels of illegitimacy above those accounted for by a core of people who formed, to borrow a rather inelegant term, a 'bastardy-prone sub-society'.[22]

Infanticide was, it seems, comparatively rare as means of coping with unwanted children.[23] As a result, such sexual activity had economic consequences, and justices were frequently alerted to illegitimacy by parishes worried about having to support a bastard child. But the impulse was godly, too, and the intervention of agents of state authority in the life of the individual dramatic. In this they might be led to apparently heartless measures. Elizabeth Laurenson alias Alscoe, in labour delivering a daughter in January 1669, was asked by the midwife 'in the extremitie of her paine' who the father was. The question was repeated several times in front of several witnesses. This was by no

---

[19] Ibid., p. 250.
[20] For a general account of these practices and associated disputes, see Ingram, *Church Courts*, chs. 6–7.
[21] D. Levine and K. Wrightson, 'The social context of illegitimacy in early modern England', in P. Laslett, K. Oosterveen and R. M. Smith (eds.), *Bastardy and its Comparative History: Studies in the History of Illegitimacy and Marital Nonconformism in Britain, France, Germany, Sweden, North America, Jamaica and Japan* (London, 1980), 158–75.
[22] P. Laslett, 'The bastardy-prone sub-society', in Laslett, Oosterveen and Smith (eds.), *Bastardy*, 217–40.
[23] K. Wrightson, 'Infanticide in earlier seventeenth-century England', *Local Population Studies*, 15 (1975), 10–22.

means a unique experience.[24] It may not have been uncommon for pregnant women to be moved on in rural England.[25] When Jane Bromefield was executed for murder in 1612, the infant bastard in her care, Thomas Lyon, threatened to become a charge on the city of Chester. His mother and father were traced, Margaret Greene and Adam Lyon of Kilshawe in Lancashire, and the infant was ordered to be passed from constable to constable back to Kilshawe.[26] In order to establish paternity detailed investigations of courtship and sexual conduct were undertaken. In fact, the punishment of bastard-bearers – by whipping and/or being sent to the house of correction – was reserved for cases where the child was likely to become chargeable.

The effect of these measures is discernible in declining illegitimacy rates, the best-studied case being the Essex village of Terling. There the hard years of the 1590s were followed by years of increased illegitimacy, but the regulatory effort and tighter social controls over entry into marriage seem to have had a long-term effect in reducing illegitimacy. In subsequent hard years – the 1620s, the early 1630s and the late 1640s – there was no similar peak in illegitimacy. Social differentiation led to 'the rejection of customary social and sexual norms by many of the more substantial villagers, and on the other hand . . . a greater willingness on their part to establish conformity to more disciplined canons of behaviour and to use both the Poor Laws and the secular and ecclesiastical courts to that end'.[27] Subsequent generations saw the nadir of English illegitimacy, as the system of social regulation was 'energized from below', by the activities of local officeholders. The low illegitimacy rates of the mid-seventeenth century thus owed very little to puritan activism prompted by the post-1649 regimes.[28] A similar campaign in Dorchester

---

[24] CCRO, MF/87/21. For other examples see L. Gowing, 'Ordering the body', in M. J. Braddick and J. Walter (eds.), *Order, Hierarchy and Subordination in Early Modern Britain* (Cambridge, forthcoming); L. A. Pollock, 'Childbearing and female bonding in early modern England', *Social History*, 22 (1997), 286–306, esp. pp. 303–4; S. Hindle, 'The shaming of Margaret Knowsley: gossip, gender and the experience of authority in early modern England', *Continuity and Change*, 9 (1994), 391–419, at pp. 402, 417 n 67.

[25] See, for example, J. Kent, 'Population mobility and alms: poor migrants in the Midlands during the seventeenth century', *Local Population Studies*, 27 (1981), 35–51, esp. pp. 37–9.

[26] CCRO, ML/6/77. It is possible that Bromefield had been paid to take the child: for an example of this from Lancashire in this period see Wrightson, 'Infanticide', pp. 16–17.

[27] Levine and Wrightson, 'Social context', quotation at p. 173.

[28] K. Wrightson, 'The nadir of English illegitimacy in the seventeenth-century', in Laslett, Oosterveen and Smith (eds.), *Bastardy*, 176–91. A similar pattern has been discerned in the Wiltshire village of Keevil: M. Ingram, 'Religion, communities and moral discipline in late sixteenth- and early seventeenth-century England: case studies', in K. von Greyerz (ed.), *Religion and Society in Early Modern Europe 1500–1800* (London, 1984), 177–93, at pp. 185–6.

in the early seventeenth century seems to have had similar effects. In Trinity parish illegitimacy rates had been higher than the national average in the years before 1611. By the 1620s they had fallen to about half, and by the 1630s about a quarter, of the national average.[29] It seems that here was an intensification of government with profound consequences for the most intimate aspects of the behaviour of the individual. It seems possible to trace actual changes in sexual behaviour to governmental initiatives. Moreover, unlike most of the policies discussed in this book, there seems to be an objective measure of efficiency: comparison of bastard births recorded in parish registers with the number that came before the courts suggests that a high proportion of bastard births resulted in official action.[30] Changing levels of prosecution almost certainly reflect, therefore, real changes in sexual behaviour. There were regional variations, however. In Cheshire, Devon and Nottinghamshire the harshest penalties were used comparatively rarely in the early seventeenth century, it seems.[31]

Punishments were reserved mainly for women, although in a number of counties it is clear that in the seventeenth century, increasingly, men were punished too.[32] There was, in the early seventeenth century, a tendency to punish the mothers for the offence (by sending them to the house of correction or by a whipping) whereas the fathers were punished for failing to meet the financial consequences of bastardy.[33] Clearly, here was a concern for order and moral reformation, the promotion of new standards of behaviour. Perhaps a particular concern, however, was with female sexuality, something manifest in attitudes towards witchcraft and female vagrants too.

Patriarchy is a term used so often that it eludes precise definition, but it might be appropriate here. The roles of men and women, old and young, were defined in relation to the household and employment

---

[29] Underdown, *Fire*, pp. 106–7.
[30] D. Levine and K. Wrightson, *Poverty and Piety in an English Village: Terling, 1525–1700* (Oxford, 1995 edn), 126–7.
[31] G. P. Higgins, 'The government of early Stuart Cheshire', *Northern History*, 12 (1976), 32–52, esp. pp. 36–7. Higgins suggests that this was a contrast with Lancashire, but Wrightson has suggested that Lancashire was also comparatively lax and that 'bastard children may have been regarded less as a source of shame than of expense and inconvenience': 'Infanticide', p. 17.
[32] Fletcher, *Reform*, p. 257.
[33] This suggestion is based on an analysis of punishments in Lancashire, Somerset, Warwickshire and Hertfordshire: W. J. King, 'Punishment for bastardy in early seventeenth-century England', *Albion*, 10 (1978), 130–51.

supported by appropriate forms of subordination.[34] These values were to be reinforced by statute in the interests of social order. But patriarchs did not simply discipline and reward, they also protected, and this was another duty of magistrates in relation to the poor. Intervention in the grain market in order to ensure a supply of cheap grain was of a piece with this generalised concern. The enforcement of these measures again reflects the potential of an active magistracy, and also the importance of discretion.

IMAGES OF DEVIANCE: BEGGARS AND WITCHES

The clearest sense of this ideal of patriarchal order is gained from visions of the epitomes of disorder: witches and vagrants. Although there clearly were witches in early modern England, historians are generally sceptical about whether they can have been guilty of the crimes of which they were actually convicted. Witchcraft can work, according to our understanding, on believing adults.[35] But belief is essential, and this seems to preclude bewitching infants, animals or inanimate objects. The issue is complicated, though, because the accused did not always, apparently, believe that they were innocent.[36] For modern historians of England and Europe, however, the question has posed itself in these terms: how did innocent people come to be convicted of this crime that they did not commit? The answers have centred on why people were accused and (less systematically in the English case) why courts would convict. Recent work has tended to offer answers of both kinds by trying to decode the threat that witchcraft posed. What were these (innocent)

---

[34] For patriarchy and social order: G. J. Schochet, *Patriarchalism in Political Thought: The Authoritarian Family and Political Speculation and Attitudes Especially in Seventeenth-Century England* (New York, 1975); S. D. Amussen, *An Ordered Society: Gender and Class in Early Modern England* (Oxford, 1988); D. Underdown, 'The taming of the scold: the enforcement of patriarchal authority in early modern England', in Fletcher and Stevenson (eds.), *Order and Disorder*, 116–36; A. Fletcher, *Gender, Sex and Subordination in England 1500–1800* (London, 1995); I. Ben-Amos, *Adolescence and Youth in Early Modern England* (New Haven, 1994); P. Griffiths, *Youth and Authority: Formative Experiences in England 1560–1640* (Oxford, 1996); M. T. Burnett, 'Master and servants in moral and religious treatises, *c.* 1580–*c.* 1642', in A. Marwick (ed.), *The Arts, Literature and Society* (London, 1990), 48–75. For some cautionary remarks based on another set of sources see J. A. Sharpe, 'Plebeian marriage in Stuart England: some evidence from popular literature', *TRHS*, 5th series, 36 (1986), 69–90.

[35] For recent work emphasising the reality of witchcraft for contemporaries see M. Gaskill, 'Witchcraft and power in early modern England: the case of Margaret Moore', in J. Kermode and G. Walker (eds.), *Women, Crime and the Courts in Early Modern England* (London, 1994), 125–45; J. A. Sharpe, *Witchcraft in Seventeenth-Century Yorkshire: Accusations and Counter Measures*, Borthwick Papers, 81 (York, 1992); R. C. Sawyer, '"Strangely Handled in All Her Lyms": witchcraft and healing in Jacobean England', *Journal of Social History*, 22 (1988–9), 461–85.

[36] Gaskill, 'Margaret Moore'.

people imagined to have done? It is here that witchcraft studies are illuminating of the history of the state, for the development of a legal code defining witchcraft as a secular crime, and the attendant willingness of courts to prosecute, is one of the most dramatic extensions of jurisdiction during our period. For that reason Larner suggested that the experience of the trials could usefully be placed in the context of a European-wide judicial revolution – an increasing insistence on the role of royal courts in regulating and settling dispute. In this sense it was representative of a larger process of state-formation.[37] The fact that this extension of jurisdiction was driven by a largely non-existent threat suggests that the imaginations that drove it are revealing of some of the inner purposes of groups in a position to achieve such an extension of authority. It was a kind of moral panic, revealing not because it was typical or normal but because it was only distantly related to an 'objective' reality. Inscribed in the witchcraft prosecutions are the lineaments of the inverse of the order that legitimate authority sought to defend. Finally, because English courts were not inquisitorial but depended for their business on matters brought before them, the trials built on a willingness to accuse. Trials became one of a number of countermeasures building on local fears and beliefs.[38]

The transformation of witchcraft into a secular crime reflects respectable fears. The statute of 1563 was probably a creation of Protestants returning from European exile from the Catholic government of Mary I. The 1604 statute, with its more developed demonological theory, is usually attributed to the influence of James I. This statute, though, seems to have come after the main bulk of trials – by the early seventeenth century prosecutions appear to have been infrequent. The decline continued throughout the century, interrupted by the rash of prosecutions associated with Matthew Hopkins in Essex in 1645 and a similar group in Kent a little later. This dissociation of statutory fears and the level of accusations is symptomatic of a bigger difference – that English witches were usually prosecuted for the harm that they did rather than for the means by which they had acquired the power to do that harm – they were prosecuted for *maleficium* rather than for making a demonic pact. Thus, although the willingness of courts to prosecute the

---

[37] C. Larner, 'Crimen Exceptum? The crime of witchcraft in Europe', in Gatrell, Lenman, Parker (eds.), *Crime*, 49–75.

[38] For some stimulating reflections on the role of legal developments in the trials in England see C. G. Unsworth, 'Witchcraft beliefs and criminal procedure in early modern England', in T. G. Watkin (ed.), *Legal Record and Historical Reality: Proceedings of the Eighth Legal History Conference, Cardiff, 1987* (London, 1989), 71–98.

crime was obviously crucial to the existence of trials, the most influential
work on English witchcraft has been that associated with the analysis of
accusations, which seem to have derived from quite different concerns.
Other aspects of the phenomenon have been re-emphasised recently,
however, particularly locating accusations in the context of widely held
beliefs about magic and healing, and possession. More than that, it has
been demonstrated that demonological interpretations of witchcraft
were more influential in England than had previously been believed.[39]

About 90 per cent of those prosecuted for witchcraft in early modern
England were women. They were also, probably, relatively poor and
old. These people were blamed for what we would probably regard as
misfortune – the death or injury of family or livestock, for example. The
components of an accusation, then, are supernatural beliefs which are
used to explain 'natural' phenomena and a suspicion, characteristically,
of marginal females. The accused had often been objects of suspicion for
a number of years prior to formal accusation and in this respect
accusations are often argued to reflect social strain. Villagers projected
the causes of misfortune onto a group with whom they felt uncomfortable.[40]

This general perception has often been extended to attribute accusations to social tensions arising from increasing economic differentiation.
The sociological explanation, briefly, is that social differentiation created a group of poor villagers with more tenuous links with their
wealthier neighbours. Increasingly, patterns of consumption demanding
competition among the well-to-do, or further productive investment, cut
across traditional communal obligations. Between 1560 and 1650 the
informal institutions offering help to the poor had broken down, and the
newer formal apparatus was not complete. It was in that period that
witchcraft accusations were most common. The very poor were whipped and sent on, or given work. 'It was the slightly less affluent neighbours or kin who only demanded a little help who became a source of

---

[39] A. Macfarlane, *Witchcraft in Tudor and Stuart England: A Regional and Comparative Study* (Prospect
Heights, Ill: 1991); K . Thomas, *Religion and the Decline of Magic: Studies in Popular Beliefs in Sixteenth-
and Seventeenth-Century England* (London, 1978), chs. 14–18. Sawyer, 'Strangely handled'; Gaskill,
'Margaret Moore'; J. T. Swain, 'The Lancashire witch trials of 1612 and 1634 and the
economics of witchcraft', *Northern History*, 30 (1994), 64–85; Sharpe, *Yorkshire*; Sharpe, *Instruments
of Darkness: Witchcraft in England, 1550–1750* (London, 1996), ch. 3.

[40] Macfarlane, *Witchcraft*, chs. 10–16. I am grateful to Lynn Botelho for pointing out to me that the
ages of only a few accused witches are known. The case that they were old, therefore, is plausible
(given other, qualitative, evidence) but unproven. I am grateful to Jim Sharpe for discussing this
issue with me.

anxiety. To refuse them was to break a whole web of long-held beliefs.'[41] Thus, the characteristic chain of events leading to an accusation involved two neighbours, close in social status. Accusations 'almost always arose from quarrels over gifts or loans in which the victim [of witchcraft] refused the witch some small gift, heard her muttering under her breath or threatening him, and subsequently suffered some misfortune'.[42] In a moral universe a cause was sought for this misfortune and the victim recalled a quarrel with a figure suspected, or capable of being suspected, of witchcraft. In a sense then, these social strains reflected, or even effected, 'a deep social change; a change from a "neighbourly", highly integrated and mutually interdependent village society, to a more individualistic one'.[43]

Accusations have characteristically been used to excavate social tensions of this kind, then. But it is equally true that the consistent attribution of blame to marginal women is revealing of another set of social relations. Marginal women were vulnerable to accusation not just because, materially, they were in a position where they might be asking frequent favours, but also because of a conceptual link between women and witchcraft: 'Popular belief, shared by men and women, was that the mysterious, harmful power that constituted witchcraft would inhere in certain women.'[44] In fact, it may have been that witchcraft and healing was a component of the by-employments available to marginal people, especially women: many practising witches probably were women.[45] As difficulties of securing prosecutions increased, these beliefs were incorporated by professional groups anxious to secure convictions. This fused popular beliefs about the witch's mark, for example, with elite misogynism. Women were active in this process, as the arbiters of local reputation through gossip and, as cases came to centre less on stock damage and more on illness, as witnesses. It was usually women who offered evidence of the witch's mark, for example. In this way women were implicated in a process that 'apparently confirmed that women were the weaker sex, more easily seduced by satanic temptation'.[46] The

---

[41] Macfarlane, *Witchcraft*, pp. 205–6.   [42] Ibid., p. 196.

[43] Ibid., p. 197. Although Macfarlane has expressed reservations about this interpretation, it has remained influential. For his reservations see Macfarlane, *The Origins of English Individualism: The Family, Property and Social Transition* (Oxford, 1978), esp. pp. 1–2.

[44] C. Holmes, 'Women: witnesses and witches', *PP*, 140 (1993), 45–78, quotation at p. 75.

[45] Swain, 'Lancashire witch trials', esp. pp. 81–2.

[46] Holmes, 'Women', p. 77. See also P. Rushton, 'Women, witchcraft and slander in early modern England: cases from the church courts in Durham, 1560–1675', *Northern History*, 18 (1982), 116–32. For other views on this issue see Gaskill, 'Margaret Moore'; Sharpe, *Instruments*, ch. 7.

participation of women in the process does not invalidate the proposition that the imagined fears from which it derived were patriarchal.[47]

It takes more than an accusation to make a trial, of course, and here the attitude of the courts was crucial. The last successful prosecution appears to have been in 1682, and the last assize trial in 1712. However, in 1751 Ruth Osborne died, having been subjected to the swimming ordeal in Tring, Hertfordshire, by a crowd convinced that she was a witch. Significantly, one of her tormentors was hanged.[48] Clearly, 'popular' beliefs about witchcraft outlived the willingness of the courts to prosecute. In part this decline in the willingness of the courts to prosecute is attributed to the spread of 'scientific' ideas among the respectable, but the chronology is difficult to match. Instead, the key influence seems to have been a specifically legal scepticism about the difficulty of proof. By 1700 this was, probably, compounded by a more general scepticism, and the development of forms of Christian faith which accorded less prominence to the devil.[49]

The most dramatic examples of this expanding social discipline were the measures put in place to deal with witches, then, and their outlines reveal the power of patriarchal ideas. An almost parallel case might be made in relation to poverty. Here an exaggerated perception of threat led to the creation of a new crime of status – that of vagrant. Vagrancy punishments were, on the whole, less severe than those for crimes to which vagrants might be thought liable – theft, for example. The crime of vagrancy was to be capable of work but unemployed and mobile – those convicted of this were guilty of a state of being rather than a crime with a particular victim. The offence was, therefore, normative and in this sense similar to witchcraft beliefs. Like witches, it seems, beggars and vagrants did not usually pose the threat which was imputed to them. Once again, then, respectable fears are inscribed with considerable clarity since these measures are more or less an unfiltered expression of normative fears rather than a response to an objective social reality.

[47] See, for example, Purkiss's readings of women's depositions as fantasies through which women relieved fears, conflicts and anxieties arising from their roles within patriarchy – as housewife and mother for example. 'Accused and accusers lived within certain definitions of female identity which were not of their own making and over which they exercised little control; these women were shaped by culture even as they struggled to shape it': D. Purkiss, *The Witch in History: Early Modern and Twentieth-Century Representations* (London, 1996), ch. 4, quotation at p. 94.

[48] W. B. Carnochan, 'Witch-hunting and belief in 1751: the case of Thomas Colley and Ruth Osborne', *Journal of Social History*, 4 (1970–1), 389–403. The last successful prosecution was that of Jane Wenham, also in Hertfordshire, in 1712: P. J. Guskin, 'The context of witchcraft: the case of Jane Wenham (1712)', *Eighteenth-Century Studies*, 15 (1981–2), 48–71.

[49] Sharpe, *Instruments*, chs. 9–11.

Vagrants were presented in literary sources, learned tracts and relatively cheap print, as being outside society. Removed from the normal means of socialisation – parish and household – and from the established conceptual hierarchies that gave shape to contemporary perceptions of order, they were objects of suspicion and of fear. Gregory King's enumeration of the population and distribution of wealth in the later seventeenth century is organised around a social hierarchy and the importance of the household. In these social accounts the vagrant poor are listed separately, outside the ranks of society and distinguished by being the only group not classified by family size.[50] Thus removed from social life it was difficult to know what they might do or what they believed in. As Juan-Luis Vives said in 1526, 'We know not according to what law or what conventions they live', or as John Gore said in the early seventeenth century, vagrants were 'without God, without magistrate, without minister'.[51] The threat they posed to society was not just physical, but normative, and this informed a number of exaggerated stereotypes. They became routinely associated with disease and sedition, as well as a whole series of crimes. But perhaps the most striking feature of this image of deviance was the counter-society that was constructed. Vagabonds were not just outside respectable society, but they were said to have their own corporations, fellowships, fraternities and companies, and they made their living from a variety of specialised trades.[52] Publications outlining these views sold well, and were no

---

[50] Reprinted in P. Laslett, *The World We Have Lost – Further Explored*, 3rd edn (London, 1983), 32–3.

[51] Quoted in A. L. Beier, *Masterless Men: The Vagrancy Problem in England 1560–1640* (London, 1985), 6.

[52] Ibid., pp. 5–8. See, for examples of this literature: A. V. Judges, *The Elizabethan Underworld: A Collection of Tudor and Early Stuart Tracts and Ballads* (London, 1930). An important part of the measures against vagrancy was a desire to control rumour. News was a valuable commodity in early modern England and it was, for example, an offence to suggest that the monarch was ill. In those circumstances vagrants and other travellers were viewed as sources of rumour and therefore politically dangerous. Thus Tudor legislation against vagrants also dealt with players and chapmen, and provost marshals were appointed to police vagrants and to control the passage of rumours. For some reflections on these issues see P. Roberts, 'Elizabethan players and minstrels and the legislation of 1572 against retainers and vagabonds', in A. Fletcher and P. Roberts (eds.), *Religion, Culture and Society in Early Modern Britain: Essays in Honour of Patrick Collinson* (Cambridge, 1994), 29–55; Beier, *Masterless Men*, pp. 96–9, 139–42, 152–3; A. Fox, 'Rumours, news and popular political opinion in Elizabethan and early Stuart England', *HJ*, 40 (1997), 597–620; L. O. Boynton, *The Elizabethan Militia 1558–1638* (London, 1967), 149, 200–2; Clark, 'Crisis contained?', p. 61; J. J. N. McGurk, 'Rochester and the Irish Levy of October 1601', *Mariner's Mirror*, 74 (1988), 57–66, at p. 58; Higgins, 'Government of Cheshire', pp. 37–8; R. Ashton, 'Popular entertainment and social control in later Elizabethan and early Stuart London', *London Journal*, 9 (1983), 3–19. There are frequent references to the dangers of false rumours in the earl of Huntington's letter book for the armada year. See, for example, HEH, HM 30881, fos. 20v, 88v–89r.

doubt of some significance to the formation of attitudes towards the problem.

The reality, as far as we can tell, was rather different. Most vagrants travelled alone or in couples. They were mainly young (40–50 per cent were under sixteen according to one sample) and male (outside London the proportion of women was rarely more than 20 per cent). The majority of vagrants were, therefore, single males: in London between 1516 and 1642 about 70 per cent; in Norwich between 1564 and 1635 the figure was about 55 per cent; in Chester, Essex, Leicestershire and Wiltshire between 1564 and 1644 about 50 per cent.[53] These were masterless men, outside the social order because they had no master and were not masters in their own household. The force of patriarchalism is reflected then, not just in the imaginings of sexual license attached to vagrant women, but to wholly anti-social values that masterless men *must* represent. It was a vision of inversion – the opposite of respectability for the young and the male. As such it was a counterpart to the witch stereotype for the old and the female. And, as with all images of deviance, we may imagine that it was self-reinforcing. Young men might have been more liable to formal prosecution as discretionary implementation of the vagrancy laws served to concentrate their effect on young adult males. Discretion served to reinforce an association between a particular kind of threat to order and a particular social group, just as marginal women were more liable than other groups to be suspected once a case of witchcraft was discovered.[54]

Even though the vagrants with which they were confronted in reality were not really like their literary image, the actions of magistrates were vigorous. As a result the 'omnibus statutory definitions of poverty were not purely theoretical'.[55] Although examples of negligence and remissness are not hard to find, evidence from Wiltshire, Essex and Lancashire in the early seventeenth century shows considerable activity in presenting and arresting the vagrant poor. In the large towns it is clear that great efforts were made to control the effects of migration, while survivals here and there show that some rural parishes were equally assiduous. This was true also of special searches. Between 1631 and

---

[53] Beier, *Masterless Men*, pp. 52–3. See also A. L. Beier, 'Social problems in Elizabethan London', *Journal of Interdisciplinary History*, 9 (1978), 203–21; P. Slack, 'Vagrants and vagrancy in England, 1598–1664', reprinted in P. Clark and D. Souden (eds.), *Migration and Society in Early Modern England* (London, 1987), 49–76; Higgins, 'Government of Cheshire', pp. 37–8.

[54] For evidence of how discretion in the implementation of the vagrancy laws might have reinforced the stereotype see Kent, 'Population mobility', p. 37.

[55] Beier, *Masterless Men*, p. 11.

1639, for example, 25,000 arrests were made, according to reports from 39 of 52 English and Welsh counties.[56] There was probably a larger number of actions behind these figures. Between 1603 and 1638, according to one analysis of constables' reports, constables whipped 982 vagrants. Of these only a minority appear in court records: 143 appeared in gaol deliveries and only 64 of them were committed for trial as felons.[57] Many others, no doubt, were pressed for service in expeditionary forces,[58] or transported. Significant numbers of poor children were shipped to Virginia and the West Indies in the 1620s, it seems.[59]

As with the poor law, however, most of this activity occurred in the period before 1640. The completion of the poor law after the restoration entailed the imposition of clear controls on migration.[60] Although there is plenty of evidence of the settlement laws being applied, there is little evidence of the ferocity which informed Elizabethan comment on vagrancy. In part this was probably a consequence of the regularisation of relations between rich and poor, but it also owed something to economic factors. Although there was a high degree of mobility among the English population of the late seventeenth and early eighteenth centuries, most of it was 'localized and basically circular'.[61] Long-distance, subsistence migration – the movement of the rootless and anonymous that had lain behind the constructions of disorder among Elizabethan and Stuart pamphleteers – was largely a thing of the past. The development was, doubtless, linked to the development of the poor law, which both discouraged movement and encouraged support in home parishes.[62] This is not to say that vagrants were unpunished in this period – they certainly were[63] – but this discipline was carried out without the shrill accompaniment of a pamphlet campaign. There were notable continuities in attitudes to the problem of poverty. For example, the paper that John Locke produced for the Board of Trade in 1697 drew on familiar ideas about poverty. It associated industry with virtue and recommended a penal element which was harsh by the standards of the day. Proposals for schooling and employment of the poor were part of a wider 'campaign for a new moral order' and 'helped

---

[56] Ibid., pp. 147–9.   [57] Ibid., p. 160.   [58] See ch. 5.
[59] Beier, *Masterless Men*, pp. 163–4.   [60] See above, pp. 116–17.
[61] P. Clark, 'Migration in England during the late seventeenth and early eighteenth centuries', reprinted in Clark and Souden (eds.), *Migration*, 213–52, quotation at p. 243; Clark and Souden, 'Introduction', ibid., 11–48, esp. pp. 29–36; J. Patten, 'Patterns of migration and movement of labour to three pre-industrial towns', reprinted ibid., 77–106; M. J. Kitch, 'Capital and kingdom: migration to late Stuart London', in A. L. Beier and R. Finlay (eds.), *London 1500–1700: The Making of the Metropolis* (Harlow, 1986), 224–51.
[62] Clark, 'Migration in England', pp. 239–44.   [63] Ibid., p. 239.

to legitimate and defend an insecure revolutionary regime'.[64] In general, an agreed set of remedies was implemented with approved rigour.

If we can conclude from this that vagrancy was no longer looming as large in contemporary imaginations the same is almost certainly true of witches. The social strains that had led to accusations were eased and the poor law machine offered a routine of relief for precisely that group that had most frequently been suspect: poor old women. It might not be too fanciful to suggest a further connection with the image of the sturdy beggar. As the limits of charity found definition in late Elizabethan statutes and pamphlets, equally important clarity was achieved in the image of the excluded. The deserving poor had a demonised Other in the morally threatening vagrant and the demonically powerful witch. This cannot be pushed too far – demonologies were more important to English witch trials than was once thought – but still the substance of the trials was *maleficium*. Restoration England does seem to have exorcised its folk devils, however, and this may be a component of the decline of the trials. Courts became less willing to convict as standards of proof rose, and it may be that this was enabled by relenting fears about social order. The dispossessed seem to have been less frightening to the propertied in later seventeenth-century England. The decline of witchcraft prosecutions, and the reduced clamour against beggars and witches, bear testimony to a more ordered world.[65]

As we have seen, regulation of the life of the poor was an issue on which national government could secure a fair degree of local cooperation. Although regular poor rates only slowly became universal, there were rapid responses from hard-pressed areas and there were also rapid responses to what was perceived to be the sharp end of the problem. Searches for vagrants, the appointment of provost marshals and the establishment of bridewells, were measures justified by the enormity of the normative threat posed by vagrancy. In confronting this threat it seems that local governors sometimes exceeded the law.[66] The alehouse in the Kentish towns was the resort of the poor migrant, providing the 'polar opposite of the aldermanic bench and the guild, the antithesis of ordered, respectable society'.[67] Seventeenth-century commentators

---

[64] A. L. Beier, '"Utter strangers to industry, morality and religion": John Locke on the poor', *Eighteenth Century Life*, 12/3 (1988), 24–41, quotations at pp. 28, 39. See J. Locke, 'An essay on the poor law' (1697), reprinted in M. Goldie (ed.), *Locke: Political Essays* (Cambridge, 1997), 182–98.

[65] For a discussion of the decline of the English trials see Sharpe, *Instruments*, chs. 9–11.

[66] J. Innes, 'Prisons for the poor: English bridewells, 1555–1800', in F. Snyder and D. Hay (eds.), *Labour, Law and Crime: An Historical Perspective* (London, 1987), 42–122, at p. 70–1; Higgins, 'Government of Cheshire', pp. 37–8; Beier, *Masterless Men*, p. 169.

[67] Clark, 'The migrant in Kentish towns 1580–1640', in Clark and Slack (eds.), *Crisis and Order*, 117–63, at p. 152.

were harsh in their views: 'alehouses are nests of Satan where the owls of impiety lurk and where all evil is hatched, and the bellows of intemperance and incontinence blown up', said Christopher Hudson in 1631. William Lambarde agreed: in alehouses 'your children and servants be corrupted in manners, bastards be multiplied in parishes, thieves and rogues do swarm the highways, the lawful pastimes of the land be abandoned, and dicing, cards, and bowling be set up in place'.[68] The 'alehouse was perceived as the command post of men who sought to turn the traditional world upside down and create their own alternative society'.[69] As we have seen, this was an exaggerated fear, and it is here that we can make a connection with beggars and witches, for these were normative crimes, ones which demanded rigorous attention. They were the most dramatic examples of a broader process of an increase in governance. The elements are by now familiar: 'a growing concern with public order generally; the development of novel attitudes towards the poor; and a religious hostility focused narrowly but with great intensity upon certain features of contemporary manners'.[70] The action was most intense, and its bases most clearly revealed, in the face of normative threat or crisis conditions.

THE CIVIL LAW: ORDER, NEIGHBOURLINESS AND HARMONY

We have already noted the centrality of patriarchal ideas to social and political thought, and it is certainly suggestive that the most dramatic extensions of administrative and legal competence between 1550 and 1640 were those made in response to groups who were thought to represent a threat to these values. But there was a high degree of participation in this process – at the very least these ideals were so widely dispersed that we might consider them normative rather than hegemonic. It has been claimed that there was a gender crisis in this period, reflected in considerable concern about the proper ordering of relations between men and women and perhaps also in increased formal punishment of women who did not conform to these standards.[71] But this was not simply an ideal imposed on women, since many women were active in propagating these ideals. So, for example, women were often important arbiters of local reputation and helped to propagate differential

---

[68] Both quoted by Clark, 'Alehouse', p. 47.   [69] Ibid., p. 48.

[70] Wrightson, 'Alehouses', p. 11.

[71] Amussen, *Ordered society*; Amussen, 'Gender, family and the social order, 1560–1725' in Fletcher and Stevenson (eds.), *Order and Disorder*, 196–217; Underdown, 'Taming of the scold'. But see the cautionary remarks in M. Ingram, '"Scolding women cucked or washed": a crisis in gender relations in early modern England?', in Kermode and Walker (eds.), *Women*, 48–80.

senses of male and female honour. Whereas male reputation depended
on a number of criteria, female honour was almost wholly concerned
with sexual behaviour. This differential standard, reflecting patriarchal
values, gave power to those women who were able to act as brokers of
local reputation.[72] Witchcraft and its prosecution also offered empower-
ment to women, as we have seen. The active role of women as arbiters of
reputation and in the prosecution of witchcraft could be the result of the
fact that 'they lived in a social world where they had to compete in
defending their own, and discrediting other women's, reputations . . . In
other words, they were competing to prove themselves in the face of a
generally misogynistic double standard applied by a male legal system.'[73] Apprentices were active in seeking protection of the courts from
abusive masters and there were informal sanctions which helped to offer
protection to wives against domestic violence.[74] Patriarchal ideals therefore offered power to women and protection to apprentices – they were
not simply a means to power for patriarchs.

This order was not only, or even ideally, imposed from outside or by
those with most to gain from its maintenance. The Wiltshire villagers
whose manifesto we considered in chapter 2 were not alone in promoting civility and neighbourliness among themselves. For them, resort to
the law was the bottom line, to be avoided if possible. In this they were
far from unique.[75] Legal process could be invoked prudentially, as an
extension of informal means of mediating conflict. Binding for peace or
for good behaviour offered a flexible means of restraining the behaviour
of individuals, giving a potentially worrying degree of discretion to
magistrates.[76] Official sanctions bore some similarities to informal sanc-

[72] L. Gowing, *Domestic Dangers: Women, Words, and Sex in Early Modern London* (Oxford, 1996), esp. ch.
   3; Gowing, 'Language, power and the law: women's slander litigation in early-modern London',
   in Kermode and Walker (eds.), *Women*, 26–47.
[73] Rushton, 'Women, witchcraft and slander', p. 131.
[74] P. Rushton, 'The matter in variance: adolescents and domestic conflict in the pre-industrial
   economy of north-east England, 1600–1800', *Journal of Social History*, 25 (1991), 89–107; E.
   Foyster, 'A laughing matter? Marital discord and gender control in seventeenth-century England', *Rural History*, 4 (1993), 5–21. On domestic violence see also Amussen, '"Being stirred to
   much unquietness": violence and domestic violence in early modern England', *Journal of Women's
   History*, 6 (1994), 70–89; J. A. Sharpe, 'Domestic homicide in early modern England', *HJ*, 24
   (1981), 29–48; Sharpe, 'Plebeian marriage'.
[75] See above, pp. 73–6. Sharpe, 'Enforcing'; Ingram, 'Communities'.
[76] J. B. Samaha, 'The recognizance in Elizabethan law enforcement', *American Journal of Legal
   History*, 25 (1981), 189–204; Wrightson and Levine, *Terling*, pp. 122–5; S. Hindle, 'The keeping
   of the public peace', in Griffiths, Fox and Hindle (eds.), *Experience*, 213–48. For the later period,
   R. B. Shoemaker, *Prosecution and Punishment: Petty Crime and the Law in London and Rural Middlesex, c.
   1660–1725* (Cambridge, 1991), ch. 5.

tions, reflecting shared values between the order of the law and of the neighbourhood.[77]

Despite what may have been a preference for informal mediation, however, resort to law in this period was not just common, but was increasingly so. In fact this disjunction was a source of uneasiness for contemporaries.[78] Detailed study of Common Pleas and King's Bench, two of the central law courts, reveals dramatic increases in levels of litigation. During the fifteenth century levels of litigation were low and there was a steady increase up to the middle of the sixteenth century. From 1560 the amount of litigation rose dramatically. By 1600 the two courts were hearing about six times as many actions as they had been at the end of the fifteenth century. Thereafter the rate of increase slowed down, but still levels of litigation doubled between 1580 and 1640. At the latter date the two courts heard perhaps fourteen times as many cases as they had heard in 1490.[79] These were the most important London courts in terms of volume of business, but the trends appear to have been similar in other courts too: a dramatic rise in volume during the reign of Elizabeth followed by deceleration or stagnation in the early seventeenth century.[80] As a result, in 1640 'there was probably more litigation per head of population going through the central courts at Westminster than at any time before or since'.[81]

Brooks' analysis of this phenomenon shows that this increase is not easy to explain in terms of procedural changes or by a transfer of business from one jurisdiction to another – it seems that there was a genuine increase in the frequency of resort to the law. The most important single factor, although by no means the only cause, was a great increase in the number of disputes over credit arrangements. Although borrowing was common in early modern England, credit facilities were limited – there were no banks and no insurance facilities to cover the costs of default. Money was sought from friends, or through

---

[77] M. Ingram, 'Ridings, rough music and the "reform of popular culture" in early modern England', *PP*, 105 (1984), 79–113; J. Walter and K. Wrightson, 'Dearth and the social order in early modern England', *PP*, 71 (1976), 22–42, esp. pp. 32–4. See also J. Kent, '"Folk justice" and royal justice in early seventeenth-century England: a "Charivari" in the Midlands', *Midland History*, 8 (1983), 70–85; T. Harris, 'The problem of "popular political culture" in seventeenth-century London', *History of European Ideas*, 10 (1989), 43–58, at pp. 49–50; Harris, *London Crowds in the Reign of Charles II: Propaganda and Politics from the Restoration until the Exclusion Crisis* (Cambridge, 1987), 19–21.   [78] Ingram, 'Communities', pp. 116–25.

[79] C. W. Brooks, *Pettyfoggers and Vipers of the Commonwealth: The 'Lower Branch' of the Legal Profession in Early Modern England* (Cambridge, 1986), 52–4.   [80] Ibid., pp. 54–7.

[81] C. W. Brooks, 'Interpersonal conflict and social tension: civil litigation in England, 1640–1830', in A. L. Beier, D. Cannadine and J. M. Rosenheim (eds.), *The First Modern Society: Essays in English History in Honour of Lawrence Stone* (Cambridge, 1989), 357–99, at p. 360.

a broker with a range of contacts who could lend, and so transactions often involved a number of separate loans. Moreover, this could be the case at every stage of a transaction, so that long chains of credit developed. Each loan was, characteristically, enforced by a bond which called for a penalty payment on default. Since a default at one point in a transaction might lead to problems elsewhere, and since the debts were not negotiable, debt litigation was common. Expanding incomes for farmers and artisans led to a multiplication of transactions and, hence, of litigation. It is these middling groups of society who made up the bulk of litigants.[82] Litigation was, therefore, closely connected with ordinary business dealings – starting an action for debt was a kind of early modern equivalent of a final demand, designed to bring pressure to bear rather than to start a protracted legal action.[83] But the cheapness of litigation also undoubtedly encouraged vexatious suits, exploiting the law to discomfort the defendant for reasons unconnected with the ostensible cause being tried, and the inflexibility of bond process encouraged hard dealing. Finally, equity courts could intervene in process on bonds where the penalty in law threatened to be too harsh, and this accentuated the multiplication of suits – the pursuit of the same cause in parallel suits to different courts. Vexatious suits and multiplication of suits were really only 'a species of flotsam and jetsam which floated in on the flood tide of litigation', but the actions of that group of litigants 'speak volumes about the legal scene during the first half of the seventeenth century'.[84]

The increase was probably disproportionately felt in London, because local jurisdictions often had territorial or other limits. For example, the Chester palatinate courts were not useful for the prosecution of debt outside the palatinate, and many borough or manor courts could only hear cases up to a certain monetary value. The significance of this limit, usually higher in borough courts, was being eroded by inflation. Elizabeth's reign also saw a dramatic expansion in the number of lawyers, many of whom had connections with particular courts, and as business increased locally it was channelled into London by these men. And just as inflation eroded the value of the limit of the jurisdiction of some courts, so it reduced the real cost of litigation in London.[85] The

---

[82] Brooks, *Pettyfoggers*, ch. 5, esp. pp. 95–6. For a general account of the expansion of marketing and associated credit litigation see C. Muldrew, *The Economy of Obligation: The Culture of Credit and Social Relations in Early Modern England* (London, 1998).

[83] See, for example, Muldrew, *Economy*, pp. 202–3.   [84] Brooks, *Pettyfoggers*, p. 111.

[85] Ibid., pp. 96–107.

cost of litigation, of course, was particularly important in deciding whether to go to court in a case of debt – was the cost of pursuing the debt in this way sufficiently low as to make economic sense? The increase in litigation was partly to do with the quickening of the economy but also 'a distinct centralization of the legal life of the realm, a shift from the provinces towards London'.[86]

Work since the publication of Brooks' pioneering study of these issues has, perhaps, modified this part of his explanation for the increase in litigation in London. It is clear that some local jurisdictions remained extremely active.[87] But in other respects the case seems to have been confirmed. The amount of litigation, the late Tudor boom and seventeenth-century decline, the relatively humble status of litigants, the sensitivity to costs and, above all, the importance of debt litigation have all been observed in these local courts. Analysis of litigation in King's Lynn, for example, seems to show that 'there was obviously little social bias in terms of who could use the law against whom' and also 'how important credit and litigation were to almost every family in the town'.[88] It will be difficult to speak with any greater certainty about the causes of the increase in litigation until we know more about these local jurisdictions, therefore, but it seems unlikely that Brooks' account will be substantially modified. Two conclusions are of particular significance here. Firstly, the volume and nature of civil litigation make it clear that the law and its use was not the exclusive preserve of any particular social group: 'it is no longer tenable to think of the English law in the eighteenth century as simply a matter of gentry hegemony over the rest of the population',[89] and this seems equally true of the earlier period. Secondly, as a result of the increase in litigation prior to 1640 'the influence of the Royal Courts in London and their agents, the common lawyers, permeated widely throughout the realm'.[90] Even if local

---

[86] Ibid., p. 96.

[87] W. A. Champion, 'Recourse to the law and the meaning of the great litigation decline, 1650–1750: some clues from the Shrewsbury local courts', in Brooks and Lobban (eds.), *Communities*, 179–98; Champion, 'Litigation in the boroughs: the Shrewsbury *curia parva*, 1580–1730', *Journal of Legal History*, 15 (1994), 201–22; Muldrew, 'Credit and the courts: debt litigation in a seventeenth-century urban community', *EcHR*, 46 (1993), 23–38; Harrison, 'Manor courts'. In fact, as Harrison shows, some manor courts retained significant criminal jurisdictions into the sixteenth century. It is not clear how far into the century he takes his case, however. Muldrew has suggested that borough courts became increasingly significant to rural society as a result of the increasing complexity of credit relations and the scale of debt litigation: 'Rural credit, market areas and legal institutions in the countryside in England, 1550–1700', in Brooks and Lobban (eds.), *Communities*, 155–77, esp. pp. 171–7.

[88] Muldrew, 'Credit', p. 36. [89] Brooks, 'Interpersonal conflict', p. 399.

[90] Brooks, *Pettyfoggers*, p. 280.

jurisdictions remained very active, the sheer volume of Westminster business, and the greater evenness of its geographical distribution, must persuade us that this was the case.

The boom in litigation was most marked in the later sixteenth and early seventeenth centuries, and litigation of all kinds seems to have been declining by the later seventeenth century. The courts were disrupted by the civil wars, but modestly increasing levels of business were reaching King's Bench and Common Pleas in the 1650s, 1660s and 1670s. Between 1680 and 1700, however, there were declines in both courts, and in King's Bench this continued through the first half of the eighteenth century. Common Pleas recovered slightly between 1700 and 1730 but both courts had reached historic low points by mid-century: 'the law as administered at Westminster was clearly at a nadir in 1750'.[91] By the end of the period covered here, then, a long-term decline in the use of the courts was under way.

In part this decline had economic origins. The last years of the seventeenth century were ones of economic dislocation and currency crisis, and this may have reduced disposable income available for litigation. The declining profitability of farming, as prices stabilised and wages began to rise, hit yeomen and husbandmen, previously prominent groups among the litigants. Particular agricultural regions also reflect this trend – for example, Norfolk's declining prosperity seems to be reflected in its declining share of litigation – while the growing numbers of urban poor resorted to cheaper local courts of requests rather than Westminster.[92] Fees were probably rising too, and lawyers returned to the provinces, from where the pursuit of actions in Westminster was more troublesome, and expensive to the client. These professional changes probably exacerbated a growing distrust of the courts at Westminster.[93] It is possible too that less tangible cultural shifts compounded these developments, as landed society withdrew from the sport, or gentlemen were less willing to have their private disputes exposed to public view. But perhaps the most important influence was changes in the ways in which credit was secured – the replacement of the bond by promissory notes – and a relaxation of the way that debts were enforced. Actions for debt had been a great majority of cases before 1640 and a sharp drop in this business had a great impact on the total volume of litigation.[94]

---

[91] Brooks, 'Interpersonal conflict', esp. pp. 360–4, quotation at p. 364.
[92] Although this was probably not an influence before the end of the seventeenth century.
[93] Brooks, 'Interpersonal conflict', pp. 367–84.   [94] Ibid., pp. 384–96.

This pattern is similar to that observed in other jurisdictions. For example, Shrewsbury litigation followed a broadly similar trend, although the decline started earlier if measured in suits *per capita*. But in Shrewsbury most of the business had been on informal agreements, especially sales credit, not on sealed obligations, and other kinds of business declined too, for example trespass and defamation. In Shrewsbury the key factor appears to have been rising legal costs,[95] but perhaps also a loss of a communal role for the court was important. The decline of Shrewsbury borough court activity was sharper than the decline at Westminster and even at the assizes, and this may point up a broader cultural change: 'If these courts to a significant extent no longer seemed appropriate for resolving personal interactions, is it possible that their communal embrace no longer seemed so legitimate?'[96] The phenomenon is so general, however, that a single explanation is difficult to provide. In Terling, Essex, the use of the law also reached a peak in the early seventeenth century, before a late seventeenth-century decline.[97] Here though the peak seems to have coincided with a period of social tension, associated with economic and social differentiation, which had eased by 1700.[98] To this general difficulty one could add, of course, the technical problems of interpretation. Changes in process or the relationship between jurisdictions could have had a dramatic impact on observed patterns of litigation. None the less, it seems that the law was available to those who might want to use it but, increasingly, fewer did.

This boom in litigation, which lasted through to the end of the period covered here, serves to temper arguments about the importance of particular social interests to the operation of local government and the courts. Although the criminal law gave life to the fears of the governing classes about, for example, vagrants and witches, the law as a whole was not the preserve of a particular social group. Legal authority was useful in all kinds of contexts. The responsiveness of the criminal law to respectable fears among a wider range of social groups is also manifest in other kinds of prosecution. There was considerable discretion involved in implementing the sanctions of the criminal law, and each time discretion was exercised at each stage of the process, broader social values were brought to bear on a particular case. Arrest, indictment and prosecution all required a degree of local initiative and the criminal

---

[95] Champion, 'Shrewsbury *curia parva*', esp. pp. 216–17.

[96] Champion, 'Recourse to the law', at p. 195. In King's Lynn the decline seems to have occurred later, in the first half of the eighteenth century: Muldrew, 'Credit', esp. pp. 26–8.

[97] Wrightson and Levine, *Terling*, pp. 113–14.   [98] Ibid., ch. 5.

process offered a number of technical or other opportunities to acquit or mitigate the sentence. Those who failed to escape at any of these points shared, broadly, similar characteristics that made them appear threatening.

At every point, evidence, social prejudice and the demeanor of opposing parties all affected the opinions of the authorities. The choices made throughout prosecution reinforced the common convictions of the propertied community: idleness, wanderlust, greed and insolence were the signposts on a road that led to anarchy and damnation. Crimes bred of these qualities were different from those born from need, confusion or intimidation. The first were committed by true criminals; the perpetrators of the second were errant brethren who might still be redeemed.[99]

Herrup is quite optimistic that the range of participation was so diverse, and the process so complex, that it cannot be reduced to the self-interest of any particular group. This seems to have been generally true, with the proviso that it was the respectable villagers who took the lead. In Terling, Essex, this group used the courts 'defensively, seeking to preserve their property, the public peace and the conventional norms of sexual behaviour'. But they could also be used 'offensively to promote new standards, new conceptions of order'.[100] The presentments made by grand juries were crucial here, offering a means by which the opinion of the respectable middling sort could be given legal power.[101]

In either case the courts were an adjunct to other means of preserving neighbourliness and order. The use of legal process was often the continuation of dispute by other means, but by the same token it was the continuation of negotiation by other means. In resorting to the law, English people invited the state in and their engagement with the formal authority of national government was intensified. In so far as the increased use of the courts represents an increase in the activity of the state, it was an increase in its collective power rather than the distributive power of the executive.[102] The state was not being consciously built or centralised, and its role was not a triumph of the centre over the localities. Instead, legal authority was an important social resource which was used to secure collective ends. The net result was a more

---

[99] Herrup, *Common peace*, p. 200. See also Samaha, 'Hanging'.
[100] Wrightson and Levine, *Terling*, p. 140.
[101] For the grand jury see Morrill, *Grand jury*. For a rather less active grand jury see S. K. Roberts, 'Initiative and control: the Devon quarter sessions grand jury, 1649–70', *BIHR*, 57 (1984), 165–77. For the increasing importance of the middling sort in the period 1550–1640 see S. Hindle, *The State and Social Change in Early Modern England c. 1550–1640* (London, 2000).
[102] See above, p. 93 for this distinction.

active legal system which regulated personal and social life to an impressive degree. But, of course, this was also an exercise of distributive power – there were groups whose position was reinforced by this, just as there were losers. In Sussex criminal prosecutions it was 'strangers and persons of marginal status [who] were exceptionally vulnerable'. It was 'those who by their crimes and their attitudes, seemed to violate the most basic rules of ethical behaviour'.[103] The vision of social and political order which drove this aspect of the 'growth of the state' was widely diffused and endorsed but was not, perhaps, unanimously supported.

Legal authority was clearly a crucial social resource for many people in early modern England, whose resort to law sanctioned its power. Participation in the initiatives outlined above was widespread and people of nearly all sorts had resort to the law to resolve civil disputes, to regulate social life or to prosecute crime. In doing so they were extending the authority of the state. This authority was something that national governments were anxious to defend.[104] The use of bonds for the peace or for good behaviour, for example, might reflect respectable local opinion, a desire to bring dispute within the bounds of civility.[105] But, on the other hand, the government's desire to end duelling or pacify territorial magnates reflects the desire to preserve, or extend, the claims of royal courts as the final arbiters of dispute. As James I pointed out in a proclamation of 1614, private settlement of disputes was not 'just and compatible with the policie of any orderly or well stayed government'.[106] In the normal run of legal business, however, resort to the courts was 'centralising' not so much in the sense that it was enforced by the centre, but in the sense that the increasing role of the courts in the resolution of disputes increased their practical authority in the localities. This state was forming rather than being built, but the process favoured some interests more than others.

At points, then, studies of the law seem to reveal a record of social discipline dominated by a gendered and class-based state. Patriarchy is a concept which can embrace both, as well as presumptions about age. But these ideals of order imposed constraints on governors as well as the governed, as the implementation of the plague measures demonstrates.

[103] Herrup, *Common Peace*, p. 200. See also Herrup, 'Law and morality'.
[104] See ch. 8 for attempts to reduce the power of clans to regulate social life independently.
[105] This case is made most fully by Hindle, 'Public peace'.
[106] J. F. Larkin and P. L. Hughes (eds.), *Stuart Royal Proclamations*, I, *Royal Proclamations of King James I 1603–1625* (Oxford, 1973), 302–8, quotation at p. 304, dated 4 Feb. 1614.

Moreover, the implementation of patriarchal ideals offered power and agency not just to heads of households. Finally, criminal and civil law was a 'multiple use-right',[107] resorted to by groups often regarded as lacking formal power. Fear of social disorder drove some radical extensions of the powers of governors. In part these were regulatory, but together they represented an intensification of government. The most dramatic examples of this intensification were the criminalisation of particular forms of poverty and the prosecution of witchcraft as a secular crime. The criminal law, as an adjunct to the law as a tool of administration, was used to safeguard the boundaries of respectable society, to preserve social order. It is worth considering criminal law in this context, therefore, but an important corrective about the role of law in general is provided by an examination of civil litigation. The law was not simply an instrument used to discipline and regulate social life from outside. Government provided a resource, and a tool that could be manipulated, even for those of fairly humble status. There was a high degree of participation at all levels of the legal system, and although increasing use of the courts ultimately reinforced the authority of the state, this was not a triumph of the centre over the localities.

Magistrates did not, therefore, act out of self-interest alone and the rhetoric of public service associated with officeholding clearly had some purchase. Moreover, the public being served was broader than the ranks of officeholders, and went beyond the male gender. There were other ways in which legitimate authority served broader interests, notably in resolving civil disputes. Indeed, in this case, it might provide a resource for the poor against the rich, although that is not easy to establish. For example, in their dispute with Thomas Egerton, first Viscount Brackley, in 1613 his tenants in Great Gaddesden were eventually drawn to arbitration. Before this was achieved, however, they had arrived at the manor court without legal counsel, claiming that they had approached learned men but none had been willing to represent them against Egerton. In fact, Egerton treated this claim as, in itself, a weapon of the weak, suggesting that it was 'but a dilatory shift'. To combat this tactic he suggested that they name anyone they would like to represent them. He would then require them to represent the tenants and to undertake their best pains to get the best possible solution for the

---

[107] J. Brewer and J. Styles, 'Introduction', in Brewer and Styles (eds.), *Ungovernable People*, 1–20, quotation at p. 20. They note the exclusion of the labouring poor from this use-right, however. See also E. P . Thompson, *Whigs and Hunters: The Origin of the Black Act* (Harmondsworth, 1975), esp. pp. 258–69.

tenants. As a result, the tenants were represented by, among others, Sir Francis Bacon, the solicitor general.[108] The need for legitimacy was, to an extent, empowering, and there was clearly a degree of negotiation here. But as Hindle has demonstrated, enclosure of common lands by means of a legal agreement, for example, might represent the acceptable face of power rather than a consensus.[109] Negotiation limits, but also favours, the relatively powerful.

In this preservation of social order the capacities of the state were considerable. Enabled by a generalised sense of the legitimacy of magisterial authority, and of the appropriateness of its application in these cases, the response was flexible. In its net effect it was considerable. It did not depend on the participation of all officeholders and was not applied equally in all details in all localities. None the less, the regulatory powers of the state expanded considerably – we may consider this an intensification of governance. It may not have been a new repertoire of measures and they may previously have been implemented by other means,[110] but as a set of state activities this is clearly an expansion, building on earlier uses of political power. The expanding range of state activities was not the result of 'central' aspiration, however, and did not require a victory over the localities. It was justified in terms of beliefs about the patriarchal basis of social order, although this did not benefit patriarchs alone and the implementation of these measures also gave force to other values, such as those of neighbourliness and harmony, for example.

FROM PATRIARCHS TO PATRICIANS: LOCAL GOVERNMENT IN RESTORATION ENGLAND

After 1660 the poor law system was nearly complete, there were few prosecutions for witchcraft and the problem of vagrancy was receding. Levels of litigation were declining, or at least ceasing to rise, although they remained at very high levels. Moral panics, dearth, pestilence, litigation: a society in which these are less prevalent is clearly one in which tensions are reduced. Restoration England was a more comfortable place for the well-off than Elizabethan England had been. This lies behind a paradox noted above. In so many ways this seems to be a

---

[108] HEH, EL 233, quotation at fo. 3. In the course of the dispute, the tenants made use of the manor court and attempted various proofs of custom in order to protect their interests.

[109] S. Hindle, 'Persuasion and protest in the Caddington common enclosure dispute 1635–1639', *PP*, 158 (1998), 37–78.   [110] McIntosh, *Controlling*; Spufford, 'Puritanism'.

'less-governed' society. Privy council oversight was gone, all courts seem to have seen less business than earlier in the century and magisterial activity was changing – petty sessions were of increasing significance and the greater gentry were beginning to withdraw from the magistracy.[111] There are institutional explanations for this contrast. For example, the administrative efficiency and probity of local governors was increasingly liable to legal review rather than privy council oversight. This was done before Kings Bench using writs of *certiorari* and *mandamus*.[112] But in part this is also an illusion caused by the success of the earlier response. Many aspects of social order had been protected by spectacular intervention, or calls for it, in the period before 1640, but in the later period these fears were met through routine, institutionalised and self-activating local means. The demons of restoration England were papists and sectaries – it was they who threatened to bring down civil confusion, not the sinful and rootless poor or the marginal driven to the exercise of supernatural power.[113]

In part this was a product of the routinisation of government by local officeholders. In 1666 the Chester corporation ordered justices to undertake monthly inspections of their wards in order to prevent the arrival of poor and potentially chargeable immigrants. Neglectful beadles were to be punished.[114] In the years that followed, routine enforcement of other civic obligations was promoted to prevent fire, or to clean the streets for example.[115] This is a minor example of a more general phenomenon, observable in rural areas too, that is the routinisation of even the lowest levels of administration in the restoration period. Overseers of the poor, surveyors of the highway, churchwardens and petty constables all seem to have acted diligently to implement legisla-

---

[111] The effectiveness of the privy council is open to question, of course: see D. Hirst, 'The privy council and the problem of enforcement in the 1620s', *JBS*, 18 (1978), 46–66; B. W. Quintrell, 'Government in perspective: Lancashire and the privy council, 1570–1640', *Transactions of the Historic Society of Lancashire and Cheshire*, 131 (1982 for 1981), 35–62, esp. pp. 39–41. For the failure to enforce accurate subsidy valuations see M. J. Braddick, *Parliamentary Taxation in Seventeenth-Century England: Local Administration and Response*, Royal Historical Society, Studies in History, 70 (Woodbridge, 1994), 105–17.

[112] N. Landau, 'Country matters: *The Growth of Political Stability* a quarter-century on', *Albion*, 25 (1993), 261–74, esp. pp. 267–9. For the legal context see E. G. Henderson, *Foundations of English Administrative Law: Certiorari and Mandamus in the Seventeenth Century* (Cambridge, Mass., 1963).

[113] See, for example, Forster's account of the shifting focus of the efforts of restoration justices, away from personal regulation to matters of routine punctuated by bouts of religious persecution: 'Government in provincial England under the later Stuarts', *TRHS*, 5th series, 33 (1983), 29–48, esp. pp. 32–8. See also Forster, *East Riding Justices of the Peace in the Seventeenth Century*, East Yorkshire Local History Society Series, 30 (1973), 65–6. For religious persecution see below, pp. 314–33.   [114] CCRO, AB/2 fo. 156v (9/11/1666).

[115] For example, CCRO, AB/2 fos. 166r (7/1/1670); 169r–169v (28/10/70); 170v–171r (13/1/71).

tion and to prosecute crime in the century after 1640, and this without much direction from the centre. In part it was to do with rewards and punishments offered by statutes, but in larger part it was to do with a more general process of regularisation in local government. Magistrates took an active role in appointing and monitoring the work of village officers and the high constables. Procedures were routinised – the use of printed warrants, for example, bears testimony to a broader process. Monthly meetings and petty sessions contributed to the sense that local government was routinely monitored. Minor officers were required to provide written answers to presentments on general as well as particular matters of local government and all areas of activity were tightened by the application of oaths. But as important as this pressure from above was the pressure from within the villages themselves. Vestries forced constables to be accountable and took the initiative in many areas of policy: local people 'acted of their own accord, without requiring prodding from higher officials'.[116] In fact, magistrates and judges were sometimes prompted by village initiatives – it was the substantial middling sort that brought business before them. 'To understand the growing power of the state in later seventeenth- and early eighteenth-century England it is thus necessary to appreciate not just the role of county elites or of the state's new bureaucrats, but also to take into account the often willing compliance of parish vestries and their officers.'[117]

What produced this willingness? In part, but only in part, it was probably force of habit.[118] More important was the fact that 'on a growing number of occasions the laws and policies of the state were viewed as serving . . . [the interests of substantial parishioners] and providing them with a means to deal with particular problems'.[119] Sporadically, this administration was capable of quite dramatic intervention in social life. During the 1650s, England stubbornly refused to be remade in a godlier image, a contrast with the progress of reform in Scotland. Catechising and preaching had a limited impact and the reformation of manners largely failed. Some initiatives were ambitious,

---

[116] J. Kent, 'The centre and the localities: state formation and parish government in England circa 1640–1740', *HJ*, 38 (1995), 363–404, quotation at p. 394. See also L. K. J. Glassey, 'Local government', in C. Jones (ed.), *Britain in the First Age of Party 1680–1750: Essays Presented to Geoffrey Holmes* (London, 1987), 151–72, at pp. 161–3. For a local example see A. Rogers (ed.), *Coming into Line: Local Government in Clayworth, 1674–1714*, University of Nottingham, Centre for Local History, Record Series, 2 (Nottingham, 1979). For printed warrants see Braddick, *Parliamentary*, p. 172 n. 23. By the 1740s, it seems, printed forms were available to constables, returning standard negatives to the fourteen enquiries routinely made of them by quarter sessions: M. G. Davies, *The Enforcement of the English Apprenticeship Laws: A Study in Applied Mercantilism 1563–1642* (Cambridge, Mass., 1956), 251. [117] Kent, 'State formation', p. 403.
[118] Ibid., p. 403. [119] Ibid., p. 395.

but they were localised and intermittent. This has been attributed to a failure of will among the godly, the rarity of godly magistrates and the lack of initiative from within villages and towns: 'Community solidarity evidently proved stronger than godly zeal.'[120] Individual puritans pursued their faith as an internal affair and activists appear to have been restrained by communal considerations. The result was that, except 'around the homes of the minority of activist J.P.s, swearers and profaners of the sabbath seem to have been less subject to molestation in the 1650s than they had been before the war; so too, once the economic crisis eased in the early 1650s, were drunks and even . . . alehouse-keepers'.[121]

After 1689 greater success seems to have been achieved, especially in London, by organised lobbies, the Societies for the Reformation of Manners. The campaign had a providential origin – it was an appropriate response to the deliverance of the nation from the popery and arbitrary government threatened by James II. But as the campaign developed prosecutions tended to centre on social regulation rather than religious reform in the strict sense. Thus, sabbath-breaking, swearing and cursing lost ground to the more generally supported campaigns against prostitution. In part, this had a practical explanation – swearing, in particular, was difficult to prosecute. It was also, though, a response to pressure from respectable inhabitants, annoyed by the disruption of their neighbourhoods caused by prostitution. In this way, it is possible to view the campaign as a response to social problems in the capital. Population growth in London continued to produce the social tensions elsewhere associated with the earlier period. Thus, the 'reformation of manners campaigns tapped into an existing (and growing) set of concerns about the state of social relations in London, and Londoners who were worried about these problems used the rhetoric of the reformers and practical support provided by the Societies to address them'.[122]

In respect of the importance of providential rhetoric and its direction against the sinful and disorderly poor this campaign resembles the

---

[120] D. Hirst, 'The failure of Godly rule in the English Republic', *PP*, 132 (1991), 33–66, at p. 60.
[121] Ibid., p. 64. For accounts giving emphasis to increased activism rather than the failure to create a new Jerusalem see A. Hughes, *Politics, Society and Civil War in Warwickshire, 1620–1660* (Cambridge, 1987), esp. pp. 282–90; Hughes, *Godly Reformation and its Opponents in Warwickshire, 1640–1662*, Dugdale Society Occasional Papers, 35 (Stratford-upon-Avon, 1993), esp. pp. 5–6, 10–18; C. D. Gilbert, 'Magistracy and ministry in Cromwellian England: the case of King's Norton, Worcestershire', *Midland History*, 23 (1998), 71–83.
[122] R. B. Shoemaker, 'Reforming the City: the reformation of manners campaign in London, 1690–1738', in L. Davison, T. Hitchcock, T. Keirn and R. B. Shoemaker (eds.), *Stilling the Grumbling Hive: the Response to Social and Economic Problems in England, 1689–1750* (Stroud, 1992), 99–120, quotation at p. 114.

earlier reformation of manners, discussed above.[123] In restoration London the procedures for the policing of immorality seem to have resembled those current in the earlier period too. During the later campaign for reformation of manners, however, there were procedural differences which seem congruent with other changes in local government in this period. Although the Societies for Reformation of Manners were dominated by respectable householders they increasingly acted by remote control, employing professional informers to do the work for them. To this extent the campaigns reflect a more general process of the 'decommunalisation' of policing. In this new context 'knowledge of the judicial system was more effective than godly zeal'. As a whole, therefore, the campaigns were 'encouraging and further institutionalising the process whereby policing was transformed from a system involving the compulsory, amateur participation of every householder in the community to one reliant by the mid eighteenth century . . . simply on the levy of an annual rate and the salaried employment of a small group of dedicated officers'.[124]

There were further important changes in the way that local government operated in this period. Regular parliamentary sittings, particularly after 1689, meant that parliament provided the obvious source of legislation. Eighteenth-century social policy proceeded by permissive parliamentary legislation which did not insist on local implementation.[125] Local interest groups sought parliamentary backing for their policy initiatives, interests to which prudent MPs were sensitive. As a result, parliament after 1689 'was evolving as an institution able to accommodate local economic and social needs through legislation, while at the same time providing a forum for the resolution of conflicts which such initiatives frequently generated'.[126] The transformation in

[123] For providentialism in the 1690s see C. Rose, 'Providence, Protestant union and godly reformation in the 1690s', *TRHS*, 6th series, 3 (1993), 151–69; T. Claydon, *William III and the Godly Revolution* (Cambridge, 1996). For dissonant voices in London's print and oral culture see R. E. Walker, '"Ordinary and common discourses": the impact of the glorious revolution on political discussion in London, 1688–1694', Ph.D. dissertation, University of Sheffield (1998). Other readings were later given greater prominence: K. Wilson, 'Inventing revolution: 1688 and eighteenth-century popular politics', *JBS*, 28 (1989), 349–86.

[124] F. Dabhoiwala, 'Prostitution and police in London, *c.* 1660–*c.* 1760', DPhil Dissertation, University of Oxford (1995), 120–40, 168–72, quotation at p. 172. For the continuities see also Shoemaker, 'Reforming'; Ingram, 'Reformation of manners'.

[125] J. Innes, 'The domestic face of the military-fiscal state: government and society in eighteenth-century Britain', in L. Stone (ed.), *An Imperial State at War: Britain from 1689–1815* (London, 1994), 96–127, esp. 104–5, 107.

[126] S. Handley, 'Local legislative initiatives for economic and social development in Lancashire, 1689–1731', *Parliamentary History*, 9 (1990), 14–37, quotation at p. 37. See also T. Keirn, 'Parliament, legislation and the regulation of English textile industries, 1689–1714', in Davison, *et al.*, *Stilling*, 1–24.

the quantity of legislation is indicative of the broader importance of this change: in 203 years from 1485 to 1688 parliament passed 2,700 acts (excluding those of the period 1640–60); in the 112 years from 1689 to 1801 it passed more than 13,600.[127] Regular parliamentary sessions also allowed for piecemeal, but cumulatively significant, reform of criminal justice designed to make it easier to bring prosecutions and to secure convictions. An important component of this was to increase the active role of government in apprehending offenders, another stage, perhaps, in the decommunalisation of the criminal law.[128] The cabinet took responsibility for managing death at Tyburn, making pardons a matter of routine business and less a product of arbitrary decision-making. This, it has been suggested, 'reflected a style of governance more closely suited to the constitutional monarchy emerging after 1689 and signaled a change in the way power was exercised and managed'.[129]

To an extent, then, that part of the state in the hands of local officeholders was 'reactive', as was parliament in relation to social and economic policy, and the degree of local initiative had increased. The success or failure of privy council policies had depended, before 1640, on local compliance. After 1660 a more regularised routine of local government gave a more 'institutional' appearance to the activities of officeholders. And now, increasingly, they were prompted by local concerns. The absence of privy council activity did not signal a reduction in the level of local government activity. The sense of increasing routinisation or decommunalisation is captured by Landau's distinction between patriarchal and patrician government, between a king in miniature and 'a legal administrator concerned with orderly government in an atmosphere more closely approximating to that of a civil service board'.[130] Commissions of the peace increased in size and their

---

[127] J. Hoppitt, 'Patterns of parliamentary legislation, 1660–1800', *HJ*, 39 (1996), 109–31, at p. 109. I am grateful to John Styles for pointing out the significance of this change to me.

[128] J. M. Beattie, 'London crime and the making of the "Bloody Code" 1689–1718', in Davison *et al.*, *Stilling*, 49–76.

[129] J. M. Beattie, 'The cabinet and the management of death at Tyburn after the revolution of 1688–1689', in L. G. Schwoerer (ed.), *The Revolution of 1688–1689: Changing Perspectives* (Cambridge, 1992), 218–33, quotation at p. 232. This depersonalisation of the pardoning process is analogous, perhaps, to the transformation of a royal debt into a public debt during the same period, for which see below, pp. 257–60, 265–8.

[130] Landau, paraphrased by L. K. J. Glassey, *Politics and the Appointment of Justices of the Peace 1675–1720* (Oxford, 1979), 163. See N. Landau, *The Justices of the Peace 1679–1760* (Berkeley, 1984), esp. pp. 1–6, 359–62. Landau's distinction is this:

> The patriarchal justice was the leader of his neighbourhood, and his leadership was based on his prestige and power as a private individual in that neighbourhood. The patrician justice was more distanced from the specific local community which he governed. Ideally, he was disinterested and therefore unaffected by the judgements and administrative

procedures became more routine, allowing, perhaps the withdrawal of leading figures.[131] This development of self-activating provincial government in relation to social and economic policy can be seen as the counterpart of the development of the more specialised fiscal and military institutions which developed in this period (considered in chapters 5 and 6). The power of subordinate officers in the excise administration was independent of their social status, and this made even clearer the distinction between political and social power. The result was that dignitaries like John, Baron Ashburnham, had to accommodate themselves to the real power of social inferiors in administrative positions. At the same time, his ability to put people into such positions – his patronage – had to be exercised with an eye to administrative effectiveness.[132] In any case, by Walpole's era 'the structural differentiation of England's central and local government had endowed central government with its own institutions to administer the concerns that were now considered national. And, likewise, local government had developed its own institutions to deal with the concerns regarded as its province.'[133] In the process, the routinisation, and formalisation of local government, and the beginning of a tendency towards elite withdrawal from active magistracy, fostered a clearer sense of the distinction between social pre-eminence and political power.

decisions that he made.... [T]he patrician model placed less emphasis on the private ties which bound the justice to his local community and more emphasis on the institutional and cultural ties which bound him to his fellow justices. The patriarchal ideal enabled the justice to think of his judicial service in the context of specific local demands ... and of his relation to specific individuals. But the patrician ideal encouraged the justice to regard his official duty as service to a wider and less limited public. So the evolution of patriarchal to patrician model governor entailed greater definition of the nature of governmental power. Local government became less an extension of myriad varieties of local authority wielded by powerful private individuals and less a rather vaguely defined control of specific and unique neighbourhoods. Instead, local government became more the execution of tasks. *Justices*, p. 360. See also Lee's distinction between social leaders (exercising authority by virtue of their birth and social status) and public persons (dependent not on social standing but on their experience of administrative and public life): J. M. Lee, *Social Leaders and Public Persons: A Study of County Government in Cheshire since 1888* (Oxford, 1963). I am grateful to John Morrill for this reference.

131 Glassey, 'Local government', pp. 159–65; J. M. Rosenheim, 'County governance and elite withdrawal in Norfolk, 1660–1720', in Beier, Cannadine and Rosenheim (eds.), *First Modern Society*, 95–125.

132 C. W. Brooks, 'John, 1st Baron Ashburnham, and the state', *Historical Research*, 60 (1987), 64–79; Brooks, 'Interest, patronage and professionalism: John, 1st Baron Ashburnham, Hastings and the revenue services', *Southern History*, 9 (1987), 64–79.

133 Landau, 'Country matters', p. 267. Although, as we will see in chapters 5 and 6, fiscal and military mobilisation still depended on participation from officeholders, and local government was not independent of central government oversight. For further discussion of this point see below, pp. 270–80.

Conclusion

The measures taken to deal with 'problems of order' between 1550 and 1640 demonstrate the potency of magisterial government. The hierarchy of local officeholders accorded closely to the hierarchy of local social status. The conduct of officeholders was tested against, and justified in terms of, the values that were thought to be constitutive of social order: the magistrate was the father of his country, the constable the representative of the village elite. These values accorded well with measures designed to preserve that social order. The evolution of the Elizabethan poor laws represented an abiding response to the changing reality and perceptions of poverty. They grew out of the innovations of active local governors and were selectively implemented throughout the country, in response to local conditions. Alongside these new arrangements some more spectacular measures of social policy were implemented, again drawing on the political resources of local government. Attempts to reform the manners of the poor were intensified, if they were not unprecedented, and it seems that the regulation of sexual relations may have had a significant effect on levels of illegitimacy. Although houses of correction and provost marshals did not deliver on the hopes that were held for them, they represent the high-water mark of an ambitious drive for social discipline. The effects of that drive were felt by large numbers of migrants, particularly young adult males, and by the parents, particularly the mothers, of illegitimate children. Not only did statute follow local practice in relation to many of these measures, but local officeholders were able to exceed their formal legal powers, drawing on a more general sense of the legitimacy of policies intended to protect the social order. The introduction of the poor law and the reformation of manners drew on the active participation not just of the gentry, but of the respectable middling sort, and the influence of these people ensured that the civil, ecclesiastical and criminal law too, were active bulwarks against the perceived threats to social order. Most

172

spectacularly, and also reflective of the broadly patriarchal uses of law and administration, witchcraft began to be prosecuted as a secular crime. However, people at almost all levels of society participated in the prosecution of other felonies and misdemeanors which were less clearly reflective of specifically patriarchal conceptions of social order. The legal process depended on participation at all levels, and this can be used as a measure of legitimacy: actions understood to be indicative of consent.

This participation was not disinterested ('autonomous'), however. The terms on which it was forthcoming served to inscribe onto administrative action the imprint of widely held social values. The other face of these disciplinary innovations was paternal protection, of course. Patriarchs had responsibilities as well as authority, as the ideal of hospitality or the practice of the plague orders demonstrates. Interventions in the grain market offered protection to the harvest-sensitive and the courts offered protection to apprentices. We might note, however, that one of the few aspects of this bundle of initiatives and measures to raise real legal queries was the policy of searches for grain – these certainly seem to have been of more concern than questions about the legality of some committals to houses of correction, for example. Thus, another one of the criteria of legitimacy, legal validity, does not always appear to have been central to the scrutiny of the activities of officeholders. Where their activities were justifiable in terms of beliefs current among the most influential groups in society at large (in particular, but not exclusively, propertied men), then legal validity was a less pressing issue. In effect, the relatively less autonomous functions of the state depended less squarely on formal legal warrant.

After 1640 these 'patriarchal' interventions became increasingly routine and less spectacular. Although local government did not become bureaucratised it became regularised to an extent that tempts some observers to describe it as 'professional'. Larger commissions of the peace with decreasing levels of participation ceded influence to conscientious minor gentry. Much activity was conducted in increasingly regular petty sessions. Poor rates became universal and the social position of virtually all the subjects of the kingdom could be assessed in relation to it, either as payers or recipients. The implementation of the settlement laws entailed, and may have been intended to enable, the monitoring of internal migration. The threat of vagrancy was receding and the chances of successfully prosecuting a witch decreasing. The reformation of manners campaigns from the 1690s onwards reflected increasing concern about the corrosive effects of sin and disorder. To that extent, they display some marked similarities with the godly magistracy of the early Stuart period. However, there were procedural innovations, reflecting changes in the policing of the metropolis more generally, which also seem to point to institutionalisation, regularisation and, even, 'professionalisation'. In particular, the societies tended to hire people with specialised knowledge to do their dirty work for them, a significant measure of 'decommunalisation' of the legal system. This was probably far less marked elsewhere, however.

It has been suggested, then, that this domestic order can usefully be described as 'patriarchal'. The visions of order that this term embraces had implications for relations between men and women, old and young and rich and poor. Patriarchal legitimations did not simply empower patriarchs, however. The role of women as arbiters of local reputation made a central contribution to the development of witchcraft prosecutions and some women were thus empowered within the limits set by the broader contours of patriarchal order. Indeed, the practice of witchcraft was itself a source of power for those excluded from influence by other means. There was also more to local government than patriarchal order. The values inscribed in the actions of the criminal law worked not just against those who threatened patriarchal order but also against strangers. Neighbourliness was a more embracing social ethic than just the proper subordination of wife to husband or servant to master, and it was of considerable importance to legal and administrative process. It was not simply a negative value either: civic initiatives included measures to prevent fire and plague, for example, terrors which struck against all groups in society. The great increase in litigation in the first part of our period bears testimony not to state building, nor even to the importance of the middling sort in promoting new standards of behaviour and civility using the resources of the state. Instead, it bears testimony to the usefulness of the law as a social resource, a means of regulating and mediating conflict and dispute. It is the net effect of the use of these resources, requiring a high degree of participation, which coloured the outcomes as patriarchal: a conscious effort of will by a particular group could not have achieved as much. Central to the success of this patriarchy was the participation of those who were formally subordinate – the middling sort, and those among women and the poor anxious to lay claim to respectability. The activities of this state favoured the interests of those with significant property and of males, but it depended on the participation of others.

The issue is also complicated by the fact that patriarchal notions changed. In particular, it seems that, in later Stuart England, the analogy between household order and political order in general was for most people looser. Many of those who had been most active before 1640 in local initiatives, and in implementing national initiatives locally, were godly magistrates, men fired by a Calvinist vision of the alliance of magistracy and ministry. It may have been that the experience of godly failure in the 1650s made such ambitions seem less plausible. We certainly hear of fewer attempts after 1660 to create a city on a hill in places like Dorchester or Gloucester. Their activities had also drawn on humanist ideals of civic activism, of course, and this may have lost purchase in the later seventeenth century.[1]

On matters in which there was material interest, or a moral consensus (or something approaching it) among governing social and political elites, innovative uses of political power could be implemented quite effectively. In some cases this normative activity led to very radical extensions of the power of the state over the individual. There is a sense with the stereotype of the witch and of the beggar of a kind of slow-motion moral panic, in which an exaggerated and inaccurate image of a marginal group assumed such significance that normal political, legal and moral categories collapsed or were over-ridden by new criminal processes. Although there is a danger of overstating the frequency with which this legislation was actually employed, these two cases do perhaps provide exemplars of the political power of this state if supported by a consensus among influential groups.

[1] This book was largely completed before the publication of P. Slack, *From Reformation to Improvement: Public Welfare in Early Modern England* (Oxford, 1998). Slack offers a more finely-grained account of public policy in relation to social order, resting on similar assumptions but drawing out the chronological and intellectual complexities more fully. He characterises periods of innovation in terms of the languages in which they were articulated and the institutions through which they were expressed. A similar exercise could be conducted for the fiscal-military state, too.

PART III

The fiscal-military state

Introduction

Political authority is, intrinsically, territorial. All political authorities are defined territorially, and they face an imperative to protect this territory. This is, in principle, an autonomous need of the state – something that operates independently of vested or sectional interests. Of course, the definition of territorial interests might create vested interests – for international traders or arms manufacturers, for example – but in the early modern period they were relatively removed from the interests of local officeholders. The administrative measures taken in the light of these imperatives were also less easy to justify in terms of their patriarchal obligations. As we will see, local officeholders acted with less alacrity in relation to these demands and this was a potentially disastrous feature of the functioning of the state in early modern England – relatively autonomous functions of government were not well served by the principal available agencies of political power.

In the sixteenth century the widespread adoption of gunpowder weapons, on land and at sea, made war technologically more complex. The skills and equipment required became more specialised and this had implications for the cost and organisation of military forces. At the same time, warfare was increasing in both frequency and intensity. The relative indifference to fiscal-military needs in the localities may have arisen from the fact that England had natural sea defences, and its consequences were certainly ameliorated by that fact. None the less, persistent attempts were made to improve the defensive and offensive capabilities of the state in England which produced considerable political friction. Activists in both local and national government, alive to the need to modernise the kingdom's military capacity, ran up against the reluctance of many local officeholders (and parliaments) to shoulder the burdens. The result was an increasing pressure on notions of service and duty to the monarchy, and an increasing stress on the necessity of military activity. It was also associated with new and more specialised

177

offices. Their effectiveness was limited, however, by problems of legitimacy. There was not a continuous local demand for their activities and
so they could not draw on a strong sense that their activities were
justified in terms of the beliefs of local society. As a result, their activities
rested more squarely on their legal warrant and this laid them open to
formal legal challenge. As a result of all this there was, before 1640, a
contrast in fortunes between the success of military-fiscal innovation,
and of innovations made to protect social order. The fiscal-military
capacity of the state was transformed in the 1640s, and this was associated with increasingly specialised institutions, legitimated with reference to ideas of necessity and national interest. In the later seventeenth
century, as we have seen, administrative innovation in relation to the
social order was relatively unspectacular. The development of the
fiscal-military state, however, was rapid and of long-term consequence.

Chapter 5 deals with the military capacity of the state. It considers
military mobilisation through officeholders – the militia and expeditionary forces – and the attempts made to mobilise naval resources in
broadly analogous ways. There were some achievements here, but it
was the military revolution of the 1640s which was the most significant
single moment in the development of the armed forces.[1] It spawned a
new, and sustained, capacity for military mobilisation and this had
implications for the role of the militia. This transformation of military
capacity rested on a transformation of the financial basis of government,
which is the subject of chapter 6. This chapter considers first the
relatively chaotic response of government to rising expenditures before
1640 and then the more rational, specialised and effective system that
emerged from the military crises of the 1640s and 1690s. It is in relation
to financial measures that issues of legitimacy were most pressing, and
chapter 6 also, therefore, considers the changing means by which these
political actions were legitimated. In all, it is argued, changes in the form
and functioning of the state in response to these pressures can be
considered to have been modernising in the Weberian sense. New,
specialised institutions, legitimated with reference to political claims of
necessity, national interest and rationality, seem closer to the model of a

---

[1] This book was completed before the publication of J. S. Wheeler's important study *The Making of a World Power: War and the Military Revolution in Seventeenth-Century England* (Stroud, 1999), with the result that I was unable to take full account of its many important research findings. Although our overall interpretations are very similar, Professor Wheeler's detailed study of financial and military matters in the mid-seventeenth century adds considerably to the brief account of that crucial period given here.

modern state than the forms of state activity called forth by problems of social order. Although we would hesitate to call the state in 1700 modern, to the extent that it was modernising it was a response to the pressure for fiscal and military mobilisation.

CHAPTER 5

The state and military mobilisation

The principal military resource in Elizabethan England was the militia, which was increasingly in the hands of the lieutenancy and this is discussed in the first section of the chapter. The impact of changing technology on early modern warfare created a pressure for specialisation – soldiers were required to deal with increasingly complicated equipment and tactical requirements. This pressure resulted in the development of trained bands from within the general muster of able-bodied men. Members of the bands carried equipment that was both expensive and technically complex, and were drilled by men with specialised knowledge. These initiatives were expressed partly in a patriarchal idiom, appealing to martial values associated with gentility – lieutenants and their deputies were, as we have seen, eminent local men whose position was justified by their social prestige. But the tasks they oversaw were also justified in a language of necessity. Doubts about the legality of these initiatives were not, apparently, assuaged by appeal to these broader beliefs, and the progress of militia reform was limited and halting. The second section briefly considers expeditionary forces, which were also the responsibility of local officeholders and which fell foul of similar tensions. The third part of the chapter examines the pressure to establish a specialised royal navy consisting of ships which were functionally distinct from the merchant ships. Here again, the pressure for specialisation and the associated costs raised legal doubts which were also not completely allayed by appeal to the language of necessity. By 1640 reform of the militia and the navy had made some progress, but these achievements were dwarfed by the massive scale of military mobilisation during the 1640s. This mobilisation permanently changed the military capacity of the state, and provided the basis for a much improved capacity to undertake military campaigns after 1640. This military revolution, and the implications it had for the militia, are considered in the final two sections of the chapter. Behind this massively improved capacity for military mobilisation lay a profound financial transformation, which is considered in chapter 6.

In response to military challenge specialised institutions developed to provide adequate defensive resources. They were not, however, entirely different from the unpaid magistracies and constabularies, and they were as dependent on local participation for their effectiveness. This participation appears to have been more difficult to secure and, moreover, the formal authority by which officeholders acted was not always clear or uncontested. Here the problem was two-fold: firstly, the powers of the lieutenancy, for example, did not have full statutory backing and were, to an extent, supplementary to existing authorities; secondly, the relationship between the powers of the lieutenancy and other bodies (quarter sessions and militia commissioners, for example) was correspondingly unclear. As a result, military reform was hampered, although not altogether stymied. Military mobilisation was grudging and this pointed up the problems of legitimating the activities of its agents, the lieutenants.

The legal position of the lieutenancy was complex. By the middle of the sixteenth century there were two parallel means of recruitment to the land forces. The crown could call on the services of individual lords and their retinues in a 'quasi-feudal' way, or could raise troops on a 'national' basis through gentry commissions.[1] The social basis of 'quasi-feudal' recruitment was disappearing, however, with the decline of great households and the crown was reluctant to support a military nobility. There was also potential for conflict between the two. From 1535 onwards commissioners were appointed to hold musters in order to check that individuals were observing their obligations under the Statute of Winchester, but in many cases they spared their own tenants or the tenants of lords who might be called on to furnish retinues of their own. The commissioners struggled with the consequences of the decline of archery too, which was the statutory basis of the obligations of many people.[2] Reforms in 1549 prefigured later changes (the appointment of lords lieutenant and a proposal to form bands of trained soldiers under

---

[1] J. Goring, 'Social change and military decline in mid-Tudor England', *History*, 60 (1975), 185–97. For this distinction see p. 188.   [2] Ibid.

the direction of professional captains),[3] but the real basis of Elizabethan activity was a statute of 1558. This brought the 'quasi-feudal' obligation within the national system by introducing a national rate for the provision of horse and armour while in the same year commissioners were instructed not to spare the tenants of lords and gentlemen in making their assessments.[4] As a consequence, a unitary national system was established, although in the emergencies of 1569, 1588 and 1599 private levies were raised as well.[5] In this sense, militia reform under Elizabeth and the early Stuarts represented a move away from dependence on the armed baronage and towards a national defence force.[6]

By 1558, then, there was a national system of recruitment, operating under gentry commissioners and regulated, in part at least, by statute. However, the main vehicle for military change in our period was the lieutenancy, 'by far the most important development in county administration during the sixteenth century'.[7] The lieutenants, as we have seen, were of very eminent status and their deputies 'were drawn from the top ranks of resident landowners'.[8] In this sense the lieutenancy was like the rest of the officeholding structure of local government: 'The lieutenancy formed part of a distinctly local power structure in which a provincial hierarchy . . . worked to preserve a traditional system of political and social values that emphasized autonomy and stability.'[9] To some extent, as we will see, these local responsibilities were in tension with the demands of the crown: activist lieutenants ran the risk of a loss of local prestige.

In seeking to improve the militia the lieutenancy pursued several related reforms, for which the legal warrant was not always clear. Musters had to be held with greater regularity, and this was to provide the basis for improvements in the number of men, quality of equipment and training. Of course these things had financial implications too, and

---

[3] For lieutenants, see A. G. R. Smith, *The Government of Elizabethan England* (London, 1967), 86–90; G. S. Thomson, *Lords Lieutenants in the Sixteenth Century* (London, 1923). For the 1549 scheme see Goring, 'Social change', pp. 194–5.

[4] This may be the origin of the distinction between the common or town armour and the private or freehold arms which a number of writers have noted: L. O. Boynton, *The Elizabethan Militia 1558–1638* (London, 1967), 249–50; D. P. Carter, 'The "exact militia" in Lancashire, 1625–1640', *Northern History*, 11 (1975), 87–106, at p. 97; A. Fletcher, *Reform in the Provinces: The Government of Stuart England* (London, 1986), 310.   [5] Goring, 'Social change', pp. 196–7.

[6] I. Roy, 'The profession of arms', in W. Prest (ed.), *The Professions of Early Modern England* (London, 1987), 181–219, makes this argument in more detail, esp. pp. 185–93.

[7] P. Williams, 'The crown and the counties', in C. Haigh (ed.), *The Reign of Elizabeth I* (London, 1984), 125–46, 275–7, at p. 126.   [8] Ibid., p. 127.

[9] V. L. Stater, *Noble Government: The Stuart Lord Lieutenancy and the Transformation of English Politics* (Athens, Ga., 1994), 11.

lieutenants had powers to raise rates. As we have seen, the lieutenancy was not simply a military institution, but its military functions involved two potentially highly unpopular tasks: the enforcement of musters and raising rates. The power to do these things did not really enjoy statutory backing and this contributed to the problems experienced by the lieutenancy, especially during the 1590s, the later 1620s and the 1630s. Those hostile to the practical implications of militia reform could appeal to law and those uneasy about the legality of the powers entrusted to lieutenants might be led to resist the practical measures of reform. The obligation to serve the monarch was Anglo-Saxon in origin, and had been extended or clarified by a number of statutes. Notable among them were the 1181 Assize of Arms, the 1285 Statute of Winchester and 1558 Statute which laid out the military obligations of every subject according to wealth and status. In practice, however, these statutory guidelines of military obligation were regularly exceeded by the lieutenants, who were acting by direct commission from the monarch in council.[10] In going 'far beyond' the statutory rates, however, it 'does not follow that they acted illegally, for the lieutenancy was given statutory recognition in 1558 and so, presumably were its virtually unlimited discretionary powers in matters of defence and security'.[11] None the less, some ambiguity attended the activities of the lord lieutenant, and this was sometimes expressed when militia obligations were pressed particularly hard. The rates made by the lieutenants and their deputies were enforceable through quarter sessions, but as the lieutenancy assumed more complete control over the militia, in the 1580s, sessions in some counties became more reluctant to offer this backing.[12]

Although lieutenants and their deputies enjoyed local status and prestige, their effectiveness was limited, at least potentially, by these legal difficulties. This, and the essential unpleasantness of their tasks, hampered attempts at practical reform. Measures of reform centred on attempts to enforce musters, to modernise weapons, and to improve training and the provision of horse. All these things were problematic. Musters were a considerable chore. A general muster of the whole county force generally took men away from work for three days, a day each side of the muster being allowed for travel. From 1573 onwards men received 8d per day, and by the early seventeenth century this had

---

[10] Boynton, *Militia*, pp. 7–12; C. G. Cruickshank, *Elizabeth's Army*, 2nd edn (Oxford, 1966), 3–13.
[11] Boynton, *Militia*, p. 72.
[12] A. H. Smith, *County and Court Government and Politics in Norfolk 1558–1603* (Oxford, 1974), esp. ch. 13. See below, pp. 187–8.

reached 1s. But it was not just expense that made the musters unpopular – the local disruption was considerable and musters were frequently postponed because of the harvest or bad weather. An alternative was to muster parts of the county separately but this gave rise to evasion. For example, arms and equipment were 'borrowed', that is the same weapons were shown in different places on different days in order to conceal shortcomings in provision.[13] In the absence of an effective system for identifying weapons it was difficult to prevent this except by ensuring that all men were mustered simultaneously.[14] Enforcement of the muster put considerable powers in the hands of lieutenants – to imprison for ten days, to impose fines of up to 40s and to punish absentees or 'querulous or mutinous' militia men at their discretion.[15] In practice, much of this was left to quarter sessions, but it again reflects the considerable personal authority of the lieutenant which was not necessarily trammelled by statute or sessions.

Musters were intended to enable the improvement of equipment and training by allowing regular inspections. 'Rapid developments in offensive weapons made a deep impression upon sixteenth-century opinion. It seemed to contemporaries that the nature of war was changing almost overnight. It seemed equally clear that England had not been keeping up with the changes.'[16] Before the late 1560s little progress had been made in modernising weapons. One of the chief concerns in this modernisation was the adoption of gunpowder weapons at the expense (ultimately) of archery. In 1567 it was proposed that the 'royal arquebusiers' should be formed, training in the use of firearms and financed by paying audiences on show-days. In 1569 a serious attempt was made to implement the scheme, funded this time by making people of particular social status participate at their own expense.[17] This was typical of Elizabethan government in many ways, in trying to link service to status. The arquebusiers scheme failed, however, and after 1569 reforming activity focused on the militia, spurred on in particular by the shortcomings in the militia revealed by the response to a rebellion in the north of the country, the rising of the northern earls. Progress in the adoption of more modern weapons was slow, however, and required constant nego-

---

[13] Boynton, *Militia*, pp. 8–30. For borrowing see also HEH, HM 30881 fo. 71r.

[14] A number of schemes to mark weapons were attempted in the early Stuart period in order to prevent borrowing, to disarm militia men when not in service and to keep track of expensive equipment: R. W. Stewart, 'Arms accountability in early Stuart militia', *BIHR*, 57 (1984), 113–17. For a crown initiative in stamping weapons in 1630s see K. Sharpe, *The Personal Rule of Charles I* (London, 1992), 489.   [15] Boynton, *Militia*, pp. 28–30.   [16] Ibid., p. 53.

[17] Ibid., pp. 59–62. For a description of this, or a similar scheme, see HEH, EL 1689.

tiation and persuasion. One problem was that archery was not obviously obsolete – early firearms were unreliable and expensive – and it was
also thought to have useful social functions. The demands changed
rapidly too. After the rising in 1569, privy council pressure aimed to
increase the numbers of calivers and pikes at the expense of archers and
men carrying bills, but by the 1580s calivers were somewhat outmoded
and there was a growing preference for muskets.[18] This was even more
true after 1613 and there was further pressure to update in the 1630s.[19]
By 1589 bows were no longer part of the standard equipment of a
company and the cost of arming a company had probably risen by 50
per cent.[20] The costs of the early Stuart improvements might therefore
be considerable in counties with an activist lieutenant.[21]

Another indication of increasing specialisation was the development
of the trained bands. In 1572 the queen sought 'a perfect knowledge' of
the 'numbers, qualities, abilities and sufficiencies' of all her subjects over
sixteen years of age. She further sought 'out of that total and universal
number . . . to have a convenient and sufficient number of the most able'
to be chosen, collected, trained, armed and equipped. This was to be
achieved 'by the reasonable charge of the inhabitants of every shire' and
to provide 'for the service and defence' of the queen, her crown and the
realm 'against all attempts, both inward and outward'.[22] In Yorkshire
and other northern counties the real impetus for reform seems to have
been postponed until the 1580s, after which the earl of Huntingdon was

---

[18] Writing to justices in 1589 about shortcomings in the arms of militia men, the earl of Huntingdon urged that the shortfalls be made up with muskets rather than more dated weapons: HEH,
HM 30881, fos. 150r–150v (29/9/1589); 151r–151v (11/12/1589).

[19] Boynton, *Militia*, pp. 64–9, 72–6, 219, 249. By 1618 the Privy Council clearly thought that the
caliver was completely outdated: *APC, 1618–1619*, p. 118 (25/4/1618). On the decline of
archery see also Cruickshank, *Elizabeth's Army*, pp. 106–8. For some failed initiatives see M. C.
Fissel, 'Tradition and invention in the early Stuart Art of War', *Journal of the Society for Army
Historical Research*, 65 (1987), 133–47. For both the persistence of archery and the continuing
pressure for modernisation, see G. P. Higgins, 'The government of early Stuart Cheshire',
Northern History, 12 (1976), 32–52, at pp. 45–6. Apparently clever innovations, such as the
Swedish 'leather' gun, took some time to prove ineffective. The leather gun was light and thus
offered considerable advantages, but the disadvantages associated with weaker barrels eventual-
ly defeated the initiative. For a discussion of their use in seventeenth-century Britain, see D.
Stevenson and D. H. Caldwell, 'Leather guns and other light artillery in mid-17th century
Scotland', *Proceedings of the Society of Antiquaries of Scotland*, 108 (1979 for 1976–7), 300–17. See G.
Parker, *The Military Revolution: Military Innovation and the Rise of the West, 1500–1800* (Cambridge,
1989), 33–5. For contemporary discussion of their use in the English civil wars see M. J.
Braddick and M. Greengrass (eds.), 'The letters of Sir Cheney Culpeper, 1641–1657', *Camden
Miscellany XXXIII*, Camden Society, 5th series, 7 (Cambridge, 1996), 105–402, at p. 179.

[20] Cruickshank, *Elizabeth's Army*, pp. 114–16.

[21] T. Cogswell, *Home Divisions: Aristocracy, the State and Provincial Conflict* (Manchester, 1998), esp. ch. 5
and Conclusion; Carter, 'Exact militia', pp. 99–105.

[22] Quoted in Cruickshank, *Elizabeth's Army*, p. 24.

an active correspondent on militia matters.[23] In general, however, the trained bands initiative probably took off earlier in most counties and is traceable to 1573, energised by fears arising from the arrival of Alva's army in the Netherlands.[24] The selection and training of a small core from within the general muster imposed yet more costs on the counties. In the 1570s the cost of equipping and training a member of the trained band was estimated variously to be between 13s 8d and £2. Given that Yorkshire, for example, was asked to produce 10,000 trained men from 1584 onwards, we can appreciate that considerable sums of money were being raised by the lieutenants on dubious legal authority.[25] Imperceptibly, we might say, a duty of service was, for many, being commuted into a cash payment to support the trained bands. The growing specialisation was also at odds with existing presumptions about the relationship between social status and service. So, for example, captains in Elizabeth's militia were admired for experience and Protestant conviction, but also for local connection. Company size reflected the status of the captain, even to the detriment of efficiency.[26]

These reforms were expensive, therefore, and there were other associated costs. In order to drill men equipped with these new weapons it was increasingly common for a muster-master with specialist knowledge to be appointed. The third earl of Huntingdon, for example, was hampered in his activities as lord lieutenant by a lack of military experience.[27] The skills required were real, of course. In September 1635, for example, Thomas Davies reported having seen two cartloads of injured men being taken away from the muster of the trained bands in Cheapside. They had been injured when a barrel of powder blew up among them 'by the necligence of some Carlesse fellowe with his mach goinge to receave Munittion'. Six had died already and forty or fifty more were 'burnte moste pittifully'.[28] Muster-masters supplemented the

---

[23] HEH, HM 30881.   [24] Boynton, *Militia*, pp. 13, 91.

[25] In Cambridgeshire it was thought to cost 1 mark per man, in Cornwall £2. The average appears to have been around £1: ibid., pp. 93, 95. For the demands in Yorkshire see Braddick, ' "Uppon this instant extraordinarie occasion": military mobilisation in Yorkshire before and after the armada', *Huntington Library Quarterly*, 61 (1998).   [26] Boynton, *Militia*, pp. 100–3.

[27] C. Cross, *The Puritan Earl: The Life of Henry Hastings, Third Earl of Huntingdon, 1536–1595* (London, 1966), 214–15, 225.

[28] HEH, EL 6547. The supply of gunpowder was in itself a difficulty: R. W. Stewart, *The English Ordnance Office: A Case-Study in Bureaucracy*, Royal Historical Society, Studies in History, 73 (Woodbridge, 1996), ch. 5. Concerns were expressed about the safety of the storage at the Tower, Cruickshank, *Elizabeth's Army*, pp. 126–9. Concern about the activities of the saltpetremen persisted throughout the period from the 1590s to the 1640s. During the latter decade it provided an opportunity to the reform-minded Hartlib circle, interested in the possibilities of manufacturing it artificially: C. Webster, *The Great Instauration: Science, Medicine and Reform 1626–1660* (London, 1975), esp. pp. 377–81.

work of the amateur captains, who were often 'absorbed in preserving their prestige' rather than in the real business of training.[29] They represented a further form of specialisation in response to military change but it was a controversial innovation – they attracted resentment and suspicion.[30] They were established by the 1580s and the council had succeeded in passing on the costs of their salary to the counties. Their appointment was at the discretion of the lieutenant and they were employed mainly to train the shot. As a result of this they also had a role in choosing men and inspecting arms and armour. But the new burden was 'generally resented and regarded as unconstitutional'. Hostility to military burdens in general sometimes came to focus on the muster-masters and refusal to pay their fees was not uncommon. In Norfolk the lieutenancy lost local support, becoming too closely associated with court policies, with outsiders such as the muster master and with the enforcement of military obligations by prerogative power in the absence of secure statutory backing.[31]

In the late 1620s men with experience in continental wars were appointed, the 'low-countries serjeants', and there were similar problems over responsibility for their wages and tensions with the local gentry.[32] A number of counties witnessed refusals to pay the muster-masters' fees in 1629.[33] In April 1635 the Shropshire grand jury presented the muster-master's salary as a grievance, claiming the office to be unnecessary. In doing so they drew on hostility in the villages and also

[29] Boynton, *Militia*, p. 106.

[30] Smith, *County and Court*, esp. pp. 277–93; T. G. Barnes, *Somerset 1625–1640: A County's Government during the 'Personal Rule'* (Chicago, 1982), esp. pp. 258–78; E. S. Cope, 'Politics without parliament: the dispute about muster masters' fees in Shropshire in the 1630s', *Huntington Library Quarterly*, 45 (1982), 271–84.

[31] Boynton, *Militia*, pp. 106–7; Smith, *County and Court*, pp. 277–93; for disputes in Somerset and Wiltshire in the early seventeenth century, ibid., pp. 336–7; Fletcher, *Reform*, pp. 314–15. For problems in Somerset in the 1630s see Barnes, *Somerset*, pp. 117–19, 263–5. In the 1630s Markham bemoaned the necessity for such an office, which demeaned military efforts by divorcing martial prowess from social prestige: Cope, 'Muster masters' fees', pp. 272–3. There was an uneasy reception of the muster master in the northern counties in May 1590. The man was recommended by the privy council but appointed by the lord lieutenant and paid by the county. Huntingdon was evidently anxious about the reception that the muster master, Captain Barton ('for his good and longe experience, and knowledge in marcyall affaiers a fytt man for that charge'), could expect: HEH, HM 30881, fos. 162v–163r. He had been careful to prepare the way for Barton in Durham too, where the muster master was well entertained. The justices there were concerned about the long-term costs of the militia, however: fo. 168r. Such schemes have precedents in the arquebusiers scheme, which had included the suggestion that old soldiers be employed to oversee training, in return for £20 p.a.: HEH, EL 1689.

[32] Barnes, *Somerset*, pp. 249–51; Carter, 'Exact militia', p. 95. For the introduction of this initiative, see B. W. Quintrell, 'Towards a "perfect militia", Warwick, Buckingham and the Essex alarum of 1625', *Transactions of the Essex Archaeological Society*, 15 (1984 for 1983), 96–105, at pp. 102–3; Fletcher, *Reform*, pp. 183–4; Higgins, 'Government', p. 45.

[33] Cope, 'Muster masters' fees', pp. 272–3.

on a long-standing sense of grievance. In fact, the issue had been avoided hitherto by not raising a rate for the muster master at all. The result was a very public division amongst the magistracy at quarter sessions, news of which quickly reached the lord lieutenant, the earl of Bridgewater, in London. The petition was denounced by the earl's steward and by one of the deputy lieutenants, but the jury was defended by other magistrates. Eventually the jurymen and two magistrates were summoned before the privy council. One of them, Sir John Corbet, was dismissed from the commission, imprisoned in the Fleet and proceeded against in Star Chamber. His chance for revenge came in 1641, when he impeached the lord lieutenant and all the privy councillors who had signed the relevant warrants.[34] This dispute reflects, to an extent, personal rivalries, but it is also indicative of how controversial militia reform could be, even when in the hands of men of established local status. The powers of lieutenants in general were, of course, a significant political issue in 1641.[35]

Reform of the horse was equally painfully achieved. In part this arose from the necessity of producing horses bred specially for war rather than agriculture, and in part because of steadily rising requirements for weapons and equipment. There is more than a suggestion, however, that the difficulties were particularly exacerbated because of the social status of those required to provide horse. Here, foot-dragging and reluctance were often led by the richest and most influential of the county gentry.[36] None the less, an overemphasis on resistance can obscure the progress that was made; indeed it might be in itself testimony to the increasing burden. One observer noted in 1586 that there were 26,000 foot and horse, organised into bands under captains, 'a thing never put into execution in any of her Majesty's predecessors' time'.[37] Further progress was made in the 1620s and 1630s, as a number of local studies show, but it was always grudging.[38]

---

[34] Ibid. For this and other disputes during the 1630s see also E. Cope, *Politics Without Parliaments, 1629–1640* (London, 1987), 98–106; Sharpe, *Charles I*, pp. 494–8.

[35] See, for example, Cogswell, *Home Divisions*, chs. 12, 13, esp. p. 278.

[36] Boynton, *Militia*, pp. 72–88; J. Goring and J. Wake (eds.), *Northamptonshire Lieutenancy Papers and Other Documents 1580–1614*, Northamptonshire Record Society, 27 (Northampton, 1975), xviii–xx; Braddick, 'Instant extraordinarie occasion'; A. J. Fletcher, *A County Community in Peace and War: Sussex 1600–1660* (London, 1975), 185–6; Carter, 'Exact militia', pp. 90–3.

[37] Quoted in Boynton, *Militia*, p. 125.

[38] Carter, 'Exact militia', pp. 89–94; G. P. Higgins, 'The militia in early Stuart Cheshire', *Journal of the Chester Archaeological Society*, 61 (1978), 39–49, at p. 44; Cogswell, *Home Divisions*, pp. 44–6; Barnes, *Somerset*, pp. 110–12, 251–3; Fletcher, *Reform*, pp. 311–14. Part of the problem was the need for special breeds of horse: P. Edwards, *The Horse Trade of Tudor and Stuart England* (Cambridge, 1988), esp. pp. 38–46.

In seeking to enforce musters, to improve weapons and the training and provision of horse, lieutenants and the privy council ran up against a brand of legalistic foot-dragging. This might tempt us to presume that the militia was doomed – the imposition of these obligations was bound to be unpopular and local officeholders unlikely therefore to cooperate assiduously. Throughout the period the gentry resisted and obstructed the imposition of obligations. In Derbyshire, for example, during the Elizabethan peace, local gentlemen hid behind their statutory obligation which was much lower than the sums being demanded by the lieutenant.[39] Rates were avoided and contested where possible. Another indication of evasion is the unreliability of muster rolls, which varied widely in form and the interpretation of such key terms as 'able'. There is evidence of concealment and evasion, driven in part by fear that muster records would serve as a precedent for other services, even in the armada year.[40] We have already noted, for example, the practice of 'borrowing' armour. Local officeholders were placed in a sensitive position between local reluctance and privy council insistence.

On the other hand, there might be a considerable pay-off for particular officeholders in seeking to implement militia reform. Part of the explanation for the success that was achieved lies in the extent to which it was possible to harness concepts of martial honour. The third earl of Huntingdon thought that if the production of horses at muster was made a matter of honour rather than duty the numbers and quality would improve considerably.[41] It is, perhaps, permissible to speculate that local gentry might be anxious to impress a man of Huntingdon's eminence, just as other local militias must have been before lesser but still important dignitaries. There was certainly a cachet to military experience and martial prowess. '[C]ontrol of the armed resources of the nation represented a crucial aspect of the obligations and responsibilities of the gentry as a social group' and, notwithstanding the role of muster masters, command lay, essentially, 'with local landowners and their families, and military rank was as often as not in direct relation to landed wealth and status'.[42] It was obviously not likely that a gentleman would bear arms under the command of a social inferior.

---

[39] Boynton, *Militia*, pp. 79–80.

[40] Ibid., pp. 40–8; Braddick, 'Instant extraordinarie occasion'. Although they are unreliable on the issue of the quantity and (particularly) quality of arms, muster rolls might still represent very full population listings: A. Chinnery, 'The muster roll for Leicestershire in 1608', *Leicestershire Archaeological and Historical Society Transactions*, 60 (1986), 25–33. For problems of ratings see below, pp. 239–41.

[41] HEH, HM 30881 fo. 79v, quoted in Braddick, 'Instant extraordinarie occasion'.

[42] P. R. Newman, 'The Royalist Officer Corps 1642–1660: army command as a reflexion of the social structure', *HJ*, 26 (1983), 945–58, p. 946.

The musters themselves were special occasions, demonstrations and reaffirmations of local hierarchy and order. The trained bands mustering and training in Cheapside in September 1635 had the privilege of being seen by the king, who dined and watched them march past.[43] 'Lieutenants feted their deputies and officers, met and socialized with many of the worthy gentlemen and yeomen of the county and displayed their "good lordship" to the shire.' 'A lord lieutenant . . . could sit in a silken tent and watch his neighbours parade respectfully by.'[44] The relationship between hierarchy and service was institutional too – in the ratings and the formal requirements for the provision of arms. In general, landowners 'probably welcomed the opportunity provided by the musters for meeting neighbours and relatives, or for renewing their acquaintance with some of the leading county families'.[45] Drawing on these values, and exploiting his own social prestige, a lieutenant could wheedle and cajole local people into more effective performance. But he had to balance this against potential unpopularity. It is clear that a number of lieutenants blew their political capital in the 1590s, 1620s and 1630s. The record shows, though, that some progress was possible. Henry Hastings, fifth earl of Huntingdon, for example, sought to cement his local status through assiduous attention to militia reform in Leicestershire and enjoyed some success in imposing burdens on the county.[46] In any case, there was not a single local interest and zealous implementation of militia reform might be seen as an opportunity by particular groups or individuals. The innovations could, clearly, cut across local interests and where they caused local difficulties legal ambiguities might make life difficult for lords lieutenant. On the other hand, reform was not impossible and it did bear fruit. Notions of honour and display might be used to justify reform and the programme could provide an opportunity for ambitious lieutenants or other local interests.

Overall, the pressure for reform was less likely to come from the provinces than was the case with measures relating to social order. The net effect of reform is difficult to gauge because the militia was never called on to fight a defensive engagement and the internal enemies, against which it was increasingly turned from the mid-seventeenth century onwards, were paper tigers. Even in the sixteenth century, the Catholic threat against which lieutenants like the third earl of Hun-

---

[43] HEH, HM EL 6547.   [44] Stater, *Noble Government*, p. 25; see also Boynton, *Militia*, p. 18.
[45] Carter, 'Exact militia', pp. 93–4.   [46] Cogswell, *Home Divisions*.

tingdon turned their attention was probably more imagined than real. Historians, therefore, have to content themselves with appraising the surviving evidence of militia administration as an indication of magisterial commitment (although this is an inaccurate measure given the unreliability of muster rolls and certificates) and the evidence of gentry wrangling caused by militia initiatives.

There were three main bouts of militia reform before 1640. Although many of these initiatives were launched in the 1570s, it seems clear that before the mid-1580s they met with footdragging and evasion. The full weight of reforming pressure was felt between 1585 and 1603. This was the first of three main bouts of militia reform before 1640. From the mid-1580s onwards, a number of counties saw considerable efforts made to improve arms and training, as well as coastal defences and beacon repair. The climax of this effort came in the armada year, when in the south of England tremendous efforts were made in all these areas.[47] Whether this effort would have sufficed if the armada had landed is unclear, of course, and opinions vary.[48] Although the efforts of magistrates in the south were impressive, those made in the north and in the inland counties (if Northamptonshire is indicative) were less impressive, or more grudging. Certainly, if the armada had landed on the north-east coast the immediate response would have been limited. What strategic use such a landing might have had is unclear, although the danger of Scottish support was evidently much on the minds of local men.[49] The patriotic fervour, and the sense of urgent necessity, clearly had limits. Indeed, even in Hampshire there was some concern that the successful mobilisation in 1588 might enter the record as a precedent. In Yorkshire in that year, evidently, more horse had been raised than the quota that the privy council had been urging over the previous few years. Local gentlemen had resisted making a certificate to this effect, however, 'leaste the same mighte remaine above of recorde as a presedent against us and the Countrie be therebie hereafter drawne to a further charge'.[50] The presentation of the war as an urgent and godly cause did not have equal purchase on all Englishmen either, because the

[47] J. S. Nolan, 'The muster of 1588', *Albion*, 13 (1991), 387–407; M. Brayshay, 'Plymouth's coastal defences in the year of the Spanish armada', *Report and Transactions of the Devonshire Association for the Advancement of Science*, 119 (1987), 169–96; J. J. N. McGurk, 'Armada preparations in Kent and arrangements made after the defeat (1587–1589)', *Archaeologia Cantiana*, 85 (1970), 71–93.
[48] G. Parker, 'If the armada had landed', *History*, 61 (1976), 358–68; Nolan, 'Muster'.
[49] Braddick, 'Instant extraordinarie occasion'; Goring and Wake, *Northamptonshire*.
[50] Boynton, *Militia*, pp. 48–9. HEH, HM 30881 fos. 149r–149v, quoted in Braddick, 'Instant extraordinarie occasion'.

armada was unlikely to land in their own back yard, or because the government rhetoric failed to persuade.[51]

There followed a 'vacation and rest'[52] before renewed interest under James I from 1613 onward. In the aftermath of the armada efforts everywhere relaxed, with the result that even the gains made in southern and maritime counties began to slip. This is of some significance, since the armada was just the most spectacular moment of 'a general European war in which Englishmen fought for nearly two decades, on the high seas, on the continent, and above all, in Ireland'.[53] At sea the story was rather different, but the achievements of the militia in these crisis years were, to say the least, qualified. The fact that pressure was eased during the 1590s and early seventeenth century reflects the political costs of this mobilisation – lieutenants drew on their own political capital while also pushing their legal rights to the limit in mobilising men and money for these campaigns. In some counties the problems that this produced were acute. In Norfolk, for example, a coastal county heavily burdened with rates for militia, coastal defences and the provision of ships, the costs of the war, passed on the through the lieutenancy, contributed to the emergence of 'court' and 'country' parties among local governors. The former centred on the lieutenancy, the latter on quarter sessions.[54] In Cheshire, effort centred on mounting campaigns to Ireland and little attention was paid to the county militia in these years.[55] Jacobean reform was associated with concerted attempts to improve drill and equipment (particularly, as we have seen, to secure the adoption of muskets in preference to calivers). It saw, at best, mixed success, with renewed disputes over muster-master's fees and marked difficulties in persuading gentlemen to produce horses. All over the country militia rates were evaded and grumbled about. Despite Jacobean exhortations to reform, the militia seems to have been in generally poor condition on the outbreak of the Thirty Years War.

The third phase of reform, the pursuit of the 'exact militia' was prompted by the Thirty Years War. It is particularly associated with Charles I although some of the initiatives predated his accession. Within the general pressure to improve drill and equipment there were three years of particularly intense activity in pursuit of the 'exact militia':

---

[51] For the latter point, see P. Croft, 'Trading with the enemy 1585–1604', *HJ*, 32 (1989), 281–302.
[52] Boynton, *Militia*, p. 212.
[53] W. MacCaffrey, 'The armada in its context', *HJ*, 32 (1989), 713–15, at p. 715.
[54] Smith, *County and Court*. This experience of polarisation contrasts sharply with that in neighbouring Suffolk: D. MacCulloch, *Suffolk and the Tudors: Politics and Religion in an English County, 1500–1600* (Oxford, 1986).   [55] Higgins, 'Militia', p. 40.

1626, 1628 and 1635. Here, again, complaints about the wide discretionary powers of lieutenants were intense. In the late 1620s they were exacerbated by the activities of lieutenants in relation to overseas expeditions and resulted in the near extinction of the institution. Renewed hostility in the late 1630s, fuelled by the costs of the Bishops' Wars and in the context of political dissatisfaction arising from other issues, left the lieutenancy with few defenders. In many counties this hostility focused on the muster-master once again.[56] All these pressures were felt by the lowliest, but crucial, officeholders. Constables throughout the country suffered from the hostility of their neighbours and sought to evade obligations or even to avoid holding office.[57]

The practical effects of the 'exact' or 'perfect' militia programme and the efforts of the later 1630s are also difficult to evaluate. In Lancashire there seems to have been a slight, unspectacular, improvement in the numbers of horse, attendance at musters and the quality of arms. Even though this imposed noticeable costs on the county there is little evidence of resistance before the late 1630s. This is a good example of the efforts of the lieutenancy, therefore. The lieutenant enjoyed good relations with his deputies and there is no evidence of a broader alienation from the lieutenancy, but even here it is not clear that the militia was 'exact' by 1640. Regular payments were made which, together with money for pressed troops, amounted to significant sums: £10,000 between 1625 and 1641 (although £4,500 of this was raised after June 1640).[58] In Essex the initiative to improve the militia offered a career opportunity to the earl of Warwick. He sought to make improvements in order to embarrass the lord lieutenant, the earl of Sussex, which he did with some success. Ultimately, he lost this private battle, but in the meantime he had made some improvements that were of long-term significance.[59] On the whole, however, it seems that the record of the militia in that county before 1640 was poor, something reflected in increasing failures to attend musters. This has been attributed to the fact that militia obligations were enforced with a lack of sensitivity to local feeling in 1625.[60] Once again, we can see that militia administrators were treading a thin line between the interests of the privy council and of their neighbours.

Considerable effort was expended in reforming the Cheshire militia

---

[56] Ibid., pp. 287–91; Cope, 'Muster masters' fees'; Sharpe, *Charles I*, pp. 494–7.
[57] J. Kent, *The English Village Constable 1580–1642: A Social and Administrative Study* (Oxford, 1986), esp. pp. 303–6.   [58] Carter, 'Exact militia', figures quoted from p. 100.
[59] Quintrell, 'Essex alarum'.   [60] Fletcher, *Reform*, pp. 306–8.

in the later 1620s, with the result that by 1629 the quotas of foot and horse were complete (the latter having been increased slightly), arms had been modernised, magazines established and the beacons repaired. However, subsequent relaxation cost the government these gains. 'By the end of 1638 the "perfect militia" was further from accomplishment than ever.' Renewed efforts from 1638 onwards met with defiance and the deputy lieutenants, forced by the privy council to keep up the pressure, eventually became uncooperative. By this time, local government was bedevilled by other problems, but the Cheshire experience does show how difficult it was to sustain a credible defence force in years of peace.[61] In other counties active lieutenancies met with serious political problems. In Somerset the feud between two prominent local men, Sir Robert Phelips and John, Lord Poulett, came to embrace militia reform and the lieutenancy's responsibilities for raising expeditionary forces, while the efforts at reform in Leicestershire were both successful and politically costly.[62]

Measuring the success of the militia programme is therefore difficult. Muster returns and militia rates suggest improvements everywhere, but also at the cost of grumbling and worse in most places. This gives grounds for positive appraisals of Caroline efforts and achievements.[63] On the other hand, however, in some counties the efforts of the lieutenancy, during both the late 1620s and the late 1630s, in relation to the militia, became conflated with other burdens imposed by war. The authority of lieutenants, billeting, the imposition of martial law, all seemed to threaten individual liberties.[64] The Bishops' Wars do not really provide the acid test of the militia either. It was not clear whether this was a defensive war, for which the trained bands could be deployed, or an expedition. In the event, the government bowed to political pressure and allowed members of the trained bands to avoid service. The result was that those felt least useful to local communities were pressed into service, with serious implications for the quality and discipline of Charles I's soldiers.[65] More generally, the political problems

---

[61] Higgins, 'Militia', pp. 41–9.   [62] Barnes, *Somerset*, ch. 9; Cogswell, *Home Divisions*.

[63] See, for example, Sharpe, *Charles I*, pp. 487–506, 541–5.

[64] For the 1620s see most recently, T. Cogswell, 'War and the liberties of the subject', in J. H. Hexter (ed.), *Parliament and Liberty from the Reign of Elizabeth to the English Civil War* (Stanford, 1992), 225–51, 313–16; P. Christianson, 'Arguments on billeting and martial law in the parliament of 1628', *HJ*, 37 (1994), 539–67; and T. G. Barnes, 'Deputies not principals, lieutenants not principals: the institutional failure of lieutenancy in the 1620s', in M. C. Fissel (ed.), *War and Government in Britain, 1598–1650* (Manchester, 1991), 58–86. For the later 1630s see V. L. Stater, 'The lord lieutenancy on the eve of the civil wars: the impressment of George Plowright', *HJ*, 29 (1986), 279–96; and Stater, 'War and the structure of politics: lieutenancy and the campaign of 1628', in Fissel (ed.), *War and Government*, 87–109.

surrounding this particular mobilisation make it difficult to evaluate the effectiveness of the militia in isolation. As in 1588, then, this does not provide the clear test that historians would like.

None the less, it is clear that seventy years of reforming effort and institutional innovation had not been entirely in vain: in 1638 returns were made of 93,718 trained foot and 5,239 horse.[66] We know little about the military effectiveness of the militia because the armada did not land and because the trained bands were largely excused service in 1639 and 1640. There is abundant evidence from around the country of at least intermittent effort and in some places at some times quite rapid improvements in the recorded capacity of the militia appear to have been made. Control of the militia was, apparently, worth fighting over in 1642. Where progress was made, the success must have owed something to the purchase of arguments of necessity. In 1588 results were achieved in the southern counties and in 1625 in Essex. By the late 1630s the evidence 'seems to suggest that the need for improved security was [also] dawning on other parts of the realm'.[67] But this achievement had come at considerable political cost, not least to lieutenants torn between their duty to their localities and to the crown. Activists seem to have made enemies, and these enemies could exploit the legal ambiguities of the powers of the lieutenancy. What to make of these problems is also unclear. The issue is complicated by the fact that hostility to militia reform was associated with periods when there were other grievances such as billeting, forced loans or ship money (as in the 1590s, the late 1620s and late 1630s). It has also become connected with the debate about the causes of the English civil war, revisionists tending to underplay either the seriousness of such discontent, or at least the seriousness of the constitutional claims made by opponents of the lieutenancy. What does seem clear, however, is that the chances of militia initiatives coinciding with perceived local needs were considerably poorer than was the case with the initiatives in relation to social order considered in the previous chapters. The other test being applied in this book is chronological, and here the answer is also fairly clear: more was achieved by way of modernising the military capacity of English government between 1642 and 1644 than had been achieved in the previous ninety years, and this improvement was sustained too.[68]

The militia was certainly unpopular, then, and most historians are

[65] M. C. Fissel, *The Bishops' Wars: Charles I's Campaigns against Scotland, 1638–1640* (Cambridge, 1994), esp. chs. 5–7.   [66] Ibid., p. 195.   [67] Sharpe, *Charles I*, p. 545.
[68] See below, pp. 213–16.

sceptical about the successes achieved. Muster rolls are unreliable guides to numbers, equipment and training, and the only meaningful test of the success of militia reform would have been an invasion. If the armada had landed the Spanish might have won, but we cannot be sure, not least because there is more to military success than supply and training. The Bishops' Wars were a special case, and it would be a mistake to make a general case from a sample of one. But the nature of the achievement is none the less revealing of more general features of early modern government. The lieutenants, although comparatively specialised in function, enjoyed power by virtue of social status and they were constrained as well as enabled by this: 'The lieutenancy's official, military function often conflicted with its informal – yet ultimately more important – local role.'[69] When there was a conflict between national and local priorities, officeholders were often unable to offer efficient service to the privy council. On the other hand, specialised agents, without local contacts, although theoretically more efficient might also, in practice, be constrained. Muster-masters exemplify this problem. Their 'standards tended to be higher', which suited the privy council, but the muster-master's 'reports to the lord lieutenant or to the council made him appear an informer who interfered with the easy-going local routine'.[70] They were disliked for their insistence and mistrusted for the fact that they profited directly from service, accused of 'mercenary motives and practices'.[71] Where there was no obvious congruence of national and local interests local officeholders might be less willing to act, but specialised officers lacked the broader legitimacy enjoyed by officeholders. By-passing the natural leaders of society carried a political cost which could over-ride the potential improvements in 'efficiency'. Overall, for defensive purposes, and within the constraints of honourable display rather than formal obligation, militia reform achieved a degree of success. This came at some political cost and was hardly dramatic, but most counties had considerably more impressive militias in 1640 than they had in 1550. Probably the most that can be said, however, is that the performance was not as bad as is sometimes suggested.

EXPEDITIONARY FORCES

By comparison with even this limited record of success the capacity of the government to mount military expeditions was woeful.[72] The re-

---

[69] Stater, *Noble Government*, p. 30.   [70] Boynton, *Militia*, p. 225.   [71] Ibid., p. 181.
[72] For what follows see also J. S. Wheeler, *The Making of a World Power: War and Military Revolution in Seventeenth-Century England* (Stroud, 1999), ch. 4.

cruitment of troops was marked by great 'irresponsibility', the supply of equipment no less so. Those responsible for transporting men and material seem to have profited considerably, and at the expense of the service. In the field corruption was rife, with captains pocketing wages and selling supplies intended for their charges. All these problems affected morale and help to explain the poor military record of the Elizabethan and Jacobean armies. This imposed more burdens on the lieutenancy too. They were responsible for impressment and for equipping the men, as well as raising money to cover most of the cost of their clothing and an allowance for their subsistence between impressment and entering the monarch's pay at the point of embarkation (coat and conduct money). Coat and conduct money was repayable, but the prospects of that happening were not always good, and the amount paid by the crown for a coat was much less than it cost. Lieutenants were also responsible for the discipline of troops, appointing provost marshals to administer martial law, and overseeing the billeting of troops on the move. Thus, expeditions made lieutenants even more unpopular than did militia reform, and it is for that reason that the institution was so unpopular in times of war.

The poor quality of recruits for foreign service is a well-remarked phenomenon. Whereas for the militia 'it was safer and cheaper to rely on prosperous citizens', this meant that the trained bands were reserved for home defence. The hard-won reforms and expensive trained bands were paid for by the counties and that was where their duties were thought to lie. By contrast, 'the worst men, poachers, thieves and drunkards, were often channelled into the expeditionary forces'.[73] It is not difficult to see how local officeholders, confronted with a demand for soldiers, were tempted to press 'village bad-boys',[74] not only resolving a potential conflict of interest but also performing what was regarded locally as a good service. The impressment of men not necessarily suited to service was, therefore, a structural problem because officeholders were using the demand to try to kill two birds with one stone. It has been suggested, in fact, that it was a conscious policy aimed at preserving domestic order.[75]

If it suited local interests, however, it was far from satisfying for the privy council and complaints were common, about both the standard of

---

[73] Boynton, *Militia*, p. 108. He notes that the preference for recruitment of the prosperous for militia service was partly to do with a fear of arming the lower orders. Cruickshank refers to the expeditionary soldiers as the 'dregs of society': *Elizabeth's Army*, p. 26.

[74] Barnes, 'Institutional failure', p. 61.   [75] Cruickshank, *Elizabeth's Army*, pp. 26–30.

recruits and their equipment.[76] In 1587, for example, the privy council complained to the earl of Huntingdon about the 'evil choice' of conscripts called for Border service and their 'impotencie of body'. The queen, he was told, had been highly offended that they 'weare not onlie for there personages so base & unhable, that they weare not thought meet to serve or worthie of her majesty's paie so as the Captens were dryven to discharge them & to receave others in there places, but also that they were sett forthe withoute anie furniture [arms] but onlie blacke bills'.[77] There were also persistent complaints about the men impressed in the East Riding during the later 1590s, when troops were regularly being mustered for service in Ireland. Henry Griffith, justice of the peace, wrote to the Council in the North in October 1596, explaining the poor performance of his division in providing men. Charged with finding twenty-eight, of whom seven were to carry muskets, Griffith viewed them and 'found them so insufficient & so unservisable (especiallie upon this shorte warninge) that we thoughte the same utterlie unmeete to be sente'. There were no muskets at all, and in the end Griffith thought it best to send money instead.[78] In April of the following year recruits sent to Chester were delayed by the weather and, eventually, returned to Yorkshire. The privy council recommended that the respite be used to make up deficiencies in their numbers and equipment.[79] In January 1599 the privy council wrote again, demanding that recruits be taken from 'hable men and thes not to be taken of the baser sort, of weake and impotent people or of vagrant and idel persons, but of chiefe men of habelitie of body'.[80] Similar complaints were made the following year, when the privy council urged officeholders to impress men 'of habilitie of bodie & liklihood, & not of loose people that are adicted to ydlenes & lewdnes & are often times taken up rather to disburthen the contrie of suche unnecessarie people than for choise of their aptnes & disposition'. They were to be properly armed too,

her majesty calling to minde the great negligence that hath bine found in divers contries of the Realme in setting forth soldiors in former service in bare &

---

[76] For a particularly well-documented case of the problems of impressing able men, which in this case led to serious political problems, see Stater, 'Plowright'; and Fissel, *Bishops' Wars*, pp. 232–8. For impressment in the Bishops' Wars more generally, ibid., pp. 222–41.

[77] HEH, HM 30881, fos. 51v–62v, quotations at fos. 56v, 57r.

[78] HEH, HM 50657, vol. I, fo. 29r. Failure to impress sufficient men could result in the impressment of minor officials instead, as George Plowright found to his cost, Stater, 'Plowright'; Fissel, *Bishops' Wars*, pp. 232–8.

[79] HEH, HM 50657, vol. I, fos. 20r–24r, 26r–27r. The list of missing armour is impressive, fo. 22r.

[80] *APC, 1598–9*, pp. 540–2. HEH HM 50657, vol. I, fos. 70r–70v.

naked sorte, wherbie they are bothe unhable to indure the cold of the contrie, & unmeete for service, & subject to take disseases and are discouraged in their service, seing other soldiours there orderlie apparelled by her majesty's care.

There was also concern about abuses by the men charged with conducting the troops to the point of embarkation, and they were, for example, suspected of allowing impressed soldiers to change places with others in order to avoid service.[81]

It was difficult to secure the cooperation necessary to send adequately equipped and able soldiers. These problems were exacerbated by corruptions in the system of supply. Heavy guns, small arms, match, shot and ancillary items such as bullet moulds and bandoliers were procured by the Ordnance Office. Although the Office was in part an outgrowth of an ancient institution, the privy wardrobe, its importance was associated with the Tudors and with the adoption of gunpowder weapons. Increasingly during the late sixteenth century the Office came to depend on contractors for these goods and gunpowder was usually procured in this way too, although it was procured under a separate contract and only part of the cost was borne by the Ordnance Office.[82] The record of the Office was not impressive, and some verdicts on its activities are particularly damning. During the 1620s, for example, it seemed 'more concerned with the improper accounting and the neglect of the ordinary equipment in the Tower than with the disgraceful and tragic inadequacies of the supplies for Cadiz and the Isle of Rhé'. At Cadiz some of the troops had arrived bearing muskets that had no touch holes and bullets that were the wrong size. Problems of corruption were considerable and the Office was further encumbered by violent internal feuds. The Bishops' Wars once again found the Office wanting.[83] More recent commentators have been more sympathetic to the pressures under which the Ordnance Office laboured. There was no long-term commitment to nurture a domestic arms industry and institutional procedures remained unsystematised. Instead, mobilisation was

---

[81] HEH, HM 50657, vol. I, fos. 89r–90r, quotations at fos. 89r, 89v. Complaints about the quality of recruits were by no means uncommon in the 1590s. For another example of the difficulties of impressment for the Irish wars see J. J. N. McGurk, 'Rochester and the Irish levy of October 1601', *Mariner's Mirror*, 74 (1988), 57–66. This demonstrates the considerable local effort of provisioning and how this was undermined by the poor quality of the recruits.

[82] G. E. Aylmer, 'Attempts at administrative reform, 1625–40', *EHR*, 72 (1957), 229–59, pp. 240–1.

[83] Ibid., pp. 240–6, quotation at p. 242. For the problems at Cadiz and Ré see R. W. Stewart 'Arms and expeditions: the Ordnance Office and the assaults on Cadiz (1625) and the Isle of Rhé (1627)', in Fissel (ed.), *War and Government*, 112–32; for the muskets and bullets see pp. 119–21. For the Bishops' Wars see Fissel, *Bishops' Wars*, pp. 90–110.

achieved in *ad hoc* ways under the immediate pressure of war. False economies abounded, such as, for example, the failure to maintain stores of arms. As a consequence, supplies had to be bought in bulk in crisis conditions, and this drove prices up. It also meant that the domestic arms industry was deprived of custom between campaigns, which hampered its development. The response in emergency conditions was frequently flexible and creative, but severely constrained by shortage of funds, inadequacies in the domestic arms industry and insensitivity on the part of Charles I in particular to these constraints. In difficult circumstances the Office often achieved considerable success in supply.[84] No one would deny that there were problems of supply, however, merely how much of the blame can be said to have rested with the Ordnance Office.

Other essential supplies were delivered to the troops by contractors and here peculation and abuse clearly affected supply. Merchants contracted to supply uniforms, for example, but were hampered by delays in payment. As a result, the practice developed whereby they were paid on exhibiting the goods in London, rather than on delivery to the troops. The temptation to deliver short-weight or sub-standard goods was considerable. The uniforms were distributed by captains who profited by returning false musters – paying someone to appear on one day, claiming and selling their uniform – or simply by failing to pass them on to the troops. There was, in short, 'a deep and universal corruption in this branch of the service'.[85] Pay was also delivered through the captains and again they were able to pocket sums paid for dead or deserted soldiers, or simply to withhold the money. It was therefore in the interests of the captains to overstate the strength of their companies. For example, at Leith in 1560 the actual strength, 5,000, appeared on paper to be 8,000. Company clerks acted, theoretically, as a check on this, but they lacked the status and desire to do so in practice. One response of government to this form of corruption was to agree a fixed rate of 'dead pays', for example sending wages for 100 men when only 94 were on the muster. This was intended to provide a means to improve the pay of the whole company, and to pay something to volunteers, but it did not satisfy captains who continued to claim extra

---

[84] Stewart, *Ordnance Office*. See also A. Thrush, 'The Ordnance Office and the navy, 1625–1640', *Mariner's Mirror*, 77 (1991), 339–54; R. W. Stewart, 'Arms and expeditions'; Stewart, 'The "Irish Road": military supply and arms for Elizabeth's army during the O'Neill Rebellion in Ireland, 1598–1601', in Fissel (ed.), *War and Government*, 16–37; M. C. Fissel, 'Introduction', ibid., 1–14.

[85] Cruickshank, *Elizabeth's Army*, ch. 6, quotation at p. 101.

dead pays and to pressure the privy council to increase the allowance.[86] The root problem was the power of the captains, something complained of by Sir Cheney Culpeper during the 1640s.[87] Military failure was not simply a matter of local foot-dragging and interest, although this is usually blamed for the poor quality of recruits and their equipment. These difficulties were exacerbated by numerous abuses in the various contracting arrangements that the government was forced to undertake. These problems, in turn, rested on such factors as financial difficulties and the rudimentary state of English arms manufacture.

Clearly the record of the lieutenancy varied from time to time and place to place, but overall most historians would judge that by 1640 it had achieved only modest success. The two great tests of the militia as a defensive force, in 1588 and the Bishops' Wars, were inconclusive, but the record in those years does not seem to have been distinguished. Away from the southern counties the militia was far from gung-ho in 1588 and in 1638 many militia men avoided service altogether. As a basis for expeditionary forces the lieutenancy continually disappointed the privy council and never provided the means for military success. Close to home, or in the face of military threat, trained and equipped troops could be summoned, but further away or in circumstances where the threat was ambiguous, cooperation was more limited. Militia mobilisation was not continuous or reliable in all circumstances, and in part this was because it demanded participation on terms which did not necessarily suit officeholders. Put crudely, conquering Ireland was a less pressing need than ridding villages of undesirables, while trained and able men were thought more suitable to be kept at home than sent on such ventures. Of course, we should be wary of holding the system to an unrealistic test – many European states faced these difficulties and encountered these political problems. In 1549 it was probably chance as much as structural capacity that led to the loss of Calais.[88] On the other hand, few would argue with the view that England had fallen behind the European pace by the 1620s.

As with poverty, the record varied from magistrate to magistrate and parish to parish, but the net effect seems clear – the institution of officeholding was better suited to implementing initiatives concerned with social order than with military innovation. As a consequence there

---

[86] Ibid., ch. 9; for dead pays see also Boynton, *Militia*, p. 194.
[87] Braddick and Greengrass (eds.), 'Cheney Culpeper', pp. 211–12.
[88] C. S. L. Davies, 'England and the French War, 1557 9', in J. Loach and R. Tittler (eds.), *The Mid-Tudor Polity, c. 1540–1560* (London, 1980), 159–85, 216–20.

was some pressure for specialisation. The lieutenancy was something of a hybrid – a specialised agency in the hands of notables whose authority rested on social pre-eminence. Military activity increasingly demanded specialised knowledge and this is reflected in the development of trained bands and the office of muster master. The costs of these specialised agencies were frequently resented, however, and they were developed to meet needs not clearly felt in many localities most of the time. To that extent they were an autonomous need of the state as a whole and they tended to outrun the capacity of the hierarchy of local officeholders to deliver on the demands. Although individuals in the locality might identify militia reform with their own interests, it was difficult to justify in the language of patriarchal authority which sustained the authority of local officeholders in general.

THE NAVY BEFORE THE CIVIL WARS

In some ways the story of naval reform is similar.[89] The mobilisation of private resources (armed merchant ships) gave way to attempts to mobilise specialised military ships. These new ships were not necessarily effective for the military challenges which confronted the government, but they were thought to be necessary – display and diplomacy were important here, therefore. The financial measures taken to support this transformation of the naval resources of the government were, notoriously, contentious. In particular, the language of necessity assumed particular prominence in attempts to legitimate the raising of ship money. The first resort of government, however, was to call for service, rather than to establish a fully state-owned fighting navy. The pressure to create specialised military bodies, therefore, ran alongside a more traditional reliance on mobilising private resources for public purposes. Thus, during the Elizabethan war with Spain private ships far outnumbered royal ships and a striking form of government by licence, 'privateering', became 'one of the main forms of English maritime activity'.[90] At sea the response of the English government to military challenge was more effective than on land, but it did not depend on the specialisation of function that had such noted political costs in the counties. Instead it rested on a congruence of public and private interest which enabled the

---

[89] For what follows see also Wheeler, *World Power*, ch. 2.
[90] K. R. Andrews, *Elizabethan Privateering: English Privateering during the Spanish War, 1585–1603* (Cambridge, 1964), 21.

effective deployment of private resources. By the 1620s, however, this relationship was breaking down and in the 1630s efforts were made to develop a more specialised royal navy. At that point some of the familiar problems associated with military activity emerged.

The early Tudors had developed something of a specialised navy, precocious among its European competitors. As the sea lanes became increasingly significant, the English crown established the infrastructure of a national navy, building thirty of its own ships by 1520, and dockyards at Portsmouth and Deptford. Further administrative developments in Henry VIII's reign meant that by 1547 'there was a navy in a sense that there was not an army'.[91] These developments were not entirely separate from the development of private shipping, however. Maritime trade in the sixteenth century was usually armed and fighting tactics did not impose constraints on ship design that demanded a separation of function between war and trading ships.

Most fighting at sea was hand-to-hand. Battle tactics, into the seventeenth century, centred on trying to board enemy ships and in this kind of warfare galleys enjoyed a considerable advantage. They were manoeuvrable and had found a simple solution to the problem of mounting guns. Heavy guns were placed in the bow, recoiling on a slide along the gangway. They were brought to bear by pointing the whole ship at the enemy, firing a volley which cleared the decks and allowed the attacker to come alongside to board. The northern seas were rougher, however, and galleys less practical than in their Mediterranean home. As a result, English shipwrights grappled with the problem of mounting guns on sailing ships. Guns were mounted forward, in imitation of the galleys, but it was also necessary to mount them low, to make them effective against galleys. This posed the problem of making holes in the hull and trying to build internal decks strong enough to carry heavy guns. Gradually ship design changed to allow for this, with watertight ports allowing fire from stern and through ports along the side. The dangers of these changes to the hull were demonstrated by the fate of the *Mary Rose*, a model royal ship which sank in 1545, having flooded through its lower gun ports. Even with gun ports, however, ships could not fire directly ahead and it was only the development of the galleon, with its low forecastle, that overcame this problem. This allowed the English to take advantage of advanced domestic iron foundries that made heavy

[91] D. Loades, *The Tudor Navy: an Administrative, Political and Military History* (Aldershot, 1992), chs. 3–4, quotation at p. 102.

guns available more plentifully and cheaply than elsewhere in Europe.[92]

These developments came at a cost, however. Armaments and internal decks reduced hold space and manoeuvrability was achieved by building with fine underwater lines. This also had implications for cargo capacity. The result was that such ships were particularly effective for carrying and defending commodities of low bulk and high value, but there were, potentially, conflicting pressures on ship design – defensive capability increasingly came at the expense of cargo space. During the sixteenth century this potential conflict was not realised because the waters of most trade routes were perilous for traders and armament mattered more than cargo space: it was only with the coming of peace in the seventeenth century that merchant ship design changed. From the mid-seventeenth century English trading ships increasingly imitated foreign designs which favoured the cheap transport of bulk commodities and, hence, diverged from a military design.[93]

Thus, although the effects were not immediately felt, there was a long-term divergence in ship design. Specialised fighting ships developed, particularly the heavily armed ships of the line and lightly armed, highly manoeuvrable, frigates. An important component of the English victory over the armada was the availability of royal ships able to fire from a distance and low. Principal ships carried heavy concentrations of guns able to fire relatively rapidly. This design had begun to develop from the 1570s onwards from the construction of the *Dreadnought*, and during the 1590s was further developed in a sustained shipbuilding programme. As a consequence, the armada campaign 'unleashed a naval arms race' and in the early seventeenth century European navies were building large, heavily armed capital ships. The *Prince Royal*, launched in 1610, was 1,900 tons and carried 55 guns. As such it was 'one of the largest warships in the world and perhaps the most heavily armed'.[94] However, although there were ships of the line capable of broadside warfare by the 1580s, this was not at the heart of naval battle tactics – the implications of this new gunnery were not immediately appreciated.[95] As a result of this, and the continued importance of

[92] N. A. M. Rodger, 'Guns and sails in the first phase of English colonization, 1500–1650', in *The Oxford History of the British Empire*, I; N. Canny (ed.), *The Origins of Empire: British Overseas Enterprise to the Close of the Seventeenth Century* (Oxford, 1998), 79–98, esp. pp. 83–6.

[93] Ibid., esp. pp. 90–1.

[94] G. Parker, 'The *Dreadnought* revolution of Tudor England', *Mariner's Mirror*, 82 (1996), 269–300.

[95] N. A. M. Rodger, 'The development of broadside gunnery, 1450–1650', *Mariner's Mirror*, 82 (1996), 301–24. The same was true of the frigate: ibid., p. 317. Both were specialised military designs, but full use of them was not made until the later seventeenth century.

fire-power to merchant shipping, the functional differentiation of merchant and fighting ships did not take place immediately. Despite the signs of specialisation of function, therefore, the continuing compatibility of the design of warships and of merchantmen in the later sixteenth century is reflected in the composition of royal fleets. The armada fleet of 1588 consisted of 23 royal ships and 79 private merchantmen. The fleet sent to Lisbon the following year consisted of 14 royal ships and 120 private vessels (see table 5.1, p. 220).

Sixteenth-century English merchants, penetrating new and more distant markets, had to defend themselves against hostile rivals and local populations.[96] Their ships were built to take arms in ways that were similar to battleships and from the reign of Henry VII onwards a bounty was paid to those who built ships of 100 tons or more to encourage this development.[97] Since the heavy ships built for trade in northern waters lent themselves well to military service there was no particular disadvantage to this arrangement, so long as mercantile and crown interests were congruent. 'Trade and plunder were inseparable in the sixteenth century' and increasingly, down to 1585, the two activities were identified with patriotism and Protestantism.[98] The relationship was not entirely easy, of course. Straightforward piracy continued to be seen as a social evil, potentially embarrassing to the crown, and there was always a potential conflict of interest in seeking to exploit private shipping. In short, because the crown did not control these resources, their deployment had to be negotiated and as a result they did not necessarily do what the crown intended. Indeed, private ships might do things that were destructive of crown aims. However, where the interests ran together a symbiotic relationship was possible – profitable to the ship owner, cheap and militarily effective for the crown.

The best example of this symbiosis was the role of privateering in the naval war against Spain. In 1588 'England could get its navy to sea faster, and keep it there longer than any other power. Its gunnery was advanced and its tactics, based upon a generation of successful privateering, innovative and effective.'[99] Privateering was not incidental to the English war effort, but integral. In theory, privateers were licensed by the High Court of Admiralty to pursue redress of a private wrong and the issue of letters of reprisal was not, therefore, an act of war. In

[96] Andrews, *Elizabethan Privateering*, pp. 34–7.
[97] B. Dietz, 'The royal bounty and English shipping in the sixteenth and seventeenth centuries', *Mariner's Mirror*, 77 (1991), 5 20.   [98] Andrews, *Elizabethan Privateering*, p. 15.
[99] Loades, *Tudor Navy*, p. 208.

war-time, though, this distinction disappeared. There was no incentive to check that the person wronged was the one who was exacting reprisal and in this way privateering was elided with the war effort more generally. It remained distinct from piracy because pirates had no commission and attacked anyone, whereas privateers attacked only designated enemies. However, privateering was equally distinct from semi-official and official action, in which the queen's interest predominated even if she did not have the biggest financial stake. By contrast, privateering 'was wholly financed and directed by private individuals'.[100] So successful was the relationship that about 100 privateering voyages set out each year during the 1590s.[101]

Of central importance to this success, therefore, was an identity of interests between the Crown and merchants, and the close relationship between merchant and military ship design. The expansion of trade prior to 1585 had led to conflict between English and Spanish traders, and there was a split among traders with Iberian interests as to whether privateering or the preservation of peaceful relations offered the best hope of advancing trade. The hawks had allies among gentlemen anxious for plunder and to pursue patriotic and Protestant glory. When war broke out those who favoured peace were able to profit, thus recovering the initial losses resulting from the disruption of trade.[102] As the war progressed the economics of privateering came to favour those who could control costs. The largest parts of the capital costs were the ship and guns, and larger ships were more expensive per ton than smaller ships. Victuals accounted for about half of the fitting-out costs. Substantial merchants already involved in armed trade could cover these costs with ordinary commerce, privateering offering a 'super-profit'. In alliance with professionals engaged in shipping, they could also control other costs – by evading Admiralty and customs exactions and driving hard bargains with crews, for example. As a result, they were less dependent on spectacular seizures and they came to dominate privateering, as enthusiastic amateurs were forced out. A corollary of the dominance of great merchants was the dominance of London, and London merchants became the principal (though not the sole) beneficiaries.[103] Not surprisingly there were non-military benefits to this activity. Privateering was, of course, of central importance to the expansion of overseas trade in the sixteenth and seventeenth centuries[104] and the profitability of privateering gave a considerable stimulus to the develop-

---

[100] Andrews, *Elizabethan Privateering*, ch. 1, quotation at p. 5.   [101] Ibid., pp. 32–4.
[102] Ibid., pp. 10–15.   [103] Ibid., pp. 45–50, chs. 4–7.   [104] For which see below, ch. 9.

ment of business skills and, especially, of shipbuilding.[105] So successful was the connection that at the end of the war the government proposed the formation of an auxiliary fleet of private ships to protect commerce in the Narrow Seas, 'tacitly admitting the inability of the royal navy to manage this duty'.[106] It was not just that the government mobilised private ships for war, then, but that the government began to lose control of maritime force.

In effect, during the sixteenth century the English navy was in many respects 'the best organised, most professional, and most "modern" navy in Europe, but it was run in ways which blurred and at times obliterated the distinctions between public and private business'.[107] However, this close relationship began to break down in the early seventeenth century, as this political alliance dissolved, and as the effect of changes in ship design and tactics began to be felt. By the end of Elizabeth's reign it was evident that the more professional and heavily armed royal navy held many privateers in contempt. Revelations of corruption in naval administration in 1618, coupled with a desire for prestige on the part of the monarch, led to a ship-building programme which concentrated on big, heavily armed ships. This did not make particularly good military sense and resulted in the neglect of the more obvious need for the smaller more mobile vessels which were still necessary for most purposes. The result was a continuing dependence on merchant auxiliaries for these other purposes, but the return of hostilities in the late 1620s revealed conflicts of interest – leading privateers wanted royal ships to defend the coasts while private ships concentrated their efforts on attacking Spanish trading interests. There was little support for an integrated effort along Elizabethan lines and, instead, what happened was that merchant ships were commandeered under royal command, their activities supplemented by 'random, small-scale privateering'. Merchants were unwilling auxiliaries in the assaults on Cadiz and Ré, and most ports were slow to respond to royal command. Meanwhile, merchant losses were considerable. Kenelm Digby's expedition to Scanderoon (Iskanderun) in 1627 epitomised the problems. It created competition for naval recruitment and the fairly modest success achieved jeopardised both the commercial interests of the Levant Company and England's diplomatic position. Clearly it was

---

[105] Andrews, *Elizabethan Privateering*, p. 230.   [106] Ibid., p. 238.
[107] Rodger, 'Guns and sails', p. 96. See also Andrews, *Elizabethan Privateering*, p. 20; G. V. Scammell, 'The sinews of war: manning and provisioning English fighting ships *c.* 1550–1650', *Mariner's Mirror*, 73 (1987), 351–67.

not a good advertisement for the Elizabethan blend of private and public enterprise.[108]

The tactical and strategic pressures for the creation of a specialised fighting navy were increasingly obvious under the early Stuarts, therefore. This posed a financial challenge, of course, and as early as 1603 there had been calls for a national rate in order to provide for the protection of trade. Letters to the counties had suggested 'there must be some certain proportion of shipping wholly assigned to guard over merchants from what ports so ever they set forth and return, which being a matter no way convenient for our own ships to attend, the uncertainty of their trade requiring sudden and chargeable going to and fro'. Calls for contributions were justified by the fact that trade was in everyone's interest, and the scheme found an echo in 1618, when contributions to take defensive measures against the Mediterranean pirates were suggested.[109] By the late 1620s there were calls for the creation of a larger royal navy and in 1628 a ship money levy was proposed – instead of supplying ships for service port towns would be asked to provide money to support the royal navy. This was not explicitly linked to a shipbuilding programme, but it is suggestive in the light of subsequent measures, and was probably a precursor to the ship money programme of the 1630s. The plan was to impose 'the burden on the whole country . . . using the proceeds for a regular fleet [and it] . . . must have seemed – indeed actually was – fairer and more efficient'.[110] The uneasy international situation and the decayed condition of the navy added to the appeal of the scheme.[111] However, the plan was dropped rather abruptly, perhaps as a result of divisions within the council as to how to proceed. There was also some local opposition, but it may just have been that an easier international situation reduced the sense of urgency. When parliament met, Charles proposed building twenty ships per year, which implied 'an annual commitment to naval

---

[108] K. R. Andrews, *Ships, Money and Politics: Seafaring and Naval Enterprise in the Reign of Charles I* (Cambridge, 1991), 140–50, quotation at p. 146. For Digby's expedition see ibid., ch. 5. For the continued commercial attractions of privateering see J. Appleby, 'A pathway out of debt: the privateering activities of Sir John Hippisley during the early Stuart wars with Spain and France', *American Neptune*, 44 (1989), 251–61; Scammell, 'Sinews'.

[109] Quoted in R. J. W. Swales, 'The ship money levies of 1628', *BIHR*, 50 (1977), 164–76, at p. 165. Some sense of the peace-time activities of the early Jacobean navy is given by E. Milford, 'The navy at peace: the activities of the early Jacobean navy: 1603–1618', *Mariner's Mirror*, 76 (1990), 23–36, an account of the fairly unimpressive operations of the navy in 1605–6.

[110] Andrews, *Ships*, pp. 140–50, quotation at p. 150.

[111] Swales, 'Ship money', pp. 166–74. The scheme gave a prominent role to the magistracy since collectors were to be appointed by the justices of the peace.

costs' in the same way that the scheme for a national rate had. In any case both suggestions reflect the fact that the Elizabethan amalgam of private and public enterprise was breaking down, and that this was recognised by influential contemporaries.[112]

Under the early Stuarts, therefore, a clearer demarcation between merchant and fighting ships was emerging. The review of naval administration in 1618 led by Cranfield probably resulted in the abandonment of the bounty paid to merchants building ships which were also serviceable in war. The bounty was restored in 1625 but applied to fewer and fewer ships so that after the restoration only the largest ships in the East India trade benefited. It was finally abandoned in the early eighteenth century, 'testimony to the professionalisation of the navy' at that point.[113] Meanwhile, under James I and Charles I royal ships became much larger, with multiple decks of guns, which inevitably meant that most of the firepower was mounted broadside. This was in part a reflection of changing battle tactics. Ships no longer bore down on the enemy firing ahead but drew up in lines of battle allowing all broadside guns to be brought to bear at once. Such ships were large and ponderous, with 'full lines to support so great a weight of metal'.[114] Thus, warships were less and less like the nimble armed merchantmen of Elizabeth's day. Meanwhile, as trade became less perilous in European waters, the competitive advantages of heavily armed English merchantmen began to disappear. Armed traders remained important in trades carrying small bulk, high value commodities in dangerous waters, notably the East India trade, but in general there was a growing separation between merchant and royal ships,[115] although the full effects of these developments were not to be felt until after 1650.[116]

The ship money fleets represent a significant initiative in the context of this breakdown of the alliance of merchant and crown shipping, but the purposes of the fleet were to some extent contradictory. The preference for large royal ships was, in part, a political rather than a simply naval matter. The large ships reflected monarchical prestige, but they

[112] Ibid., pp. 173–4.
[113] Dietz, 'Royal bounty', p. 5. See also M. Oppenheim, *A History of the Administration of the Royal Navy and Merchant Shipping in Relation to the Navy*, I, *1509–1660* (London, 1896), 37–8, 167–8, 201, 269.
[114] Rodger, 'Guns and sails', quotation at p. 95. For the *Sovereign of the Seas* see also B. W. Quintrell, 'Charles I and his navy in the 1630s', *The Seventeenth Century*, 3 (1988), 159–79, at pp. 162–3.
[115] Rodger, 'Guns and sails', pp. 90–1.
[116] Andrews, *Ships*, pp. 25–9 for the continued construction of armed merchant ships after 1618. For the divergence during the 1630s see A. Thrush, 'Naval finance and the origins and development of ship money', in Fissel (ed.), *War and Government*, 133–62, at pp. 135–7.

were ill-adapted to meeting the principal threats to English shipping.[117] The principal naval threats were the Barbary corsairs and Dunkirkers in light and manoeuvrable ships, and the expansion of the French fleet. The north African corsairs were an escalating problem in the second decade of the seventeenth century as English trade in the Mediterranean expanded, Ottoman authority in the region declined and, perhaps, improvements in ship design increased their range. Diplomatic efforts failed to control the threat and an expedition in 1616 to Algiers achieved only temporary success. Between 1616 and 1642 as many as 400 ships and 8,000 men may have been lost to the pirates.[118] Dutch rivalry led to a desire for an assertion of sovereignty over the seas and from the mid-1620s Spanish fleets posed an increasing threat. For these purposes, relatively small, fast and manoeuvrable ships were desirable: the frigates. But the shipbuilding programme was also a reflection of a desire for diplomatic prestige and leverage, particularly in the quest to recover the Palatinate.[119] Big ships helped in this respect, and did dominate the seas, although this was at the expense of effectiveness against the smaller, faster and more nimble Dunkirkers and corsairs. On the whole, building frigates appears to have been a low priority. The need for them had been recognised as early as 1624 but a plan to build them was lost in the need to mobilise for the offensive war. In the 1630s the response was poor too. Four frigates were captured and two fairly poor copies were built. Given the financial constraints, however, building frigates was probably an alternative to building capital ships with which to rival the French – it was not possible to do both. For diplomatic reasons, and for reasons of prestige too, no doubt, the government concentrated on the latter.[120]

By the 1630s, then, the potential tensions in the relationship between the public and private purposes of shipping had become quite apparent. The mobilisation of private resources directly for public service was here reaching a limit of cooperation similar to that in the case of the militia. This is one context in which to place the development of the ship money

[117] Ibid., *passim*, esp. pp. 135–7. See also A. Thrush, 'In pursuit of the frigate, 1603–1640', *Historical Research*, 64 (1991), 29–45. For a general account see D. D. Hebb, *Piracy and the English Government, 1616–1642* (Aldershot, 1994).

[118] Hebb, *Piracy*, for the scale of the losses see ch. 7 esp. pp. 137–40. For the impact of piracy on the west country see T. Gray, 'Turkish piracy and early Stuart Devon', *Report and Transactions of the Devonshire Association for the Advancement of Science*, 121 (1989), 159–71.

[119] See, in general, Andrews, *Ships*, esp. ch. 6; and Thrush, 'Naval finance'. For the latter point see Quintrell, 'Charles I', pp. 160–1.

[120] Thrush, 'Frigate', pp. 31–45. See also Hebb, *Piracy*, pp. 203–9. Dunkirkers might reach the north-east coast too: HEH, HM 50657, vol. I., fos. 51r, 53r, 66r, 67r.

fleets. Another is the long-term divergence in the design of merchant and royal shipping, which by this time was becoming quite marked. European waters were becoming safer, making cargo capacity more important than defensive capability for commercial ships. At the same time, naval design and the desire for political prestige continued to push governments towards the acquisition of large, heavily armed and specialised fighting ships.

By 1640 the king's navy consisted of forty ships, of which eleven were new and two had been rebuilt during the personal rule.[121] The actual achievement of the fleet is the subject of some debate. In the late 1620s there was already a fairly high royal tonnage by Elizabethan standards, but it was not effective against the Dunkirkers. The usual peace-time complement patrolling the Narrow Seas was only four ships: in effect the Channel had been abandoned by 1625. Thereafter, offensive capacity took precedence over defensive, whenever such a choice had to be made.[122] The navy's record was not glorious, although it provided the resources with which to exploit political divisions among the Barbary corsairs in order to secure some respite. Squadrons patrolled the Channel every year from 1635 to 1641 but their practical effect was limited. The story of Pennington's embarrassment at the Downs in 1639 is often retailed as an illustration. Charged with protecting Spanish troops being transported to Flanders, his squadron had to stand by impotently and watch a Dutch attack under the command of Tromp. He secured no more than a token acknowledgement of the sovereignty of English waters.[123]

Most commentators agree, however, that the fleet is important for what it represented, if not for what it achieved. The case of the *Sovereign of the Seas* is instructive here. Launched in 1637, 'there was no prospect of a strategic role for her to play, even if one had been intended'. She was adorned with embellishments recalling a glorious past but her purpose was unclear. Charles I had, at the last moment, insisted that her armaments be increased 'from a well-calculated 90 guns to 102, unmindful of the risks of instability which had humbled other great ships'. Yet she was also the ship of the future, 'much closer in size and design to the ships of the line of Nelson's day than to the men-of-war of Drake's'.

---

[121] Quintrell, 'Charles I', pp. 163–4. For ship-building under Charles I, see Andrews, *Ships*, pp. 148–52. [122] Thrush, 'Frigate', pp. 29–31.
[123] Andrews, *Ships*, pp. 156–8; S. Groenveld, 'The English civil wars as the cause of the first Anglo-Dutch war, 1640–1652', *HJ*, 30 (1987), 541 66, at p. 541; R. Harding, *The Evolution of the Sailing Navy, 1509–1815* (London, 1995), 55; Quintrell, 'Charles I', pp. 173–4.

Political ambition over-rode the views of conservatives in the naval administration.[124] Thus, political ambition had led to the building of a ship that was ahead of its time. But the importance of the ship money fleets lies also in the signs of a coherent attempt to break the relationship between public and private naval resources: 'this Navy, so much the King's own instrument, fashioned and wielded by him, may be seen in perspective as a significant step in the direction of a state Navy'.[125] The threat of the north African corsairs had also led to some military innovation, and two impressive expeditions were mounted, in 1616 against Algiers and in 1637 to Salé. However, again, the measures after 1640 seem more important. For example, an act of 1642 imposed a 1 per cent supplement on the customs which was to be used to protect shipping from piracy. This was to be the basis of long-term, continuous and systematic naval action against piracy.[126]

The achievements of the ship money fleets were surpassed after 1640 but they represent the first stage in the creation of a specialised, state-owned navy distinct from the merchant marine. The contrast with Elizabethan maritime resources is marked, although less so by comparison with the early Tudors. From 1550 to 1640, in response to the challenge of sea warfare, the government had responded initially, and successfully, by seeking to exploit private resources. This served to dilute the effects of early Tudor naval reform. The great successes of the 1590s though were in part a product of a chance coincidence of developments in trade, war and ship design and by the 1620s pressure for specialisation was again being felt. Military innovation was putting pressure on the government to take direct responsibility for war at sea. There was, thus, some analogy with military innovation on land. Again, the primary response was to draw on private resources and notions of service. Just as there was no fully distinct royal navy prior to 1630, and then only really a prototype, there was no standing army created in response to

[124] Quintrell, 'Charles I', p. 173. The professionals were in this regard learning from past experience: 'As is the way with military theorists, they were good at learning the lessons of the last war, but by no means percipient about the next': Rodger, 'Guns and sails', p. 95.

[125] Andrews, *Ships*, p. 159. See also Quintrell, 'Charles I', p. 174; Thrush, 'Naval finance'.

[126] Hebb, *Piracy*. For the 1642 Act see pp. 272–3. For the expedition to Salé see also Andrews, *Ships*, ch. 7. Hebb, while acknowledging the more impressive achievements of the later seventeenth century, argues that 'As long-distance trade expanded, so too did piracy cease to be a local activity or problem. The growth of England's Atlantic and Mediterranean trade brought in its train attacks on English ships by the Barbary pirates. In similar and related fashion, the navies of the great maritime nations grew from little more than occasional, coastal defence forces into permanent fleets of specially-built warships capable of mounting and sustaining blue-water operations': *Piracy*, p. 276.

the advent of gunpowder weapons. In both cases military change put pressure on the relationship between the crown and those who control-led private resources, and strained notions of obligations to aid the sovereign.

AN ENGLISH MILITARY REVOLUTION, 1640–1660

The civil war permanently changed the military and fiscal capacity of the state.[127] As we have seen, the mobilisation for the Bishops' Wars did not really change the way that things were done in any profound sense. The expedition to Ireland was mobilised as a land-based equivalent to a privateering expedition, adventurers backing military expeditions in the expectation of securing spoils.[128] But during the civil war parliament developed a financial and military apparatus, that continued to develop in the 1650s, and which allowed mobilisations different in kind from previous efforts. In essence, this centred around the creation of a standing army and a state-owned navy. In mobilising to fight Britain's civil wars the English parliament also created new fiscal instruments. These new sources of revenue and changes in borrowing were an important part of the basis for the victories of the parliamentary armies and navies of the 1640s and 1650s. More importantly, though, they provided the basis for long-term changes in the military and fiscal capacity of the English state, a capacity demonstrated during the resto-ration period and further enhanced during the 1690s. There was, by any measure, a dramatic increase in the functional effectiveness of the English state in the period after 1640.

A crude indication of the magnitude and chronology of these changes is the size of national budgets and armed forces. It seems that the proportion of national wealth commanded by national government doubled, in real terms, during the 1640s and did so again in the 1690s.[129] In the 1590s Elizabeth's total income was about £500,000 per annum.

---

[127] For what follows see also Wheeler, *World Power*, chs. 3–8.

[128] K. S. Bottigheimer, *English Money and Irish Land: The 'Adventurers' in the Cromwellian Settlement of Ireland* (Oxford, 1971). This persisted into the period of the Cromwellian conquests, of course, arrears of pay being met from the spoils of conquest.

[129] P. K. O'Brien and P. A. Hunt, 'The rise of a fiscal state in England, 1485–1815', *Historical Research*, 66 (1993), 129–76. The earlier figure is approximate and the shifting balance between local rates and national taxation means that it is difficult to read off the total cost of government from figures relating only to national taxation. None the less, the total cost of government did, undoubtedly, increase very significantly in this period. This material is discussed in M. J. Braddick, *The Nerves of State: Taxation and the Financing of the English State, 1558 1714* (Manchester, 1996), 6–12.

In the 1690s it was ten times as great.[130] This was an increase well above the rate of inflation and of population growth – there can be little doubt that the real burden of taxation per capita increased considerably in this period. At any one time during the civil wars perhaps one in ten adult males were in arms.[131] Between 1647 and 1660 the armed forces in England numbered between 11,000 and 47,000. Army officers were prominent in local government and garrisons substantially affected the religious and political lives of the areas in which they stood.[132] Although we might hesitate to describe this as a military dictatorship, it was, certainly, a large number of people to be supported from national taxation.[133] By the mid-1680s the standing army in England was nearly 20,000 strong, reaching 34,000 on the eve of the Glorious Revolution.[134] The navy was also a substantial body. During the second Dutch war the fleet was manned by 20,000 and the peace-time complement after the restoration was between 3,000 and 4,000.[135] After 1690 massive military commitment was reflected in the size of the armed forces, numbering well over 100,000. The significance of such numbers is not always clear, but one way of appreciating this commitment is that the combined population of England's seven biggest cities (aside from London) was probably smaller than the number of men in arms around 1700.[136] This was a substantial burden on an agrarian economy and, by Tudor and early Stuart standards, a miraculous governmental achievement. This was a change of capacity achieved in two stages: the 1640s and the 1690s were of at least equal significance in these terms.[137]

It is no longer plausible to suggest that anyone in England could have been unaware of the conduct of the civil war. The burden of taxation, the informal exactions of troops in billets and on the move and the material destruction in many parts of the country made it all too plain

---

[130] Braddick, *Nerves*, table 2.1; C. G. A. Clay, *Economic Expansion and Social Change: England 1500–1700*, 2 vols. (Cambridge, 1984), II, 261, 268.

[131] J. Morrill, 'Introduction', in Morrill (ed.), *The Impact of the English Civil War* (London, 1991), 8–16, at p. 9.

[132] H. M. Reece, 'The military presence in England, 1649–60', DPhil thesis, Oxford University (1981), chs. 6–7, appendix I.

[133] For the arguments against describing the regimes of the 1650s as a 'military dictatorship', see A. Woolrych, 'The Cromwellian protectorate: a military dictatorship?', *History*, 75 (1990), 207–31. Reece takes a gloomier view of the role of the army: 'Military presence'.

[134] J. Childs, *The Army, James II and the Glorious Revolution* (Manchester, 1980), 1–3.

[135] M. J. Braddick, 'An English military revolution?', *HJ*, 36 (1993), 965–75, at p. 973.

[136] For this calculation see Braddick, *Nerves*, p. 190.

[137] Ibid. For an account emphasising the importance of the 1690s see J. Brewer, *The Sinews of Power: War, Money and the English State, 1688–1783* (London, 1989).

that England might 'turn Germany'.[138] As it became clear that the war was not going to end in a season both sides regularised their exactions and both sides resorted to similar expedients. In part this helped to secure the local support that was necessary to keep an army fed and watered. Opposition to army exactions by clubmen was more likely where military authority was weak than where it was strong: strong garrisons were able to regularise their demands and offer protection from irregular demands.[139]

As the war dragged on, the more dependable parliamentary finances gave its armies a considerable military advantage. Between 1645 and 1651 nearly £5,230,000 was paid to the New Model Army from the assessment, accounting for 80 per cent of its total cost. This money, supplemented by the excise, 'was more than adequate to the task of reducing the royalist foe'.[140] Although recruitment of troopers still depended heavily on impressment, officers were positively attracted by the regularity of pay and supply. There was a problem of desertion from the lower ranks, but the royalists suffered more in this respect, in part at least because of the inferior conditions of service resulting from inferior financing.[141] Superior finances supported improved procurement and

[138] The phrase is taken from I. Roy, 'England turned Germany? The aftermath of the civil war in its European context', *TRHS*, 5th series, 28 (1978), 127–44. Some of the most graphic demonstrations of this point are D. Pennington, 'The war and the people', in J. Morrill (ed.), *Reactions to the English Civil War 1642–1649* (London, 1982), 115–36, 234–8; R. Ashton, 'From Cavalier to Roundhead tyranny, 1642–9', ibid., 185–207, 242–7; I. Roy, 'The English civil war and English society', *War and Society*, I (1976), 24–43; C. Carlton, *Going to the Wars: The Experience of the British Civil Wars 1638–1651* (London, 1992); Carlton, 'The face of battle in the English civil wars', in Fissel (ed.), *War and Government*, 226–47; R. Bennett, 'War and disorder: policing the soldiery in Civil War Yorkshire', ibid., 248–73; S. Porter, *Destruction in the English Civil Wars* (Stroud, 1994); R. Hutton, *The Royalist War Effort, 1642–1646* (London, 1982); A. Hughes, 'Parliamentary tyranny? Indemnity proceedings and the impact of the civil war: a case study from Warwickshire', *Midland History*, 11 (1986), 49–78.

[139] Clubmen were armed groups organised at local initiative to protect their localities from the depredations of the civil war armies. For the regularisation of administration see M. Bennett, 'Between Scylla and Charibdis: the creation of rival administrations at the beginning of the English civil war', *Local Historian*, 22 (1992), 191–202. For the importance of codes of conduct (and their impact on civilian relations) see B. Donagan, 'Codes and conduct in the English civil war', *PP*, 118 (1988), 65–95; Donagan, 'Atrocity, war crime and treason in the English civil war', *American Historical Review*, 99 (1994), 1137–66; Roy, 'English civil war'; R. Hutton, 'The Worcestershire Clubmen in the English civil war', *Midland History*, 5 (1979–80), 40–9; Hutton, 'The royalist war effort', in Morrill (ed.), *Reactions*, 51–66, 226–8; S. Osborne, 'The war, the people and the absence of the clubmen in the Midlands, 1642–1646', *Midland History*, 19 (1994), 85–104; R. Ashton, 'The problem of indemnity, 1647–1648', in C. Jones, M. Newitt and S. Roberts (eds.), *Politics and People in Revolutionary England: Essays in Honour of Ivan Roots* (Oxford, 1986), 117–40; Hughes, 'Tyranny'; M. Bennett, 'Contribution and assessment: financial exactions in the English civil war 1642–46', *War and Society*, 5 (1986), 1–11.

[140] I. Gentles, *The New Model Army in England, Ireland and Scotland, 1645–1653* (Oxford, 1992), 28–31, quotation at p. 31.   [141] Ibid., pp. 31–40.

supply, with the result that the parliamentary army was not forced to live off the land as outrageously as the royalists. Most importantly of all, pay was received pretty much in full. In June 1647 the army was much exercised about arrears, but at that point most arrears were for periods of service before the creation of the New Model Army, or for officers. The rank and file of the New Model had been paid nearly in full.[142] Military success was not simply purchased, of course. The New Model Army was, all the evidence suggests, fired by an unusual degree of religious piety. This, coupled with its developing record of military success, raised morale and must have contributed to the military dominance that it achieved. None the less, there is 'no gainsaying that the army owed more than a little of its success to the fact that it was relatively well-financed, clothed, provisioned and armed'.[143]

Part of this story, then, was supply. Parliament created a new system based on direct contracts with producers. It was based on prompt payment in cash and some of its achievements were quite remarkable. For example, cutlers contracted to supply 9,200 swords on 31 March 1645 had met the contract and been paid in full within sixteen days. About 200 suppliers in or near London were given contracts, producing a tremendous volume of supplies, all paid for with tax revenues. The committee of the army had a good record of driving hard bargains and paying in full for weapons and ammunition, providing considerable commercial opportunities for producers. By delivering *materiel* promptly and as appropriate, the system of provisioning 'was instrumental in achieving the victories of 1645'. Food was mainly (about 90 per cent of the time) procured locally and paid for out of the soldiers' wages. This helped relations with local populations and was, again, enabled by large and dependable tax flows.[144] In this sense, the state was more visible, affecting economic activity by commanding a measurable slice of national wealth for particular purposes. It was also more visible in the sense of acting more directly and developing specialised resources, not the least of which was an increasingly professional army.

England's armies enjoyed unprecedented military success in Britain and Ireland after the civil war, and again a significant factor in the victories was dependable supply. In 1649 a force of 12,000 men was assembled for service in Ireland and, when a contingent left Milford

---

[142] Ibid., pp. 40–7 for supply, pp. 47–52 for pay. Wheeler notes, however, that £1.3m was owing to the New Model in 1649: J. S. Wheeler, 'Logistics and supply in Cromwell's conquest of Ireland', in Fissel (ed.), *War and Government*, 38–56, at p. 40.

[143] Gentles, *New Model*, ch. 4, quotation at p. 118.   [144] Ibid., pp. 41–7, quotation at p. 41.

Haven, Bulstrode Whitelocke observed 'that no provision was wanting for the transport of this army; and there is a considerable stock of money . . . The soldiers . . . behaved themselves very civilly, and paid for what they took.' Food, military stores and £10,000 had already been sent to Dublin during April and May. Supply was to prove crucial during the following winter, ensuring the survival of Cromwell's forces, sustaining numbers by regular replacements and enabling English forces to be better equipped and provisioned than the Irish Confederates. It was the Confederate army that began to disintegrate rather than the English forces. Between 1649 and 1656, £3.5m in money and supplies was sent from England.[145] Unlike the campaigns in England, however, the army was unable to procure food supplies locally, not least because of the devastation caused by eight years of war, and vast quantities of food were sent from England. Between August 1649 and January 1650, 'England provided 16,000 men with 90 per cent of their bread, 40 per cent of their beer, 50 per cent of their cheese, and significant additional foodstuffs.' This continued too: between March and May 1650 more than 1 million pounds of oats and wheat, and 60,000 pounds of cheese were dispatched. Clothing, tents, shoes, arms and munitions were similarly procured.[146] This was the equivalent of providing food and other important commodities for two substantial towns – an enormous burden on what is normally described as an agrarian economy producing relatively slender surpluses. In the 1620s, in Germany and France, poor support had caused 'thousands of men to die of hunger, disease and exposure'. The Irish campaign, by contrast, 'demonstrated the emergence of the logistical foundation of British military power in western Europe and foreshadowed Britain's rise to world power status'.[147] The campaign in Scotland demonstrated similarly increased capacities.[148] During the 1650s there was little problem in recruiting men to serve, at least in England, since the wages and living conditions were relatively

[145] Wheeler, 'Logistics and supply', pp. 40–4 (Whitelocke quoted ibid., p. 41). Government financial reform in Cromwellian Ireland centred around trying to reduce the subsidy from England: T. C. Barnard, *Cromwellian Ireland: English Government and Reform in Ireland 1649–1660* (Oxford, 1975), 26–31.

[146] Wheeler, 'Logistics and supply', pp. 47–50. For military operations in Ireland, the military organisation of the Confederate armies and the impact on the local economy see S. Wheeler, 'Four armies in Ireland', in J. H. Ohlmeyer (ed.), *Ireland from Independence to Occupation 1641–1660* (Cambridge, 1995), 43–65; R. Loeber and G. Parker, 'The military revolution in seventeenth-century Ireland', ibid., 66–88; R. Gillespie, 'The Irish economy at war, 1641–1652', ibid., 160–80; and Ohlmeyer, 'Introduction: a failed revolution?', ibid., 1–23, esp. pp. 13–15.

[147] Wheeler, 'Logistics and supply', p. 53.

[148] J. S. Wheeler, 'The logistics of the Cromwellian conquest of Scotland 1650–1651', *War and Society*, 10 (1992), 1–18.

attractive by comparison with life among the poorer sort in civilian life. The impact of the army on local economies was restrained by regular supply, with the consequence that the depredations of troops were limited.[149] All this, to reiterate, rested on greatly increased financial potential.

Domination of the seas was also important to the parliamentary armies in Ireland, allowing secure supply lines.[150] In fact the role of the navy in the civil war has not been given the attention it deserves.[151] Naval dominance came courtesy of further important military changes. In 1642 the fleet was seized by parliament and its command and political purpose changed, but neither of these developments really affected the nature of the navy. It remained dependent on the hire of merchant shipping which remained proportionately and absolutely greater than in the ship money fleets.[152] Many of the ships employed were ones in which the navy commanders had an interest, and the activities of the fleet integrated the activities of privateers very fully. The result was that 'the borderline between official and private naval enterprise became at least as blurred as it had been during the Elizabethan war with Spain'.[153] In short, although parliament had its own Admiralty and naval administration, the Elizabethan amalgam of private and public persisted.

The navy was purged in 1648 and 1649, and in these purges corruption and political malignancy were conflated. On the whole it seems that political purification was more effective than administrative reform in this process, but it was accompanied by a dramatic transformation of the substance of the fleet.[154] The second stage of the revolution came after these purges and in the light of almost unanimous European hostility to the republican regime after 1649. Administrative reorganisation and reform of the financial procedures of the navy in the following two years provided the basis for the expansion of the fleet, and for success in battle.[155] Numbers are not always reliable in these matters,

[149] Reece, 'Military presence', chs. 1–3, 5. Problems increased in 1659 as the army increased rapidly in size and structures of command broke down, ibid., chs. 8–9.

[150] Wheeler, 'Logistics and supply', pp. 51–2.

[151] For the logistical importance of the sea lanes see, for example, J. Binns, 'Scarborough and the civil wars, 1642–51', *Northern History*, 22 (1986), 95–122.

[152] This was partly a matter of differing duties. The 1640s saw active warfare and so the more appropriate point of comparison is perhaps the 1590s, not the 1630s. As we have seen, the mobilisation in the 1590s was much like that described here. For some interesting material on the seizure of the fleet see S. J. Greenberg, 'Seizing the fleet in 1642: parliament, the navy and the printing press', *Mariner's Mirror*, 77 (1991), 227–34.   [153] Andrews, *Ships*, p. 198.

[154] Ibid., pp. 200–2.

[155] J. S. Wheeler, 'Prelude to power: the crisis of 1649 and the foundation of English naval power', *Mariner's Mirror*, 81 (1995), 148–56.

but they are quite striking here. Between 1649 and 1660, 216 ships were added, many taken as prizes but about half as the result of a massive building programme. There was clearly a decision to drop the old dependence on merchantmen and to establish a state navy.[156] In 1625 only one-sixth of Buckingham's original fleet of 90 at Ré had been owned by the king, and Charles had only 28 ships over 200 tons.[157] In 1642 he had 42 ships totalling 23,000 tons, representing in part the fruits of ship money.[158] In the period 1643–5 there were 164 state ships and pinnaces, crewed by 16,723 men, augmented by 124 hired merchantmen, crewed by 9,486 men.[159] The Commonwealth expansion appears considerable by comparison with these figures, and certainly created considerable financial strain. Whereas at Ré the fleet had been crewed by 4,000 men, the 1652 fleet required 10,024, that in September 1653 (at the height of the first Dutch war) 19,254, and that in 1655 more than 13,000. 'None of England's neighbours could match it.'[160] This fleet survived the restoration, and the building programme continued. The fleet was manned by 3,000–4,000 men during peacetime and by up to 20,000 in war.[161] In all, during the restoration period, the navy absorbed up to 20 per cent of total expenditure in any given year.[162] Again this was associated with professionalisation in the officer corps – the distinction between gentlemen and tarpaulins was becoming blurred. Moreover, the navy was 'at once the largest spending department of the state, the largest industrial concern in the country, a floating community that could be as large as many a town or county community, and, in the eyes of most Englishmen . . . the only effective and desirable defence of the nation'.[163]

After 1648 the navy was a significant political, military and commercial influence. It represented a substantial financial commitment requiring full-time administration and reliable tax revenue – it was different in kind, not just in size, from the fleets of Elizabeth, James and Charles. This transformation was of lasting significance after 1660 because the link between public and private naval resources was permanently broken (see table 5.1). The fleet grew rapidly in the Dutch and Spanish wars, with consequent implications for government spending: the correlation

---

[156] B. Capp, *Cromwell's Navy: The Fleet and the English Revolution 1648–1660* (Oxford, 1989), 4–5, 6–9. See also M. Duffy, 'The foundations of British naval power', in Duffy (ed.), *The Military Revolution and the State 1500–1800* (Exeter, 1980), 49–85, esp. pp. 51–3.

[157] Thrush, 'Naval finance', p. 135. See also the figures in Duffy, 'Foundations', pp. 49–56.

[158] Andrews, *Ships*, p. 152.   [159] Ibid., p. 191.   [160] Capp, *Cromwell's Navy*, pp. 6, 9–10.

[161] J. D. Davies, *Gentlemen and Tarpaulins: The Officers and Men of the Restoration Navy* (Oxford, 1991), 10, 13. See also S. R. Hornstein, *The Restoration Navy and English Foreign Trade 1674–1688* (Aldershot, 1991), 12–13.   [162] Davies, *Gentlemen*, p. 15n.   [163] Ibid., *passim*; quotation at p. 15.

Table 5.1. *Composition of English fleets, 1588–1692*

		Royal ships	Private vessels
1588	Armada	23	79
1589	Lisbon	14	120
1625	Cadiz	14	30
1627	Ile de Ré	10	90
1635	Ship Money	19	6
1636	Ship Money	24	3
1637	Ship Money	19	9
1638	Ship Money	24	7
1639	Ship Money	28	11
1641	Summer Guard	15	10
1642	Summer Guard	16	16
1643	Summer Guard	24	23
1644	Summer Guard	30	55
1645	Summer Guard	36	16
1646	Summer Guard	25	4
1652	Mobilisation	39	0
1653	Gabbard	25	15
1666	Four Days Battle	31	1
1672	Sole Bay	32	0
1673	Schoonveldt	49	0
1688	Dartmouth's fleet	35	0
1690	Beechy Head	56	0
1692	Barfleur	55	0

Source: R. Harding, *The Evolution of the Sailing Navy, 1509–1815* (London, 1995), 152. These figures are not strictly comparable since they include ships of differing sizes and function, and mobilisations for different purposes. None the less, the trend away from reliance on private shipping is clear.

between success in naval warfare and the availability of money is generally good. The transformation of national finances provided the means to establish this differentiation, partly necessitated by the growing differences in ship design. Heavily armed merchantmen remained economic for transporting high-value, low-bulk goods in dangerous waters, but elsewhere cheaper transport of bulky goods was important. Meanwhile, naval warfare came to centre around the broadside, with consequent advantages for very big, heavily armed ships, with very large crews.[164] Once again, the implications for domestic administration were considerable. For example, naval victories in the first Dutch war

[164] J. S. Wheeler, 'Navy finance 1649–60', *HJ*, 39 (1996), 457–66, esp. p. 457; Rodger, 'Guns and sails'.

(1652–4) 'depended on England's ability to furnish the financial resources needed to double its navy's size and the logistics to sustain it with
food, men, and munitions'.[165] From May to December 1652, measures
were rather haphazard and supply insecure, but the root problem was
money. Once this was available, after December 1652, the fleet became
more effective. In April 1653 rations were available to sustain the battle
fleet of 100 ships through to October, clearly enabling greater military
effectiveness.[166] Contrarily, the only significant naval defeat suffered by
Blake came in November 1652, when supply problems had prevented
half the fleet from sailing.[167]

The increase in the military capacity of the English state between
1642 and 1646 was a more dramatic change than anything achieved in
the preceding three generations. It rested on reform of taxation, mainly
undertaken between 1640 and 1643, which produced sums of money
vastly greater than those available to earlier regimes. Reliable flows of
money supported more effective borrowing, further increasing the military potential of the state. It is also clearly the case that the quality of
arms available, and the reliability of supply more generally, were much
improved. In terms of revenue totals and the size of the army and the
navy this discontinuity is so striking as to justify the term 'revolution'.
This is particularly the case since the new capacity was of long-term
significance – a further contrast with the paroxysms of reform which
had been undertaken since the mid-sixteenth century. It was sustained
throughout the 1640s and 1650s, supporting a record of military success
which any previous regime would have welcomed.

MILITARY AND NAVAL MOBILISATION AFTER 1660

The restoration regimes did not enjoy the same continuous access to
military resources as their interregnum predecessors, but they did enjoy
the same potential for mobilisation in times of war. A small standing
army and rather larger state navy provided the basis for this military
mobilisation.[168] Underpinning this were potentially very high-yield
taxes, largely modelled on interregnum precedents. The predictability
and scale of tax flows encouraged further developments in public

---

[165] J. S. Wheeler, 'English financial operations during the first Dutch war, 1652–54', *Journal of European Economic History*, 23 (1994), 329–43, at p. 329.   [166] Ibid., pp. 341–2.

[167] Wheeler, 'Navy finance', p. 458; Wheeler, 'Financial operations', pp. 335–9.

[168] For the long-term implications of the changes undertaken during the 1640s and 1650s see Wheeler, *World Power*.

borrowing, offering considerable security to lenders. This security was increased by reducing discretion in the order of repayment while the increasing complexity of the operations further increased the role of specialists. All this meant that the restoration regime could mobilise resources for war on a scale which had been unimaginable before 1640. The Stuart state was not the dominant military power in Europe as a consequence of these changes but was considerably closer to that position than it had been in the 1620s.

An attenuated standing army was retained after the restoration. More strikingly, perhaps, recruitment did not rest so squarely on impressment. In 1649–50 the English government had faced few problems of recruitment, given agricultural depression at home.[169] This was a contrast with the forces raised for the civil war. After 1660, conditions of service at home did not seem too unattractive to many English men. It was only service abroad in war or the distant garrisons that was a real hardship. The small standing army was not well disciplined, but on the other hand its mutinies were rarely about pay and many of its men were volunteers. In 1685 there were about 8,900 men in the English army at home and abroad (and a further 9,700 in the Scottish and Irish armies). These regular forces required an annual expenditure of £283,000, a substantial sum by early Stuart standards.[170] Increasingly, army service was professionalised, so that by 1688 Gregory King could recognise army officers as a distinct social group.[171]

The navy was not reduced at the restoration and more of the gains of the Republic were retained. At the end of the Elizabethan war with Spain privateers had been more powerful than the royal navy. The Admiralty proved unable to control and direct these private enterprises with the result that sea war 'degenerated into an indecorous scramble for private profit, a scramble in which the queen's servants had peculiar advantages, but from which the Crown itself could only lose'.[172] Privateering had prompted a shipping boom and the development of considerable private skills and experience. In 1600 Sir Thomas Wilson estimated that the merchant marine was perhaps twenty times as large as the queen's navy.[173] Thus, ironically, the privateering wars had seen

[169] Wheeler, 'Logistics and supply', p. 51.
[170] J. Childs, *The Army of Charles II* (London, 1976), ch. 2, p. 216; Childs, *The Army, James II*, pp. 1–2, 5.
[171] G. Holmes, *The Making of a Great Power: Late Stuart and Early Georgian Britain 1660–1722* (London, 1993), 75–6. See, in general, Holmes, *Augustan England: Professions, State and Society, 1680–1730* (London, 1982), chs. 8, 9.   [172] Andrews, *Elizabethan Privateering*, pp. 237–8.
[173] Ibid., p. 231.

not just the harnessing of private resources, but their preponderance: 'what was taking place was a disintegration of power'. The most graphic illustration was the proposal, noted above, to use merchant auxiliaries to protect shipping in the Narrow Seas, a tacit admission of 'the inability of the royal navy to manage this duty'.[174]

The contrast with the role of the navy after the restoration could hardly be clearer. After 1660 the navy was increasingly professionalised and it competed successfully for crews. Before 1650 merchantmen had offered much better conditions, by the eighteenth century the opposite was the case, and it may have been the 1650s that witnessed the change.[175] During the restoration period the navy was a sizeable political community whose politics were significant in themselves. More importantly, perhaps, the uses and nature of the navy were a major political issue. For example, major shipbuilding programmes were undertaken. This seemed to threaten tyranny, and there was particular suspicion of big ships which were regarded as court projects. The size of the budget increased opportunities for misappropriation and large ships were dangerous if they fell into the hands of papists, or were turned to papistical ends.[176] A recent study has shown how, between 1674 and 1688, the royal navy acted as an 'instrument of national policy', protecting trade in the Mediterranean. In this respect, the navy was the 'military corollary' of the Navigation Acts, allowing the conscious regulation of trade as a whole.[177] The expansion of the English carrying trade in the eastern Mediterranean offered tempting targets to the Barbary corsairs, and there was almost continuous war with one or other of the

---

[174] Ibid., p. 238. See also K. R. Andrews, *Trade, Plunder and Settlement: Maritime Enterprise and the Genesis of the British Empire, 1480–1630* (Cambridge, 1984), esp. p. 25.

[175] For problems of manning prior to 1650 see Scammell, 'Sinews', pp. 351–64. There was a general shortage of men in the eighteenth-century marine, and the royal navy seems to have done relatively well in competition with other employers: N. A. M. Rodger, *The Wooden World: An Anatomy of the Georgian Navy* (London, 1986), 183–8. Duffy suggests that securing sufficient manpower remained a constraint on naval activity during the eighteenth century: M. Duffy, 'Introduction', in Duffy (ed.), *Parameters of British Naval Power, 1650–1850*, Exeter Maritime Studies, 7 (Exeter, 1992), 1–13, at pp. 6–10.

[176] J. D. Davies, 'The navy, parliament and political crisis in the reign of Charles II', *HJ*, 36 (1993), 271–88. For ship-building see also Davies, 'The birth of the Imperial navy? Aspects of maritime strategy, *c.* 1650–90' in Duffy (ed.), *Parameters*, 14–38, at pp. 27–31; F. Fox, 'The English naval building programme of 1664', *Mariner's Mirror*, 78 (1992), 277–92. Such fears were of particular significance under James II, of course. In fact, fears that Catholic officers were receiving disproportionate preferment under James II (as opposed to merely being allowed to hold commissions) were probably exaggerated: L. Gooch, 'Catholic officers in the navy of James II', *Recusant History*, 14 (1977–8), 276–80.

[177] Hornstein, *Restoration Navy*, quotations at pp. 262–3, 264. For the Navigation Acts, see below, pp. 411–13.

regencies in this period. The creation of the ship money fleet had led to some military success against the corsairs[178] but this advantage was now continuously secured. It was possible to defend this shipping with reasonable success, with the result that English carriers seem to have had a competitive advantage. There was 'an emerging partnership between merchants and the state' while the navy evolved 'as an instrument designed to further the interests of both'.[179] Certainly, between 1660 and 1688 there was a heightened sense of the diplomatic and strategic usefulness of the navy. In the periods of peace between the Dutch wars 'successive regimes developed a much more formal and thorough strategy for protecting British coastal and overseas trade – notably the evolution of convoy systems, the establishment of a "western squadron" to guard trade entering and leaving the Channel and the near-permanent stationing of a fleet in the Mediterranean to guard British vessels there'.[180] There were marked developments in the convoying of merchant ships in the Mediterranean and Caribbean trades during the 1690s, building on earlier measures. Long periods of monotonous cruising increased the pressure for 'professional' standards of behaviour on navy ships.[181]

The contrast was not, of course, complete. Throughout the period 1688–1713 privateering remained an important part of the naval effort.[182] In fact, 11,000 vessels were licensed during the eighteenth century but they were no longer crucial to war efforts or to the development of trade. 'By the eighteenth century, British privateering was clearly not the "characteristic form of maritime warfare" that it had been in the 1580s and 1590s. With the development of state navies, private commissioned vessels were no longer a decisive factor in the sea war.' Indeed they were in some ways unwelcome rivals for the more important naval campaigns.[183] Further afield the reach of the state navy was limited, of course. Royal naval resources were insufficient to protect East India or Levant merchants, for example, and armed merchantmen remained important in these trades. In the Levant this would have resulted in a competitive disadvantage if company merchants had not

[178] See above, p. 211.   [179] Hornstein, *Restoration Navy*, p. 262.

[180] Davies, 'Imperial navy?', pp. 17–18.

[181] A. W. H. Pearsall, 'The royal navy and trade protection, 1688–1714', *Renaissance and Modern Studies*, 30 (1986), 109–23.

[182] W. R. Meyer, 'English privateering in the war of 1688 to 1697', *Mariner's Mirror*, 67 (1981), 259–72; Meyer, 'English privateering in the War of Spanish Succession', *Mariner's Mirror*, 69 (1983), 435–47.

[183] D. J. Starkey, *British Privateering Enterprise in the Eighteenth Century*, Exeter Maritime Studies, 4 (Exeter, 1990), quotation at p. 253.

been protected by monopoly privileges. Although, for example, the royal navy was far more likely to be able to conduct operations in the Caribbean in the 1680s than it had in the 1580s, real effectiveness at that range depended on the development of a system of advanced bases, more local sources of supply and local facilities for repair. Much of this was achieved only in the middle of the eighteenth century.[184] The western squadron, which patrolled the approaches to the Channel and the Bay of Biscay, was to become crucial to trade protection. It offered security to traders coming into and out of the Channel as well as impeding French operations in the Atlantic. As we have seen, its origins lay in the later seventeenth century, but again its perfection depended on the development of an infrastructure which was not complete until the mid-eighteenth century.[185] None the less, where the roles of merchant and royal navy had been blurred in the Elizabethan and early Stuart period they were now much more clearly differentiated. Behind this lay, among other things, a transformation of the fiscal capacity of the state. It was this that allowed the creation of a sizeable and specialised royal navy.

In 1688, before the rapid expansion of the armed forces associated with King William's Wars, Gregory King estimated that there were 5,000 families headed by naval officers, 4,000 by military officers and 35,000 by common soldiers.[186] There was a distinctive group of career soldiers, although among them were men who had bought commissions in order to secure political and social status. Clearly, military service was not simply being increasingly separated from, but was coming to be actually constitutive of, social status, a status defined in terms of a relationship to state power. Moreover, 'in the world of restoration politics . . . the navy, now the biggest and the biggest-spending department of state, was too important to be insulated from prevailing social trends or to be kept politically neutral'.[187] The development of this distinctive social group was not automatically unpopular in the localities.[188]

---

[184] C. Buchet, 'The royal navy and the Caribbean, 1689–1763', *Mariner's Mirror*, 80 (1994), 30–44. One of the principal advantages of this improving infrastructure was the benefit to the health of the crews on arrival in the Caribbean. For the importance of overseas support bases see Duffy, 'Introduction'.

[185] M. Duffy, 'The establishment of the western squadron as the linchpin of British naval strategy', in Duffy (ed.), *Parameters*, 60–81. See also Duffy, 'Introduction'.

[186] Another 50,000 families were headed by common seamen, too: reprinted in P. Laslett, *The World We Have Lost – Further Explored*, 3rd edn (London, 1983), 32–3. See also Holmes, *Augustan*, ch. 9; Roy, 'Profession', esp. pp. 193–201.

[187] Roy, 'Profession', p. 196. See also Davies, 'Political crisis'.

[188] For ideological resistance to the creation of a standing army see L. G. Schwoerer, *No Standing Armies! The Antiarmy Ideology in Seventeenth-Century England* (Baltimore, 1974).

Disciplined garrison troops offered protection (and probably business) during the civil war.[189] Their presence drove awareness of debate about 'necessity' deeper into social life and it is not clear that everyone rejected the argument.[190] During the 1650s the government was probably resented less for the role of the military within it than for its policies.[191] Certainly in the Solent the military presence in the mid and later seventeenth century was not resented.[192] It was indiscipline, rather than the military presence *per se*, which caused hostility.[193]

Based on the innovative taxes of the 1640s the military potential of the English state was transformed. The fiscal innovations are considered in detail in chapter 6, but clearly they provided the basis for specialised, and by contemporary standards, well-supplied military forces on land and at sea. The army was much reduced in size at the restoration, but the capacity for war-time mobilisation remained, and it was far superior to that enjoyed under the early Stuarts. The faltering steps towards the creation of a state-owned navy in the 1630s, although significant for what they represented, were insubstantial by comparison with the revolution in naval resources that occurred in the 1650s. This naval capacity was not so significantly reduced after 1660, and played an important role in the subsequent development of overseas trade and empire. All this had implications for the role of the militia, of course.

THE MILITIA

The militia became, increasingly, an instrument for securing domestic political order. In this function it was relatively effective, particularly

---

[189] Osborne, 'Clubmen'; Hutton, 'Clubmen'; Roy, 'English civil war'. For the potentially disruptive effects of garrisons on local social and political life during the 1650s see Reece, 'Military presence', ch. 6.   [190] Hughes, 'Tyranny'.

[191] A. Fletcher, 'Oliver Cromwell and the localities: the problem of consent', in Jones, Newitt and Roberts (eds.), *Politics and People*, 187–204; Woolrych, 'Military dictatorship?'. See also Roberts's verdict on Desborough's administration in Devon: S. K. Roberts, *Recovery and Restoration in an English County: Devon Local Administration 1646–1670* (Exeter, 1985), esp. p. 51. For a similar suggestion about troops garrisoned in Ireland in the 1620s, see G. O'Brien (ed.), *Advertisements for Ireland* (Dublin, 1623), 45, reprinted in *Irish Sword*, 73 (1992), 285. This attributes ill-discipline in part to corruptions in the system for paying troops which left them poorly supplied.

[192] A. Coleby, 'Military–civilian relations on the Solent 1651–1689', *HJ*, 29 (1986), 949–61.

[193] Bennett, 'War and disorder'; R. A. Houston, 'The military and Edinburgh society, 1660–1760', *War and Society*, 11 (1993), 41–56. Dow's discussion of the government of Cromwellian Scotland suggests that the role of the army was more complex there too. She suggests that the success of the Cromwellian regime in Scotland in establishing civilian government after the Glencairn uprising in 1653 rested on the protection of the regime by the army: F. D. Dow, *Cromwellian Scotland, 1651–1660* (Edinburgh, 1979), esp. pp. 162–4. For the unpopularity of the New Model emphasising resentment of its radical politics see Gentles, *New Model*, ch. 5.

during the 1660s, but in military terms it lost ground to a standing army. However, the most recent survey of the history of the post-restoration militia is relatively impressed by its achievements: 'the late Stuart militia was truly a militia transformed'.[194] Lieutenancy books reflect an efficiently run local administration – musters enforced, rates set and collected, a supporting staff of clerk and treasurer appointed, for example. These gains did not come primarily from institutional change, however. Although the militia was given a clear statutory base and the numbers of deputies increased, the administration was very similar to that of the early Stuart period. The key was the extent of local discretion and fairly relaxed relations between lord lieutenants and their deputies. The essence of this was a change in attitude, akin to that which supported increased levels of direct taxation.

The gentry who managed the county militias in the 1660s and 70s had lived through the turmoil of the 1640s and 1650s. From their viewpoint the local companies were a reassurance against a return to anarchy on the one hand and standing armies on the other. They had good reason to inject vigour into the prime institution that stood between their hegemony and disorder. 'Our security is the militia', Sir Henry Capel told colleagues in the Commons in 1673, 'that will defend us and never conquer us.'[195]

But it seems that the principal defensive duty was against internal subversion, not foreign invasion.

Certainly, criticism of the military performance of the militia in the 1660s and after suggests continuities with the early Stuart period. In Dorset, Somerset and Wiltshire in the 1660s and 1670s there was much foot-dragging by deputies reluctant to submit to the effort of mustering and organising companies. There were political divisions and active deputies ran up against local resentments. During the second Dutch War (1664–7) these problems escalated. Local defences were poorly organised and preparations provoked familiar grumbles. The problems were on-going, too. The record of all three militias, when 'called upon to perform serious duties in 1685 . . . was little short of appalling'.[196] This accords with the rather gloomy picture painted by Western of the performance of the militia during the second Dutch war: 'it became painfully obvious that the rather small job it was given was the largest it

---

[194] Fletcher, *Reform*, p. 324.
[195] Ibid., pp. 316–32, quotation at p. 330. For taxation, see below, pp. 276–8.
[196] P. J. Norrey, 'The restoration regime in action: the relationship between central and local government in Dorset, Somerset and Wiltshire, 1660–1678', *HJ*, 31 (1988), 789–812, esp. pp. 789–96, quotation at p. 796.

was capable of doing'. As a result, the military reputation of the militia suffered a devastating blow.[197]

Other local studies have been more sanguine, however. Stater concluded that on the whole the lieutenancy 'acquitted itself remarkably well' during the second Dutch war and, in the face of Monmouth's rebellion, 'mobilized the support of the country in the King's behalf and, despite occasional lapses on the field of battle, vindicated itself as a valuable prop of the regime'.[198] In Hampshire a hand-picked lieutenancy, backed up by an intelligence system to match that of Thurloe, responded to internal threat with at least as much success as the regimes of the 1650s had enjoyed. Before 1678 it was more effective in mobilising the local population for defensive purposes too, its hand strengthened by statutory backing for the lieutenancy and a real sense of the vulnerability of the restored regime. This responsiveness was manifest too in security scares in 1678, 1683 and 1685. It was James II's dependence on the regular forces that undid him in 1688, just as the Cromwellian regime had proved brittle by failing to secure this local support.[199] In Devon too, in the 1660s at least, the restored militia reflected social and political unity reaffirming the old order, and this was a contrast with the divisive experience of the 1650s.[200]

The Nottinghamshire militia dealt effectively with the (insubstantial) threats that it faced in the 1660s[201] and in Lancashire a smaller but more effective militia emerged. It was active throughout the restoration period and experienced none of the decay suggested by Western, despite continued problems of administration. Such difficulties were not as significant as in the earlier period, and in general the Lancashire militia appears to have been an active and important local institution. The reasons probably lay in 'Its importance both to the crown as an agency through which to preserve order and security, and to the class which controlled it as a bulwark against social revolution, which political and religious non-conformity might encourage.'[202] To judge from their militia books, Norfolk and Buckinghamshire also had active militias. In Buckinghamshire between 1677 and 1687 there certainly seem to have

---

[197] J. R. Western, *The English Militia in the Eighteenth Century: The Story of a Political Issue 1660–1802* (London, 1965), 41–8, quotation at p. 44.

[198] Stater, *Noble Government*, pp. 120, 159. See also Western, *Militia*, pp. 53–7.

[199] A. M. Coleby, *Central Government and the Localities: Hampshire 1649–89* (Cambridge, 1987), 32–41, 104–13, 179–91.   [200] Roberts, *Devon*, pp. 151–2.

[201] P. R. Seddon, 'The Nottinghamshire militia and the defence of the restoration, 1660–1760', *Transactions of the Thoroton Society of Nottinghamshire*, 86 (1983 for 1982), 79–88.

[202] D. P. Carter, 'The Lancashire militia, 1660–1688', *Transactions of the Historic Society of Lancashire and Cheshire*, 132 (1983 for 1982), 155–81, quotation at p. 177.

been frequent musters followed by a regular circuit of divisional meetings, taking place between April and July each year.[203] Deputies evidently made a variety of administrative orders at these meetings, as well as hearing grievances and handing out fines.[204] Although the list of papists' arms seized in 1678 appears unimpressive, that was probably because the threat was limited, not because the administration was negligent.[205]

There is no real agreement then, but the three western counties seem to have been less effective than most. The military effectiveness of the later Stuart militia was never really tested, and so we can give no definitive impression of it. Its performance in the face of its fairly modest tasks was creditable and, measured in terms of rates and musters, the political difficulties associated with its organisation appear to have been relatively minor. Its military function was, in any case, ancillary, and so the achievement of a paper strength of 84,000 foot and 6,000 horse in 1691 is quite impressive.[206] Where the militia showed real vigour, however, was in preserving domestic political order. In closing the first session of the Cavalier parliament Charles II asked members 'so to settle the Militia [i.e. when they got home] that all seditious insurrections may not only be prevented, to which the minds of too many are inclined, but that the People may be without reasonable apprehension of such insecurity'.[207] Even the harshest critic of the restoration militia recognises that, although 'not a serious military force' 'the militia did have their successes in dispersing unarmed worshippers, arresting lone travellers and uncovering unprotected, rusting caches of arms'. On the whole, the latter function was more important: 'the militias of the later seventeenth century were, in reality, armed emergency police forces which served primarily to deter opposition and reinforce the social hierarchy of the shires'.[208] The targets were comparatively soft, but the action could certainly be vigorous.

The post-restoration militia is generally regarded as having been more efficient than its early Stuart predecessors. In part this was associated with a change in its function as it became more clearly a political agency. 'During the first years after the restoration religious noncon-

---

[203] This discussion is based on the Buckinghamshire militia book for that period held at the Huntington Library: HEH, EL 8525. The quality of the record is poorer for the 1690s, when only particular warrants are noted, but there was energetic activity during that decade too: see below, pp. 327–30. For Norfolk see R. M. Dunn (ed.), *Norfolk Lieutenancy Journal 1660–1676*, Norfolk Record Society, 45 (1977).

[204] Notably for the production of bad horses: not everything had changed!

[205] HEH, EL 8525, fo. 86r. For the threat of popery see below, pp. 324–30.

[206] Western, *Militia*, pp. 23–4 and n. [207] Quoted ibid., p. 40.

[208] Norrey, 'Restoration regime', quotations at pp. 794, 793, 795–6.

formity and political sedition were seen as indistinguishable by many English gentry.'[209] Militias were active everywhere in the 1660s, disarming and locking up the disaffected, breaking up conventicles and so forth, but after the 1660s this activity did not always command full local support. As enthusiasm for the persecuting effort waned, there was a 'growing distaste for its function of repression' and militia activities were restricted by the need to remain close to the bounds of moderate opinion.[210] In the event, it seems, the militia became politicised. It was used in elections, to enforce purges of corporations and commissions of the peace, as well as in active repression. This, increasingly, was 'a more explicitly partisan role' than that of the early Stuart lieutenancy, and the lieutenancy itself was more carefully vetted to ensure loyalty to the current regime.[211] It was no longer 'an instrument of gentry consensus' as it had been in the earlier period. Instead, it became 'the enforcer of a system that rigidly excluded a large part of society from participation'.[212]

In this function the lieutenancy was an effective tool of royalist Anglicanism – vigorous against dissenters and Catholics, paralysed when faced by the choice between royalism and Anglicanism in 1688–9. By the 1690s the taste for very active persecution was waning, but the militia was potentially available for repression.[213] This illustrates the distance that the institution had travelled away from the Elizabethan lieutenancy by 1700. Elizabethan lieutenants like Huntingdon had been willing to hunt Catholics, some more willing than others. By the late seventeenth century they were likely to be selected because of their relative willingness to pursue repression and the lieutenancy was much more a partisan political instrument than it had been. Rather than being a manifestation of local social order the lieutenancy came to represent national political order. 'By the 1670s and 1680s the time when a lord lieutenant could be counted on to defend the interests of his county neighbours against an intrusive central government was long past. Militia obligations were enforced with more zeal, and religious dissent persecuted with little regard for social standing.'[214] Social standing was no longer a sufficient qualification, and post-restoration lieutenants

---

[209] Fletcher, *Reform*, p. 333. See J. C. D. Clark, *English Society 1688–1832: Ideology, Social Structure and Political Practice during the Ancien Régime* (Cambridge, 1985), ch. 5; J. A. I. Champion, 'Religion after the restoration', *HJ*, 36 (1993), 423–30.

[210] Western, *Militia*, pp. 57–63, quotation at p. 57. See also Stater, *Noble Government*, chs. 4–5; Fletcher, *Reform*, pp. 333–5.   [211] Stater, *Noble Government*, pp. 111, 141–4, 161–6.

[212] Ibid., pp. 111, 187. See, generally, ibid., chs. 4–6; Fletcher, *Reform*, pp. 335–48.

[213] See below, pp. 327–30, for the activities of the Buckinghamshire militia in the 1690s.

[214] Stater, *Noble Government*, p. 4.

often lacked some of the social credentials of their predecessors. But this lack was compensated for by the prestige of the office – political power helped to create social pre-eminence, rather than flowing from it.

In the period before 1640 militia reform called for the transformation of a duty of service into a payment to support a specialised corps – the trained bands. Something similar happened in relation to naval power too. Merchant ships were mobilised for war, and merchants were encouraged to build ships serviceable for this purpose, but as this system broke down, ports (and eventually the whole country) were encouraged to supply money rather than ships. In the case of the militia this commutation took place under the authority of lieutenants whose legal powers were unclear. Progress was halting and tended to come in bouts of activity, between which gains might easily be lost as the necessary weapons and skills decayed. The lieutenancy therefore had, at best, a patchy record in relation to militia reform. Its record in relation to mobilisation for foreign expeditions was worse. The pressures on the office led to the impressment of poor quality recruits whose arms and equipment were frequently inadequate. The attempt to transform the duty to supply ships into a payment to support the construction of specialised ships was equally contentious, as we will see in chapter 6. The pressure for specialisation and reform in these branches of government activity was difficult to legitimate. The costs were resented, and sometimes resisted, and the achievements seem to have been less impressive than those outlined in the previous chapters. Officeholders were more effective as agents of a patriarchal state than of a military one.

Before 1640 government in the localities depended on a network of officeholders constrained by social expectations, whose public duties were not perceived to be entirely separate from their social standing. Public and private were mingled. This did not mean that they acted out of self-interest alone – indeed, if they were accused of such a thing they lost face and prestige. It was not just a matter of successful self-presentation, however, since some magistrates clearly acted selflessly and energetically. Moreover, local opinion was not necessarily at odds with relatively disinterested administrative actions. None the less, there was a broad structural problem with meeting military demands. These arose from the territorial interests of the state as a whole, not from domestic needs transmitted to national government from the localities. These demands, as with responses to threats to the social order, were not always simple reflections of material conditions. The ships that were built in the 1630s were not necessarily those that were most useful for the most pressing naval threats – need was here defined in terms of prestige and diplomatic leverage as much as military effectiveness. On the whole, these demands were less likely to meet unqualified cooperation in any particular locality – the need, such as it was, did not necessarily bear any very close relationship to local perceptions of necessity. By contrast, social policy produced frictions only where it was forced: it was otherwise implemented, modified or ignored according to perceived local needs. No such discretion was possible with the autonomous needs of government – there was a clear bottom line, which provided a means by which to distinguish between discretion and evasion.

Some headway was made in the face of these difficulties in the years before the civil wars, but this achievement was dwarfed by the capacity for mobilisation revealed in the years after 1640. This allowed for considerably greater military success than had been conceivable a generation before. The corollary was the relative decline in the military importance of the militia, and its evolution towards an internal police force. In that function it displayed some effectiveness. It rested, however, on a transformation of the lieutenancy into a politicised office. Once again, in later Stuart England, it is possible to discern a greater separation between political and social authority. At the root of these later seventeenth-century transformations was the dramatic change in the financial basis of government activity. Once again, this was not just a difference of scale, but one of kind. Government finances were revolutionised by the experience of the 1640s, and it was this revolution which did much to remove the hindrances to the development of specialised military institutions which this chapter has revealed.

CHAPTER 6

The financing of the state

This period was a fertile one for fiscal experimentation largely, though not exclusively, driven by military needs. These experiments created complex problems of legitimation, each innovation prompting different levels of administrative, legal or political difficulty. By 1640 a complex financial structure had been erected, along Heath Robinson lines, as particular solutions were found to particular parts of the revenue problem. Part of the problem was the ineffectiveness of officeholders, who acted as tax collectors only reluctantly, and this produced a pressure for institutional innovation, including a reliance on more specialised agencies. The holders of these specialised offices and licences, however, lacked the local social reputation which could offer reassurance about their public duties. As a consequence, they were the objects of suspicion and their direct material rewards added to this. Thus, before 1640 financial administration depended either on officeholders who were half-hearted or on specialised agents whose relations with established local interests were strained. The pressure for specialisation might be taken to be a sign of pressure to modernise state forms, akin to the pressure for specialised troops and ships. However, although licensees were specialised, they were not bureaucrats. Their profit depended on forms of 'rent' rather than a salary and their personal benefit from office was unknown and difficult to regulate.

The 1640s witnessed a double transformation in the financial basis of the state. On one hand the scale of government revenues increased dramatically – a necessary condition for the military transformation discussed in the previous chapter. At the same time the proportion of total income derived from parliamentary sources also increased dramatically. Calculations of this sort are to some degree speculative but the general picture is clear – the share of national wealth successfully taxed by government roughly doubled, and the proportion of income raised through parliament rose from around 25 per cent to 90 per cent or more. After 1640, in short, the rickety structure erected between 1550 and 1640, and these licensees, were swept away, and a more coherent financial system emerged. In large part it was still in the hands of officeholders, who were now persuaded to act more 'responsibly' in relation to fiscal demands. But it also contained increasingly specialised agencies – in the customs and excise administrations, and in the machine that developed to handle public borrowing and military supply. Overall, therefore, these pressures for military and fiscal reform called forth the creation of increasingly specialised offices. The second and third sections of this chapter discuss these developments chronologically, taking first the developments between 1640 and 1688 and then the effects of the wars of the 1690s. The activities of these specialised officers, and the fiscal-military activities of local officeholders, were increasingly likely to be justified in terms of necessity, and this provides a sharp contrast with the innovations made in relation to social problems. The final section of the chapter therefore draws together these threads through a brief discussion of the relationship between fiscal-military change, specialisation and the language of political necessity.

FISCAL CHANGE IN ENGLAND FROM 1550 TO 1640: LEGITIMATION, EVASION, SPECIALISATION

In the period before 1640, however, well-established prerogative rights were pushed in new directions and a series of *ad hoc* measures was used to meet particular spending needs. The result was a bewildering variety of financial exactions, of differing constitutional and legal status, and intended for quite different purposes. The political and legal arguments prompted by apparently similar financial measures could be conducted in quite different ways, therefore, depending on the legal and political principles which had justified the levy in the first place. On the other hand, underlying all these expedients were a number of common administrative problems – for example, fixing on forms of wealth that were easy to tax, or means of administration that discouraged collusion between taxpayers and collectors.[1]

There are, therefore, a number of ways to tell this complicated story. Here, however, we will concentrate on the changing form and effectiveness of the state. Officeholders – magistrates and constables – were

---

[1] For a general account of these issues see M. J. Braddick, *The Nerves of State: Taxation and the Financing of the English State, 1558–1714* (Manchester, 1996).

reluctant tax collectors, even when the legal and political status of a tax was unimpeachable. They had neighbours before and after they raised the tax, and could not easily afford to upset local interests by vigorous administration. Many financial measures, however, also raised problems of legitimation. Where arguments were unconvincing, or debatable, this might compound the reluctance or unwillingness of local officeholders to act. As a result there was pressure for specialisation – officeholders were by-passed and agents appointed with the specific purpose of raising money – and there was a search for convincing legitimations. Many non-parliamentary sources of taxation were subject to legal challenge, for example, and the dubious legality of some kinds of revenue allowed those reluctant to pay (for whatever reason) to try to use the law to avoid payment. The motives for such resistance are difficult to gauge, of course, but we should not rule out the possibility of principled objection. Agreeing to pay a particular tax was understood to be indicative of consent – precedent might be established by such consent and it was a fear of this that led to some protracted disputes about the payment of apparently trivial sums. Overall, then, a series of *ad hoc* or particular solutions were attempted, and this produces a complex story. However, the long-term pressure is clear – it was necessary, in order to raise money, to find forms of office, modes of assessment and sources of legitimate authority for the initial grant which would carry sufficient conviction to raise the necessary sums. Before the 1640s it is the pressures rather than successful adaptation that command attention.

The legitimacy of parliamentary taxation was unquestioned in this period. An examination of the difficulties experienced in raising it is therefore particularly revealing of administrative, as distinct from political or legal, difficulty. Parliamentary taxation provided an extraordinary supplement to national coffers for military purposes. In the sixteenth century the agreed purposes for which parliamentary taxation was granted came to include peace-time military expenditure, which could be claimed retrospectively. This was probably not, therefore, a new principle of taxation: the money was not being used to subsidise ordinary, civil costs of government.[2] To an extent, then, the general consequences of changing patterns of military effort were reflected in

---

[2] G. R. Elton, 'Taxation for war and peace in early Tudor England', in J. M. Winter (ed.), *War and Economic Development: Essays in Memory of David John* (Cambridge, 1975), 33–48; G. L. Harris, 'Thomas Cromwell's "new principle" of taxation', *EHR*, 93 (1978), 721–38; J. D. Alsop, 'The theory and practice of Tudor taxation', *EHR*, 97 (1982), 1–30; Alsop, 'Innovation in Tudor taxation', *EHR*, 99 (1984), 83–93. For the interpretation here: R. W. Hoyle, 'Crown, parliament and taxation in sixteenth-century England', *EHR*, 109 (1994), 1174–96.

the use of parliamentary funds. More importantly in the present context, expeditions, particularly after 1585, required extra-ordinary revenues on a very large scale, and this effectively required the resort to parliamentary taxation.

The administrative problems experienced are well known and hardly require much rehearsal. There were two principal administrative strategies for securing direct taxation in this period. The easier was simply to impose a quota: requiring, as it may be, a county or borough to produce a certain amount of money, leaving the means by which it was actually assessed to local discretion. The alternative, and much more ambitious, strategy was to set out criteria for the assessment of individual wealth and then to impose a tax on that wealth at a consistent rate. This was what the subsidy, an 'assessed' tax, sought to do. Subsidy commissioners (usually drawn from the ranks of the justices of the peace) were required to value the wealth of local people and then to raise the tax as a proportion of that valuation. Notoriously, faced with the pressure of local expectations, their valuations of their neighbour's wealth became less and less accurate. The result was that, effectively, the tax base was contracting very rapidly. Parliaments were not necessarily eager to grant subsidies, but they did so with increasing frequency.[3] This greater willingness to grant them, however, was offset by the relentless decline in the valuations on which they were based. Here, then, is a very clear example of how the demands of military mobilisation presented considerable difficulties in securing the cooperation of local officeholders.[4]

To try to suggest that in subverting tax assessment in this way officeholders were acting out of principle would be to stretch credulity beyond reasonable limits. It is clear that many subsidy commissioners were tempted to use their influence to favour their friends or to penalise their enemies, and for all of them the line of least local resistance was to produce low valuations. None the less, it is possible to discern some sense of magisterial obligation behind their actions. Wisps of evidence about the criteria for valuation suggest that social values were important – wealth was set against the family commitments of the taxpayer, their attitude towards the poor and whether or not he or she kept good

[3] For parliaments and supply see J. D. Alsop, 'Parliament and taxation', in D. M. Dean and N. L. Jones (ed.), *The Parliaments of Elizabethan England* (Oxford, 1990), 91–116; T. Cogswell, 'A low road to extinction? Supply and redress of grievances in the parliaments of the 1620s', *HJ*, 33 (1990), 283–303. In a sense, of course, the issue of the relationship between supply and redress was one of legitimation.

[4] M. J. Braddick, *Parliamentary Taxation in Seventeenth-Century England: Local Administration and Response*, Royal Historical Society, Studies in History, 70 (Woodbridge, 1994), ch. 2.

house.[5] Clearly this suggestion should not be pushed too far, but there was something of a clash of responsibilities here. There was some disjunction between their responsibilities as tax administrators and their broader social role in the locality, and that is part of the explanation for the limited success of military mobilisation in this period.[6] The contrast is with the activities in relation to social order where the beliefs that legitimated the position of officeholders also informed the policies that they were implementing.

In the face of this reluctance, the national government was not entirely powerless. For example, the privy council sought to harness concepts of honour in persuading commissioners to be harder on their neighbours. For other levies, quite intricate games of cat-and-mouse were played. In 1586, Yorkshire justices of the peace were required to produce a horse with a petronel for the musters (and justices of the quoram to produce two) on pain of dismissal. Substantial local men who refused their obligations on 'pretence of statute' were threatened that if in such an important business 'they will so obstinatelie and preciselie do nothing but what is required by the letter of the lawe yt maye happen that the observacion of other lawes will be required of them which will touche their purses more deeplie then this thinge doth'.[7] This was pretty clearly a reference to the subsidy valuations which fell far short of the real wealth of taxpayers by the 1580s. By that time, the privy council explicitly acknowledged that the subsidy valuations bore little or no relation to the actual wealth of taxpayers, but sought to achieve some increases by threatening commissioners with the disgrace of being dropped.[8] After 1523 subsidy valuations were kept by the exchequer, and this considerably increased the potential power of the government to enforce reasonable valuations.[9] In 1563, however, assessment on oath was dropped and there was consistent hostility to the direct valuation of wealth on oath and on record. As a result, the accuracy of subsidy valuations steadily declined, and in part this was because subsidy payers were aware that the rolls were a guide to taxation of all kinds.[10] By 1589

[5] Ibid., pp. 96, 111–12.

[6] For discussion of a detailed example of this see M. J. Braddick, '"Uppon this instant extraordinarie occasion": military mobilisation in Yorkshire before and after the armada', *Huntington Library Quarterly*, 61 (1998). The issue is considered more fully below, pp. 270–80.

[7] HEH, HM 30881 fos. 19v–20r. This initiative met a dusty response in other areas of the country too: L. O. Boynton, *The Elizabethan Militia 1558–1638* (London, 1967), 87–8. A petronel was a large pistol or carbine of the late sixteenth and early seventeenth centuries, used particularly by horse-soldiers.   [8] Braddick, *Parliamentary*, pp. 105–14.

[9] Hoyle, 'Crown, parliament and taxation', pp. 1178–9.

[10] Braddick, *Parliamentary*, pp. 78–105; *Nerves*, p. 210.

the privy council was expressly disavowing the intention to have 'anie
men of wealth assessed comparablie to their livinges'. Instead, they
merely asked that they be charged with 'some mediocrity according to
their callinges'.[11] They also sought to apply the statutory rules: there was
a property qualification for justices of the peace and the council tried to
ensure that the valuations of justices in the subsidy were at that level at
least.[12] If this had any general effect, however, it can only have been to
apply some brake to the rate of decline.

One reason why taxpayers were reluctant to be raised in the subsidy
roll was that it was a guide to other rates, particularly the militia rates.
So successful, in fact, was the evasion of the subsidy that the government
sought to break this link, in order to improve militia assessments.
Paradoxically, therefore, the council and the lieutenants began to insist
that the subsidy rolls were not used as the basis of valuations. Thus, in
1584, the earl of Huntingdon wrote to the militia commissioners that in
assessing militia obligations they were 'to have regarde not to the
favorable and easie taxacion sett downe in the subsydie booke but what
there levings are inded by reasonable construction, which is the trew
meaninge of the law in that case provided'.[13] On the other hand, failure
to respond adequately to demands for private arms or loans was met
with the threat of more accurate valuation for the subsidy.[14]

Until the mid-1620s the grant of a subsidy was usually accompanied
by the grant of fifteenths and tenths, but this too was a problematic
resource. This was a quota tax and enjoyed some consequent advantages. It produced a predictable yield and as the subsidy declined its
relative importance increased. The great disadvantage, however, was
that there was very little local discretion in the allocation of the burden
because this was determined by customary arrangements. The problem
of participation here was grumbling, often very well justified, about the
unfairness of the distribution. The tax probably fell on poorer taxpayers
and the burden undoubtedly fell unevenly, as economic change affected
the distribution of wealth. As a result the allocation of the burden, dating
from the fifteenth century, became increasingly unrelated to actual
wealth. Ultimately this grumbling seems to have led to the abandon-

[11] *APC, 1588–9*, p. 414.
[12] Justices were required to hold lands worth £20 per annum in order to sit on the bench and the
privy council sought to use this to ensure that they were assessed at that sum for the subsidy:
Braddick, *Parliamentary*, pp. 105–9.
[13] HEH, HM 30881, 6r–7r. See also Boynton, *Militia*, pp. 81–2; A. J. Fletcher, *Reform in the Provinces:
The Government of Stuart England* (London, 1986), 311.
[14] A. H. Smith and G. M. Baker (eds.), *The Papers of Nathaniel Bacon of Stiffkey*, III, *1586–1595*,
Norfolk Record Society, 53 (1987 and 1988), 98, 101.

ment of the tax, at a point where its yield was worth about half as much as the fast-declining subsidy. This was a relatively serious loss for the national government.[15] These two parliamentary taxes reveal some of the purely administrative difficulties of raising money. Left to their own devices, local officeholders were reluctant tax assessors. Faced with a quota, they were immediately alert to the possibility that their quota was unfair.

These administrative difficulties were common to many rates, which all adopted one or other of these strategies. Parliamentary taxation was not the principal financial resource of government, however, and for many other rates legal objections could also be made. Military costs, as we have seen, were also passed on to the subject in indirect ways, in the commutation of militia service, or the provision of ships, into a payment. This was justifiable in terms of existing crown rights, but not necessarily completely convincingly so, and here the problems of legitimation were added to those of administration.

In the case of the militia, service was supplemented by, rather than commuted to, a payment. Although there was some statutory backing for this, the resulting militia rates were contentious. This was partly for practical and partly for principled reasons. The 1558 statute had distinguished between private arms, assessed on individuals, and parish arms assessed on areas. The assessment of each was also in different hands – the commissioners for musters assessed the parish arms, justices of the peace assessed the private arms. Initially this was a distinction without a difference – the commission of the peace and of the militia were coterminous. Increasingly, however, militia affairs were entrusted to a more restricted group, and after the 1580s, to the lieutenant and his deputies. Finally, the statute laid down the rates for the private arms but left the parish arms to the discretion of the commissioners. Several potential conflicts were created by these complications. Most importantly, as we have seen, the basis of the militia was territorial – shires, hundreds and parishes had quotas. However, because the wealthiest inhabitants, paying towards private arms, were assessed in one place only their estates elsewhere effectively escaped taxation: 'a landowner who lived in Somerset, but owned extensive estates in Wiltshire, contributed only to the Somerset forces'. Thus, some areas were forced to rate their parish arms on a reduced tax base because owners of large estates locally were paying elsewhere. In areas of the country with many large estates the problem was more pronounced. Moreover, where the

---

[15] Braddick, *Parliamentary*, ch. 1.

provision of private arms fell short, perhaps as a result of this, the extra burden was passed on to the parish arms, paid by the poorer inhabitants. These inequities multiplied as the arms rating system became the basis for other military payments such as beacons, coastal defences, muster-masters' fees and ship levies, for example. The grievances that these problems produced were exacerbated by the division of responsibility, clear by the end of the sixteenth century, between justices of the peace and the lieutenancy. The statute gave common law backing to the lieutenancy by providing for enforcement of the rates through quarter sessions. Justices and sessions, however, often had little to do with the rating of parish arms by the end of the century. As a result they were frequently unwilling to throw their weight behind the lieutenancy.[16]

In 1604 the act was repealed, and this solved one set of problems by allowing more discretion in rating, which was no longer limited by the provisions of the 1558 act. In many places a principle developed in relation to poor rates was adopted – that rates should be levied on a parish basis from both inhabitants and occupiers. This meant that owners of large estates would be rated separately wherever they held lands, but this had serious implications for the provision of private arms – because estates were parcelled out, fewer individuals in any particular place would be sufficiently rich to provide the more expensive military equipment. This led to pressure to overcome some exemptions by making the clergy and absentee landlords contribute. Moreover, the discretion now in the hands of lieutenants was disturbing, and there was pressure for new legislation. In part this was because the legal basis of the lieutenancy's actions was very unclear, still more so the authority of their deputies and captains. The 1558 statute had enjoined enforcement by quarter sessions; its repeal left the lieutenancy without this backing. Thus, repeal of the 1558 act cleared the decks but did not put the militia on a secure footing.[17] In the early Stuart period difficulties over rating

---

[16] A. H. Smith, *County and Court: Government and Politics in Norfolk, 1558–1603* (Oxford, 1974), 94–100, quotation at p. 96.

[17] Ibid., pp. 100–10. The solution to these problems seems to owe much to the ship money writs which used the poor rate principle of rating occupiers as well as inhabitants. Finally, the restoration acts ended the conflict between justices and the lieutenancy by placing the militia solely in the hands of the lieutenancy. It also gave clear statutory backing to their actions and included guidelines for the use of their powers. For evidence of resistance to militia rates see Fletcher, *Reform*, pp. 310–16; Smith, *County and Court*, esp. pp. 279–84. For opposition to the costs of muster masters see T. G. Barnes, *Somerset 1625–1640: A County's Government during the 'Personal Rule'* (Chicago, 1982), 263–4; A. J. Fletcher, *A County Community in Peace and War: Sussex 1600–1660* (London, 1975), esp. pp. 186–7 (and for the costs of beacons and watches, pp. 191–2).

were closely related to questions of legality arising from the powers of the lieutenancy. Despite their social prestige the legitimacy of the lieutenants' actions in relation to the militia was open to question. That of their appointees – deputies and muster-masters – was, by extension, even more so, since they lacked not just clear legal warrant but also social prestige.

The pressure for the creation of a specialised navy gave rise to an analogous attempt to commute an established duty of service into a payment, and here too, there were both administrative and legal difficulties. During the 1630s, for 'a tradition of augmenting the Navy in times of emergency with vessels owned and paid for by the subject was substituted the notion that the ratepayer should pay for the upkeep of the Royal fleet'.[18] Money had been raised previously to cover the cost of merchant ships levied for royal service – ship levy money – rather than to build ships – ship money. Only London actually provided ships during the 1630s, although that was what the writs demanded. The payments of the 1630s were also innovatory in that inland counties contributed alongside the maritime counties.[19] In promoting this administrative innovation old notions of service were stressed and newer legitimating languages given greater prominence. In particular, transforming a service into a payment raised the question of whether ship money was a service (the provision of ships) or a tax. In that way, it provides an example of how 'changes in the organization of war could upset a political system' since 'the law still allowed the King to conscript private ships, but did not allow him to raise money to fit out his own. It allowed him to do what he did not need to do, but did not allow him to do what he did need to do.'[20] There was ambiguity over whether ship money was a tax being raised without parliamentary consent, or a form of service for which there were precedents. The levy produced a famous legal case, brought as a result of the prosecution of John Hampden for

---

[18] A. Thrush, 'Naval finance and the origins and development of ship money', in M. C. Fissel (ed.), *War and Government in Britain, 1598–1650* (Manchester, 1991), 133–62, at p. 134.

[19] In the last years of Elizabeth's reign money rather than ships had been raised and in 1603 a rate on inland counties was proposed, although it was never put into operation: P. Williams, *The Tudor Regime* (Oxford, 1979), 76–7.

[20] C. Russell, *The Causes of the English Civil War* (Oxford, 1990), 183. See also Richard Tuck's judgement that such pressures in Europe as a whole demonstrated 'the impossibility of maintaining an effective military force within the old legal framework': *Philosophy and Government 1572–1651* (Cambridge, 1993), 224. Recent accounts of intellectual change also give great emphasis to the role of warfare in leading to changes in normative vocabularies: J. Tully, 'The pen is a mighty sword: Quentin Skinner's analysis of politics', in J. Tully (ed.), *Meaning and Context: Quentin Skinner and his Critics* (Princeton, 1988), 7–25, 289–91, esp. pp. 24–5.

non-payment, and in this case, two judges found against the king, effectively on these grounds. The writ demanded a service, but Hampden was being prosecuted for a debt – money to be paid into the king's general funds. If what the king really wanted was cash then the ship money was a tax and illegal. If it was a service, Hampden could not be prosecuted for debt.[21]

Ship money also prompted discussion, either immediately or subsequently in the 1640s, about fundamental issues of legitimacy. In particular, it gave great prominence to arguments about necessity and to questions about the relationship between the royal prerogative and common law. Prerogative power was regarded as a legitimate resource to supplement the common law in cases where the common law did not apply, such as emergency conditions. Prerogative power did not rival or over-ride common law, though, and common law provided protection for the property of the subject. If ship money could be shown to be a tax it entailed the property rights of the subject which were defended by common law. As a consequence, if it was a tax, ship money could not be raised by prerogative power. This was an example of the complexity of a constitutional consensus in which a variety of presumptions about legitimacy could be reconciled. 'In some senses the king was above the law; in other senses the law was above the king. It all depended on what was being talked about, and who was being addressed.'[22] Transforming a duty of service into a payment put considerable strain on this consensus.

In raising ship money pressure was applied to expand (as critics saw it) the range of actions falling within the bounds of the prerogative. This was done with reference to a language of necessity, yoked to arguments about reason of state, and in the context of claims about the sovereignty of the seas. Ship money, in fact, was the 'most spectacular example' of the way in which Charles I's government 'resorted on many occasions to the terminology of reason of state, *salus populi*, or interest in order to justify its actions'.[23] In pushing the bounds of legitimate prerogative action proponents of the crown's position used arguments of urgency (which prevented recourse to parliament) and necessity. Their opponents found this case so implausible that they were driven to argue that

---

[21] C. Russell, 'The ship money judgements of Bramston and Davenport', reprinted in Russell, *Unrevolutionary England 1603–1642* (London, 1990), 137–44.

[22] G. Burgess, *The Politics of the Ancient Constitution: An Introduction to English Political Thought, 1603–1642* (London, 1992), ch. 7, quotation at pp. 199–200.

[23] Tuck, *Philosophy*, pp. 212–14, 223.

the prerogative should not supplement the common law but be regulated by it – if implausible arguments could be deployed to extend prerogative powers over property then property was no longer safe.[24] Sir Roger Twysden's notes about reactions in Kent to the reading of the judges' decision on the legality of ship money in 1637 demonstrate how unease about these issues of legitimacy could reach relatively wide audiences.[25]

This conflict did not necessarily presage a collapse of the regime, but it does reflect the difficulty of legitimating this particular course of action. A functional challenge was being met by means which were greeted with grudging and partial consent. These problems of legitimation, potentially at least, threatened to limit the functional effectiveness of the response. The struggle to legitimate military reform, in this case, led to the deployment of relatively new arguments about necessity which were to acquire greater prominence subsequently, for example in the writings of Henry Parker.[26] Military reform was, to this extent, 'modernising' since it resulted in increasing specialisation and differentiation of offices and reliance on a political vocabulary more familiar to twentieth-century readers.

Much attention, probably too much, has been paid to the difficulties of collecting ship money. More recently, emphasis has rightly been placed on the financial success of the rates: between 1634 and 1638, 90 per cent of the sums assessed were collected, and they were heavy by the standards then applying. In Essex, for example, this meant that 14,500 paid towards the tax by contrast with the 3,200 whose names are recorded in the subsidy rolls of 1640.[27] None the less, full payment does not necessarily signify an absence of political or administrative difficulty,[28] and the problems with ship money are interesting for current purposes because they reveal some characteristic problems in revenue raising. It was a direct tax which was not assessed by the national

[24] Burgess, *Ancient Constitution*, esp. pp. 203–4, 208; M. Mendle, 'The ship money case, the *Case of Shipmony*, and the development of Henry Parker's absolutism', *HJ*, 32 (1989), 513–36, esp. pp. 516–20.

[25] K. Fincham, 'The judges' decision on ship money in February 1637: the reaction of Kent', *BIHR*, 57 (1984), 230–7.

[26] Tuck, *Philosophy*, pp. 227–33; Mendle, 'Ship money'; Mendle, 'Parliamentary sovereignty: a very English absolutism', in N. Phillipson and Q. Skinner (eds.), *Political Discourse in Early Modern Britain* (Cambridge, 1993), 97–119.

[27] J. S. Morrill, *Revolt in the Provinces: The People of England and the Tragedies of War 1630–1648* (London, 1999), 38–44, 181–3. Subsidy rolls probably under-recorded slightly, but the point stands.

[28] See, for example, E. Marcotte, 'Shrieval administration of ship money in Cheshire, 1637: limitations of early Stuart governance', *Bulletin of the John Rylands Library*, 58 (1975–6), 137–72.

government. Like all quota taxes, ship money produced complaints about the fairness of the allocation of the quotas. In this case, the problem was exacerbated by the fact that the rate was assessed by the sheriff alone. Sheriffs were able to use other local rates as their model, but it is clear that many of them upset important local interests. Moreover, they held office for one year at a time, so that difficulties arising from a rating might easily persist beyond the sheriff's year in office. The most successful quota taxes, those of the mid and later seventeenth century, were rated by commissions rather than individuals.[29]

These rating problems were exacerbated by legal questions, too. The precise extent of the sheriff's powers to enforce collection was unclear, and the legality of the whole exercise was questioned by some contemporaries, as we have seen. Later quota taxes were free of this difficulty because they were parliamentary in origin and, therefore, unimpeachable. It is not clear what importance to attach to footdragging and legal obstruction – whether it proceeded from principle or tight-fistedness.[30] But in the long-term context examined here, it is clear that commuting a service into a payment had political consequences, and that ship money did not enjoy the ready cooperation of local officeholders by 1639. Constables were unwilling to serve and the collection rate declined.[31] The political cost of the money received by that time was higher than for the later responses to the need for revenue.

Money could be raised for these and other purposes by a number of other means. On a number of occasions, large parts of the crown estates were sold to realise immediate supply and in the short term this was a productive strategy. In the longer term, of course, it denuded the estates and further restricted the revenues from lands.[32] Two other strategies are worth mentioning here: forced loans and coat and conduct money. Both were for extraordinary supply and both were, in theory, to be repaid, but the government's record of repayment was poor (and per-

---

[29] Marcotte suggests that dependence on the sheriff was a consequence, among other things, of the fact that ship money was a service demanded by writ, which ruled out the use of the justices or a special commission: Marcotte, 'Shrieval administration', p. 167.

[30] See, for example, the role of Lord Saye and Sele: N. P. Bard, 'The ship money case and William Fiennes, Viscount Saye and Sele', *BIHR*, 50 (1977), 177–84. The issue is discussed further in Braddick, *Nerves*, pp. 140–3, 167–8. The most comprehensive recent work on ship money is A. A. M. Gill, 'Ship money during the personal rule of Charles I: politics, ideology and the law 1634 to 1640', Ph.D. thesis, University of Sheffield (1990).

[31] J. Kent, *The English Village Constable 1580–1642: A Social and Administrative Study* (Oxford, 1986), 159–68; Morrill, *Revolt*, pp. 38–44, 181–3.

[32] R. W. Hoyle (ed.), *The Estates of the English Crown, 1558–1640* (Cambridge, 1992), esp. pp. 15–31. See also R. B. Outhwaite, 'The price of crown land at the turn of the sixteenth century', *EcHR*, 2nd series, 20 (1967), 229–40.

haps deteriorating). The forced loans rested on the long-established obligation to aid the sovereign in defence of the realm, and the transformation of this service into a money payment. They were closely related to benevolences, which were gifts rather than loans, but were otherwise similar. They were unpopular, however, for although they rested on consent, that consent could not be withheld without denying the necessity for the appeal. During the Spanish wars from 1585 to 1603, and again in the 1620s, loans were used to supplement taxation, but there was a political limit. In particular, the use of a loan virtually as an alternative to parliamentary taxation in 1626 was extremely unpopular.[33] The attempt to raise a benevolence in 1614 led prominent figures in Devon to worry about, among many other things, 'The exceeding preiudice that may come to posterity, by such a President'. They declared themselves to be willing to be forward in 'all the antient lawfull, and laudable courses of this kingdome to lay downe our goods at his Majesty's feete, for the supply of his wants'.[34] Of course, they would say that, wouldn't they? But, having said it, they were bound to obey demands for goods that could be shown to have been legitimated in that way. Legitimation was of crucial importance to administration. It provided a means both to enforce but also to resist obligations. For example, coat and conduct money was a county rate to support military expeditions. It subsidised the purchase of a coat and provided the money for the transport of troops from the county to their point of embarkation. However, it might become a contentious issue because if it was not repaid then it represented a tax raised without consent.[35]

Parliamentary taxation, militia rates, ship money, coat and conduct money, forced loans and benevolences were all revenues primarily for military purposes. There was more to military success than revenue raising, of course, but on the other hand it was a pre-requisite. Underlying the military failures of the early Stuart period was a problem of participation. In part this was to do with the difficulties of securing active service in the militia, pressing troops or preserving the alliance of merchant and royal shipping, but it was also particularly marked in the

---

[33] G. L. Harriss, 'Aids, loans and benevolences', *HJ*, 6 (1963), 1–19; R. Cust, *The Forced Loan and English Politics 1626–1628* (Oxford, 1987). For a full list and description see M. Jurkowski, C. L. Smith and D. Crook, *Lay Taxes in England and Wales 1188–1688*, Public Record Office Handbook no. 31 (London, 1998), esp. pp. xlvii–xlix, 156–90, 288–9.

[34] HEH, EL 2504. See also the reply of the magistrates in Somerset, EL 2505. Oliver St John declared it to be against law, reason and religion: EL 2506.

[35] Barnes, *Somerset*, ch. 9; M. C. Fissel, *The Bishops' Wars: Charles I's Campaigns against Scotland, 1638–1640* (Cambridge, 1994), 129–37.

raising of revenue. Parliamentary taxation was unimpeachable – there is
no evidence of anyone finding legal grounds to resist a parliamentary
tax during the seventeenth century, with the exception of two instances
in the very special case of the protectoral regime of the 1650s. However,
parliamentary forms of taxation were administratively flawed. Given
discretion, officeholders were reluctant tax collectors. With their room
for discretion reduced they were reluctant to see supply granted or
suspicious of the demand for service. In the case of non-parliamentary
taxation there were plausible ways for reluctant taxpayers to claim to be
acting in the public interest, by defending important legal rights or
principles.

It was not just for military purposes that the crown sought to increase
its revenues.[36] The principal props of the ordinary revenues were the
crown lands, the customs and the various revenues arising from tenurial
relations to the crown. There is no need to labour the point that all these
revenues suffered from similar problems. The crown lands were used
not just as a financial resource, but for patronage, and this had revenue
implications.[37] The same goes for wardship, receipts from which were
one of the most important components of the crown's vestigial 'feudal'
rights. Receipts were consistently lower than they might have been
because the profits of wardship were used as a means of political reward:
the crown gave up potential revenue, granting it instead to political
servants and friends.[38] Other income also derived from the exploitation
of these vestigial rights, such as forest fines and distraint for knighthood.
In these examples of 'fiscal feudalism' long-established (if sometimes
forgotten) legal rights were being exploited for financial reasons. Although legal, this was not necessarily popular. The customs provided
substantial sums by sixteenth-century standards, but an indication of

[36] See Braddick, *Nerves*, ch. 1. For a useful summary of the early Stuart period, with some
differences of interpretation from the account offered here, see D. Thomas, 'Financial and
administrative developments', in H. Tomlinson (ed.), *Before the English Civil War: Essays on Early
Stuart Politics and Government* (London, 1983), 103–22, 200–2. F. C. Dietz, *English Public Finance
1485–1641*, II, *1558–1641* (London, 1964) is still useful on administrative matters, despite
doubts about the accuracy of some of the figures quoted. R. Ashton, 'Deficit finance in the reign
of James I', *EcHR*, 2nd series, 10 (1957), 15–29. For attempts at reform of spending see G. E.
Aylmer, 'Attempts at administrative reform, 1625–1640', *EHR*, 72 (1957), 229–59; P. R.
Seddon, 'Household reforms in the reign of James I', *BIHR*, 53 (1980), 44–55. For a sceptical
view of the role of Cranfield in the reform of the Ordnance Office, see M. B. Young, 'Illusions of
grandeur and reform at the Jacobean court: Cranfield and the Ordnance', *HJ*, 22 (1979), 53–73.

[37] Hoyle (ed.), *Estates*. See also D. W. Hollis, III, 'The crown lands and the financial dilemma in
early Stuart England', *Albion*, 26 (1994), 419–42.

[38] J. Hurstfield, 'The profits of fiscal feudalism, 1541–1602', *EcHR*, 2nd series, 8 (1955), 53–61. For
other examples of these expedients, see Braddick, *Nerves*, ch. 4.

their inefficiency is the magnitude of the improvement of the yield by the late seventeenth century – the increase in their yield kept pace with the general transformation of the scale of public finances. They were administered by specialised agents, rather than officeholders, but they were, seemingly, drawn from the ranks of people with local influence. In general, the customs administration was 'domesticated', and this probably allowed for considerable evasion. Further complications arose from the diversity of the duties. The ancient customs and the impositions were raised without parliamentary sanction, and tonnage and poundage were parliamentary to an extent that was not clearly agreed. The right to collect impositions was tested in court, and the legality of the collection of tonnage and poundage after 1625, and particularly after 1628, was questionable. Here, again, fiscal innovation produced not just practical problems but problems relating to legal validity – the failure to secure sufficient revenues by well-established means led to experiments of more dubious legality. Meanwhile, the acceptability of the officers in the ports seems to have come at the expense of evasion.[39]

Officeholders were reluctant tax collectors, and this could be exacerbated by legal difficulties. There was a temptation, therefore, to by-pass them. Specialised revenue agents, however, were regarded with particular suspicion. Another financial innovation, the transformation of purveyance into a form of taxation, illustrates the point very clearly. The obligation to supply goods at the 'king's price' was commuted into a payment in many areas in the later sixteenth century. Firstly, counties chose to enter composition agreements to supply a specified quantity of goods at the king's price, recovering the difference between that and the market price by raising a county rate. Secondly, they chose to pay this rate directly to the Board of the Greencloth, rather than to procure the goods locally. In part this was done to restrict the activities of purveyors – outsiders of generally modest status sent into the counties to secure the supply of goods. Their activities were regarded with great suspicion and the precise extent of their powers closely checked. As Robert, earl of Leicester, Lord Steward, put it in a letter to officials in Lancashire in February 1587, her majesty had 'an especiall care that her good & lovinge Subiects shall not be greeved, Iniured & wronged by the lewde dealinges of anie her mynysters, & nowe namelie purveyers, whoe have of longe tyme (as it is supposed) under pretence of her majesty's Commission abused their office contrarye to the Lawes of the Realme'. He

---

[39] There is no modern study of the customs as a whole. For a brief account of the existing literature see Braddick, *Nerves*, ch. 3 and pp. 160–2.

encouraged the discovery of such abuses, so that prosecution might give a good example to others and took the opportunity to suggest that a composition agreement would remove the necessity of such officers, whose 'dysorders . . . hath bene long complayned of'. Such composition agreements and rates were in the control of the magistracy, and this helped to allay fears about the implications of purveyance.[40]

In Norfolk there was a heated dispute between magistrates anxious to bring purveyance under quarter sessions control and those more relaxed about the authority of the Board of the Greencloth. Achieving a composition by no means ended the difficulties and in a number of places composition agreements broke down.[41] There were also persistent problems in making the agreement stick in Yorkshire in the 1590s which were similar to those experienced elsewhere in the country. It is clear that there were difficulties over meeting a composition agreement in 1590. Edward Withes had delivered the agreed number of oxen and 'weathers', but was having difficulty collecting the money due to him. This was because, it seems, 'some have delte carfully hearin & some others of the Justices have so neglected the same as that many of the cuntrye have not yet bene sessed to contribute hearunto'. This called into question the future of the agreement, or whether some other order could be taken 'to have the Cuntrye freed from the purveyance'.[42] In December the Board wrote again calling for refusers to be summoned and threatening that the agreement might break down.[43]

Problems persisted throughout the 1590s. The Board of the Greencloth wrote in 1595, pointing out that the composition agreement to provide 200 oxen a year from Yorkshire had been reached 'for the better contentment of her majesties subiectes, & for avoyding disorder in the providing thereof (least some partes of the Shire less able might be more greived & disfurnished then others, whereby might growe anye dearth or Inhauncement of prices)'.[44] The agreement was poorly honoured in May 1597, when the man responsible for receiving the composition oxen, Richard Bland, complained of the 'slender regard' had for the Board's letters in the county. This was the more remarkable, the Board claimed, given the local benefits of composition and the fact that

[40] A. Woodworth, *Purveyance for the Royal Household in the Reign of Queen Elizabeth*, Transactions of the American Philosophical Society, 35 (Philadelphia, 1945); G. E. Aylmer, 'The last years of purveyance', *EcHR*, 2nd series, 10 (1957–8), 81–93. For Leicester's letter see HEH, EL 6276. For an example of the abuses of purveyors see the complaint of Elizabeth Shawe, widow, about the seizure of poultry from her servant on the road, 2 miles from London, in January 1599: EL 6071–75.   [41] Smith, *County and Court*, pp. 293–302.

[42] HEH, HM 50657, vol. II, fo. 8v. Wethers are male sheep.   [43] Ibid., fo. 11r.

[44] Ibid., vol. I, fo. 1r.

there was now 'no shire in England but have now due regard to the service of her majestie'. Refusers were to be summoned to answer 'their said contemptuous refusalls'.[45] In April 1598 the Board wrote to the Council in the North complaining that Serjeant Lancaster and others had been at Crestawe for four days awaiting delivery of the composition oxen. They heard nothing, however, prompting the Board to 'much marvaile that yow have soe litle care therin'. They added that they could seize 40 shillings for default of each ox 'and also send downe a purveyor with hir majesties commission which we doubt would prove very grevous to the countrie to be imposed generally upon them for the particular negligence of som private persons'. The Council in the North forwarded the letter to justices of the peace and to the defaulters in order that 'Notwithstanding all which our Care you maie perceave into what hard termes & opinion we & the Contrie are brought by suche slacknes.'[46] It seems that the Board of the Greencloth made good its threat and sent a purveyor into the county early in May.[47] None the less, in December 1598 the Council in the North found it necessary to warn local magistrates to act diligently, 'Least by disappointinge him of the money . . . the composition be dissolved and the like inconvenyence happen therbie which the contrie lately tasted of almost to the generall troble of all, but particulerlie to the hinderance of those which had ther oxen taken.'[48]

Purveyors were more like contractors than the officeholders on whom administration of the rates came to depend. Their fate reflects an abiding distrust of contractors of this kind, engaged in tax collection. Magistrates were less than willing in their cooperation with the raising of purveyance, but many were restrained in their opposition. In part this was because the alternative was probably suffering the attentions of a purveyor and because to refuse was to appear undutiful. This was particularly the case since the composition agreements had been (fairly) freely entered into in order to ease the burdens on the counties. There was a sensitive balance to be struck between scrupulous attention to legal issues (dealing 'carefully') and obstruction.[49] Left to themselves, magistrates would not have produced the goods, literally, and as a result

[45] Ibid., fos. 79r–79v. See also fos. 79r–86r, for evidence of the levying of a new rate.
[46] Ibid., fos. 72r, 73r.   [47] Ibid., fos. 74r–76r.
[48] Ibid., fo. 57r. For evidence of the rates raised see ibid., fos. 58r–65r.
[49] For similar problems elsewhere see Woodworth, *Purveyance*, pp. 32–4, 37–52; J. J. N. McGurk, 'Royal purveyance in the Shire of Kent, 1590–1614', *BIHR*, 50 (1977), 58–68. In Leicestershire the issue intersected with gentry rivals and may have helped to form a broader political consciousness: R. Cust, 'Purveyance and politics in Jacobean Leicestershire' (forthcoming). I am grateful to Dr Cust for letting me see a copy of this paper prior to publication. Some further illustration is offered by the documents reproduced in Braddick, *Nerves*, pp. 202–6.

the court resorted to the services of contractors. But the contractors had an uneasy relationship with established local officeholders. Contractors were important in other aspects of government too and, once again, their activities were regarded with suspicion. We have seen, for example, their importance in military supply, and suspicions arising from the activities of expeditionary captains.

In part, this dependence on private resources, intermediaries and contractors reflected financial weakness. The government could not create a network of officers to undertake these tasks, neither could it offer remuneration sufficient to remove the temptation to 'corruption'. Peculation was effectively institutionalised by the system of dead pays, as we have seen. Instead, the government could offer 'rents': income arising from a legally created property right. For example, the crown granted monopolies and patents, reversions in lands or offices, or wardships as means of reward.[50] This was cheap for the government and could be lucrative for the licensee, but it was wasteful of potential crown income. The problem was self-sustaining, too, because it created vested interests hostile to reform.[51] These forms of government were also relatively ineffective in securing resources, with the result that the government remained poor and committed to inefficient forms of administration. To take an extreme example, monopolies might be considered a crude form of indirect taxation since they allowed the government to profit from the production and sale of particular commodities. An individual was sold or granted a monopoly on the production or import of a commodity which could yield a profit directly (as a result of control of the trade) or indirectly (through the collection of fines for infringements). Thus, a 'rent' had been created: a legal title produced an income for its holder. It was cheap for the government, and yet a lucrative gift for the recipient. In that sense it was an effective way of rewarding service. But as a form of indirect tax it was highly inefficient. It has been estimated that, in the 1630s, monopolies yielded about £100,000 to the government at a cost of £700,000 (plus goodwill) to the country.[52] As a result the problem was perpetuated. Fiscal weakness and

---

[50] For reversions see D. Thomas, 'Leases of crown lands in the reign of Elizabeth I', in Hoyle (ed.), *Estates*, 169–90, esp. pp. 183–90. For an illuminating discussion of rent-seeking behaviour and 'corruption', see L. L. Peck, *Court, Patronage and Corruption in Early Stuart England* (London, 1990), ch. 6, esp. pp. 135–6. For dead pays see above, pp. 200–1.

[51] For the way in which fee-taking obstructed reforms aimed at improving efficiency, see Thomas, 'Financial and administrative developments', pp. 109–13; Seddon, 'Household reforms'; Aylmer, 'Attempts'. For some successes achieved during the 1630s, see K. Sharpe, *The Personal Rule of Charles I* (London, 1992), 235–42.

[52] W. R. Scott, *The Constitution and Finance of English, Scottish and Irish Joint-Stock Companies to 1720*,

dependence on contractors found a natural extension in the grant of contracts as political favours. Unable to reward loyalty directly, the government offered lucrative contracts in return. The result was that inefficiencies continued or contracts were granted which had little purpose except to reward. Similarly, the use of patents of monopoly as a means of reward was a considerable temptation – they were no cost to the crown but of considerable value to the patentee. As with many other 'revenue devices', however, there was a high political cost – hostility towards the patentees and a desire to restrict the crown's use of its power to grant monopolies.

In by-passing officeholders, national governments anxious to maximise revenue might come to depend on a variety of specialised officers or licensees. Private commercial interest was harnessed for public purposes. This was particularly true in the case of public borrowing. Financial markets were primarily organised to facilitate trade – merchants secured fairly small sums of money for short periods, and depended on their personal reputation to provide security. The crown, on the other hand, required relatively large sums, often for quite long periods, and its reputation as a creditor was very poor. As a result, the crown raised money through intermediaries – individuals like Thomas Gresham, or institutions such as the Corporation of London – with good reputations. In some cases, this obviously required the trading of favours. For example, the administration of the customs was farmed out for much of the early seventeenth century. Syndicates of merchants paid a fixed sum to the crown for the right to collect the customs for a specified period. There were administrative advantages to this arrangement. The crown received a steady income, and the farmers had an incentive to improve the yield. As a consequence, the rent could be increased each time a new lease was granted. The obvious drawback, however, was that part of the profits of the customs administration was going to private individuals, rather than to the crown. This was, after all, the reason private individuals sought the leases. One reason for the persistence of farming, and an increasingly important one, was that farmers were frequently persuaded to act as creditors to the crown. In effect, the dependence of the crown on financial intermediaries led to

3 vols. (Cambridge, 1910–12), I, ch. xi, esp. pp. 199, 222–3. Some monopolies were more benevolent measures to encourage particular trades and manufactures, in line with the justification of the power to grant them. For a sympathetic view of the grants in the 1630s, and a consideration of projects of economic improvement more generally, see Sharpe, *Charles I*, pp. 120–4, 242–62.

the persistence of a form of tax administration which, ultimately, reduced crown income.[53]

Attempts to improve the revenues before 1640 were driven most obviously by the growing cost of military preparations. There was no single response, though. There was no obvious source of revenue – land, trade, the rights of the crown – and no single institution – parliament, the lieutenancy, the tax farmers or monopolists – which offered enough money at an acceptable political cost. The result was that particular solutions developed in each case. Defensive land forces were financed through the militia, offensive through parliamentary taxation (which was supposed to provide the means to repay forced loans and coat and conduct money, too). As the need for a specialised navy became more keenly felt, privateering became less central to the efforts of government, while the levy of private ships was commuted into a money payment. For many, of course, the obligation to muster and serve had already, effectively, been commuted into a tax. In an analogous process, purveyance of many commodities in many places had come to resemble a tax, and such commutations were attended with legal doubts. The exploitation of tenurial relations and rights to regulate the economy were no less fraught.

As a result of this variety of responses the early Stuart financial system, if that is what it was, became very complex. For example, a consolidated rate for all charges was not possible because the means for enforcing the variety of payments was, if not different in every case, at least not consistent. It is for this reason that some justices of the peace, as early as 1605, were anxious that constables keep accounts for the various rates that they collected separate, 'because as the occasion for which those taxations are made are divers and several so are the means to come by them from those that refuse payment also divers, and cannot by one measure to all be compelled'.[54] Similar ambiguities operated in the customs houses too, where the same commodity might be taxed at different rates by different authorities.[55]

Officeholders were unreliable revenue agents, non-officeholders act-

[53] For a brief summary see Braddick, *Nerves*, pp. 34–7. The key works are R. B. Outhwaite, 'The trials of foreign borrowing: the English Crown and the Antwerp money market in the mid-sixteenth century', *EcHR*, 2nd series, 19 (1966), 289–305; Outhwaite, 'Royal borrowing in the reign of Elizabeth I: the aftermath of Antwerp', *EHR*, 86 (1971), 251–63; R. Ashton, *The Crown and the Money Market 1603–1640* (Oxford, 1960).

[54] Quoted in A. H. Smith, 'Militia rates and militia statutes 1558–1663', in P. Clark, A. G. R. Smith and N. Tyacke (eds.), *The English Commonwealth 1547–1640: Essays in Politics and Society Presented to Joel Hurstfield* (Leicester, 1979), 93–110, 233–6, at p. 107.

[55] Braddick, *Nerves*, pp. 49–55.

ing as revenue agents enjoyed a more limited degree of consent to the assertion of the legitimacy of their office. In securing local compliance the national government was in something of a bind. But it was not only these issues of generalised legitimacy that hampered revenue raising, there were specific legal problems, too. With the exception of the special case of the Commonwealth and Protectoral regimes, the legality of parliamentary supply was uncontested during this period. The sources of parliamentary revenue, however, were administratively flawed and, in any case, parliaments were unwilling to grant the sums that ministers thought (and most modern historians think) were necessary. These political difficulties are not the least reason why parliamentary revenue was not the sole, or even the principal, means of responding to pressures for spending. Instead, Elizabeth and the early Stuart monarchs often sought to commute services into cash payments, or to exploit prerogative and other powers for fiscal purposes. In doing this they faced a problem in convincing people that classes of actions that were essentially innovatory really could be said to lie within the ambit of existing routines of legitimation, or that they could be justified effectively in terms of beliefs current in society at large.

GOVERNMENT FINANCES *C.* 1640–1688

This complex of *ad hoc* measures and particular responses was swept away in the civil war and never recreated. It was parliament that developed the more dependable financial resources, partly as a result of the fortunes of war, which gave it secure control over fairly rich and taxable resources. The financial exactions raised were varied and their evolution was complex, but in the end two principal innovations of long-term significance were made. Direct taxation came to rest on quotas administered by commissions of local officeholders. The advantages of the quota lay in predictability and certainty of yield, and quotas had been used to apportion a number of pre-war burdens – the numbers of militiamen and horses, the fifteenth and tenth and ship money, for example. The distribution of the burden within counties and boroughs by gentry commissions offered fairly effective local mediation of the burden. Here the predecessor was the subsidy, the administration of which had always been smooth (its fatal weakness was the lack of national discipline over the yield). The assessment, therefore, was not so much a descendant of ship money as an amalgamation of the fifteenth and tenth and the subsidy. Its immediate predecessor was the £400,000 subsidy raised in 1641. At a local level its administration was related to the development of other rating systems for poor relief, purveyance and ship money, or more ancient systems.[56] This form of direct taxation persisted well into the eighteenth century, since the land tax was quickly transformed into such a quota tax after its introduction in the 1690s. The second principal innovation, alongside the greatly increased potential of direct taxation, was the successful establishment by parliament of an excise. This form of taxation was to prove of increasing financial significance in the later seventeenth century and through most of the eighteenth. In the short term, however, it was the junior partner in the finances of the 1640s and 1650s.[57] In addition to these innovations, parliament was able to derive a good income from the customs, and again this was to persist. Customs revenues expanded as quickly as revenues in general so that the proportion of total revenue derived from the customs remained the same, despite the increase in the total scale of public revenues.[58]

The sources of revenue available to the restored regime bore a striking similarity to those of the interregnum, a similarity that made many observers uncomfortable. The most effective form of direct taxation remained the assessment and it was even raised largely according to the allocation of the overall quota arrived at in 1649. John Milward was well aware of how the civil war and Commonwealth origins of taxation in the form of monthly assessments had created a prejudice against them, but was sure that the use of the terms 'royal aid' and 'further supply' in the mid-1660s had helped to overcome this.[59] In fact, the royal aid and further supply had involved some adjustment to the quotas and in a consequent dispute the corporation of Chester explicitly linked its share to the politics of the 1640s, claiming that it had been overburdened as a punishment for royalism.[60] Such suggestions were obviously embarrassing for the restored monarchy and there were

---

[56] Braddick, *Parliamentary*, ch. 3.
[57] Ibid., ch. 4. For the later importance of the excise see C. D. Chandaman, *The English Public Revenue 1660–1688* (Oxford, 1975), ch. 2; J. Brewer, *The Sinews of Power: War, Money and the English State, 1688–1783* (London, 1989).
[58] For the customs after 1649 see M. P. Ashley, *Financial and Commercial Policy under the Cromwellian Protectorate* (Oxford, 1934); Chandaman, *Revenue*, ch. 1; E. E. Hoon, *The Organization of the English Customs System 1696–1786* (New York, 1938), esp. ch. 1. There is much important detail on financial matters during the 1640s and 1650s in J. S. Wheeler, *The Making of a World Power: War and the Military Revolution in Seventeenth-Century England* (Stroud, 1999), esp. chs. 5–9.
[59] C. Robbins (ed.), *The Diary of John Milward, Esq., 1666–8* (Cambridge, 1938), p. 308.
[60] M. J. Braddick, 'Resistance to the royal aid and further supply in Chester, 1664–1672: relations between centre and locality in restoration England', *Northern History*, 33 (1997), 108–36.

attempts to avoid using the assessment. In 1663 subsidies on the old model were raised, and in 1671 a 'new subsidy' attempted. Robert Doughty, a commissioner for the 1663 subsidies in Norfolk, was anxious to promote accurate valuation on the grounds that if the subsidy failed the only viable alternative was the assessment, a commonwealth device. During the 1690s further attempts were made to avoid using quota taxation and in 1693 the Marquis of Halifax spoke passionately against the monthly assessment 'being nothing but a military contribution taken up in the civil war, and proportion to the condition of the kingdom, as it then stood forty years ago'.[61] Quota taxation was consistently proved to be the more effective form of direct taxation, however, and it remained the basis of the land tax through much of the eighteenth century.[62]

The survival of the excise was also potentially embarrassing. The word excise had been 'ungrateful' to Milward but unlike his objection to quota taxation, a change of name would not suffice to reassure him of the dangers of such taxation.[63] None the less, it was to persist. In 1660 the excises were restricted to beer and liquors, half the receipts of which were granted to the king in perpetuity as compensation for the loss of various prerogative revenues. Schemes to extend the range of commodities liable were floated, and were promoted vigorously under pressure of war-time spending during the 1660s and 1690s. These were referred to by their opponents as schemes for a general excise. Hostility to the excise was expressed in distrust of its agents and fear that long-term grants to the crown would reduce the power of parliament. These associations of the excise with tyranny and generalised threats to liberty were reinforced by its origins – opponents associated it with standing armies and the regimes of the 1640s and 1650s. Against this, however, the excises offered secure revenues attracting little hostility from tax-payers at the point of payment. In the long run the excise provided a secure basis for borrowing. As a result, the excise provided a steadily increasing proportion of the total revenues, and particularly of ordinary, peace-time revenues.[64] The customs revenue too, was improved, again by the expedient of a mixture of farming and direct collection.[65]

---

[61] Braddick, *Nerves*, p. 213.
[62] Chandaman, *Revenue*, ch. 5; Braddick, *Nerves*, pp. 95–9. For its declining relative importance see Brewer, *Sinews*, p. 95.
[63] Robbins (ed.), *Diary*, pp. 308–10. Part of this passage is quoted in Braddick, *Nerves*, pp. 220–1.
[64] Braddick, *Parliamentary*, ch. 4; Chandaman, *Revenue*, ch. 2; Brewer, *Sinews*; P. K. O'Brien and P. Hunt, 'The emergence and consolidation of excises in the English fiscal system before the Glorious Revolution', *British Tax Review* (1997), 1, 35–58.
[65] Chandaman, *Revenue*, pp. 22–36; Hoon, *Customs*, ch. 1.

A fourth major component of restoration revenues, also relatively more important in peace-time, was the hearth tax. This demonstrated some of the continuing problems of tax-raising in the changing provisions for its collection. At some points its administration was in the hands of local officeholders, but this prompted suspicions that widespread evasion and underassessment were being encouraged by officeholders sensitive to the views of their neighbours. Direct collection, however, was resented and the officers much disliked – their role in the localities was like that of specialised agents such as the purveyors before 1640. In a sense it illustrates in microcosm the larger problem in tax assessment and collection. Local officeholders were thought to be, and probably were, more sympathetic to evasion and avoidance. In response to conflicts between tax collectors and magistrates, those promoting tax collection walked a thin line between undermining magisterial authority and condoning sharp practice on one hand, or allowing evasion of taxation on the other. For example, the privy council thought that hearth tax exemptions in Chester were being granted too easily in 1671. They wrote to the mayor and magistrates complaining about the compliance and ease of churchwardens and overseers of the poor in giving certificates of exemption. Their solution was that justices should check the certificates in petty sessions before signing them, in order to check that the information was correct. As justices in the West Riding were told in relation to the excise in 1663, the privy council did not want to appear 'to give the least Countenance either to the ffarmors or their Officers in any unwarrantable actings'. On the other hand, 'it is expected that those whom his Majesty hath been pleased to trust with the Execution of the Laws should in all just cases afford that Assistance which the Lawe allowes'.[66] Specialised revenue agents, however, were objects of acute suspicion. The power of strangers to enter houses in order to count hearths was the source of great hostility and provided the context for the abandonment of the tax as a 'badge of slavery'. The hearth tax was a casualty of the Glorious Revolution, unlike both the assessment and the excise. The window tax, in some sense a replacement for the hearth tax, did not require collectors to enter houses.[67] Officeholders were unreliable in the assessment of taxation without the discipline of a quota; officers were the objects of acute suspicion and could only really operate within tightly defined legal powers.

---

[66] CCRO, ML/3/477; PRO, PC 2/56 fo. 293. This tension is examined more fully in Braddick, *Parliamentary*, ch. 5.

[67] Braddick, *Parliamentary*, ch. 5; Chandaman, *Revenue*, ch. 3. For the window tax see W. R. Ward, 'The administration of the window and assessed taxes, 1696–1798', *EHR*, 67 (1952), 522–42.

What all these sources of revenue had in common, of course, was parliamentary sanction. The administrative problems evident in the pre-civil war period had to some extent been overcome, and this was one reason for the increased revenue potential of the restoration regime. But equally important was the absence of any respectable legal argument against compliance. It was now not possible to resist payment in the localities while claiming to be defending the public interest.

There was also innovation in public borrowing in the restoration period and in some ways this involved changes parallel to those in other areas of fiscal-military activity.[68] The great volume of goods and services required by the armed forces of the 1650s, and the great flows of public money with which they were procured, resulted in some changes in the administration of supplies. In part this rested on credit arrangements, too, at least in the case of the navy – large and predictable revenues, and greater certainty about the order in which debts would be repaid increased the creditworthiness of the regime. During the 1650s the treasurers of the navy never received enough money to pay all the costs of the fleet in any given year. From 1650 onwards the debts of successive years were paid off, providing sufficient security for further credit to be advanced. It was only after 1656, when a desire to reduce taxation coincided with active war, that credit became difficult to secure. It was not until 1659, however, as cash dried up, that suppliers were 'refusing to provide services, food and material unless they received cash on delivery'.[69] It is striking, none the less, how more reliable revenues, and strict order of repayment, allowed the government to generate its own credit.

There were other long-term developments in public borrowing too. In particular, the institutional and other means by which the government found sources of loanable funds (the machinery of credit) became more complex, routine and depersonalised. During the 1640s and 1650s, institutions, like the Corporation of London or the Livery Companies, had been unwilling to act as intermediaries, and successive regimes came to rely on particularly significant individuals such as Martin Noell. Noell's position in the administration, however, gave him control over the flow of public money, so that his position was more powerful than that of, for example, Thomas Gresham in the

---

[68] These are rather technical issues and will not be narrated in full here. The best brief introduction for the period from 1660 onwards is H. Roseveare, *The Financial Revolution 1660–1760* (London, 1991), which also contains an excellent bibliography. The case made here has been outlined at greater length in Braddick, *Nerves*, pp. 37–41.

[69] J. S. Wheeler, 'Navy finance 1649–60', *HJ*, 39 (1996), 457–66, quotation at p. 465. For the level of debt see ibid., p. 460.

Elizabethan period. On the other hand, it was less independent of the government. The same was true of other individuals, like Sir Stephen Fox, who dominated government credit operations during the 1660s on the basis of his administrative position. The government was not merely exploiting the credit of private merchants, but by ceding positions in the financial institutions of government it was possible to reinforce the financial power of these men. The restoration regime was able to draw on the credit of the Corporation of London once again, and on other large corporations such as the East India Company, but another notable innovation was the role of the goldsmith bankers. These men had developed deposit banking businesses and thereby had access to large pools of loanable funds, and began to take on business as government creditors. Here, the relationship between the development of public borrowing and the private money market was very close. The net effect of these changes was an increasing specialisation in the machinery of government credit.[70]

The instruments of credit, the specific agreements which tempted lenders to become government creditors, also evolved. Early Stuart borrowing had ultimately depended on the security of the word of the monarch, and repayment was uncertain. In the 1650s, as we have seen, the navy board began to offer repayment in strict order – debts were paid off in the order in which they had been taken on – and this considerably improved the attractiveness of government credit. This improved security came at the expense of royal power to use repayment as means of political leverage. During the 1660s further steps were taken in this direction by the exchequer, which began to offer repayment of its short-term debts in strict order. This was done by issuing, along with a traditional exchequer tally which recorded the debt, a numbered repayment order which gave a guarantee as to when the debt would be paid off. The credibility of these repayment orders depended on enforceability, of course, and parliaments began to guarantee this through powers of appropriation (granting a tax for a particular purpose) enforced by audit (the power to check that money granted for a particular purpose

[70] See Roseveare, *Financial Revolution*, ch. 2; G. O. Nichols, 'English government borrowing 1660–1688', *JBS*, 10/2 (1971), 83–104; Nichols, 'Intermediaries and the development of English government borrowing: the case of Sir John James and Major Robert Huntingdon, 1675–79', *Business History Review*, 29 (1987), 27–46. For the goldsmith bankers see also W. A. Shaw, 'The beginnings of the national debt', in T. F. Tout and J. Tait (eds.), *Historical Essays by Members of Owens College, Manchester* (London, 1902), 391–422, at pp. 407–14. For Martin Noell see Braddick, *Nerves*, 37–8.

had indeed been used in that way).[71] Once again, increased security for lenders came at the expense of monarchical or ministerial flexibility in the use of public revenues.

There was another major innovation in the instruments of credit in the 1660s, which ended in disaster, but which had implications for the future. The exchequer began to issue fiduciary orders, credit notes which were not secured against any particular revenue, but against the credit of the exchequer in general. These circulated quite widely, and their popularity led to an over-issue. The ability of the exchequer to guarantee all this credit became suspect, and the value of the orders collapsed. In 1672 repayment of the orders was halted, in the notorious Stop of the Exchequer. The principal casualties of this were the bankers, who had taken up much of the credit. The way in which they were compensated was very significant, however. Instead of cash repayment of all or some of their money, they were offered annuities – credit instruments with a face value equivalent to the sum of money they were owed which gave an annual return on this 'loan'. What had been short-term advances were thereby transformed into long-term debt – the government now had a debt which had no particular date for redemption, but which was an annual charge on the revenues. These 'Bankers' Annuities' were popular, and it seems that some people tried actively to increase the amount of this kind of debt that they held. In that sense the debacle of the Stop gave rise to an experiment in borrowing that foreshadows the better-known innovations of the 1690s.[72]

A consequence of these changes was to reduce the personal role of the monarch and over the long term this is symbolised by the transformation of a royal debt into a national one. Early Stuart borrowing had been dependent for its security on the word of the monarch and it had been raised through the good offices of individuals or corporations bribed or coerced into acting. The institutionalisation and depersonalisation of credit relationships made lending to the government increasingly attractive and creditors, by the 1690s, were acting voluntarily in the expectation of secure returns. This was underpinned by the availability of large and dependable tax revenues. However, these developments also drew on developments in the private money market.

---

[71] H. Roseveare, *The Treasury: Evolution of a British Institution* (London, 1969), 60–1; Nichols, 'Government borrowing', pp. 96–8. For the constitutional implications see J. P. Kenyon, *The Stuart Constitution, 1603–1688: Documents and Commentary* (Cambridge, 1966), esp. pp. 388–96.

[72] J. K. Horsefield, 'The "Stop of the Exchequer" revisited', *EcHR*, 2nd series, 35 (1982), 511–28; Nichols, 'Government borrowing', pp. 98–102.

Without increasingly sophisticated banking and insurance markets, and the development of the stock market, government debt could not have developed as quickly as it did.

The middle and third quarter of the seventeenth century, then, had seen significant innovations in government borrowing, which were predicated on secure income. Appropriation, audit and assignment made government credit more attractive during the 1660s. On the other hand, much of this borrowing amounted to anticipation of a fixed future sum (especially of the royal aid and further supply, for example) rather than a permanent debt. More importantly, although the crown had little room for manoeuvre over repayment, the debt remained a royal rather than a national one, ultimately dependent on the creditworthiness of an individual. As one commentator put it in 1737, the security for such loans was as dependable 'as the Breath in a Man's Nostrils'.[73] The regimes of 1660–88 were much better equipped to bear the short-fall between income and expenditure than those of the early seventeenth century, but they still depended on anticipation of particular revenues either by appropriation or through tax-collection syndicates. However, secure and renewable revenues enabled, in the 1650s and 1660s, changes in public credit that were significant features of the 'financial revolution'.

There were other signs of the development of specialised fiscal-military institutions too. As we have seen, the improved revenues on which public credit rested depended to a large extent on the assessment – local officeholders, disciplined by the quota, followed parliamentary command in raising taxation. But, alongside the magistracy, another specialised institution was developing – the excise. These dramatic changes, which meant that the restored monarchy had fiscal and military resources beyond the capacity of the early Stuarts, required not just the cooperation of the parliamentary and officeholding gentry, but were also associated with the creation of more fully bureaucratic forms of local administration.

From the 1640s on the excise had not been staffed by ordinary officeholders but by specialised officers – there was no such thing as an assessment man, but everyone knew what an exciseman was. Although the formal means of collection varied – sometimes the tax was farmed and sometimes it was in commission – beneath this layer of manage-

---

[73] P. G. M. Dickson, *The Financial Revolution in England: A Study in the Development of Public Credit 1688–1756* (London, 1967), 16.

ment there are signs of continuity. Changes of administration in the 1650s and 1660s seem to have occurred while collection remained dependent on the same substratum of officers. Following the resumption of direct collection of the excise in 1683, an initial dependence on the farmers' local organisation gave way to concerted reform. Unsuitable officers were weeded out and salaries were increased in the expectation that improved administration would increase the yield and more than cover the increased costs. Promotion by merit and training, combined with adequate salaries, further stimulated efficiency. Officers were expected to be full time, to be employed away from their place of birth and to be moved frequently. After 1687 they were also encouraged by comprehensive accident insurance and superannuation.[74] The result was a precocious bureaucracy and one which achieved notable increases in yield. In 1690 there were 1,211 full-time employees in the excise department.[75]

Men in such positions legitimated their authority in ways that were quite different from the authority claimed by magistrates. Their authority depended on knowledge, precision and the application of impersonal norms, rather than on a broadly conceived 'natural' and personal authority. The excise administration saw the creation of a new social role in the localities, that of the neutral, bureaucratic officer applying standard and rationalised rules to his conduct. This precision and professionalism was part of a wider intellectual movement, but it had the advantage of countering suspicions of corruption and arbitrary power that had attended the activities of monopolists, farmers and excisemen. By the mid-1680s an elaborate system of rides (regularised routes followed by the officers when assessing and collecting the excise) had been established which allowed for the oversight of the work of officers. As Charles Davenant put it, without such frequent circuits 'the inferior officers would have run into sloth, and the superior into corruption'. Accurate gauging of production was 'a way of maximising revenue without endangering political legitimacy'. It allowed excisemen to ensure that they could, if necessary, charge everything that was due – not a drop more or less. In this way it helped to ensure the legitimacy of collection 'by countering the fear that the officers could wield extensive and arbitrary powers'. A part of this process was the creation of a new social role for the exciseman.

---

[74] Chandaman, *Revenue*, pp. 72, 74.   [75] Braddick, *Parliamentary*, ch. 4; Brewer, *Sinews*, p. 66.

Avoiding local connections was a matter of maintaining the claims of autonomy, rationality, objectivity and, therefore, legitimacy against both a venal,
local corrupting of the national uniformity of the Excise and the claims of
excessive state intervention raised by its opponents. These rational, bureaucratic practices had to be lived out and performed in public by the exciseman.
This meant a careful modulation of language and feeling, a process of self-
fashioning.

The requirements of this new social role were outlined in print in 1697
by Ezekial Polstead, writing on the basis of his experiences as an
exciseman in South Wales. Its essence was precision, accuracy and
professionalism. Excisemen had to 'present themselves' as holders of
social positions dependent on 'knowledge and employment, rather than
on the personal or family wealth that would allow other sorts of position
to be bought'. The self that Polstead described was an ideal to which real
individuals could not, of course, really conform and Polstead's text is
partly ironic in tone. However, it was also the case that individual
magistrates could not really live up to the ideal that was set for them,
either. What was particularly striking about this new social role was that
it was 'an identity shaped by being a professional state official', applying
impersonal, mathematical rules indifferently.[76]

Clearly there were new political issues to go along with these new
institutions. The excise was thought to pose a threat to liberty quite out
of proportion to its yield and this was surely a response to the nature of
its administration. There were two principal causes. On one hand, there
was a concern that the 'easiness' of the tax, and the fact that its receipts
could be increased, made it a dangerous resource to hand over to the
executive. Thus, parliament might inadvertently grant away one of its
principal sources of power.[77] Secondly, and more significant for our
purposes, the agencies of collection were distrusted. Specialised revenue
agents, and licensees, had been the objects of suspicion before the civil
war, as we have seen. A corrupt servant represented an inversion of
good order: it might be significant, therefore, that 'rough ridings' were
used to punish both monopolists and those transgressing norms of
sexual propriety.[78] Placing the rider backwards meant that the mount
was in charge – the rider could not control the horse and was in for a
rough ride. This may have evoked an image of a wife dominating her

---

[76] M. Ogborn, *Spaces of Modernity: London's Geographies, 1680–1780* (London, 1998), quotations at
pp. 172, 173, 187, 191. For the role of the exciseman see esp. pp. 185–94. See also Ogborn, 'The
capacities of the state: Charles Davenant and the management of the Excise, 1683–1698',
Journal of Historical Geography, 24/3 (1998), 289–312.   [77] Braddick, *Nerves*, pp. 148–9.
[78] Braddick, *Nerves*, frontispiece.

husband or a servant deceiving his or her master. The initial response to excisemen seems to have been similar – they were described in terms of a biblical plague, as caterpillars, frogs or locusts. This violent language was reserved for those clearly profiting from activity as revenue agents, such as monopolists – it does not seem to have been used against constables or magistrates acting as tax collectors. The resonance, presumably, was of an invasion from outside, devouring local crops to the peril of the inhabitants. A clue to the rationale for this hostility is provided by Heal's observation that there was in early modern England 'an aristocratic or elite ethos in which honour accrued to acts of beneficence and shame to forms of avarice'.[79] Magisterial tax collectors exercised beneficence through indulgence and a relatively relaxed view of the regulations. Excisemen pressed the letter of the law out of self-interest, to the point where they might be suspected of cozening both the king and the country. One defence against charges of corruption was precision about the task in hand – expressed in our terms as professionalisation, specialisation and bureaucratisation. The 'bureaucratisation' of the excise can be seen, therefore, as a means of legitimation. Of course, another safeguard was magisterial oversight of their actions, something which often caused friction between excisemen, magistrates and the privy council.[80]

Alongside the developing corps of specialised military personnel discussed in the previous chapter, therefore, there was in later seventeenth-century England a growing body of full-time administrators. The customs administration employed 1,313 full-time officers in 1688,[81] and it was more than just a revenue service. After 1660 the tariffs were more consciously manipulated to promote trade and domestic manufactures, not simply to raise revenue. As an instrument of trade policy the customs administration was required to implement large numbers of regulations and this added considerably to the complexity of an officer's life.[82] This resource was an essential prerequisite for the establishment of the navigation system, which regulated the trade of the expanding empire.[83] Military supply was also improved in the later Stuart period. The

---

[79] F. Heal, *Hospitality in Early Modern England* (Oxford, 1990), 389.
[80] Braddick, *Parliamentary*, pp. 211–20.   [81] Brewer, *Sinews*, p. 66.
[82] Braddick, *Nerves*, pp. 120–3; Hoon, *Customs*, pp. 26–7. Their activities in imposing quarantine measures may have been significant too: E. A. Carson, 'The customs quarantine service', *Mariner's Mirror*, 64 (1978), 63–9. Or perhaps not: P. Slack, *The Impact of the Plague in Tudor and Stuart England* (Oxford, 1990), ch. 12; Slack, 'The response to the plague in early modern England: public policies and their consequences', in J. Walter and R. Schofield (eds.), *Famine, Disease and the Social Order in Early Modern Society* (Cambridge, 1989), 167–87.
[83] See below, ch. 9.

development of a system of salaries in the Ordnance Office overcame the difficulties associated with a fee'd administration and an ethos of public service began to pervade the office.[84] This did not occur overnight, of course, and problems outside the office remained – awkward divisions of responsibility, shortages of storage and loading facilities, for example.[85] Since not all the problems of early Stuart supply had been due to the shortcomings of the Ordnance Office, remedy required more than reform of that institution. None the less, by 1714 offices were not regarded as property, there was no trade in them, life tenures had been abolished, a 'rudimentary' salaried structure had been established and a 'permanent civil service of clerks was also taking root under the principal officers'. All this was associated with 'a new spirit of public service'.[86] During the seventeenth century military supply had come to depend increasingly heavily on contracting, as purveyance for military supply became less important. From 1699 contracts were publicly advertised, reducing the corruptions of the system and offering the possibility of reducing costs.[87] As with the financial developments, this must have depended, to an extent, on economic developments occurring independently of changes in administration.

The 1660s saw something of a still-born financial revolution. This implied a reduction in the personal authority of the monarch in that it appeared to transform the royal debt into a public debt. The security offered to lenders was improved by reducing the scope for 'preference' in repayment, and part of this increased security rested on parliamentary powers of audit and appropriation. The power of the monarch, as medievalists would surely point out, was not 'personal' in a literal sense, and had been tied to a sense of the public good for some time. But here, the location of this political authority was abstracted still further – the security of the debt was increasingly dissociated from the word of any individual. It lay, instead, with the state. There is an analogy with the transformation of the military resources, too. Before 1640 military effort on land and sea had depended substantially on private resources mobil-

---

[84] H. C. Tomlinson, 'Place and profit: an examination of the Ordnance Office, 1660–1714', *TRHS*, 5th series, 25 (1975), 55–75; Tomlinson, *Guns and Government: The Ordnance Office under the Later Stuarts*, Royal Historical Society, Studies in History, 15 (London, 1979).

[85] H. C. Tomlinson, 'The Ordnance Office and the navy, 1660–1714', *EHR*, 90 (1975), 19–39.

[86] Tomlinson, *Guns*, ch. 2, quotations from p. 17. For an impression of a day's business, see N. A. M. Rodger, 'The Ordnance Board in 1666', *Mariner's Mirror*, 62 (1976), 91–4.

[87] J. D. Alsop and K. R. Dick, 'The origins of public tendering for royal navy provisions, 1699–1720', *Mariner's Mirror*, 80 (1994), 395–402. For rising standards of administrative probity in general, see G. Holmes, *Augustan England: Professions, State and Society* (London, 1982), ch. 8.

ised with reference to obligations to serve the monarch. After 1660 military service was more frequently voluntary and undertaken as a kind of employment. Arguments of military necessity were taken more seriously in parliament and, apparently, in the localities. Again, this was dissociated from personal obligations to serve the monarch. It is possible, then, that an impersonal sense of the state was pretty widely understood in late seventeenth-century England. Certainly, these new, more differentiated institutions of government were not regarded as the king's, and their purposes not restricted to his. For example, commercial policy was more self-consciously pursued, exploiting new fiscal and military resources.[88] In many ways, then, the central features of the 'fiscal-military' state, and many of the political issues raised by its power, were visible before 1688.

MILITARY AND FISCAL MOBILISATION: 1688 AND ALL THAT

These developments were to be the basis for further innovations after 1688. The changes in borrowing suggested by the reforms of the 1650s and 1660s, and the institution of the excise, became steadily more important, while the size of the military mobilisation was staggering by comparison with what had gone before. The story has been well told in many places but it is worth singling out some of the developments that were most innovatory. During the Nine Years War there were on average nearly 117,000 men in military service each year (more than 40,000 in the navy and over 76,000 in the army). This necessitated annual average spending of nearly £5.5m. Thus, even though taxes produced £3.64m per annum, the government quickly ran into debt. The War of Spanish Succession saw over 135,000 men in arms (about 43,000 in the navy and 93,000 in the army), at a cost of £7.06m per annum. Tax revenues now reached £5.36m per annum but even this could not save the government from accumulating still larger debts. By the end of the Nine Years War the debt was £16.7m. It was reduced to £14.1m by the outbreak of the War of Spanish Succession, but by 1713 had climbed again, reaching a dizzying £36.2m.[89]

The armies, fleets and taxes were more like Cromwell's than Cromwell's had been like Charles I's, although they were bigger. But it was the debt, and the way that it was managed, that represented the most dramatic departure – it is the changes in this area that justify the use of

---

[88] See below, ch. 9.   [89] Brewer, *Sinews*, p. 30.

the term 'Financial Revolution'.[90] These changes were closely associated with effective parliaments[91] – offering consent, long-term security for credit and the necessary funding to cover the debt. Granted the existence of these preconditions, the startling innovations of the 1690s were a product of the war years. The expenses of the war were grievous, and the response of government, facing a ceiling on its capacity to tax, was to borrow directly from the public. Although this strategy remained consistent, the means by which the potential creditors were induced to lend varied considerably, and, in the aftermath of the War of Spanish Succession, the government was left with some difficult problems.

Developments in public borrowing, as we have seen before, stimulated but also depended upon developments in private finance. Early Stuart governments were handicapped in their dealings with the money market by the inadequacy of existing credit instruments for government purposes, whereas the explosion of national debt after 1690 was considerably aided by developments in private finance.[92] The rapid development of a stock market and of instruments of private finance such as annuities, insurance and mortgages, created a financial market from which governments could draw very considerable sums. The remarkable developments of the financial revolution from 1690 onwards were those relating to the instruments and machinery of long-term credit. A variety of forms of government borrowing – lotteries, stocks, a tontine – offered combinations of security, returns and liquidity which attracted investment from large numbers of private creditors: the day of the intermediary was gone and access to the fruits of government credit was available much more widely. A number of substantial debts were launched in order to raise specific sums, and the handling of the complex arrangements for lotteries, tontines and issues of stock became, increasingly, a matter for the Bank of England rather than for the exchequer. In fact, the Bank itself was in origin a means to secure loans. Creditors were lured to supply a loan of £1.2m in 1694 with the promise that, if half of the sum was raised within a specific time then those subscribers would be incorporated as a Bank. Once established, the Bank rapidly began to offer other sums to the government, both long and short term, and in this way institutionalised the role that the goldsmith bankers had per formed a generation earlier. The incorpor-

---

[90] For the following paragraphs see, in general, Dickson, *Financial Revolution*, esp. chs. 1–4. For the effectiveness of taxation after 1690 see D. W. Jones, *War and Economy in the Age of William III and Marlborough* (Oxford, 1988), esp. pp. 66, 70–3.   [91] Dickson, *Financial Revolution*, p. 14.
[92] Ibid., pp. 40–1.

ation of the New East India Company and of the South Sea Company represented similar initiatives: stock in the companies was issued on the basis of a government charter in return for advances or credit to the government.[93]

These operations were increasingly sophisticated, and will not be narrated here, but there are a number of features of these innovations crucial for our purposes. In particular, the creation of these very specialised institutions to handle public finance greatly increased the effectiveness of credit raising. The security offered to creditors was improved by technical developments in the instruments of credit, which have to be seen in relation to the development of the private money market, and in the routinisation and institutionalisation of borrowing. Repayment of the capital sum or payment of interest was the subject of formal guarantee, the role of political influence much reduced. Behind this, though, lay the more fundamental fact that it depended on confidence in the future revenue of the regime. An effective and predictable tax regime was the asset against which, ultimately, the government was securing its credit.

It should be clear that this process had started before 1690, and we might also note that most debt in the 1690s was short term, secured in ways familiar from at least the 1660s. During the 1690s long-term borrowing was 'expensive, small in its relative amount and tentative and experimental in form'. By 1702 long-term borrowing only accounted for £6.9m of a total expenditure of £72m. By contrast, £32m had been raised in short-term loans between 1688 and 1697 alone.[94] As in the 1660s, over-borrowing by means of tallies led to a collapse in their value and in 1697 Bank of England stock was offered in return for the tallies in order to forestall a credit crisis. In 1710 a similar operation took place when a floating cash debt was exchanged for South Sea Company stock.[95] These measures are reminiscent of the issue of the Bankers' Annuities to redeem the fiduciary orders that could not be honoured in the 1660s,[96] and in other ways short-term borrowing in the 1690s was familiar in form and in the problems that it posed. The exchequer began to issue paper bills on the credit of the exchequer in general, and these bills began to circulate like money. Other departments adopted similar measures, notably the navy board, and there was a lively market in these bills. The roots of much of this also lay in the 1660s. Moreover, powers of appropriation and audit, the principle of strict repayment and the

---

[93] Ibid., ch. 3.   [94] Ibid., pp. 47, 343.   [95] Ibid., pp. 64–7, 343–57.   [96] See above, p. 259.

existence of secure tax revenues were essential prerequisites for these developments, and their origins also lie earlier in the century. The scale of borrowing, however, was remarkable, and the institutionalisation of a national debt, as opposed to a royal one, decisive.

The distinctiveness of the developments after 1690 therefore lay in the variety of instruments of credit and the development of very specialised machinery of credit, and these developments were particularly significant in respect of long-term borrowing. There was an explosion of public debt, a great increase in the range of government creditors, and the means of inducement and administrative measures to control it were largely present by the 1720s, at least. There was subsequent development, of course; after 1714 the problem of government was to reduce the cost of servicing this massive debt, rather than to secure further credit, and a number of innovations were made in this direction. Most important for present purposes, though, were the implications for legitimate authority. In this complicated story the fate of government borrowing was closely connected with the development of private finance, in both the instruments of public credit and the institutional means available for bringing borrower and creditor together. Behind this lay the question of security – these elaborate credit mechanisms depended on making government security attractive in order to secure voluntary participation in government lending. The expansion of the tax base of government in the 1640s was crucial to this and so too was the process by which, in stages from the 1660s onwards, control of the flow of these funds was taken out of the control of the monarch by means of appropriation and audit. In this way the royal debt became a national debt, and 'it is with the national debt that modern finance begins'.[97] This fundamental transformation effectively depersonalised the responsibility for the debt and hence, it might be suggested, for the finances as a whole. It was this depersonalisation that had persuaded Clarendon that such measures were 'introductive of a commonwealth'. The necessities of war in the 1640s, 1660s and 1690s had stimulated a notable growth of specialised, differentiated institutions of fiscal-military administration.

---

[97] Ashton, *Crown and Money Market*, p. 187. For some reflections on the influence of Dutch finance on these developments see M. 't Hart, '"The Devil or the Dutch": Holland's impact on the financial revolution in England, 1643–1694', *Parliaments, Estates and Representation*, 11 (1991), 39–52. Considerable political advantages accrued from a dependence on market rates for determining the returns on public loans, a fact made clear by comparison with the rather different pattern of borrowing in France: D. R. Weir, 'Tontines, public finance, and revolution in France and England, 1688–1789', *Journal of Economic History*, 49 (1989), 95–124.

Aside from the debt, much about the 1690s was familiar – in a sense it was more of the same. But it was so much more that it might no longer have been the same. During the 1690s, for the second time in forty years, government income rose much more quickly than the economy grew.[98] During the 1690s the capacity to tax seriously affected patterns of demand in the economy because supplies were secured abroad. In effect, a huge amount of demand was exported and not the least serious effect of this was a currency crisis at home.[99] The role of the navy in trade protection continued to develop, and this was associated with increasing 'professionalisation'.[100] In 1710 the British government supported 300,000 men, either in its own army and navy or with subsidies, a significant number beside a total population at that time of about 5.23m.[101] In that year military spending represented about 10 per cent of national income.[102] These are crude indicators of how 'big' the early eighteenth-century state had become. In some ways, the scale of these operations is more easily appreciated by looking at the more marginal aspects of the problem, the adoption of uniform dress for a large percentage of the adult male population, for example.[103] Such complexity inevitably reduced the personal role of the monarch.[104] The pressure for military change had, by this time, resulted in the creation of specialised institutions, and these institutions mobilised men and money in enormous quantities. More direct government, in this sense, was more effective government, too. So striking was this that the government's employees became a recognisable interest group. From 1650 onwards, but particularly after 1690, parts of the state represented a more clearly recognisable apparatus outside civil society. Not the least important feature of this was the rapid development of the excise administration, but it was manifest in many areas of fiscal and military activity.[105] This was quite different from the growth of the state prior to

[98] P. K. O'Brien and P. A. Hunt, 'The rise of a fiscal state in England, 1485–1815', *Historical Research*, 66 (1993), 129–76. [99] Jones, *War and economy*.

[100] A. W. H. Pearsall, 'The Royal Navy and trade protection, 1688–1714', *Renaissance and Modern Studies*, 30 (1986), 109–23.

[101] Brewer, *Sinews*, p. 42; E. A. Wrigley and R. S. Schofield, *The Population History of England and Wales, 1541–1871: A Reconstruction* (Cambridge, 1989), table 7.8. [102] Brewer, *Sinews*, p. 41.

[103] B. Lyndon, 'Military dress and uniformity 1680–1720', *Journal of the Society for Army Historical Research*, 54 (1976), 108–20. For an impression of the organisational difficulties associated with the campaign in Ireland in 1690 see K. Ferguson, 'The organisation of King William's army in Ireland, 1689–1692', *Irish Sword*, 18 (1990), 62–79. For the low countries see J. Childs, *The Nine Years' War and the British Army 1688–1697: The Operations in the Low Countries* (Manchester, 1991), esp. ch. 2.

[104] J. B. Hattendorf, 'English governmental machinery and the conduct of war, 1702–1713', *War and Society*, 3 (1985), 1–22. [105] Brewer, *Sinews*, ch. 3. See also Holmes, *Augustan*, ch. 8.

1640, which was most manifest in the efforts of officeholders, labouring away under their stacks of statutes.

We have noted in several places the emergence of a clearer distinction between social and political authority in later seventeenth-century England. The routinisation of local government, the modulation from patriarch to patrician, was associated with elite withdrawal from local office. The development of specialised military and financial institutions, dependent on knowledge and expertise rather than status, is a more marked example of the same thing. This might create tensions – it is one way, for example, of reading the frictions that emerged between magistrates and excisemen which were reflected in magisterial obstruction of the excise administration, sympathetic readings of the laws relating to exemptions and sometimes overt sympathy with hostility to the excise officers. Magistrates were not always able to have their way in these disputes and the privy council was willing to back tax collecting agents against the 'natural' leaders of local society. For some people, the growing importance of these agencies of the fiscal-military state might entail the discomfort of complying with the political and administrative authority of their social inferiors.[106] The creation of specialised offices led to a clearer differentiation of state agencies, and a sharper distinction between political and social authority.

FISCAL-MILITARY CHANGE, SPECIALISATION, NECESSITY AND AUTONOMY

Throughout chapters 5 and 6 we have seen how increasing functional effectiveness in relation to fiscal-military mobilisation was associated with the creation of specialised institutions, and that it increasingly implied a transformation of the perceived nature of political authority. It was associated, in particular, with a more impersonal sense of political authority and was justified not with reference to the obligations of an individual (such as a patriarch) but with impersonal claims of precision and necessity. The growth of the fiscal-military state created new social roles, justified by distinctive kinds of legitimation. Essential to an understanding of the phenomenon, therefore, is a discussion of the linguistic

---

[106] For the tensions between magistrates and excisemen see Braddick, *Parliamentary*, pp. 195–7, 211–20. For the conflict between social and administrative authority see also the tribulations of John, first Baron Ashburnham, in the later seventeenth and early eighteenth centuries: C. Brooks, 'John, 1st Baron Ashburnham, and the state, *c.* 1688–1700', *Historical Research*, 60 (1987), 64–79.

resources which justified and explained (and therefore enabled) the growth of fiscal-military power. This is, of course, a very complicated set of issues and the brief discussion that follows is by no means definitive. It does, however, illustrate how the growth of the fiscal-military state was quite distinct from the growth of the patriarchal state.

As we have seen, fiscal-military reform before 1640 was haphazard and *ad hoc*. It consisted, frequently, of commuting services into payments, or seeking to establish new functional capacities within existing legitimations. In both respects, activists enjoyed measured success, at some political cost. Discussion of these problems is complicated by the knowledge that a civil war broke out in 1642, and assertions about the significance of abstract questions of legitimacy are often related to explanations of the causes of the civil war. But another way of looking at these issues is to suggest that there was a problem of presentation in commuting services into payments. In effect, a new class of action – raising a rate for the support of a national navy – was legitimated with reference to an existing political language. To the extent that everyone recognised this language there was a consensus, but to the extent that some people thought that this new action did not fall within its remit, there was not. Put more bluntly, at issue in Hampden's case was whether or not people had to pay ship money. The terms in which the debate was conducted reflected general agreement as to the principles by which such a question might be decided, but on the practical issue – of whether to pay or not – there was fundamental disagreement.[107]

Clearly, therefore, there were problems of legitimation consequent on these innovations, although they were not necessarily harbingers of civil war. Holmes has suggested that financial expedients of the period 1558 to 1640 were justified with reference to three abstract principles: absolutist theory, prerogative rights and the claim to transcendent rights in particular circumstances.

A necessitous king attempted a number of fiscal expedients and sought to legitimize them by appeals to forms of argument that, while rooted in traditional language, were concretized and thus transformed. Royal prerogative was

---

[107] See above, pp. 241–3. For the consensus prior to 1625 see Burgess, *Ancient Constitution*, esp. chs. 5–6. For consensus prior to 1637 see Sharpe, *Charles I*, esp. pp. 714–30. Burgess explores the ways in which fundamental consensus allowed for conflict and for diversity of principled opinion. The debates about ship money, for example, did not represent 'a clash of absolutists and constitutionalists. Rather, we are witnessing increasingly divergent interpretations of a commonly accepted framework': ibid., p. 209. The point here, and not one to which Burgess would necessarily object, is that conflict short of a civil war might still reflect potentially serious problems of legitimation.

taking precise shape and was substantially intruding into the previously opaque borderland between amorphous rights of the crown and rights of the subject.[108]

In response theories of property hardened and closer thought was given to the circumstances in which taxation should be granted. The argument was also more difficult to make because of the success with which ideals of commonwealth had been propagated to officeholders. This gave them further reason to protect their localities from unwanted or unnecessary burdens.[109] After 1640, or more particularly 1660, such arguments were a thing of the past – revenue was parliamentary and there was no mileage in raising legal objections.

Policy initiatives represented new classes of administrative action, expressions of power. Successful implementation therefore required both legitimation at a general, abstract level and also that the specific powers and practical role of administrative officers should be regarded as legitimate. This required legitimation both of an abstract kind and a recognition of the legitimacy of the agents responsible for its actual exercise. Before 1640 military and fiscal innovation faced difficulties in both respects, which limited the effective power of the state. Officeholders were reluctant agents of fiscal and military reform but more specialised revenue agents were regarded with acute suspicion. In order to meet demands for credit, and in order to sustain a naval presence, governments harnessed private resources – drawing on the creditworthiness of great merchants or building coalitions of interest with the owners of armed trading ships. Problems in all these respects provided an incentive for institutional innovation – to find better ways of securing revenue, men or ships.

In seeking this innovation, it seems, activists emphasised 'necessity' – a common need which overrode the particular interest of any group or individual. This is more properly the subject of another study, of course, but the increasing purchase of these languages is suggestive. Necessity, in the sense intended here, represents a claim about the autonomous needs of the state. As a legitimation for a form of office, however, it was quite different from the beliefs in terms of which the authority of magistrates was justified. Viroli has argued that in late medieval and early modern Italian discourse it is possible to discern a conflict between

---

[108] C. Holmes, 'Parliament, liberty, taxation and property', in J. H. Hexter (ed.), *Parliament and Liberty from the Reign of Elizabeth to the English Civil War* (Stanford, 1992), 122–54, 299–304, at p. 137.

[109] Ibid. Holmes is careful to argue that these intellectual developments were connected with broader developments too, in the common law, for example, and cannot be reduced simply to reflections of fiscal needs and resistance to them.

definitions of politics as the art of good government and politics as the art of preserving a state. The former was primarily concerned with the preservation of a *respublica*, 'in the sense of a community of individuals living together in justice', the latter with the preservation of a regime. It is the triumph of the latter, with its potential for instrumentality and amorality, which led to the devaluation of the art of politics.[110] This distinction bears some resemblance to the distinction made here between the patriarchal claims on political power (the politics of good government) and fiscal-military claims (the politics of the state).

An important sub-text in calls for military reform in the early Stuart period was this kind of political necessity. The need for defensive innovation in Elizabethan England was also urged with reference to threats to the true religion, life and liberty, but because the basis for these preparations was local the response was modulated by the immediacy with which the threat was perceived in any particular place. In the privy council correspondence relating to these issues, however, we can discern the presence of a language of state – an impersonal political entity to be defended[111] – although, of course, it took its place alongside more familiar arguments stressing the gratitude of the subject for beneficent monarchical rule.[112] In the periods of active warfare in the 1590s and 1620s, and in the context of the ship money levies, rate payers, conscripts and militia men were confronted with claims about necessity and their material consequences.[113] Debates in the later years of the 1620s, and in particular those surrounding the Petition of Right, reflected stresses on existing practice. Arguments about necessity and reason of state certainly figured in these debates.[114] The experience of the ship

---

[110] M. Viroli, *From Politics to Reason of State: The Acquisition and Transformation of the Language of Politics 1250–1600* (Cambridge, 1992), esp. pp. 2–3.

[111] For privy council rhetoric and its measured practical effect see Braddick, 'Instant, extraordinarie occasion'. Some of the usages cited in M. C. Questier, *Conversion, Politics and Religion in England, 1580–1625* (Cambridge, 1996), 5–7 are also suggestive. For the increasing importance of the idea of the state see Q. Skinner, *The Foundations of Modern Political Thought*, 2 vols. (Cambridge, 1976); and Skinner, 'The state', in T. Ball, J. Farr and R. L. Hanson (eds.), *Political Innovation and Conceptual Change* (Cambridge, 1989), 90–131. For a general account of the pressure placed on notions of legality by the need for (especially military) spending see C. Russell, 'Monarchies, wars and estates', in Russell, *Unrevolutionary*, 121–36, esp. pp. 126–7.

[112] See, for examples of this, Hoyle, 'Crown, parliament and taxation', pp. 1191–6; Braddick, *Parliamentary*, pp. 110–11.

[113] Burgess, *Ancient Constitution*.

[114] Tuck, *Philosophy*, ch. 6, esp. pp. 118–19; Burgess, *Ancient Constitution*, pp. 179–202; Cogswell places the political difficulties of the 1620s parliaments in a similar context: of trying to fight an expensive war within the constraints of established and agreed practice. He suggests that 'Compulsory billeting and martial law introduced many contemporaries to constitutional questions': 'War and the liberties of the subject', in Hexter (ed.), *Parliament and Liberty*, 225–51,

money controversy gave currency to the language of necessity, and this language was picked up by Parker during the 1630s, for example. Allied to his conviction that sovereignty lay with parliament, this heightened sense of 'the necessary superiority in extreme situations of the executive over the legislative function' led to his peculiar assertion of a 'parliamentary absolutism' in the 1640s.[115]

In both the 1620s and the 1630s, the language of necessity and reason of state was linked to military and fiscal mobilisation and in both cases it was only imperfectly believed. It was probably during the 1640s, in the face of military mobilisation on an unprecedented scale, that this language acquired real purchase.[116] During the civil war, arguments of necessity were not new, but they must have become much more pressing in English villages. 'In the course of the war people came to reflect on profound questions of legality, justice, necessity and tyranny. The experience of war made these notions obviously partisan and contested.' As a result of the local experience of war, conflicts were recast in a 'politicized form', the war saw 'the creation of a specialized "political sphere" of life'.[117] The language of reason of state has a long genealogy in humanist thought, descending in particular from Tacitean scepticism, but the experience of the 1640s was, it has been suggested, formative for the European tradition as a whole. The agents of the revolutionary regimes 'were notable for the extent to which the ideas and the vocabulary of the new humanism of Tacitism and *raison d'état* were allowed a free rein in the fundamental politics of a major European state'. In the period prior to the civil war pressure for military change had placed great strains on constitutionalist arguments and, throughout

313–16, at p. 241. See also P. Christianson, 'Arguments on billeting and martial law in the parliament of 1628', *HJ*, 37 (1994), 539–67; J. A. Guy, 'The origins of the petition of right reconsidered', *HJ*, 25 (1982), 289–312. Christianson suggests, in effect, that the pressure of war had forced a consideration of the relationship between Roman law and common law.

[115] For the importance of necessity to the ship money issue see Mendle, 'Ship money', pp. 516–20. For Parker see Mendle, 'Parliamentary sovereignty', quotation at p. 98. See also Mendle, *Henry Parker and the English Civil War: the Political Thought of the Public's 'Privado'* (Cambridge, 1995). Parker's views about reason of state are also discussed by Tuck, *Philosophy*, pp. 226–33. Parker was even led to argue that legality was not the issue in the 1640s, since parliament was clearly the body best able to discern what was the national interest, ibid., p. 228.

[116] Tuck, *Philosophy*, ch. 6.

[117] A. Hughes, 'Parliamentary tyranny? Indemnity proceedings and the impact of the civil war: a case study from Warwickshire', *Midland History*, 11 (1986), 49–78, quotations at p. 71. Pre-civil-war developments were also related to military needs, of course. The issue is given lengthier consideration by Tuck, *Philosophy*, see esp. pp. 223–5. For civil war urgency, see, for example: R. Ashton, 'From cavalier to roundhead tyranny, 1642–9', in J. Morrill (ed.), *Reactions to the English Civil War 1642–1649* (London, 1982), 185–207, 242–7; Braddick, *Parliamentary*, pp. 278–9.

Europe, rulers urged necessity in trying to overcome constitutional constraint,[118] but the trauma of the English civil war seems to have been of particular significance in giving currency to these arguments.

It is important to note, of course, that the relationship between the development of political languages and of political institutions (as defined here) was reciprocal. The roots of reason of state lie not simply in the need for fiscal-military mobilisation but also in developments within humanism, in a desire to seek wisdom through the renunciation of passion, or of beliefs that induced conflict. These exercises of self-control were viewed by Grotius and Hobbes as the basis for political life – self-government was the basis of secure civil government, and this represented a political principle. Reason of state, as an idea, can be located within a genealogy of humanist thought, but it was sharpened and developed in the light of political circumstance. These arguments 'played a vital role in the construction of the effective modern states which had begun to occupy Europe, and lay siege to an entire world, by 1650'. They were particularly useful in legitimating the innovations associated with changing patterns of warfare and the attendant fiscal demands. This pressure for administrative innovation, it is claimed, led to an 'attack on constitutionalism and its replacement by a modern, instrumental and often unscrupulous politics'.[119]

It is clearly the case that political languages, as resources for political actors, have lives of their own. Indeed that is, to an extent, the reason that they can serve to legitimate particular acts. On the other hand, as resources, they acquire value through use, and reason of state and necessity enjoyed particular purchase in explaining and justifying fiscal-military innovation. None the less, this was an affinity, not a perfect correlation. Confessional issues were also important to the preservation of regimes, and the language of the state is evident in relation to these claims too. Contrarily, the power to override constitutional constraint in response to military change was not justified solely with reference to reason of state. In fact, it is more than possible that Filmer's patriarchal political vision was worked out as early as the late 1620s or early 1630s, in the context of constitutional concerns attendant on the problems of military mobilisation.[120] None the less, military challenge was creating a pressure for more specialised, differentiated institutions legitimated with

---

[118] Tuck, *Philosophy*, esp. pp. 223–32, quotation at p. xvi.
[119] Ibid., quotations at pp. xii, xiv.
[120] I am grateful to Prof. Linda Peck for pointing this out to me. See Tuck, *Philosophy*, p. 262.

reference to a language of necessity more familiar to modern eyes than the offices and languages of the patriarchal state.

Gauging the extent to which these ideas were diffused is, of course, very difficult. Much of the massively increased revenue of the post-1640 state was secured through the county gentry and virtually all of it was parliamentary. To this extent it seems to have depended as much on changing attitudes as on new institutions. During the civil wars, tax collection in England and Wales almost certainly did not rest primarily on force. In fact, violent resistance was unusual in the period from 1640 to 1660 and it is striking how often accounts of such resistance mention the presence of soldiers: collection by soldiers did not always produce violence but violence was often associated with collection by soldiers. Indirectly, of course, the soldiery was crucial since the alternative to payment of taxation was not non-payment but free quarter. Necessity had a literal meaning here that it had plainly lacked for many ship money payers in the 1630s. If this was the bottom line, however, far more immediate in most cases was the threat of distraint. The legality of the excise was not tested in court, although payment evidently stopped in 1659 during the taxpayers' strike. In 1655 Peter Wentworth threatened to challenge the Protector's right to collect assessments but was dissuaded at the last moment. This suggests that the prospect of taxpayers successfully resisting payment through the courts was not good. Collection during the period from 1640 to 1660 rested far more on the force of law than on the force of arms, although the presence of the soldiery lent urgency to arguments of necessity.[121]

This was even more clearly the case after the restoration – parliamentary grant lent unimpeachable legality to the demand and much reduced the possibilities for resistance in the localities. The puzzle, then, is why so much taxation was granted. We are not in a position to answer this question with any certainty, but Robert Doughty's remarks as a subsidy commissioner in 1663 might reflect a more general sense. His address took as its theme the responsibility of the governed to support the governors as the reciprocal obligation for the protection they gave to the governed. This was, he said, 'a truth, if not agreed on, assented to on all sides during our late uncivil civil wars when almost all things were

---

[121] M. Bennett, 'Contribution and assessment: financial exactions in the English civil war 1642–46', *War and Society*, 5 (1986), 1–11; see also Braddick, *Parliamentary*, chs. 3, 4, Conclusion; Braddick, *Nerves*, pp. 146–7.

controverted', the difference being over which took precedence. He went on to argue that 'our kings (as well ancient as modern) have in their straits and necessities, which their own revenues (though great) could not sufficiently provide against, had constant recourses (first or last) to their people in Parliament'. The rest of the address emphasised the advantages of the subsidy over rival forms of taxation, rather than seeking to justify taxation in itself. Here was a magistrate willing to throw his weight behind taxation, informed directly by the experience of civil war. It was then that 'some men's self-preservation or worse ends disguised under that pretence, made them warp from' the fundamental, reciprocal obligations of governors and governed.[122] This seems to bear the stamp of reason of state and provides quite a contrast with subsidy addresses before 1640.[123] We need to know more about the rhetorics of magistracy in the later seventeenth century, but in other respects at least Doughty was representative of the 'obscure, hard-working country justice' who was indispensable to 'the expansion of the English state and the solidifying of England's landed order during the trying times under the last Stuart monarchs'.[124]

Doughty's attitude to taxation apparently reflects debate at more exalted political levels, which seemed to focus on how to tax, and who was to control the revenues, rather than on whether to tax. In urging accurate valuation of the first two subsidies in 1663, the privy council had suggested that adequate supply would confound those 'who aim to lessen the supplies for public occasions as a means to make all things revert to the late confusions'. Disappointed with the yield of the first two, they renewed their efforts for the third and fourth subsidies. Their disappointment derived, they said, from the fact that they had hoped to 'have brought this kind of tax into usefulness and reputation'.[125] In

---

[122] J. M. Rosenheim (ed.), *The Notebook of Robert Doughty 1662–1665*, Norfolk Record Society 54 (1989), 123.

[123] For subsidy addresses prior to 1640 see those of Nathaniel Bacon and Thomas Wentworth quoted in Braddick, *Parliamentary*, pp. 110–14. For the rhetoric of early Stuart magistracy (in which reason of state does not figure prominently) see F. Heal and C. Holmes, *The Gentry in England and Wales 1500–1700* (London, 1994), 177–84; R. Cust and P. Lake, 'Sir Richard Grosvenor and the rhetoric of magistracy', *BIHR*, 54 (1981), 40–53.

[124] J. M. Rosenheim, 'Robert Doughty of Hanworth, a restoration magistrate', *Norfolk Archaeology*, 38 (1983), 296–312, quotation at p. 309. See also Goldie's suggestion that the lesson of the civil war and revolution, which was well taken by the English, was that 'It now seemed incontrovertible that the crown's supremacy was the foundation of the gentry's own authority': M. Goldie, 'Restoration political thought', in L. K. J. Glassey (ed.), *The Reigns of Charles II and James VII and II* (Basingstoke, 1997), 12–35; 253–6 at p. 12.

[125] PRO, PC 2/56 fos. 259r–259v at fo. 259v; PC 2/57, fo. 17v. See also Braddick, *Nerves*, chs. 6–7.

parliament and print arguments of national economic interest, necessity and reason of state seem to have had increasing importance.[126]

To an extent we are entitled to read a change of attitude from the practical record. Parliament granted, and officeholders collected, unprecedented sums of money through the restoration period. Moreover, although there is plenty of evidence of debate about the form of taxation – quota or assessed, on land or on other forms of wealth and so on – there is little evidence of debate about the need for taxation. Even in the numerous letters arising from Chester's dispute about the royal aid and further supply during the 1660s, many of them between the corporation and its representatives in London, there is no hint that the tax was too heavy or unnecessary. Instead, the consistent line was that the city was paying disproportionately. This was only to be expected in official letters to the privy council or treasury, but if resentment at the very demand for taxation had been a significant factor in motivating opposition one would expect at least some hint of it among the surviving correspondence.[127] Magistrates did lead resistance to forms of taxation which they did not control, and local courts were sometimes suspected of being too sympathetic to disgruntled taxpayers, but there is little evidence of such resistance to assessments, the land tax or the window tax. Generous interpretation of the rules of assessment allowed evasion to become avoidance, perhaps, but the quotas limited the damage caused by local discretion.[128] The puzzle remains, therefore, why parliament agreed to grant quota taxation in such quantities. By its very nature, much of the evidence is inconclusive, but the suggestion arises from the cumulative evidence of compliance that the parliamentary and officeholding gentry were more 'responsible' in the later seventeenth century.[129]

Before 1640 the fiscal-military functions of the English state were not well served by the agents on whose shoulders the burden of administration fell. The civil war and the defensive requirements of the republican regime led to a transformation of military potential. Behind this lay the creation of new fiscal instruments which were of lasting significance. Much of this was retained after 1660, and parts of it further developed.

---

[126] This is one of the themes of S. C. A. Pincus, 'Neither Machiavellian moment nor possessive individualism: commercial society and the defenders of the English commonwealth', *American Historical Review*, 103 (1998), 705–36. It is explored more fully in Pincus, 'From holy cause to economic interest', in S. Pincus and A. Houston (eds.), *A Nation Transformed? The Modernity of Later Seventeenth-Century England* (Cambridge, forthcoming). I am grateful to Professor Pincus for allowing me to consult this paper prior to publication. [127] Braddick, 'Royal aid'.
[128] Braddick, *Nerves*, ch. 9. [129] The phrase is taken from Fletcher, *Reform*, p. 360.

The result was that, in 1689, there was a substantial capacity for mobilisation which was once more dramatically increased. To a significant extent this rested on more direct forms of government and more specialised agencies, much more recognisably 'modern' than their early Stuart predecessors. These new institutions were justified with reference to a more thoroughly developed sense of the autonomous needs of the state, while the nationalisation of military effort simultaneously increased the effect of such arguments. Meanwhile the transformation of a royal debt into a national one represented a significant depersonalisation of political authority. Growing effectiveness was associated in the long run with the development of specialised agencies of government. Employees increasingly replaced licensed or commissioned agents, and these employees had more specialised functions. In this sense, the state was more clearly differentiated.

This institutional differentiation seems also to have been associated with changing perceptions of the nature of political authority. The dynastic and religious idiom remained important, but the instruments of fiscal and military action were not simply the king's. The identification of national interests was implicit in the criticism that the Williamite regime was following another national interest. Ultimately, the sources of legitimacy were monarchical and religious and William's claims to the throne were expressed in providential, not contractual, terms.[130] But, in practice, parliament was thought by many to be the appropriate body to ensure that the purposes to which the revenues and armed forces were put were the proper ones. We can also point to the record of the parliamentary and county gentry in supporting fiscal and military effort, a record which suggests a greater acceptance of arguments of necessity. An important feature of this was the dependence on parliamentary resources. In the later sixteenth century, and during the early seventeenth, arguments of necessity were urged by the privy council to a series of local governors, to whom the arguments made more or less sense. After 1642, military effort was financed through parliament and carried out by armed forces wholly owned by the national government. Reason of state had, by the restoration, ceased to be disreputable and had become instead a normal measure of policy. Arguments of national

---

[130] T. Claydon, *William III and the Godly Revolution* (Cambridge, 1996); J. C. D. Clark, *English Society 1688–1832: Ideology, Social Structure and Political Practice during the Ancien Régime* (Cambridge, 1985), esp. chs. 3, 5.

interest, alongside those of necessity, if they could be carried in parliament, automatically had an impact throughout the country as office-holders and taxmen responded to statutory requirements.[131]

[131] For the growing importance of arguments of national interest and changing justifications for war, see Pincus, 'Machiavellian moment'; Pincus, 'Holy cause'. It is reflected too in the development of the navigation system, see below, pp. 411–13. For the close relationship between East India Company merchants and national government in the restoration period see A. A. Sherman, 'Pressure from Leadenhall: The East India Company lobby, 1660–1678', *Business History Review*, 50 (1976), 329–55.

Conclusion

Pressure for military reform was intermittently intense and had significant fiscal consequences. There was, throughout Europe, for much of this period a tendency for armies and navies to become larger, for military equipment to become technologically more complicated and for warfare to become tactically more sophisticated. As a consequence, armies and navies became more expensive and more troublesome to organise. There are difficulties in applying the concept of a 'military revolution' to the whole of Europe since the chronology was varied and reform did not always deliver military advantage. For individual states, however, the issues are clearer – it is possible to find decisive moments of military innovation and to chart the effect of administrative and institutional change on military effectiveness. In England there had been a round of investment in up-to-date fortifications and warships under Henry VIII. A bout of more consistent pressure was applied from the later sixteenth century onwards, and after 1580 in particular. But this pressure for change posed problems of legitimation that ultimately restricted the effectiveness of reform. During the 1640s, however, rapid and lasting change occurred which transformed the capacity of governments to mobilise for war.

On land, reform came through the militia and the lieutenancy. The development of select, trained bands from within the general muster had the effect of transforming, for most people, a duty of personal service into a payment. Rather than appear personally, people supported the activities of trained bands through militia rates. This transformation was not complete, however. Richer inhabitants continued to offer service, being required by statutes of apparel to provide horse, for example. Moreover, alongside the common armour most counties had bands of private armour, again provided by individuals who were exempt from rates to support the common armour. These innovations, which involved the acquisition of more expensive firearms and equip-

281

ment as well as breeds of horse only really useful for warfare, imposed considerable costs. The practical complexities of ratings in such diverse ways could also be formidable. Above all, however, it is clear that consent was not unqualified; local resistance to this mobilisation is well remarked and the progress of improvement was, at best, halting. More than this, there were concerns about the legality of these innovations. The commutation of a service into a payment was controversial, of course, and it was administered, increasingly, by lieutenants whose formal powers were unclear. In the 1580s the office appears to have been regarded as a response to emergency conditions, but it was to become a permanent feature of county life. Lieutenants came to exercise extensive powers with questionable legal authority. In general they enjoyed a high degree of respect and consent, but activists ran the risk of prompting questions about the legal basis of their activities.

The success of this reform effort is difficult to appraise because the defensive forces were seldom tested. Historians have concentrated, therefore, on the effort expended by officeholders and on the official records of militia activity – muster rolls and letter books of lieutenants. These are problematic sources, of course. In the armada year, mobilisation in the south was effective by these criteria, although we will never know whether it would have been sufficiently effective to withstand Spanish forces if they had landed. In the north, however, it was far less effective, reflecting again some of the difficulties of transforming the duty of service in these ways. In the Bishops' Wars the opposite was true – there was much reluctance for the trained bands from the south to be deployed against the Scots. In the meantime, in the absence of any very obvious threat, reform had prompted contestation, and the summoning of parliament in 1640 led to the escalation of complaints against the powers of lieutenants. Thus, militia reform suffered from practical and formal difficulties in the localities, as well as, in the end, more generalised concerns about the ultimate source of the authority of the lieutenancy. The administration was in the hands of officeholders whose credentials for rule were good, but whose actions were constrained. In so far as innovation was explicitly justified it was done in a language of necessity – the territorial imperative of political authority. But this language of national danger simply lacked purchase or was refracted, in times of actual danger, through institutions that were regional rather than national in their competence. The way in which resources were tapped still reflected the origin of the militia in an obligation of service, and the established limits of this obligation (within particular localities or for particular purposes, such as Border defence, for example) limited the effectiveness of the mobilisation.

Two functions that were subsequently separate were conflated in the militia – defence and policing. The emergency for which lieutenants had been thought necessary was domestic subversion as much as foreign invasion. It was on this policing function that the militia was subsequently to concentrate, with some effectiveness but at the expense of consensual support. Military functions became concentrated in specialised agencies supported by national taxation. In the body granting these taxes the language of national interest and necessity had more purchase, while parliamentary sanction conferred unimpeachable legal sanction upon taxes to support national military action. Local militia rates were devoted primarily to the threat of domestic subversion. More explicitly military functions fell into the hands of garrisons of soldiers, a by-product of the changes in mobilisation that occurred during the 1640s.

Expeditionary forces had a poor record before 1640, except in Ireland, and even there the military record was to be dramatically improved after 1640. The problems were two-fold – recruitment was not opposed in the localities so much as subverted to serve other purposes; and the government did not have at its disposal forms of taxation that produced sums on the scale now thought necessary. The result was poor quality recruits with supplies of inadequate quantity and unreliable quality. Reform of taxation in the period 1640–43, with subsequent modifications, provided the basis for reliable military supply on a hitherto unattainable scale. The result was larger armies, which were better paid and supplied, and were to a remarkable degree able to attract volunteers. Much of this rested on an adjustment within existing constraints – a combination of the virtues of the quota (fifteenth and tenth) and the magisterial commission (the subsidy) in the assessment. At a local level it probably rested on the development of agreed rating systems for the poor rate and ship money. But there were also two quite distinctive features of revenues after 1640. First, they were derived from a narrower range of exactions sanctioned in a far more uniform way. Secondly, there was, among them, at least one form of taxation that was remarkably bureaucratic – the excise. Following from, and related to, the financial weakness of the Elizabethan and early Stuart armies was the problem of supply. The Ordnance Office was forced into complex solutions to the problems of supply, depending on expertise that disappeared when peace came. Here, too, the later seventeenth century saw significant regularisation and the capacity for continuous performance.

Modern bureaucratic standards were not achieved in the age of Pepys (or of Walpole), but the notion of public service in our sense was probably less alien to later Stuart officials of the Ordnance than it had been earlier.

Before 1640, governments faced pressure for spending on a number of fronts and a series of *ad hoc* measures were used to meet them. Part of the cost of military modernisation was met by passing on the burden directly to the localities – by demanding the presentation of armed and trained men rather than the money to recruit them. Expeditions were also funded from parliamentary taxation and by local levies, repaid out of parliamentary taxation, to cover the cost of delivery of the men. Similarly, pressure for household spending led to the transformation of purveyance into a cash payment, although in most counties both goods and money were supplied most of the time. General funds were supplemented by extending vestigial feudal rights or prerogative powers to regulate trade or reward invention. In order to pay for naval modernisation, another service, the provision of ships in time of war, was transformed into a payment – ship money – in order to put a royal fleet to sea on a regular basis. After 1640, virtually all money came through parliament from three sources – customs, excise and 'assessments' – paid as taxes to support patterns of expenditure increasingly determined in parliament. By comparison, early Stuart finances look like a patchwork of remedies each of which had particular problems.

The naval resources of the state were also transformed, again with long-term effects. During the armada campaign the government successfully mobilised merchant ships. Developments in trade favoured the design of armed trading ships which were not dissimilar to warships. In wartime armed trade shaded into war anyway, and the ships were easily converted for military service. The aspirations of traders, their methods and the resources at their disposal offered the prospect of a harmonious relationship with the government. This was, to an extent, institutionalised in the bounty paid to merchants to construct ships of a size that would be useful in battle. The relationship broke down in the 1620s as tensions began to emerge between the strategic interests of the government and the activities of individual merchants, while merchant ship design began to diverge from that of warships. This did not simply reflect the material realities of seventeenth-century warfare, any more than the poor law was a straightforward response to poverty. The issue is not so much the practical usefulness of these new warships as that activists successfully argued that there was a need for them. Greater difficulty in mobilising them from civilians, and the pursuit of a broader programme of naval reform, led to the transformation of ship money in the 1630s. It became a national rate deployed directly to the service of a national navy. Locally, this initiative was in the hands of the sheriffs and constables, but their specific competence was much questioned, while the whole project raised questions of legitimacy and led to close scrutiny of the legal warrant for such activity. These can be overstated, of course, and the functional effectiveness of the measures was reasonably impressive. However, like the perfect militia, there was evidently a high political cost. After 1649, naval ship-building was undertaken on a national basis but under parliamentary control, and funded from the resources already outlined. The ships that were built were increasingly specialised in function, the design of warships and of merchant ships continuing to diverge. As a result, in European waters, merchant ships were likely to be protected by naval convoys rather than by their own armaments. This specialised state navy, more clearly differentiated from the merchant marine, became a tool of more self-conscious manipulation. Here was an obvious means of pursuing the 'national interest'.

Magisterial authority was not particularly effective for military or fiscal mobilisation. Where discretion was constrained, or where magistracy was by-passed altogether (as in purveyance) there were problems of informal legitimacy and a consequently greater dependence on, and scrutiny of, legal warrant. In the end, there was a shift towards specialised agencies but their powers were specified by statute and their activities overseen by magistrates. There was close scrutiny of their legal warrant and their remuneration and terms of employment were systematised. Specialised revenue officers were more likely to be salaried or fee'd than to be operating by licence and this regularisation of the profits of office may have helped to mute the description of such agents in terms of a biblical plague. Professionalisation in these revenue offices, and in the central bureaucracy, can be understood in terms of legitimation too: the development of salary and superannuation structures, and attempts to ensure accuracy in valuation also operated to counter charges of corruption. It is for this reason – their association with professionalisation and specialisation – that military and fiscal functions were particularly important in the emergence of the 'modern' state defined in terms of specialised, bureaucratic, differentiated institutions. The legitimation of these activities was also associated with more 'modern' languages, those describing an impersonal state, necessity and autonomous, 'national' interests.

PART IV

The confessional state

Introduction

In a sense, religious policy flowed from a similar generalised sense of the need for order to that which informed the measures outlined in Part II. Indeed, one of the most influential discourses of magistracy, and one which drove much social activism among officeholders, was a godly one. The 'animating spirit' of Puritans in local government was 'a profound veneration for order and a strong disposition towards obedience: the double need to obey God and his earthly representatives, and in turn to exact the obedience due from inferiors'. Magistrates such as John Newdigate and Richard Grosvenor were clearly driven by a vision of magistracy in which the battle against sin and the promotion of true religion occupied a central place.[1] But there was also a more specific problem of religious order facing early modern governments and that was the 'confessionalisation' of politics. Political legitimacy was claimed to rest in part upon the defence of the true religion, defined in doctrinal and liturgical terms. There was a consequent pressure to define these terms and to enforce conformity to them. The importance of religion to political legitimacy meant that the religious policy of the government was also strongly affected by external considerations. This duality is clear in a privy council letter, dated 15 October 1599, sent to the justices in Yorkshire. It expressed concern at 'the great declininge of her majesty's subjects in these north partes from the religion established and from there due allegiance'. This was to be explained 'partley by reason of there not reparinge to the churche & partley by the seditious

---

[1] P. Collinson, *The Religion of Protestants: The Church in English Society 1559–1625* (Oxford, 1982), 152–3. V. Larminie, *Wealth, Kinship and Culture: The Seventeenth-Century Newdigates of Arbury and their World*, Royal Historical Society, Studies in History, 72 (Woodbridge, 1995), ch. 10; P. Clark, '"The Ramoth-Gilead of the Good": urban change and political radicalism at Gloucester 1540–1640', in P. Clark, A. G. R. Smith and N. Tyacke (eds.), *The English Commonwealth 1547–1640: Essays in Politics and Society Presented to Joel Hurstfield* (Leicester, 1979), 167–87, 253–60; D. Underdown, *Fire from Heaven: The Life of an English Town in the Seventeenth Century* (London, 1992); P. Slack, *Poverty in Early-Stuart Salisbury*, Wiltshire Record Society, 31 (Devizes, 1975).

perswasions of Jesuits & popishe priests sent from beyond the seas'. The result was the 'great dishonor of allmighty god the discontentment of her majesty & danger of the state'.[2]

In administrative terms this posed some fundamental tasks. Domestically it was imperative to enforce church attendance and to ensure that what was done there conformed to national policy. But there was an important corollary to domestic purity – the necessity of defending against foreign infection. In the 1590s, for example, the privy council was concerned that the children of the 'better sorte' were being sent abroad for their education 'under Coullour of languages to be learned'. The threat was clear: 'it is daylie by dangerous experience founde that theducation of such in forraine partes doe breede much corruption in Religion and manners'.[3] Abroad, they fell into 'conversation with English Trators and fugitives' and among them 'the most dangerous persons that come over to attempt most devillishe practices agaynst her majesty & the state'. One remedy was to lie in the examination of all arrivals from overseas by gentlemen living near the coast, with the help of the vice-admiral or his deputies, 'one of the said gentlemen . . . alwayes [to] remayne at the severall ports' of Yorkshire, Cumberland, Westmorland and Northumberland. It is accompanied by instructions for enforcement at Hull and its creeks.[4] Each gentlemen was to be there three days each week and to stay anyone not known to be an honest merchant 'or that shall not geve good or undouted testimonie unto you of their good behavior & good affection in religion & dutie to her majesty' and the reasons for their journey. A record was to be kept of all movements, and report made to the Council in the North every twenty days. All those who were not merchants or mariners in the queen's navy were to be stopped and searched, the findings being reported to the Council in the North. Lastly, it was to be publicised in all ports and creeks that no landing was to be allowed on the coast or in the creeks, unless forced by weather. Infringement was to be punished by forfeiture of the ship and cargo and imprisonment at the queen's pleasure.[5]

This programme was ambitious in the extreme, requiring a considerable commitment of time and energy on the part of voluntary office-holders. Clearly their willingness to cooperate would depend on their own perception of threat – either of the general atmosphere of the times

[2] HEH, HM 50657, vol. I, fo. 68r.   [3] Ibid., vol. II, fo. 13r. 31 December 1593.
[4] Ibid., fo. 16r. 16 February 1594[5]. A 'creek' is here an administrative term – a subordinate port in the customs administration. The customs administration was divided into head ports, each responsible for ports and creeks below it.   [5] Ibid., fo. 16v.

or of the intentions of local people. The stakes were particularly high in relation to Catholicism from the 1570s onwards, especially after 1585, and the loyalty of the north of England was a particular concern,[6] so the preceding examples are not 'typical' of the normal level of concern. We might distinguish here between a political pressure for conformity and an evangelical pressure for true profession. 'Their interests might co-incide from time to time, notably in moments of extreme political crisis' but more normal was the tendency for the two perceptions to drift apart. 'Paradoxically, the very act of enforcement by the State then had the effect of promoting conformity as a political necessity rather than a religious one.'[7] But if the fears were only particularly exaggerated at specific moments, they none the less drove regimes to demand some extremely ambitious programmes, enforcing protestations and engagements across their whole territory, for example, in times of acute danger.[8]

The legitimation of the regime with reference to a particular religious identity, and the administrative consequences of that identity, did not always sit so easily with local beliefs. Lay influence over the institutions of secular government and over the church gave force to local beliefs about appropriate religious practice. These local views were not necessarily at odds with national policy, of course, but the fact that they might be was a source of considerable anxiety at times. Lay influence also ensured that generalised notions about religious order were difficult to enforce. The divisions within and between local communities were reproduced at the centre of government too, so that what was to be imposed was not always clear – it is difficult to say with any certainty what 'official policy' was for much of the time, still less to define 'Anglicanism' as a confession. Still less was it clear whether what was wanted was uniformity or conformity, or whether conformity ruled out supplementary beliefs and practices.[9] The term confessional state is an imperfect one, therefore, but it is intended to capture the sense that political power was legitimated with reference to a particular (though variable) set of doctrinal beliefs and liturgical practices and that this had

---

[6] See, for example, C. Cross, *The Puritan Earl: The Life of Henry Hastings Third Earl of Huntingdon 1536–1595* (London, 1966), esp. chs. 6, 7.

[7] M. C. Questier, *Conversion, Politics and Religion in England, 1580–1625* (Cambridge, 1996), 166.

[8] D. Cressy, 'Binding the nation: the Bonds of Association, 1584 and 1696', in D. J. Guth and J. W. McKenna (eds.), *Tudor Rule and Revolution: Essays for G. R. Elton from his American Friends* (Cambridge, 1982), 217–34. See also P. Collinson, 'The Elizabethan exclusion crisis and the Elizabethan polity', *Proceedings of the British Academy*, 84 (1993), 51–92, esp. pp. 62–71.

[9] C. Russell, *The Causes of the English Civil War* (Oxford, 1990), ch. 4; Questier, *Conversion*, esp. ch. 6.

administrative consequences. These demands were relatively autonomous, and frequently removed from immediate local interests. In these circumstances, as with fiscal-military measures, local discretion could not always be harmonised with the spirit of the measures being taken – here, local divergence from national norms was more likely to be viewed as evasion than discretion.

CHAPTER 7

The claims of the confessional state: local realities

The promotion of the true religion was perceived to be of crucial importance ideologically but in practice it proved impossible to achieve. The imposition of a confessional identity posed particular problems because it should, ideally, have forced a matter of conscience. This was difficult enough, but made impossible by the fact that the government did not control the means by which this might, theoretically, have been done. Considerable lay influence in the church and secular administration reduced the capacity of regimes to propagate the true religion, to restrict the propagation of rival versions and to punish heterodoxy. In fact, one of the well-remarked features of the Elizabethan and early Stuart church was the scope for lay initiative. Such initiative was by no means universally subversive of official policy, of course, but the existence of powerful lay interests in the government of the church significantly reduced the direct authority of its head, allowing for significant local initiative and a considerable capacity for local evasion of unwelcome directives from the centre. The influence of local dissenters, Catholic and Protestant, and the wider obligations of neighbourliness, seem to have undercut the perception of threat. These difficulties made uniformity impossible to achieve and made relatively narrow conformity difficult to sustain. Indeed, voluntary religion was a feature of the development not just of Catholic and Protestant dissent, but of Anglicanism too. All this was exacerbated, of course, by the fact that there was little more agreement about the nature of the true religion in the highest councils of the church and state than there was in the kingdom at large. The result was that, although England was Protestantised by 1640, it was by no means uniform in religion. The explosion of sectarian activity during the 1640s and 1650s exacerbated the problem, while also sharpening the fears of orthodox churchmen and politicians about the social consequences of religious dissent. In restoration England the demons in the minds of the respectable were not so much witches or vagrants as seminary priests, Jesuits and Protestant sectaries. The structural problems hampering the pursuit of uniformity persisted, however, and concerted attempts to eradicate dissent by force came in paroxysms of vigorous but ineffectual activity. Ultimately, sporadic persecution gave way to a limited toleration of forms of dissent which were not thought to be corrosive of social and political order.

THE INFLUENCE OF THE LAITY

Lay initiative was particularly significant for the future of England's religion, not just because of the central place accorded to religious belief by contemporaries but also because of the difficulty of reaching a consensual view about what was desirable. To call for the promotion of true religion was to start an argument, not to end one, and the argument was likely to be particularly heated because the stakes were so high. Disagreement split not just parishes but the privy council. Few issues can have led a privy councillor to be as blunt as Grindal was in 1576 when he wrote to the queen, 'Bear with me, I beseech you, Madam, if I choose rather to offend your earthly majesty than to offend the heavenly majesty of God.'[1] Not only, then, were there large numbers of people with the capacity to affect religious policy, but there was, among this group, a high degree of highly principled disagreement. This discussion deals with the reformation as an administrative and political problem, rather than as a debate about the nature of the true religion and the correct route to salvation. This is, therefore, a partial and slanted view of the subject, but it is not an insignificant one. We noted in chapter 2 how religion impinged upon an already unstable international scene. Sixteenth and seventeenth-century experience furnished many examples of the domestic dangers of religious heterodoxy and all states needed a religious policy. However, because it was so important, it was extremely difficult for governments to achieve their ends. A matter of conscience is no simple administrative problem. We will here consider how the Elizabethan and early Stuart regime coped with the challenge, and how the manner of this coping reveals further aspects of the structure and functioning of the Elizabethan and early Stuart state.

Some of the highest praise attaching to official religious policy attests

---

[1] Quoted in P. Collinson, 'The downfall of Archbishop Grindal and its place in Elizabethan political and ecclesiastical history', in P. Clark, A. G. R. Smith and N. Tyacke (eds.), *The English Commonwealth 1547–1640: Essays in Politics and Society Presented to Joel Hurstfield* (Leicester, 1979), 39–57, 219–27, at p. 44.

to a genius for compromise. For example, the 1559 Prayer Book fudged the central issue of the nature of the communion. It took a conservative phrase from the 1549 Prayer Book suggesting the real presence and yoked it to a phrase from the 1552 Prayer Book suggesting that the communion was a memorial only. Thus, as he or she received the bread, the communicant would hear the words 'The body of our Lord Jesus Christ, which was given for thee, preserve thy body and soul unto everlasting life (1549). Take and eat this in remembrance that Christ died for thee, and feed on him in thy heart by faith with thanksgiving (1552).' This has been described as a 'masterpiece of theological engineering'.[2] Similarly, although there are sharp disagreements about how to interpret early Stuart religious policy, in one sense they amount to an argument about who, Calvinists or their opponents, represented the moderate, compromise position.[3] The Elizabethan settlement had opponents, both Catholic and Protestant, since it represented something of a *via media* between available forms of religion – well short of Genevan Calvinism and also of the emergent Catholicism of the counter reformation. The settlement, like most policies, was the product of negotiation between a number of interests in the light of a number of political options. However, this is not the end of the story because legislated policy was subject to further mediation and negotiation in the locality, when its enforcement was handed over to local officeholders. We need to consider how religious policy evolved over the following years, and one way of doing this is to follow the progress of opponents of the settlement. The spread of puritanism, the survival of unreformed Catholicism and the spread of reformed Catholicism reflect (to a degree to be discussed below) a failure of enforcement. The reasons for this failure highlight the weakness of the state as a means to achieve the implementation of an unpopular policy, and so illustrate very clearly how the

---

[2] D. MacCulloch, *The Later Reformation in England 1547–1603* (London, 1990), 30.

[3] The origin of this debate can be found in N. Tyacke, 'Puritanism, Arminianism and counter-revolution', in C. Russell (ed.), *The Origins of the English Civil War* (London, 1973), 119–44, 270–1. For its subsequent development see esp. P. White, 'The rise of Arminianism reconsidered', *PP*, 101 (1983), 34–54; Tyacke, 'The rise of Arminianism reconsidered' with a rejoinder by White, *PP*, 115 (1987), 201–29. For some important later contributions see K. Fincham and P. Lake, 'The ecclesiastical policies of James I and Charles I', in Fincham (ed.), *The Early Stuart Church, 1603–1642* (London, 1993), 23–49, 251–6; A. Milton, 'The Church of England, Rome and the True Church', ibid., 187–210, 282–5; N. Tyacke, 'Anglican attitudes: some recent writings on English religious history, from the reformation to the civil war', *JBS*, 35 (1996), 139–67. For opposing views see P. White, 'The *via media* in the early Stuart church', in Fincham (ed.), *Early Stuart Church*, 211–30, 285–9; K. Sharpe, *The Personal Rule of Charles I* (London, 1992), ch. 6; G. W. Bernard, 'The Church of England, c. 1529–c. 1642', *History*, 75 (1990), 183–206.

participatory nature of the administration gave local groups a fair degree of political power and autonomy.

The two main tasks to be achieved were, firstly, to establish and maintain discipline within the clergy and, secondly, to discipline the laity, enforcing attendance at church and preventing the promotion of worship outside it. We have already noted the difficulty of defining 'official policy', but in order to highlight the importance of lay influence over the development of the church, we will assume for a moment that there was a 'government view'. In order to enforce it, clearly the government would need to control appointments in order to control what was said in the churches and to ensure that the official religion was propagated. The second priority was to make sure that the laity heard the message and did not hear supplementary or alternative messages. This was to be enforced by positive promotion of orthodox belief and practice, and the persecution of those who opposed its propagation. The church courts and the secular authorities could prosecute dissent, while unorthodox ministers could be ejected. But persecution, in so far as it rested on cooperation locally, was problematic: 'puritans' and Catholics alike had powerful protectors. On the other hand, attempts at persecution by bodies acting more directly in response to archiepiscopal or royal authority were a much-resented intrusion into local life. In this context the emergence of separate and semi-separate communities of belief with their own institutional support represents an administrative failure.

There were a variety of sources of lay influence in church affairs. Most importantly, the right of presentation to clerical livings – the advowson – was often held by members of the laity. These rights might have originated in the foundation of a church to cater for the tenants of a manor or have been passed on to laymen with the lands of dissolved monasteries. As a consequence of this latter development, many benefices became 'impropriate' and by the late sixteenth century perhaps a third of all presentments were in lay hands, some of them Catholic.[4] This prompted Hill to suggest that:

Something very like a *cujus regio* settlement grew up in England after the Reformation, quite unintended by the government, as a result of the combination of lay patronage with a serious cleavage . . . within the class of lay patrons. So patrons would be likely to favour the religious tendency which suited them

[4] C. Hill, *Economic Problems of the Church from Archbishop Whitgift to the Long Parliament* (Oxford, 1956), 54; R. O'Day, *The English Clergy: Emergence and Consolidation of a Profession 1558–1642* (Leicester, 1979), ch. 6.

and a seventeenth-century character writer could take it for granted that for the humble villager 'his religion is part of his copyhold, which he takes from his landlord and refers it wholly to his discretion'.[5]

In practice, however, the significance of lay patronage might have been more limited than this suggests. For example, the precise rights of the patron varied from case to case. In most instances the bishop had to approve candidates and, of course, candidates had to have been ordained.[6] The choice was not an entirely free one, therefore.

None the less, from the point of view of a government trying to build a pliant and disciplined clergy, the alienation of the right to nominate candidates for presentment was, potentially at least, a considerable handicap. In the later sixteenth century, as religious identities hardened, advowsons were held by Catholics who were no longer reconciled to the church and had retreated into recusancy. On the other hand, the crown also used advowsons to reward courtiers and great nobles such as Leicester, Bedford, Warwick and Pembroke, all men with relatively radical sympathies, who were thus able to propagate their own views. In fact, on the whole, there is little evidence of a very coherent campaign by puritans to exploit the patronage system, although in some places and under some patrons this was the case.[7] The crown's patronage was coordinated by the lord keeper but was not manipulated to promote a coherent religious policy so much as to respond to political pressures at court – the influence of the bishops over the distribution of this patronage was reduced by comparison with that of influential courtiers. Clerical patronage was a political resource for the crown and others, and an important property right for many laymen, and so the prospects of close control over appointments to clerical livings were very remote indeed.[8]

A second very serious administrative problem for the crown (or, to put it another way, source of influence for the laity) related to the revenues of the church. The collection of tithes had often come under the control of the laity, a development with implications for clerical

[5] Hill, *Economic Problems*, p. 55.
[6] R. O'Day, 'The law of patronage in early modern England', *Journal of Ecclesiastical History*, 26 (1975), 247–60; O'Day, *English Clergy*, chs. 4–5.
[7] O'Day, *English Clergy*, chs. 7–8. For examples of Catholic families with patronage to church livings see W. J. Sheils, *The Puritans in the Diocese of Peterborough 1558–1610*, Northamptonshire Record Society, 30 (Northampton, 1979), 39. The diocese of Peterborough also furnishes an example of a fairly systematic attempt to use rights of patronage to secure particular doctrinal ends: ibid., pp. 36–40.
[8] O'Day, *English Clergy*, ch. 9; O'Day, 'Law'; O'Day, 'Ecclesiastical patronage: who controlled the church?', in F. Heal and R. O'Day (eds.), *Church and Society in England: Henry VIII to James I* (London, 1977), 137–55, 197.

living standards and so for the recruitment of ministers. Tithes were collected on income directly from the land (crops and livestock), from the fruits of manufacture and from mixed sources such as the produce from livestock (cheese, wool and milk, for example). As economic activity became more complex, so too did the calculation of these tithes and in many cases a composition was made whereby a single cash payment was received. This *modus decimandi* varied from parish to parish, but in a period of inflation it might saddle an incumbent with a fixed income of declining value. This problem was exacerbated by the impropriation of benefices. This meant that some of the tithes in many livings went to the impropriator rather than to the incumbent. Many impropriators may have been conscientious about the distribution of these impropriated tithes but often they were not. Impropriations were regarded as property rights like any other, and the incumbent might be viewed as exactly that: an encumbrance on the value of the benefice. Local studies have shown that in the same area rectors, whose tithes were not impropriate, enjoyed richer livings than vicars, those whose tithes were impropriate.[9] Clerical income also derived from glebe holdings, but they had often entered into leases allowing others to farm their land, and these agreements too, could cause economic problems in a period of inflation.[10] There was then, a dual pressure on clerical incomes in this period: inflation and the capacity of the laity to take a portion of clerical income.

The effects of this varied considerably. Clergy who collected their own tithe and farmed their own glebe were in a much better situation than vicars dependent on unfavourable commutations and leases who were also losing a part of the living to an impropriator. It is not easy to generalise, therefore, but it is clear that some ministers were paid a pittance.[11] This posed a problem in attracting high quality candidates. One of the features of the clergy in this period was the improvement in educational qualifications. This has been referred to as 'professionalisation' and, more recently and more cautiously, as 'graduatisation'. In the late sixteenth century there was a shortage of qualified candidates, a problem exacerbated by the poverty of many livings. In fact, it may have

[9] Hill, *Economic Problems*, ch. 5; F. Heal, 'The economic problems of the clergy', in Heal and O'Day (eds.), *Church and Society*, 1–14, 188. For a local study see M. L. Zell, 'Economic problems of the parochial clergy in the sixteenth century', in R. O'Day and F. Heal (eds.), *Princes and Paupers in the English Church, 1500–1800* (Leicester, 1981), 19–43, esp. pp. 33–5.
[10] Heal, 'Economic problems'.
[11] Ibid.; Zell, 'Economic problems'; O'Day, *English Clergy*, ch. 13. For the problems of supply and the rising educational standards of the clergy see ibid., chs. 10–14.

been the rising expectations of an educated (and often married) preaching ministry which made clerical poverty appear to be an increasing problem. On average the value of benefices appears to have kept pace with inflation.[12] In any case, lay control over the economic resources of the church and over the right to present candidates to livings obviously represented a considerable power to affect the development of the church.

A consequence of the loss of control of economic resources by the clergy was the exacerbation of the economic difficulties of some of the clergy in this period. This, in turn, made it difficult to provide good livings that would support a well-qualified preaching ministry. Some of the solutions to this set of problems were to establish supplementary institutions – prophesyings, exercises, lectureships – which provided preaching to the laity and income to preachers. However, these were often lay initiatives, backed by wealthy patrons or godly corporations, and therefore reduced episcopal and crown control of what was preached.[13] Again, this did not necessarily mean that official religious policy was subverted. For example, the most common form of lecture in the period before 1640 was the lecture by combination where a number of beneficed clergy lectured in rotation and attended one another's lectures. These initiatives were undertaken with episcopal blessing, and by men who, because they held benefices, were vulnerable to episcopal pressure should that be necessary. Lecturers were not necessarily a free-lance clergy beyond episcopal control.[14] Similarly, prophesyings – meetings of clergy to expound and discuss scripture before a lay audience – were usually supplementary, rather than rival, to the activities of the parish churches. By the mid-1570s, however, influential churchmen were increasingly suspicious of such initiatives. A conflict between those

---

[12] O'Day, *English Clergy*, chs. 4, 10–14. For 'graduatisation', see P. Collinson, 'Shepherds, sheepdogs and hirelings: the pastoral ministry in post-reformation England', in W. J. Sheils and D. Wood (eds.), *The Ministry: Clerical and Lay*, Studies in Church History, 26 (Oxford, 1989), 185–220. For some sceptical reflections on 'professionalisation' see M. Hawkins, 'Ambiguity and contradiction in "the rise of professionalism": the English clergy, 1570–1730', in A. L. Beier, D. Cannadine and J. M. Rosenheim (eds.), *The First Modern Society: Essays in English History in Honour of Lawrence Stone* (Cambridge, 1989), 241–69. For a case study see R. B. Manning, *Religion and Society in Elizabethan Sussex: A Study of the Enforcement of the Religious Settlement 1558–1603* (Leicester, 1969), ch. 9. On rising expectations, see Heal, 'Economic problems'; Zell, 'Economic problems', esp. pp. 40–1. For calculations of the average value of benefices see Hill, *Economic Problems*, pp. 117–21; Zell, 'Economic problems', pp. 35–40.

[13] C. Hill, *Society and Puritanism in Pre-Revolutionary England* (London, 1964), ch. 3; Hill, *Economic Problems*, esp. pp. 106–8, ch. 13; P. S. Seaver, *The Puritan Lectureships: The Politics of Religious Dissent 1560–1662* (Stanford, 1970), chs. 3–4.

[14] P. Collinson, 'Lectures by combination: structures and characteristics of church life in seventeenth-century England', *BIHR*, 48 (1975), 182–213; O'Day, *English Clergy*, pp. 99–102.

anxious to suppress them, and those who supported the initiatives as likely to promote the preaching of the gospel, provides the context for the fall of Grindal.[15] Here is another indication of how such divisions operated at the heart of the national government as well as in the parishes – it is not easy to discern a consistent 'government line' on these issues.

As a result of the economic problems of the church the difficulty of establishing a preaching ministry was increased. Frustration with these shortcomings, and a desire to improve the income for the preaching clergy, led to lay initiatives which further increased the influence of the laity. In particular, the endowment of lectureships offered a potential threat to episcopal control. In general, it became difficult to distinguish 'between voluntary societies within or alongside the church and alternative or rival churches taking shape outside it and in total rejection of it'. It was the interaction with official policy which determined whether or not such voluntarism evolved into separatism – it was frequently a 'rudderless drift' rather than a coherent choice.[16] Lay initiative did not automatically produce religious pluralism, therefore, but it did reduce the direct control of the head over the development of the reformed religion in England. And it did suggest that uniformity would not be easily achieved in the parishes or the church as a whole. Responses to particular godly initiatives, or to attempts at episcopal control, could produce serious local divisions.[17] The promotion of Protestantism in England was dependent on lay initiative.[18]

Of course, it was not just in the positive promotion of Protestantism that lay initiative was important. The other side of the process – disciplining the laity and clergy – lay within the purview of the church courts. They dealt with a number of offences not cognisable at common law, some of which offered a means of preserving social order. For example, the jurisdiction of the archidiaconal courts extended not just

---

[15] Collinson, 'Downfall', p. 43; P. Clark, 'The prophesying movement in Kentish towns during the 1570s', *Archaeologia Cantiana*, 93 (1977), 81–90; Manning, *Religion*, ch. 4. Pressure to raise clerical standards was not always restricted to the narrowest group of the godly: J. Goring, 'The reformation of the ministry in Elizabethan Sussex', *Journal of Ecclesiastical History*, 34 (1983), 345–66.

[16] P. Collinson, 'The English Conventicle', in W. J. Sheils and D. Wood (eds.), *Voluntary Religion*, Studies in Church History, 23 (Oxford, 1986), 223–59, at p. 227.

[17] P. Collinson, *The Religion of Protestants: The Church in English Society 1559–1625* (Oxford, 1982), ch. 6; Collinson, 'Cranbrook and the Fletchers: popular and unpopular religion in the Kentish Weald', in P. N. Brooks (ed.), *Reformation Principle and Practice: Essays in Honour of Arthur Geoffrey Dickens* (London, 1980), 171–202.

[18] See, for important case studies, C. Cross, *Urban Magistrates and Ministers: Religion in Hull and Leeds from the Reformation to the Civil War*, Borthwick Papers, 67 (York, 1985); Manning, *Religion*.

over matters of ecclesiastical discipline but the regulation of moral and sexual behaviour of the laity. Although the punishments inflicted by the courts aimed to shame rather than to inflict physical pain this made them no less potent in the attempt to combat vice.[19] Church court business was divided between 'office' business (analogous to a criminal jurisdiction) and 'instance' business (cases brought by individuals, akin to civil suits in the secular courts). In both cases, the effectiveness of the courts rested, as in the secular courts, on participation. Much of the office business depended on the activities of churchwardens who, like constables, were subject to local pressures. Officers of the court sought out offences but their detection depended, ultimately, on the willingness of churchwardens to report offences in response to visitations. Instance business, of course, depended on private initiative. These courts, like their secular counterparts, were therefore open to local influence and opinion. They were, as we have seen, integral to the reformation of manners discussed in chapter 4, and this activism in relation to moral and sexual regulation has contributed significantly to their rehabilitation in the eyes of historians.[20] In some cases, it is clear, the courts were dominated by evangelicals who used them to promote reform, but it was not just evangelicals who had influence. They did not represent a single local community, therefore, but neither were they simply the tools of the godly or of episcopacy.[21] Reform and discipline through the courts

---

[19] J. H. Baker, *An Introduction to English Legal History*, 3rd edn (London, 1990), ch. 8; J. H. Baker, 'Criminal courts and procedure at common law, 1500–1800', in J. S. Cockburn (ed.), *Crime in England 1550–1800* (London, 1977), 15–48, 299–309, at p. 32. For their role in attempts to reform manners see in particular M. Ingram, *Church Courts, Sex and Marriage in England, 1570–1640* (Cambridge, 1987); Ingram, 'Reformation of manners in early modern England', in P. Griffiths, A. Fox and S. Hindle (eds.), *The Experience of Authority in Early Modern England* (London, 1996), 47–88; F. Dabhoiwala, 'Prostitution and police in London, *c.* 1660–*c.* 1760', DPhil Dissertation, University of Oxford (1995).

[20] See, in particular, Ingram, *Church Courts*. For an outline of the hierarchy of courts and their jurisdiction, and for further reference see M. Ingram, 'Puritans and the church courts, 1560–1640', in C. Durston and J. Eales (eds.), *The Culture of English Puritanism* (London, 1996), 58–91, 288–95, esp. pp. 60–1.

[21] Goring, 'Reformation'; Collinson, 'Cranbrook'; M. Spufford, 'Can we count the "Godly" and the "Conformable" in the Seventeenth Century?', *Journal of Ecclesiastical History*, 36 (1985), 428–38, at pp. 430–4. For the ecclesiastical commissions see P. Clark, 'The ecclesiastical commission at Canterbury, 1572–1603', *Archaeologia Cantiana*, 89 (1974), 183–97; C. Cross, 'Sin and society: the northern high commission and the northern gentry in the reign of Elizabeth', in C. Cross, D. Loades and J. J. Scarisbrick (eds.), *Law and Government under the Tudors: Essays Presented to Sir Geoffrey Elton Regius Professor of History in the University of Cambridge on the Occasion of his Retirement* (Cambridge, 1988), 195–209. The church courts were not entirely unresponsive to episcopal initiative, of course. For a local example, see J. A. Vage, 'Ecclesiastical discipline in the early seventeenth-century: some findings and some problems from the archdeaconry of Cornwall', *Journal of the Society of Archivists*, 7 (1982), 85–105.

might fall foul of conservatism and indifference, or a preference for local order over full conformity.

Episcopal visitations depended on the reliability of churchwardens. Churchwardens might themselves be heterodox[22] and were often as sensitive to local expectation as their secular counterparts, the constables. Failures to present, or inaccurate and partial responses to visitation articles, represented the same sort of negotiation between 'concepts of order' as we have noted in secular administration. Similarly, churchwardens, who were drawn from among the ranks of the middling sort, might have been reluctant to present the offences of the gentry.[23] Once again, however, there is a danger of overstatement. It has been suggested that we might view the growth of sectarianism as a consequence of the failure of some churchwardens to maintain communal commitment to the parish church, rather than emphasising the influence of heterodox churchwardens.[24] Local initiative did not automatically lead to the growth of sects, neither was it untrammelled. The church courts did have an effect on religious practice as a functioning part of the ecclesiastical machine. Steady pressure to uphold the standards of Protestant faith and Christian morality had an effect even though there were lapses in individual cases. 'The approach of the judges may be described as broadly consensual, marching slightly in advance of popular attitudes to effect steady if unspectacular improvement.' The slowness of the process was partly a result of weaknesses in procedure but also owed something to the ethos of canon law, which inclined towards 'the medicinal rather than retributive purposes of ecclesiastical discipline'.[25]

Ultimately, then, the imposition of much religious policy rested on the spiritual equivalent of constables. The secular arm, too, had a role in this. For example, the stepping-up of the campaign against recusancy after 1581 was associated with a shift of responsibility for prosecuting recusants from churchwardens to justices of the peace.[26] But the willingness to impose these disciplines was not simply a matter of relations between orthodox officers and the heterodox – many officeholders were

---

[22] For example, see C. Marsh, '"A Gracelesse and Audacious Companie"? The family of love in the parish of Balsham, 1550–1630', in Sheils and Wood (eds.), *Voluntary Religion*, 191–208, pp. 204–5.

[23] J. S. Craig, 'Co-operation and initiatives: Elizabethan churchwardens and the parish accounts of Mildenhall', *Social History*, 18 (1993), 357–80; E. Carlson, 'The origins, function and status of the office of churchwarden, with particular reference to the diocese of Ely', in M. Spufford (ed.), *The World of Rural Dissenters, 1520–1725* (Cambridge, 1995), 164–207; Manning, *Religion*, esp. pp. 22–5, 131–2.   [24] Carlson, 'Churchwarden'.

[25] Ingram, 'Puritans', esp. pp. 69–75, quotation at p. 73.   [26] Manning, *Religion*, p. 25.

themselves heterodox. It has been estimated that in Sussex in the 1560s between 39 per cent and 50 per cent of the officeholding class could be defined as 'Catholics'. The control of the commission of the peace and of the lieutenancy only gradually passed into the hands of a dependably Protestant group.[27] At every stage in the propagation of official religion and the discipline of the laity, significant lay influence gave force to local standards of religious behaviour.

THE PROGRESS OF PROTESTANTISM AND THE FAILURE OF UNIFORMITY

The progress of Protestantism is difficult to judge, but there were some tangible achievements, and some impressive initiatives, during the later sixteenth and early seventeenth centuries. We have already noted the rising standards of clerical education and the spread of the preaching ministry. Progress in these areas varied from place to place, and was probably quicker in the south of England, but certainly by 1603 England was a Protestant country.[28] For those too young or poorly educated to benefit from sermons and lectures a vast number of catechisms were produced. More than 280 different catechitical works were published between 1549 and 1646 and it has been calculated that about 1.25m such works were in circulation in the early seventeenth century, in a population of 4m. In a sense this represents a recognition of the failure of official Protestantism and, once again, a significant part of this output was not official in origin. Nevertheless, it represents a huge effort of propagation.[29] There is good evidence that by 1640 there was a developing commitment to worship according to the Prayer Book and of high

[27] Ibid., chs. 11–12, figure quoted from p. 129. In Norfolk the process of purging the commission of Catholic recusants continued into the later 1580s at least: A. H. Smith, *County and Court: Government and Politics in Norfolk 1558–1603* (Oxford, 1974), 81–6. See also P. Williams, *The Tudor Regime* (Oxford, 1979), 271–2. In a number of counties the purging of Catholics from the commissions did not occur before the 1570s or 1580s: C. Haigh, *English Reformations: Religion, Politics and Society under the Tudors* (Oxford, 1993), 278–9.

[28] For rising standards see O'Day, *English Clergy*; Zell, 'Economic problems'. In Elizabethan Leicestershire one-fifth of incumbents had BA degrees. By the mid-seventeenth century nearly all had BAs and two-thirds had MAs: J. H. Pruett, *The Parish Clergy under the Later Stuarts: the Leicestershire Experience* (Urbana, 1978), 175.

[29] I. Green, '"For Children in Yeeres and Children in Understanding": the emergence of the English catechism under Elizabeth and the early Stuarts', *Journal of Ecclesiastical History*, 37 (1986), 397–425, figures at pp. 400, 425. See also Green, *The Christian's ABC: Catechisms and Catechizing in England c. 1530–1740* (Oxford, 1996), 45–79 and appendix I, for a discussion of the volume and significance of publication prior to 1640. For the efforts of the Northern High Commission in such initiatives see R. W. Hoyle, 'Advancing the reformation in the North: orders from York High Commission, 1583 and 1592', *Northern History*, 28 (1992), 217–27.

rates of attendance at official worship.[30] Just as the gap between the godly and the established church was not unbridgeable, so there is increasing evidence that there were points of contact between the educated Protestants and their less-well-educated brothers and sisters.[31] The pressure for clerical conformity also increased as the supply of ordinands began to catch up with demand. As career prospects diminished so the pressures for conformity increased.[32] Lay initiative was central to this, but that did not lead automatically to sectarianism and disunity.

All this having been said, however, lay initiative made conformity difficult to achieve and uniformity a very distant prospect indeed. This was as obvious to many contemporaries as it is to modern historians. For much of the time 'Tensions between the requirements of politicians and churchmen explain better than pure provincial localism or bungling officialdom the slow and uncertain spread of English Protestantism, or at least the ease with which its dispersal could be resisted.' There was a political emphasis on the need for conformity, but this fell far short of evangelicals' requirements about the acceptance of new concepts of grace. Pressure could be brought to bear to secure a conformity which was acceptable in political terms but which did not satisfy the evangelical Protestant conception of what it meant to forsake Babylon. The difference was between a 'political rhetoric of unity' and the 'Reformed evangelical rhetoric of grace and renewal'. Confessional identities were more complex and unstable than fully reformed or wholly Catholic, therefore. A corollary of this instability was that 'there was in this period no such thing as a unitary English Catholicism... In that there was an "English Catholicism" it was a series of dissident oppositional expressions of religious motive (linked by a common reliance on Rome).'[33]

[30] J. Maltby, '"By this Book": parishioners, the Prayer Book and the established church', in Fincham (ed.), *Early Stuart Church*, 115–37, 264–9. In Southwark relatively high rates of participation in the key services of the liturgical calendar seem to reflect 'a consensus of what were the basic constituents of lay church life in the neighbourhood': J. Boulton, *Neighbourhood and Society: A London Suburb in the Seventeenth Century* (Cambridge, 1987), 275–88, quotation at p. 288.

[31] P. Lake, 'Deeds against nature: cheap print, Protestantism and murder in early seventeenth-century England', in K. Sharpe and P. Lake (eds.), *Culture and Politics in Early Stuart England* (London, 1994), 257–83, 361–7; Lake, 'Popular form, puritan content? Two puritan appropriations of the murder pamphlet from mid-seventeenth-century London', in A. Fletcher and P. Roberts (ed.), *Religion, Culture and Society in Early Modern Britain: Essays in Honour of Patrick Collinson* (Cambridge, 1994), 313–34; Lake, 'Puritanism, arminianism and a Shropshire axe-murder', *Midland History*, 15 (1990), 37–64. See also Spufford (ed.), *Rural Dissenters*; E. Duffy, 'The godly and the multitude in Stuart England', *Seventeenth-Century Studies*, 1 (1986), 31–55.

[32] I. Green, 'Career prospects and clerical conformity in the early Stuart church', *PP*, 90 (1981), 71–115.

[33] M. C. Questier, *Conversion, Politics and Religion in England, 1580–1625* (Cambridge, 1996), esp. ch. 6, quotations at pp. 10, 167, 204.

The development of Catholicism was shaped in part by the administrative capacities of the state and by these conflicting political and evangelical aims. This is true in two ways: the slow and patchy progress towards the eradication of forms of medieval religion now defined as inimical; and the failure to repel the advance of reformed Catholicism in the later sixteenth century. The first of these failures has been touched on above in the slow progress of Protestantism and the difficulties of establishing a preaching ministry. As Protestantism made progress, however, it became clear that it was not taking everyone along with it – as Protestantism emerged so too did a positive commitment to Catholicism. This added to the disciplinary problems of the church and secular government, which was now required to prosecute Catholics. Churchwardens were reluctant to present their neighbours or their social superiors, and justices of the peace seem to have been less than rigorous in these duties.[34] Officeholders might themselves have been sympathisers or actual recusants. For example, Sir Thomas Bishop, a justice of the peace and commissioner for the discovery of recusants and seminary priests in Sussex during the 1590s, 'had living under his own roof a recusant gentleman whose son was a priest and who had smuggled two priests into London from Cornwall'. Henry Spiller, the exchequer clerk in the lord treasurer's remembrancer's office, with responsibility for all the financial business arising from recusancy fines was himself at the centre of a Catholic network and may well have held Catholic opinions.[35] But such administrative 'failings' were not necessarily problematic because it was still possible to enforce the degree of conformity demanded by political rhetoric. On the other hand, heavy-handed intervention by the ecclesiastical authorities might be resented on jurisdictional grounds.[36] There were some characteristic weaknesses of the ecclesiastical administration in this respect, which helped to mould the development of English Catholicism. The chief effect of the penal laws on the Catholic gentry was, eventually, to exclude them from office. They remained protected from financial and other penalties by virtue of their social pre-eminence.

Thus, Catholicism was shaped by institutional and administrative

[34] Manning, *Religion*, ch. 7. Questier, *Conversion*, pp. 128–49, offers a rounded picture of exchequer pressure and the limits of its achievements.

[35] Manning, *Religion*, p. 157; Questier, *Conversion*, p. 163. Questier notes, however, that this did not necessarily interfere with his implementation of the bureaucratic processes of the exchequer: ibid., pp. 162 6.

[36] Manning, *Religion*, chs. 5–6. See for similar tensions in other contexts: A. Foster, 'The clerical estate revitalised', in Fincham (ed.), *Early Stuart Church*, 139–60, 269–75; P. S. Seaver, 'Community control and puritan politics in Elizabethan Suffolk', *Albion*, 9 (1977), 297–315.

factors. Survivalism was patterned in such a way as to affect the impact
of the revival when it came, so that the Catholic community came to
centre on the households of rich recusant landowners. It was these
people who had been able to withstand the pressures exerted by the
penal laws and they were now able to support and harbour the seminarists and priests representing the missionary effort in England. This
seigneurial religion was the heart of a community which included those
of lower social status, of course, but the centrality of the gentry and
aristocracy to the protection and fostering of Catholicism reflected the
capacities and limitations of the English state.[37] Around this core of a
fully separate, increasingly sectarian, Catholicism there was a penumbra of church papistry, partial and occasional conformity.[38]

In practice, the Catholic community during the 1590s seems to have
adopted a quietist position, eschewing resistance and contesting control
of loyalist rhetoric.[39] The issue is complicated, however, by divisions
within the Catholic community and the association of the mission with

---

[37] For seigneurial Catholicism and the missionary effort, see J. Bossy, *The English Catholic Community,
1570–1850* (London, 1975), chs. 1–8; Bossy, 'The character of Elizabethan Catholicism',
reprinted in T. Aston (ed.), *Crisis in Europe 1560–1660: Essays from Past and Present* (London, 1965),
223–46; Bossy, 'The English Catholic community, 1603–25', in A. G. R. Smith (ed.), *The Reign of
James I and VI* (London, 1973), 91–105, 233–6. For local examples see J. A. Hilton, 'Catholicism
in Elizabethan Durham', *Recusant History*, 14 (1977), 1–8; Hilton, 'Catholicism in Jacobean
Durham', ibid., 78–85; Hilton, 'Catholicism in Elizabethan Northumberland', *Northern History*,
13 (1977), 44–58. For the importance of survivalism see C. Haigh, 'The continuity of
Catholicism in the English reformation', *PP*, 93 (1981), 37–69; Haigh, 'From monopoly to
minority: Catholicism in early modern England', *TRHS*, 5th series, 31 (1981), 129–47; Haigh,
'The fall of a church or the rise of a sect? Post reformation Catholicism in England', *HJ*, 21
(1978), 181–6; A. D. Wright, 'Catholic history, north and south', *Northern History*, 14 (1978),
126–51. Haigh's view that the missionary achievement was fairly unimpressive has been
questioned by P. McGrath, 'Elizabethan Catholicism: a reconsideration', *Journal of Ecclesiastical
History*, 35 (1984), 414–28; and by A. D. Wright, 'Catholic history, north and south, revisited',
Northern History, 25 (1989), 120–34. For Catholicism among the lower orders see B. G. Black-
wood, 'Plebeian Catholics in the 1640s and 1650s', *Recusant History*, 18 (1986–7), 42–58.
[38] Wright, 'North and south'; A. Walsham, *Church Papists: Catholicism, Conformity and Confessional
Polemic in Early Modern England*, Royal Historical Society, Studies in History, 68 (1993); P. R.
Newman, 'Roman Catholics in pre-civil war England: the problem of definition', *Recusant
History*, 15 (1979–80), 148–52.
[39] Bossy, *Community*; 'Elizabethan'. For some thoughts on Catholic resistance to the increasing
tendency to conflate 'loyal' with 'Protestant' see G. Brennan, 'Papists and patriotism in
Elizabethan England', *Recusant History*, 19 (1988–9), 1–15. See also P. J. Holmes, *Resistance and
Compromise: The Political Thought of Elizabethan Catholics* (Cambridge, 1982); C. Hibbard, 'Early
Stuart Catholicism: revisions and re-revisions', *JMH*, 52 (1980), 1–34, esp. pp. 30–1. The
ambiguities of Catholic political attitudes are explored by A. Pritchard, *Catholic Loyalism in
Elizabethan England* (Chapel Hill, 1979). His account, however, tends to assume that individuals
adopted coherent and consistent positions either of loyalism or opposition. More recent work
has emphasised how the situation was ambiguous for individuals too: see, for example, S.
Kaushik, 'Resistance, loyalty and recusant politics: Sir Thomas Tresham and the Elizabethan
state', *Midland History*, 21 (1996), 37–72.

more radical political views.[40] Moreover, there are a variety of possible positions between quietism and resistance, and there may have been many other Catholics like Sir Thomas Tresham who occupied this grey area.[41] On the whole, however, it seems clear that relations between Catholics and Protestants in the country were less tense than the wilder rhetoric of anti-popery would have led us to believe. The principal form of pressure on English Catholics was the imposition of fines for non-attendance at church. These recusancy fines, however, were evaded, and the impact of sequestration (the seizure of goods) was mediated in the light of local circumstances.[42] In part, this was a matter of deliberate policy because the fines came to be seen as a financial resource as much as a means to the conversion of Catholics – heavy-handed administration would have killed, if not a golden goose, at least one that produced reasonably nutritious eggs.[43] Similarly, the disarming of recusants was implemented fitfully and half-heartedly, reflecting intermittent privy council interest in the issue.[44]

An illustration of local hostility to heavy-handed implementation of recusancy fines is provided by the disturbances that took place in 1600 at Childwall, Lancashire, disturbances in which non-Catholics were involved. During the 1590s the pressure of visitations had led to the first presentments of recusants in the area, immediately revealing a sizeable Catholic presence. The attempt to arrest Ralph Hitchmough for non-payment of a fine coincided with the funeral of another recusant which was being attended by non-recusants. Hitchmough was rescued and there were reprisals against his persecutor, William Brettergh, whose cattle were maimed. When he indicted rioters at the assizes he suffered further reprisals along with another actively anti-Catholic officeholder. The disturbances represented as much an expression of neighbourly

---

[40] See for example, Bossy's discussion of the archpriest controversy (1598–1602) and the later 'Chalcedon issue' (1625–31) in which issues to do with ecclesiastical discipline intersected with political loyalties in complicated ways: *Community*, chs. 2–3; '1603–1625', pp. 96–8; Questier, *Conversion*, chs. 5–6.

[41] Kaushik, 'Tresham'. See also I. D. Grosvenor, 'Catholics and politics: the Worcestershire election of 1604', *Recusant History*, 14 (1977–8), 149–62. Tresham is also discussed by Pritchard, *Loyalism*, pp. 49–56.

[42] J. J. La Rocca, 'Time, death, and the next generation: the Elizabethan recusancy policy, 1558–1574', *Albion*, 14 (1982), 103–17; Hibbard, 'Early Stuart Catholicism'; A. Dures, *English Catholicism 1558–1642: Continuity and Change* (London, 1983), 28–34. For case studies see V. Burke, 'The economic consequences of recusancy in Elizabethan Worcestershire', *Recusant History*, 14 (1977–78), 71–7; Manning, *Religion*, chs. 7–8.

[43] J. J. La Rocca, 'James I and his Catholic subjects, 1606–1612: some financial implications', *Recusant History*, 18 (1986–87), 251–62; Questier, *Conversion*, pp. 163–5.

[44] B. W. Quintrell, 'The problems and practice of recusant disarming, 1585–1641', *Recusant History*, 17 (1984–5), 208–22.

resistance to strict and divisive administration as they did Catholic resistance to persecution.[45] In fact, the brunt of persecution was borne by the seminarists and the Jesuits, and their harbourers – here were people less protected by notions of neighbourliness and who were not perceived in terms of a range of local relationships. It is also important to remember that they were executed for treason rather than for their religion.[46] This hints at a duality in the perception of the nature of the threat of Catholicism which was to become more marked later in the century. It was popery rather than recusancy that threatened domestic political and social order – the real threat was foreign infection and most lay Catholics suffered under the penal laws rather than the treason laws.[47]

The relatively flexible use of the penal laws in this period, of course, also reflects differing ambitions. There were those who doubted the efficacy of force in affecting conscience and others who were primarily concerned with political loyalty. A desire to convert undoubtedly existed, but this did not necessarily entail a commitment to persecution.[48] It has been suggested, for example, that the imposition of the oath of allegiance in 1606 was a means to toleration, offering security to those willing to pledge political loyalty, rather than a measure of persecution.[49] But the oath posed a very painful series of questions, and for many Catholics it was impossible to accept toleration on these terms.[50]

The importance of lay initiative may also have carried within it the

[45] R. G. Dottie, 'The recusant riots at Childwall in May 1600: a reappraisal', *Transactions of the Historic Society of Lancashire and Cheshire*, 132 (1982), 1–28.
[46] For the sufferings of the laity see P. McGrath and J. Rowe, 'The imprisonment of Catholics for religion under Elizabeth I', *Recusant History*, 20 (1990–1), 415–35, although the authors do not really explore whether the imprisonments were for religion or for treason. A number of the examples of Catholic laity imprisoned relate to bringing in seminarists, papal bulls, circulating books or dealing with priests. One joiner was imprisoned for, among other things, refusing to say what he would do if the pope sent an army against England. None the less there are some examples of imprisonments for non-attendance at Church or for hearing mass: pp. 420–1. The distinction between religion and treason is, of course, a fine but important one.
[47] Hibbard, 'Early Stuart Catholicism', esp. pp. 20–1.
[48] For the theory of intolerance see C. Russell, 'Arguments for religious unity in England, 1530–1650', reprinted in Russell, *Unrevolutionary England*, (London, 1990), 179–204; M. Goldie, 'The theory of religious intolerance in restoration England', in O. P. Grell, J. Israel and N. Tyacke (eds.), *From Persecution to Toleration: The Glorious Revolution and Religion in England* (Oxford, 1991), 331–68. For force and conscience see B. Bradshaw, 'Sword, word and strategy in the reformation in Ireland', *HJ*, 21 (1978), 475–502; J. J. La Rocca, '"Who Can't Pray With Me, Can't Love Me": toleration and early Jacobean recusancy policy', *JBS*, 23/2 (1984), 22–36. For the desire for genuine conversion, see Questier, *Conversion*, ch. 5.   [49] La Rocca, 'Toleration'.
[50] M. C. Questier, 'Loyalty, religion and state power in early modern England: English Romanism and the Jacobean oath of allegiance', *HJ*, 40 (1997), 311–29. See also W. B. Patterson, *King James VI and I and the Reunion of Christendom* (Cambridge, 1997), ch. 3.

seed of Protestant separatism. Puritanism was not a doctrinal position but a position in relation to the prevailing orthodoxy within the established church. Evangelists could be driven to relatively fuller withdrawal from, or engagement with, the established church according to official liturgical and doctrinal initiatives. It was not an automatic or easy step to take, but if they withdrew they might do so with the potential to promote their own version of the true faith among these forms of voluntary religion, which were supplementary to those of the established church. It is not safe to assume that anyone involved in such schemes had only a provisional commitment to the established church, still less that they were opposed to it.[51] Orthodoxy was constructed continuously and in conversation with heterodoxy. Neither was religious pluralism as destructive of social order as many contemporaries feared. In the parishes it was, it seems, quite possible for the godly to cohabit with the ungodly for much of the time.[52] But there was, by the late Elizabethan period, a set of institutions and a degree of lay control within the church, which gave, potentially at least, an organisational base for rival forms of Protestant practice. Those who, at particular moments or in response to particular policies, found themselves opposed to official religious policy had alternatives open to them.

Measures of success or failure are difficult in all the areas of government activity but here the problem is particularly marked. The evidence is extremely difficult to interpret, of course, and very partial. But even if it was very good there is no simple taxonomy of belief against which the beliefs of the population can be measured and neither is there a clear and consistent sense of what was being aimed at. While in one context it has been said that there were no Catholics in England in 1560, it is now frequently said that there were hardly any Protestants either.[53] Protestant jeremiads offer support to those pessimistic about, or unimpressed by, the achievement, while the minority status of Catholicism within a

[51] P. Collinson, 'A comment: concerning the name puritan', *Journal of Ecclesiastical History*, 31 (1980), 483–8; Collinson, 'The cohabitation of the faithful with the unfaithful', in Grell, Israel and Tyacke (eds.), *Persecution to Toleration*, 51–76; Collinson, 'Downfall'; Collinson, *Religion*, ch. 6. A similar conclusion can be drawn from P. Lake, 'The significance of the Elizabethan identification of the Pope as Antichrist', *Journal of Ecclesiastical History*, 31 (1980), 161–78. For a local study see Sheils, *Peterborough*, esp. chs. 3–5.

[52] D. Plumb, 'A gathered church? Lollards and their society', in Spufford (ed.), *Rural Dissenters*, 37–62; C. Marsh, 'The gravestone of Thomas Lawrence revisited (or the Family of Love and the local community in Balsham, 1560–1630)', ibid., 208–34. For the intellectual positions on this issue see Collinson, 'Cohabitation'.

[53] Bossy, *Community*, ch. 8; for a blunt statement approaching the latter position see P. Collinson, *The Birthpangs of Protestant England: Religious and Cultural Change in the Sixteenth and Seventeenth Centuries* (London, 1988), ix.

generation or so of the beginning of the process of Protestantisation offers support to those who see that process as a 'howling success'.[54] The difference is whether we are looking for whole-hearted Protestantism or conformity. It is not clear which of these yardsticks to apply because it is not clear which the privy council or the episcopacy would have applied. In short, there is no very clear contemporary aspiration against which the achievement can be measured. None the less, by 1603 it is possible to see a number of developments broadly acceptable to the head of the church, as well as some more worrying signs. The reduction of Catholic separatism to a rump and the restriction of the mission to a network of gentry and aristocratic households represented a measure of success against which must be set the increasing size of the counter-reformation Catholic community.[55] On the other hand, while Protestant evangelism had made considerable ground in the generation after 1570 this owed a considerable debt to lay initiatives which were not fully amenable to episcopal control. Protestant separatism was not inevitable, but it was a feature of Elizabethan religious life. The promotion of a particular view of Protestantism could not be achieved by a simple act of will by the crown, any more than it had been in the 1530s.

By the start of the Stuart period, Catholicism and, perhaps to a lesser extent, Protestant separatism, had an organisational basis beyond the control of the established church or secular authorities. Moreover, lay influence in the church impeded the authority of its head and meant that royal or archiepiscopal initiatives faced a degree of internal resistance. There are signs of the relative weakness of the government under James I. The Hampton Court conference, called after the accession of James I to discuss divergent views about the future of the English church, failed to achieve the hoped-for agreement. The subsequent attempt to enforce conformity through the 1604 canons met resistance in parliament, particularly the Commons.[56] Not all bishops were willing to enforce conformity to the Thirty Nine Articles drawn up by Archbishop Parker in 1563, and regarded by many as the cornerstone of Anglican doctrine. They preferred instead a more conciliatory approach, and in Northamptonshire a petition against deprivations of 'painful' ministers (that is, relatively godly preachers) was signed by

---

[54] Haigh, acknowledging the conformity of the bulk of the English population by 1603, is unimpressed: 'Some reformations', *Reformations*, p. 295. See also Haigh, 'Puritan evangelism in the reign of Elizabeth I', *EHR*, 92 (1977), 30–58. For broadly the same phenomenon as a 'howling success' see D. MacCulloch, 'The impact of the English reformation', *HJ*, 38 (1995), 151–3, at p. 152.   [55] For the success of the mission, see Bossy, *Community*, ch. 8.

[56] R. Lockyer, *The Early Stuarts: A Political History of England 1603–1642* (London, 1989), 105–10.

deputy lieutenants and justices of the peace.[57] It seems that the ecclesiastical policy of James I was, subsequently, more conciliatory, taking account of the existence of hotter Protestantism and the influence of the laity in church government.[58] Calvinists were powerful within both secular and ecclesiastical institutions.[59] At the same time, the pressure to step-up the persecution of Catholics after the gunpowder plot soon gave way to a more relaxed regime in the implementation of the penal laws against the Catholic laity.[60] There were also more straightforwardly political difficulties. For example, the commons were hostile to pluralism and non-residence. The temptations of holding more than one living were increased by the poverty of many livings and yet, because property rights were affected, the Commons were unwilling to support the obvious solution – to re-endow the church by returning impropriations.[61] Fundamental difficulties may have been left unaddressed as a result of these kinds of difficulty.

Charles I and William Laud were associated with a more aggressive assertion of order. A concerted drive for conformity and discipline, which seems to have chimed at some level with the secular political views of Charles I, resulted in some change. But this came at a high political cost. A particularly revealing episode in this is the attempt to restore the dignity of the clergy. Laudianism was associated with a desire to enhance episcopal authority and this was, in part, a financial issue. The clash over the Feoffees for Impropriations symbolises the broader struggle to establish the control of the head over the members. The Feoffees had formed a trust to purchase impropriations, and to receive donations, with which to supplement the livings of worthy ministers and lecturers. In other words, the financial problems of the church were being addressed by lay interests, with a view to raising the standards of preaching. However, such a lay initiative, entirely outside of episcopal

---

[57] K. Fincham and P. Lake, 'The ecclesiastical policy of King James I', *JBS*, 24 (1985), 169–207, at pp. 176–7. For the varied local response to the enforcement of the 1604 canons see Fincham, 'Ramifications of the Hampton Court Conference in the Dioceses, 1603–1609', *Journal of Ecclesiastical History*, 36 (1985), 208–27. See also O. U. Kalu, 'Continuity and change: bishops of London and religious dissent in early Stuart England', *JBS*, 18/1 (1978–9), 28–45.

[58] For the Jacobean consensus, see Fincham and Lake, 'Ecclesiastical policy of James I'. The energy for the enforcement of the 1604 canons seems to have run out quite rapidly: Fincham, 'Ramifications'.

[59] Tyacke, 'Puritanism'; P. Lake, 'Calvinism and the English church, 1570–1635', *PP*, 114 (1987), 32–76.

[60] La Rocca, 'Financial implications'; La Rocca, 'Toleration'; Dures, *English Catholicism*, pp. 47–51. Questier is more sceptical on this point, citing increasing levels of conformity at the exchequer in the years following the plot: *Conversion*, p. 137.

[61] Lockyer, *Early Stuarts*, pp. 107, 110–14. For this tension more generally, see Hill, *Economic*, ch. 6.

control, was anathema to the Laudian order and the Feoffees were prosecuted in the court of the exchequer for creating an illegal corporation.[62] A similar desire for uniformity and order in the church led to the attempt to regulate lectureships.[63] The use of high commission and star chamber to punish non-conformity, the licensing of some sabbath-day recreations, pressure to improve the fabric of churches and to position the communion table altar-wise all suggested to hotter Protestants a similar willingness to persecute worthy Christians.[64]

In this policy the Laudian claim was to the heritage of the true Church. Calvinists, it was suggested, were innovators, pulling the Church of England away from its purity. Naturally enough, the Calvinist response was to accuse the Laudians of the same thing. Under Charles and Laud, it was said, innovations were being made which smacked of popery and threatened the gains of the reformation. A nearly parallel debate is being conducted among modern historians, between those who see Laudians as guardians of a moderate tradition that can be traced back to Henry VIII and those who see them as innovators against a broadly based and well-established Calvinist domination of the early Stuart church. The debate is the more heated because it is intimately connected with the debate about the causes of the English civil war.[65] It seems clear, however, that the aspiration for order was unrealisable. Few would disagree that such an aspiration was expressed, that some opposition met attempts to implement it and that, by 1640, it had not succeeded. The apologias for Laud follow two lines: that he was the moderate; and that opposition did not necessarily presage civil war. For our purposes, however, these are not the main issues.

The liturgical developments of the 1630s, like the programme to restore and enhance the fabric and furniture of the parish churches, met with some

---

[62] See Hill, *Economic*, ch. 11.

[63] Hill, *Society*, ch. 3. For a thorough discussion of these initiatives which, controversially, seeks to discount the claim that Laud was their architect see J. Davies, *The Caroline Captivity of the Church: Charles I and the Remoulding of Anglicanism 1625–1641* (Oxford, 1992), ch. 4.

[64] For critical accounts of the Laudian or Caroline regime in the dioceses see Fincham, 'Episcopal government, 1603–1640', in Fincham (ed.), *Early Stuart Church*, 71–91, 259–62; Fielding, 'Arminianism in the localities: Peterborough diocese 1603–42', ibid., 93–113, 262–4; Foster, 'Clerical estate'. For the desire for order and uniformity see Fincham and Lake, 'Ecclesiastical policies of James I and Charles I'; and P. Lake, 'The Laudian style: order, uniformity and the pursuit of the beauty of holiness in the 1630s', in Fincham (ed.), *Early Stuart Church*, 161–85, 275–82. For some of the conflicts arising from the attempt to restore clerical dignity see Hill, *Economic*, ch. 14.

[65] This point is also made by P. Lake, 'Defining Puritanism – again?', in F. J. Bremer (ed.), *Puritanism: Transatlantic Perspectives on a Seventeenth-Century Anglo-American Faith* (Boston, 1993), 3–29, at pp. 28–9. Tyacke's interpretation was launched on the public stage in a volume devoted explicitly to the origins of the civil war: see above, n. 3.

opposition but certainly not with universal antagonism. Responses to particular initiatives varied from diocese to diocese, even from parish to parish; different reactions to, and perceptions of, changes may be explained as much by personal and regional factors – the preferences and tact of bishops and clergymen, the variety of local custom and practice – as by clearly defined theological alignments.[66]

The impossibility of achieving uniformity is the point here, not the extent or seriousness of opposition, nor who had the better claim to orthodoxy. The failure of uniformity should not surprise us, and probably would not have surprised most contemporaries, but it was clearly at variance with some official statements of intent. Hotter Protestants had protectors. For example, Henry Sherfield has achieved a degree of fame he can hardly have anticipated as a result of his prominence in the controversy over the early Stuart church. In October 1630 he broke a window in St Edmund's church, Salisbury, a response to what he regarded as idolatry. He was a prominent godly magistrate, associated with an ambitious programme of social and religious reform in the city and typifies the socially active, but essentially conservative, godly magistrates described by Collinson.[67] Such men were not puritan revolutionaries except in so far as their religious opinions could not be held within the bounds of the established church. Sherfield had the support of the mayor and persuaded the earl of Dorset to speak to Charles I on his behalf.[68] The Calvinist bishop, John Davenant, cooperated in the prosecution, and he had earlier forbidden the churchwardens to replace the window with plain glass, questioning the authority of the vestry to make such an order.[69] However, although he initiated the prosecution he was probably not a willing party – it seems clear that he was pushed into doing so by the dean.[70] Not only, then, were powerful secular interests sympathetic to Sherfield but it seems that the bishop was also unwilling to persecute such a figure. The problems of enforcing strict conformity to a particular vision of the true religion are plain.

By 1640 religious pluralism seems to have been quite marked. It is certainly uncontentious to claim that, encouraged by gentry protection

---

[66] Sharpe, *Charles I*, p. 345.

[67] P. Slack, 'Religious protest and urban authority: the case of Henry Sherfield, iconoclast, 1633', in D. Baker (ed.), *Schism, Heresy and Religious Protest*, Studies in Church History, 9 (Cambridge, 1972), 295–302; P. Slack, *Poverty and Policy in Tudor and Stuart England* (London, 1988), 184; Slack, 'The public conscience of Henry Sherfield', in J. Morrill, P. Slack and D. Woolf (eds.), *Public Duty and Private Conscience in Seventeenth-Century England* (Oxford, 1993), 151–71, esp. pp. 168–71; Collinson, *Religion*, ch. 4 (for Sherfield see pp. 147–9). [68] Sharpe, *Charles I*, p. 347.

[69] Ibid., p. 346.

[70] Tyacke, 'Anglican attitudes', pp. 164–5. Slack also suggests that Davenant was reluctant: 'Religious protest', pp. 298–9.

and a degree of toleration at court, Catholicism was entrenched by that date.[71] This lent credence to anti-Catholic scares. It also seems plausible that, during the 1630s, Protestant separatism increased. By then there had been 'an accommodation of voluntary religious forms within the Church of England over a period of two or three generations'.[72] Forms of piety supplemental to those available through the church were common and tolerated. This might not have made congregationalism inevitable[73] but it made narrow uniformity impossibly difficult to attain. Recent work has demonstrated how forms of dissent were integrated into local social life. Familists in Elizabethan Cambridgeshire, for example, were churchwardens and seem to have had protectors even at court.[74] Many such groups existed in a condition of semi-separatism, that might turn into separatism in response to changes in official policy. During the 1630s ten separatist congregations were active in London, and there were others in Kent and East Anglia.[75] On either wing, then, uniformity was challenged. These groups have attracted more than their fair share of attention, at the expense of conforming prayer book Protestants, but it is still worthy of note that religious diversity was (probably unavoidably) a fact of national life by 1640.

Lay initiative exercised a profound influence over the development of religious practice in England and, under certain circumstances, this might represent evasion of official policy. Religious plurality was a measure, among other things, of political failure and this failure had, in part, an institutional explanation. The significance of this failure has been given much emphasis recently in explaining how Stuart government, in all three kingdoms, broke down and how English people overcame profoundly held beliefs about the inviolability of monarchical authority. As negotiations between interested parties reached deadlock it was religious anxieties and hopes that drove the activist minorities on.[76] Of course, these concerns were not narrowly religious. Religious ideas provided a means for understanding and justifying all aspects of social, economic and political life, as we have seen. Religion was central

---

[71] For Caroline recusancy see Dures, *English Catholicism*; T. S. Smith, 'The persecution of Staffordshire Roman Catholic recusants: 1625–1660', *Journal of Ecclesiastical History*, 30 (1979), 327–51.

[72] Collinson, *Religion*, p. 250.   [73] Ibid.

[74] C. W. Marsh, *The Family of Love in English Society, 1550–1630* (Cambridge, 1994). See, more generally, Spufford (ed.), *Rural Dissenters*.

[75] S. Doran and C. Durston, *Princes, Pastors and People: The Church and Religion in England 1529–1689* (London, 1991), 111.

[76] J. S. Morrill, 'The religious context of the English civil war', reprinted in Morrill, *The Nature of the English Revolution: Essays by John Morrill* (London, 1993), 45–68.

to the legitimation of political authority and hence religious issues were, crucially, political. This divisiveness was multiplied by the attempt to impose conformity on three kingdoms simultaneously – those of a like mind on religious issues made common cause across national boundaries.

In these ways, then, the failure of religious uniformity was central to the breakdown of government in 1640. It was not only, but in significant part, an institutional failure. The participation of local elites in fostering conformity and persecuting non-conformity was not forthcoming. Lay influence in the church handicapped episcopal authority while religious diversity was reflected at all levels of secular administration from court to constable. In such circumstances the pursuit of narrow conformity was almost certainly doomed and in this sense it was not the failure of enforcement that caused the breakdown so much as the very attempt. Vested interests here cut across official aspirations with disastrous effects and thus religious policy invites comparison with fiscal and military policy.

By the same token, it provides a contrast with the relative success of social and economic policy. To return to Sherfield, it was his iconoclasm, not his social activism that got him into trouble. His radicalism was doctrinal, not social, and his activities in response to social order were in fact quite respectable. Indeed, Chief Justice Richardson defended him by saying that 'he hath done good in that City since I went that circuit; so that there is neither Beggar nor Drunkard to be seen there'.[77] Both his social activism and religious radicalism sprang from a religious imperative but it was only as a social reformer that Sherfield was in tune with the spirit of national administrative prescription. As such, his initiatives in relation to social order did not pose the problem to his superiors that Sherfield the religious reformer did. The relatively autonomous functions of state, such as the promotion of the 'true religion', for example, were those least closely connected with the collective interest of officeholders and their constituency. They seem also to have been implemented less fully than those relating more directly to those collective interests, such as the preservation of local social order, about which there was a much greater coincidence of opinion among the better sort.

---

[77] Quoted in P. Slack, 'Poverty and politics in Salisbury, 1597–1666', in P. Clark and P. Slack (eds.), *Crisis and Order in English Towns 1500–1700: Essays in Urban History* (London, 1972), 164–203, at p. 184.

DISSENT, POPERY AND PERSECUTION IN LATER
SEVENTEENTH-CENTURY ENGLAND

During the 1640s and 1650s religious pluralism increased dramatically. The Church of England was dismantled and the Presbyterian system constructed in its place enjoyed, at best, a shadowy existence. Censorship collapsed too, contributing to the proliferation of sects to which much attention has been paid. Presbyterians, the religious radicals of the 1630s, were in the conditions of the 1640s relatively conservative. They sought to restrict the freedom of individuals and congregations to interpret scripture without external discipline. For others, this attempt at discipline was merely popery on a smaller scale.[78] The worst fears of the respectable were, it seemed, to be realised. Thomas Edwards's best-seller, *Gangraena*, catalogued the threats to society posed by this proliferation of sects while the descriptions of Ranters and Familists in contemporary polemic suggest that they offered a religious counterpart to the secular threat of the vagrant. During the 1650s the Quakers epitomised the dangers of this sectarianism – individuals responding directly to what they perceived to be God's will, with no intercession. Priestly control of the sacred had, as it turned out, been permanently damaged, and religious pluralism was a fact of English life thereafter. It has been suggested that even the activities of the commissions for better propagating and spreading the gospel in Wales, in handing initiative to the local middling sort, helped to sow the seeds for the development of Methodism in the eighteenth-century Glamorgan.[79]

But the challenge to 'the respectable puritans of the Parliamentarian majority' did not come from religious radicals alone. It also 'came from the passive strength of Anglican survivalism'.[80] With the restoration of the monarchy came the restoration of a Church of England demanding a high degree of conformity to official doctrine. 'The strength of the Anglican reaction lay not exclusively, or even principally, in the response of a gentry who craved the return of a hierarchical Church which would shore up a hierarchical government and society, but in the popularity of traditional religious forms at all levels

---

[78] M. J. Braddick and M. Greengrass (eds.), 'The letters of Sir Cheney Culpeper, 1641–1657', *Camden Miscellany XXXIII*, Camden Society, 5th series, 7 (Cambridge, 1996), 105–402, at pp. 138–9, 144–5.

[79] T. Edwards, *Gangraena* (London, 1646). S. K. Roberts, 'Godliness and government in Glamorgan, 1647–1660', in C. Jones, M. Newitt and S. Roberts (eds.), *Politics and People in Revolutionary England: Essays in Honour of Ivan Roots* (Oxford, 1986), 225–51.

[80] J. Morrill, 'The church in England, 1642–9', in Morrill (ed.), *Reactions to the English Civil War 1642–1649* (London, 1982), 89–114, 230–4 at p. 90.

of society.'[81] The existence of 'parochial Prayer Book Protestantism' before the civil war is also, now, receiving attention. Maltby has recovered a strand of parish conformity that could be held with commitment by rich and poor. It drew on a positive commitment to conformist vestments, burial rites and even altar rails (although not those of the popish Arminians).[82] This was a measure of the success of the official reformation and provides a context for the survival of 'Anglicanism', but the fact that until recently it received comparatively little attention is testimony to the failure of uniformity.

The restored Church of England was apparently committed to the pursuit of, at least, conformity, building on 'Anglican survival' during the 1640s and 1650s. During that period there had been large numbers of ejections, but they were not all for matters of doctrine. Many other clergymen hung on – pluralists retained at least one of their livings, while others ejected from one living were able to secure another. Of 2,780 clergy ejected, perhaps 1,180 continued to serve. In 1649 perhaps two-thirds or three-fifths of livings were in the hands of clergy who had held them in 1642. These men had often been educated under the relatively hot Protestant Abbott rather than Laud, and the Anglican reaction at the restoration is difficult to attribute to a vengeful Laudian clergy.[83] It has been suggested that even during the 1650s, when candidates for the ministry had to appear before thirty-eight 'triers' in London, many new clergymen were essentially conservative. The post-restoration ejections were more effective. The first ordinations in the 1660s reflected aspirations for a relatively broad church settlement, but a conservative backlash in the Cavalier parliament produced, among other things, an Act of Uniformity that resulted in 900 ejections or resignations.[84] The corollary of disciplining the clergy was, of course, to discipline the laity, and the Cavalier parliament enacted a series of measures designed to reduce non-conformity: the Corporation Act,

---

[81] Morrill, 'Church in England', p. 91, taking issue with the interpretation advocated by I. M. Green, *The Re-Establishment of the Church of England 1660–1663* (Oxford, 1978). The Devon grand jury, for example, roused itself from its customary sloth to achieve this restoration: S. K. Roberts, 'Initiative and control: the Devon quarter sessions grand jury, 1649–70', *BIHR*, 57 (1984), 165–77, pp. 166–7. See also R. Clark, 'Why was the re-establishment of the Church of England possible? Derbyshire: a provincial perspective', *Midland History*, 8 (1983), 86–105.

[82] Maltby, 'By this Book'.

[83] I. M. Green, 'The persecution of "scandalous" and "malignant" parish clergy during the English civil war', *EHR*, 94 (1979), 507–31, figures at pp. 508, 525. See also Morrill, 'Church in England', pp. 100–3.

[84] Green, *Re-Establishment*, esp. ch. 2. Green's argument about where the pressure for strict conformity originated is questioned by Clark, 'Derbyshire'; and by Morrill, 'Church in England'.

1661; the Quaker Act, 1662; the Act of Uniformity, 1662; the Conventicles Act, 1664; the Five Mile Act, 1665; and the Second Conventicles Act, 1670.[85]

This discipline over the clergy and the laity was informed by practical and principled hostility to religious plurality. There were three strands to Anglican arguments for intolerance. First there was the political concern that religious dissent might breed sedition. Secondly, there was an ecclesiological concern to promote order and decency in public worship. Thirdly, there was a desire to bring dissenters conscientiously to believe the orthodox tenets of Anglican doctrine. This latter argument was based on the assumption that coercion was only effective in tandem with education and that belief was voluntary. It is important to note that those who argued in this way would have resisted the description of their policies as 'persecution': that term was reserved for those who suffered for the true faith.[86] The attempt to establish order and uniformity therefore, could proceed from practical concerns for political order[87] or from a more principled desire to promote the true religion. To an extent this seems to represent a sharpening of attitudes as a result of the experience of civil war and the explosion of sectarian religion with which it had been associated.

The issue of religious order goes to the heart of political argument after the restoration. During the 1650s Edward Spanne had offended the worthies of Chester corporation with his 'many horrid Blasphemies', but there was more at stake too. He was a man 'soe farre from having a tend[er] Conscience as to be w[i]thout Conscience towards God or towards men'.[88] Despite being bound to 'shew and performe all due reverence and duty' towards the governors of the city, he had publicly stated that 'the sword and mace usually carried before the mayor should be layd in the Channell very shortly for all that Mr Mayor or his great horse or the Haltermen [Aldermen?] his brethren could doe'. He was also said to be a 'contriver and spreader of false Newes' and had spoken out against taxes being levied on the city.[89] This radicalism seems to have proceeded from religious beliefs, for he had powerful protectors

---

[85] This code was subsequently strengthened by the Test Acts of 1673 and 1678. For summaries of the provisions see G. Holmes, *The Making of a Great Power: Late Stuart and Early Georgian Britain, 1660–1722* (London, 1993), 455, 457.

[86] Goldie, 'The theory of religious intolerance'.

[87] See, for example, the suggestion of a fortieth article of Anglican faith, acknowledging a religious duty of obedience to the monarch: R. Beddard, 'Of the duty of subjects: a proposed fortieth article of religion', *Bodleian Library Record*, 10 (1978–82), 229–36. It was this genuine conviction in the duty of obedience which posed such an acute problem of conscience for Tory Anglican clergy after 1689.   [88] CCRO, ML/3/352.   [89] CCRO, ML/3/361.

arguing for the freedom of his conscience.[90] But clearly it was the practical consequences of his beliefs for political order and decency which most concerned the city's governors. Religion was an institutional interest, a style of discourse and a mode of power relations, and 'debates about religion were ultimately debates about power and social authority'.[91] The fusion of religious and political concerns is manifest in the term 'popery', which often did not really connote a doctrinal position at all. '"Papists are enemies not because they are erroneous in religion but because their principles are destructive of the government" said one MP. "Popery in a great measure is set up for arbitrary power's sake; they are not so forward for religion" said another.'[92]

In many localities there was, after the restoration, a revival of the earlier pattern of semi-separatism, many dissenters finding ways of conforming occasionally. Again this may have resulted from political calculation – a desire to evade the restrictions on officeholding – or from a genuine desire to continue to reform the church from within.[93] This attitude was matched by those within the church willing to pursue comprehension, but was regarded with acute suspicion by others. After the concession of limited toleration for particular kinds of dissent high churchmen remained acutely suspicious of occasional conformity, 'what they perceived as its hypocritical, blasphemous use of religion to evade the law'. More importantly, 'it was based on their adherence to the ancient concept of the interdependence of Church and State, that the welfare and security of the one was the vital concern of the other, and that political rights should be reserved for those who were constant in

---

[90] CCRO, ML/3/362, 374.

[91] J. A. I. Champion, 'Religion after the restoration', *HJ*, 36 (1993), 423–30, esp. pp. 429–30, quotation at p. 429. See also G. Schochet, 'From persecution to "Toleration"', in J. R. Jones (ed.), *Liberty Secured? Britain Before and After 1688* (Stanford, 1992), 122–57, 356–62, esp. pp. 128–30.

[92] J. Miller, 'The potential for "absolutism" in later Stuart England', *History*, 69 (1984), 187–207, quotations at p. 187.

[93] See, for example, J. D. Ramsbottom, 'Presbyterians and "partial conformity" in the restoration church of England', *Journal of Ecclesiastical History*, 43 (1992), 249–70; N. E. Key, 'Comprehension and the breakdown of consensus in restoration Herefordshire', in T. Harris, P. Seaward and M. Goldie (eds.), *The Politics of Religion in Restoration England* (Oxford, 1990), 191–215; D. L. Wykes, 'The church and early dissent: the 1669 return of nonconformist conventicles for the archdeaconry of Northampton', *Northamptonshire Past and Present*, 8 (1991–2), 197–209. Spurr argues that this parish puritanism should caution against an assumption of the inevitability of separatism: J. Spurr, 'From puritanism to dissent, 1660–1700', in Durston and Eales (eds.), *English Puritanism*, 234–65, 316–20. The practice is also noted by Hurwich, but in the context of the increasing pressure placed on dissent by prosecution: J. A. Hurwich, '"A Fanatick Town": the political influence of dissenters in Coventry, 1660–1720', *Midland History*, 4 (1977), 15–47; Hurwich, 'Dissent and Catholicism in English society: a study of Warwickshire, 1660–1720', *JBS*, 16/1 (1976), 24–58.

their loyalty to both'.[94] The central issue here was hypocrisy. The true church had a real obligation to promote true religion and to allow occasional conformity was to allow hypocrisy to flourish. At the same time dissenters might welcome persecution as testimony to their steadfastness and integrity in the pursuit of the true religion. To them too, occasional conformity could represent a repugnant hypocrisy.[95] Many of the religious radicals of the interregnum had been committed to uniformity too, although there was an increasing scepticism about the use of force to achieve it.[96] Toleration was opposed by many people in restoration England, therefore, and this fed a suspicion of comprehension or indulgence. A softening of views might concede fundamentals of Anglican or dissenting belief and was opposed from both wings, but this was in tension with a shared sense of the desirability of uniformity, too. Principled commitment to intolerance in a situation of pluralism was, of course, a recipe for considerable conflict.

To many people, for at least some of the time, Protestant dissent posed at least as great a threat to political order as did Catholicism. And like the fear of popery, this was partly derived from an interpretation of international politics. It helps to explain, for example, domestic attitudes towards the Dutch. The memory of the sects of the 1640s and 1650s was fresh in many minds, and associated with social disorder and republicanism. These domestic fears were, in the 1660s, allied with suspicion that the Dutch aspired to the creation of a universal dominion based upon control of international trade. Their republicanism and universal aspirations were attacked as 'popery' – authority hostile to that of kings – and they were said to be implicated in republican plots at home. The second Dutch war, then, involved a trading hostility but was not straightforwardly a 'trade war'. Domestic opinion resembled the anti-popery of the 1620s which was expressed as a desire for an active foreign policy.[97] Non-conformity at home clearly posed a threat to established

---

[94] J. S. Flaningham, 'The occasional conformity controversy: ideology and party politics, 1697–1711', *JBS*, 17 (1977–8), 38–62, quotations at p. 46.

[95] I am grateful to Justin Champion for making this point to me. Such a line of reasoning led Lancashire Quakers to be suspicious of compromises promoted by the metropolitan organisation: N. Morgan, *The Lancashire Quakers and the Establishment, 1660–1730* (Halifax, 1993).

[96] A. Zakai, 'Religious toleration and its enemies: the independent divines and the issue of toleration during the English civil war', *Albion*, 21 (1989), 1–33.

[97] S. C. A. Pincus, *Protestantism and Patriotism: Ideologies and the Making of English Foreign Policy* (Cambridge, 1996), chs. 11–16. See also P. Seaward, 'The House of Commons Committee of Trade and the origins of the second Anglo-Dutch war, 1664', *HJ*, 30 (1987), 437–52. For the 1620s see T. Cogswell, *The Blessed Revolution: English Politics and the Coming of War 1621–1624* (Cambridge, 1989); Cogswell, 'Phaeton's chariot: the Parliament-men and the continental crisis in 1621', in J. F. Merritt (ed.), *The Political World of Thomas Wentworth, Earl of Strafford, 1621–1641*

social and political order.[98] The religious order of the parish became a point of conflict, around which alternative visions of social and political order were articulated. The failure of comprehension or the necessity of intolerance could cause deep divisions within Protestantism.[99]

There were some familiar administrative difficulties in the pursuit of religious intolerance and the active propagation of the Anglican message, however. Lay patronage within the church remained as dominant as it had been in the earlier period. In 1742, 26 per cent of advowsons were in clerical hands, less than 10 per cent in crown control and over 53 per cent in lay hands. Many of these lay patrons were of non-noble status, the majority, in fact, not being baronets or knights. There may have been some change since 1660 but it is likely that this is a fair reflection of the situation throughout that period.[100] In Leicestershire between 1660 and 1714 about 15 per cent of advowsons were controlled by the crown, and 10 per cent by the bishops and corporate bodies. The rest were held by individual members of the laity.[101] Nationally, the crown had to lobby individuals to create an interest, in much the same way that an electoral interest in parliament was established – influential private interests were wooed and cajoled to use their influence in support of the government.[102] This lay influence must have reduced the power of those seeking uniformity, although little attention is paid to these issues by historians of the restoration period. Leading gentry recusants in Monmouthshire were certainly able to use their control of advowsons in the late seventeenth and early eighteenth centuries to promote the careers of sympathisers or those opposed to persecution.[103] The associated problems of clerical poverty persisted too, although clerical living standards were improving in Leicestershire.[104] The response to such problems, as in the earlier period, drew on the commitment of the laity. For example, Queen Anne's Bounty, which established a fund to supplement the income of the poorest clergy attracted

(Cambridge, 1996), 24–46; C. Russell, 'Sir Thomas Wentworth and anti-Spanish sentiment, 1621–1624', ibid., 47–62.   [98] Champion, 'Religion after the restoration'.

[99] See D. Beaver, 'Conscience and context: the popish plot and the politics of ritual, 1678–1682', *HJ*, 34 (1991), 297–327; J. Barry, 'The parish in civic life: Bristol and its churches, 1640–1750', in S. J. Wright (ed.), *Parish, Church and People: Local Studies in Lay Religion 1350–1750* (London, 1988), 152–78; Barry, 'The politics of religion in restoration Bristol', in Harris, Seaward and Goldie (eds.), *Politics*, 163–89; M. Goldie and J. Spurr, 'Politics and the restoration parish: Edward Fowler and the struggle for St Giles Cripplegate', *EHR*, 109 (1994), 572–96.

[100] D. R. Hirschberg, 'The government and church patronage in England, 1660–1760', *JBS*, 20 (1980), 109–39, figures quoted from p. 111.   [101] Pruett, *Leicestershire*, p. 60.

[102] Hirschberg, 'Patronage'.

[103] J. R. Guy, 'The Anglican patronage of Monmouth recusants in the seventeenth and eighteenth centuries', *Recusant History*, 15 (1979–81), 452–4.   [104] Pruett, *Leicestershire*, ch. 3.

considerable lay support.[105] In Bristol, the corporation supported lectureships which became a bulwark of Anglicanism and a source of
income for poor clergymen.[106] Church courts remained active in a
number of dioceses, not just in relation to testamentary, matrimonial
and sexual business but also in matters of discipline.[107] In these courts,
too, local influence probably mediated the impact of persecution.[108]

Before the civil war the division between conformists and dissent was
not absolute, as we have seen. This continued to be the case. For
example, it has been suggested that in Wiltshire parish Anglicanism was
engaged and independent-minded: partial conformity was not necessarily a reflection of the failure of Anglicanism but of a continuing commitment to it.[109] The success of measures against non-conformity depended
on the willingness of secular authorities to give teeth to national legislation: national panics did not necessarily find a resonance in all localities.[110] The Buckinghamshire visitation of 1669, for example, revealed
the existence of conventicles in many villages. Some 'pretend the authority of the spiritt from whom they presume for impunity', while others
took comfort from 'the King's indulgence'. In virtually all cases, the
names of conventiclers were well known and there was a strong conviction throughout the returns that vigorous action by the civil authorities
would have been sufficient to extinguish the conventicles. As Thomas
Cookson put it:

if the rigour of the law (which is the life of the law) was diligently and duly
executed by the assistance of the civil magistrates (especially against the
speakers in those conventicles and the owners or possessors of those houses or

---

[105] I. Green, 'The first years of Queen Anne's bounty', in O'Day and Heal (eds.), *Princes and Paupers*,
231–54.   [106] Barry, 'Politics', pp. 165–6.

[107] J. Walsh and S. Taylor, 'Introduction: the Anglican church in the "long" eighteenth century', in
J. Walsh, C. Haydon and S. Taylor (eds.), *The Church of England c. 1689–c. 1833: From Toleration to
Tractarianism* (Cambridge, 1993), 1–64, pp. 5–6. See also Pruett, *Leicestershire*, pp. 19–20 and
passim.

[108] See, for example, M. G. Smith, *Pastoral Discipline and the Church Courts: the Hexham Court
1680–1730*, Borthwick Papers, 62 (York, 1982).

[109] D. A. Spaeth, 'A common prayer? Popular observance of the Anglican liturgy in restoration
Wiltshire', in Wright (ed.), *Parish*, 125–51.

[110] See, for example, T. Harris, 'Was the Tory reaction popular?: attitudes of Londoners towards
the persecution of dissent, 1681–6', *London Journal*, 13 (1988), 106–20. This is not to suggest that
the success of persecution depended on a triumph of central will over the locality. It is quite
clear that in many counties there were magistrates and constables who were more than willing
to prosecute dissenters. The relationship could work in the other direction too, local plots
feeding national fears of disorder, as in the case of the Kaber Rigg plot in Cumbria in 1663: P.
D. Clarke, 'The sectarian "threat" and its impact in restoration Cumbria', *Transactions of the
Cumberland and Westmorland Antiquarian and Archaeological Society*, 88 (1988), 161–75. See also M.
Mullett, '"Men of Knowne Loyalty": the politics of the Lancashire borough of Clitheroe,
1660–1689', *Northern History*, 21 (1985), 108–36, esp. pp. 109–10.

barnes wherein they exercise) those conventicles would in a short tyme without danger to church or state be suppressed.

To an extent, then, the survival of public and identifiable dissent seems to have rested on local indulgence, although whether Cookson's faith in the potential of suppression was justified must remain a matter of speculation.[111]

The fear of dissent, like the fear of popery, might not be identified with local dissenters who were often well known and to some extent assimilated into local social networks. This is demonstrable even in the case of the most reviled of all late seventeenth-century dissenters, the Quakers. The early Quakers were represented in pamphlets as a fundamental threat to decency and to both social and political order.[112] The treatment of James Nayler provides eloquent testimony to that hostility. In 1656 he rode into Bristol on an ass, in imitation of Christ's arrival in Jerusalem, to demonstrate the Quaker belief that Christ was in all human beings. Others regarded this gesture with horror, and he was convicted of 'horrid blasphemy'. The severity of the physical punishment to be inflicted upon him took parliament some time to consider. Following the restoration, this level of fear was sustained and there was clearly a local constituency for decisive action against the Quakers in a way that there was not in the case of Catholics.[113] Their views were radical in social terms, and Quakers are often noted to have refused to respect some of the standard signifiers of social status in early modern society.[114] In Evesham the Quakers drew their support from those marginalised or excluded from established local influence.[115] But even in the case of the Quakers there is plenty of evidence of local support, protection and mitigation of the penal code. In Lancashire there is clear evidence of hostility to the Quakers during the 1650s and early 1660s, but in the end '[c]o-existence . . . overcame conflict' as Quakers and their neighbours found ways to avoid conflict over the taking of oaths or

[111] J. Broad (ed.), *Buckinghamshire Dissent and Parish Life 1669–1712*, Buckinghamshire Record Society, 28 (1993), 1–72, quotations at pp. 7, 10, 12.

[112] B. Reay, 'Popular hostility towards Quakers in mid-seventeenth-century England', *Social History*, 5 (1980), 387–407. Reay demonstrates the existence of considerable animosity but does not convincingly demonstrate its ubiquity.

[113] B. Reay, 'The authorities and early restoration Quakerism', *Journal of Ecclesiastical History*, 34 (1983), 69–84.

[114] Reay, 'Popular hostility'. They were also radical in relation to law reform: R. M. Rogers, 'Quakerism and the law in revolutionary England', *Canadian Journal of History*, 22 (1987), 149–74. See also C. Holmes, *Seventeenth-Century Lincolnshire* (Lincoln, 1980), 205 6.

[115] S. Roberts, 'The Quakers in Evesham, 1655–1660: a study in religion, politics and culture', *Midland History*, 16 (1991), 63–85.

the payment of tithes.[116] The Lancashire book of sufferings, the Quaker's testimony to the trials of following their consciences, provides evidence of sympathetic treatment at the hands of constables and even of constables paying fines due out of money that they owed to persecuted Quakers. Sympathetic neighbours cushioned the impact of the persecution, which came to depend on the activities of informers rather more than it did on constables.[117] In Derbyshire, too, there is evidence of neighbourly cooperation over the swearing of oaths and the payment of tithes.[118] Detailed study of Quaker communities has revealed that, like less dangerous dissenters, they were drawn from all ranks of local society, and were integrated into local social networks.[119]

The result was partial and sporadic persecution, even of what was thought in the abstract to be one of the most threatening forms of dissent. We have already noted the partial conformity of the 'parish puritans', inheritors of the Presbyterian and semi-separatist tradition. In London a high degree of participation in the implementation of the law and a reluctance to prosecute dissent seem to have limited the effectiveness of persecution. Here, too, resort was made to informers, and the participation of tory politicians in organising pope-burning processions may have been a conscious attempt to instil a sense of the church in danger.[120] In Coventry dissenters were not removed from borough office and in Preston vigorous initial purges had given way by the 1670s to a degree of co-existence in corporation office.[121] The returns of dissenters and Catholics in Worcestershire presentments seem too low to be credible, suggesting that both enjoyed some local protection.[122] In

---

[116] N. Morgan, 'Lancashire Quakers and the oath, 1660–1722', *Journal of the Friends' Historical Society*, 54 (1976–82), 235–54, quotation at p. 254. See also Morgan, *Lancashire Quakers*.

[117] A. B. Anderson, 'A study in the sociology of religious persecution: the first Quakers', *Journal of Religious History*, 9 (1976–7), 247–62, esp. pp. 254–9. Anderson properly notes that this might not be a disinterested impression.

[118] H. Forde, 'Friends and authority: a consideration of attitudes and expedients, with particular reference to Derbyshire', *Journal of the Friends' Historical Society*, 54 (1976–82), 115–25.

[119] B. Stevenson, 'The social and economic status of post-restoration dissenters, 1660–1725', in Spufford (ed.), *Rural Dissenters*, 332–59; Stevenson, 'The social integration of restoration dissenters, 1660–1725', ibid., 360–87. In York there was a trend towards membership of a wider group of respectable godly people: D. Scott, *Quakerism in York 1650–1720*, Borthwick Papers, 80 (York, 1991). This kind of acceptability was less eagerly embraced by the Lancashire Quakers: Morgan, *Lancashire Quakers*.

[120] T. Harris, 'Tory reaction'. In Clitheroe, for example, persecution offered a means to establish one's own credentials: Mullett, 'Clitheroe', pp. 109–10.

[121] Hurwich, 'Coventry'; M. Mullet, '"To Dwell Together in Unity": the search for agreement in Preston politics, 1660–1690', *Transactions of the Historic Society of Lancashire and Cheshire*, 125 (1974), 61–81.

[122] J. S. Leatherbarrow, *Constables' Presentments in the Diocese of Worcester, c. 1660–1760*, Worcestershire Historical Society, Occasional Publications, 1 (Halesowen, 1977), 14–16.

general, Protestant dissent seems to have been treated with some discretion and sensitivity in the localities, despite the very clear threat that was perceived from some forms of dissent in the abstract.

The impact of persecution varied from time to time and from place to place, depending on the commitment of local officeholders. In Norfolk, between 1660 and 1676, it is the 'Norfolk leadership's moderation towards religious dissenters' which is most manifest in militia activities. Repression was intermittently enforced and was often prompted from above. But action could also be energetic in moments of particular tension, such as the month of the 'northern plot' of 1663, during the second Dutch war, or in 1666 when the discovery of papists in the army coincided with news of the fire of London.[123] In Somerset, Wiltshire and Dorset during the 1660s and 1670s, the gentry on the benches were far from unanimous. Conflicting messages from national government were received by officeholders who were far from united in their commitment to revenge and persecution. '[H]arrassment . . . depended entirely upon the disposition of the local magistrates, deputy-lieutenants and militia officers. The many Council orders . . . calling for care and vigilance from militia and magistracy, were often misinterpreted as a cue for gratuitous thuggery, but many justices refused to wage open war on the nonconformists.'[124] Even those committed to persecution might be hampered by legal doubts, or legal challenge from dissenters.[125] In these two decades the equivocal position of national government, 'the sensitivity of many justices to the unpopularity of persecuting drives against Protestants, and the mixed religious and political outlooks represented on the bench, meant that there was no persistent attempt to wipe nonconformity off the face of the English landscape'.[126] Attempts to establish conformity among borough officeholders enjoyed similarly mixed success.[127] A survey of eight counties (including Wiltshire) across the country has produced similar conclusions regarding the enforcement,

---

[123] R. M. Dunn (ed.), *The Norfolk Lieutenancy Journal 1660–1676*, Norfolk Record Society, 45 (1977), 10–11 and references noted there.

[124] P. J. Norrey, 'The restoration regime in action: the relationship between central and local government in Dorset, Somerset and Wiltshire, 1660–1678', *HJ*, 31 (1988), 789–812, at pp. 804–5.

[125] See for example, the legal doubts about how to proceed against dissent expressed by the corporation of Chester between 1667 and 1670: ML/3/407, 427, 467, 468. One decision was whether to proceed by enforcing oaths or by employing the conventicle acts. Morgan detects a shift from one to the other as the conventicle acts provided alternative grounds for prosecution: Morgan, *Lancashire Quakers*, esp. pp. 123–4. Such a shift seems to have been taking place in Chester. For the sophistication of legal resistance to religious persecution see, for example, Anon., *The Only Legal Answer which Constables and Churchwardens May Give . . .* (London, 1680).

[126] Norrey, 'Restoration regime', p. 808.   [127] Ibid., pp. 809–12.

specifically, of the Conventicle Acts. They were not, 'it would seem . . . systematically enforced in the 1660s or 1670s. The story is rather one of localised battles between particular groups of dissenting congregations and either individual JPs or a few strongly motivated justices.' Campaigns once launched were difficult to sustain.[128] Hampshire, where persecution was very effective, appears to have been rather the exception than the rule.[129] If the mid-century had improved the 'responsibility' of magistrates in relation to fiscal and military matters, it appears to have done rather less for a commitment to uniformity. We noted above an important consequence of this: that an insistence by national government on reliability in these matters among its officeholders necessarily made officeholding less socially representative. The pursuit of exclusivity was inevitably politicising, whether it meant purges of magisterial benches, of town corporations or politically informed selections of deputy-lieutenants. For example, in 1696 Captain John Tyringham was recommended to the earl of Bridgewater, the energetic lord lieutenant of Buckinghamshire, on the grounds not only that he was 'well Qualified for that Service [and] is seldom from home', but also because 'I am satisfied that [he] is well affected to the present Government'.[130]

Dissent in the abstract was quite frightening, it seems, but local indulgence of particular dissenters seems to have been quite usual. The same appears to be true of the relationship between fear of popery and the treatment of recusants. The threat of popery appeared very real in the late seventeenth century but it was not, it seems, directly associated with a fear of the domestic recusant population. Fear of popery and its near twin 'arbitrary government' animated much political debate in the years after 1660. The threat was European in origin – driven by concerns about the advance of the Catholic reformation. 'The hard fact behind . . . lurid and frequently wildly exaggerated reports [of Catholic victories and atrocities] is that the century from 1590 to 1690 saw European Protes-

---

[128] A. J. Fletcher, 'The enforcement of the conventicle acts 1664–1679', in W. J. Sheils (ed.), *Persecution and Toleration*, Studies in Church History, 21 (1984), 235–46, quotation at p. 245.

[129] Although not entirely different – there was a local constituency for intolerance, but also a counter-pressure to limit the effects of persecution. Persecutors were also hampered by the 'recalcitrance, cowardice, corruption or complicity of lesser officials': A. M. Coleby, *Central Government and the Localities: Hampshire 1649–89* (Cambridge, 1987), 133–41, 200, 235–6, quotation at p. 140.

[130] HEH, EL 9417. For the anti-Catholic activities of the Buckinghamshire militia in the 1690s see below pp. 327–30. For the political manipulation of the bench see L. K. J. Glassey, *Politics and the Appointment of Justices of the Peace 1675–1720* (Oxford, 1979); N. Landau, *The Justices of the Peace 1679–1760* (Berkeley, 1984). For the politicisation of the lieutenancy, V. L. Stater, *Noble Government: The Stuart Lord Lieutenant and the Transformation of English Politics* (Athens, Ga., 1994); for parliament, M. A. Kishlansky, *Parliamentary Selection: Social and Political Choice in Early Modern England* (Cambridge, 1986).

tantism reduced by armed force from almost one half to one fifth of the land area of the European continent.'[131] This fear of Catholicism abroad helps to explain why such heat was generated by such a small domestic group. By 1680 it seems likely that little more than 1 per cent of the population of England and Wales was Catholic.[132] None the less, part of the concern was that official policy soft on Catholicism might open the flood-gates to counter-reformation. During the third Dutch war (1672–4) opinion shifted decisively in that direction – it was French absolutists not the Dutch republicans who threatened England's destruction.[133] This explains the apparent paradox, that the persecution of Catholics at home receives such little attention from modern historians – there does not seem to have been much. In part this was probably because in most places Catholics were thin on the ground and well known locally. But it also points up the need to distinguish between fear of popery and fear of Catholics. Certainly, the Catholic laity were not much persecuted in this period. For example, between 1660 and 1671, when £4m or £5m might have been collected in recusancy fines, only £146 15s 7d had actually been received at the exchequer. Thereafter, the rate of the fines increased, and the possibility of the imposition of fines seems to have been occasionally used to intimidate Catholics or to extort money from them, but even in the 1680s the sums raised were nowhere near the amount that might have been exacted under the law.[134] In Wigan there was a remarkable degree of practical religious toleration for local Catholics, under the protection of the Bradshaigh family. The breakdown of this toleration was the result of the intrusion of more aggressive anti-recusancy policies from the county at large. Disorder occurred in 1681 as a crowd protected a poor widow from distraint, in a demonstration of solidarity reminiscent of that at Childwall in 1600.[135]

[131] J. Scott, 'England's troubles: exhuming the popish plot', in Harris, Seaward and Goldie (eds.), *Politics*, 107–31, at p. 114.

[132] Bossy, *Community*, pp. 187–90. Miller estimated that there were around 60,000 Catholics in restoration England, about 1 or 1.2 per cent of the population. Particular county studies had produced estimates of between 0.4 and 1.5 per cent: J. Miller, *Popery and Politics in England 1660–1688* (Cambridge, 1973), 9–12. The difficulty of counting Catholics is partly one of definition, of course, and these figures could probably be inflated if church papists were included. Hurwich, estimates the Catholic population of Warwickshire at 2.1 per cent but thought that this could be increased to 6 per cent if occasional conformists were included: 'Dissent', p. 30.

[133] S. C. A. Pincus, 'From butter boxes to wooden shoes: the shift in English popular sentiment from anti-Dutch to anti-French in the 1670s', *HJ*, 38 (1995), 333–61.

[134] Miller, *Popery*, esp. pp. 62–3, 106, 142, 145–6, 191–3.

[135] M. Mullett, '"A Receptacle for Papists and an Assilum": Catholicism and disorder in late seventeenth-century Wigan', *Catholic Historical Review*, 73 (1987), 391–407. For the Childwall disorder see above, pp. 305–6. See also W. J. Sheils, 'Catholics and their neighbours in a rural community: Egton Chapelry, 1590–1780', *Northern History*, 34 (1998), 109–33.

During anti-Catholic scares in the late 1670s Catholic priests and places of worship were attacked, and worshippers prevented from attending, but the lay Catholic community appears to have suffered relatively lightly. In the nationwide panic of 1678–9 it is perhaps significant that fear of foreign invasion figures prominently in the rumours that were circulating.[136] Crowds burned the pope in effigy and demonstrated, but 'there was little or no violence against Catholics'.[137] The English Catholic community was, as we have seen, small and it was also, on the whole, quiescent. Priests and courtly Catholics were perceived to be agents of foreign popery rather then domestic threats in the straightforward sense. Popery in this sense, of a foreign threat to English religion (and liberties), was what Presbyterians often seemed to threaten. It was something rather different from recusancy. Fear of popery was of tremendous significance in national politics; fear of recusants of relatively little significance.[138] The distinction between popery and Catholicism is not entirely clear, of course, and being friendly to English Catholics might be interpreted as acting as an agent of international popery. In the Welsh marches, fears of Catholicism were fuelled by local conversions. Among their persecutors, former Catholics were prominent perhaps, it has been suggested, because they were more aware than other Protestants of how tenuous the hold of Protestantism was in the area.[139] None the less, the distinction between fear of popery and fear of Catholics helps to explain why heated

---

[136] Miller, *Popery*, pp. 159–62. The Irish fright of 1688 centred around the intentions of Catholic soldiers rather than local recusants: G. H. Jones, 'The Irish fright of 1688: real violence and imagined massacre', *BIHR*, 55 (1982), 148–53. However, it should also be noted that there were also rumours of stores of arms at Catholic houses. For other accounts of crowd actions which seem to confirm the relative infrequency of attacks on the Catholic laity see T. Harris, *London Crowds in the Reign of Charles II: Propaganda and Politics from the Restoration until the Exclusion Crisis* (Cambridge, 1987); Harris, 'Tory reaction'; M. Knights, *Politics and Opinion in Crisis, 1678–81* (Cambridge, 1994); J. C. H. Aveling, *The Handle and the Axe: The Catholic Recusants from Reformation to Emancipation* (London, 1976), 215–21. The anti-Catholic crowds in London in the later 1680s seem to have concentrated on the destruction of property and disruption of worship, rather than on attacks on persons: T. Harris, 'London crowds and the revolution of 1688', in E. Cruickshanks (ed.), *By Force or by Default? The Revolution of 1688–1689* (Edinburgh, 1989), 44–64, esp. pp. 47–9, 51–5.   [137] Miller, *Popery*, pp. 182–9, quotation at p. 182.

[138] See, for example, the verdict of Holmes that 'what was so feared was not recusancy but *popery* – the one being seen as a local and essentially religious manifestation, the other as an international phenomenon, which in its English guise was perceived as strongly political and primarily metropolitan', Holmes, *Making of a Great Power*, p. 121. This is a central theme of Miller, *Popery*. For the earlier period see above, pp. 303–6. 'Political' is here a loose term, of course: Champion, 'Religion after the restoration'.

[139] P. A. Jenkins, 'Anti-popery on the Welsh marches in the seventeenth century', *HJ*, 23 (1980), 275–93.

national political debate did not produce a concomitant commitment to persecution in the localities.

By 1688, then, England was probably no more uniform in religious belief and practice than it had been in 1660. Fear of popery was extremely important to the loss of domestic support that James II's regime could command, and was deliberately manipulated by the Orangist propagandists after 1689. The providential delivery of the English, and the rescue of domestic liberties, was central to the legitimation of the new regime. According to the Bill of Rights, James II, his judges and (evil) advisers, had 'endeavour[ed] to subvert and extirpate the Protestant religion and the laws and liberties of this Kingdom'.[140] William and Mary guaranteed their safety and this sense of divine providence suffused the propaganda of the new regime.[141] This image was central to the public justification for Reformation of Manners, as we have seen. In some ways this initiative came to deprive the Anglican church of its claim to moral leadership, but in its early stages the campaigns built on a longer pattern of the Anglican use of providence and pressure for moral reform.[142]

Despite this triumphant providential Protestantism, recusant families in many localities must have established a *modus vivendi* with their neighbours. There are hints of this, for example, in the response of the Buckinghamshire militia to disarm papists in late February 1696.[143] This followed the revelation, in February, of the 'Fenwick conspiracy' to assassinate William III. The discovery of the plot was followed by over 300 arrests and the adoption by both Houses of a proposal for an 'Association' to defend the king. Sir John Fenwick later implicated prominent government figures in his confession, but this was disregarded.[144] None the less, the plot excited some energetic action in Buckinghamshire. The earl of Bridgewater, Lieutenant of the Buckinghamshire militia, was a strong supporter of the Association[145] and

---

[140] SR, VI, pp. 142–4.   [141] T. Claydon, *William III and the Godly Revolution* (Cambridge, 1996).

[142] Above, pp. 168–9. For Anglicans, providence and moral reform see J. Spurr, '"Virtue, Religion and Government": the Anglican uses of providence', in Harris, Seaward and Goldie (eds.), *Politics*, 29–47; Spurr, 'The church, the societies and the moral revolution of 1688,' in Walsh, Haydon and Taylor (eds.), *Church of England*, 127–42. For the revolution as a crisis of popery and arbitrary government, see Scott, 'England's troubles', esp. pp. 108–15.

[143] For the privy council orders of 24 February 1696 see HEH, EL 9545, 9546.

[144] See Holmes, *Making of a Great Power*, pp. 198–9.

[145] HEH, EL 9415, Buckingham to Francis Duncombe, 3 March 1996. For the larger campaign, see D. Cressy, 'Binding the nation: the bonds of association, 1584 and 1696', in D. J. Guth and J. W. McKenna (eds.), *Tudor Rule and Revolution: Essays for G. R. Elton from his American Friends* (Cambridge, 1982), 217–34, esp. pp. 226–33.

surviving papers of the earl contain drafts of address and association from this time.[146] The language of the Association and the subsequent action of the militia are revealing.

The Association spoke of 'a horrid and detestable Conspiracy formed and carried on by Papists and other wicked & traiterous persons for Assassinating your Majesty's Royall person, in order to Incourage an Invasion from France to subvert our Religion, Laws & Liberty from which it has pleased God to deliver your Majesty & these Kingdoms'. The members of the militia went on to beseech 'Almighty God to grant your Majesty long Life to reign over us, & to perfect our Deliverance from Popery and Slavery'. Moreover, as testimony to 'Our Zeal for the preservation of your Majesty's Sacred Life & of the peace and quiet of the Kingdom', they bound themselves to do their utmost to defend the king's 'sacred person and Government against the late King James, & all his adherents' since 'your Majesty is Rightful & Lawful King of these Realms'. If the king did come to a violent end, 'which God forbid', they further engaged to secure the succession.[147] Subscription to the Association subsequently became a test of loyalty, affecting the decision of the lieutenancy as to whether to seize arms or not; 86 justices of the peace and 104 deputy lieutenants lost office for failing to subscribe, or failing to subscribe sufficiently quickly.[148]

The campaign to seize papists' arms in Buckinghamshire reveals a rather less impressive record.[149] In part this was because the local Catholic threat appears to have been unimpressive. Bridgewater was informed on 3 March that the deputy-lieutenants had met and three days later was contacted directly by a prominent local recusant, Robert Throckmorton, who requested that he be allowed to stay at home with his sick wife, or at least near by, she 'havving binn lately lyke to Dye and continuing still ill'.[150] He had heard that papists were to be seized and offered instead to stay at home but to attend the deputy-lieutenants at the least notice. He claimed to have been keen to avoid public affairs since the accession of the new King and was grateful to William III for failing to enforce the penal laws since then. His fellow Catholics, he hoped

are all as ready as I am to declare theyr publick Thancks and acknoledgements with a detestation of and Abhorrence of the late intended villany which practices being directly oposite to the fundamentals of Christiannity, and to the

[146] HEH, EL 9568, 9569.   [147] HEH, EL 9568.   [148] Cressy, 'Binding', p. 230.
[149] A list of seizures made in 1678, among these papers also makes less than impressive reading: HEH, EL 8525, fo. 86r.   [150] HEH, EL 9416, Robert Throckmorton to earl of Bridgewater.

Lawes of nature and nations, and tending to the dissolution of humane society, ought to be abhorred by all men of Religion, honor or understanding.[151]

Thomas Ligor, a deputy lieutenant, wrote to Bridgewater on 21 March to report that he had not found any dangerous papists, 'but if any thing occurs wherein I can be servisable to the King or Government I shall do it to the utmost of my power'.[152] Elsewhere, other deputy-lieutenants found the local Catholic population small, poor and unthreatening.[153]

In fact, the local Catholic and non-conforming population were familiar and the deputy-lieutenants were able, for example, to check their findings with the land tax commissioners (who charged papists double). Not only, then, were Catholics (and Quakers and Anabaptists) small in number and largely quiescent, they were also familiar. A number of letters state, specifically, that there were no 'dangerous' papists. For example, the two Catholics who refused to sign the Association in Henry Paggett's division were 'not thought to be designers against the Government by those that know them'.[154] By the same token, those who might be a threat were also well known. Peter Tyrill, Robert Chapman and Francis Duncombe reported that all the papists in their division were 'inconsiderable' except Sir Edward Longueville, who had gone abroad some months previously.[155] John Gadsden, a miller, on the other hand, was reported to have 'a very ill Caracter and is a very dangerous person and was very buisy in the Popish Plott in King Charles the Seconds time'. Gadsden, however, had clearly left his home 'for feare of being taken up upon some matters against the Government (as I am informed by his Neighbours)'. He was also, apparently, easily found since the deputy was able to report having had him taken into custody.[156]

In comparing the Bonds of Association promoted in 1584 and in 1696 Cressy has suggested that the later exercise was 'more ambitious and less discriminating'. It depended on the whole machinery of government, rather than on a number of prominent individuals cajoled by the privy council. In a sense, then, it serves as an illustration of the routinisation of local government. 'The county elite could still take the oath in a formal setting, as assizes or sessions, but parish officers took the associ-

---

[151] HEH, EL 9423, Robert Throckmorton to Cousin Lattin, 17 March 1696. We might wonder, of course, about the significance of the fact that a copy of this letter found its way into Bridgewater's hands.   [152] HEH, EL 9425.   [153] HEH, EL 9418, 9422, 9429, 9432–3, 9435–8.
[154] HEH, EL 9432, Henry Paggett to earl of Bridgewater, 20 May 1696.
[155] HEH, EL 9418, Peter Tyrill *et al.* to earl of Bridgewater, 7 March 1696. Two other influential Catholics were listed: Sir John Fortescue (who was 'Lunatick') and Sir Robert Throckmorton, whose strenuous attestations of loyalty have already been noted.   [156] HEH, EL 9427.

ation to the rest from door to door, like travelling salesmen.'[157] The
records of the land tax and of this routine administration of the Bond of
Association provided a means of testing the political commitments of
county society. Buckinghamshire's was an active militia, with the records of this administration to hand. Throckmorton, for example, in
spite of his sick wife, protestations of loyalty and an offer to take the oath
of allegiance was placed in custody in London.[158] The correspondence
demonstrates that a number of horses were, indeed, seized, and the
Association was actively promoted. Yet the overwhelming impression is
the absence of a serious threat. The local recusant (and, less clearly,
non-conformist) population was well known and not much feared.
These recusants, at least, were quite different from the image of popery
that was a standard of political polemic. This adjustment to the fact of
religious diversity was not a reflection of 'official policy'. Religion
remained central to the legitimation of political authority. This fact, and
the dominance of religion as a 'social ideology', has led to the suggestion
that 'all forms of radicalism in early-modern England had a religious
origin'.[159] Others have questioned the totality of the claim, not its
essence: 'religion' remained central to 'political' legitimation after
1688.[160] Locally, however, toleration of religious pluralism had been
developing for some time.

After the Glorious Revolution a further 400 clergymen were ejected
as non-jurors – those who in conscience could not swear an oath of
allegiance to the new monarchs whose tenure of the throne, they
suggested, breached the divine right of kings.[161] Toleration after 1689
was not indifference, therefore. The concession of toleration represented a preference among influential Anglicans for schism outside the

---

[157] Cressy, 'Binding', p. 234.

[158] HEH, EL 9428. For the offer to take the oath of allegiance, see EL 9424.

[159] J. C. D. Clark, *English Society 1688–1832: Ideology, Social Structure and Political Practice during the Ancien Règime* (Cambridge, 1985), p. 277.

[160] For some cautionary remarks see J. Innes, 'Jonathan Clark, social history and England's "Ancien Règime"', *PP*, 115 (1987), 165–200, esp. pp. 186–94. Colley has given considerable emphasis to the 'absolute centrality of Protestantism to British religious experience in the 1700s and long after', noting that it 'is so obvious that it has proved easy to pass over'. An emphasis on divisions within Protestantism threatens to 'obscure what was still the most striking feature in the religious landscape, the gulf between Protestant and Catholic'. This is central to her account of eighteenth-century political culture too: L. Colley, *Britons: Forging the Nation 1707–1837* (London, 1994), 18–19. For Clark's response to Innes see 'On Hitting the Buffers: the Historiography of England's Ancien Règime. A Response', *PP*, 117 (1987), 195–207, esp. pp. 198–200.

[161] Doran and Durston, *Princes*, p. 158. For Divine Right theories see Clark, *English Society*, pp. 121–41.

church rather than within it. Their unyielding attitude towards division within the church had, in the end, caused the failure of comprehension.[162] Comprehension had failed, persecution did not seem to work and so indulgence may have been the next viable alternative.[163] In fact, toleration is a misleading term. What the measures actually did was to suspend some of the penalties for dissent for certain categories of dissenter.[164] Protestant dissenters were relieved from the penalties of the 1670 Conventicles Act and the necessity of church attendance imposed by the 1559 Act of Uniformity. Freedom of worship was granted, but only in licensed meeting houses, which had to be left unlocked during service (hardly a provision that suggests a relaxed attitude towards dissent). Ministers were relieved of the penalties of the Act of Uniformity, the Five Mile Act and the Conventicles Acts provided that they accepted the doctrinal statements of the Thirty Nine Articles (although special provision was made for Quakers and Baptists). Above all, however, papists and Unitarians were excluded from the benefits of the Act which also failed to remove the Test Acts. All Protestant dissenters were, therefore, confronted with the familiar civil disabilities. As one recent survey has concluded 'Nonconformist worship remained subject to a number of petty and annoying restrictions, and a whole range of civil disabilities prevented dissenters from attending the universities or holding military or civil office.'[165]

The toleration that was established was not, therefore, an official recognition that religious and political authority were unconnected. Instead, toleration licensed dissenting practice while sustaining civil

[162] J. Spurr, 'The Church of England, comprehension and the Toleration Act of 1689', *EHR*, 104 (1989), 927–46. For Anglican attitudes towards schism, see Spurr, 'Schism and the restoration church', *Journal of Ecclesiastical History*, 41 (1990), 408–24. On the dangers to the church of comprehension see also Schochet, 'Persecution'.

[163] Schochet, 'Persecution'. Greaves suggests that it came to be recognised that persecution caused rather than combatted plotting: R. L. Greaves, 'Conventicles, sedition and the Toleration Act of 1689', *Eighteenth Century Life*, 12/3 (1988), 1–13. See also Greaves, 'The organizational response of nonconformity to repression and indulgence: the case of Bedfordshire', *Church History*, 44 (1975), 472–84. The measure is placed in a broader context by N. Tyacke, 'The rise of puritanism and the legalizing of dissent, 1571–1719', in Grell, Israel and Tyacke (eds.), *Persecution to Toleration*, 17–49.

[164] Greaves, 'Conventicles', p. 1; Schochet, 'Persecution', pp. 152–6. See also Tyacke, 'Dissent', pp. 39–43.

[165] Doran and Durston, *Princes*, p. 120. For the Toleration Act see E. N. Williams (ed.), *The Eighteenth Century Constitution 1688–1815: Documents and Commentary* (Cambridge, 1960), 42–6. See also J. W. Martin, 'Toleration 1689: England's recognition of pluralism', in G. J. Schochet, P. E. Tatspaugh and C. Brobeck (eds.), *Restoration, Ideology, and Revolution* (Washington, DC, 1990), 67–82.

disabilities. It was a recognition of the fact of plurality, akin to the local accommodation suggested by the Buckinghamshire example, not an assertion that dissent was politically harmless. Indeed, it almost certainly was not regarded as harmless. The point has been made elsewhere, and a full discussion would take us well beyond the bounds of the present study, but an indication of the position is provided by legislation of the early eighteenth century. This legislation put the narrowest possible interpretation on toleration while also reflecting the continued suspicion of occasional conformity.[166] The Occasional Conformity Act (1711), for example, imposed fines on those holding military or civil office who attended conventicles and made continuance of their office conditional upon taking Anglican communion three times each year. To prevent the growth of nonconformity the Schism Act (1714) required teachers and schoolmasters to conform and receive a licence from their bishop before establishing a school. Such licences were to be granted only to those who had taken Anglican sacrament within the previous year, made a declaration against transubstantiation and taken the oaths of supremacy and allegiance. Those evading these provisions were liable to imprisonment.[167] Thus, the religious identity of the state was clear but so too was the existence of plurality. The Schism Act, for example, excluded teachers at Oxford and Cambridge, and tutors in noble households, from its provisions.[168] In the late 1670s the number of Protestant dissenters may well have been 220,000, at the beginning of George I's reign it was probably 400,000.[169] Persecution served political ends and flowed from political fears but it had, obviously, failed to establish conformity.

The pursuit of relatively narrow conformity was more often initiated from the centre than the locality, but it usually enjoyed some local support. Its effect was to politicise some of the institutions of local government, in particular the lieutenancy, which became instruments for the pursuit of a vision ascribed to only by sections of the constituencies which were being served. Persecution was in tension with comprehension at all levels of restoration society, and there were principled reasons for adhering to one side or other of that debate. On the side of

---

[166] Tyacke, 'Dissent'; Schochet, 'Persecution'. It was only really in the nineteenth century that religious liberty emerged from within toleration: R. K. Webb, 'From toleration to religious liberty', in Jones (ed.), *Liberty Secured?*, 158–98, 362–7. For the continued importance of the identity of the confessional state before that date see Clark, *English Society*.

[167] Williams, *Eighteenth Century Constitution*, pp. 334–7, 337–40.

[168] Ibid., p. 339.

[169] Holmes, *Making of a Great Power*, pp. 459–61.

persecution, however, was the assertion of the need for conformity for reasons of state. The prosecution of dissent could plausibly be promoted as a political necessity, particularly at moments of international tension. Persecution failed, and Anglicanism developed alongside other forms of religious practice, despite the wishes of some of its most influential thinkers.

Conclusion

Initiatives in relation to religious order provide a contrast with both fiscal-military and patriarchal initiatives. In 1558 we are told, England was a predominantly Catholic country; a generation later registered recusants were a tiny proportion of the population and by 1640 there was clearly a body of committed 'Anglican' opinion. Certainly by 1603 England was a Protestant country and, accepting the revisionist case about the slowness of Protestant reformation in the first three-quarters of the sixteenth century, this represents a remarkable achievement in the generation after 1570. By the stricter test applied by a number of activists, however, English people were conformist rather than fully reformed and uniformity was clearly beyond the capacity of this state. There were groups outside the church and others who only remained within it conditionally. A problem here was that there were numerous competing versions of orthodoxy, which were continually contested and redefined – orthodoxy was not *agreed* at any level of the state. What was to be imposed was by no means clear and this added to the institutional problem that local preference and initiative were embedded in the organisation of the church. In this sense, the experience resembles that of military-fiscal reform. Many of the initiatives here were 'central': definitions of orthodoxy were being propagated from the head of the church downwards and outwards in same way that the primary initiative in military reform came from national rather than local government. The problem of compliance was just as difficult, and was exacerbated by the fact that national government did not control the apparatus of the church, nor could it prevent the establishment of alternative institutions. Religious peace depended on a complex consensus which could be disrupted by undue pressure for greater uniformity. Religious imperatives were, then, relatively autonomous, not deriving very directly from the immediately perceived interests of local elites.

All this might have been acceptable in functional terms as a *de facto* adjustment to the reality of religious diversity. However, regimes were, to an extent, prisoners of their own rhetoric. Having justified the political order as a guarantee of true religion it was almost inevitable that they would have to take measures to define and impose true religion. This is a crude summary, of course, but it is an important corrective to what might be taken to be the materialism of much of the argument presented so far. It might have been inferred from the preceding account that legitimating languages merely follow and acquire appeal from their use in solving functional problems. But the opposite was also true, that strategies of legitimation might become autonomous, requiring particular functional initiatives in order to appear credible.[1] More than this, they might be sincerely intended – individuals might genuinely believe their rhetoric and take its obligations seriously. Magistrates were under pressure to remain in place during outbreaks of the plague and defenders of the faith felt, periodically, a pressure to define and propagate the faith that they were defending. But, given the institutional limitations and the ambition of the task the attempt to define and propagate orthodoxy was bound to cause problems.

After 1640 the history of religious persecution offers a sense of continuity – the stated aspirations of activists outran the administrative capacity of government by a considerable distance so that an uncomfortable gap continued to open between the pretensions of the confessional state and local political and social realities. The exceptions were the sporadic efforts to suppress dissent, associated in particular with the remodelled militia. We noted in chapter 4 how the threat of beggars and witches seems to have receded in restoration England. In their place as the most frightening threats to social order stood the sectaries, harried by the increasingly politicised lieutenancy. Local militias, unimpressive as military forces, seem to have been run more systematically and to have shown intermittent relish for their internal policing duties. In general, these persecuting initiatives were rather more top-down than they were bottom-up: Catholics and parish puritans seem to have been regarded with less concern in particular localities than popery and Presbyterianism in the abstract. Even in the case of the Quakers there is

---

[1] See Skinner's argument that: 'even if the agent is not in fact motivated by any of the principles he professes, he will nevertheless be obliged to behave in such a way that his actions remain compatible with the claim that these principles genuinely motivated him': Q. Skinner, 'Some problems in the analysis of political thought and action', reprinted in J. Tully (ed.), *Meaning and Context: Quentin Skinner and his Critics* (Princeton, 1988), 97–118, 309–11, quotation at p. 116.

clear evidence of closer integration into local social networks than was compatible with sustained and effective persecution and this was even more true of recusants and Presbyterians. Presumably this goes part of the way to explaining why comprehension was frightening both to high Anglicans and to some dissenters, since it threatened a dilution of the true religion through accommodation with those in error. Increasingly, however, it appeared that the battle against Protestant dissent was a losing one, and at the end of our period the quest for uniformity was decisively and publicly abandoned. There was no real institutional innovation in order to achieve Anglican uniformity, despite these administrative problems. Instead, it was the ambition that changed. Limited toleration after 1689 can be seen as a recognition of the permanence, if not the desirability, of the gap between the claims of the confessional state and the more practical accommodations that were being reached in many localities.

PART V

The dynastic state

Introduction

Previous chapters have dealt with the intensification of government in the English core, but perhaps more dramatic was the extension of London's political authority, throughout Britain and Ireland and across the Atlantic. State formation in early modern England was not simply a matter of central will or direction. Influential groups in the localities made use of legitimate authority in ways which served their interests, but also called the state into action. This is a helpful perspective from which to view the extension of the authority of the Tudor and Stuart state too.[1] The peripheries of the empire were not simply coerced by the centre and in Britain and the Atlantic world at large activists made use of crown authority as a source of legitimate political power. The process of state formation, as in England, was intimately connected with the processes of elite formation – access to political power, the holding of office, was integral to the social status of gentlemen and the middling sort. Social differentiation was reflected in, and compounded by, the distribution of political power. The emphasis of this discussion will be on the propagation of an idea of civility, which supported the interests of

---

[1] There is, of course, a difficult terminological problem here. Previous chapters have explored the development of the state in early modern England, not the English state. In describing the increasing dominion over trade and territory coordinated from London the term 'dynastic' state will be preferred. Through this period an increasingly large area was subject to political authority coordinated from London, but this authority was not English. What gave it coherence (in so far as it possessed any) was the identity of the crown, not membership of a nation. The overarching identity of 'the state coordinated from London' was dynastic rather than ethnic, although of course the term elides a complex set of constitutional relationships. Its interests were defined in dynastic and religious terms as much as in national terms. The term 'English' is also inappropriate since, as the territories that it governed extended further and further beyond the English core, the variety of regional elites on which it depended increased. 'British' is little better. Before 1707 (or 1801) 'British' is constitutionally inaccurate and in any case it seems that relatively few subjects of the Tudor and Stuart crowns took the British identity seriously before 1700. By 1700, 400,000 people who were later to be Americans or West Indians were also subject to the authority of the English monarch and Virginians, for example, claimed to be English rather than British or American.

elite groups in stable agrarian societies. In the respective national historiographies this is often referred to as Anglicisation, but as we will see, not all the English were civil and by no means all the proponents of civility were English. One important dimension of a discussion of the emergence of empire is cultural, therefore – the emergence and consolidation of elites bound together in part by ideas of civility. The hub of these commercial and cultural developments was London, and so we might say that all the subjects of the Tudor and Stuart crown 'lived in London's provinces, whether in rural England, provincial towns or transatlantic colonies'.[2]

Although empire was not a product simply of coercion of the peripheries by the centre, however, metropolitan power was by no means always harmonised with particular local interests. Again, as in England, some interests of state (or empire) were transcendent, or autonomous, and cut across local interests. Here the 1640s were of great significance for the development of the empire, for the military revolution which took place in that decade at the centre of the Stuart state greatly enhanced the power of the centre to coordinate the nascent empire, and to coerce recalcitrant groups within it. It was in that decade that English arms came to dominate in Britain and Ireland, and the fiscal and military instruments were created which would provide the means to a more coherent regulation of empire. However, within the umbrella of the mercantilist empire local political arrangements continued to develop along lines analogous with those in the English core. In the English case there was a complex relationship between the autonomous needs of the state and the social and ideological interests of the elites upon which government depended. This duality was equally apparent in these wider territories between, on one hand, autonomous, 'imperial' interests protected by force and, on the other, the developments encouraging the willing cooperation of local elites which underpinned stable domestic governance in the provinces and colonies.

---

[2] The phrase is taken from I. K. Steele, 'The empire and provincial elites: an interpretation of some recent writings on the English Atlantic, 1675–1740', *Journal of Imperial and Commonwealth History*, 8/2 (1980), 2–32, quotation at p. 3. Steele uses it in a more limited sense, to capture the similarities of experience between transatlantic colonies and the English provinces. London's role in this respect was not unique. Across Europe composite monarchies were developing and at their heart lay capital cities (Stockholm, Vienna, Madrid, Paris) whose populations were increasing despite a general stagnation in population growth in the seventeenth century. 'To these capitals were drawn every kind of resource which the provinces had to offer; from them radiated the power and prestige of their imperial rivalries': J. Robertson, 'Union, state and empire: the Britain of 1707 in its European setting', in L. Stone, (ed.), *An Imperial State at War: Britain from 1689–1815* (London, 1994), 224–57, quotation at p. 233.

Although these developments were, in a sense, part of a single phenomenon, a broad Westward Enterprise, the discussion here is divided between two chapters. Chapter 8 discusses elite formation and state formation in England, Wales and Scotland. The first section offers a brief discussion of the relationship between ideas relating to governance, civility and order which were thrown into sharper relief at the margins of the Tudor and Stuart state. The second section examines the integration of the English peripheries and the Welsh principality into the Tudor state. The third section discusses the processes of elite formation and state formation in Scotland and the Anglo-Scottish Borders. The development of the first British empire rested not simply on expansion into the Atlantic, Mediterranean and Asian worlds but also on the creation of a British state at its core. In Britain elite interest increasingly bound authority in those territories to the crown – elite formation and state formation were complementary processes. In Ireland and the settlements in the Americas, however, new elites were created, and the development of the dynastic state appears rather different. Chapter 9 accordingly gives an outline of the development of Tudor and Stuart government in Ireland and the earliest stages of the development of the British empire.

CHAPTER 8

Elite formation and state formation in England, Wales and Scotland

The ideas which compounded the authority of local elites, and bound them to the authority of the state, can be subsumed within the concept of 'civility'. At the margins of the territories of the English and Scottish crowns were areas thought to fall short of ideals of civility, and therefore to represent problems of government and order. The maintenance or establishment of political order in these areas was a matter, therefore, of the promotion of civility. This process, in the English and Scottish peripheries, and in Wales, was a means by which influential local groups could consolidate, and legitimate, their social position. This was not a matter of Anglicisation, however, since it emanated from two distinct centres – both England and Scotland confronted the problem of incivility, and their interests came together over the problem of the Borders. The first section of the chapter briefly considers the notion of civility, and its relationship to the ideas of 'order' which lay behind much of the governmental activity examined in chapters 3 and 4. The second section considers the integration of Wales and the English peripheries into the Tudor state. In the final sections, similar processes in Scotland are briefly considered, along with the problem of the Highlands and the Borders, where the civilising projects of Britain's two lowland states intersected. It is at these margins that many contemporary perceptions about the basis of political order were thrown into sharpest relief.

GOVERNMENT, CIVILITY AND ORDER

Government in the English core depended to a considerable degree on the voluntary action of elites for whom political authority was a useful resource: it rested on a mutuality of interests. Local offices were conceived of in terms of wider social roles and legitimated with reference to a

340

set of values that underpinned a broader sense of social order. Relations between those playing particular social roles – between husband and wife, father and son, master and servant, magistrate and neighbours – were frequently spelled out in prescriptive literature. An important part of the definition of these offices was, therefore, to embed them in a wider web of social relationships in which particular forms of behaviour were expected from those in particular social positions. Local offices were part of a broader 'interaction order', in which the proper relations of authority and subordination were expressed in the performance of the correct forms of politeness.[1] Thus, the extension of the territorial boundaries of the English state was not simply a jurisdictional matter, but also one of cultural expansion – the extension of the authority of the English crown into its peripheries was regarded as a broader programme to promote civility, entailing social and economic reform as well. Political order was being created as part of a larger interaction order, in which characteristic means of legitimation would make sense.

Some of the clearest statements of these broader concerns of governance were actually made in relation to Ireland and the Americas, where new social orders were being consciously fostered. Edmund Tremayne, advocating government in Ireland along English lines in 1573, was not suggesting merely constitutional and institutional change, but a transformation of the economic and social underpinnings of Irish governance. In this he had much in common with other sixteenth-century commentators, and it is worth considering his diagnosis in some detail. The essence of Irish rule, he suggested, was the domination of an area, often the size of an English shire, by a single man, often chosen by election rather than succession. Although the successor was usually chosen from among the kin of his predecessor it was, in general, 'he that hathe showed himself most mischevous in murderinge, spoilinge & burninge dothe sonest atteyne to the government'. Supported by warlike followers, 'he useth the inferior people at his will & pleasure . . . without any meanes to be withstanded or againesaid'. Disputes were settled by Brehon law ('nothinge agreeing with the lawes of England'),

---

[1] Pursued at greater length in M. J. Braddick, 'Administrative performance: "face", dignity and the effectiveness of political authority in early modern England', in M. J. Braddick and J. Walter (eds.), *Order, Hierarchy and Subordination in Early Modern Britain* (Cambridge, forthcoming). For the 'interaction order' see E. Goffman, 'The interaction order', *American Sociological Review*, 48 (1983), 1–17. Goffman discusses 'public order' (in the sense of orderly relations between individuals in public rather than public safety) in *Behaviour in Public Places: Notes on the Social Organisation of Gatherings* (New York, 1969), chs. 1–2, see esp. pp. 8–10, 22–4. For a fuller account of his thought see T. Burns, *Erving Goffman* (London, 1992), ch. 2; and P. Drew and A. Wootton (eds.), *Erving Goffman: Exploring the Interaction Order* (Oxford, 1988).

lords used considerable discretion and sought revenge without commission from the queen. The result was 'to drawe all love & feare & consequentlie all aucthoritie from the prince & turneth it to the great lord of the Cuntrey for in good reson men do moste feare love & obey them who be in state to do them most good or harme'.[2]

The problem of governing Ireland lay not just in local social structure, law and customs, however, for these practices had corrupted the English already in Ireland. They abused their inferiors and in doing so acted as 'an absolute governor in his owne Cuntrie'. In competition with one another for influence they had not failed to adopt any Irish characteristics and, although they retained some of the marks of civility such as holding estates by succession, they sought pliant tenants-at-will to provide a basis for this absolute territorial authority. This had dire implications for husbandry, since lords sought obedient tenants

withoute regard to make himself stronge by his Tenants Whereof it followeth that thenglishe pale is marvilously weakened for strengthe of men. And thereof also it ensueth that the Tenants nether buylde, nor repayre their houses Make neither gardens orchards nor meadowes repaire no inclosures nor in effect do any thing els that may be to the bettering of their Tenements.

The English lords, he thought, had more regard for the authority of the crown, but were otherwise indistinguishable in their pursuit of local power. Faction multiplied, 'thaucthoritie Royall of the Crowne of England' was diminished, the force of the law between great and small taken away and the revenue difficult to collect. In all, 'the verie office of a prince' was threatened, while the cost to the crown was considerable. Finally, and again not untypically, Tremayne suggested that the Irish were not only disposed to popery, but were virtually unchristian, since they 'Murder Robbe Ravishe burne & spoile, marry & unmarry at their pleasures with pluralities of wyves without any grudge of conscience that is able to abashe any christian harte'.[3]

In principle, Ireland, being an island very much like 'England', should have been able to yield the same commodities, from the land and from the sea, but this required heavy investment from the queen and considerable strength of purpose. The main problem was tyranny, and to overcome this Tremayne suggested the establishment of three presidencies in Munster, Connacht and Ulster, liasing closely with the deputy in Leinster and, through him, with London. Backed by strong

[2] HEH, EL 1701 fo. 1r. See also D. B. Quinn, *The Elizabethans and the Irish* (Cornell, 1966), esp. ch. 5. Tremayne is quoted at pp. 35–6.   [3] HEH, EL 1701 fo. 1v–2v.

garrisons they would have as their priority the regularisation of relations between landlord and tenant 'So as there maye be a certentie what the one shall give & the other take', and defining the limits of the authority of the lords. Lending certainty to tenurial relations was an essential precursor to agricultural improvement, since it was tenants and farmers that 'give fode to the land'. In these ways, by offering security and improvement, Ireland could be made to yield a rate to support the garrisons and the horseboys, kearns and gallowglasses that plagued Irish society could be returned to productive work. As a result, the queen would garner glory; the poor Irish tenants and farmers, and the inhabitants of the towns, would get justice and order; and the English exchequer would be saved money. Significantly, Tremayne did not think that this planting of civility would, or should be, introduced at the expense of the Irish. He was aiming to establish a powerful local elite, whose position was harmonised with the authority of the crown. There should be 'No intention of any Usurpacion or inequalitie But as her majestie is the naturall lieg sovereign of bothe the Realmes so shold there be made no difference of Subjects So farre forthe as bothe shall showe like obedience to her Majesties lawes.'[4] Clearly the fruits of civil, orderly government and the associated spread of good husbandry should be attractive to all.[5]

It need hardly be said that this is not necessarily a trustworthy description of sixteenth-century Irish society, but it is revealing of the self-image of an Elizabethan activist in Ireland.[6] A campaign for orderly

[4] HEH, EL 1701 fo. 3r–4v. For Tremayne see C. Brady, *The Chief Governors: The Rise and Fall of Reform Government in Tudor Ireland, 1536–1588* (Cambridge, 1994), esp. pp. 140–3; and Brady, 'The decline of the Irish Kingdom', in M. Greengrass (ed.), *Conquest and Coalescence: The Shaping of the State in Early Modern Europe* (London, 1991), 94–115, at pp. 100–1. For more general context see Quinn, *Elizabethans*, esp. ch. 5; and N. P. Canny, *The Elizabethan Conquest of Ireland: A Pattern Established 1565–76* (Hassocks, 1976), ch. 6. For examples of similar views see ibid.; Canny, 'Rowland White's "Discors touching Ireland", *c.* 1569', *Irish Historical Studies*, 20 (1976–7), 439–63; and Canny, 'Rowland White's "dysorders of the Irisshery"', *Studia Hibernica*, 19 (1981 for 1979), 147–60. For the economic potential of Ulster in the early seventeenth century see R. Gillespie, *Colonial Ulster: The Settlement of East Ulster, 1600–1641* (Cork, 1985), ch. 1.

[5] See Canny, *Elizabethan Conquest*, ch. 4, for the practical effects of the desire to create islands of civility. For a review of the recent literature relating to the 'colonisation' of Ireland, emphasising the variety of means by which lands changed hands, piecemeal and to the benefit of a variety of groups in Irish society, see R. Loeber, *The Geography and Practice of English Colonisation in Ireland from 1534 to 1609*, Irish Settlement Studies, 3 (Dublin, 1991).

[6] But historians do often take a dim view of Gaelic social relations, in particular the means by which security was achieved amidst competing petty lordships through the imposition of the burdens of 'coyne and livery' on the unfortunate tenantry. See, for example, Canny, *Elizabethan Conquest*, ch. 1; and Brady, 'Irish kingdom', p. 97. For descriptions of Gaelic economy and society more generally see K. W. Nicholls, *Land, Law and Society in Sixteenth-Century Ireland* (Dublin [1976]); and D. B. Quinn and K. W. Nicholls, 'Ireland in 1534', in T. W. Moody, F. X. Martin and

social relations underlay the measures of the Elizabethan 'reformation of manners', as we have seen, and in that sense this manifesto is a reflection of similar concerns. The concern for social order was exaggerated by the perception of how very different was the organisation of Irish society but also, increasingly, by a gathering sense of the failure of reformation there. Similar concerns were expressed in the Act of 1536 uniting Wales and England. The preamble referred to the difficulties arising from differences in rights, laws, customs and speech between the English and Welsh. An explicit aim was to extirpate 'sinister usages and customs', which was probably a reference to legal customs which had contributed to 'lawlessness' in the past.[7] Again, however, the concern was not just with laws and jurisdiction, but with social practices. For example, partible inheritance was to be replaced by primogeniture, and all judicial and administrative proceedings were to be conducted in English. A corollary of that, of course, was that no-one using 'the Welsh speech or language shall have or enjoy any manner of office . . . unless he or they use the English speech or language'.[8] Clearly, government in these 'peripheries' was a matter not just of 'centralisation' but of the creation of the social basis for governance along English lines.

This was not straightforwardly a matter of Anglicisation, however. It was applied to areas within England, and was promoted by, for example, lowland Scots as well as by lowland English. Thus, the regal union of 1603 between England and Scotland, meant that the Anglo-Scottish Borders were no longer a frontier zone between the two kingdoms. One of the purposes pursued by James VI and I in promoting closer union was 'utterlie to extinguishe as well the name, as substance of the bordouris, I meane the difference betwene thaine and other pairts of the kingdome'.[9] Among the opponents of closer union noted by Pont, one of its advocates, were papists and 'theeves . . . and assassinats stealing and driving away whole heards of cattell, a late and ordinary traffique and trade without controll, or feare of punishment, inured and bred from their cradle in this marchandise, assayling quiet and peaceable men by night and stripping them both of their cattle and other goods'. Thirdly, there were 'fierce and insolent governours and pettie

F. J. Byrne (eds.), *A New History of Ireland*, III, *Early Modern Ireland 1534–1691* (Oxford, 1978), 1–38. The 'exploitative' element of the demands of the chiefs has another context: K. Simms, 'Guesting and feasting in Gaelic Ireland', *Journal of the Royal Society of Antiquaries of Ireland*, 108 (1978), 67–100; and R. A. Dodgshon, 'West Highland chiefdoms, 1500–1745: a study in redistributive exchange', in R. Mitchison and P. Roebuck (eds.), *Economy and Society in Scotland and Ireland 1500–1939* (Edinburgh, 1988), 27–37.

[7] G. Williams, *Renewal and Reformation: Wales c. 1415–1642* (Oxford, 1993), 268.

[8] Quoted ibid., p. 269.   [9] *HMC, Salisbury*, 16, p. 405.

princes possessing large territories in the places most remote and abandoned of justice'. There, they were able to 'tyrannise over their tenants' and 'will be brought to any conformity but with an high and strong hand'. As things stood, if they were brought to book 'they so pester and throng the places of judgement with their clients, followers and friends that many times they prove terrible even to the judges themselves'.[10]

The parallels with Tremayne's view of the Irish are striking, but it was not just the English who would benefit from reform. Pont noted that the cattle thieves lived 'between the skirts of the Scottish and English pale', and there were other threats to Scottish order. For example, in addition to the 'wild and savadg Irish of the English dominion', there were the 'Hebrediani' of the Scottish Islands 'who for the most part are enemies also to tillage, and weare out their dayes in hunting and idleness after the maner of beasts'. The problem was common to both kingdoms, since the Irish fled justice to the Isles and the Hebrediani fled in the opposite direction. The problem of the petty princes ('seldome justice can be had against them') was particularly felt in Scotland.[11] James proclaimed high hopes of reform, 'entending that the bounds possesst by those rebellious people, being in fertilitie and all other benefits nothing inferiour to many of the best parts of the whole Ile, shall be no more the extremities, but the middle, and the Inhabitants thereof reduced to perfect obedience'.[12] A case can be made, therefore, that this was a process best understood as lowland versus highland, of settled, lawful societies against upland clan societies.[13] In fact such border areas comprised about half of the territories of the Tudor state and the implication is that the traditional English historiography, emphasising developments in lowland England, distorts our perception of the development of the Tudor (and Stuart) state.[14] The

[10] R. Pont, *Of the Union of Britayne*, reprinted in B. R. Galloway and B. P. Levack (eds.), *The Jacobean Union: Six Tracts of 1604*, Scottish History Society, 21 (1985), 1–38, at pp. 21–3.

[11] Ibid., p. 22.

[12] J. F. Larkin and P. L. Hughes (eds.), *Stuart Royal Proclamations*, I, *Royal Proclamations of King James I 1603–1625* (Oxford, 1973), 18–19, dated 19/5/1603.

[13] For a discussion of this perspective, derived from Pocock, see B. Bailyn and P. D. Morgan, 'Introduction', in Bailyn and Morgan (eds.), *Strangers within the Realm: Cultural Margins of the First British Empire* (Chapel Hill, 1991), 1–31.

[14] S. G. Ellis, 'England in the Tudor state', *HJ*, 26 (1983), 201–12; Ellis, *The Pale and the Far North: Government and Society in Two Early Tudor Borderlands* (Galway, 1988); Ellis, *Tudor Frontiers and Noble Power: The Making of the British State* (Oxford, 1995); and Ellis, 'Tudor state formation in the shaping of the British Isles', in S. G. Ellis and S. Barber (eds.), *Conquest and Union: Fashioning a British State, 1485–1625* (London, 1995), 40–63. It has been suggested, in fact, that this emphasis compounds a Whiggish preoccupation with progress, J. C. D. Clark, 'English history's forgotten context: Scotland, Ireland, Wales', *HJ*, 32 (1989), 211–28.

Scottish state also shared in this experience, confronting relatively less 'well-governed', highland borderlands.[15]

In the British case the spread of good governance into the border-lands was associated with the spread of the English language and models of English governance. This was seen as crucial to the incorporation of Wales, as we have seen, and Pont saw the spread of English as a hopeful sign of the future success of union. Already, 'by the litle commerce the English have had with the Scot (albeit many discordes and jars have interrupted it) their tounge is now growen familiar and naturall, not onelie to the chief parts of Scotland but even to the Orchades and the iles of Zetland or Thule, the utmost bounds of the Scottish dominion'.[16] The advance of the authority of London was reflected in the retreat of the Celtic languages, from a point in 1500 when, perhaps, only about two-thirds of the inhabitants of Britain and Ireland spoke variants of the English language.[17]

The expansion of the Tudor and Stuart states was partly a cultural project, and one that found local support among the inhabitants of the Scottish and Irish 'pales'. To this extent it was akin to the intensification of magisterial government in the English core which, as we have seen, had a strong 'moral' content. Indeed, even the English gentry had to be reminded, in 1614, that 'private challenges and combats' were 'not just or compatible with the policie of any orderly or well stayed govern-ment'. Underlying this concern was a fear of lawlessness: 'what purpose serve the Lawes of God, the provisionall instructions of men, and the course of ordinarie Justice in the Common wealth . . . if it be free for Subjects out of the distemper of their owne distempered conceits, either to rate the quality of the wrong supposed or the satisfaction that belongs to it?'.[18] The disorder of the Irish was connected with perceived impro-prieties in gender relations there, again suggesting connections with the

[15] A. Grant, 'Scotland's "Celtic Fringe" in the late middle ages: the Macdonald Lords of the Isles and the Kingdom of Scotland', in R. R. Davis (ed.), *The British Isles, 1100–1500: Comparisons, Contrasts and Connections* (Edinburgh, 1988), 118–41; J. W. M. Bannerman, 'The Lordship of the Isles', in J. M. Brown (ed.), *Scottish Society in the Fifteenth Century* (London, 1977), 209–40. For a brief account of the history of the Lordship of the Isles, see J. Munro, 'The Lordship of the Isles', in L. MacLean (ed.), *The Middle Ages in the Highlands* (Inverness, 1981), 117–29.

[16] Pont, *Union of Britayne*, p. 23.

[17] J. Morrill, 'The British problem, *c.* 1534–1707', in B. Bradshaw and J. Morrill (eds.), *The British Problem c. 1534–1707: State Formation in the British Archipelago* (London, 1996), 1–38, 273–81, at p. 2. For the decline of Celtic languages over a longer period see V. E. Durkacz, *The Decline of the Celtic Languages: A Study of Linguistic and Cultural Conflict in Scotland, Wales and Ireland from the Reformation to the Twentieth Century* (Edinburgh, 1983).

[18] Larkin and Hughes (eds.), *Royal Proclamations*, I, pp. 302–8, quotations at pp. 303–4. I am grateful to Anthony Milton for this reference.

agenda of patriarchal government we have examined in England.[19] The pastoral economy of the fenlanders helped to persuade William Camden in 1585 that they were 'a kind of people according to the nature of the place where they dwell rude, uncivill, and envious to all others whom they call *upland-men*'. William Dugdale seems to have held a similar view, more than a century later, remarking of the Great Level that it was 'until of late years, a vast deep fen, affording little benefit to the realm, other than fish or fowl, with overmuch harbour to a rude, and almost barbarous, sort of lazy and beggarly people'.[20] This was not an 'English' view in the sense of a national programme, then. And, of course, there was more to the subordination of Ireland, the incorporation of Cornwall, Wales and the Borders, and the promotion of union with Scotland, than a moral project. Diplomatic and strategic consideration and the pursuit of profit by individuals were also of central importance. But these templates for government in newly incorporated areas are revealing of many of the underlying presumptions of the proponents of order and civility. To an extent they parallel the images of deviance associated with the prosecution of witches and vagrants – exaggerated accounts of the normative threat posed by those outside the bounds of civil society. Such images were promoted by activists seeking to define a problem and to promote a governmental solution to it.

ELITE FORMATION IN ENGLAND AND WALES

In England, local elites at both village and county level found the exercise of political power helpful to their own position – the process of state formation went hand-in-hand with the process of elite formation. Almost everywhere else under the Tudor and Stuart crown local elites found mutualities of interest in supporting this programme of civility. In Wales, local elites seized on the opportunities offered by London government with considerable alacrity. The 'acts of union' between England and Wales were actually measures of jurisdictional regularisation.

---

[19] Although there was general agreement that the disorders of Irish society related in part to disorders in gender relations, there was no consistent account of what, specifically, those disorders were: C. Carroll, 'Representations of women in some early modern English tracts on the colonization of Ireland', *Albion*, 25 (1993), 379–93. See also W. Palmer, 'Gender, violence and rebellion in Tudor and Early Stuart Ireland', *Sixteenth Century Journal*, 23 (1992), 699–712. Gender roles were also important in defining racial difference in the Americas: K. M. Brown, *Good Wives, Nasty Wenches and Anxious Patriarchs: Gender, Race, and Power in Colonial America* (Chapel Hill, 1996), chs. 1–3; M. B. Norton, *Founding Mothers and Fathers: Gendered Power and the Forming of American Society* (New York, 1996), 5–7.

[20] Quoted in H. C. Darby, *The Draining of the Fens*, 2nd edn (Cambridge, 1956), 23 and n.

Wales was shired, justices of the peace appointed and MPs elected. It was, thus, a matter of bringing Wales fully within the ambit of English legal and political practice. Tudor propagandists undoubtedly overstated the benefits that this brought to the Welsh, but modern historians tend to echo the generally positive account of these measures.[21] The effect was not instant, however. The Tudor settlement built on processes of reform already at work and, on the other hand, took some time to take full effect in a country with poor communications and many isolated communities.[22] Although in theory, as we have seen, the application of English law was associated with the use of the English language, in practice the change was less dramatic. The use of English did build on a pre-existing trend for Welsh officeholders to function in Welsh, English and Latin, but it is likely that discretion was used in allowing the continued use of Welsh in court.[23]

The Tudor settlement was a success, however, in securing the interests of both the crown and the local gentry. It 'marked a turning-point rather than a starting-point and signified the coming of age of the Welsh *uchelwyr* [gentry] in a new politically unified realm'.[24] The adoption of shire government offered to the Welsh gentry greatly improved avenues for political advancement.[25] The Council in the Marches and shire government offered the promise of order and administrative effectiveness too. There was some concern at the apparent anomalies of the constitutional arrangements, but this was not a nationalist rejection so much as a desire for tidiness – the attack on the Council in the Marches in 1641 was not led by Welsh MPs.[26] The gentry adopted the ideals of

---

[21] See, for example, the accounts in P. Jenkins, *A History of Modern Wales, 1536–1990* (London, 1992); J. G. Jones, *Wales and the Tudor State: Government, Religious Change and the Social Order 1534–1603* (Cardiff, 1989); Jones, *Early Modern Wales, c. 1525–1640* (London, 1994); W. S. K. Thomas, *Tudor Wales: 1485–1603* (Llandysul, 1983); Williams, *Renewal*.

[22] Jones, *Wales and the Tudor State*.

[23] Ibid., ch. 2 esp. p. 21. On the adoption of English in the courts see P. R. Roberts, 'The Welsh language, English law and Tudor legislation', *Honourable Society of Cymmrodorion Transactions* (1989), 19–75; M. E. Jones, '"An Invidious Attempt to Accelerate the Extinction of Our Language": the abolition of the Court of Great Sessions and the Welsh language', *Welsh Historical Review*, 19 (1998), 226–64, esp. pp. 229–34. For the use of interpreters in court see J. G. Jones, *Law, Order and Government in Caernarfonshire, 1558–1640: Justices of the Peace and Gentry*, University of Wales, Studies in Welsh History, 12 (Cardiff, 1996), 69–71.

[24] Jones, *Wales and the Tudor State*, ch. 2, esp. p. 37; Jones, *Caernarfonshire, passim*, and esp. pp. 207–8.

[25] W. R. B. Robinson, 'The Tudor revolution in Welsh government, 1536–1542: its effects on gentry participation', *EHR*, 103 (1988), 1–20.

[26] P. Williams, *The Council in the Marches under Elizabeth I* (Cardiff, 1958); Williams, 'The attack on the Council in the Marches, 1603–1642', *Transactions of the Honourable Society of Cymmrodorion* (1961), 1–22; P. Roberts, 'Wales and England after the Tudor "union": crown, principality and parliament, 1543–1624', in C. Cross, D. Loades and J. J. Scarisbrick (eds.), *Law and Government under the Tudors: Essays Presented to Sir Geoffrey Elton Regius Professor of History in the University of*

order and gentility disseminated by Tudor government, ideals that were assimilated into the bardic poetry that they patronised. Ultimately, Welsh ideals of gentility lost their distinctive character.[27]

The union was a political success, and there was no Welsh rebellion against, for example, the reformations of the sixteenth century. The success rested on the ready cooperation of Welsh elites, something that did not come at the expense of Welsh cultural identity – many Welsh landowners continued to act, initially at least, as patrons of the bards.[28] But economic change favoured the consolidation of landholding and the reformation was associated with a revitalisation of religious life and further bound the gentry to the Tudor regime.[29] Meanwhile, the gentry built up English connections through marriage and education. In fact, there was not so much a Welsh gentry as three distinct sets of Anglo-Welsh gentry. Welsh families on the north coast had close commercial and social links with Chester, those in mid-Wales with Shrewsbury and those in South Wales with Bristol.[30] The Tudor settlement was a means by which they could preserve their social position and increasingly they were divided from a conservative and monoglot peasantry. Thus, 'One of the most remarkable features of the history of Wales in the sixteenth century is the ease with which its traditional social structure was adapted and used to serve the needs of the new independent sovereign state which was established in the 1530s.' In the later seventeenth century and into the eighteenth the correspondence of the Glamorganshire gentry reflects an almost complete lack of interest in the uplands.[31] As a consequence of this assimilation, by the later sixteenth century the

Cambridge on the Occasion of his Retirement (Cambridge, 1988), 111–38. For parliamentary representation see P. S. Edwards, 'The parliamentary representation of the Welsh boroughs in the mid-sixteenth century', *Bulletin of the Board of Celtic Studies*, 27 (1976–7), 425–39.

[27] J. G. Jones, *Concepts of Order and Gentility in Wales, 1540–1640* (Llandysul, 1992); Jones, 'Concepts of order and gentility', in Jones (ed.), *Class, Community and Culture in Tudor Wales* (Cardiff, 1989), 121–57.   [28] Jones, *Wales and the Tudor State*, p. 35.

[29] For the success of the Reformation see ibid.; G. Williams, *Wales and the Reformation* (Cardiff, 1997); B. Bradshaw, 'The Tudor reformation and revolution in Wales and Ireland: the origins of the British problem', in Bradshaw and Morrill (eds.), *British Problem*, 39–65, 281–4; C. Brady, 'Comparable histories?: Tudor reform in Wales and Ireland', in Ellis and Barber (eds.), *Conquest and Union*, 64–86. D. Walker, 'The Reformation in Wales', in D. Walker (ed.), *A History of the Church in Wales* (Penarth, 1976), 54–78, is a useful short treatment.

[30] Jenkins, *Modern Wales*, p. 4. For gentry marriages in the first half of the sixteenth century see W. R. B. Robinson, 'The marriages of knighted Welsh landowners, 1485–1558', *National Library of Wales Journal*, 25 (1988), 387–98. Robinson raises the interesting question of whether the willingness of Welsh knights to take English wives was matched by a willingness on the part of English knights to take Welsh wives: ibid., p. 389.

[31] Jones, *Wales and the Tudor State*, p. 117; P. Jenkins, *The Making of a Ruling Class: The Glamorgan Gentry 1640–1790* (Cambridge, 1983), ch. 1.

Welsh literary tradition *was* in decline, deserted by increasingly large numbers of the natural leaders of society. Social differentiation here had a linguistic dimension, too.[32] Meanwhile, poets were 'quick to sense and to reinforce the emphasis on the duties of magistracy'. In place of the old martial values Bardic eulogies now 'hymned the role of the gentleman as a conscientious magistrate, legally knowledgeable, and administering justice even-handedly'.[33]

Gentry society in Wales could, clearly, be accommodated to the authority of the English crown. This compatibility was cemented by underlying similarities of social structure. The Welsh 'peasantry' resembled the English middle and lower orders. It is possible to discern the equivalents of yeomen, active in manorial, hundredal and petty juries and, less frequently, on quarter sessions and assize juries. Some were as wealthy as the poorest of the gentry. Below them was the bulk of the population, equivalent to the English husbandman, engaged in mixed farming. The regulation of service, wages and the implementation of the poor law all reflect the English pattern of paternal control and flexible administration. Although mainly monoglot Welsh speakers these people did not inhabit a single Welsh world, but a series of segmented, local worlds.[34] A study of Denbighshire in the 1590s suggests that by that time English patterns of crime and prosecution were current in Wales too. As in England there is evidence of corruption of the legal process and of a preference for non-legal means of dispute resolution. None the less, in all 'a picture emerges . . . of a relatively law-abiding society in which the community did turn to the watch, the local constable and the justices to protect both their property and their peace. The authorities were helped with pursuit and search with what may seem surprising eagerness.'[35] Welsh towns, although small and poor by comparison with their English equivalents, were similar in many ways, sharing the same fluctuations in economic fortunes. The good times, when they did come, arrived on the back of regional specialisation in agriculture, as in England, and on integration with the English economy.[36] In all these ways, then, Wales

---

[32] For social differentiation, see Williams, *Renewal*, ch. 17. For education and cultural change with consequent pressure on the Welsh literary tradition see ibid., ch. 18.

[33] F. Heal and C. Holmes, *The Gentry in England and Wales, 1500–1700* (London, 1994), 179. See Jones, *Order and Gentility*; Jones, 'Order and gentility'.

[34] B. E. Howells, 'The lower orders of society', in Jones (ed.), *Class*, 237–59. For constables in Caernarfonshire in this period see Jones, *Caernarfonshire*, pp. 48–53. This account reveals problems of administration akin to those experienced in England as, for example, in the hostility that constables met in imposing financial obligations: ibid., pp. 136–8.

[35] N. M. W. Powell, 'Crime and criminality in Denbighshire during the 1590s: the evidence of the records of the Great Sessions', in Jones (ed.), *Class*, 261–94.

[36] M. Griffiths, '"Very Wealthy by Merchandise"? Urban fortunes', in Jones (ed.), *Class*, 197–235.

seems to have been assimilated to the Tudor state without major conflict.

One of the key ingredients of the successful integration of Wales was the existence of a gentry which could identify its collective interests with those of Tudor government. In part this was facilitated by the Tudor appeal to a British heritage that was meaningful in Wales, a clear contrast to the promotion of Britishness in Scotland. In Wales, furthermore, the Tudor state was not in competition with other sources of administrative and political authority, again a contrast to Scotland where the independent apparatus of government and justice offered a means to local influence after the departure of the court to London. Early modern London had a substantial Welsh population, the social status and wealth of which reflected that of the city as a whole and which was not marked out by residence in particular areas. Wales did not have its Edinburgh, and a broad cross-section of Welsh society was drawn into participation in a wider Anglo-Welsh world.[37] Of course, this begs further questions about the medieval history of Wales, the development of a gentry class and the absence of alternative power-centres.[38]

In any event, this integration did not come at the expense of a Welsh identity. Although the gentry adopted English, around 90 per cent of the population in the seventeenth century was Welsh speaking.[39] The future of the language was threatened by the use of English as the language of government, although the use of Welsh to propagate the gospels helped to preserve its vitality.[40] The assimilation of the Welsh gentry to the Tudor state did, therefore, pose a threat to the survival of the language but, even among the English speaking population, a sense of Welshness was preserved. In boroughs, schools and Jesus College, Oxford, Welsh identity was preserved within the institutional framework of the larger Tudor world.[41] An indication of the extent of political assimilation is that the political history of Wales during the 1640s and 1650s can be

[37] E. Jones, 'The Welsh in London in the seventeenth and eighteenth centuries', *Welsh History Review*, 10 (1981), 461–79.

[38] For some reflections on the contrasting heritage of Wales and Ireland, see Bradshaw, 'Wales and Ireland'. In part, of course, the sixteenth-century assimilation of Wales rested on earlier conquest: I am grateful to Professor Dan Beaver for making this point to me.

[39] P. Jenkins, 'A new history of Wales', *HJ*, 32 (1989), 387–93, at p. 388.

[40] Roberts, 'Welsh language'; P. Jenkins, 'The Anglican church and the unity of Britain: the Welsh experience, 1560–1714', in Ellis and Barber (eds.), *Conquest and Union*, 115–38; G. Jones, *The Gentry and the Elizabethan State* (Llandybie, 1977), 88–9, 91–2. To this extent the survival was fortuitous: in Ireland and Scotland the promotion of the reformation in English contributed substantially to the decline of Gaelic languages: Durkacz, *Decline*. See below, pp. 383–4. For the importance of governmental support for modern Welsh see J. Aitchison and H. Carter, 'Rural Wales and the Welsh language', *Rural History*, 2 (1991), 61–79.

[41] Jenkins, 'New history'.

treated in terms similar to those used of English counties.[42] But this institutional development (the history of the state) is separate from the development of the nation.[43] There was clearly a local demand for more regular government under the Tudor and Stuart crown which cannot easily be presented as centralisation or Anglicisation. It is permissible, perhaps, in these respects, to liken the Welsh experience to that of the peripheries of England. It has been suggested, for example, that by 1600, in terms of its *political* culture, Wales may not have been a greater variation on the English norm than Norfolk or Lancashire.[44]

It is easy to exaggerate the importance of the jurisdictional peculiarities of the English peripheries. By the Elizabethan period the great palatinate jurisdictions are best seen as local expressions of royal authority rather than delegations of it. They, and the regional councils, offered a means of bringing the benefits of royal government to populations physically distant from the privy council and the Westminster courts. The incorporation of the palatinates was essentially a jurisdictional matter with which local elites could co-operate, as the resort to their courts declined.[45] The appointment of justices of the peace and the election of MPs from Cheshire built upon similarities of social structure and cultural values which supported the English polity elsewhere. It was informed by new views of sovereignty, but its success depended on the participation of the gentry, alive to the possibilities offered to them by fuller participation in the institutions of the Tudor state. Moreover, jurisdictional changes overlay broader continuities in the social and political life of the gentry so that, once again, incorporation did not mean an end to particularism.[46] As we will see, it was as much the Cumberland gentry as the London government that sought to pacify the surname groups on the Cumberland Borders in the later sixteenth century.

[42] A. M. Johnson, 'Wales during the commonwealth and protectorate', in D. Pennington and K. Thomas (eds.), *Puritans and Revolutionaries: Essays in Seventeenth-Century History Presented to Christopher Hill* (Oxford, 1978), 233–56.

[43] For a similar view see J. Morrill, 'The fashioning of Britain', in Ellis and Barber (eds.), *Conquest and Union*, 8–39, esp. pp. 38–9. See also Jones, *Gentry and Elizabethan State*, esp. pp. 90–2.

[44] Morrill, 'Fashioning', p. 18. For an account of the Lancashire commission of the peace, downplaying Lancastrian exceptionalism see D. J. Wilkinson, 'The commission of the peace in Lancashire, 1603–1642', *Transactions of the Historic Society of Lancashire and Cheshire*, 132 (1983), 41–66.

[45] W. J. Jones, 'Palatine performance in the seventeenth century', in P. Clark, A. G. R. Smith and N. Tyacke (eds.), *The English Commonwealth 1547–1640: Essays in Politics and Society Presented to Joel Hurstfield* (Leicester, 1979), 189–204. For the Council in the North see R. R. Reid, *The King's Council in the North* (London, 1921); for that in the Marches see Williams, *Council in the Marches*; Williams, 'Attack'.

[46] T. Thornton, 'The integration of Cheshire into the Tudor nation state in the early sixteenth century', *Northern History*, 29 (1993), 40–63.

In Cornwall a similar observation holds. The most isolated English county and, in its western extremities, as remote from London as the Cumbrian Borders, Cornwall was home to a large population of non-English speakers. Even in 1640 many west Cornish did not speak English and were regarded by neighbouring Devonians as foreigners, not just strangers.[47] But despite jurisdictional particularities, Cornish society was similar enough to other parts of England to support magisterial government: 'The structure of Cornish society, by which I mean the classes, their character and relations to one another, was not essentially different from that of the rest of England.'[48] The more general case being made here is that the survival of a very distinct Cornish popular culture does not seem to have affected the political integration of Cornwall into the Tudor and Stuart state. 'Within the county, the gentry ruled, as within every shire in England. They were the backbone of the government of the country: its effective political class.'[49] Remoteness meant that the Cornish gentry were closely interrelated, and the jurisdiction of the Duchy cut rather across that of the county, but none the less Cornwall is recognisable as a county community like any other in England.[50] The creation of fifteen parliamentary boroughs between 1545 and 1603 bears testimony to its assimilation.[51] As English (indeed European) trade was reoriented towards the Atlantic so too were strategic and political interests. By 1700 Cornwall was definitely not at the outer edge of the interests of the crown.[52]

[47] M. J. Stoyle, '"Pagans or paragons?": images of the Cornish during the English civil war', *EHR*, 111 (1996), 299–323. For the survival of Cornish see esp. pp. 300–1. Rowse was rather more sceptical about the survival of Cornish which, he thought, was 'fast dying' by 1600: A. L. Rowse, *Tudor Cornwall: Portrait of a Society* (London, 1941), esp. pp. 21–4. Coate and Duffin are also cautious on this point: A. Duffin, *Faction and Faith: Politics and Religion of the Cornish Gentry before the Civil War* (Exeter, 1996), 2; M. Coate, *Cornwall in the Great Civil War and Interregnum 1642–1660: A Social and Political Study* (Oxford, 1933), 2–3.   [48] Rowse, *Tudor Cornwall*, p. 77.

[49] Ibid., p. 83.

[50] See, for example, Duffin, *Faction*. And the duchy, of course, helped to integrate the county into the English patronage system: ibid., pp. 3–4; G. Haslam, 'The Elizabethan Duchy of Cornwall, an estate in stasis', in R. W. Hoyle (ed.), *The Estates of the English Crown, 1558–1640* (Cambridge, 1992), 88–111; Haslam, 'Jacobean phoenix: the Duchy of Cornwall in the principates of Henry Frederick and Charles', ibid., 263–96. For the relative isolation and high degree of in-marriage in Cornwall see Duffin, *Faction*, ch. 1. High rates of marriage within a county have been observed elsewhere, of course: J. S. Morrill, *Cheshire 1630–1660: County Government and Society during the English Revolution* (Oxford, 1974), 15–16; A. Everitt, *The Community of Kent and Great Rebellion 1640–60* (Leicester, 1966), 42–3.

[51] Coate, *Cornwall*, p. 18. By 1625 there were forty-two borough members and two knights of the shire in the county, 'a representation quite disproportionate to the size and population of the county': ibid., p. 17.

[52] For later peripheralisation see S. Fisher and M. Havinden, 'The long-term evolution of the economy of south-west England from autonomy to dependence', in M. A. Havinden, J. Quéniart and J. Stanyer (eds.), *Centre and Periphery: A Comparative Study of Brittany and Cornwall & Devon* (Exeter, 1991), 76–85.

In late medieval Durham, magnate power was, according to James's influential study, based on territory and following.[53] Tenancies were let on easy terms and social mobility was possible for those who could make a profit from their holdings. The political education and political world of the magnates centred around the household, and the great noble households offered employment and influence to ambitious local people. This magnate society was able to mobilise considerable forces in rebellion in 1569 but the defeat of that rising created a power vacuum that was filled by the new gentry. These men tended to be more closely integrated into national life by their educational experience at the Inns of Court or the universities and their political interests were more ideological. They had a more entrepreneurial attitude to estate management, preferring to derive a revenue rather than to build a following. Their relationships with their inferiors were contractual rather than those of personal service. At the same time, commercial interests in Newcastle and the coalfields also generated political and social change.

Another agent of change in the region was the reformation. The bishops of Durham had possessed extensive lands in the area and controlled considerable power and patronage, but their influence had been limited by their origins. As outsiders their appeal had been to the crown rather than to a local following and they had, as a result, been the representatives of the crown interest in the region. Following the collapse of the great noble houses in the aftermath of the rising this potential power was increasingly realised and the politics of the region were increasingly dominated by the church. This impact was two-fold, as it was elsewhere in England. On the one hand, the reformation promoted obedience and loyalty while, on the other, the growth of religious pluralism destabilised politics. During the 1630s active government under Bishop Neile led to political conflict: he was insensitive to local feeling, eager to increase clerical influence in civil administration, and had a narrow view of orthodoxy. By this time, then, Durham's politics were not very different from those elsewhere in the country, both in issues and form. In the early sixteenth century Durham had been a lineage society, characterised by bounded horizons and particularised modes of thought. It had been dominated by great magnate households and followings, encouraging personalised loyalties and an honour code centring on personal ties. By 1640 it was a civil society, characterised by 'generalised discourse and the universally valid view-

[53] M. James, *Family, Lineage and Civil Society: A Study of Society, Politics, and Mentality in the Durham Region 1500–1640* (Oxford, 1974).

point'. These intellectual and political changes were encouraged by gentry education in public institutions influenced by renaissance and reformation thought. It was underpinned by the spread of a more contractual view of relations with the tenantry and the influence of the new commercial society developing in the coalfield.[54] The defeat of the northern earls was a significant moment in this process, but clearly Durham was not integrated into the Tudor state and governed by force of arms.[55]

In Wales and the English peripheries then, the increasing authority of the English crown came in tandem with the spread of magisterial government. It depended on a mutuality of interests between crown and local elites and this worked by a mixture of means. Social and commercial ties bound the gentry of the regions of England more closely to London, the Inns of Court and the universities, where broader political interests were encouraged. At the same time, the institutions of royal government offered a means of cementing local social influence and status, and the resolution of local conflict. It was further encouraged by the reformation, which again gave both material and intellectual grounds for cooperation. But this integration did not come at the expense of local identity among the gentry, or at the expense of particularism, and it evidently did not depend on the homogenisation of the population below the level of the gentry. The persistence of linguistic difference among the Welsh or Cornish peasantry did not prevent the assimilation of those regions to shire government.

STATE FORMATION AND ELITE FORMATION IN SCOTLAND

In Scotland these processes did not lead so clearly towards integration, or met with greater obstruction. In Scotland, in fact, a Francophile elite offered a credible alternative to the English alliance while the existence of an independent educational, legal, religious and political system offered alternatives to integration. The union with Scotland was, to a large extent, a matter of dynastic and political contingency, as we will

---

[54] Ibid. See also James, *Society, Politics and Culture: Studies in Early Modern England* (Cambridge, 1986), esp. chs. 7, 8, 9. For the social and economic development of the coalfield see D. Levine and K. Wrightson, *The Making of an Industrial Society: Whickham 1560–1765* (Oxford, 1991).

[55] In contrast to the argument of Webb about 'the military nationalization of England and the militant organisation of its emerging empire, from the royal arquebusiers' defeat of the northern earls' tribesmen in 1569 down to the imperial compromise between the armed executive and the civil legislatures in 1681': S. S. Webb, *Lord Churchill's Coup: The Anglo-American Empire and the Glorious Revolution Reconsidered* (New York, 1995), ix.

see. To describe these variations, as in the case of Wales and the English peripheries, is to beg a question about developments in the preceding periods, but the discussion here will centre on the period from around 1550 to around 1707.

In lowland Scotland, as in lowland England, a number of processes were already under way before the Union of the Crowns which made Scottish political society potentially assimilable to the Tudor or Anglo-Scottish Stuart state: much of what is later identifiable as 'Anglicisation' actually had its roots within Scottish society prior to 1603 and, of course, long before the Union of 1707. In part this was a product of the development of greater civility among the Scottish aristocracy (which in some accounts of Scottish history amounts to a taming of them).[56] In any case, it brought the culture and manners of many Scottish landowners closer to the European mainstream than had hitherto been the case and like England, Scotland had its own centres of 'civility'. At the same time, other aspects of Scottish government became more routinised – for example, taxation, parish poor relief and the work of justices of the peace (at least in their non-judicial functions). But this was complicated by at least two factors. Firstly, civility appealed differentially, spreading new forms of behaviour among the lowland aristocracy more quickly than among the Highlanders. As a result, the cultural divide noted by John Fordun in the late fourteenth century, hitherto visible but not unbridgeable, was exaggerated.[57] Secondly, after 1603, the progress of civility was encouraged by, and served the purposes of, a monarch no longer resident in Scotland. The connections between the cultural and legal changes, and the assimilation of Scotland into a 'British' state, thus became more complex.

The development of 'civil' government opened a frontier within Scotland. In the sixteenth century the differences between highland and lowland were not as marked as they later became. Dependants in clan society were linked by consanguinity but this kinship was often pretended.[58] Clan chiefs offered protection and justice in the same way as feudal lords in the lowlands, but there was not necessarily a tenurial relationship between them. In fact, clansmen might be tenants of other

[56] This idea is debunked by J. Wormald, 'Taming the magnates?', in K. J. Stringer (ed.), *Essays on the Nobility of Medieval Scotland* (Edinburgh, 1985), 270–80.

[57] For the highland–lowland divide in Fordun's time see R. Nicholson, *Scotland: The Later Middle Ages* (Edinburgh, 1974), esp. pp. 204–7.

[58] R. A. Dodgshon, '"Pretence of blude" or "place of thair dwelling": the nature of the highland clans, 1500–1745', in R. A. Houston and I. D. Whyte (eds.), *Scottish Society, 1500–1800* (Cambridge, 1989), 169–98. For kinship in Scotland at large, J. Wormald, 'Bloodfeud, kindred and government in early modern Scotland', *PP*, 87 (1980), 54–97, esp. pp. 66–71.

chiefs and chiefs might be powerful but landless. At the same time, there were feudal relationships between chiefs and the crown which gave chiefs a degree of control over their land enabling them to parcel it out between their tenants and clansmen. Finally, succession to the chiefdom was increasingly, by 1550, following the feudal (rather than Gaelic) principle of primogeniture.[59] In the lowlands feudal tenures were important, but kinship was also extremely significant. Although it was something of a fiction, the language of kindred was common throughout Scottish society. The practical significance of distant kinship was limited, but the language of kinship was so important that it affected the way in which lordship was described. Bonds of manrent, assuring protection and service, were analogous to kin relationships – they related less to land grants and more to 'the personal relationship between the lord and his friends and dependants'.[60] In these respects, then, there was common ground between highland and lowland: 'The differences in social structure between agrarian society in the Highlands and lowlands were . . . mainly ones of emphasis – highland society was based on kinship modified by feudalism, lowland society on feudalism tempered by kinship.'[61] The differences between highland and lowland lay more in language, dress and manners than in these aspects of social structure.

An example of the similarities between the two regions, and the processes by which they became more distinct, is provided by the history of feuding. The late survival of the bloodfeud in Scotland marks it out as a society in which political authority was relatively poorly institutionalised. In this respect, highland and lowland societies were reasonably similar. The feud was not unique to Scotland, by any means, but it is well documented and provides a window onto a broader process of cultural change, both an 'internalisation of obedience' and a 'retreat into respectability'.[62] The feud offered a kind of personal justice, often ended by arbitration, into which was built the concept of 'assythment' – compensation for the wrong committed. Thus, feuding could serve to control and resolve conflict, and was a supplement to legal process since arbitration to end the feud might well include legal settlement. There

[59] T. C. Smout, *A History of the Scottish People 1560–1830* (London, 1972), 41–3.
[60] Wormald, 'Bloodfeud', p. 71.
[61] Smout, *Scottish People*, p. 43. For a similar account of Scottish Border society which emphasises the intertwining obligations of kinship and feudal landholding, see T. I. Rae, *The Administration of the Scottish Frontier, 1513–1603* (Edinburgh, 1966), 4–11.
[62] M. E. James and J. Sharpe, quoted by K. M. Brown, *Bloodfeud in Scotland 1573–1625: Violence, Justice and Politics in an Early Modern Society* (Edinburgh, 1986), 270.

were close connections between the principles and practice of the feud and legal procedure, not least in the way that compensation was built into formal legal settlement.

There was, in the late fifteenth and early sixteenth centuries, some 'peace within the feud' in Scotland – feuding and kin relations operated to contain and resolve conflict in a way that was analogous to good lordship.[63] But in the late sixteenth-century 'Indian summer' of feuding, this peace within the feud became less well remarked. The intensity of feuding, and the violence related to it, seem to have increased, probably fuelled by social, religious and political tension in a period of weakened religious and political authority. It has been estimated that 365 feuds, a minimum figure, erupted in Scotland between 1573 and 1625, most of them before 1610.[64] 'Religious disunity and crown weakness coupled with socio-economic problems facing the landed community created strains which a feuding society was ill-equipped to cope with, and it fragmented into endemic feuding and violence.'[65]

It is all the more striking, therefore, that as a system of civil and criminal justice, the feud seems to have disappeared rapidly in the early seventeenth century. As late as 1592 James VI recognised the justice inherent in the feud by approving a bond of manrent as assythment of a slaughter. At the end of that decade, however, an act was issued condemning settlement of feuds in which slaughter was involved. This preference for public over private justice was supported by the professional lawyers. By the late sixteenth century sons of landowners were increasingly well educated, and those with a university education were most likely to prosper in government and administration. This professionalisation at first assimilated the principle of the feud. For example, judges set the level of assythment, thus professionalising the arbitration to end a feud. A broader process of cultural change created a 'milieu in which formality, the forms and procedures of the law, the written authenticated record, had an appeal and an authority which would in the end far outweigh the amateur justice of lord and kin'. This extended to criminal justice too.[66]

By the mid-seventeenth century this process was well advanced, and

---

[63] Wormald, 'Bloodfeud'.

[64] Brown, *Bloodfeud*, p. 5. This may have been an illusion caused by changing levels of government concern, of course. It is likely, however, that the declining levels of reported feuds did reflect pretty accurately declining levels of actual feuding.   [65] Ibid., p. 266.

[66] Wormald, 'Bloodfeud', pp. 85–92, quotation at p. 91. There was also a huge increase in levels of civil litigation in the later sixteenth century. I am grateful to Dr Julian Goodare for pointing this out to me.

the parliament of 1649 legislated against the feud in terms that were wholly hostile. This seems to have reflected the opinions of the Coven-anters, the Calvinist opponents of Charles I. Church and state united in punishing law-breaking as a sin rather than a crime against humans.[67] But the feud was, in practice, in decline before that date. The decline was a response, it has been suggested, to the disorder that feuding had produced in the latter half of the sixteenth century. Political stability was sought by middling groups in town and country, by the church and by the king. But 'Much more politically important was the attitude of the nobility who had no interest whatsoever in prolonging violence, and who . . . were fully prepared to work with the King in finding a more acceptable level of peace.'[68] This was a matter of choice, not coercion.

This, in effect, changed the nature of justice – making it routine and bringing it within the ambit of royal authority. As a result, recent work on the Scottish bloodfeud has placed it in the context of state forma-tion.[69] The triumph was not one of state over society, though; instead, it was the triumph of a particular set of cultural values. The changes in attitude 'created a new milieu in the lowlands, in which men thought with pride of their modern civilized society and looked back with horror to the barbarities of the past'. But the impact was regional: 'with a decline in the bloodfeud in the lowlands went an increase of suspicion and hatred of the highlander, and men looked sideways to the highland area of their country without understanding, but with embarrassment, fear and violent hostility'.[70]

Civil government was developing in Scotland independently of 'Eng-lish' authority, and it was not a product of monarchical ambition alone. It was not a triumph of centre over the localities, but its uneven development did open, or at least give greater definition to, a frontier in Scotland between the Highlands and the lowlands. This 'depersonalisa-tion' of justice is not attributable to the successful ambition of the Stuart monarchs.[71] The nobility dominated Scottish politics throughout the seventeenth century, as they had done in the fifteenth, and government depended on mutual interest rather than a victory by the crown over the magnates.[72] None the less, the spreading influence of legal redress did serve the interests of the crown and ran alongside more self-consciously

[67] Ibid., pp. 93–4.   [68] Brown, *Bloodfeud*, p. 268.   [69] Ibid.; Wormald, 'Bloodfeud'.
[70] Ibid., p. 97.   [71] Ibid., pp. 95–6.
[72] Wormald, 'Taming?'; J. Brown, 'The exercise of power', in Brown (ed.), *Scottish Society in the Fifteenth Century* (London, 1977), 33–65. For an overview of aristocratic power in seventeenth-century Scotland see K. M. Brown, *Kingdom or Province? Scotland and the Regal Union, 1603–1715* (London, 1992), 33–47.

designed regularisation of government. For example, Scottish legislation in the later sixteenth century followed that of much of Europe in
seeking to control vagrancy and provide relief for the deserving. The Act
of 1575 was 'an almost exact copy' of the English statute of 1572
although its effect was probably much more limited.[73]

Law was an instrument of government in early modern Europe. In
Scotland, as in much of England, justice was administered through
franchises and this had the effect of limiting the direct administrative
influence of the crown. 'In the Highlands the king had no sources of
revenue and no power: he could persuade, influence, offer inducements
for action, and impose penalties on clan leaders if they strayed beyond
their own areas, but he could not command or tax.' In the lowlands
many great nobles had hereditary legal courts which excluded royal
jurisdiction.[74] The most substantial of these private jurisdictions were
the regalities, in which the lord could hear not just minor cases but the
four pleas of the crown: murder, rape, arson and robbery. Treason was
not included, but regality courts could repledge cases – a lord could
claim the right to hear the case of any person from within his jurisdiction
who had been before another court. There were also lesser baronial
jurisdictions covering a variety of criminal and civil matters.[75] By comparison, royal justice and administration were institutionally underde-
veloped. In the early seventeenth century, at least by 1609, a remedy
was sought in the appointment of justices of the peace, albeit with more
limited powers than their English counterparts. As James I put it in his
speech to the judges in Star Chamber on 20 June 1616, 'government by
justices is so laudable and so highly esteemed by me, that I have made
Scotland to be governed by justices and constables as England is'. There
may have been some grounds for this claim. The system of justices, and
below them constables, was operating in most of Scotland by 1613 and
although they did not supersede the baronies and regalities, they were
significant in promoting non-judicial administration. As such, they were
resented by many among the nobility but by 1630 there was a positive
local demand for more justices.[76] The growth of the poor law provides

[73] R. Mitchison, 'North and south: the development of the gulf in poor law practice', in Houston
and Whyte (eds.), *Scottish Society*, 199–225, at p. 200. Dr Goodare is more impressed than
Professor Mitchison by the spread of the poor law, particularly in the towns. The date frequently
given for the act, 1574, is an error – the published acts did not modernise dates. I am grateful to
Dr Goodare for discussing this issue with me.   [74] Mitchison, 'North and south', p. 201.

[75] Rae, *Frontier*, pp. 14–15.

[76] M. Lee, Jr, *Government by Pen: Scotland under James VI and I* (Urbana, 1980), 125–8; Lee, *The Road to
Revolution: Scotland under Charles I, 1625–37* (Urbana, 1985), 94, 237. James' speech quoted from
J. R. Tanner (ed.), *Constitutional Documents of the Reign of James I: A.D. 1603–1625* (Cambridge,

an index, therefore, of the growth of the effectiveness of this non-judicial administration. Further developments took place in the 1650s, as the English government sought to build up dependable local government following the Glencairn rising against the Cromwellian regime.[77]

None the less, James had been exaggerating when he boasted of the achievements of justices, and an indigenous institution, the Kirk sessions, was probably more important to programmes of moral reform. The sessions also had responsibility for the poor as a Christian duty,[78] and the development of the role of the justices of the peace took place alongside these bodies. From 1617 onwards efforts were made to increase the role of the justices of the peace, and bad harvests in the early 1620s led to attempts to increase compulsory poor rates. However, the relative weakness of local administration was painfully apparent in the subsistence crisis of 1623, when privy council proclamations 'should more realistically be regarded as appeals' demonstrating 'the limited authority of the Council and lack of a coherent framework of local government'. The action that was taken was insubstantial, and there was some active hostility to the privy council programme.[79] At the mid-century though, the Kirk took a more active role in civil government and the effectiveness of local institutions improved. After legislation in 1649 church courts were responsible for the poor law and active everywhere except in the Highlands. Regular rates were collected, although whether this was on the basis of assessments was left to the discretion of the presbyteries. Over the next forty years parish relief extended throughout the lowlands and measures against vagrancy were implemented. In the hard years of the 1690s the response of local government was better, although patchy. By this date it is relatively easy to distinguish a closely governed lowland region from highland areas where poor relief was not administered, where private jurisdictions persisted and the feud remained important in the resolution of disputes.[80]

The increasing formality of poor relief and dispute resolution suggest

---

1952), 20. See also J. Goodare, 'The nobility and the absolutist state in Scotland, 1584–1638', *History*, 78 (1993), 161–82, esp. pp. 175–8; Mitchison 'North and south', p. 202.

[77] F. D. Dow, *Cromwellian Scotland, 1651–1660* (Edinburgh, 1979), esp. pp. 162–4, 178–81.

[78] L. Smith, 'Sackcloth for the sinner or punishment for the crime? Church and secular courts in Cromwellian Scotland', in J. Dwyer, R. A. Mason and A. Murdoch (eds.), *New Perspectives on the Politics and Culture of Early Modern Scotland* (Edinburgh, 1982), 116–32; W. Makey, *The Church of the Covenant 1637–1651: Revolution and Social Change in Scotland* (Edinburgh, 1979). See below, pp. 366–7.

[79] Lee, *Government by Pen*, pp. 215–17. Quotation from Mitchison, 'North and south', p. 205.

[80] Ibid., pp. 206–14. For the extension of the authority of justices of the peace at mid-century see Goodare, 'Absolutist state', p. 176. For the poor law see R. A. Cage and R. Mitchison, 'Debate: the making of the old Scottish poor law', *PP*, 69 (1975), 113–21.

processes quite similar to those producing an intensification of government in England. They were expressed through different institutions –
notably the Kirk sessions – but they drew on similar strands of thought –
not least Calvinism – which fired many godly magistrates in England.
Although there is some evidence of borrowing from English models, this
was more like an indigenous process than an English imposition. The
Scottish witchhunts also reveal developments parallel to, but separate
from, those in England. There is some similarity in the patterns of
accusations in England and Scotland, although in Scotland a higher
proportion of the accused were men. The reputation of the witch spread
further but the misfortunes that promoted accusations were similar. The
chronology of their rise and fall was also broadly the same. In Scotland,
however, the legal system had an inquisitorial element. In particular,
prior to criminal trial, Kirk sessions sought out offenders. In the Highlands, where there were fewer sessions, there were also fewer accusations
than in the lowlands and it seems that the inquisitorial elements of
Scottish procedure could lead to an escalation of witchhunts as the
accused named accomplices. This helps to explain the greater numbers
of witches in Scotland as a whole than in England. Under torture
Scottish witches revealed a stronger role for the devil, and this may also
reflect the greater power of the Kirk in propagating educated beliefs.
English confessions about the devil were similar, but less frequent.[81]

Most significantly of all, though, for present purposes, the degree of
central oversight in Scotland was much greater. Every case had to go
through parliament or privy council, and so the imprint of political
concerns is much clearer.[82] As a result, the 'fit' between the chronological patterns of trials and high politics is better in Scotland, although it
would probably be an exaggeration to say that the prosecution of
witches was consciously manipulated. Concerns about the legitimacy of
various regimes, notably that of James VI and of the Covenanters,
found more direct expression in witchhunting, and to this extent legitimacy was established by contrast with the inversion of respectable and
legitimate power. Thus, between 1591 and 1597 the most extensive
hunt responded quite directly to the king's wishes 'and served to demonstrate his concern for the safety of the realm'.[83] Levels rose again during
the 1620s, peaking in the last months of 1628 and 1630. Further peaks in
1649 and 1661 fell close to changes of regime and Larner suggested that

---

[81] I am grateful to Dr Julian Goodare for discussing this issue with me.
[82] C. Larner, *Witchcraft and Religion: The Politics of Popular Belief* (Oxford, 1985), 69–78.
[83] C. Larner, *Enemies of God: The Witch-Hunt in Scotland* (Oxford, 1983), 69.

on both occasions they were consciously manipulated for political purposes.[84] 'Between 1680 and 1735 the witch-belief disappeared almost
without comment from the cognitive map of the ruling class, and retired
to the secret, uncharted areas of peasant exchange.'[85] Thus, overall,
witchhunting in Scotland coincided with the dominance of the political
ideologies of divine right kingship and the godly state. Its role in
legitimating those ideas is more clearly revealed than in England because of the higher degree of control exercised over the process by the
institutions of national government. It is thus easier to place the Scottish
hunts in the context of state formation. More precisely, the pattern of
trials offers a way of examining the attempt to christianise the peasantry
and to establish the legitimacy of institutions of dispute resolution.

Scottish government then was moving towards institutionalisation in
ways analogous with developments in England and elsewhere in
Europe. It was not a matter of English imposition, in fact in the case of
witchcraft the influence was more significant in the other direction.[86]
Similarly, the lawyers who helped to bring an end to the feud formed a
powerful interest group resisting institutional unification of the two
kingdoms.[87] As in England, regularisation of government prior to 1640
was not driven primarily by warfare. Indeed in Scotland warfare had
very little to do with it. It is noticeable too in the institutionalisation of
aristocratic politics, although here the relationship with England is
important: it was partly a consequence of absentee government.[88]

From the 1580s onwards the frequency and level of taxation increased rapidly. In the process it was established that the government
had the right to tax and that this taxation should be granted by a

---

[84] Ibid. p. 73, 197–9; Larner, *Witchcraft*, p. 78. For the latter peak see B. P. Levack, 'The great
Scottish witch-hunt of 1661–1662', *JBS*, 20 (1980), 90–108. For an interesting recent contribu-
tion to discussion of Scottish witchcraft, see J. Goodare, 'Women and witch-hunt in Scotland',
Social History, 23 (1998), 288–308.   [85] Larner, *Enemies*, p. 79.   [86] Larner, *Witchcraft*, ch. 1.

[87] See A. Murdoch, 'The advocates, the law and the nation in early modern Scotland', in W. Prest
(ed.), *Lawyers in Early Modern Europe and America* (London, 1981), 147–63. For the defence of
Scottish legal independence see B. P. Levack, *The Formation of the British State: England, Scotland, and
the Union 1603–1707* (Oxford, 1987), esp. ch. 3.

[88] For the late sixteenth-century position and attempts to increase the effective authority of the
crown see M. Lee, Jr, *John Maitland of Thirlstone and the Foundation of Stewart Despotism in Scotland*
(Princeton, 1959). For his views on the consequences of absentee government and the development of more institutionalised forms see Lee, *Government by Pen*, and *Road to Revolution*. Many of
the central arguments are summarised in Lee, 'James VI's government of Scotland after 1603',
Scottish Historical Review, 55 (1976), 41–53; Lee, 'Charles I and the end of conciliar government in
Scotland', *Albion*, 12 (1980–1), 315–36; Lee, 'Scotland and the "general crisis" of the seventeenth
century', *Scottish Historical Review*, 63 (1984), 136–54; and Lee, 'Scotland and the "general
crisis"', in R. A. Mason (ed.), *Scots and Britons: Scottish Political Thought and the Union of 1603*
(Cambridge, 1994), 41–57.

parliament or convention.[89] This prompted, in the late sixteenth century, attempts to revise the basis of assessment. Tax was raised from three separate sources: burghs, lay land and church benefices. The assessments of benefices and lay lands, however, were based on outdated, notional values which bore an inconsistent relationship to actual values. This was made the more unfortunate by changes in landholding. For example, many church lands were now held by feuars – tenants whose services to their lord had been commuted into a single cash payment (the feu). Feuars were not liable to tax, therefore, and this exposed their superiors to an increasing problem. The resolution of the problem was to establish the principle that a benefice holder unable to meet his tax demand could charge his vassal. But to do this, some more up-to-date value of the church lands had to be found. Similarly, teinds (tithes) which were previously exempt from taxation were brought within its scope, but again the basis for taxation was unclear and inconsistent. In practice, though, these many inequalities were quite welcome, since they imposed a political ceiling on tax demands to the double benefit of those underrated. Reform was not entirely successful in this period and once again the 1640s were important in the development of a more powerful Scottish state.[90]

The difference between the two periods lies, perhaps, in the source of the pressure for reform. Before 1603 the pressure came from the declining value of other revenues, especially the crown lands.[91] For the Covenanters it was war ('the need for troops was paramount'), and this was sufficient pressure to break through this rickety structure.[92] The covenanting revolution was important, then, in stimulating institutional change in Scotland. It was driven both by the demand for military mobilisation and by an assault on sin. The active government that these pressures produced led to the creation of a committee structure and a far greater intervention in local societies, a 'dynamic' that resulted in politicisation and polarisation in the Gaelic areas. It was driven by two of the pressures that were central to the development of the state in

[89] J. Goodare, 'Parliamentary taxation in Scotland, 1560–1603', *Scottish Historical Review*, 68 (1989), 23–52, at p. 23. Parliament was not a nugatory body. For example, the Lords of the Articles, who discussed business before putting it before parliament, provided a forum for discussion not simply a means of managing parliament. In so far as they were a means of management they reflect the strength rather than the weakness of the institution: Brown, *Kingdom*, pp. 16–20. For a particular example see J. Goodare, 'The parliament of 1621', *HJ*, 38 (1995), 29–51. For the Lords of the Articles see also Brown, 'Exercise of power', pp. 45–6.

[90] For tax reform see R. S. Rait, *The Parliaments of Scotland* (Glasgow, 1924), ch. 8, esp. pp. 495–6.

[91] Goodare, 'Taxation', p. 46.   [92] Ibid., p. 47.

England in this period: war and reformation.[93] Institutional change was marked during the Cromwellian occupation too, again driven by similar pressures. The conquest was defensive in origin, the Cromwellian re-gimes not holding a particular brief to reform and improve the Scots. However, the pressure to raise money and troops and to combat vice led, once again, to governmental intervention in local life. Attempts were made once more to introduce shire government along English lines, for example. English judges seem to have been less willing to countenance witch prosecutions than their Scottish predecessors, but much of the effort to expunge sin was expressed through indigenous institutions, in particular the Kirk sessions.[94]

These changes – the reduction in importance of private jurisdictions, the expanding claims of royal justice and administration, pressure for fiscal reform – suggest that the Scottish state was developing in ways analogous to some other European states. Feuing changed the relation-ship between lord and vassal, parliament secured a regular role in government and acted as a channel for the influence of an increasingly reconstituted aristocracy. And, although they continued to dominate Scottish society and political life, the aristocracy did so on the basis of a new relationship to the crown.[95] The relative weaknesses of the judicial and administrative powers of the justices were partly a consequence of the existence of other local jurisdictions, but also of the importance of the Kirk.

Alongside regularisation of government Scottish historians have dis-cerned something akin to the rise of the middling sort in England. The feuing of lands gave control of the land to a larger class of people and they profited from the price rise. Theirs was a commercial interest in the land, while their superiors' interest was jurisdictional. The ceding of

[93] For the governmental impact of the Covenanters see A. I. Macinnes, 'The Scottish constitution, 1638–1651. The rise and fall of oligarchic centralism', in J. S. Morrill (ed.), *The Scottish National Covenant in its British Context* (Edinburgh, 1990), 106–33; Macinnes, 'Scottish Gaeldom, 1638–1651: the vernacular response to the covenanting dynamic', in Dwyer, Mason and Murdoch (eds.), *New Perspectives*, 59–94; M. Lynch, *Scotland: A New History* (London, 1992), 252–3; E. M. Furgol, 'Scotland turned Sweden: the Scottish Covenanters and the military revolution, 1638–1651', in Morrill (ed.), *Covenant*, 134–54.

[94] For government in Cromwellian Scotland see Dow, *Cromwellian Scotland*; D. Stevenson, 'The effects of revolution and conquest on Scotland', in Mitchison and Roebuck (eds.), *Economy and Society*, 48–57; Stevenson, 'Cromwell, Scotland and Ireland', in J. Morrill (ed.), *Oliver Cromwell and the English Revolution* (London, 1990), 149–80; D. Hirst, 'The English republic and the meaning of Britain', in Bradshaw and Morrill (eds.), *British Problem*, 192–219, 300–14. For the importance of Kirk sessions see Smith, 'Sackcloth for the sinner'; and for Kirk sessions in a broader context see below, pp. 366–7.

[95] Goodare, 'Absolutist state'. For aristocratic power see Brown, *Kingdom*, pp. 33–47.

commercial control, however, had serious economic consequences, since the cash payments due from feuars were fixed. In the later sixteenth century Scotland experienced rapid inflation which steadily reduced the value of these cash payments. As the nobility coped with the effects of the declining value of these rents, and the pressures on spending created by increased taxation and the need for conspicuous consumption, feuars prospered. These effects were not felt on other estates where many rents were paid in kind and were therefore inflation-proof. Feuing, though, did create a prospering middling sort, some of whom began to assume the manners and status of lairds, and the rise of smallholders was not limited to the lowlands.[96] As a result, Scottish agriculture can no longer be represented as static and unchanging in the centuries prior to union and industrialisation. On the other hand, the extent of this change was limited by comparison with the English experience in this period and by comparison with what was to come in the later eighteenth century.[97] Accepting this reservation though, it seems clear that the balance of social relations was changing in Scotland prior to 1700.

The economic developments within agrarian society went alongside administrative developments in a way reminiscent of what we have seen in England and Wales. They were associated with the development of

---

[96] For the rise of the middling sort see Makey, *Church of the Covenant*, pp. 1–6. For feuing see M. H. B. Sanderson, *Scottish Rural Society in the Sixteenth Century* (Edinburgh, 1982); Sanderson, 'The feuing of Strathisla: a study of sixteenth-century social history', *Northern Scotland*, 2 (1974–5), 1–11. C. Madden, 'The feuing of Ettrick forest', *Innes Review*, 27 (1976), 70–84, shows how feuing in the fifteenth century later had disastrous effects. For the Highlands, see A. I. Macinnes, 'From clanship to commercial landlordism: landownership in Argyll from the seventeenth to the nineteenth century', *History and Computing*, 2 (1990), 176–81. For aristocratic indebtedness see K. M. Brown, 'Aristocratic finances and the origins of the Scottish revolution', *EHR*, 104 (1989), 46–87; Brown, 'Noble indebtedness in Scotland between the reformation and the revolution', *Historical Research*, 62 (1989), 260–75. For an account which acknowledges the significance of feuing but also gives greater emphasis to the period after 1690 in the rise of the middling sort see Smout, *Scottish People*, esp. pp. 127–8.

[97] For a measured view of the importance of agrarian change in the sixteenth and seventeenth centuries see T. M. Devine, *The Transformation of Rural Scotland: Social Change and the Agrarian Economy, 1660–1815* (Edinburgh, 1994), ch. 1; Devine, 'Social responses to agrarian "improvement": the highland and lowland clearances in Scotland', in Houston and Whyte (eds.), *Scottish Society*, 148–68; and Devine, 'The making of an industrial and urban society: Scotland 1780–1840', in R. Mitchison (ed.), *Why Scottish History Matters* (Edinburgh, 1991), 59–67. A broadly similar line is taken by Houston and Whyte, 'Introduction: Scottish society in perspective', in *Scottish Society*, 1–36. For the relative underdevelopment of Scottish agriculture in the Highlands see also A. Morrison, 'The question of Celtic survival or continuity in some elements of rural settlement in the Scottish highlands', in L. Laing (ed.), *Studies in Celtic Survival*, British Archaeological Reports, 37 (Oxford, 1977), 67–76. For the persistence of peasant farming in the north-east see I. Carter, 'Social differentiation in the Aberdeenshire peasantry, 1696–1870', *Journal of Peasant Studies*, 5 (1977), 48–65.

shire government to which reference has already been made, but also with the development of the Kirk. Kirk sessions offered a political resource for the middling sort and the impact of the Calvinists' 'obsessive concern' for all areas of human conduct served to wreak its 'silent havoc' on the balance of local social relations. 'The English justices were the antennae of the monarchy; James seems to have seen the Scottish elder in the same role.' The impact of Calvinist activism along with the development of more minor offices of administration and justice therefore constituted the second element of a 'silent revolution' in Scotland, in which the middling sort acquired greater political importance.[98] Although this was marked in the period before the covenanting revolution the subsequent development of administration and the continuing rise of the professions in Scotland meant that the rise of the middling sort occurred over the whole century.[99]

The period between the reformation and the Union of 1707 'was clearly of vital importance in the making of modern Scotland'. It saw a 'strengthening of royal authority and the associated development of Scotland's distinctive legal institutions', as well as the establishment and increasing influence of the reformed Kirk. It also saw the growth of education, the establishment of the poor laws, agrarian change and signs of early industrialisation.

And yet on the other hand, the same period witnessed Scotland's political marginalisation, the removal to London of the apex of the political and social order, and Scotland's eventual absorption as a junior partner in the larger political unit of the United Kingdom. Similarly Scotland was increasingly incorporated into a larger economic and social system in which the centre of gravity lay far to the south.[100]

But the development of Scottish institutions and the process of absorption into a British state were separate processes. In the period between

---

[98] Makey, *Church of the Covenant*, pp. 6–12, quotations at pp. 7, 11. For studies of the activities of particular sessions see J. Di Falco, 'Discipline and welfare in the mid-seventeenth century Scots Parish', *Records of the Scottish Church History Society*, 19 (1977), 169–83; and M. F. Graham, *The Uses of Reform: 'Godly Discipline' and Popular Behaviour in Scotland and Beyond, 1560–1610* (Leiden, 1996); and, for the later period, L. Leneman and R. Mitchison, 'Acquiescence and defiance of church discipline in early-modern Scotland', *Records of the Scottish Church History Society*, 25 (1993), 19–39. We should note that there were godly magistrates among the nobility too: K. M. Brown, 'In search of the godly magistrate in reformation Scotland', *Journal of Ecclesiastical History*, 40 (1989), 553–81.

[99] For a general account of the rise of the middling sort see Lynch, *Scotland*, pp. 247–62; and Lynch, 'Response: old games and new', *Scottish Historical Review*, 73 (1994), 47–63.

[100] K. E. Wrightson, 'Kindred adjoining kingdoms: an English perspective on the social and economic history of early modern Scotland', in Houston and Whyte (eds.), *Scottish Society*, 245–60, quotation at p. 250.

the Union of the Crowns and the Union of 1707 the Scottish aristocracy remained just that, while the political idea of Britain remained confused and lacking in broad appeal either in Scotland or England.[101] Those Scottish aristocrats who did adopt the manners current in the English court exacerbated their financial problems and alienated their inferiors in Scotland.[102]

There is enough here to suggest that a process of state formation was under way in Scotland independent of that in England. It drew on similar European developments but was expressed in distinctive ways, through institutions peculiar to Scotland. Certainly these developments were clearly in train before the Union of the Crowns and so these processes were not, straightforwardly, Anglicising. However, they did create the possibility (although not necessarily the likelihood) of coalescence. They built on values associated with Protestantism and were propagated in the English language. As a result the Anglophone, educated Scottish landowning class could have some common ground with their English counterparts. There was a British Protestant tradition on which proponents of union could draw.[103] It is equally true, however, that they could be in competition: the Scottish lawyers favoured civility but opposed union.[104] To a considerable extent, then, these were parallel developments to those in England, not an extension of them. The development of Scots law and of the poor law certainly occurred in response to influences common to, rather than emanating from, England. For example, we have noted many times the significance in England of a Calvinist vision of godly magistracy in pushing forward the bounds of government activity. The influence of the Kirk is hardly less important in Scottish political life.[105]

[101] For the failure of Anglicisation among the Scottish aristocracy see K. M. Brown, 'Courtiers and cavaliers: service, Anglicisation and loyalty among the Royalist nobility', in Morrill (ed.), *Covenant*, 155–92; Brown, 'The origins of a British aristocracy: integration and its limitations before the treaty of Union', in Ellis and Barber (eds.), *Conquest and Union*, 222–49; Brown, 'The Scottish aristocracy, Anglicisation and the court, 1603–1638', *HJ*, 36 (1993), 543–76; and Brown, 'The vanishing emperor: British kingship and its decline', in Mason (ed.), *Scots and Britons*, 58–87. The term 'Anglicisation' is, perhaps, inappropriate: Morrill, 'Fashioning', p. 26.

[102] D. Stevenson, 'The English devil of keeping state: élite manners and the downfall of Charles I in Scotland', in R. Mason and N. Macdougall (eds.), *People and Power in Scotland: Essays in Honour of T. C. Smout* (Edinburgh, 1992), 126–44; Brown, 'Aristocratic finances'.

[103] J. Dawson, 'Anglo-Scottish Protestant culture and integration in sixteenth century Britain', in Ellis and Barber (eds.), *Conquest and Union*, 87–114; R. Mason, 'The Scottish reformation and the origins of Anglo-British imperialism', in Mason (ed.), *Scots and Britons*, 161–86.

[104] For the legal lobby and the union see Levack, *Formation of the British State*, esp. ch. 3. See below, p. 370.

[105] For some stimulating reflections on these ambiguities, see A. H. Williamson, 'A patriot nobility?: Calvinism, kin-ties and civic humanism', *Scottish Historical Review*, 72 (1993), 1–21.

However, although the Scottish state was developing independently, the political lives of the two kingdoms were increasingly interconnected. These developments were not designed solely by Stuart monarchs, still less imposed by the English, but they were of use to the Stuarts who were increasingly identified in Scotland with the English. This became crucial when the regime identified itself explicitly with policies for which there was little local support. For example, Charles I launched a highly unpopular ecclesiastical policy and his revocation scheme exemplified measures which elaborated upon this broader process of unification and reorientation towards royal jurisdictions. Under the scheme all grants of church and crown lands made since 1540 were to be revoked, something which affected up to half the landed income in Scotland. The lands were not to be taken back, compensation was to be offered for losses that accrued and in fact most of the grants were simply to be confirmed. The intention was to enable a restoration of the value of teinds (tithes). It was a political disaster, however, because Charles refused to give such undertakings in advance of the surrender of the lands – instead he expected landowners simply to recognise that he had the power to do this.[106] The effect of these measures was ultimately to be disastrous in Scotland, England and Ireland. The Covenanting revolution helped to precipitate a crisis in all three kingdoms and was to lead, eventually, to conquest, military occupation and a concerted attempt to use state power to achieve social transformation. The restoration of the relatively loose Union of the Crowns in 1660 did not conceal the fact that the politics of the two kingdoms were inextricably linked. Charles II was less concerned than either James VI and I or Charles I had been to achieve a uniformity of ecclesiastical practice, but issues such as exclusion clearly reverberated in Scotland. English 'whigs' were so-named after a Scottish political position, of course.[107]

The fact that political life in the two kingdoms was closely interlinked did not mean that full integration was inevitable. Many Scots aristocrats took commissions in the British army, and they were to vote overwhelmingly for union in 1707.[108] The commercial arguments were complex, however. An English survey of Anglo-Scottish trade in the mid-1660s revealed that the balance was in favour of the Scots, contrary to

---

[106] For a concise description of the revocation scheme see A. Hughes, *The Causes of the English Civil War* (London, 1998), 36.   [107] Brown, *Kingdom*, ch. 6. Morrill, 'British problem', pp. 34–6.

[108] K. M. Brown, 'From Scottish lords to British officers: state building, elite integration and the army in the seventeenth century', in N. Macdougall (ed.), *Scotland and War, AD 79–1918* (Edinburgh, 1991), 133–69.

contemporary wisdom on the issue. This discovery may have proved decisive in firming up the resolution of the Council of Trade against a relaxation of the 'mercantilist' line being taken by the English, protecting English interests in Anglo-Scottish trade.[109] On the other hand, the failure of the Darien venture, an attempt by a Scottish trading company to establish a New World colony, while causing much resentment about the apparent neglect of Scottish trading interests, also served to illustrate how much better Scottish merchants might have fared within a British mercantile world. There was the basis for cooperation between a British executive and important groups within the Scottish political elite, therefore, but this was by no means complete. For example, tariff concessions were negotiated to protect the Scottish salt and coal producers suggesting that union was not in the direct interest of these two crucial industries.[110] Clearly the economic interests were not all in one direction. Commercial interest was important in the debate, although there is plenty of evidence of popular hostility to the English.[111] The Darien venture itself was understood in part as a means of protecting Scottish independence against the threat of the creation of a Universal Monarchy. The model was of a seaborne empire like that of the Portuguese or Dutch.[112] And, of course, built into the shape of the union that was made were the vested interests of other groups among Scotland's political elites – protection for its separate legal and religious institutions, for example.[113] Recent explanations for the acceptance of the union have

[109] D. Woodward, 'Anglo-Scottish trade and English commercial policy during the 1660s', *Scottish Historical Review*, 56 (1977), 153–74.

[110] C. A. Whatley, 'Salt, coal and the union of 1707: a revision article', *Scottish Historical Review*, 66 (1987), 26–45.

[111] For a measured account of the economic argument see T. C. Smout, 'The road to union', in G. Holmes (ed.), *Britain after the Glorious Revolution 1689–1714* (London, 1969), 176–96. For the limits of that explanation and an account of anti-English sentiment see M. Goldie, 'Divergence and union: Scotland and England, 1660–1760', in Bradshaw and Morrill (eds.), *British Problem*, 220–45, 314–16.

[112] D. Armitage, 'The Scottish vision of empire: intellectual origins of the Darien venture', in J. Robertson (ed.), *A Union for Empire: Political Thought and the British Union of 1707* (Cambridge, 1995), 97–118. For developments towards a Scottish empire see also Armitage, 'Making the empire British: Scotland in the Atlantic world 1542–1717', *PP*, 155 (1997), 34–63; and Armitage, 'Greater Britain: a useful category of historical analysis?', *American Historical Review*, 104 (1999), 427–45. For the only other attempt to establish a Scottish trading company in the Atlantic trades see R. Law, 'The first Scottish Guinea Company, 1634–9', *Scottish Historical Review*, 76 (1997), 185–202. Union with England could also be represented as a defence for Scotland against the threat of Universal Monarchy: J. Robertson, 'An elusive sovereignty: the course of the union debate in Scotland 1698–1707', in Robertson (ed.), *Union for Empire*, 198–227, and for Universal Monarchy see S. Pincus, 'The English debate over Universal Monarchy', ibid., 37–62.

[113] For the religious compromise see C. Kidd, 'Religious realignment between the restoration and the union', in Robertson (ed.), *Union for Empire*, 145–68. For the attitudes of two influential

tended to centre on such political considerations. For example, it has recently been suggested that the proposals derived from the need to manage the Scottish parliament more effectively.[114] That close political relations should lead to union in 1707 owes much to political contingency, therefore, and perhaps to political jobbery.[115] Similar apparent convergence between Dutch and English interests in the 1650s had led first to proposed union and then, within a year, to war.[116] On the other hand, the convergence does underline the extent to which Scottish social, economic and political life had been civilised, and that convergence can be understood in a wider European context. Scottish and English intellectuals lived in a larger European world.[117] The process of state formation in Scotland and the origins of the union with England and Wales, however, have separate explanations – there were two centres of civility in Britain, and its propagation was not simply a matter of 'Anglicisation'.

LOWLAND AND HIGHLAND IN SCOTLAND AND ENGLAND

As we have seen in the context of the feud, one effect of the regularisation of government in Scotland was to 'open a frontier' in the Scottish kingdom, an area of contest between these values and the values of Gaelic, or upland, Scotland. In these areas they were more clearly a matter of 'central will' against local practice. Here were issues on which lowland Scots and lowland English could come close to unity, and it is perhaps not surprising that the civilising of the margins of political authority received some prominence in the pro-union propaganda in the years around 1603. It has also been suggested that in response to rising population and prices, and expanding commercial opportunity,

lawyers, see B. P. Levack, 'Law, sovereignty and the union', in Mason (ed.), *Scots and Britons*, 213–37.
[114] D. Hayton, 'Constitutional experiments and political expediency, 1689–1725', in Ellis and Barber, *Conquest and Union*, 276–305.
[115] For a recent and characteristically vigorous version of the jobbery explanation see B. P. Lenman, 'Union, Jacobitism and enlightenment', in Mitchison, (ed.), *Why Scottish History Matters*, 48–58. Whatley inclines towards the same view: 'Salt, coal and the union'. Goldie offers a revealing account of one strand of the debate, revealing the political considerations that lay behind a rapid change in the mood of parliament between 1702–3 (a revolt against English rule) and the vote for union in 1707: Goldie, 'Divergence'. For a brief summary, again inclining towards a political explanation, see A. I. Macinnes, 'Early modern Scotland: the current state of play', *Scottish Historical Review*, 73 (1994), 30–46.
[116] For the oscillations in Anglo-Dutch policy see S. Groenveld, 'The English civil wars as the cause of the first Anglo-Dutch war, 1640–1652', *HJ*, 30 (1987), 541–66.
[117] R. L. Emerson, 'Scottish cultural change 1660–1710 and the union of 1707', in Robertson, *Union for Empire*, 121–44.

the parallels between the economic and social histories of England and Scotland are more marked than has usually been acknowledged.[118] Lordship in the Highlands and Ireland was eroded not just by government pressure, but by monetisation and the impact of the market economy. The more rapid disappearance in Ireland was a result of the greater intensity of both processes.[119] The intensification of royal authority offered a resource for Gaelic chiefs too, and the nature of their lordship was affected by their relationship to the power of the state. The Campbells, in particular, straddled two worlds and this is reflected in the invention of their genealogies. They continued to portray their lordship in terms of established Gaelic traditions, although in reality the basis of their power was being transformed.[120] The Covenanters' demands for money, men and ideological conformity led to polarisation within the clans and the emergence of political divisions based on ideological principle. As a result of such divisions clan chiefs became oriented towards Scottish national politics and this accelerated their assimilation with lowland landed society. New standards of consumption, and absenteeism, led to financial pressures and reorientation of attitudes towards the land. Increasingly the chiefs sought revenues rather than followers, and in this they were supported by less eminent figures in clan society.[121]

[118] Wrightson, 'Adjoining kingdoms'.

[119] For an overview see A. I. Macinnes, 'Crown, clans and fine: the "civilizing" of Scottish Gaeldom, 1587–1638', *Northern Scotland*, 13 (1993), 31–55. For economic change see R. Mitchison and P. Roebuck, 'Introduction', in Mitchison and Roebuck (eds.), *Economy and society*, 1–13, at 1–2. For the effects of commercialisation on Gaelic lordships in Scotland see Dodgshon, 'Redistributive exchange'; Dodgshon, 'Agricultural change and its social consequences in the southern uplands of Scotland, 1600–1780', in T. M. Devine and D. Dickson (eds.), *Ireland and Scotland 1600–1850: Parallels and Contrasts in Economic and Social Development* (Edinburgh, 1983), 46–59; Dodgshon, 'West highland and Hebridean settlement prior to crofting and the clearances: a study in stability or change?', *Society of Antiquaries of Scotland Proceedings*, 123 (1993), 419–38; Houston and Whyte, 'Introduction'; Devine, 'Social responses'; Macinnes, 'Clanship to commercial landlordism'. For a brief overview see T. M. Devine, *Clanship to Crofter's War: The Social Transformation of the Scottish Highlands* (Manchester, 1994), ch. 1; and for an account emphasising economic transformation rather than government action, I. Donnachie, 'Economy and society in the 17th century in the highlands', in L. Maclean (ed.), *The Seventeenth Century in the Highlands* (Inverness, 1986), 52–9. For Ireland see P. J. Duffy, 'The territorial organisation of Gaelic landownership and its transformation in County Monaghan, 1591–1640', *Irish Geography*, 14 (1981), 1–26; H. Morgan, 'The end of Gaelic Ulster: a thematic interpretation of events between 1534 and 1610', *Irish Historical Studies*, 26 (1988), 8–32.

[120] J. Dawson, 'The fifth Earl of Argyle, Gaelic lordship and political power in sixteenth-century Scotland', *Scottish Historical Review*, 67 (1988), 1–27; W. Gillies, 'The invention of tradition, highland-style', in A. A. Macdonald, M. Lynch and I. B. Cowan (eds.), *The Renaissance in Scotland: Studies in Literature, Religion, History and Culture Offered to John Durkan* (Leiden, 1994), 144–56. For the MacKenzies see F. J. Shaw, 'Landownership in the Western Isles in the seventeenth century', *Scottish Historical Review*, 56 (1977), 34–48, at p. 35.

[121] Macinnes, 'Scottish Gaeldom'. See also Macinnes, 'The impact of the civil wars and interregnum: political disruption and social change within Scottish gaeldom', in Mitchison and Roebuck (eds.), *Economy and Society*, 58–69; Shaw, 'Landownership'.

Changing patterns of social and political authority were interrelated and, both before 1650 and after 1660, did not really proceed from England in any meaningful sense. But they did help, increasingly, to define the 'Highland' problem of the Borders, Highlands and Islands.

In the years following the Union James oversaw a concerted attempt to pacify the Borders and the Highlands. Between 1606 and 1610 a Border commission brought decisive political and military commitment to bear, substantially achieving the transformation of the Borders into the Middle Shires. Many of the Grahams, the Border surname group most famously associated with disorder, were transplanted to Ireland, an unsuccessful policy but one which reflects the determination of government.[122] Similar policies were attempted in the Isles – a plantation of Gentleman Adventurers of Fife in 1598, for example. Once again it is evident that a common set of techniques existed to deal with what were perceived to be common problems. Plantation in the Highlands was unsuccessful, however, and instead the government sought to exercise authority through local noblemen. Thus, commissions of fire and sword were issued. Most notably, however, an expedition led by Lord Ochiltree in 1608 captured a number of chiefs who were taken to Edinburgh. Ultimately they agreed to the Statutes of Iona, which stand as something of a manifesto for the programme of civility – they epitomise a broader process by which the chiefs and their followers were to be reformed. They sought to regularise landlord–tenant relations; to tie clan chiefs to closer relations to the Scottish privy council; to promote churches; to encourage the education of elder sons; to discourage temporary marriages; and to restrict the import of alcohol and the movement of masterless men and itinerant bards. The importance of the Statutes of Iona has probably been exaggerated – this is but one episode in a much longer programme. They built, for example, on the extension to the Highlands in 1587 of the 'general bands', which made the chiefs directly responsible for the conduct of their followers. But this was a law and order policy congruent with the simultaneous attack on feuding and, as we will see, similar measures in Ireland.[123] An important feature of the statutes was that they were not hostile to the authority of

---

[122] R. T. Spence, 'The pacification of the Cumberland Borders, 1593–1628', *Northern History*, 13 (1977), 59–160, esp. pp. 110–14; Ellis, *Pale*, pp. 27–8.

[123] See Lee, 'James VI's government', pp. 49–53; Brown, *Kingdom*, pp. 91–2. For the more general process see Macinnes, 'Crown, clans and fine'; J. Goodare, 'The Statutes of Iona in context', *Scottish Historical Review*, 77 (1998), 31–57. For the Kirk in the Highlands see J. Kirk, 'The Kirk and the highlands at the reformation', *Northern Scotland*, 7 (1986), 1–22; Kirk, 'The Jacobean church in the highlands, 1567–1625', in MacLean (ed.), *Seventeenth-Century Highlands*, 24–51. For Jacobean policy in the Highlands see Lee, *Government by Pen*, esp. pp. 44–5, 75–6 and 81–2.

chiefs, in fact it made the chiefs responsible for the conduct of their followers.[124] Again, this bears some similarity to the policy, for example of surrender and regrant, which would have stabilised, rather than abolished, Gaelic lordships in Ireland.[125] The aggressive policies towards the Highlands after the restoration were an extension of the general air of menace produced by the government of Lauderdale. Highland lawlessness was a pretext rather than a cause of the introduction of garrisons, the establishment of the militia and the fairly ruthless use of law and bonds to quell disorder. In all this the chiefs were compliant, but the attack on the 'problem' served broader political purposes.[126]

The problem of the Borders was common to both England and Scotland, of course, and as we have already seen a similar process occurred on the English side. In England the need for security against the Scots had led to the delegation of royal authority to powerful local magnates. Underpaid by the crown in the sixteenth century, men such as Lord Dacre were forced to cultivate personal followings in order to wield authority. The result was that they came to appear 'over-mighty', and often became embroiled in local factional rivalries in a way wholly inconsistent with the ideals of disinterested magistracy propagated by the privy council. These conditions of life on the marches applied to about half the territories of the Tudor crown.[127] However, the development of these personal followings was, in itself, destabilising. On 1 April 1557 Thomas Wharton complained to the high sheriff and justices of the peace of Northumberland about their inaction in relation to an affray at Berwick in which the mayor was killed. He also reported rumours that bands of men were arming themselves in preparation for the sessions.[128] Writing to the Council in the North two weeks later he reported that attempts to take bonds from those involved had been unsuccessful. The summons 'they have disobeyed and not appeared accordingly, to the noe litle mervaile of the obedient subiects in these parts but have kept in great bands in armor together'. It had become

---

[124] Ibid., p. 80.   [125] For surrender and regrant see below, pp. 380–1.

[126] A. I. Macinnes, 'Repression and conciliation: the highland dimension 1660–1688', *Scottish Historical Review*, 64 (1986), 167–95.

[127] S. G. Ellis, 'A border baron and the Tudor state: the rise and fall of Lord Dacre of the North', *HJ*, 35 (1992), 253–77. For the medieval border see D. Hay, 'England, Scotland and Europe: the problem of the frontier', *TRHS*, 5th series, 25 (1975), 77–91. For an account of the longer history of the English clans, see R. Robson, *The Rise and Fall of the English Highland Clans: Tudor Responses to a Mediaeval Problem* (Edinburgh, 1989).

[128] HEH, HM 41954, p. 19. See also *APC, 1556–58, passim*. For fuller description of this feud see M. M. Meikle, 'Northumberland divided: anatomy of a sixteenth-century bloodfeud', *Archaeologia Aeliana*, 5th series, 19 (1991), 79–89.

clear that this was related to a feud between the Carrs and the Herons, and Giles Heron, treasurer of Berwick, was named as a second fatality. The Herons claimed that they had the support of the justices and their armed assailants had fled into Scotland.[129] Family loyalties were enmeshed with local office and justice difficult to secure because of the presence of the border. At the root of the feud lay a disputed inheritance, apparently, and in the conditions of Border life such disputes could easily escalate. It was feared that this 'perillous . . . seed' of malice and hatred being sown was 'like to take roote if the same be not hastilye mett withall & prevented by grudges and hatred growing upon the premises almost throughout the whole Countrye the most part of Gentlemen thereof being as it were divided into two parts'. This was especially dangerous given the sensitive state of relations with Scotland.[130] Sessions were cancelled, but still three gentlemen, including Sir John Forster, arrived with 250 armed men.[131] In the end, it seems, the parties were persuaded to pursue an arbitrated settlement before the queen's officers, which quietened the feud temporarily, but the instability of political life on the Borders is plain.[132]

This was an exceptional bloodfeud, for the length and consistency with which loyalties were sustained. It may also have reflected broader shifts in the politics of the region, a developing division between the old order of Percy adherents and a new gentry order of men dependent on direct crown patronage.[133] However, the insecurity of Border life more generally, arising from the threat of raids from Scotland, had led to the evolution of relations between Border magnates and their tenants based on protection and security. A characteristic, though very varied form of tenancy, 'tenant-right', seems to have been offered on preferential terms in return for the promise of military service, for example.[134] In

[129] HEH, HM 41954, p. 21.

[130] Justices of the peace for Northumberland to the Privy Council, 3 April 1557, HEH, HM 41954, pp. 25–9, quotation at p. 27.

[131] Justices of the peace for Northumberland to Wharton, 2 April 1557, HEH, HM 41954, pp. 30–2. For the behaviour and factional involvements of Forster, a notorious Elizabethan warden, see S. J. Watts with S. J. Watts, *From Border to Middle Shire: Northumberland 1586–1625* (Leicester, 1975), ch. 5; C. Cross, *The Puritan Earl: The Life of Henry Hastings, Third Earl of Huntingdon, 1536–1595* (London, 1966), ch. 6. Concern about his behaviour in the late 1580s was related to fears about the security of the border: HEH, HM 30881, fos. 45r–50v. His career is discussed in M. M. Meikle, 'A godly rogue: the career of Sir John Forster, an Elizabethan border warden', *Northern History*, 28 (1992), 126–63.   [132] HEH, HM 41954, pp. 32–5.

[133] Meikle, 'Anatomy'.

[134] R. W. Hoyle, 'Lords, tenants and tenant-right in the sixteenth century: four case studies', *Northern History*, 20 (1984), 38–63; Hoyle, 'An ancient and laudable custom: the definition and development of tenant-right in north-western England in the sixteenth century', *PP*, 116 (1987), 24–55. McDonnell disputes his claim that tenant-right was a recent invention: J. McDonnell, 'Antecedents of border tenant right', *Northern History*, 30 (1994), 22–30. The importance of

Cumberland, protection was offered by the surnames but this protection could come at a high cost to the tenantry. Agricultural productivity was low. Partible inheritance led to fragmentation of holdings and population pressure and arable cultivation was limited not just by geography but by the problem of security. The response to population pressure was therefore restricted to the extension of cultivation and this further destabilised the region by leading to disputes between surnames. By-employments were limited and the most important were reiving and blackmail. During the 1590s conditions worsened as international tensions added to the insecurities of Border life and population pressure resulted in further resort to reiving and blackmail.[135]

The instability and poverty of Border society was a product of the interconnection of political and economic influences. However, following the Union of the Crowns in 1603 'the Border problem melted like snow on the Cheviots in spring'.[136] In north Cumberland, the core of the problem on the English side, this was achieved by a number of means. Much of the initiative, however, rested on Cumbrian concern at the 'blight of lawlessness'.[137] Even the Grahams showed a degree of acquiescence. Building on this local feeling, the government undertook a concerted programme of pacification. The most recalcitrant offenders were executed, others (including the Grahams) transported or pressed for service in Ireland. The local nobility, anxious to increase estate revenues, implemented the government-inspired plan for agrarian improvement. The areas cleared were settled by lowland husbandmen and towns were founded in order to foster trade. Religion, education and apprenticeship were corollaries of all this. On the Scots side the methods entailed more force and less persuasion, but it was a similar programme, aimed at the transformation of a society. For example, the enforcement of primogeniture was an adjunct to the establishment of law and order.[138] Within four years of James's accession to the English throne

military service has been questioned by M. L. Bush, 'Tenant right under the Tudors: a revision revised', *Bulletin of the John Rylands Library*, 77/1 (1995), 161–88. See also Watts, *Border to Middle Shire*, pp. 70–1.

[135] R. T. Spence, 'The Graham clans and lands on the eve of the Jacobean pacification', *Transactions of the Cumberland and Westmorland Antiquarian and Archaeological Society*, 80 (1980), 79–102. This probably was a real deterioration, rather than just an increase in government concern. For transhumance see J. McDonnell, 'The role of transhumance in northern England', *Northern History*, 24 (1988), 1–17. The social context of raiding in the late medieval period is discussed by P. J. Bradley, 'Social banditry on the Anglo-Scottish border in the late middle ages', *Scotia*, 12 (1988), 27–43.

[136] A. Calder, *Revolutionary Empire: The Rise of the English-Speaking Empires from the Fifteenth Century to the 1780s* (London, 1981), 108.   [137] Spence, 'Pacification', p. 157.

[138] Ibid., esp. pp. 156–7.

the Cumberland Borders had been transformed. The old Border society was gone, largely unlamented. In its place came 'the provincial England of noble and gentry landowners and administrators and the Established Church, grafted onto the surviving surnames and their pastoral economy to form a new Border society on the pattern of the settled English shires'.[139] Cumberland did not become a model shire, of course. The progress of established religion remained slow and the region continued to support a highly organised horse-stealing business well past the Union of the Crowns.[140] None the less, Cumberland came to be recognisable as a variation on the general theme. Part of the success of this programme depended on the fact that the border disappeared. Scots Border commissioners co-operated with English Border officials and gentry in tackling Border crime.[141] The pacification continued by an amalgam of similar means.

In Northumberland, too, pacification came quickly, again through deportation and vigorous prosecution.[142] Here, the Border uplands were only one of three regions, regarded with some hostility by those living on the lowlands. The gentry of the lowlands, although drawing relatively poor incomes from relatively poor agriculture, were not unlike their fellows in other counties. They were poorly rather than un-educated and although there was a shortage of preachers the propagation of the Protestant faith had made some headway. The sense of the lawlessness of the Northumberland Borders was exaggerated by the lowland gentry for their own purposes and it seems that in the uplands the surnames had had their day before the 1590s. This was because belonging to a surname involved embroilment in feuds without offering full protection and security. The end of the Border, and with it the peculiarities of local government, led pretty quickly to a normalisation of local politics which came to centre instead around gentry faction. In Northumberland this did disrupt the administrative and legal activities of quarter sessions, however. Land values rose in areas previously subject to raids and by 1611 'the overwhelming majority of the inhabitants of Northumberland were as law-abiding and deferential towards those in authority as people in any part of England'.[143] Although Scots reivers continued to raid in

---

[139] Ibid., p. 160.

[140] S. M. Keeling, 'The reformation in the Anglo-Scottish border counties', *Northern History*, 15 (1979), 24–42; M. A. Clark, 'Reformation in the far north: Cumbria and the Church 1500–1571', *Northern History*, 32 (1996), 75–89; P. Edwards, *The Horse Trade of Tudor and Stuart England* (Cambridge, 1988), esp. pp. 135–9. For religious practice in the Cumberland uplands see also Spence, 'Graham lands', pp. 81–2.   [141] Spence, 'Pacification', p. 156.

[142] For the following see Watts, *Border to Middle Shire*.   [143] Ibid., p. 179.

Jacobean England, the very vigorous action of the Border commissioners seems to have had a rapid effect on crime levels and gentlemen
could make their careers by promoting order through quarter sessions.
Overall, then, the experience of Northumberland offers some support
for James's contention in 1607 that the Middle Shires were

> planted and peopled with Civilitie and riches: their Churches begin to bee
> planted, their doores now stand open, they feare neither robbing nor spoiling
> and where there was nothing before heard nor seen in those parts but blood-
> shed, oppressions, complaints and outcries, they now live every man peacably
> under his owne figgetree, and all their former cryes and complaints turned
> onely into prayers to God for their King under who they enjoy such ease and
> happy quitenesse.[144]

The fruits of Anglo-Scottish cooperation were being reaped before the
Union.[145] Looking at the Borders as whole Fraser traced the ending of
disorder, at least as it is recorded in the privy council registers and the
state papers, to 1611: 'it had ended almost overnight, in one murderous
decade at the start of the seventeenth century'.[146]

There were at least two centres of civility in Britain – the lowlands of
England and Scotland – and the associated programme of political and
tenurial reform could be attractive to elite groups at the margins of
crown dominions. The integration of the English and Scottish peripheries was not simply, or even mainly, a matter of coercion. The concerns
of those promoting civility in England and Scotland came together over
the Border problem and also in Ireland. Separating the development of
the Scottish state, and of Scottish civility, from the national question
reveals the extent to which the vision enunciated in the wake of the 1603
Union of the Crowns had been fulfilled. Inside or outside a union
eighteenth-century Lowlanders would have regarded their Highland
neighbours as barbarous.

[144] Quoted ibid., p. 157.
[145] D. L. W. Tough, *The Last Years of a Frontier: A History of the Borders in the Reign of Elizabeth* (Oxford,
1928), esp. pp. 264–78; Rae, *Frontier*, ch. 9 and esp. pp. 232–3.
[146] G. M. Fraser, *The Steel Bonnets: The Story of the Anglo-Scottish Border Reivers* (London, 1989), 376.

CHAPTER 9

London's provinces: state formation in the English-speaking Atlantic world

In Ireland and the American colonies, for different reasons, local elites did not provide the basis for civil government. In Ireland the attempt to foster a sister kingdom, dominated by an indigenous elite whose interests could be served through the Tudor or Stuart crown, was a failure. The principal stumbling block was the failure of the reformation, which in contemporary English thinking necessitated the creation of a securely Protestant elite. In America, colonies of white settlement sought to erect new social orders in the 'wilderness'. As these colonies developed they came to resemble modified versions of English culture, with social and political orders conceived and protected in similar ways. To that extent, the development of these settlements was similar to the development of the patriarchal state in England. And, as in England, these settlements were established within the shell of a developing imperial system, something which grew out of the English military revolution. The first section of this chapter considers the failure of the kingdom of Ireland; the second, the earliest stages of the development of the empire and of the American colonies. In this first phase of the development of the empire private initiative was extremely important, and the empire was certainly not the result of a concerted act of will. The third section briefly outlines the development of more coherent imperial oversight in the later seventeenth century, a development which built on the transformation of English fiscal-military resources in the 1640s.

THE FAILURE OF THE KINGDOM OF IRELAND

In Ireland a concerted attempt to create a sister kingdom foundered on the failure of the reformation, which put what turned out to be an insurmountable obstacle in the way of coalescence. The natural gov-

379

ernors in Ireland, although clearly tempted by features of the Tudor political order, were increasingly alienated by religious difference and, ultimately, were elbowed aside by incomers. None the less, during the sixteenth century, in general, the attempt to foster the development of a civil society in Ireland proceeded by reform rather than conquest.

In Ireland the authority of the early Tudors depended on the cooperation of leading Gaelic chiefs and of the community of Old English – descendants of the English settlers of the middle ages. Here, however, coalescence failed, for both groups were unmoved by the Protestant reformation and Gaeldom in particular was resistant to the new standard of civility. As a consequence, attempts at closer government became increasingly associated with moral and religious claims quite alien to much of the population of Ireland. A solution to this was perceived to lie in plantation, an ambitious project to remake Irish society in a better image. Thus, although there were always elite groups in Ireland willing to accommodate themselves to royal authority, these mutualities of interest are less remarked upon than episodes of vigorous and, ultimately, brutal intervention. This intervention increasingly aimed at the creation of a new elite, more suitable for the exercise of civil governance than the Gaelic and Old English elites. This marked the Tudor failure in Ireland.

In 1541 Henry VIII was declared king of Ireland and this, it has been suggested, represented a real change in the attitude of the crown. Government would no longer proceed through the loose association with the Kildare magnates, but a programme of civil and governmental reform would be undertaken, bringing to the Irish the benefits of Tudor rule. In this, the crown had potential allies in the inhabitants of the pale, the area of secure crown authority around Dublin. Henceforth Tudor rule was not to be achieved by conquest but by 'constructing a model constitution in Ireland through the gradual introduction of the same legal, social and political institutions that had shaped England into a stable and orderly polity'.[1] The preferred method was, then, to secure the cooperation of existing elites in transforming the basis of political authority in Ireland, and this was not a forlorn hope. Many Gaelic lords entered surrender and regrant agreements, surrendering their land titles which were to be regranted so that the lands were held from the Tudor

[1] See B. Bradshaw, *The Irish Constitutional Revolution of the Sixteenth Century* (Cambridge, 1979); Bradshaw, 'Cromwellian reform and the origins of the Kildare rebellion, 1533–34', *TRHS*, 5th series, 27 (1977), 69–93; C. Brady, 'The decline of the Irish kingdom', in M. Greengrass (ed.), *Conquest and Coalescence: The Shaping of the State in Early Modern Europe* (London, 1991), 94–115, p. 96.

crown and conformed to English law. Chiefs were attracted to such agreements because secure title offered certainty about their rights to land and over their tenantry. Tenants, for their part, were grateful for a formal limitation on the collection of military obligations, known collectively as 'coign and livery'. But the attempt to feudalise relationships in this way cut across other aspects of Gaelic practice, notably partible inheritance and tanistry (means of deciding succession to chiefdoms other than by primogeniture). In place of these practices it sought to promote political stability by insisting on primogeniture. It was this, rather than the assertion of royal authority, that prompted resistance.

Of course, failing effective cooperation, the exercise of force was the alternative. This is the fundamental tension in the discussion of Irish history, between those accounts emphasising attempts to create a kingdom and those which emphasise the colonial experience following from conquest and colonisation.[2] During the 1540s and 1550s, in response to political problems, garrisons were established in the Gaelic midlands. This pacification was associated also with settlement – the so-called Laois–Offaly plantation. Meanwhile, the programme of surrender and regrant was accompanied by encouragement to adopt English language, dress and manners and attempts to introduce shire government represented the effort to remake Irish society in an English image.[3] This strategy, of settlement, was further enabled by the insistence on legal formality in landholding. Support in Ireland was fostered among Old English inhabitants of the pale who favoured civil reform and who could also hope to build up estates by testing legal title and buying up forfeited lands. Thus, the introduction of English legal practices was an opportunity not just for new immigrants but for others among the Irish population. One of the principal sources of support for civil reform in

---

[2] For influential contributions to this debate see K. S. Bottigheimer, 'Kingdom and colony: Ireland in the westward enterprise 1536–1660', in K. R. Andrews, N. P. Canny and P. E. H. Hair (eds.), *The Westward Enterprise: English Activities in Ireland, the Atlantic, and America 1480–1650* (Liverpool, 1978), 45–64; N. Canny, *Kingdom and Colony: Ireland in the Atlantic World 1560–1800* (Baltimore, 1988); J. Ruane, 'Colonialism and the interpretation of Irish historical development', in M. Silverman and P. H. Gulliver (eds.), *Approaching the Past: Historical Anthropology Through Case Studies* (New York, 1992), 293–323; H. Morgan, 'Writing up early modern Ireland', *HJ*, 31 (1988), 701–11; M. Perceval-Maxwell, 'Ireland and the monarchy in the early Stuart multiple kingdom', *HJ*, 34 (1991), 279–95. For an attempt to alter the terms of the debate see C. Brady and R. Gillespie (eds.), *Natives and Newcomers: Essays on the Making of Irish Colonial Society 1534–1641* (Dublin, 1986).

[3] G. A. Hayes-McCoy, 'The royal supremacy and ecclesiastical revolution, 1534–47', in T. W. Moody, F. X. Martin and F. J. Byrne (eds.), *A New History of Ireland*, III, *Early Modern Ireland 1534–1691* (Oxford, 1978), 39–68, esp. pp. 48–52; Hayes-McCoy, 'Conciliation, coercion, and the Protestant reformation, 1547–71', ibid., 69–93, esp. pp. 76–9.

Ireland, in fact, was the Old English community, marked out by its loyalty to royal authority in Ireland.[4]

In some areas of Ireland the problem was not so much the introduction of these practices, but their revival. Elizabethan pundits were often concerned that lords of Anglo-Norman descent had become Gaelicised. In this there was some justification, and modern historians tend to discuss Gaelic and Gaelicised Ireland together. The waning of Anglo-Norman influence in the later middle ages had led to a Gaelic revival which had embraced Anglo-Norman lords. By the later sixteenth century it was being suggested that the means by which the Anglo-Norman practices could be revived was through provincial presidencies. In the 1560s, under the Sussex administration, these aspirations were expressed in a fairly coherent programme. Sussex oversaw the completion of the Laois–Offaly plan, the desire to establish presidencies and a concerted attempt to stabilise the Gaelic chiefdoms.[5]

In this latter respect his principal target was Shane O'Neill, who had assumed the earldom of Tyrone according to Gaelic practice rather than by primogeniture. The military commitment to confront O'Neill imposed financial costs on the Pale which were met without resort to parliament and this led to resistance. The Old English leaders, offended by the financial measures, appealed over the head of the governor, directly to the court. This undermined, fatally, the reforming initiatives not just of Sussex but also those of his successors, Sidney and Perrot. By this time the attempt to promote civil government through existing local elites was facing increasingly complex problems. Surrender and regrant suited lords, elder sons and tenants, and to some extent built on tendencies already observable in Gaelic chiefdoms. But they acted against the interests of younger sons and the mercenary and professional soldiers who profited from tanistry and coign and livery. Thus, Shane O'Neill could find allies in resisting the measures.[6]

---

[4] Changes in landholding in Ireland in the sixteenth century occurred by a variety of means, piecemeal and to the benefit of a variety of ethnic groups: see R. Loeber, *The Geography and Practice of English Colonisation in Ireland from 1534 to 1609*, Irish Settlement Studies, 3 (Dublin, 1991). For the attitude of the palesmen see C. Brady, *The Chief Governors: The Rise and Fall of Reform Government in Tudor Ireland, 1536–1588* (Cambridge, 1994), esp. ch. 6; and Brady, 'Conservative subversives: the community of the pale and the Dublin administration 1556–86', in P. J. Corish (ed.), *Radicals, Rebels and Establishments* (Belfast, 1985), 11–32.

[5] For the presidencies see N. P. Canny, *The Elizabethan Conquest of Ireland: A Pattern Established 1565–76* (Hassocks, 1976), ch. 5; B. Cunningham, 'Native culture and political change in Ireland, 1580–1640', in Brady and Gillespie (eds.), *Natives and Newcomers*, 148–70, 229–32; L. Irwin, 'The Irish provincial presidencies: 1569–1672', *Stair* (1980), 19–21; and Tremayne, cited above pp. 342–3.

[6] For Shane O'Neill's rising see Hayes-McCoy, 'Conciliation, coercion', pp. 79–86. For the palesmen see Brady 'Irish kingdom', pp. 107–8.

At the same time, it was clear by the 1570s that the progress of Protestantism in Ireland was slow. After 1570, most historians would agree, Catholics were a minority in England but at that date reformation had made little progress among the Gaelic, Gaelicised or Old English populations. It has been suggested that the reformation down to 1547, while not particularly popular in Ireland, was not fatally divisive. Religious reform had some supporters in the Pale and reactions to the dissolution can be understood in secular terms relating to concerns about the distribution of the spoils. The royal supremacy was not unpopular. Thereafter, however, the promotion of reform was associated with coercion rather than persuasion, and this gradually alienated more and more of the Old English and Gaelic population.[7] The date for the failure of reform has, subsequently, been pushed further back. Elizabethan conquest was not followed by a consistent policing effort or by a sufficient effort at evangelisation. The counter-reformation arrived at the end of the sixteenth century and Protestant success was a possibility until then at least.[8] From the 1590s, however, there was a polarisation of Ireland's religious life; as the second reformation took hold in the Protestant church the influence of Calvinist theology led to the definition of the Catholics in Ireland as not simply unreformed but beyond reformation. There was an associated tendency for Protestantism to become more inward looking, abandoning evangelisation. At the same time, the counter-reformation mission enjoyed much more success among the populations ignored or poorly catered for by the Protestant church.[9] An important difference between the two reform efforts was the willingness of the Catholic church to use Gaelic in order to propagate its message, and this is one plausible explanation for the difference between the fate of reform in Wales and Ireland. In Ireland the generally approved strategy of the use of the vernacular to

[7] B. Bradshaw, 'The Edwardian reformation in Ireland, 1547–1553', *Archivium Hibernicum*, 34 (1977), 83–99; and Bradshaw, 'Sword, word and strategy in the reformation in Ireland', *HJ*, 21 (1978), 475–502. See also K. S. Bottigheimer, 'The reformation in Ireland revisited', *JBS*, 15/2 (1976), 140–9.

[8] N. Canny, 'Why the reformation failed in Ireland: *Une question mal posée*', *Journal of Ecclesiastical History*, 30 (1979), 423–50. His suggestion that the reformation did not fail until the early nineteenth century has not commanded general acceptance. The chronology suggested by Bottigheimer represents the rough consensus: 'The failure of the reformation in Ireland: *Une question bien posée*', *Journal of Ecclesiastical History*, 36 (1985), 196–207. For the failure of evangelisation see S. G. Ellis, 'Economic problems of the church: why the reformation failed in Ireland', *Journal of Ecclesiastical History*, 41 (1990), 239–65.

[9] A. Ford, 'The Protestant reformation in Ireland', in Brady and Gillespie (eds.), *Natives and Newcomers*, 50–74, 219–21; P. Kilroy, 'Protestantism in Ulster, 1610–1641', in B. Mac Cuarta (ed.), *Ulster 1641: Aspects of the Rising* (Belfast, 1993), 24–36, 192–5; Bottigheimer, 'Failure'. For the counter-reformation see C. Lennon, 'The counter-reformation in Ireland 1542–1641', in Brady and Gillespie (eds.), *Natives and Newcomers*, 75–92, 221–4.

promote reform was in tension with a perception that Gaelic was a language of treachery and deceit.[10]

As a result of the failure of the reformation in Ireland it was, by the early seventeenth century, an unusual place by European standards. It represented a major exception to the general rule that the religion of the populace should be the religion of the ruler. In practice, the tension was not fatal, because Catholicism could still be reconciled to loyalty to the crown (as in England, in fact). That 'Gallican' position was encouraged by some among the counter-reformation missionaries.[11] But the emergence of this religious divide compounded the alienation of the Old English, previously the natural allies of reform and royal authority. They remained loyal, but were increasingly resentful of the costs of establishing order by military means and were excluded from public office as the government turned to new, Protestant, settlers.[12] By the mid-Elizabethan period the reform effort was confronting increasingly intractable problems. The failure of reform prompted rebellion which drew the English crown into more expensive and intrusive solutions to the problem of governing Ireland: conquest and colonisation. The failure to establish English norms of political behaviour helped to prompt the Fitzgerald rebellion of 1579. The earl of Desmond joined

---

[10] For the intermittent use of Gaelic to propagate Protestantism, and the comparison with Wales see M. Mac Craith, 'The Gaelic reaction to the reformation', in S. G. Ellis and S. Barber (eds.), *Conquest and Union: Fashioning a British State, 1485–1625* (London, 1995), 139–61; C. Brady, 'Comparable histories?': Tudor reform in Wales and Ireland', ibid., 64–86; B. Bradshaw, 'The Tudor reformation and revolution in Wales and Ireland: the origins of the British problem', in B. Bradshaw and J. Morrill (eds.), *The British Problem c. 1534–1707: State Formation in the British Archipelago* (London, 1996), 39–65, 281–4. For attitudes towards Gaelic see Mac Craith, 'Gaelic reaction', p. 140; B. Mac Cuarta, 'A planter's reaction to Gaelic culture: Sir Matthew de Renzy, 1577–1634', *Irish Economic and Social History*, 20 (1993), 1–17, at pp. 11–13; for the later seventeenth century see T. C. Barnard, 'Protestants and the Irish language, c. 1675–1725', *Journal of Ecclesiastical History*, 44 (1993), 243–72. Obviously there is more to the comparison with Wales than the use of the vernacular. For a full treatment see G. Williams, *Wales and the Reformation* (Cardiff, 1997). Gaelic was used in Scottish evangelisation too: P. Jenkins, 'The Anglican church and the unity of Britain: the Welsh experience, 1560–1714', in Ellis and Barber (eds.), *Conquest and Union*, 115–38, esp. 122–4; Mac Craith, 'Gaelic reaction', pp. 140–44; V. E. Durkacz, *The Decline of the Celtic Languages: A Study of Linguistic and Cultural Conflicts in Scotland, Wales and Ireland from the Reformation to the Twentieth Century* (Edinburgh, 1983), 9–14. It was also used by Irish priests seeking converts to Catholicism in the Scottish Highlands: Macinnes, 'Catholic recusancy and the penal laws, 1603–1707', *Records of the Scottish Church History Society*, 23 (1987), 27–63, at pp. 30–1.

[11] J. Bossy, 'Catholicity and nationality in the north European counter-reformation', in S. Mews (ed.), *Religion and National Identity*, Studies in Church History, 18 (Oxford, 1982), 285–96. See also C. Ryan, 'Religion and state in seventeenth-century Ireland', *Archivium Hibernicum*, 33 (1975), 122–32; Mac Craith, 'Gaelic reaction', esp. pp. 154–7.

[12] Brady, *Governors*, ch. 6; Brady, 'Conservative subversives'; Canny, *Kingdom*, ch. 2; A. Clarke, 'Colonial identity in early seventeenth-century Ireland', in T. W. Moody (ed.), *Nationality and the Pursuit of Independence* (Belfast, 1978), 57–71.

the rebellion and in doing so appealed to religion as a justification. This goes some way to explaining the prevarication of other Irish leaders and the determination of the English response. Military defeat led to plantation on a larger scale in Munster – the heartland of Desmond's support.[13] Conquest led to financial costs and the introduction of new settlers, a potential threat to existing interests in Ireland.

The response to English reform and English force was not straightforward, therefore. The Old English, as we have seen, lost influence in government but remained loyal despite their Catholicism. In Gaelic Ireland there was no unified response either. Although some historians have found evidence in Bardic literature of a Gaelic rejection of alien authority and intrusion into Irish lands, this does not appear to have been a consensual position. The work of other poets reflects more measured responses, including the assimilation of English officeholding and Protestant virtue as qualities worthy of praise.[14] Even those poets who seem to have had a 'nationalist' viewpoint apparently abandoned resistance in favour of accommodation.[15] Of course, political relations within Gaeldom were not stable and the prospects of a pan-Gaelic alliance remote. It is also clear that, during the sixteenth and seventeenth centuries, divisions within Gaeldom were increasing under the impact of the reformation and the extension of state authority both in Ireland and Scotland.[16]

By the Elizabethan period, then, the means by which government operated in Ireland were complicated by the failure of the Old English

---

[13] For the Fitzgerald rebellion see Hayes-McCoy, 'Conciliation, coercion', pp. 86–91.

[14] For the rejection, see B. Bradshaw, 'Native reaction to the westward enterprise: a case-study of Gaelic ideology', in Andrews, Canny and Hair (eds.), *Westward Enterprise*, 65–80. For the ambiguities of reactions see N. Canny, 'The formation of the Irish mind: religion, politics and Gaelic Irish literature, 1580–1750', *PP*, 95 (1982), 91–116; M. O'Dowd, 'Gaelic economy and society', in Brady and Gillespie (eds.), *Natives and Newcomers*, 120–47, 226–9; M. O Riordan, 'The native Ulster mentalité as revealed in the Gaelic sources', in Mac Cuarta (ed.), *Ulster, 1641*, 66–91, 200–5; Cunningham, 'Native culture'; Mac Craith, 'Gaelic reaction'; Gillespie, *Ulster*, pp. 150–2. Gaelic landowners seem to have adopted some of the values of English estate management too: P. J. Duffy, 'The territorial organisation of Gaelic landownership and its transformation in County Monaghan, 1591–1640', *Irish Geography*, 14 (1981), 1–26.

[15] Bradshaw, 'Native reaction'.

[16] See, for example, A. I. Macinnes, 'Gaelic culture in the seventeenth century: polarization and assimilation', in Ellis and Barber (eds.), *Conquest and Union*, 162–94; and Macinnes, 'The impact of the civil wars and interregnum: political disruption and social change within Scottish gaeldom', in R. Mitchison and P. Roebuck (eds.), *Economy and Society in Scotland and Ireland 1500–1939* (Edinburgh, 1988), 58–69. For religious and political divisions within Scottish Gaeldom see E. M. Furgol, 'The highland Covenanter clans, 1639–1651', *Northern Scotland*, 7 (1987), 119–31; A. F. B. Roberts, 'The role of women in Scottish Catholic survival', *Scottish Historical Review*, 70 (1991), 129–50; and Roberts, 'Aspects of highland and lowland Catholicism on Deeside', *Northern Scotland*, 10 (1990), 19–30.

or the Gaelic lords to make common cause with the crown. On the other hand, the alternative, expensive conquest and the introduction of settlers, the New English, further exacerbated tensions.[17] In general, however, there was a trend towards more interventionist government. It has been argued that it is possible to isolate shifts of policy such as a move from robe to sword in the government of Ireland, or of a decisive switch towards conquest in the 1560s and 1570s. However, it has proved difficult to isolate such clear turning points and Brady has shifted attention towards the structural difficulties facing the agents of the English crown, the viceroys. Developments in Irish government represented a negotiation between vested interests there – the Old English, the Dublin administration and Gaelic lords – and the English government. If the viceroy was not amenable to their pressure these groups appealed over his head to the English court (there was no Irish court to which such appeal could be made). Viceroys, appointed by the English crown, had no local power base but did have extensive executive authority. A paradox of Irish government in this period was, therefore, that viceroys were very vulnerable to attacks on their authority at the English court, rather than in Ireland. Later viceroys came to defend themselves from this by developing programmes of reform that would impress at home, even though such programmes cost them support in Ireland. But at the same time the temptation to develop support among the communities in Ireland often cut against the consistent pursuit of such programmes. The changing face of English government in Ireland did not reflect a switch from soft to hard government so much as a modulation of the priorities facing all viceroys. As a result of these complexities, and the continued failure of reform, viceroys tended to become more concerned with security, achieved by conquest and settlement, and less concerned with reform. In any case, overall, reform failed. Viceroys had 'aimed to fashion a kingdom of Ireland, and had laid instead the foundations of a colony'.[18]

There was, in the later sixteenth century, an escalation of rebellion. But this was not a measure of the success of Elizabethan conquest so

---

[17] Brady, *Governors*, ch. 6.

[18] Ibid. See also Brady, 'Court, castle and country: the framework of government in Tudor Ireland', in Brady and Gillespie (eds.), *Natives and Newcomers*, 22–49, 217–19, quotation at p. 49. See also Brady and Gillespie, 'Introduction', ibid., 11–21, 215–16; Brady, 'England's defence and Ireland's reform: the dilemmas of the Irish viceroys, 1541–1641', in Bradshaw and Morrill (eds.), *British Problem*, 89–117, 287–93. This is a critique of earlier work by Bradshaw and Canny. See especially Bradshaw, 'Robe and sword' and Canny, *Elizabethan Conquest*. The differences of approach between Bradshaw and Canny are reviewed by H. Pawlisch, *Sir John Davies and the Conquest of Ireland: A Study in Legal Imperialism* (Cambridge, 1985), ch. 1.

much as an indication of the complexities of reform.[19] The O'Neill rebellion leading to the outbreak of the Nine Years War is a good illustration of this. Hugh O'Neill was, in some ways, a good prospect for royal authority. His claim to the earldom of Tyrone, which he made good in 1585, was recognised by the crown because it came through his father Matthew, who had been excluded by Shane in contravention of a surrender and regrant agreement. Hugh's succession, therefore, was a potential vindication of primogeniture over other forms of succession. He had spent much of his youth in wardship in England and was familiar with the Protestant settler interest. His ambition appears to have been the creation of a palatine jurisdiction, something to which the English crown should not necessarily have been hostile. However, in pursuing this ambition he upset not just the O'Neills but also minor officials whom he sought to exclude from local influence. As this dispute escalated he appealed to Catholic sentiment (rather unconvincingly to some, it seems) and to Spain. In pressing the nuclear button in this way, however, he ensured that a vigorous reaction would proceed from London. Eventual military victory was followed by a comprehensive attempt at settlement.[20] In general, rebellion in sixteenth-century Ireland was less a nationalist rejection of alien rule than an expression of magnate politics akin to the rebellions of Tudor England. It was supported by personal followings and informed by ideals of honour emphasising personal ties rather than the virtues of loyalty to the state.[21]

The crucial event in the end of Gaelic Ulster was the flight of the earls in 1607, because this created the power vacuum which was filled by Protestant settlement. The reasons for the flight of the earls in 1607 are not entirely clear. They seem to have continued to plot against the crown, seeking and receiving Spanish support, and were probably right to fear retribution from London. It was a political decision taken as a temporary expedient, but it was to have lasting effects by paving the way to a further programme of plantation.[22] It was this, rather than government pressure, commercialisation or religious change that signalled the

---

[19] See Brady, 'Irish kingdom', pp. 106–10; and Brady and Gillespie, 'Introduction', pp. 12–15.

[20] N. Canny, 'Early modern Ireland, *c.* 1500–1700', in R. F. Foster (ed.), *The Oxford Illustrated History of Ireland* (Oxford, 1992), 88–133, esp. 112–13.

[21] See, for example, Bradshaw, 'Wales and Ireland', pp. 61–2. For honour codes see W. Palmer, 'That "Insolent Liberty": honor, rites of power and persuasion in sixteenth-century Ireland', *Renaissance Quarterly*, 46 (1993), 308–27. For the English comparison see M. E. James, *Society, Politics and Culture: Studies in Early Modern England* (Cambridge, 1986), chs. 8, 9.

[22] J. McCavitt, 'The flight of the earls, 1607', *Irish Historical Studies*, 29 (1994), 159–73, and the references there. For the plantation, McCavitt, 'The political background to the Ulster plantation, 1607–1620', in Mac Cuarta (ed.), *Ulster, 1641*, 7–23, 188–92.

end of Gaelic Ulster. Until that point, the Gaelic chiefdoms had adapted quite successfully to the pressures of military and political change.[23] By 1630, however, 34,000 settlers had been planted in Ireland to secure the Protestant interest, a goal pursued also by the use of church property to further Protestantism. But this movement of population was not simply an act of state, it drew on existing patterns of migration, and the effects of plantation depended partly on the nature of the migration that it encouraged.[24] Gaelic legal codes were discountenanced and titles to land were only recognised if they were proved good in common law. Alongside the religious and legal instruments of civility went administrative and political regularisation – county divisions, sheriffs, justices of the peace and assizes. And, of course, garrisons. All this signalled 'a process of centralization which was pursued relentlessly by the government in Ireland after its military victory'. This was reinforced by martial law, imposed by provosts marshal and a strict application of the Oath of Supremacy.[25] These new disciplinary measures were unpopular with the Old English but, in general, leaders of Gaelic and Old English communities sought to work within the system. In Munster, Catholics served as justices of the peace and sheriffs.[26] But in a sense the spread of these forms of dispute resolution were a means of subduing Ireland, more effective and more durable than force of arms. English law was

[23] H. Morgan, 'The end of Gaelic Ulster: a thematic interpretation of events between 1534 and 1610', *Irish Historical Studies*, 26 (1988), 8–32. See also M. O'Dowd, 'Land and lordship in sixteenth- and early seventeenth-century Ireland', in Mitchison and Roebuck (eds.), *Economy and Society*, 17–26.

[24] For this perspective on plantation see N. Canny (ed.), *Europeans on the Move: Studies on European Migration 1500–1800* (Oxford, 1994), esp. chs. 4–6; Canny, *Kingdom*, ch. 3; Canny, 'Dominant minorities: English settlers in Ireland and Virginia, 1550–1650', in A. C. Hepburn (ed.), *Minorities in History* (London, 1978), 51–69; Canny, 'Migration and opportunity: Britain, Ireland and the New World', *Irish Economic and Social History*, 12 (1985), 7–32; P. Robinson, *The Plantation of Ulster: British Settlement in an Irish Landscape 1600–1670* (Dublin, 1984); and for Munster, M. Mac Carthy-Morrogh, *The Munster Plantation: English Migration to Southern Ireland 1583–1641* (Oxford, 1986), esp. pp. 279–81. One component of the failure of efforts to create a new society in the later seventeenth century was a broader shift in the patterns of migration and opportunity available to English, Scots and Welsh: T. C. Barnard, 'New opportunities for British settlement: Ireland, 1650–1700', in *The Oxford History of the British Empire*, I, N. Canny (ed.), *The Origins of Empire: British Overseas Enterprise to the Close of the Seventeenth Century* (Oxford, 1998), 309–27.

[25] N. Canny, 'Irish resistance to empire? 1641, 1690, 1798', in L. Stone (ed.), *An Imperial State at War: Britain from 1689–1815* (London, 1994), 288–31, quotation at p. 292. For legal reform and the development of local administration see J. McCavitt, '"Good Planets in Their Several Spheares" – the establishment of the assize circuits in early seventeenth-century Ireland', *Irish Jurist*, new series, 24 (1989), 248–78; R. Gillespie, 'Harvest crises in early seventeenth-century Ireland', *Irish Economic and Social History*, 11 (1984), 5–18, at pp. 14–15; Brady, 'Court, castle and country', pp. 38–40. For the role of the presidencies in fostering the resort to law see Irwin, 'Irish presidencies', esp. p. 20. The shallow roots of (or perhaps hostility to) the English legal system helps to explain the absence of witch trials in Ireland, despite the evident presence of witch-beliefs there: E. C. Lapoint, 'Irish immunity to witch-hunting, 1534–1711', *Eire-Ireland*, 27 (1992), 76–92.   [26] Mac Carthy-Morrogh, *Munster*, pp. 268–72.

deliberately fostered in this way, justified by the doctrine that conquest had made English law prior. Native practices and rights were recognised only where they did not conflict with common law principles. This doctrine was subsequently applied in a variety of colonial contexts.[27]

Even though Stuart policy turned increasingly to plantation, it was still possible for aspects of normal social and political relations to develop. Relations between native and newcomer in the planted areas were not necessarily hostile. Irish landowners adopted English dress, manners and housing, and in Munster these developments gave it the appearance of a 'slightly raffish county on the English Borders'.[28] In Ulster, too, natives came to accommodations with the newcomers and 'English' culture spread there as well, involving the coexistence of both native and newcomers' customs.[29] Looked at in one way this represented the failure of plantation to remake society, but it also represented the development of means of coexistence.[30] Settlers did not create model villages and seem to have had relatively complex relationships with the natives. Their suitability as agents of moral reform rather depended on their own background, and the experience varied from place to place.[31]

[27] Pawlisch, *Sir John Davies*.

[28] M. Mac Carthy-Morrogh, 'The English presence in early seventeenth-century Munster', in Brady and Gillespie (eds.), *Natives and Newcomers*, 171–90, 230–4, quotation at p. 190. By 1641 Munster was developing commercial and cultural links with south-west England: Mac Carthy-Morrogh, *Munster*. Close connections developed with Wales too: 'It is clear that as in the days of the Celtic saints, the Irish sea in the eighteenth century was a pathway rather than a moat': P. Jenkins, 'Connections between the landed communities of Munster and South Wales, *c.* 1660–1780', *Journal of the Cork Historical and Archaeological Society*, 84 (1979), 95–101, quotation at p. 101.

[29] Gillespie, *Ulster*, chs. 5–6; Gillespie, 'Destabilizing Ulster, 1641–2', in Mac Cuarta (ed.), *Ulster, 1641*, 107–21, 208–10; Robinson, *Plantation*, esp. chs. 5–8; B. S. Blades, 'English villages in the Londonderry plantation', *Post-Medieval Archaeology*, 20 (1986), 257–69, esp. pp. 265–7. See also Canny, *Kingdom*, ch. 2; R. Gillespie, 'Continuity and change: Ulster in the seventeenth century', in C. Brady, M. O'Dowd and B. Walker (eds.), *Ulster: An Illustrated History* (London, 1989), 104–33.

[30] For the suggestion that the experience in Ulster reflects a common 'Celtic' heritage see J. M. Hill, 'The origins of the Scottish plantations in Ulster to 1625: a reinterpretation', *JBS*, 32 (1993), 24–43. For the insecure beginnings of the migrant society in Ulster see McCavitt, 'Political background'.

[31] N. Canny, 'The marginal kingdom: Ireland as a problem in the first British empire', in B. Bailyn and P. D. Morgan (eds.), *Strangers within the Realm: Cultural Margins of the First British Empire* (Chapel Hill, 1991), 35–66, esp. pp. 40–53; Robinson, *Plantation*, esp. chs. 5–8; Gillespie, *Ulster*, esp. chs. 5–6; and Blades, 'English villages'. For the moral shortcomings of migrants to Virginia and Ireland see also N. Canny, 'The permissive frontier: social control in English settlements in Ireland and Virginia, 1550–1650', in Andrews, Canny and Hair (eds.), *Westward Enterprise*, 17–44. For studies of the attitudes of one (unusual) settler see R. Loeber, 'Civilization through plantation: the projects of Matthew de Renzi', in H. Murtagh (ed.), *Irish Midland Studies: Essays in Commemoration of N. W. English* (Athlone, 1980), 121–35; and Mac Cuarta, 'De Renzy'. For the symbolic significance of settlement patterns in another context, see R. A. Dodgshon, 'The Scottish farming township as metaphor', in L. Leneman (ed.), *New Perspectives in Scottish History: Essays in Honour of Rosalind Mitchison* (Aberdeen, 1988), 69–82.

Militant anti-settler sentiment seems to have derived not from local experience but from the ideas of Catholic exiles on the continent.[32]

These developments were cut short by the 1641 rebellion against the English crown. The unpopularity of Strafford, the lord deputy during the 1630s, was to a considerable extent religious in origin. It was attempts at forced conversion, associated with claims to novel powers by the Dublin government, that led to a conservative rebellion. Unable to appeal over Strafford's head, Irish leaders rebelled in 1641. Their target, however, was innovation rather than British authority *per se*, but in rebelling they unleashed forces which they could not control. Popular hostility to settlers from Scotland and England led to attacks which, although wildly exaggerated by contemporary English accounts, were definitely violent. As a result 'a conservative uprising, aimed at curbing the power of the administration in Dublin, had by 1642 become a revolutionary movement intent on reversing every achievement of the state authorities in Ireland'.[33] For the settlers this rising was a surprise. They had not been particularly aware of themselves as an embattled minority, their houses had not been fortified and, encouraged by a sense of the superiority of their society, they had not perceived a threat from the native population.[34] The impact of the rising, however, was catastrophic. It immediately became assimilated to an anti-Catholic tradition and very quickly became a focus for sectarian conflict.[35] Thereafter the Protestant interest sought to secure its position quite self-consciously and the policies of the English government were increasingly clearly colonial. The Irish were no longer regarded as barbarians to be reformed but as perfidious Catholic reprobates, potential agents of foreign subversion, to be controlled. Natives and newcomers were now clearly marked out from one another.[36]

---

[32] For the militancy of the exiles see G. Henry, 'Ulster exiles in Europe, 1605–1641', in Mac Cuarta (ed.), *Ulster, 1641*, 37–60, 195–200. Not all exiles were militant, of course: Mac Craith, 'Gaelic reaction'. For the political acquiescence of native Catholics see Lennon, 'Counterreformation'; Gillespie, 'Continuity and change', pp. 113–17; Ryan, 'Religion and state'.

[33] Canny, 'Resistance to empire?', quotation at p. 299; Canny, 'Marginal kingdom', pp. 53–9; Canny, 'What really happened in 1641?', in J. H. Ohlmeyer (ed.), *Ireland from Independence to Occupation 1641–1660* (Cambridge, 1995), 24–42. For a brief account of outbreak and escalation of the rising see M. Perceval-Maxwell, 'Ulster 1641 in the context of political developments in the three kingdoms', in Mac Cuarta (ed.), *Ulster, 1641*, 93–106, 205–8. For the escalation of the violence see H. Simms, 'Violence in County Armagh, 1641', ibid., 122–38, 210–13.

[34] Canny, 'Dominant minorities'. For the surprise of settlers at the outbreak of the rising see A. Clarke, 'The 1641 rebellion and anti-popery in Ireland', in Mac Cuarta (ed.), *Ulster, 1641*, 139–57, 214–18, at pp. 148–9; Gillespie, 'Destabilizing Ulster'; Canny, 'Marginal kingdom', pp. 53–9.

[35] Clarke, '1641 rebellion'; T. C. Barnard, '1641: a bibliographical essay', in Mac Cuarta (ed.), *Ulster, 1641*, 173–86, 223–8.

[36] Clarke, '1641 rebellion'; R. Gillespie, 'The end of an era: Ulster and the outbreak of the 1641

When the English response came, in 1649, it was on the basis of a radically improved capacity for financial and military mobilisation, and Catholic unity could not be maintained. Once again, large-scale military activity was followed by a comprehensive attempt at settlement. The Cromwellian regime, backed up by overwhelming military force, undertook 'nothing less than the erection of a completely new society in the place of the old which it set out to destroy'.[37] Those investing in the conquest, the adventurers, were not necessarily making a shrewd economic investment and were probably motivated by a godly view of the necessity of reform.[38] The land was comprehensively surveyed with this aim in mind and large numbers of Catholic proprietors dispossessed and resettled west of the Shannon. In 1641, 59 per cent of the land had been in the possession of Catholics, by 1659 this had fallen to less than 20 per cent.[39] The reformed Catholic church was destroyed, its priests hunted, and a concerted attempt was made to endow a Protestant church. Attendance at Protestant service became compulsory. This was a formidable, if unappealing, achievement. But the roots were shallow.[40]

The restoration brought the end of military government and the incorporating union, but it did confirm the Protestant presence as an essentially colonial one.[41] On the other hand, Catholic landownership

---

rising', in Brady and Gillespie (eds.), *Natives and Newcomers*, 191–213, 235–7; Canny, *Kingdom*, ch. 4; 'Marginal kingdom', pp. 59–66. For the development of a distinctive 'Protestant interest' (as opposed to an English or Irish interest) see T. C. Barnard, 'The Protestant interest', in Ohlmeyer (ed.), *Ireland*, 218–240. For the 1641 rising as a transformative event see Ohlmeyer, 'Introduction: a failed revolution?', ibid., 1–23; Barnard, 'Conclusion. Settling and unsettling Ireland: the Cromwellian and Williamite revolutions', ibid., 265–91.

[37] Canny, 'Resistance to empire?', p. 300. For the possibilities of a Confederate victory, particularly in the 1640s see S. Wheeler, 'Four armies in Ireland', in Ohlmeyer (ed.), *Ireland*, 43–65. For the Confederate adjustments to the demands of modern warfare, see R. Loeber and G. Parker, 'The military revolution in seventeenth-century Ireland', ibid., 66–88. For the dolorous effects on the Irish economy, which had implications for the local supply of the armies see R. Gillespie, 'The Irish economy at war, 1641–1652', ibid., 160–80.

[38] K. Lindley, 'Irish adventurers and godly militants in the 1640s', *Irish Historical Studies*, 29 (1994), 1–12.

[39] S. J. Connolly, *Religion, Law and Power: The Making of Protestant Ireland 1660–1760* (Oxford, 1992), 13 quoting K. S. Bottigheimer, *English Money and Irish Land: The 'Adventurers' in the Cromwellian Settlement of Ireland* (Oxford, 1971), 141–2. See also Bottigheimer, 'The restoration land settlement: a structural view', *Irish Historical Studies*, 18 (1972–3), 1–21; J. G. Simms, *The Williamite Confiscation in Ireland, 1690–1703* (London, 1956). The effects of changes in ownership may have been limited by the persistence of tenancies. Certainly there is evidence of Catholic sub-tenancies: see for example, Robinson, *Plantation*, pp. 183–4.

[40] For a summary of the limitations of Cromwellian reform see D. Stevenson, 'Cromwell, Scotland and Ireland', in J. Morrill (ed.), *Oliver Cromwell and the English Revolution* (London, 1990), 149–80. For a fuller account see T. C. Barnard, *Cromwellian Ireland: English Government and Reform in Ireland 1649–1660* (Oxford, 1975).

[41] J. Morrill, 'The British problem, *c.* 1534–1707', in Bradshaw and Morrill (eds.), *British Problem*, 1–38, 273–81, p. 37.

began to recover, reaching 22 per cent by 1688.[42] In part this was because Cromwellians sold up, disappointed by their experience in Ireland. Although the extent of the dispossession of Catholics may have been exaggerated, however, these land distributions did change the tenurial basis of landholding, so that the 'tribal' basis of Gaelic lordship disappeared. Meanwhile Catholics re-entered trade and, alongside the Protestants, began to further various projects of 'Anglicisation'. They successfully lobbied government for a conciliatory policy with studied declarations of loyalty, while the spread of manor courts and English ideals of estate management continued apace.[43] And, importantly, the ambiguous position of Presbyterians in Ireland meant that relations remained more complex than simply Catholic versus Protestant.[44]

There is little doubt that this quiescence was, at least in part, prudential but it also owed something to constitutionalism. The hopes of the Catholic elites for improvement were gradualist and the eruption of rebellion in the 1680s was prompted by external events rather than internal tensions. In general, 'Catholics as well as Protestants in Ireland benefited from the prosperity of the restoration years.'[45] However, the conversion to Catholicism of James II opened up avenues of advancement far more quickly than could have been hoped. Cautious about redistributing land, James was quick to promote Catholics in office. This was regarded as providential and rapidly seemed to threaten the Protestant interest with extinction, particularly in the light of the vigorously

---

[42] Connolly, *Religion*, p. 147, quoting Simms, *Williamite Confiscation*, p. 195. For an overview of developments in restoration Ireland see Barnard, 'Settling and unsettling Ireland'.

[43] Canny, 'Resistance to empire?' For rural social relations see M. Mac Curtain, 'Rural society in post-Cromwellian Ireland', in A. Cosgrave and D. McCartney (eds.), *Studies in Irish History Presented to R. Dudley Edwards* (Dublin, 1979), 118–36. For the changing opportunities presented by settlement in Ireland see Barnard, 'New opportunities'. See also W. J. Smyth, 'Making the documents of conquest speak: the transformation of property, society, and settlement in seventeenth-century Counties Tipperary and Kilkenny', in Silverman and Gulliver (eds.), *Approaching the Past*, 236–90, esp. pp. 286–8. In Ulster economic opportunities continued to present themselves as trade grew and rents remained low: Gillespie, 'Continuity and change'; Gillespie, 'Landed society and the Interregnum in Ireland and Scotland', in Mitchison and Roebuck (eds.), *Economy and Society*, 38–47. Irish Atlantic trade was on a significant scale, particularly from the 1680s onwards: R. C. Nash, 'Irish Atlantic trade in the seventeenth and eighteenth centuries: legal and illegal trade', *William and Mary Quarterly*, 42 (1985), 329–56. For further cautionary remarks about the extent of dispossession, and for the point about the 'tribal' authority of Gaelic lords, see K. McKenny, 'The seventeenth-century land settlement in Ireland: towards a statistical interpretation', in Ohlmeyer (ed.), *Ireland*, 181–200.

[44] J. Smyth, 'The communities of Ireland and the British state, 1660–1707', in Bradshaw and Morrill (eds.), *British Problem*, 246–61, 316–18; Gillespie, 'Continuity and change', pp. 124–9. For the growth of Protestant dissent in the 1640s see P. Kilroy, 'Radical religion in Ireland, 1641–1660', in Ohlmeyer (ed.), *Ireland*, 201–17. For the eighteenth century see Connolly, *Religion*, ch. 5.   [45] Canny, 'Resistance to empire?', p. 302.

Catholicising policies of the earl of Tyrconnel, James's lord deputy.[46] His policies seem to have unnerved the conservative Catholic leadership while an awareness of them augmented political unease in England. Moves to cancel the Cromwellian land settlement meant that, after the Protestant victory, land was once again an issue. Ironically, then, it was the attempt to normalise relations in Ireland, by restoring government to the natural (Catholic) leaders of Irish society, that brought down James's regime there.[47] By 1703 only 14 per cent of the land of Ireland was in Catholic hands, although this survival reflected the failure of more ambitious plantation schemes. It was Irish Protestants who pressed for a Protestant standing army, a strengthened and Protestant state and a regular, Protestant, Irish parliament. The role of the London government was really to restrain the most extravagant anti-Catholic demands. An indication of the Protestant attitude towards Catholicism is the complexion of the Irish campaign for the reformation of manners, which conflated sin with poverty but also with Catholicism, and in the light of providential deliverance sought to attack other kinds of heterodoxy.[48] In 1690, therefore, Irish Catholic leaders

grasped at the opportunity provided them to improve upon their position but in the course of doing so they always acted within the law. Instead of rebelling against the state that had been instituted by British authority in Ireland they were in fact taking the instruments of the state into their own hands, and they sought to prove their responsibility in their new role in their efforts to prevent unlicensed assault upon the Protestant population of the country such as had occurred in 1641.[49]

Like previous rebellions, then, it is a misreading to suggest that this was aimed against crown authority in any straightforward way. It resulted, however, in the establishment of a Protestant domination of Irish life that was more clearly colonial. This was not necessarily imposed by English will, of course, but it was reflected in the loss of legislative independence. Clearly the Irish kingdom was a lost ideal.[50]

All this should not necessarily suggest that relations in Ireland were, thereafter, marked by continual conflict. 'Ireland in the century or so

---

[46] For Tyrconnel's policies see J. Miller, 'The Earl of Tyrconnel and James II's Irish policy, 1685–1688', *HJ*, 20 (1977), 803–23; and for their conservative legal and constitutional basis see T. C. Barnard, 'Scotland and Ireland: the late Stewart monarchy', in Ellis and Barber (eds.), *Conquest and Union*, 250–75.   [47] Barnard, 'Scotland and Ireland', esp. pp. 273–5.

[48] T. C. Barnard, 'Reforming Irish manners: the religious societies in Dublin during the 1690s', *HJ*, 35 (1992), 805–38.

[49] Canny, 'Resistance to empire?', quotation at p. 304. See also Ryan, 'Religion and state'.

[50] Smyth, 'Communities of Ireland'; P. Kelly, 'Ireland and the Glorious Revolution: from kingdom to colony', in R. Beddard (ed.), *The Revolutions of 1688* (Oxford, 1991), 163–90.

following the restoration is best seen as first and foremost a part of the European ancien régime.' It was pre-industrial, power was in the hands of a mainly landed elite, ties of patronage and clientage predominated over horizontal solidarities and popular protest was expressed within this political idiom. As in most of the rest of Europe, political participation was restricted according to religious identity and, although it did have built-in conflicts which were not common to the rest of Europe, the position of the Protestant elite was not necessarily that of a wary, embattled colonial presence. Indeed, that elite was internally divided along religious lines.[51] Despite the civil and religious disabilities of its Catholic population, Ireland in the seventeenth and eighteenth centuries was 'an ordered and relatively harmonious community which enjoyed a modest prosperity as a generally contented partner within a broader British jurisdiction'. Friction arose most frequently because of the exclusion of Irish people from privilege and patronage rather than because they were 'opposed to the source of that patronage, which ultimately was the British crown'.[52] The tenantry was not simply differentiated by religion either.[53] To that extent, then, Ireland had accepted important elements of the civilising project. Increasingly, thereafter, Catholics were regarded with scorn rather than concern.[54]

In Ireland then, reform had failed to make a reality of the kingdom invented in 1541, and the 'cardinal fact' of early modern Irish history was the refusal of the Old English elite to support reform and the progress of reformation.[55] The reasons for this, and the point at which the breakdown was complete, are matters of debate. But for the present purposes it draws attention to the common theme of this discussion of state formation in Britain and Ireland. In England and Wales it was the adoption by the gentry of ideals of government promoted by Tudor propagandists that enabled integration. The existence of cultural and linguistic diversity was not, in itself, an unassailable obstacle. In Scotland, by contrast, these developments, and the linguistic common ground between the lowlands and England, did not provide a basis for easy integration following the Union of the Crowns. Here the existence

---

[51] Connolly, *Religion*, quotation at p. 2.
[52] Canny, 'Resistance to empire?', p. 290. See Connolly, *Religion*, ch. 6, for the use of the law, and accommodations of formal codes to local conditions. Again, the experience is not completely unlike that in England.
[53] M. Cohen, 'Peasant differentiation and proto-industrialisation in the Ulster countryside: Tullylish, 1690–1825', *Journal of Peasant Studies*, 17 (1990), 413–32.
[54] D. W. Hayton, 'From barbarian to burlesque: English images of the Irish, *c.* 1660–1750', *Irish Economic and Social History*, 15 (1988), 5–31.   [55] Clarke, '1641 rebellion', pp. 142–3.

of a separate state created alternatives for those seeking more active government and created powerful vested interests. In Ireland the absence of viable institutional alternatives did not compensate for the absence of an activist, Protestant, reforming gentry: in the end the kingdom came to resemble a colony. The roots of these differences, it need hardly be said, lie much deeper than the period being considered here.

Coalescence in Britain and Ireland was not an unqualified success, therefore. But an important feature of the experience outlined here is the extent to which lowland Englishmen could make common cause with lowland Scots and (to a lesser extent) Old English, in seeking to promote new standards of civility. Civilising the Highlands was an interest shared by the governments of London, Edinburgh and Dublin partly because of the close links between Irish and Scottish Gaeldom. In the later sixteenth century the settlement of the Highlanders in Ulster served to destabilise politics there, a development exacerbated by the influx of Highland mercenaries during the same period.[56] As a consequence, the Borders, Highlands and Gaelic and Gaelicised Ireland represented a common 'problem'. In all three areas a problem of 'order' became identified (with varying degrees of inaccuracy) with differences in language, law and custom. Several 'frontiers' were 'opened', between discordant images of social and political order. The most dramatic closure of a frontier was that in the Borders, which were rapidly pacified after 1603 and where new tenurial relations were adopted with alacrity. In the Highlands and Islands change occurred more slowly. There, 'the political frontier . . . did not finally close until after the Jacobite rising of 1745, when the government outlawed Gaelic, disbanded the clans, and refused to tolerate lordly power'.[57] The achievement of the dominance by the Protestant elite, which had come to be the form assumed by civility in Ireland, was sealed by the Williamite conquest. Nationalist historiographies emphasise resistance and discordance. For example, in Scotland the association of these policies with the Stuarts leads to a description of the process as one of Anglicisation, something of an irony given the later identification of the support for the Stuart pretenders with Scottish and Highland loyalties. That 'Anglicisation' should lead to

[56] G. Hayes-McCoy, 'The completion of the Tudor conquest and the advance of the counter-reformation, 1571–1603', in Moody, Martin and Byrne (eds.), *Early Modern Ireland*, 94–141, esp. pp. 98–9, 111–12; Morgan, 'End of Gaelic Ulster'; Brady, 'Sixteenth-century Ulster and the failure of Tudor reform', in Brady, O'Dowd and Walker (eds.), *Ulster*, 77–103, esp. pp. 90–3.
[57] J. Ohlmeyer, '"Civilizinge those rude partes": colonization within Britain and Ireland, 1580s 1640s', in Canny (ed.), *Origins of Empire*, 124–47, quotation at p. 145.

union was probably contingent. In Ireland it was religious differences, ultimately, that determined that civility would be achieved by dispossession – a Protestant Ireland, one in which the Tudor reformation had succeeded, might have adapted to these social changes within a Union. In any case, the means by which these areas were brought within the ambit of London's authority are recognisable – through the willing participation of local elites in a programme promoting commerce, and social, legal and religious order. Only in Ireland could that elite be said to have been consciously created by an expansionist government and even there attempts to foster coalescence had been the first resort.[58]

By 1640 the cultural and social values and assumptions necessary to support government along English lines had been widely diffused in Britain and Ireland. In Scotland, and even more in Ireland, however, the process was not smooth and was reinforced by conscious and aggressive policy. The image of planting is revealing of the general aspiration – it was not to dominate by occupation but to cultivate civilised society. In the 1640s and 1650s the Hartlib circle saw in plans for plantation the possibility of ridding England of the poor. This was the root of the suggestion in 1649 'for erecting an Office for sending the Poore into Plantations abroad, which will ... [among other things] rid the Country of the unprofitable and begging men and Children'. But this was part of a larger vision of 'improvement'. It was hoped that such schemes would make better people of the poor of England by planting them in a soil more suitable for them – these schemes aimed at 'improoving of Poore by way (among other things) of transplanting the worst Persons to become better in another soile'. This would make better use both of them and of that soil, and the image recalls the larger concern of the Hartlib circle with agricultural improvement. Of course this was not necessarily the case, as experience showed, but in both Ireland and America plans to improve the land were also thought to be means to establish civil and godly society.[59] The clash of honour codes between Irish Gaelic chief and Elizabethan servitor was reminiscent of the conflict of ideals in the north of England in the same

---

[58] For accounts of the 'civilisation of Gaeldom' emphasising commercial and religious pressures in addition to governmental policy see the works cited above, ch. 8 nn. 119–21, and C. W. J. Withers, *Gaelic Scotland: The Transformation of a Culture Region* (London, 1988).

[59] HP, 28/1/28b, Samuel Hartlib's Ephemerides, 1649; 28/2/52a, Samuel Hartlib's Ephemerides, 1653. For the larger context see C. Webster, *The Great Instauration: Science, Medicine and Reform 1626–1660* (London, 1975), esp. ch. 5. For the defeat of such hopes see Canny, 'Permissive frontier'; Barnard, 'New opportunities'. For plantation and profit see R. Gillespie, 'Plantation and profit: Richard Spert's tract on Ireland', *Irish Economic and Social History*, 20 (1993), 62–71. See above pp. 344–7.

period.[60] During the medieval expansion of Europe, ethnicity was defined in terms of custom, law, manners and religion, rather than in terms of race.[61] These things were mutable and in the early modern period considerable energy was spent on trying to achieve such mutation. National and racial perspectives cannot do justice to what lowlanders in England, Scotland, Ireland and Wales were trying to achieve.[62] Neither was this process, which drew on renaissance and reformation ideals, in a European diplomatic context, 'English' in origin or design. It was a process within England as well as within Scotland, Wales and Ireland, although at some points (immediately after 1603 or during the Cromwellian occupation of Ireland and Scotland) some of its features were directed by an English regime. Still less was it the product of a 'British policy'.[63] Civility was a broader process, involving mutualities of interest between dominant groups and crown authority, both within England and other parts of Britain and Ireland.

TOWARDS A BRITISH EMPIRE

The creation of the first British empire, as we have known since the days of Seeley, was not an act of central will. Similarly, the authority of the crown in its American colonies was not simply imposed. Elites in the colonies of settlement had vested interests which could be protected by crown authority, and mutualities of interest with the metropolitan authority. In these settlements the programme of civility was propagated in ways that shored up the interests of developing local elites and which bore considerable similarities to the activities of the

[60] Palmer, 'Rites of power', adapting the work of M. E. James, for example, *Society, politics and culture*.

[61] R. Bartlett, *The Making of Europe: Conquest, Colonization and Cultural Change 950–1350* (London, 1993), ch. 8.

[62] For a critique of nationalist approaches to the history of states, J. Morrill, 'The fashioning of Britain', in Ellis and Barber (eds.), *Conquest and Union*, 8–39, esp. pp. 38–9.

[63] The limits of British policies are much written about. See H. Morgan, 'British policies before the British state', in Bradshaw and Morrill (eds.), *British Problem*, 66–88, 284–7; D. Hirst, 'The English republic and the meaning of Britain', in Bradshaw and Morrill (eds.), *British Problem*, 192–219, 300–14; S. Barber, 'Scotland and Ireland under the Commonwealth: a question of loyalty', in Ellis and Barber (eds.), *Conquest and Union*, 195–221; J. Morrill, 'A British patriarchy? Ecclesiastical imperialism under the early Stuarts', in A. Fletcher and P. Roberts (eds.), *Religion, Culture and Society in Early Modern Britain: Essays in Honour of Patrick Collinson* (Cambridge, 1994), 209–37. For the limited appeal of the British vision of James VI and I see, in particular, J. Wormald, 'The creation of Britain: multiple kingdoms or core and colonies?', *TRHS*, 6th series, 2 (1992), 175–94; B. P. Levack, *The Formation of the British State: England, Scotland, and the Union 1603–1707* (Oxford, 1987); K. M. Brown, 'The vanishing emperor: British kingship and its decline', in R. A. Mason (ed.), *Scots and Britons: Scottish Political Thought and the Union of 1603* (Cambridge, 1994), 58–87.

patriarchal state in England. None the less, these developments took place within the shell of a developing fiscal-military empire, the interests of which overrode the interests of particular colonies. As in England, therefore, there was a potential tension between the interests that bound local elites to the crown and the autonomous interests of the state which could, at particular times or in particular ways, make that relationship more difficult.[64]

The expansion of overseas trade, and the first steps towards settlement in the Americas, proceeded in ways that were, in some sense, analogous to the means by which the practical authority of the Tudor and Stuart state was intensified in its core areas. In particular, activists played an important role in lobbying for the use of state power in new territories and new functions. In this case, the extension took place as a result of the 'variable interplay of state control and individual initiative in which great men at Court and in the councils of the realm performed an indispensable rôle as intermediaries'.[65] The trading companies chartered in the period between 1550 and 1640 represented a technique whereby national government, at little cost to the exchequer, could act to promote the expansion of English commerce. In fact, so successful was the strategy that by the 1580s it was only trade with France, Scotland and Ireland that was not in the hands of a company.[66]

Companies overcame a number of problems associated with new trades. In many cases the commercial risks were high – the markets for English goods and the English market for the expected imports equally uncertain. To these commercial risks were added others, real and imagined. For example, political relations between the governments of the two areas might be poorly established and merchants unsure that their property and persons were secure. Similarly, in many trades English merchants were entering into more or less direct competition with traders from other European countries and this also posed a threat to commercial interests. As a result, merchants entering these new and

---

[64] The perspective adopted here is similar to the arguments developed independently by Professor Elizabeth Mancke. See, for example, 'Another British America: a Canadian model for the early modern British empire', *Journal of Imperial and Commonwealth History*, 25, 1 (1997), 1–36; and 'Elites, states, and the contest for Acadia' (forthcoming). I am grateful to Professor Mancke for many helpful discussions of these issues and for letting me see this paper prior to publication.

[65] K. R. Andrews, *Trade, Plunder and Settlement: Maritime Enterprise and the Genesis of the British Empire, 1480–1630* (Cambridge, 1984), 15.

[66] C. G. A. Clay, *Economic Expansion and Social Change: England 1500–1700*, 2 vols. (Cambridge, 1984), II, 193–200, esp. pp. 197–8; W. R. Scott, *The Constitution and Finance of English, Scottish and Irish Joint-Stock Companies to 1720*, 3 vols. (Cambridge, 1910–12), II, Divisions i and ii. See also G. V. Scammell, *The English Chartered Trading Companies and the Sea* (London, 1983), 5–13.

uncertain trades developed particular techniques of organisation. Merchants banded together into guild-style organisations in order to negotiate with foreign governments, establishing 'stranger communities' and taking responsibility for their relations with local populations. Associated with such functions might be controls over price and quality. Such extra-commercial activity might impose an extra overhead on merchants, however, and they sought to defend their position and to secure their returns through privileges granted by the government. With or without a monopoly, the power of such regulated companies was much enhanced by a charter.[67]

All these related problems meant that these ventures were risky, and capital was hard to find. In response to this difficulty a characteristic form of funding developed which spread the risk – the joint-stock. A permanent fund of capital was established from individual investments, and profits were shared according to the proportion of the total stock held by each individual. This spread the risks while still offering the possibility of attractive returns. In many cases a new stock was created for each voyage, rather than creating a permanent fund, but in either case, again, the security was further enhanced if a government charter could be secured. There was then a fundamental difference between the joint-stock and the regulated companies. In the latter case, merchants traded on their own account under the umbrella of a protective organisation. In the former case, the company traded as a corporate body. Joint-stock ventures helped to establish the most exotic trades of the sixteenth and seventeenth centuries, companies being established to trade with Guinea, Muscovy, the Levant, Virginia, the East Indies, West Africa and Hudson's Bay. The East India Company, in particular, provides an illustration of the dangers of these trades. The search for the north-west passage was driven by a desire to secure a share of this trade without interfering with established Portuguese control of trade routes while the rivalry with the Dutch traders is typified by the reaction to the

---

[67] For the general argument here see also M. J. Braddick, 'The English government, war, trade, and settlement, 1625–1688', in Canny (ed.), *Origins of Empire*, 286–308. For studies of particular companies see K. N. Chaudhuri, *The English East India Company: The Study of an Early Joint-Stock Company 1600–1640* (London, 1965); P. Croft, *The Spanish Company*, London Record Society (London, 1973); K. G. Davies, *The Royal African Company* (London, 1957); R. W. K. Hinton, *The Eastland Trade and the Common Weal in the Seventeenth Century* (Cambridge, 1959); P. Lawson, *The East India Company: A History* (London, 1993); E. E. Rich, *Hudson's Bay Company, 1670–1860*, I, *1670–1763* (New York, 1961); A. C. Wood, *A History of the Levant Company* (Oxford, 1935); T. S. Willan, *The Early History of the Russia Company, 1553–1603* (Manchester, 1956). For an overview see Clay, *Economic Expansion*, II, pp. 191–202; Davies, *African Company*, pp. 16–38.

Amboyna 'massacre'.[68] The crown could help to promote trade in these circumstances by granting charter rights, particularly monopoly rights.

This kind of relationship created a situation in which the use of political power and armed force were intimately connected with commercial activities. In response to the diplomatic weakness of the Russian crown in the 'time of troubles', the English government, perhaps improbably, showed some interest in establishing a protectorate over northern Russia in order to protect English commercial interests. Behind this policy lay the Russia Company.[69] The acme of this kind of arrangement was the East India Company which, for much of its history, 'was a state within a state'. After 1709 its total trading capital was loaned to the government and the interest was met by assigning the profits of salt and paper duties directly to the company.

The possession of a legal monopoly by the Company firmly and unambiguously debarred the entry of competitors in the home market. The Company could rely on the diplomatic support of the Crown and its ministers to bring pressure on foreign European governments to subdue small rival companies on the Continent. In India and elsewhere in Asia, it had established a number of trading settlements which possessed semi-sovereign status, distinguished by an elaborate procedure of government, courts of law, a municipal system, and military force. [T]he Company's organisational structure and bureaucratic apparatus shared many of the attributes of a great department of state.[70]

In these respects, the East India Company, although unusually durable and powerful, reflects a more general feature of commercial and imperial expansion. But there were a number of failed projects and there was no overall plan. English commercial interests grew out of a loose process of trade, plunder and settlement. In the Caribbean it was the outcome of that 'crabwise scuttling motion of small groups taking precarious hold on unoccupied islands'. In fact, attempts to establish a company to coordinate and protect this process foundered on political difficulties.[71] In general, 'the evidence we have hardly ever shows the

---

[68] Lawson, *East India Company*, pp. 7–8, 31–2. Fear of Dutch aggression, for example, played a part in the shift of East India Company attention towards India, and in the decision to fortify the factory at Bombay: G. Z. Refai, 'Sir George Oxinden and Bombay, 1662–1669', *EHR*, 92 (1977), 573–81, at pp. 573, 576.

[69] C. Dunning, 'James I, the Russia Company and the plan to establish a protectorate over north Russia', *Albion*, 21 (1989), 206–26.

[70] K. N. Chaudhuri, *The Trading World of the English East India Company, 1660–1760* (Cambridge, 1978), 20.

[71] K. R. Andrews, 'The English in the Caribbean, 1560–1620', in Andrews, Canny and Hair (eds.), *Westward Enterprise*, 103–23, quotation at p. 103. For the process more generally see Andrews, *Trade*. For the failure of the West Indies company, see J. C. Appleby, 'An association for the West Indies? English plans for a West India Company, 1621–29', *Journal of Imperial and Commonwealth*

crown – or ministers on its behalf – taking the initiative, but rather responding more or less helpfully to private projects'.[72] These mercantile interests drew the government in, defining new commercial and territorial opportunities in terms of dynastic, religious or national interest and thereby driving an extension of the territorial reach of the state. Clearly, this was not simply a product of executive or central will.[73]

The crown was fostering trade, then, by creating a 'rent': a premium on the value of trade was produced by creating a legal title in it, effectively excluding competition. In this sense, trading companies were one more concessionary interest among many, akin to some of the unpopular financial expedients of the period. We saw in chapter 6, for example, how in order to raise revenue the government granted patents of monopoly. These patents were extremely unpopular and, in 1624, legislation was passed to prevent grants to individuals. Obviously, this allowed continued grants to trading companies, but the legislation was circumvented by the creation of largely fictitious corporations.[74] The result was a continued general antipathy towards monopolies, although most public attention was directed at domestic patents. In many cases trading privileges benefited a very small number of people: in 1604 the Russia trade was handled by fifteen members and the Eastland trade by thirty; a century later the Levant company had 200 members of whom only 50 were trading and the Hudson's Bay company had only 35 shareholders.[75] Merchants excluded from privileged trades were often hostile to these privileges and there was pretty continuous resistance to chartered trading rights. These companies had something of a life-cycle, therefore. For new trades the political purchase of these objections was limited, but as the commerce became more routine, so the arguments in favour of privilege became less compelling. Such hostility could be politically significant. In fact, it has been suggested that opposition to concessionary interests was a significant factor in the outbreak of the

History, 15 (1987), 213–41. For similar problems in the Guiana trade, hampered also by diplomatic imperatives, see J. Lorimer, 'The failure of the English Guiana ventures, 1595–1667 and James I's foreign policy', *Journal of Imperial and Commonwealth History*, 21 (1993), 1–30. Scammell, *Trading Companies*, has some graphic examples of failed initiatives. See Scammell, 'English in the Atlantic islands' for another example.   [72] Andrews, *Trade*, p. 360.

[73] For examples of particular individuals see H. R. Huttenbach, 'Anthony Jenkinson's 1566 and 1567 missions to Muscovy reconstructed from unpublished sources', *Canadian-American Slavic Studies*, 9 (1975), 179–203; Refai, 'Sir George Oxinden'.

[74] For monopolies see J. Thirsk, *Economic Policy and Projects: The Development of a Consumer Society in Early Modern England* (Oxford, 1978); Scott, *Joint-Stock Companies*, I, chs. 6, 9, 11; K. Sharpe, *The Personal Rule of Charles I* (London, 1992), 120–4, 242–62.

[75] Scammell, *Trading Companies*, p. 12.

civil war, and there is surely some truth to the suggestion.[76] However, there were a variety of concessionary interests, which could be mutually contradictory, and so the politics of concessions were not straightforwardly a matter of beneficiaries versus the excluded.[77] For our purposes, however, we can note influential hostility to corporate privilege.

The activities of these trading companies, and of privateers and contraband traders, created a permanent English presence overseas. These interests were also crucial to the first steps in American settlement. The original interest of settlements in Terra Florida and at Roanoke was almost certainly that they would provide the basis for privateering raids against the Spanish treasure fleet.[78] These returns were much more promising than the settlements further north, lacking such resources and offering only the hope of agricultural development.[79] The Atlantic winds circulated in such a way that the Spanish fleet went out via the Canaries, returning northwards through the Florida channel and thence eastwards for home.[80] Privateering was one of the surest ways of recouping the costs of settlement and of offering a living to colonists. Virginia did not, of course, prosper in this way and was saved instead by tobacco. But Jamaica did depend on privateering for much of its early history before sugar and slaves provided the means to prosperity.[81] The first successful settlements in North America – in Virginia and

[76] R. Brenner, *Merchants and Revolution: Commercial Change, Political Conflict, and London's Overseas Traders, 1550–1653* (Cambridge, 1993).

[77] For some observations along these lines see R. Ashton, 'Conflicts of concessionary interest in early Stuart England', in D. C. Coleman and A. H. John (eds.), *Trade, Government and Economy in Pre-industrial England: Essays Presented to F. J. Fisher* (London, 1976), 113–31. There are broader grounds on which to question Brenner's interpretation too. For example, it is not easy to see the politics operating at an individual level: can it be shown that an individual's political position arises from his economic interest rather than some other element of his socialisation. Similarly, the variety of economic activities undertaken by particular individuals might make it difficult to define them as, primarily or exclusively, new merchants. For criticisms along these lines see J. Morrill, 'Conflict probable or inevitable?', *New Left Review*, 207 (1994), 113–23.

[78] Canny, *Kingdom*, ch. 1; J. H. Parry, 'Introduction: the English in the New World', in Andrews, Canny and Hair (eds.), *Westward Enterprise*, 1–16, esp. pp. 1–2; C. Shammas, 'English commercial development and American colonization 1560–1620', ibid., 151–74, at p. 154. For the importance of privateering and the contraband trade to the establishment of viable settlements in the Caribbean see also N. Zahedieh, 'The merchants of Port Royal, Jamaica and the Spanish contraband trade', *William and Mary Quarterly*, 3rd series, 43 (1986), 570–93; Zahedieh, '"A frugal, prudential and hopeful trade": privateering in Jamaica', *Journal of Imperial and Commonwealth History*, 18 (1990), 145–68.

[79] K. O. Kupperman, 'Errand to the Indies: puritan colonization from Providence Island through the Western Design', *William and Mary Quarterly*, 3rd series, 45 (1988), 70–99.

[80] A. W. Crosby, *Ecological Imperialism: The Biological Expansion of Europe 900–1900* (Cambridge, 1993), 109–10. See also N. A. M. Rodger, 'Guns and sails in the first phase of English colonization, 1500–1650', in Canny (ed.), *Origins of Empire*, 79–98, at p. 88, and map 1.1.

[81] Zahedieh, 'Privateering in Jamaica'; 'Merchants of Port Royal'. The profits of sugar planting in the 1650s were exceptional, and the result of the disruption of the Brazil trade: J. R. Ward, 'The

Massachusetts Bay – were funded on a joint-stock basis by chartered companies. Clearly this owed much to the Elizabethan experience.[82]

Joint-stock organisation could finance colonial ventures, then, and to a significant extent it was commercial interests that provided the impetus for colonisation.[83] But this was not the only way in which familiar techniques established English jurisdiction in unfamiliar territory. In 1632 Lord Baltimore was given control of the new territory of Maryland by a charter explicitly based on the Durham palatinate charter of the fourteenth century. Baltimore and his heirs were created lords and proprietors with extensive powers to establish a political society in the wilderness. They could grant titles to land with manorial rights, incorporate towns, create ports and raise revenues. Most remarkably of all, perhaps, given seventeenth-century attitudes, they were given the right to license religious worship. As a sign of fealty they were to deliver two arrows each year to the monarch. This was to be a political society, too, however. In exercising these powers the lords were to seek the advice and assent of freemen. It is tempting to see here an expanding range of indirect rule – the fourteenth-century margin had been Durham, that of the seventeenth century was Maryland. In bringing these margins under royal authority there were considerable formal similarities.[84]

In 1625 company government in Virginia collapsed, leading to the assumption of direct responsibility by the crown. Thus, a third general form of colony was born – alongside company and proprietary government there was now direct royal authority. Virginia's early history was very troubled, and the colony survived only with great difficulty. Part cause and part consequence of the problems was the dissatisfaction of the settlers themselves. In response to their demands for a greater economic and political stake in the settlement the company offered guarantees of a determination to create 'a flourishing state … [and] a laudable form of Government by Majestracy and just laws'.[85] This was the so-called 'Great Charter', but it was not enough to bring respectability to the company's record in Virginia. Internal divisions weakened the capacity of the company to resist criticism. The company was in debt, reports of hardship and disorder circulated in London and, the final

profitability of sugar planting in the British West Indies, 1650–1835', *EcHR*, 2nd series, 31 (1978), 197–213.

[82] For the Providence Island Company see K. O. Kupperman, *Providence Island 1630–1641: The Other Puritan Colony* (Cambridge, 1993).

[83] For a brief account of the commercial context of colonisation see Shammas, 'Commercial development'.

[84] For Maryland see D. B. Quinn (ed.), *Early Maryland and the Wider World* (Detroit, 1982).

[85] R. M. Bliss, *Revolution and Empire: English Politics and the American Colonies in the Seventeenth Century* (Manchester, 1990), 11.

straw, in 1622 news reached home of an Indian 'uprising'. Indians responded with hostility to the spread of white settlement along the James River. An attack was launched on 22 March 1622 in which 350 colonists died. Bloody reprisals followed and the damage done threatened the colony's survival once more. James I put the colony under a temporary commission, allowing privy council oversight, and announced the intention to issue a new charter. In 1625 direct royal government was instituted.[86] This confirmed the emerging consensus, that these settlements represented an extension of the English polity.[87]

Thus, within the expanding world of English overseas trade there developed civil societies recognisable as variants of those in Britain and Ireland. The process as a whole did not represent the execution of a central design and did not proceed as a consequence of the interests of the centre alone. By 1640 these commercial settlements were clearly recognised, in some cases at least, to be outliers of English society, although central coordination of local political life was loose at best. In part the recognition of the colonies as extensions of the English polity was the product of sentiment in the colonies themselves – there was a local demand for settled forms of government. A recent study has shown how in five colonies (Virginia, Massachusetts, Barbados, Maryland and Jamaica) there was a trend towards a tripartite colonial administration – governor, council and assembly. The council and the assembly in each case formed a bicameral legislature. This was not a response to a central blueprint, however. In each case the route to this form of government was different, except in the fundamental point of responding to pressure from the colonists. As the government in London recognised that colonisation required private resources and initiative it also recognised the need to secure the cooperation of the colonists. The result was the development of a series of assemblies.[88]

In these assemblies local elites sought to assert their status and thereby enhanced the separation within assemblies between appointees and representatives. In the early seventeenth century it had been presumed

---

[86] Ibid., pp. 10–15, 18–21. For the uprising, see R. Middleton, *Colonial America: A History, 1607–1760* (Oxford, 1992), 35–6. Although this represents a recognition of the need to govern overseas settlements, it does not really mark the opening of a new chapter in imperial history: Andrews, *Trade*, p. 13.

[87] See, for example, A. Fitzmaurice, 'The civic solution to the crisis of English colonization, 1609–1625', *HJ* 42 (1999), 25–51. For some historiographical reflections see D. Armitage, 'Greater Britain: A useful category of analysis?', *American Historical Review*, 104 (1999), 427–45, at pp. 433–6.

[88] Y. Man, 'English colonization and the formation of Anglo-American polities, 1606–1664', Ph.D. dissertation, Johns Hopkins University (1994).

that the ideal form of government was conciliar – a governor and appointed councillors – but by 1640 the tripartite model had become established, and in 1660 it became the acknowledged basis of colonial government. This was a convergence though, from different starting points. In Virginia and Massachusetts it mimicked the constitution of the mother company (general meetings of stockholders) whereas in Maryland it grew out of manorial society (assemblies of freemen). It was not consciously modelled on the home government, although once established the similarity was pleasing.[89] The process is testimony, however, to the demand for settled government as settlements became societies.[90] These societies grew out of American soil, but in the light of British or Irish experience and precedent. It is in this sense that 'British history' can be further widened to include the transatlantic British world.[91]

The influence of the English heritage and of English political presumptions to the development of American society has recently attracted much attention. In part the American similarity was not a survival of the presumptions of the original settlers but a product of later mimesis, as complex societies sought models for their political and social order.[92]

[89] Ibid.

[90] J. P. Greene and J. Pole, 'Reconstructing British–American colonial history: an introduction', in Greene and Pole (eds.), *Colonial British America: Essays in the New History of the Early Modern Era* (London, 1984), 1–17, esp. pp. 14–15.

[91] F. J. Bremer, 'A further broadening of "British" history?', *HJ*, 36 (1993), 205–10. For accounts of 'British history' see S. G. Ellis, 'The concept of British history', in Ellis and Barber (eds.), *Conquest and Union*, 1–7; Morrill 'British problem'; J. G. A. Pocock, 'The Atlantic Archipelago and the War of the Three Kingdoms', in Morrill and Bradshaw (eds.), *British Problem*, 172–91, 299–300. As Ellis points out (p. 5), Ireland is as 'British' in many ways as Wales, Scotland or England, despite its political independence. Early America might be said to bear some similarity in that respect: see Armitage, 'Greater Britain', pp. 433–8.

[92] This is a complex question. For some influential views see T. H. Breen, 'Persistent localism: English social change and the shaping of New England institutions', *William and Mary Quarterly*, 3rd series, 32 (1975), 3–28; Breen, 'Creative adaptations: peoples and cultures', in Greene and Pole (eds.), *Colonial British America*, 195–232; Breen (ed.), *Shaping Southern Society: The Colonial Experience* (New York, 1976); Breen (ed.), *Puritans and Adventurers: Change and Persistence in Early America* (Oxford, 1980); I. K. Steele, *The English Atlantic 1675–1740: An Exploration of Communication and Community* (Oxford, 1986); Steele, 'The empire and provincial elites: an interpretation of some recent writings on the English Atlantic, 1675–1740', *Journal of Imperial and Commonwealth History*, 8/2 (1980), 2–32; Steele, 'Empire of migrants and consumers: some current approaches to the history of colonial Virginia', *Virginia Magazine of History and Biography*, 99 (1991), 489–512; J. M. Sosin, *English America and the Restoration Monarchy of Charles II: Transatlantic Politics, Commerce and Kinship* (Lincoln, Nebr., 1980); J. P. Greene, *Peripheries and Center: Constitutional Development in the Extended Polities of the British Empire and the United States, 1607–1788* (London, 1987); Greene, *Pursuits of Happiness: The Social Development of Early Modern British Colonies and the Formation of American Culture* (Chapel Hill, 1988); Greene, *Negotiated Authorities: Essays in Colonial Political and Constitutional History* (London, 1994); Canny, *Kingdom*, ch. 4. For the later evolution of English gentility among Virginian planters see M. H. Quitt, 'Immigrant origins of the Virginia gentry: a study in cultural transmission and innovation', *William and Mary Quarterly*, 3rd series, 45 (1988), 629–55.

Models of civility in these colonies, although clearly owing much to English models, were to a considerable degree the product of local conditions. Settlers heading for the New World, or Ireland, took with them presumptions gained from their background in the Old World. These presumptions will have varied, of course, across time, region of origin and social status. As a consequence 'The culture of an emigrant heading for Virginia in 1607 was not the same as that of one going to South Carolina in 1680 or to Georgia in 1750.'[93] What the settlers found on arrival also varied considerably – climate, topography, indigenous populations and disease environments, for example, could all have substantial effects on the development of settlements. In seeking to recreate the Old World in the New, therefore, colonists drew upon diverse local experiences and responded to conditions with which they were not necessarily familiar – not least, of course, racial diversity. In understanding social order in the light of such racial diversity, differences in the gender ordering of society were important – the disorders of Irish, or American Indian, society were frequently thought to lie in the sexual division of labour, or in the behaviour of women towards men.[94] But in the diversity of responses to these situations there was something irreducibly 'English' – these settlers 'undoubtedly considered themselves representatives of a general English culture'.[95] In the first generation of settlement, therefore, in which the majority of migrants were English,[96] colonies took on the appearance of aspects of English regional cultures. So, for example, 'If the Chesapeake's landscape and climate was unfamiliar, nevertheless conventional attitudes about the social order, the locus of political power, hierarchy, government, justice, property, marriage, the family, gender relations, and religion left immigrants in no doubt that they had arrived on "English ground in America".'[97]

[93] Breen (ed.), *Shaping*, p. 5. A similar point emerges from Allen's study of English settlement in Massachusetts: 'The inhabitants of our five Massachusetts towns had essentially reproduced what they wanted – the ordering of life as they knew it before their emigration. They had recreated the diversity of local England in the New England countryside': D. G. Allen, *In English Ways: The Movement of Societies and the Transferral of English Local Law and Custom to Massachusetts Bay in the Seventeenth Century* (Chapel Hill, 1981), 205. See also Allen, 'A tale of two towns: persistent English localism in seventeenth-century Massachusetts', in H. C. Allen and R. Thompson (eds.), *Contrast and Connection: Bicentennial Essays in Anglo-American History* (London, 1976), 1–35; D. H. Fischer, *Albion's Seed: Four British Folkways in America* (Oxford, 1989).

[94] K. M. Brown, *Good Wives, Nasty Wenches and Anxious Patriarchs: Gender, Race, and Power in Colonial America* (Chapel Hill, 1996), chs. 1–3; M. B. Norton, *Founding Mothers and Fathers: Gendered Power and the Forming of American Society* (New York, 1996), 5–7.   [95] Breen (ed.), *Shaping*, p. 14.

[96] Much Scottish emigration was absorbed by the movement of population to Ireland: D. Armitage, 'Making the empire British: Scotland in the Atlantic world 1542–1717', *PP*, 155 (1997), 33–63, at p. 46.

[97] J. Horn, *Adapting to a New World: English Society in the Seventeenth-Century Chesapeake* (Chapel Hill, 1994), 427.

Of central importance to the ways in which colonists made the New World orderly was the importation of English law, government and ideas about legitimate political authority. 'The fabric of English society and culture was maintained by the transfer and adaptation of English values, norms and attitudes, which represented major continuities between life in the Old World and the New.'[98] These issues are complex, and the subject of much debate, but one thread of recent argument has been the ways in which 'patriarchal' authority was reconceived and embodied in a variety of New World contexts. In the Chesapeake colonies the imbalance in the sex ratio, high mortality rates and dispersed settlement made patriarchal order more difficult to attain than in Massachusetts Bay and the Plymouth colony.[99] The presumptions from English culture which were drawn upon in the two places were quite different – in the Chesapeake individualism and competition, in Massachusetts and Plymouth, order, hierarchy and communitarian ideals. Both were, in some sense, 'English', but they were radically simplified versions of aspects of seventeenth-century English society.[100]

Order was brought to the Chesapeake through the importation of English law, the establishment of county courts and a pattern of government which presumed that patriarchal authority was the basis of social and political stability.[101] This patriarchal order seems to have differed from that emerging in New England where 'heads of households bore heavy responsibilities and were closely supervised by public officials'. In the Chesapeake households were less stable and authority understood and expressed in different ways. This 'placed less onerous burdens on male residents and [courts] were less inclined to intervene in disorderly households'. The distinction may have reflected a broader difference in (gendered) understandings of political order. In the north a patriarchal system developed, in which both political and household relations were conceived of in patriarchal terms – a view of political life most associated with the thought of Robert Filmer. In the south, patriarchy was central to the prevailing view of household order, but did not offer a model for political life. Power was gendered, the preserve of males, but among men it was legitimated by contract rather than appeal to a patriarchal

---

[98] Ibid.
[99] Greene, *Pursuits*, ch. 1. Norton notes that concern was expressed in New England in the 1630s that dispersed settlement might militate against the maintenance of household order: *Founding Mothers*, pp. 38–9.　[100] Greene, *Pursuits*, ch. 1.
[101] Horn, *Adapting*, pp. 355–49; W. M. Billings, 'The transfer of English law to Virginia, 1606–50', in Andrews, Canny and Hair (eds.), *Westward Enterprise*, 215–44, esp. pp. 222–42; Brown, *Good Wives*, chs. 1–3.

order, in a way that predicted the arguments of John Locke.[102]
Chesapeake society was probably no less like Old England than Massachusetts Bay was,[103] and was quite like developing societies in Ireland,
the Caribbean and the mainland colonies founded in the later seventeenth century.[104]

Greater stability was brought to Virginia's politics through the
emergence of a planter elite by the early eighteenth century,[105] but these
patriarchal estate owners were operating in a very different environment from estate owners at home. In part it rested on invented gentility[106] and it had to take account, increasingly, of the presence of black
slaves. The labour shortage in early Virginia was a shortage not simply
of hands, but of willing hands: the settlers had not been socialised to
perform agricultural labour.[107] The development of estates depending
on slave labour created a problem of social order without direct parallel
in England. A crucial moment in the construction of a vision of social
order which comprehended this racial dimension was Bacon's rebellion
of 1676. In the aftermath of the rebellion, order was brought to gender
and race relations through the affirmation of a white, patriarchal conception of social and political order.[108] Eighteenth-century Virginia
plantations were interracial patriarchies.[109] To this extent the patriarchal order in 'the south' was similar to that emerging in the plantation
societies of the Caribbean.[110] Indeed planter society in South Carolina
drew not simply on an English heritage but on the heritage of English
presumptions transmuted by the experience of the sugar islands.[111] Here
then is another level of complexity in the development of new regional
varieties of 'Englishness' (and, increasingly 'Britishness'): the mutual
influence of colonies on one another, alongside the continuing recipro-

---

[102] Norton, *Founding Mothers*, quotations at p. 292.

[103] Greene, *Pursuits*, chs. 1–2. Horn's study suggests that the lack of order in the Chesapeake has been overstated, see *Adapting*, esp. ch. 8 and for a comparison with England, p. 380.

[104] Greene, *Pursuits*, esp. pp. 38–52.

[105] B. Bailyn, 'Politics and social structure in Virginia', reprinted in Breen (ed.), *Shaping*, 193–214.

[106] Quitt, 'Virginia gentry'.

[107] E. S. Morgan, 'The labour problem at Jamestown, 1607–18', reprinted in Breen (ed.), *Shaping*, 17–31.   [108] Brown, *Good Wives*, esp. chs. 5–6.

[109] G. W. Mullins, 'The plantation world of William Byrd II', reprinted in Breen (ed.), *Shaping*, 156–84.

[110] The classic Caribbean study is R. S. Dunn, *Sugar and Slaves: The Rise of the Planter Class in the English West Indies, 1624–1713* (Chapel Hill, 1972). For the comparison, see Greene, *Pursuits*, esp. pp. 38–52.

[111] R. S. Dunn, 'The English sugar islands and the founding of South Carolina', reprinted in Breen (ed.), *Shaping*, 48–58.

cal influences between individual colonies and the mother country.[112]

These new societies developed towards English models, but by diverse routes and in the light of distinctive local experiences.[113] This ambiguous cultural experience is reflected too in the ambiguous political relationship between metropole and colony. But these political tensions were not the product of a necessary conflict of interest, and are analogous to forms of conflict within England. On the one hand, colonial elites depended on the metropolis for the legal validity of their actions and for more general legitimating beliefs. On the other hand, however, these local accommodations also drew upon and responded to particularist impulses and interests. Their position might be likened to that of English corporations, dependent on the crown for their legal existence but also jealously protective of that existence, not least, but not only, in response to perceived threats from the crown.[114] Boroughs increasingly employed recorders to advise them on legal issues and to represent them in London. Colonial authorities employed agents in a similar role from early in their history.[115] The power of governments in America derived from English grants and was legitimated in ways familiar from the English case.[116] Similar ambiguities arose from the evolution of local institutions. For example, the Virginia law code was the product of *ad hoc* and pragmatic appropriations from English law, in the light of local conditions. Untrained settlers, brought up in an English culture of marked legalism, responded eclectically to local difficulties using local legislative authority and, eventually, produced a written legal code. This was administered through a system of courts familiar from England.[117] The defence of such locally grown codes, developed independently of English direction but drawing upon English procedures

---

[112] For the connections between the colonies and Britain, see Steele, *English Atlantic*; Sosin, *English America*. For a review of more recent work in this field see Steele, 'Migrants and consumers'. The implications that this has for 'British' history are suggested by Armitage, 'Greater Britain', esp. pp. 433–8.

[113] Greene, *Pursuits*, chs. 1–2; Breen (ed.), *Shaping*; Breen (ed.), *Puritans and Adventurers*.

[114] D. H. Sacks, 'The corporate town and the English state: Bristol's "little businesses"', 1625–91', *PP*, 110 (1986), 69–105; M. J. Braddick, 'Resistance to the royal aid and further supply in Chester, 1664–1672: relations between centre and locality in restoration England', *Northern History*, 33 (1997), 108–36.

[115] For recorders see W. R. Prest, *The Rise of the Barristers: A Social History of the English Bar 1590–1640* (Oxford, 1986), esp. pp. 140–52. For the first generation of colonial agents see G. J. Milne, 'New England agents and the English Atlantic, 1641–1666', Ph.D. dissertation, Edinburgh University (1993). [116] Norton, *Founding Mothers*, esp. pp. 298–305.

[117] Billings, 'Transfer of English law'. For some interesting reflections on the significance of the export of the office of sheriff throughout the British empire, at a time when the office was of declining significance at home, see M. C. Noonkester, 'The third British empire: transplanting the English shire to Wales, Scotland, Ireland and America', *JBS*, 36/3 (1997), 251–84.

and ideas, became an issue of 'periphery rights'. The ambiguity of defending such rights from the metropolis (which was also understood to be the ultimate source of their authority) was considerable.[118]

These are issues of very considerable complexity, then. Discussions of them have addressed, explicitly or not, the roots of American identity and political independence. Here, though, we can emphasise some fundamental agreements. The importance of English models of pro-cedure and the use of legitimating beliefs common to English political culture made these polities dependent to some extent on the metropolis. Tied by trade and kinship, elites on both sides of the Atlantic belonged to a common culture, but this culture was not simply 'English'. Patterns of thought, and of administrative action within the colonies were similar to those of magistrates in England.[119] Within the shell of an expanding imperial government, coordinated by specialised and differentiated institutions of government concerned with military and commercial interests, there developed polities recognisable as variants of English prescription. Within England we can recognise the existence of both patriarchal and fiscal-military states and the same is true of the Atlantic world at large. Fiscal-military developments at home helped to foster imperial interests abroad, but the development of the empire of settle-ment was also guided by ideals of governance: these colonies were recognised to be polities.

THE GROWTH OF IMPERIAL REGULATION

Local initiative was crucial in the establishment of the first settlements and in the construction of local social and political orders. As a result of such private initiative, rather than an imperial plan, the commercial and territorial interests of the English crown in 1640 were much more widely spread than they had been ninety years earlier. This was reflected, to a degree, in attempts to regularise the oversight of these interests. After 1640 there developed more specialised agencies responsible for coor-dinating and protecting these interests. Once again, this is a develop-ment linked to the process of state formation at home, and in particular the consequences of the military revolution of the 1640s. All the colonies – proprietary, company or royal – owed their legal existence to the crown. Regulation of their activities therefore depended on the king-in-

---

[118] Greene, *Peripheries*, ch. 2.
[119] See for example, Horn, *Adapting*, ch. 8; Brown, *Good Wives*, chs. 3, 6; Norton, *Founding Mothers*, ch. 7.

council and, in practice, on sub-committees of the privy council. The history of these councils is tangled, with a variety of committees and commissions created to deal with trade or plantations or both. Their lives were often brief and their activities obscure but the very complexity of the arrangements suggests a lack of coherence and commitment at the centre.[120] From the 1620s onwards then, a series of mayfly committees burst briefly but, no doubt, brilliantly, to life. There was a trend, however, for them to last longer. In particular, a commission for the plantations was established in 1634, recommissioned in 1636, and was in continuous existence thereafter until at least 1641. On the whole, though, the government in London, despite some grand statements of intent, was not particularly interventionist in relation to the internal lives of these colonies before 1640.

The trend towards direct oversight and, indeed, direct authority, accelerated after 1640. In 1643 parliament assumed the role previously taken by the king-in-council. The Warwick commission, as it is known to historians, was given power to call before it any inhabitants of America or owners of land there who were within 20 miles of its meeting; to make use of all books and papers relating to the colonies; to appoint governors for the plantations; to remove and replace existing officers; and to assign powers to secure better government in them. In fact, these powers were not exercised in full and did not exceed the powers given to the 1634 commission.[121] Warwick was convinced of the importance of the plantations, not least the importance of the sugar and tobacco trades to providing war-time revenue. In general, however, the committee acted with restraint, seeking to cooperate with established colonial authorities. This was true even in the case of Virginia, despite Governor Berkeley's 'notorious royalism'. 'Under the oversight of the Earl of Warwick's committee for plantations . . . the empire continued to work in familiar ways.'[122]

After 1650 the trend towards more coherent oversight and regulation was more marked. The Navigation Act of 1651 signalled a new, more ambitious approach towards the regulation of trade. It made blanket provision for the regulation of trade to be undertaken directly by government. As a result, the importance of privileged corporate bodies receded considerably. It was aimed at the promotion of shipping as much as anything else, and recent work has emphasised how the

---

[120] C. M. Andrews, 'British committees, commissions, and councils of trade and plantations, 1622–1675', *Johns Hopkins University Studies in Historical and Political Science*, series 26, nos. 1–3 (1908).   [121] Ibid., pp. 20–3.   [122] Bliss, *Revolution*, pp. 49–52, quotations at pp. 49, 51.

measures sought to chastise the Dutch for their errant religion and corruption of republican ideals.[123] We should be wary, therefore, of reading this legislation as straightforwardly imperial. None the less, in requiring that all commodities be brought to England from their country of origin or first port of shipment, and that the ships carrying the goods be either from England or the country of production, this did demonstrate a new level of intervention. African, Asian and American goods were to be carried in English ships only. Above all, the legislation can be seen as a reflection of a larger shift from a contractual empire to a legislative one. A more coherent programme of regulation was envisaged, and was to be undertaken more directly. Crown oversight of trade was no longer mediated by privileged corporate bodies.[124] The shift was confirmed by further legislation in 1660 and 1663.

Enforcement of these measures was imperfect, of course, but it depended on some of the new instruments of power discussed chapters 5 and 6. Specifically, the regulations required regular oversight of trade, and this was provided by the increasingly significant customs service. The difficulties of the customs officer's job were multiplied by the baffling range of regulations that were imposed from the mid-seventeenth century onwards.[125] Secondly, the navy was increasingly able to provide the protection of trade which merchants had previously provided themselves. As we have seen, it was from this point on that warship design began to diverge from the design of merchantmen. In European waters, even the western Mediterranean, English trading interests were protected increasingly by the royal navy.[126]

In these circumstances it became more difficult to justify the creation of concessionary interests and the activities of trading companies were increasingly restricted. A case in point is the demise of the Eastland Company which withered away as more direct forms of government activity became preferred. The Navigation Act was a blow to the company but more significant in this case was the increasing power of the navy. Among the chief commodities of the Baltic trade were naval stores and the build-up of the navy after 1650 made these strategically more significant and a more direct interest of the crown. Moreover,

---

[123] S. C. A. Pincus, *Protestantism and Patriotism: Ideologies and the Making of English Foreign Policy, 1650–1668* (Cambridge, 1996), ch. 4. For the ways in which Cromwell's contemporaries and successors dealt with the tensions inherent in the pursuit of empire by a republic see D. Armitage, 'The Cromwellian protectorate and the languages of empire', *HJ*, 35 (1992), 531–55.

[124] Bliss, *Revolution*, pp. 58–60.

[125] E. E. Hoon, *The Organization of the English Customs System, 1696–1786* (New York, 1938), ch. 1.

[126] Above, pp. 222–5.

naval penetration of the Baltic meant that the navy could take over the duties of protection and representation previously undertaken by the company. Although the company was restored in 1660 its trade was opened up to non-members in 1673 when naval trades were removed from its privileges. This reflected the needs of the royal navy and behind it was the Council of Trade and Plantations. The company lived on for a further twenty-five years, but in the end its principal expenses were dinners.[127] During the Elizabethan and early Stuart period the crown 'sat at the centre of a web of rights and privileges which were designed to guide the self-interest of individuals into channels profitable to the commonwealth'.[128] This government by delegation was largely super-seded by the development of the navigation system: 'the conduct of mercantile affairs was progressively taken over by the central organs of government at Whitehall – or rather ... it was resumed by Whitehall, for the Crown had always been responsible for it even when it exercised its responsibility by delegation'.[129]

It was not just the Navigation Act that signalled a new intent: 1650 also saw the creation of the Council of Trade. This was one of a number of bodies established to provide coherent oversight of trade and overseas settlements. It had a regular membership and paid secretary, and was succeeded by a number of fairly active committees of the Council of State.[130] This intent reinforced that of the Navigation Act, and after the restoration the trend towards more permanent bodies continued. A Council for Trade and Plantations was in existence from 1660 to 1665. Separate Councils were subsequently established, that for Trade in 1668, for Plantations in 1670. They were amalgamated in 1672 in a Council that is often seen as the crucial development of imperial administration. A special building was planned and a budget of £7,400 included £6,400 for salaries.[131] From 1675 administration was in the hands of the Lords of Trade, acting under a similar remit, and who were in turn succeeded by the Board of Trade in 1696. The latter body oversaw trade and colonial affairs until 1782.[132] A corollary of the navigation system was, then, the development of regular and coherent

---

[127] Hinton, *Eastland Trade*, chs. 7, 8, 11. [128] Ibid., p. 71.

[129] Ibid., p. 121. For the later, but in some ways analogous, demise of the Royal African Company see Davies, *African Company*, pp. 38–46, and ch. 3.

[130] Andrews, 'British committees', ch. 2. For the secretary of the 1650 committee, see C. Webster, 'Benjamin Worsley: engineering for universal reform from the Invisible College to the Navigation Act', in M. Greengrass, M. Leslie and T. Raylor (eds.), *Samuel Hartlib and Universal Reformation: Studies in Intellectual Communication* (Cambridge, 1994), 213–35.

[131] R. P. Bieber, 'The British plantation councils of 1670–4', *EHR*, 40 (1924), 93–106; Andrews, 'British committees', chs. 4–5. [132] Andrews, 'British committees', ch. 5.

oversight of trade and the colonies. This was also accompanied by more deliberate manipulation of customs duties in the interests of trade. Rates were set in such a way as to encourage the import of raw materials and the export of manufactured goods, or to discourage the import of manufactures, for example.[133]

These changes persuade some historians that an important shift had taken place in English colonial and foreign policy, that it was oriented towards the protection of trade and that it was pursued by naval means. It is not necessarily reflected in programmatic foreign policy, but in the kinds of decisions that were made when the government did act. There seems to have been a tendency to prefer trading interests as strategic goals and naval war as the means to those ends.[134] Certainly commerce was an important strategic asset and international conflicts increasingly centred around trade as well as territory.[135] Others have been more sceptical about the coherence of the programme, or have located attacks on trade in the context of means of affecting the power of European rivals for essentially political or religious purposes: a war involving trade is not necessarily *about* trade.[136] Moreover, the imposition of direct control over the nascent empire was not uniform and in new or more distant trades the role of trading companies persisted – most notably the East India company's continued importance in the East. None the less, the new instruments of state power provided new means to coordinate the developing empire.

In a way the experience of the American colonies after the mid-1670s was analogous to that of English localities closer to home, and this may also suggest that claims for an imperial vision in the modern sense are overstated. There is evidence of a strong desire on the part of the crown

---

[133] M. J. Braddick, *The Nerves of State: Taxation and the Financing of the English State, 1558–1714* (Manchester, 1996), 120–3.

[134] D. A. Baugh, 'Maritime strength and Atlantic commerce: the uses of "a grand marine empire"', in Stone (ed.), *Imperial State*, 185–223; and 'Great Britain's "blue-water" policy, 1689–1815', *International History Review*, 10 (1988), 33–58.

[135] N. Zahedieh, 'Overseas expansion and trade in the seventeenth century', in Canny (ed.), *Origins of Empire*, 398–422. For a clear statement of the mercantilist interpretation of war in the later seventeenth century see C. Wilson, *Profit and Power: A Study of England and the Dutch Wars* (London, 1957).

[136] J. Black, *A System of Ambition? British Foreign Policy, 1660–1793* (London, 1991); D. Massarella, '"A world elsewhere": aspects of the overseas expansionist mood of the 1650s', in C. Jones, M. Newitt and S. Roberts (eds.), *Politics and People in Revolutionary England: Essays in Honour of Ivan Roots* (Oxford, 1986), 141–61. For the latter point see Pincus, *Protestantism*. See also P. Seaward, 'The House of Commons Committee of Trade and the origins of the second Anglo-Dutch war, 1664', *HJ*, 30 (1987), 437–52. The description of this empire as one of 'gentlemanly capitalism' is also of relevance here: P. J. Cain and A. G. Hopkins, 'Gentlemanly capitalism and British overseas expansion, I, The old colonial system, 1688–1850', *EcHR*, 2nd series, 39 (1986), 501–25.

to exert closer control over the internal affairs of the colonies. Pressure was brought to bear on a number of corporate colonies to surrender their charters and submit to direct royal authority. In the royal colonies of Virginia and Jamaica the role of legislative assemblies was restricted and measures taken to strengthen the hands of the governors. Thus, in Virginia, the governor sought a permanent revenue that would free him from dependence on the assembly and in the later seventeenth century the Lords of Trade considered extending Poynings's law to Virginia and Jamaica. This was a practice imposed on Ireland whereby legislation in the Irish parliament required the prior consent of the English privy council. In New York and Maryland, authoritarian governors pursued strong executive authority. *Quo Warranto* proceedings were commenced in relation to a number of colonial charters. Rhode Island, Connecticut and New Jersey all accepted royal government, and Carolina was on the verge of doing so in 1689. The grand vision seems to have been the consolidation of all the colonies into three or four vice-royalties 'on the Spanish model'. The most spectacular step in this direction was the creation of the Dominion of New England, incorporating eight previously separate colonies. [137]

There are two observations to be made here, however. Firstly, it was not necessarily imposed from outside: 'The fact is that many colonists were anxious for closer union with the home government.' Local merchants sought closer commercial links and better relations with Whitehall. None the less, in Massachusetts, Virginia and Maryland the mid-1670s also witnessed hostility to narrowly based governments. The strengthening of the authority of governors was not universally popular, and this helps to explain the second general observation about the tightening of colonial administration: it did not last. The political crisis of 1688–9 saw a great variety of responses in the colonies, but in all cases they were not simply a product of events in England. Broadly speaking, the planter societies in the West Indies emerged with close ties to London, ensuring prosperity to the big sugar planters. On the mainland a looser relationship emerged, as colonists successfully secured a greater degree of political and economic independence.[138] Claims that this was

---

[137] R. S. Dunn, 'The Glorious Revolution and America', in Canny (ed.), *Origins of Empire*, 445–66, quotation at p. 452. For some sceptical reflections about the absolutist intent behind similar initiatives under Charles II, see J. Miller, 'The crown and the borough charters in the reign of Charles II', *EHR*, 100 (1985), 53–84. Of course, James II makes a more convincing absolutist than Charles II, but even so the potential for absolutism in England in the 1680s was limited: Miller, 'The potential for "absolutism" in later Stuart England', *History*, 69 (1984), 187–207.

[138] Dunn, 'Glorious revolution', quotation at p. 453.

a military empire, based on coercion from London, are surely over-stated,[139] but there was an imperial shell, and imperial office clearly provided employment for men with military backgrounds.[140]

If the Glorious Revolution brought an end to interventionist royal government in the colonies it did not signal the end of the aspiration to coherent management from London. The navigation system persisted, overseen by the Board of Trade. Recent work has reminded us how central mercantile imperial interests were to the state in eighteenth-century Britain. They were an important means by which the sinews of power were drawn and a significant end to which these ideological, fiscal and military interests were deployed.[141] For their part, the colonists were tied into a wider Atlantic world by links of commerce and kinship. Eighteenth-century American society clearly bore the stamp of a British heritage and this was true also of its political culture. In constitutional and political thought Americans followed (or believed that they did) English precept.[142] The failure of later Stuart 'absolutism' in America seems to have been followed, as in England, by a more settled period of cooperation and incorporation. This was the underlying and, ultimately, more successful process.

Thus, the later seventeenth century saw the government undertaking much more direct control of overseas trade and settlement. But there were continuities too, in that new chartered companies were established and new proprietary colonies founded. Despite signs of energised administration in London, there is no record of any official communication between the crown and the Massachusetts Bay Company between 1666 and 1674.[143] The recall of the Bermuda charter was not followed by vigorous action, and proprietary charters were granted not just in the 1660s (to New York, Carolina and the Bahamas) but also in 1681 (to William Penn). Moreover, trading companies were chartered to reinvigorate the West African trade and to open up the far north of America

---

[139] For the 'garrison government' thesis see, in particular, S. S. Webb, *The Governors-General: The English Army and the Definition of Empire, 1569–1681* (Chapel Hill, 1979). For a discussion see the debate with R. R. Johnson in *William and Mary Quarterly*, 3rd series, 43 (1986), 408–59.

[140] For the latter point see Armitage, 'Greater Britain', p. 442.

[141] J. Brewer, *The Sinews of Power: War, Money and the English State, 1688–1783* (London, 1989); L. Colley, *Britons: Forging the Nation 1707–1837* (London, 1994).

[142] Greene, *Pursuits*; Greene, *Peripheries*; Greene, *Negotiated Authorities*; Sosin, *English America*; Fischer, *Albion's Seed*; Steele, *English Atlantic*. For an overview of the colonial economy see J. McAllister, 'Colonial America, 1607–1776', *EcHR*, 2nd series, 42 (1989), 245–59.

[143] Dunn, 'Glorious revolution', pp. 447–8. For parallel arguments about institutional forms in Britain and Ireland in the early sixteenth century see S. G. Ellis, 'The destruction of the liberties: some further evidence', *BIHR*, 54 (1981), 150–61.

(the Hudson's Bay Company). Elsewhere – in the Levant and the East Indies – the power of the companies persisted, and the Darien venture is testimony to the hold of such ideas among progressive Scots. There were, thus, limits to the capacity of the home government to take direct responsibility for trade and settlement. In areas very distant and/or densely populated by complex societies, the purchase of the new instruments of state authority was limited. A significant example here might be the Levant Company's control over the embassy at Constantinople. Financial support for the embassy had come from an import duty levied on company members. The crown had taken over the levy without taking responsibility for the embassy (a not insignificant fact in Bates's celebrated refusal to pay the duty).[144] The company retained considerable actual authority over the appointment down to 1687. It was only then, with the appointment of Sir William Trumball, that 'a commercial agent masquerading as an ambassador' was transformed into 'a servant of the Crown sent primarily for political and diplomatic business'.[145] The company had a nominal authority well after that.

None the less, in the later seventeenth century well-established trades and settlements were subject to direct government. Underwriting this was a much-increased capacity to mobilise armed force and to exert it over an increased area. Bacon's rebellion against autocratic governorship in Virginia in 1676, provoked also by alleged mishandling of Indian relations, was put down by a force including 14 royal ships and 1,300 English troops. This was a quite amazing transformation. In 1625, as we have seen, it had proved beyond the capacity of the English government to deliver men to Cadiz with bullets that would fit in their guns.[146] This is the strength of the claim that England's was an empire of domination and that 1676 marked the end of American independence.[147] The increased fiscal and military capacity was a product of the same transformation of the 1640s and 1650s that had allowed the Cromwellian conquests of Ireland and Scotland. It has been suggested that techniques of garrison government, honed in these areas, were subsequently

---

[144] P. Croft, 'Fresh light on Bates's case', *HJ*, 30 (1987), 523–39.

[145] A. C. Wood, 'The English embassy at Constantinople, 1660–1762', *EHR*, 40 (1925), 533–61, quotation at p. 545. For the renewal of a charter for the Greenland Company in 1692 see Scott, *Joint-Stock Companies*, II, p. 379.

[146] S. S. Webb, *1676: The End of American Independence* (New York, 1984), 12. Elsewhere in North America British interests were upheld in alliance with the Iroquois. For the failure of the Cadiz expedition see above, p. 199; R. W. Stewart, 'Arms and expeditions: the ordnance office and the assaults on Cadiz (1625) and the Isle of Rhé (1627)', in M. C. Fissel (ed.), *War and Government in Britain, 1598–1650* (Manchester, 1991), 112–32.   [147] Webb, *1676*.

exported.[148] The forcible seizure of Jamaica in 1655 and of New York in 1664 bear further testimony to the increasing military reach of the metropolitan government. The military outposts of the English crown in the later seventeenth century were Tangier and Bombay, acquired as dowry from Catherine of Braganza. In the event they were of little value. Tangier was less important to the support of the Mediterranean squadrons than had been hoped and Bombay was sold to the East India Company, which was better equipped to hold it.[149] None the less, this was a far cry from the position under Mary Tudor when the outposts were Berwick and Calais.

This same capacity for increased mobilisation had allowed for domination within Britain and Ireland, where coalescence failed. But a similar repertoire of techniques and ideas was used in all cases. It has been persuasively argued, in fact, that it was Elizabethan policies towards Ireland that established the pattern of British imperialism more generally. Plantation as a technique developed in Ireland and many early adventurers in America had cut their teeth on speculations in Ireland. The ideology which justified attempts to remake society in Ireland was exported to the Americas where, it was perceived, the Indians shared many of the shortcomings of the Irish. Indeed, all this expansion can be seen as part of a general 'Westward enterprise'.[150] It was not simply a matter of force, expropriation and profiteering, however. The formation of a political elite sharing the generalised vision of an orderly polity was an integral part of the process. In Ireland, the Catholicism of the Old English ruled them out, although in many other respects they were promising candidates. Force was the bottom line, then, but if things had gone differently, as they did in Cornwall, Wales, the Borders and lowland Scotland, the outcome might have been different.

---

[148] Webb, *Governors-General*.

[149] For the role of Tangier in the protection of English Mediterranean interests see S. R. Hornstein, *The Restoration Navy and English Foreign Trade, 1674–1688: A Study in the Peacetime Uses of Naval Power* (Aldershot, 1991), ch. 5. See also E. Routh, 'The English occupation of Tangier (1661–1683)', *TRHS*, 2nd series, 19 (1905), 61–78; Routh, 'The English at Tangier', *EHR*, 26 (1911), 469–81. For the costs of Tangier see C. D. Chandaman, *The English Public Revenue, 1660–1688* (Oxford, 1975), appendix 3. For Bombay see Lawson, *East India Company*, p. 47. For private initiative in the transformation of Bombay into an armed fort see Refai, 'Sir George Oxinden'.

[150] There is a large body of work comparing attitudes to native Irish and the North American Indians. See, in particular, Canny, *Elizabethan Conquest*, ch. 6; Canny, *Kingdom*, ch. 2. For attitudes towards the Indians see P. C. Mancall, 'Native Americans and Europeans in English America, 1500–1700', in Canny (ed.), *Origins of Empire*, 328–50.

Local elites were thought to provide the basis of good governance throughout the English-speaking Atlantic world. But this mutuality of interest only emerged from stable societies practising settled agriculture within a framework of recognisable legal process. In this sense, the government of, say, Virginia and Massachusetts was, by the later seventeenth century, quite like the government of Hertfordshire or Kent. Where the conditions did not exist for this happy result they could be fostered by forms of delegated authority, and this persisted in trades and areas of the world where the English government exercised limited leverage. But, and finally, that leverage was increasing, and the trades and areas beyond the reach of English government were fewer and more distant than had been the case in 1550. The intensification of government in the core, particularly in fiscal and military terms, had increased the radius of English authority. Government by delegation receded and the capacity of metropolitan government to pursue its wishes by force dramatically expanded.

Conclusion

One of the most striking developments of this period was the rapidly increasing extent of Tudor and Stuart authority. In this larger world – in London's provinces in Britain, Ireland, America, Africa and India – all the processes outlined in the previous chapters were present and similar arguments hold. It is difficult to discern a blueprint or identify an architect and the whole process, although it increased the power of the centre, was not dictated by the centre. Although it was, in the end, civil war that transformed the capacity to mobilise men and money, this new capacity was also deployed externally. Military force was an important enabling factor in the expanding territorial reach of the dynastic state. But this expansion was not solely a military phenomenon and it was enabled and prompted in other ways too. Territory was acquired by means of marriage as well as war, and the territorial interests of the crown were related to the dynastic interests of its wearer. In Britain and Ireland crown authority was extended through dynastic politics. Elsewhere it was trade that seemed to drive the process and as a result of the opening of the Atlantic world and Asian routes, trade became as important as territory in dynastic competition. In some areas this could mean the acquisition of territory but, in general, commanding a share of these prestigious and profitable new trades required more than military conquest. That the geographical scope of the authority of the crown increased is an obvious fact, but it was not a simple or homogenous process.

In Wales incorporation was successful, based on the willing participation of the indigenous elite, and the effect of the institutional changes of the 1530s and 1540s bears comparison with the fuller integration of the English marches. In Scotland state formation was a parallel but largely separate process. English influences were felt in policy initiatives, but so too were broader European processes (of which English innovations were themselves a local variant). As in Wales, then, there was the possibility that Scottish elites might identify their interests with the Stuart state following the dynastic union of 1603. Unlike Wales, however, there was another institutional structure that offered a vehicle for elite ambition – the Scottish kingdom. That the Union of the Crowns was followed by a fuller political union was probably contingent, and the development of the Scottish state was not an imposition from England. The end of the feud, the progress of civility, the subjugation of Gaeldom were all processes that owed little or nothing to English initiative and it was the Covenanters, rather than Cromwell, who brought the military revolution to Scotland.

In Ireland the attempt, in 1541, to create a kingdom was followed by a century of unsuccessful reform aimed at making Irish society resemble more closely 'civil' norms. Crucially, however, the natural local agents of such reform, the palesmen, became alienated from the Dublin government which fell increasingly into the hands of new English and Scots settlers. In effect, the English crown sought to create an institutional basis for the government of the whole island and there is considerable evidence that it might have found allies among Old English and Gaelic Irish in making that institutional structure work. But this alliance was fatally disrupted and in that process the failure of the Protestant reformation in Ireland was crucial. As a mutuality of interests failed to develop so force became more important and Ireland came steadily to resemble a colony rather than a kingdom. The rising in 1641 was probably not intended by its leaders to be a revolt against the Protestant interest but that became an important element of it, and it was certainly how it was perceived outside Ireland. Military control was established during the 1650s and government was subsequently dominated by Protestants who were, on the whole, newcomers. In this sense, the Irish experience was more like that of a colony than a sister kingdom, although in other ways life in Ireland was much like that in other parts of Europe. In any case, in Ireland, as in Scotland, the increased military capacity of the English government was important. It underwrote the Protestant interest in Ireland and, in the 1690s, focused Scottish minds on the dangers that a Jacobite rising posed to all Scottish interests.

Mutualities of interest between the crown and local elites developed to some extent in all areas of Britain and Ireland, but, where they conspicuously failed to support civil governance, force intervened. None the less, Scottish participation in union could be reconciled with important elements of elite interest, notably trade, and if it was the 'greatest political job of the eighteenth century' these mutualities of interest were crucial to its success. In Wales and the margins of the English kingdom this was even more the case. In promoting this coalescence, languages of Protestantism and of civility were of crucial, and transnational importance: not only did Elizabethan descriptions of the Irish sound like Stuart descriptions of Indians in Virginia, but they bear comparison both with the attitudes of lowland Scots to their Highland neighbours and with the normative threat imputed to the vagrant poor in the English core. Plantation was seen as a solution to the problem of order in Ireland, America and on the Isle of Lewis, while the transplantation of the Grahams or of the vagrant poor was a solution to problems in England.

We noted above that states do not possess a 'monopoly of the means of legitimate violence' but that they do claim to be arbiters of what kinds of violence are legitimate.[1] Making such a claim stick is in part a cultural programme. In all the territories of the Tudor and Stuart crown means of enforcing this claim are observable. In England we might point to the use of recognisances to control interpersonal violence or proclamations against duelling; in the Borders and Highlands, to measures to control feuds. Statements about ideal political order in these areas described a system of social positions and status roles. These social roles were described in terms of generalised expectations and norms. Order lay in the relations between these roles – what was being described was an 'interaction order' in which decency and civility were sustained through proper displays of deference and obligation. For this reason the crown was not infinitely flexible about the elites with which it co-operated – in Ireland and America civil orders were consciously fostered as a means to securing an acceptable political order.

Political relations and offices were only a dimension of this wider interaction order. A general feature of the expansion of the Tudor and Stuart state was that it entailed these larger cultural claims. The introduction of magisterial government and arable husbandry were a central component of the attempt to bring order to Ireland and the Borders, for example. A final observation to be made here is that while coercion was clearly a matter of political will, coalescence occurred, to an extent, independently of political purposes. The transformation of Gaeldom was partly the result of the interventions of the lowland states, particularly under Elizabeth and under the Covenanters, but it was also a product of broader changes in economic and social life. The passing of Gaelic manners, dress and attitudes towards the land was not simply a

[1] Above, p. 18.

matter of external, political, imposition, still less of English imposition.

Before 1640 the growth of the empire of trade and settlement was driven by private enterprise. The leaders of the trade, plunder and settlement of the Elizabethan and early Stuart period were activists seeking crown licence to pursue private interests. License was granted as a result of the congruence of these interests with the larger claims of the Tudor and Stuart state – to protect and further the true religion at the expense of the Spanish or Dutch, for example. Before 1640 this energy was poorly coordinated. The crown lacked the means – military and institutional – to undertake colonisation and trade war across the Atlantic, and instead, English influence spread by private initiative under licence from the crown. Capital for colonising ventures was raised by chartered companies and these bodies, along with numerous individuals, pursued armed commercial competition with trading rivals. In these transatlantic colonies, and in the military outposts established in Africa and Asia, military force was crucial but before 1640 it was exercised largely by proxy.

The transformation of the military capacity of the English state in the 1640s allowed for a more direct role in this exercise of trade, plunder and settlement. As in the English core the role of government by licence was being reduced. It was also associated with more coherent oversight, epitomised by the ambition expressed in the Navigation Acts or the new councils for trade and plantations. Underpinning this new ambition was increased military capacity, but also an expanded bureaucracy – the enforcement of the navigation system rested as much on the customs administration as on the navy. Over these longer distances the necessary force continued to be exercised by proxy – notably by the East India Company – but the difficulty of justifying the privileges of these companies increased as trades became more secure and better established. This is one reason why, within European waters, trading monopolies disappeared. A second reason was that the state-owned navy could now offer military protection in European waters, excluding the eastern Mediterranean. In a sense this represents a degree of 'modernisation' – a differentiation of function and bureaucratic specialisation – but it also has a spatial context. The radius of more direct forms of government control had increased and pushed government by licence to further corners of the globe, but they had not been eliminated – it was not simply a matter of one superseding the other. None the less, the increasing importance of direct government control underwrote a re-orientation of trade 'policy', with the adoption of more effective government protection and promotion of trade. On the other hand, the existence of the means to achieve these things might have encouraged their more conscious manipulation – this process created new opportunities. The pressure for this was not necessarily new to the later seventeenth century, but the means by which it was achieved were.

As settlements in north America matured into societies their institutional arrangements became more complex and this occurred within the shell of increasingly specialised metropolitan institutions. Elites defined themselves as Englishmen and within the protective shell of a 'modernising' imperial state local patriarchal orders, upheld by relatively undifferentiated magistracies, developed. Tied to England by kinship, trade and strategic interest the inhabitants of the new world adopted what they took to be the manners and society of England. That they were often misinformed or mistaken was not because they were hostile to the idea of being English. In a number of new or distant trades and colonies, however, semi-private trading companies remained the guarantee of security and government. Within Britain and Ireland, and across the oceans, the political influence of London extended by a mix, varied in each case, of elite interest and executive force. Its coordination was institutionalised as increasingly direct forms of government. In so far as force was important, the transformation of the military capacity of the English state in the 1640s was crucial, but the British empire was not simply the result of an effort of military will. Its origins and governance also rested on processes of commercial and cultural development which were encouraged by governments, but which did not originate with them. Military force was important in making political authority stick, but on the whole the transoceanic empire rested on elite coalescence and a perceived community of interest.

In nationally based historiographies the growth of the British state and the British empire are often seen as measures of centralisation and such accounts often emphasise conflict between the executive and local authorities. However, in seeking to explain the expanding territorial reach of the political power exercised under the Tudor and Stuart crowns an emphasis on elite interests seems to explain more than a concentration on national identities. Of crucial importance to these developments were ideas and processes that were not English, or even governmental, in origin. Social differentiation, humanism, Calvinism and commercial ambition, for example, were features of European life at large, and were not created by governments. But governmental power increased as elites seeking to benefit from, or participate, in these developments drew on political resources to further their interests. This provided further opportunities to local elites. Forms of government within territories resembled the undifferentiated magistracy of the English core, but overall there was a notable development of specialised, differentiated, imperial institutions responsible for the oversight of this expanding empire of trade and settlement. On the other hand, there were dangers in trying to govern against the interests of local elites, both in England and the British world at large, as James II discovered to his cost.[2]

The propagation of civility under the crown was a process which found support among sections of the elites across the English-speaking Atlantic world. But the military revolution of the 1640s delivered into the hands of Stuart governments the means for the subjugation of rival powers in Britain and Ireland and even across the Atlantic. Developments towards a British state and, hence, a British empire, were not simply a matter of English political will but neither were they the result of wholly peaceful coalescence. As English trade and territory expanded, and colonies matured, the new instruments of fiscal and military power provided the means by which they could be coordinated and protected, but also coerced. In the Atlantic world at large, just as in the English core, there were elites with differing interests and differing degrees of power. Local elites throughout the Atlantic world, from Kent to Jamaica, were confronted by an increasingly well-armed crown. But force was not all, in Kent or Jamaica. State formation in the English-speaking Atlantic world is a relatively new subject of study, but it seems clear that it proceeded by means that were not totally unlike state formation in the English core.

---

[2] Webb notes, in the context of a discussion of an earlier attempt to institute direct rule, that although pressure could be applied in various ways, '"the most popular and well-principled men" of New England . . . must choose to do the crown's business because it enhanced their own stature, increased their colonies' security, and promoted trans-Atlantic commerce and trade': S. S. Webb, *1676: The End of American Independence* (New York, 1984), 237.

Conclusion: actions without design, patterns without blueprints

> Mankind, in following the present sense of their minds, in striving to remove inconveniences, or to gain apparent and contiguous advantages, arrive at ends which even their imaginations could not anticipate . . . and nations stumble upon establishments, which are indeed the result of human action, but not the execution of any human design[1]

> [In order to] account for structural change it has to be shown how social groups as collective actors exercise pressure on existing constraints and, through acting upon interests of their own and by mobilising distinctive resources, make use of the enabling aspects of the environment.[2]

This has been a study of state formation in early modern England. The state consisted of a network of offices exercising political power co-ordinated under the Tudor and Stuart crown. It has not been defined in terms of particular institutional forms, or functions, but in terms of the kind of power that these offices embodied. No single will or interest lay behind the use that was made of these offices. Instead, agency was given to the state by activists, both officeholders and those who could influence them. These people responded to the problems and opportunities that they perceived around them by designing and implementing political innovations. However, although there was no architect or overall blueprint – this was not state building – it is still possible to discern and explain patterns in the outcomes of these innovations. There were consistent patterns in the way that political power was embodied in the villages and wards of the early modern English-speaking world.

One way of discerning patterns in this process is by distinguishing

---

[1] A. Ferguson, *An Essay on the History of Civil Society* (1767), quoted in C. Brady, *The Chief Governors: The Rise and Fall of Reform Government in Tudor Ireland, 1536–1588* (Cambridge, 1994), ix.

[2] R. Axtmann, 'The formation of the modern state: a reconstruction of Max Weber's arguments', *History of Political Thought*, 11 (1990), 295–311, quotation at p. 295.

general pressures for innovation – the effects of revolutions in prices, commerce and military technology, as well as the consequences of the reformation. The price revolution led to increased differentials in wealth, increased poverty and migration and, ultimately, to economic specialisation and differentiation. The reformation had implications for the nature of political authority and its purposes, as well as leading to a greater sensitivity to lapses in morality or religious observance. Such concerns could become enmeshed with responses to some of the consequences of the price revolution. But religious change also affected the international order which was also being transformed by the expansion of Europe's trading world and by changes in military technology. The religious pretensions of the state imposed considerable burdens on the government.

Political innovations were not, of course, straightforward reactions to material conditions. Political initiatives, and the administrative routines to which they gave rise, reflected the interests of those who promoted them, and social interests therefore patterned state activity. Political actors, however, were also constrained by the need to legitimate their initiatives – to justify and explain them in terms of beliefs in society at large, and the formal requirements of office. Each of these pressures was responded to by different groups at different times, and was legitimated with reference to different sets of beliefs. The form and function of the state were shaped by the collective interests of those who could define political issues and administrative responses to them, therefore, but also by the political languages available to justify and lend credibility to their actions. The absence of design, and the fact of complexity, do not imply the absence of pattern. By adopting a broad definition of the state it is possible to place in perspective the role of class, gender and religious interests, and of military mobilisation, in the development of the state; the importance of particular periods, such as the 1640s and 1690s; and to locate this important period in relation to developments in the preceding and succeeding periods.

In order to do this we have distinguished between four crystallisations of power within the whole network of offices exercising political power. Each was distinguished by the forms of office, the purposes for which power was used, the interests at stake and the languages which proved most effective in legitimating these actions. In the case of the patriarchal state, we have seen that relatively undifferentiated offices were deployed to sometimes spectacular effect in dealing with perceived threats to the social order. The measures were legitimated with reference to a view of social order which was, broadly speaking, patriarchal. It was these ideas which gave definition to both 'social problems' and their solution, therefore. The impetus came from the localities at least as much as from the centre and the uses of state power were clearly patterned by social interest – by powerful groups in the hierarchies of class, gender and age. Although these measures cannot be considered 'modernising', their impact on the lives of particular individuals was sometimes dramatic. Within the period covered by this book the crucial periods in their development were probably the 1590s, 1620s and 1640s, although there were important developments in the post-restoration period and during the 1690s too.

The various 'states' discussed in the preceding pages vary in each of these respects – chronology, autonomy, the relationship between centre and locality, and the degree of modernisation. In response to military change measures were taken which were modernising – the development of specialised, differentiated institutions, legitimated with reference to modern languages of politics. These innovations were more often driven from the centre than the localities, and the most important periods in their development were the 1640s and 1690s, although the 1590s and 1620s were also important. By comparison with the patriarchal state, the fiscal-military state was relatively autonomous. Clearly, some social interests could benefit from the growth of fiscal and military power. For many members of existing social elites, however, the development of these offices, exercising power based on knowledge and expertise rather than birth and status, was a challenge. The confessional state was also relatively autonomous – the pursuit of true religion could cut across status hierarchies, and jeopardise the position of otherwise powerful people. Like the fiscal-military state, the impetus for innovation was more often central than local, but its legitimation and purposes, by contrast, can hardly be considered modernising. Looked at from the perspective of the entire territories governed under the authority of the crown – the point of view of the dynastic state – elements of all these things are repeated in all areas. In all of London's provinces we can see the mix of interest and local initiative associated with the patriarchal state in the English core. But in the development of the imperial shell of the navigation system, and in the creation of elites in areas where coalescence failed, the experience is more closely related to that of the fiscal-military state. For the development of the relatively autonomous imperial shell the 1640s and 1690s were particularly significant, but the chronologies of development in other respects vary from place to place.

These four crystallisations of power offer a way of examining the pressures that shaped state formation in the period from about 1550 to about 1700. They were not actually, of course, separate entities and to concentrate on only one would be to misunderstand not only the whole, but the part that was being examined. John Churchill's rise to prominence from the minor gentry was a result not of military service, but of connection. It was his skill at taking advantage of those opportunities that came his way as a young courtier that enabled him to rise from the lowly position of page to James, duke of York, to commander of the allied armies in the Low Countries between 1702 and 1711. His great military victory at Blenheim in 1704 decisively halted the military advance of Louis XIV, and was both rewarded and commemorated in the construction of Vanbrugh's Blenheim Palace in Oxfordshire. Both the victory, and the construction of the house, rested on the capacity of the fiscal-military state. An important dimension of Churchill's career was 'imperial', and many of his military associates were subsequently important in the administration of transatlantic empire. But for the duke of Marlborough, as he became, this was an extension of a remarkable court career. The house itself typified the 'formal house' of the English countryside in the seventeenth century. It inscribed onto the landscape a concern for patriarchal order, manifest in both the park and the house itself. Such houses encapsulated a belief that 'a hierarchy under a single head was the only right order for society', a belief reflected in the orderly arrangements of internal rooms: internal design differentiated male from female space, relatively public and private apartments and the worlds of the master and the servant. The chapel was the symmetrical counterpart of the kitchen, a juxtaposition of spiritual and bodily nourishment 'which may have amused Vanbrugh'.[3] Fiscal-military triumph was here expressed in the idiom of patriarchal authority, within a protestant, monarchical order. Not only did the house give material expression to religious, dynastic, patriarchal and fiscal-military power then, but it did so in a style that reflected independent (and European-wide) movements in architectural taste. In distinguishing general pressures for political innovation and general types of response, this study has been making analytic distinctions that would not necessarily have corresponded to contemporary consciousness. And the cultural influences that shaped these developments – humanism, reformation, Calvinism,

---

[3] J. R. Jones, *Marlborough* (Cambridge, 1993); S. S. Webb, *Lord Churchill's Coup: The Anglo-American Empire and the Glorious Revolution Reconsidered* (New York, 1995); M. Girouard, *Life in the English Country House: A Social and Architectural History* (London, 1978), quotations at pp. 145, 156.

commercial expansion, military revolution and so on – were, like those that shaped Blenheim Palace, common to much of Europe.

The argument is not that these particular categories should be more widely employed, but that the study of state formation as that term has been interpreted here offers the possibility of a more satisfactory overall account of the development of the English state. The argument is about the ways in which political power was used, how its forms were continuously modulated and how patterns in that process can be explained. These four crystallisations of power – fiscal-military, patriarchal, confessional and dynastic – offer ways in which to characterise particular uses of political power and the language in which they were justified. The terms, however, are anachronisms: they can describe a pattern of action in terms comprehensible to us, but they cannot explain the consciousness of the actors themselves. Moreover, as a result of changing functional form and legitimating languages, other terms might be more appropriate for other periods. For example, the language of mercantilism was, by 1700, brought to bear on poverty. The 1696 examination of the poor law was conducted by the Board of Trade, the body also responsible for the oversight of imperial trade and settlement. At that point, therefore, we might discern the presence of a mercantilist state, with its own distinctive institutional forms and legitimating languages, with some of the functional purposes previously characterised as belonging to a patriarchal state.[4] Similarly, the Stuart state might be said to have given way not to a Hanoverian state, but to a British one. For other periods, or other questions, different distinctions might be developed.

The essential point is not, therefore, the usefulness of these particular terms (patriarchal, fiscal-military, confessional and dynastic), but a methodological claim about how to analyse the development of the state. Conceiving of offices as social roles integrates intellectual and administrative history, and the abstract order of the state with the actual experience of political authority, thus drawing attention to the ways in which ideas and values can drive political action. Wrightson has complained about the 'enclosure' of English social history,[5] but there is an even more general problem, that social, political and intellectual histories have become entirely separate enterprises. This division of labour

---

[4] I owe this observation to Dr Clive Holmes.
[5] K. Wrightson, 'The enclosure of English social history', reprinted in A. Wilson (ed.), *Rethinking Social History: English Society 1570–1920 and its Interpretation* (Manchester, 1993), 59–77.

has impoverished our understanding of political power.[6] This account
has been partial in that respect – much more could be said about the
development and everyday use of political languages and about the
representation of political authority in face-to-face contexts. Such a
history would add considerably to the account given here. For example,
new languages and understandings of the natural or political world must
also have created important resources for activists and, although there
has been substantial work on the rhetorics of magistracy in the early
seventeenth century, there is no corresponding body of work on the later
period.[7] Moreover, implicit in this argument about the institutional
development of the English state has been an account of the effect of
resistance – both routine resistance to routine expressions of political
power and awareness of the potential for more spectacular resistance.[8] A
more explicit discussion of contested legitimacy could encompass a
reading of recent work on the meaning of 'opposition' in early Stuart
England, and consideration of the role of legal validity in legitimating
political power provides a means to connect the account of administrative change given here with the political and constitutional history of the
period.

An account of the development of the state could therefore be
connected with a wider political, cultural and intellectual history. It
could also be connected with a wider 'material' history. A fuller understanding of political power would integrate it with the history of the
other resources available to political activists. For example, the widening sphere of print communication and the development of a civil
society in which political discourse flourished, a 'coffee house culture',
offered new opportunities to activists and must have affected the ways in
which state functions and forms were negotiated. In short, changing

[6] In a sense the explanation for institutional change advanced here provides a counterpart to
Skinner's explanation of the process of ideological change. Skinner argues that authors manipu-
late the conventions of prevailing ideologies and textual practices – the commonly understood
meanings of normative terms – in order to achieve particular ends. In doing so, they create
ideological change by lending new meanings to those terms. Here the emphasis is on officeholders and political activists rather than on theorists, and on their manipulation of conceptions
of office as the motor of institutional change, but this might be seen as a different aspect of the
same set of transactions. See J. Tully, 'The pen is a mighty sword: Quentin Skinner's analysis of
politics', reprinted in Tully (ed.), *Meaning and Context: Quentin Skinner and his Critics* (Princeton,
1988), 7–25, 289–91.

[7] F. Heal and C. Holmes, *The Gentry in England and Wales 1500–1700* (London, 1994), esp. ch. 8; R.
Cust and P. Lake, 'Sir Richard Grosvenor and the rhetoric of magistracy', *BIHR*, 54 (1981),
40–53; R. Cust (ed.), *The Papers of Sir Richard Grosvenor, 1st Bart. (1585–1645)*, Record Society of
Lancashire and Cheshire, 134 (Stroud, 1996).

[8] For further reflections on this issue see my essay in M. J. Braddick and J. Walter (eds.), *Order,
Hierarchy and Subordination in Early Modern Britain* (Cambridge, forthcoming).

perceptions of the sphere of legitimate political power did not arise simply from attempts to justify political innovation: they are neither internal to government, nor simply a rationalisation of new 'material' circumstances. A history of the state, as that term is understood here, should be part of a wider cultural history. Naturally, such a project is more ambitious than has been attempted here, but would represent a fuller study of the genetic material from which the state was embodied.

Alongside this larger methodological purpose, however, this book has been particularly concerned with a range of questions arising from the historiography of seventeenth-century England. One such question is the relationship between centre and locality and the effect of that relationship on the development of the state. Clearly, political innovation did not emanate from Whitehall or Westminster alone, and the exercise of political power was not something done by the centre to the locality. Innovation was the product, in many cases, of activists whose names are now lost to us. The functional and institutional form of the state was the product of negotiation, as activists sought means to legitimate innovations in the exercise of political power. In the case of some uses of state power the pressure was, more generally, from the centre than from the localities – for example, in the case of military reform, the defence of strategic interests or the drive for religious orthodoxy. On the other hand, the patriarchal state and the patriarchal orders in London's provinces across Britain, Ireland and the Americas owe much more to local initiative and interest.

A second important question relates to the degree of autonomy of the state, and if it was not driven from the centre alone, this process was, clearly, shaped by the interests of powerful social groups. The primary means by which these interests were brought to bear was not through the contest for constitutional power, but in the routines of government in the localities. The process of state formation reflected differentials in power consequent on the distribution of access to office. Policies launched from the privy council table or the royal court had a far more real prospect of national application than those originating in vestries and wards in London and the provinces. Those with access to local office, by the same token, had a greater capacity to influence administrative development than those outside the ranks of local officeholders. The range of people in a position to influence administration directly was not great. It ran from the middling sorts in parishes and wards to territorial magnates at the privy council table with the result that initiative was not restricted to a homogenous elite. However, it was, on the whole, limited to protestant men with property whose social and political position was justified with reference to an ethic of social respectability which can be understood to have been, broadly, patriarchal. But these social interests were more clearly expressed in relation to some kinds of political challenge – notably in relation to social order rather than attempts to enforce official religious belief or deal with the consequences of changes in military technology and organisation. Commercial expansion, of course, also reflected social interests, although they were not necessarily the same as those that lay behind the growth of the patriarchal state.

The power of these vested interests was constrained by the process of legitimation. In a sense these pressures reflected an 'objective' reality – the poor, Jesuits and wars did exist – but what counted in practice was contemporary perception of the urgency of the problem or the attractiveness of the opportunity. The *Sovereign of the Seas*, the show-piece ship built for Charles I, was not a straightforward response to military needs, and in fact was quite inadequate to the task of meeting the main naval challenges confronting English shipping. Similarly, responses to social problems were not unmediated responses to changing material conditions: social order is not a matter simply of material conditions, or simply of ideas, but of ideas about material conditions. We might also point to the gap between the fear of popery and the reality of recusancy. Of course, the definition of such 'problems' was also patterned, in terms of dominant discourses and by the differential power of particular groups to decide what was, and what was not, a problem worthy of public response.[9] However, these discourses also constrained those seeking to exercise political power, providing a yardstick against which to measure the conduct of individual officeholders. To this extent, legitimation was a source of autonomy in the state – in all cases the exercise of political power was coloured by the consequences of legitimating it with reference to wider beliefs and values.

A third important question relates to the modernity, and modernisation, of the seventeenth-century state. Particular languages, and forms of office, were more effective in legitimating responses to functional challenges than to others. The definition of offices reflected other kinds of social power, but was constrained by the need to legitimate political innovation; and there was an affinity between particular kinds of legitimation and particular uses of political power. Some forms of office – some embodiments of the state – approximated more closely to the

---

[9] For 'non-decisions' as exercises of power see S. Lukes, *Power: A Radical View* (London, 1974), esp. ch. 7.

Weberian ideal-type of modern state forms than others. Before the 1640s the undifferentiated local offices which dominated the English localities performed much more effectively in some ways than in others. In general, they found it easier to meet local concerns for order and provision for the poor than they did to conform to demands for orthodoxy in the church. The most divisive issue of all, because less easily evaded, was the variety of fiscal and military duties they were being required to impose. Here were the demands most removed from local needs, the most 'autonomous' needs of the state.

However, throughout the period, fiscal-military innovation called forth forms of administration which were specialised, and more suited to these autonomous functions. The problems of finding ways to legitimate these offices was acute and the outbreak of civil war may not have been related to these problems. What is clear is that a consequence of the civil wars was to break these constraints and in the long run this produced more modern forms of office. From the mid-century onwards there was an increasing tendency to legitimate fiscal-military offices by imposing tight controls on their exercise. In order to overcome suspicions about self-seeking and corruption in officeholders, impersonal rules were imposed which left (or were intended to leave) little room for discretion, and these political actions were also legitimated in modern languages – of necessity and reason of state, for example. Modernisation, in this case, took the form not just of specialisation and differentiation, but also of increasing coordination, reflected in the decline of forms of government by licence. The greater distinction between social and political authority seems also to have been a feature of other forms of officeholding in the later seventeenth century, too. However, although the experience of the 1640s was 'modernising', the state in 1700 was only modernised in limited senses. The continuities in magisterial government, and the relatively limited development of the fiscal-military state before 1689 (and the importance of the magistracy within it) should caution us against pushing that argument too far. So too, should the continuing pretensions of the confessional state

An account of modernisation draws attention to the role of war in state formation and in particular, therefore, to the importance of the 1640s and 1690s to the development of the English state. But modernisation is by no means the only important issue raised by the study of the seventeenth-century state. Those who felt the impact of state authority most sharply in this period were probably not taxpayers or conscripts. Instead they were people like Elizabeth Laurenson alias Alscoe, in labour delivering a daughter in February 1669, asked by the midwife 'in the extremitie of her paine' several times in the presence of witnesses who the father was.[10] Suspected witches, those inhabiting houses visited by the plague, or young adult males on the roads in search of work were all subject to increasingly coordinated measures of social discipline. At particular moments those holding religious beliefs thought to be threatening to social and political order were also subject to dramatic exercises of state power. If we are concerned with the question of the relationship between the power of the state and the life of the individual, then, it is not the most modern aspects of the early modern state that demand our attention. And for the development of these other uses of political power other periods than the 1640s are also important – the 1590s and 1620s, for example. However, looking at the whole network of political power over the entire period we can, despite these complexities and reservations, discern two broad and relatively distinct phases of development. Before 1640 the most striking and effective innovations were those made in relation to social problems. After 1640 it is the development of the fiscal-military functions of the state that commands most attention.

   This analysis has been concerned with modulations and changes in functional efficiency which necessarily take place over relatively long periods of time, and the development of the state cannot be said to have hinged on a single moment of definitive reform. This, of course, raises a question about the usefulness of the overall chronological boundaries adopted here. The beginning and end points adopted for this study encompass a long trend in the relationship between population and resources, with the consequent effects on social relations. With the benefit of hindsight we can say that it was in the 1560s that the protestant identity of the state was settled, and the roots of the expansion of overseas trade also lie in the later sixteenth century. The dynastic union of England and Scotland can also be comprehended within these chronological limits. However, for Ireland and Wales the 1530s would make a more obvious starting point. The account of the development of the state navy should really start in the 1530s rather than the 1630s, although the enormous Henrician effort was not built on resources as durable as those developed in the seventeenth century. None the less, no particular claim is being made here for the importance of 1550 or 1700 as terminal dates and this analysis could, clearly, be extended both

---

[10] See above, p. 143.

forwards and backwards. Many of the initiatives of social regulation in the period 1550–1640 have precedents from the fourteenth and fifteenth centuries. On the other hand, the fiscal and military changes of the 1640s, while important both in quantitative and qualitative terms, were overshadowed by the massive increase in the size of the revenues and military forces in the 1690s. Such a periodisation thus pays attention to an important period of structural change but in the context of an awareness of the longer history of magisterial government and the importance of later periods in the development of bureaucratic government. The more important point, however, is again methodological – by concentrating on the continuous pressure for political change, and the consequent modulation of institutional forms in dialogue with wider intellectual changes, connections with preceding and succeeding periods are made easier.

Institutional change was the outcome of negotiating legitimate responses to political problems and opportunities. The terms of these negotiations, and their effects, were very different in 1700 from those in 1550 and in some ways these can be said to have been modernising. They are not best described as the outcome of 'state building' or 'centralisation', however. These developments derived from pressures throughout the political system and they could be relatively autonomous – certainly an important part of the legitimation of public power was the disavowal of private benefit and interest in its exercise. None the less, the definition of opportunities and challenges, and the capacity to make suggestions as to how to meet them, was in the hands of dominant social groups. Greater dominance delivered, within limits, greater influence over administrative innovation. In embodying the state contemporaries drew upon the social interests and beliefs which they found around them. 'Structural change' in the state was the net effect of the ways in which individuals took advantage of political, social, cultural and linguistic resources in order to legitimate acts of political power. There were patterns in the outcome of these negotiations even though they lacked an overall design. They produced innovations which were of long-term significance, and transformations that were in some sense modernising. And written into the process of state formation were the interests of dominant groups – particularly adult, propertied, protestant males – even though their command of political power was neither exclusive nor complete.

Index